M. Mignet

The History of Mary, Queen of Scots

M. Mignet

The History of Mary, Queen of Scots

ISBN/EAN: 9783337323905

Printed in Europe, USA, Canada, Australia, Japan

Cover: Foto ©ninafisch / pixelio.de

More available books at **www.hansebooks.com**

THE HISTORY

OF

MARY, QUEEN OF SCOTS.

By F. A. MIGNET,

MEMBER OF THE INSTITUTE, AND OF THE FRENCH ACADEMY; SECRETARY OF
THE ACADEMY OF MORAL AND POLITICAL SCIENCE.

SEVENTH EDITION.

LONDON:
RICHARD BENTLEY AND SON,
Publishers in Ordinary to Her Majesty the Queen.
1887.

PREFACE.

THE History of Mary Stuart has been written many times; and each successive publication has thrown fresh light upon the subject. At the present day, the number of new documents which have been added to those already known, enable us to relate its vicissitudes in a more complete and truthful manner. In 1734, Keith inserted in his History of Scotland some very valuable papers relating to the reign of Mary Stuart, from the birth of that princess until her flight into England. In continuation of his sober narrative, and in support of his candid and sagacious opinions, Robertson published several documents which he had extracted from the national archives of England and Scotland. The extensive collections of Anderson and Goodall contained all the Acts relating to the memorable discussion which took place at York and Westminster, in 1568, before the Commissioners of the artful Elizabeth, between Mary Stuart and her subjects, regarding the assassination of Darnley. Finally, the important works of Digges, Murdin, Haynes, and Hardwicke, compiled from the State Papers of England, together with the no less interesting publication of Jebb, and the Memoirs of Castelnau de Mauvissière, as enlarged by Le Laboureur, assisted the student to pursue the history of the captive Queen to her death.

This mass of documents has been very largely increased of late years. In Great Britain, Mr. George Chalmers has written a

Life of Mary Stuart, based upon documents in the State Paper Office. Sir Henry Ellis and Mr. Thomas Wright have published a number of the letters of Queen Elizabeth and the principal personages of her time. Sir Cuthbert Sharpe has narrated, from inedited manuscripts, the progress of the Catholic insurrection in the North of England in 1569, which was occasioned by Mary Stuart's imprisonment, and intended to secure her liberation. Mr. Patrick Fraser Tytler, the last, the most voluminous, and the most learned of the historians of Scotland, has drawn from the political archives of England all the papers which escaped the notice of his predecessors, and has thus completed the histories of Keith and Robertson, and the collections of Haynes, Murdin, and Hardwicke. The despatches of the various English ambassadors and agents have enabled him to relate the whole life of Mary Stuart in more striking colours, and with greater animation of detail. In France, the Correspondence of Francis II., collected and edited by M. Louis Paris; the Diplomatic Correspondence of Lamothe Fénelon, extending from 1568 to 1574, during the first six years of Mary Stuart's captivity, which has been printed by Mr. Purton Cooper; the letters of Noailles, Montluc, Paul de Foix, Du Croc, Castelnau de Mauvissière, the Baron D'Esnéval, Aubespine de Chateauneuf, and others, which M. Teulet has just published, and which embrace, as it were, the existence of Mary Stuart from 1542 to 1587; and lastly, the Correspondence of Mary Stuart herself, in seven volumes, completed by the unwearied research and skilful care of Prince Labanoff—would have left us nothing further to desire with regard to the history of that Queen and her times, if we had possessed the Spanish documents which have reference to them both. Philip II., the great head of Catholicism in Europe, was constantly mixed up with the religious and political affairs of Scotland and England, under Mary Stuart and Elizabeth, and never ceased to take part in the long and terrible rivalry of the two creeds and the two Queens. In 1832, Don Tomas Gonzalez published for the Royal Academy of History at Madrid, some extracts from the correspondence of the Spanish Ambassadors in England between the years 1558 and 1576. I have been able to do more, by means of despatches copied from the Archives of Simancas. The confidential letters of Philip II., the Duke of Alva, and the Spanish Ambassadors, in England, at Rome, and in France, from 1558 to 1588, have enabled me more rightly to understand the attempts of the Catholic party in Great Britain, and the plans of Mary Stuart, during the nineteen years of her captivity, when she conspired to secure her own freedom by driving Elizabeth from her throne.

Aided by these materials, and also by the numerous works published during and after the sixteenth century, upon the political events and religious changes of Scotland and England, I have composed this history. In the years 1847—1850, I published a series of articles upon this subject in the *Journal des Savants*, taking Prince Labanoff's vast collection as the basis of my work. These articles, which were similar to those that appeared in 1846 upon Antonio Perez and Philip II., have been entirely recast in the work which I now publish under the form of a continuous narrative. After a short description of the previous condition of Scotland, my narrative commences with the minority of Mary Stuart, and terminates with the expedition of the Invincible Armada, sent by Philip II. to avenge the death of that Queen, and to dispossess the Protestant Elizabeth of the throne of England. I hope I have succeeded in giving a complete sketch of this long and pathetic episode in the great revolutions of the sixteenth century.

AUGUST 8, 1851.

TRANSLATOR'S PREFACE.

NEARLY twelve months ago, I made a proposition, to M. Mignet, to publish an English translation of his forthcoming History of Mary, Queen of Scots. My offer was accepted, and M. Mignet, with great kindness, promised to forward to me the proof-sheets of his work, as he received them from the printer, and also to sanction my translation by sending me a letter of approval. This letter, unfortunately, did not arrive in time for insertion in the first volume; and I now publish, in its stead, a note which I have since received from M. Mignet:—

'MONSIEUR, *Paris*, 14 *Août*, 1851.

'J'AI adhéré bien volontiers à la proposition que vous m'avez faite de traduire l'*Histoire de Marie Stuart*, dont les feuilles vous ont été transmises à mesure qu'elles étaient imprimées, afin que les deux éditions, Française et Anglaise, pussent paraître en même temps.

'Je me félicitais que cet ouvrage trouvât, en vous, un traducteur habile qui saurait le reproduire avec un soin exercé, une ferme précision, une fidélité élégante. Tout ce que j'attendais, Monsieur, est heureusement réalisé dans le premier volume de votre traduction que vous m'avez envoyé avec une obligeance si empressée, et que je viens de lire avec une entière satisfaction. Je vous remercie d'avoir si bien rendu dans votre langue un ouvrage dont le sujet a pour votre pays un intérêt encore plus grand que pour le mien ; et je vous prie d'agréer aussi les assurances de ma haute considération.

'MIGNET.'

I am glad to find that several eminent critical authorities participate in the high opinion which I entertain of the literary merit and historical value of this work; and I am proud to have introduced to English readers a book in every respect worthy to rank with Thierry's 'History of the Norman Conquest,' and Guizot's 'History of the English Revolution.'

In conclusion, I have to express my obligations to Miss Ross, for a translation of the last two chapters, which I was unable, from want of time, to execute myself.

ANDREW R. SCOBLE.

London, August 25th, 1851.

CONTENTS.

CHAPTER I.

INTRODUCTION.   PAGE

Scotland before the reign of Mary Stuart—Wars with England for the maintenance of her independence—Conflicts of her Kings and Barons—Her condition at the death of James V. and accession of Mary Stuart. . . 1

CHAPTER II.

FROM THE ACCESSION OF MARY STUART TO HER RETURN FROM FRANCE INTO SCOTLAND.

Minority of Mary Stuart—War with England—Mary is sent to France—Regency of Mary of Lorraine—Marriage of Mary Stuart—Her pretensions to the crown of England—Origin and progress of Protestantism in Scotland—Treaty of Berwick—Death of the Regent—Treaty of Edinburgh—Mary Stuart becomes a widow, and returns to Scotland. . . . 14

CHAPTER III.

FROM MARY'S RETURN INTO SCOTLAND TO HER MARRIAGE WITH DARNLEY.

Policy pursued by Mary Stuart—Concessions to the Protestant party.—Lord James Stuart appointed Prime Minister—Disgrace of the Hamiltons—Rebellion of the Earl of Huntly—Negotiations for the Queen's second marriage.—Her rupture with Murray—His conspiracy—Marriage of the Queen to Lord Darnley. 63

CHAPTER IV.

FROM MARY'S MARRIAGE WITH DARNLEY TO THE MURDER OF RICCIO.

Effect produced in England by Mary's marriage—Negotiations for the marriage of Elizabeth—Coolness between Elizabeth and Mary—Murray's revolt, defeat, and flight into England—Influence of Riccio—Attempts to restore Catholicism in Scotland—Darnley's jealousy of Riccio—Conspiracy against Riccio—League between Darnley and Murray—Murder of Riccio—First captivity of the Queen. 101

CHAPTER V.

FROM THE ASSASSINATION OF RICCIO TO MARY'S MARRIAGE WITH BOTHWELL.

Mary's reconciliation with Darnley—Pardon of Murray and the other exiles—Punishment of Riccio's murderers—Birth of the Prince Royal of Scotland—Mary's aversion to Darnley—Her attachment to Bothwell—Her illness—Plots against Darnley's life—His alarm and illness—Pardon of Riccio's murderers—Murder of Darnley—Public indignation—Trial and acquittal of Bothwell—His marriage with the Queen. 131

CHAPTER VI.

FROM MARY'S MARRIAGE WITH BOTHWELL TO HER FLIGHT INTO ENGLAND.

League of the nobility against Mary and Bothwell—Applications to Queen Elizabeth for assistance—Attack of Borthwick Castle—Mary's flight to Dunbar—Entry of the confederates into Edinburgh—Mary levies an army—Her defeat at Carberry Hill—Her separation from Bothwell—She yields to the confederates, is led captive to Edinburgh, and finally imprisoned in Lochleven—Government of the Lords of the Secret Council—Arrest and confessions of Bothwell's accomplices—Deposition of the Queen—Coronation of James VI.—Murray is appointed Regent—Conduct of Queen Elizabeth—Behaviour of Murray—Convocation of Parliament—Flight and fate of Bothwell—Mary escapes from Lochleven, and collects an army at Hamilton Castle—Battle of Langside—Defeat of the Queen's army—Her flight into England. 178

CHAPTER VII.

FROM MARY STUART'S ARRIVAL IN ENGLAND TO THE RETURN OF MURRAY TO SCOTLAND.

Arrival of Mary Stuart on the English frontier—Her detention at Carlisle—Plans of Elizabeth—Mission of Middlemore—His propositions are rejected by Mary Stuart—Her appeal to the Princes of the Continent—She accepts the arbitration of Elizabeth—Suspension of hostilities in Scotland—Conference at York—Position, character, and wishes of the Duke of Norfolk—His secret negotiations with Lethington and Murray—Transfer of the Conference from York to Westminster—Accusation of Mary Stuart—Her defence—Rupture of the Conference—Murray returns to Scotland. . 225

CHAPTER VIII.

FROM MURRAY'S RETURN TO SCOTLAND TO THE EXECUTION OF THE DUKE OF NORFOLK.

Mary's efforts to restore her party in Scotland—Murray's activity and energy—Proposed marriage of Mary to the Duke of Norfolk—Negotiations on the subject—League of the nobility against Cecil—He joins Norfolk's party—

CONTENTS. xi

PAGE

Secret intrigues of Norfolk in Scotland—Convention at Perth—Alarm and anger of Elizabeth—Norfolk and his friends retire to their estates—Arrest of Norfolk—Catholic insurrection in the North of England—Defeat of the Insurgents—Assassination of Murray—Insurrection of Mary Stuart's party in Scotland—Invasion of the English border—The Earl of Lennox appointed Regent—Negotiations for Mary's liberation; they are broken off—Conspiracy of Mary Stuart and the Duke of Norfolk—Mission of Rodolfi—Discovery of the conspiracy in England—Trial and condemnation of Norfolk —His execution and Mary's distress. 263

CHAPTER IX.

FROM THE EXECUTION OF THE DUKE OF NORFOLK TILL THE FORMATION OF THE PROTESTANT LEAGUE.

Alliance between England and France—State of parties in Scotland—Assassination of Lennox—The Earl of Mar appointed Regent—Massacre of St. Bartholomew—Its effects on Elizabeth's policy—Killegrew is sent into Scotland—Death of Mar and Knox—Morton appointed Regent—Treaty of Perth—Resistance of the Castilians—Capture of Edinburgh Castle—Death of Lethington—Execution of Grange—Position of Mary Stuart—Morton resigns the Regency—Destruction of the house of Hamilton—Esmé Stewart arrives in Scotland, and becomes the King's favourite—Judgment and execution of Morton—Catholic conspiracy for Mary Stuart's Restoration—Raid of Ruthven—Flight of Lennox—Deliverance of James VI.—Fears of Elizabeth—Her negotiations with Mary Stuart—Projected expedition against England—Elizabeth's rupture with the King of Spain—Formation of a Protestant League to protect the life of Elizabeth—Mary Stuart offers to join it—Leicester is sent to the Netherlands with an army—League to oppose a Catholic invasion of Great Britain. 322

CHAPTER X.

FROM THE FORMATION OF THE PROTESTANT LEAGUE TO THE FRUSTRATION OF BABINGTON'S CONSPIRACY.

Severity of Mary Stuart's treatment—Her complaints against her son—Her residence at Tutbury and Chartley—New schemes of the Catholic party on the Continent—Projected assassination of Elizabeth—Babington enters into the conspiracy—Mary Stuart's ignorance of the plan for Elizabeth's murder —Walsingham's efforts to involve Mary Stuart—Proceedings of Philip II. —Letters of Babington to Mary—They are communicated to Walsingham —Arrest of Babington and his friends—Mary is transferred to Texall— Trial and execution of Babington and his accomplices—Mary Stuart's death is resolved upon. 373

CONTENTS.

CHAPTER XI.

FROM THE FRUSTRATION OF BABINGTON'S CONSPIRACY TO THE DEATH OF MARY STUART.

Deliberations of the English Privy Council—Appointment of a High Court of Justice—Transference of Mary Stuart to Fotheringay Castle—Mary refuses to appear before the Court—She at last resolves to defend herself—Her accusation and defence—Her discussion with Burghley—Her condemnation—Elizabeth hesitates to execute the sentence—Intervention of the Kings of France and Scotland to save Mary's life—Elizabeth signs her death-warrant—Paulet refuses to put Mary Stuart to death clandestinely—Mary's execution. 401

CHAPTER XII.

CONCLUSION.

Effect produced by Mary Stuart's execution—Elizabeth's pretended indignation—Anger of the Kings of France and Scotland—Elizabeth pacifies them—Philip II. resolves to avenge Mary's death—His preparations to invade England—The Invincible Armada—Its defeat—Triumph of Protestantism in Great Britain—Summary of Mary Stuart's life and character. . . 442

HISTORY

OF

MARY, QUEEN OF SCOTS.

CHAPTER I.

INTRODUCTION.

Scotland before the Reign of Mary Stuart—Wars with England for the Maintenance of her Independence—Conflicts of her Kings and Barons—Her Condition at the Death of James V. and Accession of Mary Stuart.

UNTIL the time when England and Scotland were united together under the name of Great Britain, no country in Europe was more disturbed by foreign invasion and domestic warfare than Scotland. Under none of her national Kings did she undergo so many revolutions, or present a series of such tragical catastrophes as under Mary Stuart. This Queen, whose life was a tissue of misfortunes from beginning to end, was scarcely six days old when she was called to the throne. Compelled ere long to fly her kingdom, she married the heir to the crown of France, who died when she was eighteen years of age. Left a widow in early youth, she returned into Scotland, where the Protestant revolution had just taken place, and where she found the ancient untractableness of the feudal barons augmented by all the fanaticism which is inspired by a sudden change in religious belief. In a very short time, she was imprisoned, deposed, and proscribed; and, in order to escape from the violence of her subjects, she fell into the power of her neighbours, who kept her in captivity for nineteen years, and finally beheaded her upon the scaffold.

In relating, after so many others, her touching and tragical history, I shall endeavour to depict its occurrences in all their reality, and to leave no uncertainty as to their true causes. To the documents which have recently been employed or discovered, I shall add others, hitherto unpublished. Thus provided with more complete materials than any of my predecessors, I shall, perhaps, be able to shed some new light upon the obscurer points of the subject. Free from all prepossession on either side, I shall be neither the apologist nor the traducer of this lovely Queen, who possesses a host of passionate admirers even at the present day. I shall not judge Mary Stuart as she would be judged by a Catholic or a Protestant, a Scotchman or an Englishman. With the calm impartiality of history, I shall strive to show how far her misfortunes were merited, and how far they were the result of necessity, by giving such an explanation of her position and conduct, as shall be devoid at once of indulgence and of harshness. In the first place, however, it is indispensably necessary briefly to describe the political state of Scotland, and the spirit of the Presbyterian revolution, both of which exercised great influence upon the destiny of Mary Stuart.

Situated at the northern extremity of the island of Britain, with a surface diversified by mountains, lakes, and plains; cold, poor, and warlike; Scotland had uniformly succeeded in defending herself against the different conquerors who had successively occupied the southern portion of the island. In ancient times, she had escaped from the Roman yoke; from the arms of the Saxons, Angles, and Danes, at the period of the Germanic invasions; and from the dominion of the Anglo-Normans, during the feudal period. Her rude and intrepid inhabitants were divided into clans, governed by the head of the family or tribe, whom his followers served with fidelity, and for whom they would willingly sacrifice their lives. All the members of the same clan bore the same name; and between clan and clan were entertained, for injuries inflicted, and murders committed, those hereditary feelings of vengeance, those deadly hatreds, which form one of the principal characteristics of that primitive state of society in which the family constitutes the only bond of association. A remnant of the ancient Gallic race, they possessed an enterprising character, a quarrelsome disposition, indomitable courage, changeful tastes, and almost equally changeless manners. At the time of Mary Stuart, they still retained the language, the costume, the organization, and, to some extent, the arms of the Celtic tribes.

During the period which elapsed from the end of the eleventh century, until nearly the end of the thirteenth, their national Kings had admitted, or allowed to penetrate into the Lowlands of Scotlands, some fugitive Saxons and adventurous Normans, who had established themselves there less as conquerors than as colonists. At about the same time, the feudal system of the Germanic nations was introduced, beside the patriarchal system of the Gallic tribes, which had continued to prevail among the

Grampian Mountains in the north, and the Cheviot Hills in the south, as well as throughout the marshy lands which divided Scotland from England. From this period, there existed in this small kingdom two peoples, two languages, two states of society, two forms of organization. The old Celtic race kept to the mountainous country; the Germanic race of the Anglo-Saxons and Normans occupied the plains. The wild *Highlanders*, as they were called, spoke Gaelic; the armed colonists of the Lowlands spoke English. The former continued to live in clans, the latter under the institutions of feudalism; and while the first recognized no bond but that of family relationship, the others acknowledged all the political and territorial framework of a military society.

War, so to speak, was of permanent existence in Scotland, where very few towns were built, but which literally bristled with fortresses, into which the inhabitants of the country used to retire whenever a private feud broke out. To the quarrels, which were of continual occurrence between clan and clan, as well as between the Highlanders and Lowlanders, were added foreign wars of no mean importance. The Anglo-Norman Kings, who had invaded Ireland and conquered Wales, aspired to become the masters of Scotland also. They would thus have reduced under their sway all that portion of the British Isles in which the Gallic race still maintained its independence. Several times had they entered into Scotland victoriously, and even seemed to have completely established themselves therein under Edward I. and Edward III., in spite of the heroic efforts of Wallace, and the obstinate resistance of Robert Bruce. In all probability they would, at this period, have annexed Scotland to England, if they had not been compelled, to employ all their forces in the defence or aggrandisement of their possessions on the Continent. The long wars which they waged against the Kings of France, for more than a century, prevented them from completing the conquest of Ireland, and consolidating that of Scotland. Thus we find, that in 1357, when David II. was restored to the throne so gloriously founded by his father Robert Bruce, the national independence of Scotland had been placed beyond dispute, and was no longer menaced by the Kings of England.

France had largely contributed to insure this great result. Exposed to the continual attacks of the same enemy, she had contracted an alliance with Scotland, which lasted from the thirteenth century until the end of the sixteenth, and was of equal advantage to both countries, as it enabled each in turn to get rid of the English. This alliance was carefully maintained by the Kings of France, who sent assistance to the Scotch when they were in peril, and received support from the Scotch in their own wars; who surrounded themselves by a Scottish guard, gave titles and lands to several members of the important houses of Stuart, Douglas, and Hamilton; and opened their court as an asylum or a school to those of the Scottish nobility who came to the Continent in search of refuge or education. It lasted until the end of the sixteenth century, and exercised no slight influence upon the destiny of Mary Stuart, by rendering her a Frenchwoman by her birth, her education, her first marriage, and her manners; and by originating that spirit of insurrection among the high aristocracy of Scotland, which reached so inordinate a height during the minority and absence of this princess.

The five kings who preceded Mary Stuart upon the throne, in obedience to the general tendency which prompted every State to a concentration of authority, had vainly endeavoured to subject this formidable nobility to the monarchical sway. A political struggle had then commenced between them and the great barons, which took the place of the national conflict between the Scotch and English. The great barons, many of whom were at once heads of clans and feudal lords, had considerable forces at their disposal. The chieftain of the Black Douglas clan alone, who held the Scottish marches in the south, had from one thousand to fifteen hundred horsemen as his ordinary escort, and could at any time bring an army of forty thousand men into the field. The Kings, on the contrary, possessed neither permanent troops, nor financial resources. Their strength consisted entirely in the royal title, which was not, however, always respected; and their principal means of action was the fleeting and changeable attachment of the great families, whom they employed as checks upon each other. Notwithstanding this limited power, the daring dynasty of the Stuarts, who had succeeded, by marriage, to the throne of Robert Bruce, laboured almost incessantly, from 1423 until 1542, to diminish the influence and humble the pride of the high aristocracy.

This difficult task was commenced by James I. On his return to Scotland, after twenty years of captivity in England, he took the English government for his model, and endeavoured to establish it in his own country. In order to overawe all resistance, he made an expedition into the Highlands, and seized no fewer than forty chiefs of clans. He next attacked several of the great lords who ruled over their possessions as absolute sovereigns,—thus striking a heavy blow at the two aristocracies whose existence hampered the exercise of the royal authority. He also interdicted the confederations of the barons; divided the Parliament of Scotland, which had previously formed a single House in which the nobility predominated, into two Houses; provided for the more vigorous administration of justice, by bringing under its cognizance, at assizes held four times a year throughout the kingdom, those disputes which it had been customary to settle by an appeal to arms; and resumed from their unlawful or rebellious possessors those counties and domains which they had either usurped from the crown or employed in opposition to its interests. But the nobles, alarmed at his innovations and severity, arrested further proceedings by an assassination. A plot was formed against him, and the conspirators, having surprised him at Perth, murdered him on the night of the 20th of February, 1436.

All the changes which he had introduced into the State disappeared during the minority of his son, James II.; who, however, resumed his father's plans as soon as he became of age. The Earl of Douglas, the most powerful baron of the south, had made a league with the Earl of Crawford, who possessed great influence in the east, and with the Earl of Ross, who was equally strong in the north. James II., having failed to induce him to renounce this confederation, stabbed him with his own hand in Stirling Castle, whither he had come in reliance upon a safe conduct. After this act of treason and violence, an implacable war arose between the Stuarts and Douglases, who marched against each other at the head of equal forces. The two armies, each consisting of forty thousand men, met on the banks of the river Esk. Either the Stuarts must crush the Douglases, or the Douglases dispossess the Stuarts. The Stuarts gained the victory, in consequence of the dread felt by the nobility of the power of that haughty and ambitious house, which, if it had been victorious, would have threatened them with a more formidable yoke than that of the reigning family. James of Douglas, abandoned by a portion of his troops, was defeated, dispossessed, and banished. With him fell the branch of the Black Douglases; and their possessions were divided between the Red Douglases of the Angus branch, the Hamiltons in the west, and the Scotts of Buccleuch in the south,—three families which rose upon the ruins of the conquered clan, but none of which ever obtained the same importance.

The enterprising James II. did not long survive this success, which rendered him very formidable to his nobility. He was killed in 1460, at twenty-nine years of age, by the bursting of a cannon at the siege of Roxburgh. This fate probably saved him from one similar to that which his father had experienced, and which vas reserved for his son. James III., left a minor, continued the work of his two predecessors as soon as he became old enough to govern. But he acted without discernment and energy. Surrounded by ministers and favourites sprung from the lower ranks of the people, he delegated his authority to persons who endangered, instead of increasing it. Instead of dividing the nobility, he united them against himself, and displayed as much timidity as incapacity in meeting their attacks. In 1482, the Scottish barons deprived him of his vulgar favourites, whom they hanged upon the bridge of Lauder; and in 1488, they gave him battle at Sauchie, and slew him in his flight.

Alarmed or admonished by their unhappy fate, James IV. did not follow the footsteps of his ancestors. He made terms with the Scottish nobility, whom they had attacked, and effected a reconciliation with the Kings of England, whom they had warred against. He then took advantage of this internal tranquillity and external peace to strengthen his kingdom and extend its civilization. He had married the daughter of the politic Henry VII. of England, who had just brought to a conclusion the violent civil wars between the Houses of York and Lancaster, and who readily perceived the advantages which would accrue to his insecurely established sovereignty from such an alliance. The Tudors, whose dynasty was founded by Henry VII., entertained new views with regard to Scotland. They had no intention to incorporate it violently with, or subject it feudally to, England, as the Plantagenets had previously attempted to do. But they were anxious to bring it into alliance with England by marriages and treaties, and thus to withdraw it from that connection with France, which, for two centuries, had so powerfully contributed to frustrate the plans of their predecessors, both at home and on the Continent. To effect the political assimilation of the two countries, and thus prepare the way for their territorial junction —such was the plan which Henry VII. inaugurated by the marriage of his daughter Margaret with James IV., and by a treaty of alliance offensive and defensive, which was the first wound inflicted on the ancient union of Scotland and France. But Henry VIII., who possessed neither the skilful dexterity nor the politic foresight of his father, soon thwarted his intentions. In 1513, he compelled James IV. to form a fresh alliance with

France, and to take up arms against him. The war had, it is true, an issue fatal to the King and nobility of Scotland, who, for once, acted in concert. James IV. was totally defeated. He fell on the battle-field of Flodden, with ten thousand of his troops, among whom were two bishops, two mitred abbots, twelve earls, thirteen lords, five eldest sons of peers, and many nobles of inferior rank. The kingdom fell into the greatest disorder under his young successor, James V., who was under two years of age when he ascended the throne.

During the long minority of James V., the great families of Scotland contended furiously with each other for the supreme authority, and combats between their different factions were of frequent occurrence, even in the streets, of Edinburgh. The Hamiltons and Red Douglases, however, possessed most influence in the country. The chieftain of the former was the Earl of Arran, the nearest heir to the crown after the Stuarts; while the latter obeyed the Earl of Angus, who had married the widow of James IV., and the sister of Henry VIII. The family of the Hamiltons was, in general, faithful to the French policy; while that of the Douglases supported, and strove to extend, English influence throughout the country. After many years of opposition, the two factions entered into a league at the expense of the monarch. The young prince was kept under such strict tutelage that he resembled an actual captive. This led him to conceive an implacable hatred for the Scottish nobility; and to the systematic project for its humiliation which had been pursued by his predecessors, he added an earnest desire to be revenged upon it. As soon as he had succeeded in shaking off the yoke of the Earl of Angus, who governed in his name, he marched against him, and compelled him to seek refuge in England, where this chieftain of the Red Douglases lived an exile during the lifetime of James V.

The impetuous James V. displayed more boldness than his forefathers had shown in restoring the general authority of the crown, and reducing the anarchical power of the nobility. He humbled the Red Douglases as effectually as his great-grandfather, James II. had humbled the elder branch of the family. He next made an expedition to the southern frontier of his kingdom, where the warlike clans of the Hepburns, Homes, Scotts, and Kers, were living in complete insubordination; took their castles, seized their chieftains, and punished their disobedience. He succeeded in inspiring universal dread of his authority and rigour; punished the murders, which were of constant occurrence among his rude and hot-headed subjects;

visited with severe penalties the house-burning and cattle stealing, which had become a common practice in the country; improved its judicial institutions, favoured mental cultivation, gave a stimulus to various kinds of trade, and rendered the internal peace of the nation so secure that it was said on every hand, that 'the furze-bushes kept the cows.'

All these changes were, however, ephemeral. Effected only on the surface of Scottish society, they were not allowed time to penetrate to its depths. Henry VIII. contributed largely to prevent this. This headstrong and imperious prince was desirous that the King, his nephew, should adopt all his plans, both political and religious. When he seceded from the Church of Rome, he urged James V. to introduce into his kingdom, the same change of religious faith which he had just accomplished in his own. He perceived that it was impossible for Scotland to remain Catholic, at the time when England was becoming Protestant, without resuming those continental alliances which his father and himself had been so anxious to break off, and without giving rise to fresh causes of enmity which would renew and aggravate the ancient hostility of the two nations. He, therefore, made most tempting proposals to his nephew, and offered him his eldest daughter in marriage.

James V. hesitated for a moment.[1] The extreme corruption of

[1] He felt great aversion towards the Archbishop of St. Andrews, James Beton, or Beaton, son of the laird of Balfour. Ample evidence of this is supplied by an instruction of James V., inserted by M. Teulet in the two volumes of *Pièces et documents inédits relatifs à l'histoire d'Ecosse au XVI. siècle, tirés des archives et bibliothèques de France*, recently published by the Bannatyne Club. In this instruction, which was prepared for the agents sent by James V. to the Pope, this prince states that during his minority, the Archbishop abused his power in order to enrich himself and his relations; and that, though sprung from a small and poor family, he had married his niece to the chieftain of the Hamiltons, the Earl of Arran, cousin to the King, and the nearest heir to the throne. He adds:—
'Quant nous sommes veneus à l'aige que nostre auctorité estoit entre nous mains, ledict archevesque, portant impatientement d'estre bouté hors de ce gouvernement et auctorité où il estoit paravant, par la richesse et soubstance qu'il avoit amassé et accumelé cidevant par l'usage de nostre auctorité et tuelles aultres subtiles moyens, solicitoit et convenoit (réunissoit) unge grand parte des seigneures, barons et subjectes, et est venu, en manière de guerre, luy-mames en personne avecques eux, et nous a asseigé aprement et activelment par unge pièce de temps, dedans nostre chastiau d'Edinburgh, et nous tenoit là-dedans, jusques à ce que, pour la sauveté de nostre vie et pour éviter grandes dangiers et péricules, nous estions forcés et compellés, contre nostre intention et voloir, de mettre nostre person, auctorité et gouvernement de nostre royalme en ses mains et aucunes aultres ses collèges, estant avec luy par son solistation, a l'èvre desquelles le Comte d'Angus, son frère et oncle, estiont principaulx, lesquelles sont et ont esté par longe temps nous (nos) rebelles évecques (avec) nous (nos) enemys d'Engleterre, lesquelles

the Scottish clergy, who united to the laxity then universally charged against churchmen, the gross habits and violent manners of the Scottish nobility, made the King incline towards a reformation. The immense property possessed by the clergy also tempted him. He even permitted the poet, Sir David Lindsay, and Dr. George Buchanan, to publish satires against the monks and priests, which obtained a large share of public favour. But he quickly changed his mind. He saw, or it was explained to him, that by humiliating the clergy he would strengthen the nobility, and that the property of the former of these bodies could not be taken from it, without passing, in great measure to the second. To act thus, would be to thwart the projects of his predecessors, and to disavow his own previous actions,—to abandon the plan which had been pursued for more than a century with regard to the nobility, in order to adopt one diametrically opposed to it. James V. further consided that the clergy, in whose ranks resided nearly all the talent in the kingdom, and who supplied the majority of men competent to exercise high civil functions, would, by their disappearance, plunge Scotland in ignorance, and deprive him of all counterpoise to the parliamentary, as well as territorial, influence of the feudal aristocracy. The primate Beaton, Archbishop of St. Andrews, and the other bishops, furnished him with another reason for leaving them alone, by offering him in the name of the clergy, an annual subsidy of fifty thousand crowns out of the rents of the Kirk,[1] which was destined to satisfy his covetousness, and aid him to defend himself against Henry VIII., if that prince became discontented and declared war.

Compelled to choose between the ruin of the Catholic Church and the humiliation of the feudal nobility, James V. resolved to persevere in the latter course, but in rejecting the oppressive friendship of Henry VIII., it became necessary for him to recur to the protective alliance of Francis I. He was therefore forced to return to the ancient policy of his family and country. In 1536, he proceeded to France in order to consummate his marriage with Magdalen, the daughter of Francis I.[2] This princess

---

sont la principale cause et occasion des grandes dommages que nous et nostre dict royalme a sustenu de par nous dictes enemys d'Engleterre.' Pp. 97, 98. This document, which extends over pages 95—108, is exceedingly interesting and valuable.

[1] Memoirs of Sir James Melvil of Halhill, p. 4. (Lond., 1683.)

[2] M. Teulet has published a project of marriage with Mary of Bourbon, daughter of the Duke de Vendôme, whom James V. visited in September, 1536, in disguise, and whom he did not marry, because she did not please him (vol. i. pp. 109-121), and some curious documents relative to his residence and expenses in France. from the end of December, 1536, until April, 1537 (vol. i. pp. 122-126).

dying a few months after her marriage, he took as his second wife, during the year following, Mary of Lorraine, widow of the Duke of Longueville, and sister of Duke Francis of Guise. This union was indicative of the policy which he intended to pursue, both with regard to the religious innovators, whose doctrines were secretly gaining ground in Scotland, and to the territorial nobles, who endured with impatience the pressure of his authority. He persecuted the Protestants by stringent laws and cruel executions, and extended his violence to the chief families of the kingdom. Every suspicion of a conspiracy on the part of the latter was followed by condign punishment. Goaded to the last degree of irritation and hatred, the nobles only awaited an opportunity for giving expression to their feelings regarding James V. Such an opportunity quickly presented itself.

Henry VIII. renewed his solicitations to the King of Scotland to unite with him in introducing the Reformation into his country. He even proceded to York, where James V. had promised to meet him. But for six days the uncle waited in vain for his nephew, and furious at this want of respect, immediately declared war against him. This was a perilous moment for James V. He could not repulse the King of England without the armed assistance of the Scottish nobles, who were more disposed to cripple his strength than to render him victorious. This feeling was soon manifested. When the English retired into their own country, after having ravaged the frontiers of Scotland, the Scottish nobles refused to pursue them beyond the border, declaring to James V. that this war was injurious to the interests of the kingdom; and that, moreover, the retreat of the enemy rendered its continuation useless. Their bold defection plunged the unfortunate monarch into deep dejection. He nevertheless prepared an expedition against England, intrusting the command to Oliver Sinclair, whom the nobles detested as a favourite of the King and friend of the clergy, and who advanced by the western frontier at the head of ten thousand men. The Scottish army, having met five hundred English near the eastern extremity of Solway Frith, fled before them, preferring to humiliate the King by suffering a defeat, rather than strengthen him by gaining a victory which would turn to the advantage of his authority. The ignominious and significant defeat of Solway Moss drove James V. to despair. Fever seized him, and he died on the 14th of December, 1542, in the Castle of Falkland, in the thirty-first year of his age. A few days before his death he learned that his wife had just given birth to a daughter at Linlithgow; and, referring to the fact that a granddaughter of Robert Bruce had brought the crown of Scotland into the Stuart family, he said mournfully : ' It came by a woman, and it will go by one.'[1] This daughter was Mary Stuart, born on the 8th of December, 1542.

At the time when this Queen, whose long minority was destined to restore and extend the anarchical domination of the nobility, ascended the throne, the work of transformation undertaken by the five Kings who had preceded her, had made externally little progress. The ancient condition of Scotland was hardly at all changed. Few towns had been enlarged, and very few built, although the country still bristled with fortresses. The clans and fiefs subsisted in all their primitive vigour. They found no counterpoise either in the commons, who had not yet received sufficient development, or in the monarchy, which had not yet become sufficiently powerful. The Kings had, indeed, attempted to introduce into Scotland some general organization of the state, but without the success which had attended similar efforts in other countries. The legislative power, the national forces, and the judicial authority—which last remained hereditary, not only in the domains of the barons, but also in the royal districts, where it was exercised by the officers called seneschals, bailiffs, or stewards,[2]— were retained in the hands of the nobility, who directed the Parliaments, sat in the tribunals of justice, composed the feudal army, and even obtained the provostship of the towns.

The Parliament of Scotland consisted of a single assembly. King James I. had for a time divided it into two Houses, like the English Parliament; but this innovation had not been continued: Restored to its ancient form, the Parliament of Scotland formed the Great Council of the country, in which the lords spiritual and temporal, the deputies of the burghs, and the officers of the crown deliberated in common. The landed aristocracy greatly predominated in it. By an arrangement peculiar to Scotland, a small

---

[1] 'It will end as it began; the crown came by a woman, and it will go by one; miseries approach this poor kingdom; King Henry will labour to make it his own, by arms or by marriage.'—Keith's History of the Affairs of Church and State in Scotland, p. 22. (Edinb., 1734.)

[2] See the *Estat et Constitution du Royaulme d'Escosse en Janvier*, 1559. This document is printed in pp. 223-242 of the *Négociations, lettres, et pièces diverses relatives au règne de François II.*, published by M. Louis Paris in the large collection of inedited documents respecting the history of France (Paris, 1841). It is signed by J. Makgill, clerk of the register, and J. Bellenden, justice-clerk. The barons, seneschals, bailiffs, stewards, and provosts of towns had both civil and criminal jurisdiction. (Ib. pp. 229-233.) 'Tous lesquels seneschaulx ont leurs offices en héritage du père au fils, et ainsi de degré en degré.' (Ib. p. 229.) 'Chacuns lesdits officiers ont leurs offices en héritages.' (Ib. p. 233.)

Council of thirty-two members was detached from the greater one, under the name of the *Committee of the Lords of the Articles*, which prepared all the business which was to be discussed during the session. This Committee directed the Parliament by which it was elected.

The Kings of Scotland had attempted to institute some general administration of justice superior to that of the feudal barons. This was at first itinerant, at assizes held every three months, in the different parts of the kingdom, by the *Lords of Session*, who were created by James I. It became stationary under James IV., by the establishment at Edinburgh of the *Court of Daily Council*. Finally, it was rendered still more complete by James V., who founded the *College of Justice*.[1] But, as it was still administered by the nobles themselves, it remained in too great dependence upon their passions and quarrels. Where there is no impartial public influence, there can be no respected general justice. Justice then becomes nothing more than a form of oppression; and the strong use it to crush the weak.

In Scotland, at this time, the Kings had not succeeded in organizing any public influence to support them. Possessed of very moderate revenues, they were not able to maintain any permanent troops.[2] Their army had remained feudal. At the first signal, all those who owed military service flocked to their standards, to remain a very short time. The Kings had neither forces sufficient to crush the nobility, nor any regular administration which they could substitute for their disorderly authority. Compelled to employ the territorial barons against each other, they dispossessed those who opposed them, to aggrandize those

[1] 'Les derniers et suprêmes juges en le royaulme sont les *Seigneurs de la Session*, aultrement nommés le *Collége de Justice*. . . . Lesdits seigneurs sont au nombre de quinze, sçavoir est un président et aultres sept tousjours de l'estat spirituel, et sept aultres gens laïques.' (Ib. p. 231.) If within three days after the commission of a crime, the barons, bailiffs, seneschals, and stewards, do not punish its perpetrators, 'leur jurisdiction est pour ce expirée, et partant sont tenus de mettre ès mains de la suprême justice les dits meurtriers et mutillateurs.' (Ib. p. 232.)

[2] In 1551, the king's revenue amounted only to ninety thousand crowns, according to a Venetian ambassador. 'Sono piu abondanti d'huomini che di richesse, perche il re non ha 90^m scudi d'entrata.' Relatione d'Inghilterra et Scotia di Messer Daniele Barbaro, che fu ambasciatore al re Edouardo del 1551, et poi Patriarche eletto d'Aquileia. (Nat. Lib. Paris, MS. Saint Germain, No. 793, fol. 29.) According to Lethington, Mary Stuart's Secretary of State, she derived, in 1563, an annual income of two hundred thousand crowns from Scotland. He made this statement to the Spanish ambassador, Quadra, who wrote to Philip II.: —'Dixome que vale dozientos mille escudos de renta, lo que su ama possee en Escocia.' (Quadra to the King. MS. Despatch, March 18, 1563. Archives of Simancas.)

who were favourable to them. They thus varied the distribution of the power of the aristocracy without weakening it as a whole; and instead of breaking in pieces the framework of feudalism, they filled it up in a different manner. The consequence was that they merely changed their antagonists. They had indeed endeavoured to render the royal domain inalienable, to recover the usurped rights of the crown, to abolish the hereditary guardianship of the frontiers, to diminish as much as possible the number of hereditary offices, and to interdict all confederations of the barons; but, yielding to the irresistible influence of usage and necessity, they had distributed the property which they had confiscated, restored the titles which they had withdrawn, continued the hereditary offices which they had interdicted, and most of them had found themselves unable to prevent the leagues which they had condemned.[1]

Of the five Kings who occupied the throne before Mary Stuart, two had been assassinated, James I. and James III.; two had fallen in battle, James II. and James IV.; and the last, James V., had died of despair at beholding himself deserted by his nobility, whom he had hoped to subjugate, and at finding himself defeated at the moment when he believed his triumph secure. All the five had fallen victims to the antagonism of the Scottish aristocracy, or to the hostility of England. Placed in circumstances too powerful for them to resist, they had all, while still young, lost their lives in battle or by conspiracy. The

[1] The state of Scotland at the middle of the sixteenth century, is thus described by the Venetian ambassador, Barbaro:—' In questo regno ci sono grandi dissensioni civili per la potentia et odii perticulari dei signori. Usano due lingue; una i domestici, et questa poca lontana dall' Inglese; l'altra, i selvaggi che del tutto parlano diversamente. Governa il Re col consilio dei principi; usano le legge civili; fanno i parlamenti al modo Inglese. Sono piu abondanti d'huomini che di richesse, perche il re non ha 90^m scud d'entrata, et sono tanti che si alla sprovista comparessa un essercito di 50^m persone, non passarebbono dieci hore, che trovaria rencontro. Danosi i segni coi fumi sopra i monti. Corrono al romore armati di camiscia di maglia, di celata, lancia et spada una mano et mezza, laquale pero manegiano con una destramente. Giunti al luogo del combattere, lasciano i cavilli, quali sono del vincitore, perche non si partono di luego finche si combatte. Hanno per ogni lega due fortezze o rocche dove ricorrono le genti a salvarsi ne primi impeti delle questioni private. Il paese non ha terra murata d'importanza. Quando il regno e sotto governatori per esser el re pupillo, il governatore e' como re assoluto, tira l'entrate et commanda, et quando restituisce el regno non e obligato a render conto de cosa alcuna. . . . Li Scocesi hanno più giuste cause di venir ad assaltar l'Inghilterra che Inglesi la Scotia, perche il paese da se e' poverissimo, et gli huomini di sua natura poco industriosi se dilletano più presto di latrocinii che di fatiche.' Relatione d'Inghilterra et Scotia di Messer Daniele Barbaro. (Nat Lib. Paris, MS. Saint Germain, No. 793, fols. 29 and 30.)

oldest of them had not completed his forty-first year, and all had left infants to succeed them. During five successive and prolonged minorities, there had been not merely a suspension of the royal work, but even a paralysis of the monarchy. The nobles regained all the power they had lost, and Scotland relapsed into her former disorders. It was thus that, in spite of their plans and efforts, these five Kings, by allowing the same state of society to subsist, handed down to each other the same dangers. These dangers were multiplied in the case of Mary Stuart, during whose minority such a revolution was effected in the religious belief of the nation, as added fresh causes of insubordination and conflict to those already in existence. The Protestant Reformation occurred to strengthen and extend the anarchy of the aristocracy.

CHAPTER II.

FROM THE ACCESSION OF MARY STUART TO HER RETURN FROM FRANCE INTO SCOTLAND.

Minority of Mary Stuart—War with England—Mary is sent to France—Regency of Mary of Lorraine—Marriage of Mary Stuart—Her Pretensions to the Crown of England—Origin and progress of Protestantism in Scotland—Treaty of Berwick—Death of the Regent—Treaty of Edinburgh—Mary Stuart becomes a Widow, and returns to Scotland.

MARY STUART was the first woman who ever occupied the throne of Scotland; and to the weakness attaching to her sex she added that of her tender age. The regency of the kingdom, which would naturally be of long duration under a Queen who was scarcely six days old when she succeeded her father, was contended for by Cardinal Beaton, Archbishop of St. Andrews,[1] whose rank as primate placed him at the head of the Scottish Church, and by James Hamilton, Earl of Arran, and heir presumptive to the crown, who was supported by the majority of the barons. The head of the nobility gained an easy victory over the head of the clergy. The Earl of Arran was intrusted by the assembled Parliament with the regency of the kingdom, and

---

[1] It even appears that he induced the dying King, some few minutes before he expired, to sign a blank paper, which was afterwards converted into a will, in which the Archbishop was appointed tutor to the young Queen, and Governor of the kingdom. The Earls of Argyle, Huntly, and Arran were named as his councillors and assessors in the administration. This will was published at Edinburgh, but its provisions were not carried into effect by the nobility, who would probably not have obeyed it, even if they had not doubted its authenticity. (Keith, p. 25.)

the guardianship of the young Queen. Mary Stuart was thereupon crowned, on the 9th of September, 1543, at Stirling, by Cardinal Beaton.

From this period were formed, and called into action, those two parties which were destined to dispute with each other for the power, the person, and the inheritance of Mary Stuart, and to seek the support of England and France respectively in their undertaking. The first faction, composed originally of the greater part of the nobility who were now restored to the possession of their independence, withdrew the government entirely from the hands of the second, which consisted of the clergy, and was directed by the discontented primate,[1] in concert with the Queen Dowager, at this moment perfectly powerless. Henry VIII. did not fail to seize an opportunity so favourable for the accomplishment of his designs upon Scotland. Some years before he had offered his daughter Mary in marriage to James V., and he now demanded the hand of Mary Stuart for his son, the Prince of Wales.[2] This proposal was as politic as it was opportune. By the union of the heiress of Scotland with the heir of England, the union of the two countries would be effected naturally and without difficulty. But Henry VIII. caused the failure of his own project. His fiery spirit, which could neither suffer delay, nor brook uncertainty, rendered him at once too impatient and too exacting. He claimed the guardianship of the young Queen until she had reached a marriageable age, and meanwhile he required that several of the strongest fortresses in the kingdom should be placed in his hands. This was not attempting the conquest of the kingdom, as the Edwards had done, but confiscating the monarchy, and placing Scotland under the provisional sequestration of England.

This unwise precipitancy, and an unreasonable exaction justly offensive to Scottish pride, were very injurious to Henry VIII., who soon found himself compelled to diminish his pretensions. He contented himself with requiring that Mary Stuart should be sent into England when she had attained the tenth year of her age, that she might there espouse the Prince of Wales, as soon as it was possible for the marriage to be celebrated. A treaty was

---

[1] The Cardinal, who had invited the Duke of Guise to come in arms and assume the government of the kingdom, was himself placed in custody of Lord Seton, at Blackness Castle. (Keith, p. 27.)

[2] This was foreseen by James V., whose last words were, 'Miseries approach this poor kingdom; King Henry will labour to make it his own, by arms or by marriage.' (Keith, p. 27.)

concluded upon these conditions, on the 1st of July, 1543. But even this treaty was repugnant to the mind of the nation, and influenced Scotland strongly in favour of an alliance with France. The Earl of Arran, whose family had always been friends of France, and whom the interests of his ambition alone had momentarily biassed in favour of England, now joined the Queen Dowager, from whom he as yet feared nothing, and the Cardinal Primate, who had ceased to be formidable. This junction once more produced a sudden change in the policy of Scotland. The treaty with Henry VIII. was annulled five months after it had been concluded, and a close alliance with France was signed at Edinburgh, on the 15th of December, by the Regent and Estates of Scotland, who ratified, in the name of Mary Stuart, all the treaties which had been entered into between the two countries since the time of Robert Bruce.

War with England was thus rendered inevitable. Henry VIII., furiously incensed, immediately declared it; and sent into the Frith of Forth a fleet which ravaged its coasts, and even threatened to burn the city of Edinburgh. A short time afterwards, an English army crossed the southern frontier, and repeatedly laid waste the Scottish territory. To demand Mary Stuart in marriage in this violent manner, was to render it certain that he would not obtain her. By this impolitic war, Henry succeeded only in inspiring the Scotch with an universal hatred of the English, whose party dwindled rapidly away; induced them to summon auxiliary troops from France, and excited a violent persecution of the religious reformers, who were attached to his cause, and whose leaders, already numerous, were taken in the Castle of St. Andrews, and sent to work in chains in the French galleys. He died in January, 1547, very far from attaining the object he had so long pursued, having failed in his attempts to unite the two houses of the Stuarts and the Tudors, and thus to blend into one the two kingdoms of Scotland and England.

The Duke of Somerset, the maternal uncle of Edward VI., and Protector of the kingdom during his minority, carried on the plans of the late King with equal vigour. During the year in which Henry VIII. died, he entered Scotland at the head of an army, which he offered to lead back into England if the Scotch would promise that their Queen should not be sent to the Continent until she was of marriageable age, and if they would break off all connection with France. But the latter preferred to fight rather than submit to English dictation, and on the 10th of

September, 1547, they fought and lost the battle of Pinkie. This fatal defeat, which cost them more than ten thousand men, opened Scotland to their inveterate enemies. The English advanced as far as Leith, and subsequently established themselves in the southern part of the country, where they took up a strong position, and received the submission of the principal lairds of the warlike districts of that frontier.

Weakened, but nothing daunted, by this great reverse, the national party in Scotland had recourse to France, which alone was able effectually to protect their country against the arms of England. In order to interest her in their cause by other than political reasons, they were ready to offer her that which the English so ardently desired,—the guardianship and the inheritance of Mary Stuart. This princess, now nearly six years of age, had hitherto resided in Stirling Castle, with her two governors, the Lords Erskine and Livingston. After the battle of Pinkie, she was removed from that fortress, which was in danger of being attacked, to the monastery of Inchmahome, situated in a little island in the lake of Menteith,[1] which was less exposed to the incursions of the English army. The Queen Dowager, in concert with the Regent, then conceived the twofold plan of sending her daughter to the Continent, and affiancing her to the young Dauphin of France, who was about the same age as herself. The overtures which this politic princess made on the subject to the Scottish nobility and the court of France, were eagerly received by both parties;[2] for all found their advantage in the scheme. The kingdom would acquire a protector capable of maintaining its independence; the Queen Dowager hoped she would ere long be appointed Regent; and the court of France expected to find, in an indissoluble alliance, the certain means of keeping England in check. But none derived greater advantages from it than the nobility of Scotland, whose turbulent predominance could not fail to gain strength from the absence of Mary Stuart, and her marriage in a foreign land.

As soon as this project had been adopted by both parties, Henry II., who had succeeded Francis I., three months after the accession of Edward VI., sent a fleet into the Forth, manned by six thousand men, and provided with an excellent train of artillery, under the command of André de Montalembert, Lord of Essé. This leader of the auxiliary troops, when introduced into the Scottish Parliament, announced that the King his master,

[1] Tytler's History of Scotland (Edinb., 1846), vol. iv., p. 409.
[2] Ibid., vol. iv., p. 410.

happy to cement the ancient union of the two countries by the marriage of their two heirs, willingly undertook to defend Scotland, and to educate the young Queen at his court, and solemnly pledged himself to respect the laws and liberties of the kingdom.[1] This transaction completely disconcerted the plans of the Lord Protector, who had conquered Scotland without making her yield, and who, by devastating her territory, had only alienated her still more from England. He immediately published a manifesto, in which he disavowed any other design than that of uniting the two countries by a marriage, upon a footing of perfect equality, and under the common denomination of Britain. He declared that he was desirous thereby to put an end to the wars which had so long raged between them, to their mutual disadvantage. But his political reasonings met with no greater success than his military expeditions. The Duke of Somerset then attempted to prevent the young Queen of Scotland from proceeding to France. He despatched a fleet under the command of Admiral Clinton[2] to intercept her passage, feeling certain that whichever of the two countries obtained the guardianship of her person, would be finally placed in possession of her kingdom.

The Queen Dowager, by the prudence and wisdom of her measures, preserved her daughter from this danger. She quickly conducted the young Mary from Inchmahome to Dumbarton, whither had proceeded, with no less haste than secrecy, the French Admiral Villegagnon, accompanied by four galleys, intended to convey her to France. The young princess embarked on board the royal galley with her two governors, her natural brother, Lord James Stuart, who was then seventeen years of age, and four companions of her own age belonging to the noble families of Fleming, Seton, Beaton, and Livingston. They were called the four Marys, because they all bore the same name. The little fleet, with its precious freight on board, left the western coast of Scotland on the 7th of August, a short time before the English squadron arrived at St. Abb's Head to oppose its departure. After a pleasant voyage, it arrived in safety in the harbour of Brest on the 13th of August. Mary was conducted to Saint Germain, where the court at that time resided, and was received and treated as a daughter by Henry II. He assigned her a household worthy her rank, and had her brought up with his own children.[3]

All was now consummated. As the policy of union had not succeeded between Scotland and England, the old policy of rivalry

---

[1] Tytler, vol. iv., p. 417.   [2] Ibid.   [3] Ibid., vol. iv., p. 418.

and animosity was resumed, to be practised during all the rest of
the century, sometimes with violence and sometimes with craftiness. After Mary Stuart's departure for the Continent, hostilities
continued for two more years against her kingdom.[1] But the war
changed its character, now that the Scotch had been reinforced
by French troops. The English were defeated, lost most of the
positions which they had occupied since the battle of Pinkie, and
decided to evacuate the Scottish territory, and conclude a peace,
which was signed at Boulogne on the 24th of March, and proclaimed at Edinburgh on the 20th of April, 1550. They were
not, however, the less detested by their neighbours, all whose
antipathies they had reawakened by a war of nine years' duration.

The ten years which followed the peace of 1550 witnessed the
progress, establishment, and fall of the French dominion in Scotland. The Queen Dowager, whose ambition equalled her address,
then aspired to govern her daughter's kingdom. In her efforts to
obtain the regency she displayed the same ability which she had
used to secure a close alliance between France and Scotland, and
to contrive the marriage of Mary Stuart with the Dauphin. She
had no difficulty in securing the interested support of Henry II.
This prince, at whose court her two brothers, Duke Francis of
Guise and the Cardinal of Lorraine, possessed great influence,
placed the dukedom of Chatelherault at the disposal of the Earl
of Arran, if the chieftain of the Hamiltons would resign the
regency. Mary of Lorraine also gained over the nobility by
making them offers which tempted their avidity; the Protestant
party, which was already considerable, by showing great toleration
for their doctrines; and the Earl of Huntly, who was the chief
of the Gordons and the most powerful noble in the North, by
promising to give him the earldom of Murray, and to create his
eldest son Earl of Rothsay. At the same time she obtained for
herself the tutelage of her daughter as the first step towards the
administration of the kingdom. But it was not until after four
years of intrigues and efforts that she attained her object. In the
spring of 1554 the feeble Earl of Arran surrendered to her the
regency, in exchange for which he received the duchy of Chatelherault and a handsome pension from France. He kept Dum-

[1] The events of this war are related in a very lively, detailed, and interesting
manner in a little book of 119 pages, 12mo., printed some year after, and entitled,
'Histoire de la Guerre d'Escosse, traitant comme le royaume fut assailly et en
grand partie occupé par les Anglois, et depuis rendu paisible à sa reyne, et reduit
en son ancien estat et dignité. Par Jean de Beaugué, gentilhomme François. A
Paris, pour Gilles Corrozet, en la grand' salle du Palais, 1556.' I am indebted
for this book to the kindness of M. de Montalembert.

barton Castle until the Queen became of age, was acknowledged to be the second person in the kingdom, and in the event of Mary Stuart's death would have succeeded to the throne. Mary of Lorraine, in the presence and with the consent of the estates of Scotland, received from her daughter, then nearly twelve years of age, the title and authority of Regent.[1]

This able princess had now reached the end which she had never ceased to pursue. She had hitherto made no mistakes, which are more easily avoided when we desire than when we possess, when we aspire to rule than when we govern. When she stood in need of every one's favour, she was careful to keep on good terms with all. But this ceased to be the case as soon as she had acquired the royal authority. Influenced by a bias which it would have been difficult to avoid, she displayed too much favour towards France, to which country she owed her elevation. She conferred several of the great offices of the kingdom upon Frenchmen, giving the authority of Vice-Chancellor to M. de Rubay, the post of Comptroller to M. de Villemore, the government of Orkney to M. de Bonton, and leaving the general conduct of affairs to M. d'Oysel, who was her confidential adviser in all matters of state.[2] This administration of Scotland by foreigners

[1] Tytler, vol. iv., pp. 429, 430.

[2] This was one of the principal complaints which the Scottish lords, after their insurrection in 1559, preferred against the administration of the Regent. They thus refer to the subject: 'Magnum Schotiæ sigillum rectrix tantisper penes se esse voluit donec ex Parisiensi senatu advocatus Rubœus quidam in Schotiam est accersitus. Is postquam appulit, ad perstringendos popularium oculos, Cancellarii quidem nomen Huntlæo Comiti ... restitutum est ... ita quidem ut titulo tenus Huntlæus esset Cancellarius, re autem ipsâ Rubœus. Villamoro cuidam Gallo primi ordinis magistratus demandatus est, quem nos a subducendis rationibus regiis computorum rotulatorem dicimus. D'Oyzillus, ad cujus nutum omnia gerebantur," &c. *Manifesto addressed by the Lords of the Congregation to the Princes of Christendom in* 1559, printed by M. Teulet in his *Pièces et documents inédits relatifs à l'histoire d'Ecosse*, vol. i., pp. 416-419. In page 416 it is also stated: 'Visum est ut, quemadmodum regni totius habenas Galla in manibus haberet, ita etiam inferiora reipublicæ munera Galli obirent.'

The office of *Comptroller*, bestowed upon M. de Villemore, was the most important financial office in Scotland. 'Le controlleur est général recepveur des droits appelés la propriété, laquelle gist ès fruitz, rentes et revenuz ordinaires des duchés, comtés, seigneuries et aultres terres propres à la couronne, soit uniz ou non uniz à icelle. ... Aussi est ledit controlleur recepveur général de toutes les grandes coutumes, de toutes et chacunes villes, ports et havres de ce royaulme.' *Estat et Constitution du royaulme d'Escosse*, in page 224 of M. Paris' volume of *Néjociations, &c., sous François II.*

The other financial office was that of *Treasurer*. 'Le trésorier a géneralle intromission et charge sur les casualités, lesquelles consistent ès droitz et prouffitz qui, par accident et adventure, viennent à la couronne.' Ibid., p. 225. Among these were confiscations, fines, inheritances by bastardy, &c

was unwise and dangerous. It excited the jealousy of the Scottish nobility, who willingly accepted assistance from France, but could not tolerate her dominion.

The rupture did not, however, immediately break out between the French and the Scotch. The Regent still continued to treat all those with consideration whose assistance she needed to secure the marriage of her daughter with the Dauphin, and to defend Scotland against England. The situation of this latter country had totally changed since the accession of Mary Tudor to the throne. The new Queen, undoing, with as much hardihood as hatred, the religious work begun by her father, Henry VIII., and extended under her brother, Edward VI., had violently restored Catholicism. Next, by her marriage with Philip II., she had united England to the vast possessions of the sovereign of Spain, the Two Sicilies, the duchy of Milan, the Netherlands, and America. This union, which was equally alarming to both France and Scotland, could not fail momentarily to draw closer the ties which connected them with each other. It prevented the Catholico-national party from standing aloof from the Regent, and the Anglo-Protestant party from entering into communication with a Queen, who persecuted their religion in England, and with a King, who was its most implacable adversary on the Continent. It also rendered more indispensable and pressingly urgent the marriage of the Queen of Scotland to the Dauphin of France, in order to oppose one alliance to the other.

The mental and personal attractions of Mary Stuart were early developed. She was tall and beautiful.[1] Her eyes beamed with intelligence, and sparkled with animation. She had the most elegantly-shaped hands in the world.[2] Her voice was sweet, her appearance noble and graceful, and her conversation brilliant. She early displayed those rare charms which were destined to make her an object of universal admiration, and which rendered even her infancy seductive. She had been brought up with the daughters of Catherine de Medici, and under the superintendence of the learned Margaret of France, the sister of Henry II.,[3] the

---

[1] 'Venant sur les quinze ans sa beauté commença à paroistre, comme la lumière en beau plein midy.' *Vies des dames illustres, Marie Stuart*, in vol. v., p. 83 of the *Œuvres complètes du Seigneur de Brantôme* (Paris, 1823).

[2] Ibid., vol. v., p. 86.

[3] All these princesses were learned. Brantôme says of Elizabeth of France, who married Philip II., in 1559: 'Elle avoit un beau sçavoir, comme la reyne sa mère l'avoit faicte bein estudier par M. de Sainct-Estienne son précepteur.... Elle aymoit fort la poësie et à la lire.' Vol. v., p. 140.

Of Margaret of France, who, in 1572, married the King of Navarre, afterwards

protectress of Michel de l'Hôpital, and who subsequently married the Duke of Savoy. The court, in the midst of which Mary Stuart had grown up, was then the most magrificent, the most elegant, the most joyous, and we must add, one of the most lax, in Europe. Still retaining certain military customs of the middle ages, and at the same time conforming to the intellectual usages of the time of the *renaissance*, it was half chivalric and half literary,—mingling tournaments with studies, hunting with erudition, mental achievements with bodily exercises, the ancient and rough games of skill and strength with the novel and delicate pleasures of the arts.

Nothing could equal the splendour and vivacity which Francis I. had introduced into his court[1] by attracting thither all the principal nobility of France, by educating as pages therein young gentlemen from all the provinces,[2] by adorning it with nearly two hundred ladies belonging to the greatest families in the kingdom,[3] and by establishing it sometimes in the splendid palaces of Fontainebleau and Saint Germain, which he had either

---

Henry IV. of France, he says : ' Elle se plaist fort aux lettres, . . . aussi peut-on dire d'elle que c'est la princesse, voire la dame qui soit au monde la plus eloquente et la mieulx disante. . . . Elle-mesme compose tant en prose qu'en vers. . . . Ses compositions sont très-belles, doctes, et plaisantes.' Ibid., vol. v., pp. 158, 159, and 160.

Of Claude of France, who married the Duke of Lorraine, he says: ' En son sçavoir et bonté elle resembloit sa tante.' Ibid., p. 242.—This aunt was Margaret of France, daughter of Francis I., who married the Duke of Savoy in 1559, and of whom Brantôme says: ' Elle avoit beaucoup de science, qu'elle entretenoit tousjours par ses continuelles estudes les après-disnées, qu'elle apprenoit des gens sçavants, qu'elle aymoit par-dessus toutes sortes de gens. Aussi l'honoroit-on comme leur déesse et patronne.' Ibid., p. 230.—' Sopra tutto erudita, e ben dotta nella lingua latina, greca, et anche italiana.' Narrative of Marino Cavalli, in the *Relations des ambassadeurs Vénitiens*, published by N. Tommaseo, vol. i., p. 284 (Paris, 1838).

[1] Consult the lives of Anne of Bretagne and Francis I., in the fifth and second volumes of Brantôme, for information regarding the new court commenced by the one, and carried to its highest pitch of splendour by the other. Francis I. always kept open table. Brantôme says, ' Il y avoit sa table, celle du grand maistre, du grand chambellan et chambellans, des gentilshommes de la chambre, des gentilshommes servans, des valets de chambre, et tant d'autres et très-bien servies que rien n'y manquoit, et ce qui estoit très-rare, c'est que dans un village, dans des forêts, en l'assemblée, l'on y estoit traité comme si l'on fust esté dans Paris.' Vol. ii., p. 211. ' Dans les festes où il avoit tournois, combats, mascarades, &c., il donnoit de grandes livrées aux hommes et aux dames.' Ibid., p. 209.

[2] These pages numbered one hundred and thirty under Francis I. and Henry II., and every year fifty of them left the royal service to enter the army. Henry II. used to call them ' son plus beau haras.' Brantôme, vol. ii., pp. 353, 354.

[3] ' D'ordinaire pour le moins sa court estoit pleine de plus de trois cents dames et demoiselles.' Ibid., vol. v., p. 66.

built or beautified on the banks of the Seine, and sometimes in the spacious castles of Blois and Amboise, which his predecessors had inhabited, on the banks of the Loire. A careful imitator of his father's example, Henry II. kept up the same magnificence at his court, which was presided over with as much grace as activity by the subtle Italian, Catherine de Medici; whose character had been formed by Francis I., who had admitted her into the *petite bande de ses dames favorites*,[1] with whom he used to hunt the stag, and frequently sport with alone in his pleasure-houses! The men were constantly in the company of the women; the Queen and her ladies were present at all the games and amusements of Henry II. and his gentlemen, and accompanied them in the chase.[2] The King, on his part, together with the noblemen of his retinue, used to pass several hours every morning and evening in the apartments of Catherine de Medici. 'There,' says Brantôme, 'there were a host of human goddesses, some more beautiful than the others; every lord and gentleman conversed with her whom he loved the best; whilst the King talked to the Queen, his sister, the Dauphiness (Mary Stuart), and the princesses, together with those lords and princes who were seated nearest to him.'[3] As the Kings themselves had avowed mistresses, they were desirous that their subjects should follow their example. 'And if they did not do so,' says Brantôme, 'they considered them coxcombs and fools.'[4] Francis I. had taken as his mistresses, alternately, the Countess de Chateaubriand and the Duchess d'Etampes; and Henry II. was the chivalrous and devoted servant of the Grand Seneschal of Normandy, Diana of Poitiers. But besides their well-known amours, they had other intrigues;[5] and Francis I., in his unblushing licentiousness, prided himself on training the ladies who arrived at his court.[6] His second in this work of debauchery and corruption was Mary Stuart's uncle, the opulent and libertine Cardinal of Lorraine.[7] Such was the

---

[1] Brantôme, vol. v., pp. 34, 35. [2] Ibid., vol. ii., pp. 354, 355, and 357.
[3] Ibid., vol. ii. p. 358.
[4] Ibid., vol. vii., p. 538. Speaking of Francis I., he adds: 'Et bien souvent aux uns et aux autres leur en demandoit les noms, et promettoit de les y servir.'
[5] 'Mais il ne s'y arresta pas tant,' says Brantôme of Francis I., 'qu'il n'en aymast d'autres.' Vol. ii., p. 326.
[6] Ibid., vol. vii., pp. 538, 539.
[7] 'J'ay ouy conter que quand il arrivoit à la cour quelque belle fille ou dame nouvelle qui fust belle, il la venoist aussitost accoster, et, l'arraisonnant, il disoit qu'il la vouloit dresser de sa main. Quel dresseur! . . . Aussi pour lors disoit-on qu'il n'avoit guères de dames ou filles résidantes à la cour ou fraischement venues qui ne fussent desbauchés ou attrapées par son avarice ou par la largesse dudit M. le Cardinal; et peu ou nulles sont-elles sorties de cette cour femmes et filles de bien.' Ibid., vol. vii., p. 540.

court which furnished Brantôme with the majority of those examples which he has commemorated in his *Dames Galantes*, and of the laxity of which we may form some conception from the following verses, addressed to a lady by Henry II.'s own almoner, the poet Mellin de Saint-Gelais:—

> 'Si du parti de celle voulez être
> Par qui Vénus de la cour est bannie,
> Moi, de son fils ambassadeur et prêtre,
> Savoir vous fais qu'il vous excommunie
> Mais si voulez à leur foy être unie,
> Mettre vous faut le cœur en leur puissance
> Pour répondant de votre obeïsance ;
> Car on leur dit qu'en vous, mes demoiselles,
> Sans gage sûr, y a peu de fiance,
> Et que d'Amour n'avez rien que les ailes.' [1]

It was in this school of elegance and depravity, which produced Kings so witty and vicious, and princesses so amiable and dissipated, that Mary Stuart received her education. During her childhood she only derived benefit from it, although she could not fail to perceive what was evil, and afterwards to imitate it; for what we see, is sure eventually to influence what we do. But then she profited simply by the charms and instruction diffused throughout this agreeable and literary court, in which the King's daughters devoted themselves to the study of languages, and cultivated a taste for the arts, and every prince had his poet; Francis I., Marot; Henry II., Saint-Gelais; Charles IX., Ronsard; Henry III., Desportes.[2] She resided there whilst that literary revolution was attempted, which, separating poetry from the simple form which it had assumed in the middle ages, in order to assimilate it to the classic mould of antiquity, deprived it of its originality, without imparting to it grandeur, and could not fail to be ephemeral, although it was advised by Joachim du Bellay, effected by Ronsard, favoured by the Chancellor de l'Hôpital, admired by Montaigne, and applauded by the whole court of Henry II.[3] Ronsard, who had lived in Scotland for three years as page to James V., was teacher of poetry to Mary Stuart, and one of her most ardent admirers.

She early displayed the varied gifts of her rich and charming nature. At ten years of age she astonished all who knew her by

[1] Quoted by M. Sainte-Beuve, in the 44th page of his *Tableau historique et critique de la poésie Française et du théâtre Français au seizième siècle*. Paris, 1828.

[2] See M. Sainte-Beuve's above-mentioned work, not only for details regarding the poetry of that time, but also respecting its introduction into the court.

[3] This revolution is admirably described by M. Sainte-Beuve, who has written its history, displayed its causes, and estimated its character, in pp. 54-108 of his book.

her maturity, and wrote to the Queen Dowager about the affairs of Scotland with delicate and precocious good sense.[1] When thirteen years old, she recited a Latin speech of her own composition in presence of the King, the Queen, and the whole court, in the hall of the Louvre.[2] Fully able to exercise discretion, she never divulged the political secrets confided to her by her mother,[3] to whom the Cardinal of Lorraine thus wrote: 'Your daughter has so increased, and indeed increases daily in height, goodness, beauty, wisdom, and virtues, that she is as perfect and accomplished in all things honest and virtuous as it is possible for her to be; and there is no one like her to be found in this kingdom, either among noble ladies or others, of whatever low or mean condition and quality they may be: and I am constrained to tell you, madam, that the King takes such a liking to her, that he often passes his time in chatting with her for the space of an hour; and she knows quite well how to entertain him with good and wise conversation, as if she were a woman twenty-five years of age.'[4] Her education was attended to with extreme care, and had added varied talents to her natural graces. Besides Latin, which she thoroughly understood and spoke fluently, she had considerable knowledge of history, knew several living languages, excelled in music, sang very agreeably to her own accompaniment upon the lute, and composed verses which received the praise of Ronsard and Du Bellay.[5] Lively and open in disposition,

[1] See vol. i., pp. 5-7 of the *Lettres, Instructions, et Mémoires de Marie Stuart, publiés par le Prince Alexandre Labanoff.* London, 1844.

[2] Brantôme, vol. v., p. 83.

[3] 'J'ay veu l'ayse que aviès de ce que je tiens les choses qu'il vous plaist me mander secrètes; je vous puis asseurer, madame, que rein qui viendra de vous ne sera sceu par moy.' Mary Stuart to Mary of Guise, Queen Dowager of Scotland, in Labanoff, vol. i., pp. 5, 6.

[4] Labanoff, vol. i., pp. 9, 10.

[5] 'Elle se naturalisa si bien Françoise qu'on pouvoit dire qu'elle n'estoit pas seulement la plus belle, mais la plus polie de tout son sexe, dans la langue et dans la belle gallanterie.' *Mémoires de Castelnau de Mauvissière,* vol. i., p. 528 (Brussels, 1731). 'Elle aymoit la poësie et les poëtes, mais surtout M. de Ronsard, M. du Bellay, et M. de Maisonfleur, qui ont fait de belles poësies et élégie pour elle. Elle se mesloit d'estre poëte, composoit des vers, dont j'en ai vu aucuns de beaux et très-bien faits. Elle chantoit très-bien, s'accordant avec le luth, qu'elle touchoit bien joliment de ceste belle main blanche et de ces beaux doigts si bien façonnez.' Brantôme, vol. v., pp. 84-86. The following are some of the verses which Ronsard and Du Bellay have left us regarding her:—

'Au milieu du printems entre les liz naquit,
Son corps qui de blancheur les liz mesme veinquit,
Et les roses, qui sont du sang d'Adonis teintes,
Furent, par sa couleur, de leur vermeil depeintes;

amiable and insinuating in character, she was at once the ornament and the darling of the court. The Cardinal of Lorraine announced to his sister the ascendency which she had obtained there in these words: 'I can truly assure you, madam, that there is no one more beautiful or more virtuous than the Queen, your daughter; she governs both the King and the Queen.''

When this charming princess was nearly fifteen years of age, Henry II. began to urge her marriage with the Dauphin. On the 31st of October, 1557, he wrote to the Parliament of Scotland to invite them to fulfil their pledge on this subject. The Parliament, which met at Edinburgh on the 14th of December, acceded to his wishes, which the Regent contrived to render agreeable to them, and appointed nine Commissioners to go to Paris to sanction

---

Amour de ses beaux traits luy composa les yeux,
Et les Grâces, qui sont les trois filles des cieux,
De leurs dons les plus beaux cette princesse ornèrent,
Et pour mieux la servir les cieux abandonnèrent.'
(Ronsard, *Œuvres*, vol. viii., p. 19.)

The following are from Du Bellay, *Œuvres*, pp. 504, 507 :—

I.

' Toy qui as veu l'excellence de celle
Qui rend le ciel sur l'Escosse envieux,
Dy hardiment, Contentez vous, mes yeux,
Vous ne verrez jamais chos plus belle.

II.

' Celle qui est de cette isle princesse
Qu'au temps passé l'on nommoit Caledon,
Si en sa main elle avoit un brandon,
On la prendroit pour Venus la déesse.

III.

' Par une chaîne à sa langue attachée
Hercule à soy les peuples attiroit ;
Mais ceste-cy tire ceulx qu'elle voit,
Par une chaîne en ses beaux yeux cachée.

IV.

' En vostre esprit le ciel s'est surmonté ;
Nature et art ont en vostre beauté
Mis tout le beau dont la beauté s'assemble.'

All her contemporaries unite in praising the mental and personal charms of Mary Stuart. In 1554, the Venetian John Capello thus writes regarding her: ' Gli (*i. e.* the Dauphin) fu data per moglie la regina de Scozia, che gia altre fiate fu condotta in Francia, la qual e bellissima et di maniera tale costumata, che porge maraviglia a chiunque considera la qualità sue. E anco il Delfino molto se non contenta, e prende gran piacere nel ragionare e ritrovarsi con esso lei.' Tommaseo, *Relations des Ambassadeurs Vénitiens*, vol. i., p. 374.

[1] Labanoff, vol. i., p. 36.

this marriage in the name of Scotland, and be present at its celebration. These Commissioners were the Archbishop of Glasgow, the Bishop of Ross, the Bishop of Orkney, the Earls of Rothes and Cassillis; Lord James Stuart, the commandant of Saint Andrews, then twenty-six years of age; Lords James Fleming, George Seton, and John Erskine of Dun.[1] They were directed, in conformity with their instructions, to do nothing until they had obtained from both the Queen and the Dauphin a promise to preserve the integrity of the kingdom, and observe its ancient laws and liberties. When this formality had been gone through, the contract was drawn up on the 19th of April, 1558, on the following conditions: the eldest son sprung of this marriage was to be King of France, and, if daughters only were born, the eldest of them was to become Queen of Scotland, to receive 400,000 crowns as a daughter of France, and not to marry without the consent of both the estates of Scotland and the King of France; the Dauphin was to assume the title and arms of King of Scotland, and, if he died after his accession to the throne of France, the Queen his widow was to receive a jointure of 600,000 livres.[2]

Five days afterwards the marriage was celebrated with the greatest pomp in the cathedral of Notre Dame. The Cardinal of Bourbon gave the nuptial blessing in presence of the King, the Queen, the princes of the blood royal, and the chief nobility. As soon as the ceremony was concluded, the young bride, whose example was followed by the Scottish Commissioners, hailed the Dauphin King of Scotland; and during several days, a succession of festivities rendered Paris a continual scene of activity and joy.[3] All classes vied with each other in celebrating the grandeur and happiness of that brilliant princess, who seemed destined to be the fortunate possessor of two crowns, and who, in less than ten years, lost them both, and fell into an abyss of calamities.

The Court of France itself contributed to produce this result by teaching her that duplicity and deceitfulness which were subsequently so fatal to her. Not satisfied with securing, by this marriage, the alliance of Scotland, which thus became involved in the war of France against England and Spain, Henry II. was

---

[1] Keith, p. 72. Tytler, vol. v., p. 26.
[2] Keith, p. 74, and Appendix, p. 17, where the contract is printed.
[3] *Cérémonies du mariage de monseigneur le dauphin avec la royne d'Escosse, &c.*, extracted from the sixth volume of the Registers of the Hôtel de Ville of Paris, in the national archives of France, and published by M. Teulet in the *Pièces et documents inédits relatifs à l'histoire d'Ecosse*, vol. i., pp. 292-303.

anxious to insure his possession of that kingdom if Mary Stuart died childless. He hoped thereby to prevent the accession of the Hamiltons to the throne, and to annex to France a country which had always revolted against the idea of its incorporation with England. On the 4th of April, 1558, fifteen days before Mary Stuart accepted the conditions proposed by the Commissioners of the Scottish Parliament, she affixed her name at Fontainebleau to two secret acts of the most perilous importance. The first of these acts was a full and free donation of Scotland to the Kings of France in consideration of the services which those monarchs had at all times rendered to Scotland by defending her against the English, her *ancient and inveterate enemies*, and especially for the assistance which she had received from King Henry II., who had maintained her independence at his own expense during the minority of her Queen.[1]

The second act[2] seemed framed merely to meet the case of the non-execution of the first, in which she also conveyed to him any claims which might accrue to her upon England and Ireland. The usufruct of the kingdom of Scotland was granted to the King of France, until he should have been repaid the sums which he had expended in her defence. Estimating these sums at a million of pieces of eight, which Scotland, in her existing state of poverty, could not restore, Mary Stuart ordained that the King of France should have the enjoyment of her kingdom until they were entirely liquidated. With the consent of her uncles, the Duke of Guise and the Cardinal of Lorraine, whose opinion she had consulted on the matter, she thus placed Scotland in pledge for debts which Scotland had never accepted.

Equally injudicious and inexecutable, such acts as these could not be useful to the King of France, and might greatly compromise the Queen of Scotland, who was taught on that same day to despise her pledged word, to make light of her obligations, and thus to enter upon a course fraught with disaster. In fact, on the 4th of April, she signed a secret protest against the solemn engagements into which she entered, fifteen days afterwards, in presence of the Scottish Commissioners. Annulling beforehand

---

[1] This act, extracted from the National Archives of France (Trésor des Chartes, I., 679, No. 59), was published for the first time in 1838 at the end of the first volume of the *Correspondance Diplomatique* of Lamothe Fénelon, p. 425. It will also be found in Prince Labanoff's Collection, vol. i., p. 50.

[2] This is also extracted from the National Archives (Trésor des Chartes, I., 679, No. 60); and it will be found in Lamothe Fenelon's Correspondence, vol. i. p. 427; and in Prince Labanoff's Collection, vol. i., p. 52.

the consent which she will have to give to the articles drawn up by the estates of her kingdom, in conformity with its laws, she states in this protest that she intends to dispose of her inheritance like a true Queen, without allowing it to fall into the hands of any one of the nobles of the country, and that she is desirous *to bind, join, annex, and unite the kingdom of Scotland to the crown of France.* She adds that she is compelled to appear to submit to the conditions which her subjects exact from her, because she is far from her country, because she is not in possession of its strongholds, and because she fears that otherwise troubles would arise and cause her ruin.[1]

Thus, by an act of weakness and of treason, did Mary Stuart —whom we cannot fairly charge with this fault, so young was she and submissive to the will of others,—enter upon life and royalty. But she remembered this detestable lesson only too soon. The Scottish Commissioners, far from suspecting that their Queen had utterly disregarded her oaths and arbitrarily disposed of their country, returned to Scotland to obtain sanction for the transactions of the 19th of April. They were ratified by the Parliament in December, 1558, and the matrimonial crown was bestowed upon the Dauphin. It was also decided that, in future, all acts should be published in the name of Francis and Mary, King and Queen of Scotland, Dauphin and Dauphiness of Vienne.[2]

This marriage marked the culminating point of French influence in Scotland; but no sooner had it arrived at this, its furthest limit, than it began rapidly to decline. Scotland had reaped its advantages, and now perceived its inconveniences only. She felt that her independence, though protected from English aggression, was threatened by France, and she felt quite as adverse to the domination of one foreign power as of another. On her side, Mary of Lorraine, now that she had attained all her ends, having deprived the Earl of Arran of the regency, married her daughter to the most powerful prince in Europe, and placed Scotland under the protection of France,—was less careful in her conduct towards those whom she thought she no longer needed either to employ or to fear. She placed all her confidence in

---

[1] This was published in 1693, in Leonard's *Recueil des Traités de Paix,* vol. ii., p. 510, to which it was communicated by MM. Godeffroy. It is also to be found in Lamothe Fénelon's Correspondence, vol. i., p. 429; and in Prince Labanoff's Collection, vol. i., p. 54.—Keith was aware of the existence of these three acts, as he refers to them in p. 73 of his history.

[2] Keith, pp. 76, 77. Tytler, vol. v., pp. 29, 30.

her fellow-countrymen, and thus offended the jealous and suspicious nobility of Scotland, who were, both by nature and education, inclined to dislike and oppose her. The principal barons, with the Duke of Chatelherault and the Earl of Huntly at their head, had already manifested their distrust during the war waged by the French and Scotch against England and Spain. Assembled at Kelso, they refused to enter the English territory, alleging that they had no interest to assume the offensive, and that they should content themselves with repulsing the enemy if he should attack their kingdom.[1]

This beginning of disagreement was soon carried further. Seven months after the marriage of the Queen of Scotland to the Dauphin of France, Mary Tudor died, and her death put an end to the close connection between Spain and England. It moreover caused the second fall of Catholicism in the latter country, which was then exceedingly variable in its religious opinions, and whose faith seemed to depend upon the will of its sovereigns. The daughter of Catharine of Aragon was succeeded by the daughter of Anne Boleyn, who lost no time in restoring the faith of her father Henry VIII., and her brother Edward VI. The accession of Elizabeth to the throne, in November 1558, changed both the situation of Mary Stuart with regard to England, and the dispositions as well as the relations of parties in Scotland. As Elizabeth had been declared a bastard when her mother was beheaded, the Court of France considered her incapable to rule, both on account of her birth and her religion. In the interested judgment of that Court, Mary Stuart, a direct descendant of Henry VII., through his eldest daughter, Margaret Tudor, the wife of James IV., was the legitimate heir to the crown of England. With even greater imprudence than had been displayed in the matter of the secret acts of Fontainebleau, Henry II. caused the Dauphin to quarter the arms of England[2] with

[1] Tytler, vol. v., pp. 24, 25.
[2] See pp. 436-459 of the documents published by M. Teulet, for the complaints of Elizabeth on this point, contained in the *Responsum ad protestationem quam orator regis Gallorum, nomine sui principis, serenissimæ Angliæ reginæ obtulit xv Aprilis*, 1560.—She bitterly complained that the injury had been done her of suspending the arms of England on the stage where sat the judges of the tournament in which Henry II. was killed, and that they were borne publicly on that day by the heralds of the Dauphin's band; that after the death of Henry II., Francis II. and Mary Stuart had called themselves *rex et regina Franciæ, Scotiæ, Angliæ et Hiberniæ*; that they had quartered the arms of England with those of France in their chambers, chapels, wardrobes, &c.; and that on the entrance of Mary Stuart into Chattelherault, on the 23rd of November, 1559, a triumphal arch

those of Scotland, and thus gave rise to the formidable conflict between her and Elizabeth.

What was the character of this princess, whose hostility the Court of France did not fear to excite against Mary Stuart, and who, from that moment, became her rival both as a Queen and a woman? High-spirited, imperious, and extremely proud, with great energy, astuteness, and capacity, Elizabeth had long been compelled to dissimulate her feelings and her religious faith during the terrible reign of her sister, who would have proscribed her but for the support given her by Philip II. She had lived at a distance from the Court, under strict surveillance, and had thus acquired those habits of deception, which combined in her with the haughty and violent passions she inherited from her father. Giovanni Michele, the Venetian Ambassador, in 1556, thus describes this princess, then twenty-three years of age, a short time before she ascended the throne: 'She is no less remarkable,' he says, 'in body than in mind, although her features are rather agreeable than beautiful. She is tall in person and well made; her complexion is brilliant though rather dark. She has fine eyes; but above all, a splendid hand, which she is very fond of showing. She possesses great tact and ability, as she has abun-

---

had been erected, upon the two gates of which these two inscriptions had been placed:—

    Gallia perpetuis pugnaxque Britannia bellis
    Olim odio inter se dimicuere pari.
    Nunc Gallos totosque remotos orbe Britannos
    Unum dos Mariæ cogit in imperium.
    Ergo pace potes, Francisce, quod omnibus annis
    Mille patres armis non potuere tui.

    Ardebat bellis, cum te, Francisce, salutat
    Nascentem, cunis Gallia fausta tuis.
    Pace alitur, cum te regem, Francisce, salutat
    Auspiciis regni faustior illa tui.
    Nec mirum; tibi regna tuo sunt omnia jure,
    Dote, aut æternis subdita fœderibus.

Killegrew and Jones had given Elizabeth an account of this entrance in their despatch, dated from Blois, November 29, 1559, and printed in Forbes, vol. i., p. 266.

It is a curious fact that, at the time when the King of France and the Queen of Scotland set up these pretensions to the throne of England, Philip II., after having endeavoured to induce Elizabeth to marry him, became her advocate with the Pope, that he should not declare her a schismatic, and demanded that, in any case her kingdom should be bestowed on no one but himself.

dantly proved by the wise way in which she has conducted herself in the midst of the suspicions of which she was the object, and of the perils which surrounded her. She surpasses the Queen, her sister, in her knowledge of languages. Besides English, Spanish, French, Italian, and Latin, which she knows as well as her sister, she has no slight acquaintance with Greek. She is haughty and high-spirited. Although born of a mother beheaded for adultery, she esteems herself no less highly than the Queen, her sister, and considers herself equally legitimate. It is said that she is very much like the King, her father, to whom she was always very dear on that account, and who had her as well educated as the Queen, and made an equal provision for them both in his will.'[1] To the most solid learning Elizabeth united the most agreeable accomplishments. She was an excellent musician, and danced to perfection.[2] Certain gifts of person, great mental attractions,[3] all the adornments of a brilliant education, much originality without sufficient grace, and the resources of a lively and strong imagination rendered her remarkable as a woman, whilst her acute and penetrating judgment, her unwearied application, her

---

[1] 'Tenuta non manco bella d'animo che sia di corpo, ancora che di faccia si può dire che sia più tosto gratiosa che bella. Ma della persona è grande et ben formata, di bella carne ancor che olivastra, belli ochi et sopra tutto bella mano della quale ne fa professione, d'uno spirito et ingegno mirabile, il che hà saputo molto ben dimostrare con l'essersi saputa, nei sospetti et nei pericoli nei quali s'è trovata, ben governare. Supera la regina nella cognitione della lingue; perch' oltra che con la latina habbia congionta non mediocre cognitione della greca. Parla di più che non fa la regina l'italiana nella quale si compiace. È superba et altiera, che se bene sà d'esser nasciuta d'une tal madre publicamente decapitata, però non si reputa ne stima manco che faccia la regina, ne si tiene per manco legitima. Se tiene superba et gloria per el padre, al quale dicono ch'è anco più simile, et per cio gli fù sempre cara, et fatta nodrire da lui come fù la regina et nel testamento cosi beneficata come quella.' Relatione del clarissimo Giovanni Michele, tornato della serenissima regina Maria d'Inghilterra, l'anno 1557. MSS. of the National Library of Paris, depart. Saint-Germain Harlay, Supplement, No. 225, 4to, fol. 184 recto et verso.

[2] 'Elle prend grand plaisir au bal et à la musique. Elle me dict qu'elle entretenoit pour le moins soixante musiciens; qu'à sa jeunesse elle avoit fort bien dansé, et qu'elle composoit les balets, la musique, et les jouoit elle-mesme et les dansoit.' Manuscript Journal of Hurault de Maisse, ambassador from Henry IV. to Elizabeth, in 1596, a short time before the Peace of Vervins, fol. 391, verso, in the archives of the French Foreign Office.—' Elle me dict que quand elle vint à la couronne qu'elle sçavoit six langues mieux que la sienne; et parceque je luy dis que c'estoit une grande vertu à une princesse, elle me dict que ce n'estoit pas merveille d'apprendre une femme à parler, mais qu'il y avoit bien de plus à faire à luy apprendre à se taire.' Ibid., fol. 410, verso.

[3] 'Elle est vive du corps et de l'esprict et adroitte à tout ce qu'elle faict.' Ibid., fol. 286, verso.

haughty and politic disposition, and her active ambition destined her to be a great Queen.

On the day of her accession she displayed those qualities which characterized all the rest of her life. She took possession of the throne as a matter of course, and passed from oppression to command without either surprise or uneasiness. Adopting the policy which was destined to constitute the glory of her reign, she pursued it assiduously, but without precipitancy. We cannot say that she was a zealous Protestant; but she was averse to Catholicism as the religion which had oppressed her youth, and still menaced her crown. She felt more disposed to detest than to contest it. She said that she had read neither Luther nor Calvin, but St. Jerome and St. Augustine, and she considered that the points of difference between the various Christian communities were of very little importance.[1] She therefore restored Protestantism rather from policy than conviction,[2] in order to give the direction of affairs and the government of the State to her own party, and withdraw it from her adversaries.

She immediately surrounded herself with men of great ability or entire devotion to her service. Her two principal advisers were Lord Robert Dudley, one of the sons of the Duke of Northumberland, whom she appointed her Master of the Horse, and who remained her favourite as long as he lived; and William Cecil, whom she made Secretary of State, and who was her prime minister for forty years. Careful to retain those whom she had chosen, she was always well served. She never permitted her favourites to become for a single moment her masters, and her most experienced ministers were never more than her useful instruments. On all occasions, though she sought counsel, she

---

[1] 'Elle me dict que s'il y avoit deux princes en la Chrestienté qui eussent bonne volonté et du courage, qu'il seroit fort aisé d'accorder les différends de la religion, qu'il n'y avoit qu'un Jésus Christ et une foy, et que tout le reste dont on disputoit n'estoit que bagatelle... Elle me jura n'avoir leu aucun des livres de Calvin, mais qu'elle avoit veu les pères antiques et y avoit prins grand plaisir, d'aultant que ces derniers sont pleins de disputes et de contentions et les aultres n'ont que bonnes intentions.' MS. Journal of Hurault de Maisse, fols. 282-284.

[2] A year and a half after her accession to the throne, she tried to pass herself off as a Catholic at heart to Quadra, Bishop of Aquila, the chaplain of Philip II., and his ambassador at London. She was desirous thereby to conciliate the good opinion of the Spaniards, and if necessary, to obtain their assistance against France and Scotland. 'Vino à decirme,' writes Quadra to Philip II., '*que ella era tan Catolica como yo*, y que hacia a Dios testigo de que lo que ella creia no sea diferente de lo que todos los catolicos de sa reyno creian.' The Bishop of Aquila having asked her why she thus concealed her religion, 'respondió me que era forzada *ad tempus*.' MS. Despatch, 3rd June, 1560.

acted upon her own decisions. Her will, guided solely by either calculation or interest, was sometimes slow, often audacious, always sovereign. In less than a month after she had succeeded Mary Tudor, the Spanish ambassador wrote to Philip II. :—'She is held in incomparably greater dread than was the Queen her sister. She orders and does whatever she pleases, just as absolutely as the King her father.'[1] Speaking of herself, with a full consciousness of what she was, and what she could effect, Elizabeth said about this time 'that she would let the world know that there was in England a woman who acted like a man, and who was awed neither by a Constable of Montmorency like the King of France, nor by a Bishop of Arras like the King of Spain.'[2]

Such was the Queen whose ardent animosity Mary Stuart was ill-advised enough to provoke, and who thenceforward became the supporter of all the religious dissenters and discontented politicians of Scotland. These two classes rapidly increased in numbers and influence; as the Regent, Mary of Lorraine thought, after the marriage of her daughter with the Dauphin, that it was less necessary for her to act with tolerance towards the reformed party, and that she might with impunity neglect the high nobility. She governed according to the counsels, and aided by the soldiers, of France,[3] which was then as much detested in Scotland as England had been in other times. But what chiefly emboldened Mary of Lorraine to pursue this course, was the accession of her son-in-law and daughter to the throne of France.

Henry II. died on the 10th of July, 1559, from a lance wound received in a tournament, and left the crown to the young Francis II., who was completely under the influence of Duke Francis of Guise and the Cardinal of Lorraine, the brothers of the Regent of Scotland. Although a general peace had been concluded three months previously (on the 2nd of April), at Cateau-Cam-

[1] 'Paraceme que es muy mas temida que su hermana sin ninguna comparacion, y manda y hace lo que quiere tan absolutamente como su padre.' Despatch of December 14th, 1558, from the Count of Feria, Philip II.'s Ambassador at London. MS. Archives de Simancas. Estado Inglaterra, fol. 811.

[2] This is what she said to the Marquis of Moreto, who had come in the name of the Duke of Savoy to ask her in marriage for the Duke of Nemours: 'Dice Morata que le dixo la reyna que ella havia conoscer al mundo que aqui havia uña muger que obraba como hombre, y que en Inglaterra no hay condestables ni obispo de Arras.' MS. Despatch from Quadra to Granvella, 30th December, 1560. Archives de Simancas, fol. 815.

[3] Manifesto addressed by the Lords of the Congregation to the princes of Christendom, extracted from the Archives of the French Foreign Office, Correspondence with England, vol. xxi., and published by M. Teulet, in his *Pièces et documents inédits relatifs à l'histoire d'Ecosse*, vol. i., pp. 414-428.

bresis, and Elizabeth had been included in the treaty, Mary Stuart had not ceased to bear the arms of England, and still retained the title of Queen of England and Ireland.[1] This vain and rash usurpation determined Elizabeth, on her side, to sustain the members of the high aristocracy and the professors of the reformed religion, who reconstructed the English party in Scotland. From this moment commenced, between the barons of the country and the foreign soldiers, between the Protestants and the Catholics, the agitation of the great question whether the aristocracy or the monarch should gain victory; whether the old or the new faith should prevail. The absence of Mary Stuart, and the imprudence of Mary of Lorraine, largely contributed to decide it in favour of the feudal aristocracy and the Presbyterian Church, which soon became predominant in the kingdom.

This revolution must be briefly described. The Protestant party, which took so large a part in the misfortunes of Mary Stuart, had slowly gained ground in Scotland, where it had been cruelly persecuted during the lifetime of James V. This King detested it as heretical, and dreaded it as anti-national; he perceived in it an enemy to the old Church and an auxiliary of England. Before deriving its religious constitution from Geneva, the Protestantism of Scotland had borrowed its first articles of faith from Germany, and was originally inspired by the spirit of Luther. As early as 1525, an act of Parliament had prohibited the introduction into the kingdom of the writings of this formidable innovator, and had proscribed his doctrines. But neither laws nor penalties had been able to arrest the progress of these powerful and life-giving truths which had been embraced and maintained, even unto the death, by abbots, priests, Benedictine monks, canons of St. Andrews, and gentlemen of rank and influence. The King's own confessor, Seton, who had shown some disposition to approve them, was compelled to fly to England in order to avoid being burned at the stake, where, during the year 1539 alone, seven martyrs to Protestantism lost their lives. In 1541, the Parliament enacted that no person, under pain of confiscation and death, should contest in anything the authority of the Pope.[2]

But matters assumed an altogether different aspect shortly afterwards, under the regency of the Earl of Arran. This noble-

---

[1] M. Teulet's *Pièces et documents inédits relatifs à l'histoire d'Ecosse*, especially pp. 440, 441, 455, 456. *Responsum ad protestationem*, &c. by Queen Elizabeth.

[2] For the history of this period see Keith, Appendix, pp. 1-12; the Wodrow Society's edition of the Works of John Knox, vol. i., pp. 1-76; M'Crie's Life of Knox, 3rd edition, vol. i., pp. 1-37; and Melvil's Memoirs, vol. i., pp. 1-12.

man, whose interest had at first led him to act favourably towards England, agreed with the Lords of the Articles to authorize the reading of the Bible in the vulgar tongue, and tolerate the preaching of the evangelical innovators. One of these, George Wishart, then returned from England, whither he had fled for refuge, and spread the doctrines of the Reformation all over Scotland. Among his disciples was the famous John Knox, whose forerunner he was in the propagation and establishment of Protestantism. He was a man of elevated mind, strong affections, and rather ascetic devotion; and he combined extreme gentleness with the most earnest convictions.[1] He had preached with great success at Montrose, Dundee, Perth, and Ayr against the doctrines of the Romish Church and the disorderly lives of the clergy. He had met with the zealous support of the Earl of Glencairn, the Earl Marshal;[2] Sir George Douglas, brother of Archibald, Earl of Angus;[3] the Lairds of Brunston, Long Niddry, Ormiston, Calder, and Loch Norris.[4] The reconciliation of the Earl of Arran with Cardinal Beaton had not arrested their progress, although the repentant head of the State no longer favoured them, and the unscrupulous head of the Church left no means untried to crush them. An attempt was even made to assassinate Wishart; but it had not succeeded, and he never after preached unless surrounded by a circle of barons and armed men. At length, however, he was surprised by night at Ormiston by Earl Patrick Bothwell[5] with a detachment of soldiers, and placed in the hands of Cardinal Beaton, who caused him to be burned alive on the 28th of March, 1546. His death excited to the highest degree the hatred of the Protestant party against the Cardinal, whom sixteen determined men, led by Norman Lesly, the eldest son of Earl of Rothes,[6] surprised in his turn in the castle of St. Andrews,

---

[1] Knox's History of the Reformation, vol. i., p. 125, et seq. M'Crie, vol. i., pp. 41-43.

[2] Alexander, fifth Earl of Glencairn, died in 1574. Knox, vol. i., p. 72, note 4, and p. 127. William, fourth Earl Marshal, died in 1581. Ibid., p. 126, note 2.

[3] Ibid., p. 77 and p. 135, note 5.

[4] Alexander Crichton, laird of Brunston, in Mid-Lothian. Hugh Douglas, laird of Long-Niddry. Ibid., p. 134, note 3, and p. 136. John Cockburn, laird of Ormiston, in East Lothian. Ibid., pp. 134, 135, note 3. James Sandilands, laird of Calder, in West Lothian, and Knight of St. John of Jerusalem. Ibid., p. 249, note 2. George Crawfurd, laird of Loch Norris in Ayrshire. Ibid., p. 127, note 1.

[5] Third Earl of Bothwell, and father of the celebrated James Bothwell, who plays so prominent a part in this history.

[6] George Lesly, third Earl of Rothes. The Leslies settled in Scotland as early as the twelfth century.

murdered him with fanatical ferocity, and then hanged his body ignominiously from the battlements of the fortress.[1]

This crime excited universal horror, and did very great injury to the Protestant cause. The leaders of this party—among whom was Knox, of whom Wishart had take an affectionate farewell just before he was captured, saying to him: 'Return; one is sufficient for a sacrifice,'[2]—became the objects of more violent persecution than ever, shut themselves up in the castle of St. Andrews, were taken prisoners after a siege of five months, and sent over to France. There they were kept in cruel captivity, and their enfeebled party had not regained its strength until Mary of Lorraine found it necessary to show it favour in order to obtain the regency for herself, and govern Scotland undisturbed. Then it had assumed new vigour, and Knox, who had passed several years in chains on the French galleys,[3] had returned to animate it with his spirit, and inspire it with his own boldness.

This adventurous reformer was at that time in the prime of life, and had acquired, by his talents, his services, and his sufferings, immense influence in Scotland. Born in 1505, educated at the grammar-school of Haddington, and afterwards at the University of St. Andrews,—where with Buchanan, he had studied theology under John Major, who had imbibed the independent doctrines of D'Ailly and Gerson in France,—he had become the wandering disciple of Wishart, and the prisoner of Henry II. Of the three languages cultivated by the literary men and reformers of his day, he knew Latin only in his youth; and it was not until after 1534 that he studied Greek, then recently introduced into Scotland, by a professor who had come from France; and in 1550 he learned Hebrew on the Continent, when the conclusion of peace had put an end to his captivity.[4] In possession of these three instruments of innovation, with extensive religious knowledge at his command, animated by an ardent mind, inspired by indomitable zeal, endowed with fascinating eloquence and a dauntless character, he consecrated himself to the service of his cause wherever it stood in need of him. He had gone to England to assist in the Reformation which been greatly promoted there by

[1] Knox, History of the Reformation, vol. i., pp. 139-177. Keith, pp. 41-43.

[2] 'Nay, returne to your bairnes, and God blisse you: ane is sufficient for a sacrifice.' Knox, vol. i., p. 139.

[3] 'Knox, with some others, was confined on board the galleys, bound in chains, and in addition to the rigours of ordinary captivity, exposed to all the indignities with which Papists were accustomed to treat those whom they regarded as heretics.' M'Crie's Life of Knox, vol. i., pp. 67, 68.

[4] M'Crie's Life of Knox, vol. i., pp. 4-8.

Edward VI.[1]; had left that country when Queen Mary restored Catholicism; had gone to rule a church of English refugees at Frankfort, and had next proceeded to Geneva, where he had as his master and friend Calvin, whom he equalled in inflexibility and surpassed in energy.[2] The tolerant policy of Mary of Lorraine having thrown open his country in 1555,[3] he returned thither and prepared himself to become the religious organizer and moral regenerator of Scotland.

Knox's first step was to induce the adherents of the reformed religion to cease attending, as they had hitherto done, at the ceremonies of the established Church, and to separate themselves openly from the Catholics. At the same time, he gained over to his doctrines three young men of great influence, who were destined to play an important part in the affairs of their country. Lord James Stuart,[4] the natural brother of the Queen, and Prior of St. Andrews, a man no less remarkable for the high qualities of his character and the vigour of his mind, than for his elevated rank, embraced Protestantism with Lord John Erskine,[5] and Archibald, Lord Lorn, son of the Earl of Argyle.[6] Two of these were subsequently Regents of Scotland, under the titles of Earl of Moray, and Earl of Mar. In conjunction with other powerful barons, such as the Earl of Glencairn, the Earl Marshal, Sir James Sandilands, called Lord St. John because he had been Prior of the order of St. John of Jerusalem, and Erskine of Dun,[7] they formed themselves, by Knox's advice, into religious congregations; and solemnly pledged themselves to maintain and propagate the preaching of the Gospel. The clergy, thinking to intimidate Knox, cited him to appear at Edinburgh. The bold reformer went thither, but with the intention of publicly advocating the reformed faith. During ten days, he preached both in morning and afternoon, to an immense crowd, attracted by his eloquence and pleased by his expositions; and no one ventured

[1] M'Crie's Life of Knox, vol. i., pp. 78-122.
[2] Ibid., vol. i., pp. 122-150. Tytler, vol. v., p. 34.
[3] Tytler, vol. v., p. 34. M'Crie, vol. i., p. 176.
[4] Son of James V. and Margaret Erskine, daughter of Lord John Erskine, Earl of Mar, and born in 1533.
[5] Third son of the above-named Earl of Mar. He succeeded to his father's title in 1565. M'Crie, vol. i., p. 178. Knox, vol. i., p. 249.
[6] A member of the Anglo-Norman family of Campbell, which settled in Scotland during the twelfth century under Malcolm IV. He succeeded his father as fifth Earl of Argyle in 1558.
[7] Laird of Dun in Forfarshire, between Montrose and Brechin. He was one of the earliest and most zealous advocates of the Reformation in Scotland.—Knox, vol. i., p. 59, and p. 249, note.

to oppose him.¹ The people, who were greatly excited by his sermons, dispersed the annual procession in honour of St. Giles, the patron of the town, and threw the statue of the saint into the lake.²

After having thus diffused the new doctrines amongst the nobility and people, it only remained for him to obtain their sanction by the government. Knox hoped to succeed in this, and presented a requisition to this effect to the Regent. But she received it with the most scornful disdain,³ and declared that it was time to arrest the progress of a revolution which threatened both the creed of the Church and the organization of the State. The clergy had no difficulty in persuading her that it was necessary to use severe measures against Knox, and the innovations of which he was the seditious propagator; and she readily authorized them to prosecute and condemn this formidable adversary, whom they had attempted to have assassinated in the county of Angus.

Knox's courage consisted in braving dangers when it was advantageous to do so, but certainly not in yielding to them. He combined prudence with his enthusiasm, and exposed or withdrew himself according to circumstances. Seeing that the time for effecting the change which he desired in the religion of his country had not yet arrived; he retired from before the storm which was ready to burst over him, and proceeded once more to Geneva, where he was invited to become a pastor.⁴ Sentence of death was passed upon him, and he was burnt in effigy at the High-Cross of Edinburgh.⁵ Emboldened by his condemnation and flight, the Catholic party hoped they would be able equally to intimidate the other preachers of reform, who were traversing the country in all directions. John Douglas, a Carmelite convert to Protestantism, and chaplain of the Earl of Argyle, took Knox's place as pastor of the congregation at Edinburgh: Paul Methven preached publicly at Dundee; the Englishman John Willock was actively employed in diffusing evangelical doctrines in the counties of Angus and Mearns; other ministers were gaining converts in other districts,⁶ and private meetings continued to be held all over the kingdom, at which the best-informed member of the congregation used to read passages of Scripture, and follow his reading by pious exhortations. The Regent summoned all these propagators of a

---

¹ M'Crie, vol. i., p. 183. Knox, vol. i., pp. 251-252.
² Knox, vol. i., pp. 260, 261. Tytler, vol. v., pp. 35, 36.
³ Knox, vol. i., p. 252. M'Crie, vol. i., pp. 186, 187.
⁴ M'Crie, vol. i., pp. 189, 190. Knox, vol. i., pp. 252, 253.
⁵ M'Crie, vol. i., p. 190. Knox, vol. i., p. 254.   ⁶ Keith, pp. 64-65.

prohibited creed to appear before her and give an account of their conduct. They came, but accompanied by so strong a body of gentlemen of their party, that the Regent thought it wise merely to direct them to proceed to the frontier districts. This order they did not obey. One of the barons of the west, Chalmers of Gathgirth, stood up in the midst of his party, and boldly denounced the persecutions to which they were subjected by the clergy. 'The bishops,' he said to the Regent, ' oppress us and our poor tenants to feed themselves: they trouble our ministers, and seek to undo them and us all. We will not suffer it any longer.' At these words, his companions, who had hitherto stood uncovered, proudly put on their steel caps, with an air of defiance.[1]

The Regent was constrained to grant them tacit toleration. But ere long at the suggestion of Knox, who, from his retreat, continued to direct their movements, the Protestant barons and gentlemen met together on the 3rd of December, 1557; determined by a *Covenant* openly to practise their worship, and to denounce no less openly the ceremonies of the old religion; and formed an insurrectionary government in the State under the name of the *Lords of the Congregation*.[2] The Earls of Glencairn, Argyle, and Morton; Lord James Stuart, the Prior of St. Andrews; Erskine of Dun, and others, were the principal Lords of the Congregation,[3] which placed the new religion under the protection of a new power.

It was some time before the two parties thus organized came into open collision. The Regent continued to temporize with the Protestants until she had married her daughter to the Dauphin, and the union of Spain with England had ceased by the death of the Catholic Mary and the accession of the Protestant Elizabeth to the throne. But then she threw off the mask. During the early months of 1559 she became involved in the dangerous designs of the court of France, which was desirous to secure to Mary Stuart the possession of England as well as of Scotland, by the assistance of the Catholics of the two kingdoms. Accordingly the Regent, ratifying by her authority the decisions of a synod of bishops, condemned all the innovations which had been introduced into Scotland, and exacted the complete restoration of religious uniformity.[4] To this declaration of intolerance the Protestant party replied by a threat of revolt.

[1] Tytler, vol. v., p. 40.
[2] This first Covenant is in Keith, p. 66. Knox, vol. i., p. 273. Keith, pp. 68-69.
[4] Knox, vol. i., pp. 291-294. M'Crie, vol. i., pp. 248-255.

The war thus declared on both sides was not long in breaking out. Several towns, and among others, Dundee, Montrose, and Perth, had openly embraced the reformed faith. Knox had hastened from Geneva at the summons of the Lords of the Congregation, and early in May, 1559,[1] he returned to Scotland to remain there during the rest of his life. His bold denunciations of the ceremonies and institutions of Catholicism produced such an effect that a mob of what Knox calls 'the rascal multitude,' began to break the images, pull down the convents, and destroy the monuments of the ancient faith. This devastation commenced at Perth,[2] and was soon imitated in other places; and the Regent, in her anger, threatened to raze that town to its very foundations, and sow it with salt.[3]

She accordingly assembled her forces and prepared to attack Perth, which the Lords of the Congregation resolved to defend. She, however, entered the town in consequence of an arrangement, the conditions of which she did not observe. Then the army of the Congregation, at the head of which were Lord James Stuart, the Earl of Argyle, and Sir William Kirkaldy, Laird of Grange,[4] one of the most valiant and experienced soldiers in Scotland, advanced from St. Andrews to Perth, which they recaptured on the 25th of June. They anticipated the Regent at Stirling, of which they took possession, secured Linlithgow, and marched upon Edinburgh, into which city they entered on the 30th of June. The capital of the kingdom fell into the hands of the Protestants, and there, as in every other place through which the army of the Congregation passed, and where its ministers preached, the revolution was effected by the destruction of monasteries, the overthrow of altars, the breaking of images, and the violent cessation of the Catholic form of worship.[5]

During this struggle, which was destined to be decisive, the Protestants applied to Elizabeth for aid, while the Regent urged Henry II. to send her some assistance. Meanwhile, an armistice until the 10th of January, 1560, was concluded on the 20th

[1] M'Crie, vol. i., pp. 237-246. Knox, vol. i., p. 318.
[2] M'Crie, vol. i., pp. 257-260. Knox, vol. i., pp. 321-323. Keith, pp. 84-85.
[3] Knox, vol. i., p. 324. Tytler, vol. v., p. 59.
[4] Eldest son of James Kirkaldy of Grange, Grand Treasurer of James V. Laird William's barony was in Fife, about a mile to the N.E. of Kinghorn. He was one of the first Scottish barons who embraced the reformed faith: and he had long taken a prominent part in all the religious and warlike affairs of Scotland. He was made prisoner in the castle of St. Andrews, sent over to France, and imprisoned at Mont St. Michel. See Knox, vol. i., *passim.*
[5] Knox, vol. i., pp. 336-364. M'Crie, vol. i., pp. 259-276. Keith, pp. 90-94.

of July,[1] and both parties pledged themselves not to molest each other in the exercise of their faith. The Lords of the Congregation agreed to evacuate Edinburgh, from which they withdrew on the 25th of July, 1559, and into which the Regent promised not to introduce any French garrison. The time of the armistice was employed by both parties in organizing and augmenting their forces. Henry II. was just dead, and the armies of France, rendered inactive by the peace of Cateau-Cambresis, seemed to be more than ever at the disposal of Mary of Lorraine, whose daughter had now ascended the throne of that powerful country. A small body of troops was immediately sent to her, and the court of France, which was governed by her two brothers, prepared to equip an expedition under the command of the Marquis d'Elbeuf. Francis II. despatched M. de Bethencourt to Scotland with eighty thousand livres.[2] He also wrote a threatening letter to the Prior of St. Andrews,[3] and instructed Bethencourt to declare publicly that he would spend the crown of France rather than not reduce Scotland to obedience.[4]

Whilst the Regent was garrisoning Leith with the troops she had received from France, and restoring its fortifications so as to command the Frith of Forth and guard the approach to Edinburgh on that side, the Congregation was by no means inactive. Knox proceeded secretly to Berwick,[5] to confer with Sir James Crofts, the English governor of that place, of whom he requested ships to place Dundee and Perth in safety, soldiers to resist the French troops, and money to supply the poor nobility with means to remain in the field. He moreover wrote to Cecil that their destruction would entail the ruin of his mistress, and besought him in the most pathetic language to induce her to support them. 'The gentlemen in these lower parts,' he said, 'will put themselves in readiness to enterprise the uttermost, if ye will assist with them; and, therefore, in the bowels of Christ Jesus, I require you, Sir, to make plain answer what they may lippen (trust) to, and at what time their support shall be in readiness.'[6]

[1] This armistice, in eight articles, is given in Keith, pp. 98-99.
[2] Paris, *Négociations, &c., relatives au règne de François II.*, pp. 12-17.
[3] Tytler, vol. v., p. 98.
[4] 'Lord Bettancourt bragged in his credit, after he had delivered his menacing letter to the prior (Lord James Stuart), that the King and his council would spend the crown of France, unless they had our full obedience.' MS. Letter from Knox to Cecil, 15th August, 1559, quoted by Tytler, vol, v., p. 95.
[5] MS. Instructions, State Paper Office, quoted in Tytler, vol. v., pp. 85-86.
[6] MS. letter, State Paper Office, Knox to Cecil, 15th August, 1559; quoted in Tytler, vol. v., p. 95.

Cecil entertained the same views as Knox, and had already expressed them to Elizabeth, before the Reformer's letter reached him. On the 5th of August, with that political sagacity which for forty years he devoted to the service of his sovereign, he drew up a *Memorial of certain points meet for the restoring of the realm of Scotland to the ancient weale.* ' It is to be noted,' he says in this document, ' that the best worldly felicity that Scotland can have is either to continue in a perpetual peace with the kingdom of England, or to be one monarchy with England. If the first be sought, then must it necessarily be provided that Scotland be not so subject, as it is presently, to the appointments of France, the ancient enemy of England. As long as Scotland is at the command of the French, there is no hope to have accord long betwixt these two realms.' In order to liberate the Scotch from this influence, Cecil advised the Queen his mistress to send them some assistance, and pointed out the measures which the estates of Scotland ought to take—measures which tended to the expulsion of the French troops, the exclusion of foreigners from all public employments and military commands, the formation of a council of government independent of the Queen, and, if Mary would not accept these conditions, the transference of the sovereign authority to the nearest heir to the crown. He concluded with these words: ' And then may the realm of Scotland consider, being once made free, what means may be devised through God's goodness, to accord the two realms to endure for time to come at the pleasure of Almighty God, in whose hands the hearts of all princes be.'[1]

Elizabeth hesitated. A year had not yet elapsed since her accession to the throne, upon which she did not feel herself quite firmly established. She had no liking for the Presbyterian Reformation, which destroyed all hierarchy in the Church, and introduced a spirit of faction into the State. To her dread of this subversive Protestantism was united bitter hatred of the man who was its chief promoter; for Knox had deeply wounded her royal pride by a violent treatise which he had published against the government of women, during the reign of Mary Tudor.[2] Moreover, the recent treaty of Cateau-Cambresis seemed to interdict her from any act of hostility with regard to France and Scotland. However, as she was always guided by present expediency, and as Francis II. and Mary Stuart had freed her from her

---

[1] Keith, Appendix, pp. 23-24.
[2] This treatise was entitled, 'The first Blast of the Trumpet against the monstrous Regiment of Women.'

obligations towards them by disallowing her right to the crown of England, and usurping her title, she determined to defend the confederated lords. She thus entered upon a course of action which she continued to pursue during the whole of her life, and which was diametrically opposed to her doctrines, though entirely in conformity with her interests.

But the first assistance which she gave to the Scottish insurgents was rendered in a very feeble and covert manner. Sir Ralph Sadler was despatched to them with a subsidy of 3000*l.* and made an agreement with them that they should transfer the supreme power from Mary of Lorraine to the Duke of Chatelherault, who had been induced to join their cause by his son, the Earl of Arran, then recently returned from France, where he had been deprived of the command of the Scottish guard, in consequence of his having become a Calvinist.[1] The confederates now summoned the Regent to suspend the fortification of Leith; and as she replied that her daughter, whose authority she represented, had no need of the permission of her subjects to fortify one of the ports of her kingdom,[2] they again took the field on the 15th of October, 1559, with an army of twelve thousand men; and on the 16th they once more took possession of Edinburgh without opposition. They immediately established two councils, the formation of which announced their intention to govern the State and overthrow the Church. The first, or political, council was composed of the Duke of Chatelherault, the Prior of St. Andrews; the Earls of Arran, Argyle, and Glencairn; the Lords Ruthven, Boyd, and Maxwell; the Laird of Dun, Kirkaldy of Grange, Henry Balnaves, and John Haliburton, the Provost of Dundee; whilst Knox, Goodman, and the Protestant Bishop of Galloway were members of the second, or religious, council.[3] Four days afterwards they all met in public assembly, and took a resolution of extreme boldness which was the prelude to those violent measures which characterized the reign of Mary Stuart. They deposed the Regent, whom they informed of her deposition in the following terms: 'We, our Sovereign Lord and Lady's true barons and lieges, suspend, for most weighty reasons, any authority you have by reason of our Sovereign's commission granted unto your Grace, in the name and authority of our Sovereigns, whose council we are of native birth, in the affairs of this our common weal.'[4] To their disobedience they gave the name of fidelity, and to their usurpation of power the appearance of justice.

[1] Tytler, vol. v., pp. 91-92.   [2] Ibid., p. 92.   [3] Ibid., pp. 101-102.
[4] The whole of the document is in Keith, p. 105.

After having thus organized their plans, they marched upon Leith, but they were defeated by the French, and compelled a second time to abandon Edinburgh, during the night of the 5th of November.[1] Queen Elizabeth then resolved to assist them in a more formal and effective manner. William Maitland, Laird of Lethington, who had resigned his office of Secretary of State to the Regent, in order to devote his talents and experience to the service of the Congregation, was despatched to London to beseech the Queen to send a fleet and army to Scotland, unless she wished to see that kingdom speedily subjected to France, and her own right to the crown of England attacked.[2] Lethington was the most intelligent, skilful, persuasive, and versatile politician in Scotland.[3] He succeeded in convincing Elizabeth of her true interest: and she accordingly sent the Duke of Norfolk to Berwick, where he concluded, in her name, a defensive alliance with Maitland, Balnaves,[4] Pittarow,[5] and Ruthven,[6] who acted as commissioners of the Congregation. It was agreed that the Queen of England should furnish assistance to the Duke of Chatelherault and his party until they should have expelled the French from the country, and that the Duke of Chatelherault and his party should join their forces to those of the Queen of England, if she were attacked by France. In order that this treaty might not give grounds for a charge of rebellion against the confederates, and of disloyalty against Elizabeth, the subjects of Mary Stuart concluded it in the name of their Sovereign, and promised to preserve intact their obedience to her in all things that did not tend to subvert the ancient laws and liberties of the land.[7]

This intervention of England in the affairs of Scotland excited the surprise of the Court of France, which, after having had the imprudence to provoke Elizabeth's hostility, demanded the reasons of her conduct. But Elizabeth was always able to find plausible

[1] Tytler, vol. v., pp. 106-107.   [2] Ibid., vol. v., p. 109.
[3] The barony of Lethington was an old and massive tower in East Lothian, about a mile to the south of Haddington.—Knox, vol. i., p. 137, note 2.
[4] Master Henry Balnaves was one of the earliest and most strenuous supporters of Protestantism in Scotland. He was made prisoner at the Castle of St. Andrews in 1547, taken captive into France, and confined in the Castle of Rouen. He was an advocate, and became one of the Lords of Session in 1558. He died in 1570.—Knox, vol. i., *passim*.
[5] Sir John Wishart, Laird of Pittarow, was one of the principal barons of the reformed party. Mary afterwards appointed him Comptroller.—Knox, vol. i., pp. 274-337, and vol. ii., p. 311, note 1.
[6] Lord Patrick Ruthven, Provost-elect of Perth, from 1554 until his death in 1566. An ardent supporter of the reformed faith.—Knox, vol. i., p. 337, note 1.
[7] Keith, pp. 117-119.

reasons to justify actions which were advantageous to her. She boldly replied that she could not consider the nobility and people of Scotland as rebels; that, on the contrary, she regarded them as faithful subjects of the crown, since they had run the risk of offending the King of France in order to maintain the rights of his wife, their Sovereign. 'And truly,' she added, 'if these barons should permit the government of their kingdom to be wrested out of their hands during the absence of their Queen; if they tamely gave up the independence of their native country, whilst she used the counsel, not of the Scots, but solely of the French, her mother and other foreigners being her advisers in Scotland, and the Cardinal and Duke of Guise in France, it were a good cause for the world to speak shame of them; nay, if the young Queen herself should happen to survive her husband, she would in such a case have just occasion to condemn them all as cowards and unnatural subjects.'¹

In execution of the treaty of Berwick, an English fleet entered the Forth during the spring of 1569, and an army of six thousand infantry and two thousand cavalry marched into Scotland under the command of Lord Grey. It was joined at Preston by eight thousand confederates, with the Duke of Chatelherault at their head.² The French could now no longer make head against forces so far superior to their own. They fell back upon Leith, and shut themselves up in that town, which guarded the Frith of Forth and formed the port of Edinburgh. Blockaded by sea and closely invested by land, they sustained a memorable siege in Leith. They made several vigorous sorties, and long resisted the attacks of the enemy with brilliant valour. But the court of France sent them no reinforcements. It was prevented from doing so by the impoverished state of its finances,³ and by the struggle which had just commenced in that kingdom between the Protestants and the Catholics, between the princes of the house

---

¹ MS. letter, State Paper Office, 17th February, 1560, backed by Cecil; Answer made to the French Ambassador, by Sir William Cecil.—Quoted in Tytler, vol. v., pp. 115-116.

² Tytler, vol. v., p. 117.

³ When sending the 80,000 livres, of which Bethencourt had brought 40,000 in July, 1559, Francis II. had said that it would be out of his power to do more, on account of ' les grandes et incroyables sommes de deniers qu'il estoit contrainct payer et desbourser pour l'effect et exécution des choses promises par le traicté (de Cateau Cambresis): principalement pour payer les gens de guerre qui estoient dedans les places qui se doivent rendre, et se descharger des estrangers, tant de pied que de cheval ... payement aussi des mariages de mesdames ses filles et sœur.' Négociations, &c., relatives au règne de François II., p. 12.

of Bourbon and those of the house of Lorraine. The conspiracy of Amboise, discovered in the month of March, had compelled the Duke of Guise and the Cardinal of Lorraine to defend themselves, and had thus prevented them from succouring their sister, the Regent of Scotland. This compulsory desertion rendered the position of the besieged troops in Leith still less tenable; for all the nobility including the Earl of Huntly, the head of the Catholic party,[1] had set their faces against the presence and domination of foreigners.

The Bishop of Valence Montluc, sent by Mary Stuart and Francis II. to gain time by negotiating a reconciliation between the Regent and the insurgent nobles, failed in his mission.[2] The Regent herself was not more fortunate in a conference which she had with some of the confederates, who specially insisted upon the evacuation of the kingdom by the French.[3] At length this princess, overwhelmed by fatigue and anxiety, fell mortally ill. She caused herself to be conveyed to Edinburgh Castle, where she was received by Lord Erskine. There, feeling that her dissolution was at hand, and that her death had been hastened by the troubles of the kingdom, the sorrows of dispossession, the cares of defence, and the grief she had felt at being placed between the opposite requirements of the Scotch, whom she wished to satisfy, and of the French, whom she was obliged to obey,—she desired to have one more interview with the leaders of the confederates before she died. The Duke of Chatelherault, the Earls of Argyle, Marshal, and Glencairn, and Lord James Stuart, immediately repaired to the Castle. The Regent received them with all her former cordiality and natural kindness of heart. She spoke to them in mournful language of the unhappy state of the kingdom, which she had governed for several years in union and prosperity; expressed her regret that she had been compelled to obey the orders she had received from France; advised them to send away both the French and English troops, but recommended them to prefer the alliance of that country which could not endanger their national independence. After this wise advice, which she was at liberty to give, but which she had not been at liberty to follow, she embraced and kissed them all, and extended her hand to those nobles of inferior rank who had accompanied

---

[1] Tytler, vol. v., p. 118.
[2] MS. letter, State Paper Office, Lethington to Cecil, 26th April, 1560. Tytler, vol. v., p. 119.
[3] MS. letter, State Paper Office, Lethington to Cecil, 14th May, 1560. Tytler, vol. v., p. 121.

them. These farewells of a dying Queen, nearly all whose faults were the work of others, and whose good sense and amiability led her to forget all hostility upon her death-bed, touched their hearts and they took their leave in tears.[1]

Mary of Lorraine did not long survive this affecting scene. She died on the 10th of June, 1560. After her decease, legal authority was entirely wanting to the French, as there was no longer any Regent, and the Queen was absent from the country. They were now also as devoid of means as of right to continue the struggle, hard pressed as they were in Leith, and unable to reckon on reinforcements from France, then a prey to intestine divisions and paralyzed by the commencement of a civil war. Peace thus became inevitable, and it must be concluded upon such conditions as the Scottish confederates might impose.

A treaty was accordingly negotiated at Edinburgh between Cecil and Nicholas Wotton as Elizabeth's commissioners, and the Bishops of Valence and Amiens, La Brosse, D'Oysel, and Randan, as commissioners of Mary Stuart and Francis II. It was signed on the 5th and 6th of July, and contained the following clauses: the French troops were to evacuate Scotland; the fortifications of Leith to be demolished; the sovereigns of France cease to bear the arms and title of King and Queen of England; the Duke of Chatelherault and other Scottish nobles who possessed property in France to have restored to them the lands and titles of which they had been deprived since their rebellion; the high offices of Chancellor, Treasurer, and Comptroller to be conferred not upon ecclesiastics but upon laymen; and the guardianship as well as the administration of the kingdom never to be again intrusted to foreign soldiers and dignitaries. The conduct of affairs was to be confided to a council of twelve members, seven of whom were to be nominated by the Queen, and five by the estates of the realm; and this council was instructed to introduce a better system into the government of the country. It was also agreed that a free Parliament should assemble in the month of August.[2]

Such were the principal stipulations of the treaty of Edinburgh, which marked the defeat of France and the triumph of England in Scotland. It changed the government from royal to aristocratic. It prepared the way for the overthrow of the ancient religion by the victorious efforts of the adherents of the Reforma-

---

[1] MS. letter, State Paper Office, Randolph to Cecil, 8th June, 1560. Tytler, vol. v., pp. 121-122. Keith, pp. 127-128.

[2] All these documents are in Keith, pp. 130-142.

tion, and thus secured to the feudal aristocracy the support of the Presbyterian democracy. The two commissioners of Queen Elizabeth perceived the great utility such a treaty would be to her, and in the letter in which they announced its conclusion, they expressed their opinion, 'that the treaty would be no small augmentation to her honour in this beginning of her reign; that it would finally procure that conquest of Scotland which none of her progenitors, with all their battles, ever obtained, namely, the whole hearts and goodwills of the nobility and people, which surely was better for England than the revenue of the crown.'[1]

Now that the domination of strangers had been overthrown in Scotland, it remained for the confederates to consummate the religious revolution. The Lords of the Congregation closely kept up their league until this great work was accomplished. During the period which elapsed between the signature of the treaty, which had freed them from all resistance, and the assembling of the Parliament which was to end their labours, they agitated the country in order to render it universally favourable to their plans. Their preachers were sent all over the kingdom,[2] and when the Parliament met, an immense majority of its members declared their determination to alter the religious constitution of Scotland.[3] The inferior nobles, who had long neglected to attend, made their appearance on this extraordinary occasion, and resumed the right of voting. The ecclesiastical benches were almost deserted,[4] as the greater number of the bishops and abbots who were members of the House, did not choose to be present at the destruction of their Church. The Lords of the Articles were nearly all chosen from among the Congregation, and the Parliament opened under the presidency of Lethington, whose character adapted itself to every situation, and who was destined long to employ his talents in the service of the victorious cause. The royal power was represented by the dumb and insignificant insignia of a crown, mace, and sword, placed upon the empty throne.[5] Absent and enfeebled, the sovereign authority had become incapable of directing and restraining that revolutionary assembly, which was commissioned to conclude the work pursued, for more than twenty years, by the Reformers, with various vicissitudes, but continual progress. A violent petition of the most zealous Reformers, approved if

[1] MS. letter, State Paper Office, Cecil and Wotton to Queen Elizabeth, 8th July, 1560. Tytler, vol. v., p. 128. [2] Keith, p. 145.
[3] Their names are given in Keith, pp. 146-147.
[4] Tytler, vol v., p. 135. [5] Ibid.

not composed by Knox, demanded of the Parliament to restore the primitive discipline established by the apostles, to proscribe the Romish Church, to suppress the Catholic clergy, to condemn the doctrine of transubstantiation and the adoration of the body of Jesus Christ under the form of bread, to denounce the merit of works, purgatory, pilgrimages, and prayers to departed saints; in a word, to abolish all those sacraments and ceremonies of the Romish Church, which were attacked by nearly all the Reformers of Europe, and to deprive the clergy for ever of the right to sit and vote in the Great Council of the Nation.[1] Most of these imperious injunctions were obeyed. The Parliament satisfied the Reformers by adopting their faith, and pleased the nobility by granting them a share of the property of the clergy.

Application was then made to the reformed ministers for a Confession of Faith, which they drew up in four days. This confession was based upon the Apostles' Creed, and was very similar to the Articles of the Church of England in the reign of Edward VI. The doctrines asserted in it were nearly the same as those held by Calvin; and the Parliament ratified it on the 17th of August, almost by acclamation.[2] The only temporal lords who did not approve of it, were the Earls of Cassillis and Caithness; and among the spiritual lords, there were only the Primate Archbishop of St. Andrews, and the Bishops of Dumblane and Dunkeld, who, without refusing to reform existing abuses, required time to effect these reforms with maturity and reflection.[3] The victorious Reformers became, as it too frequently happens, intolerant in the extreme. By successive acts, they abolished the Catholic faith and the Papal jurisdiction in the kingdom; and enacted terrible penalties against all who should celebrate or attend mass, condemning them, for the first offence, to confiscation of their property, for the second, to banishment, and for the third, to death.[4]

The ministers of the new Church of Scotland next prepared the *Book of Discipline*, which was intended to regulate their system of ecclesiastical government. They disapproved of the Anglican almost as much as of the Romish hierarchy, and called it a remnant of superstition and idolatry offensive to all godly men. Thus, whilst they prescribed obedience to princes and magistrates, and denounced, as enemies alike to God and man,

---

[1] Tytler, vol. v., pp. 137-138. Keith, p. 149.
[2] Knox, vol. ii., pp. 95-123. Keith, pp. 149-150.
[3] Tytler, vol. v., p. 141.
[4] These acts are given in Keith, p. 151. Knox, vol. ii., pp. 123-130.

all who should attempt to abolish the *holy state of civil policies*,[1] they did not recognize, as was the case in England, the head of the State to be the head of the Church. The religious sovereignty belonged to the people, who were the source of all ecclesiastical authority. They alone appointed the ministers by election; but those elected by any Christian society, before they were admitted to the ministry, were publicly examined by the ministers and elders of the congregation, upon the fundamental points of faith, and the differences of doctrine between the Romish and Presbyterian Churches. After this examination, without even receiving any imposition of hands, they were introduced among the brethren, and took the service of that church to which they had been appointed. They administered the sacraments of baptism and the Lord's Supper; preached the Word of God, and read the Common Prayers as well as the Holy Scriptures. This last duty was performed by simple 'readers,' in places where there were no regularly-constituted pastors. Deacons were also elected to receive the revenues and distribute the alms of the Church.

The kingdom was divided into ten districts, over which ten ministers were to be placed with the title of superintendents.[2] Over these districts they were appointed regularly to itinerate, for the purpose of preaching three times a week, of providing for the complete establishment of all the churches, of observing that the ordinary ministers led a regular life and received a sufficient income, of inspecting the manners of the people, and of taking care that the poor were supplied with alms, and that the young received instruction.[3] It was in obedience to the Book of Discipline that those parish schools were formed, to which Scotland was subsequently indebted for the general diffusion of knowledge among the inferior classes of her population, and for the prosperity which has thereby accrued to the country. 'It was necessary,' such are nearly the words of the Congregation, 'that care should be had of the virtuous and godly education of the youth, wherefore it was judged in every parish to have a proper schoolmaster, able to teach at least the grammar and Latin tongue, where the town was of any reputation. But,' it adds, ' in land-

---

[1] Tytler, vol. v., p. 141. Knox, vol. ii., chap. 24.
[2] The stations of these superintendents were at Orkney, Ross, Argyle, Aberdeen, Brechin, St. Andrews, Edinburgh, Jedburgh, Glasgow, and Dumfries. Knox, vol. i., pp. 203-204.
[3] For details regarding the organization of the Scottish Church, see Knox, vol. pp. 185-258, and Tytler, vol. v., pp. 144-146.

wart (that is, country parishes), where the people convened to doctrine only once in the week, there must either the reader or the minister take care of the youth of the parish, to instruct them in their rudiments, and especially in the catechism of Geneva.'[1]

A Book of Discipline, which devoted the property of the Catholic clergy to the service of the reformed faith, the education of the people, and the support of the poor, and which exposed laymen of every rank to the severe censure of the pastors, was not at all pleasing to the nobility, whom it deprived of both wealth and power. It did not, consequently, obtain the same unanimous approbation as the Confession of Faith. Several barons refused to subscribe it, and others evaded signing it although they had expressed their adherence to it.[2] They wished to keep the property that they had taken, and were not anxious, as they said, alone to 'bear the barrow to build the houses of God.'[3] But with the exception of this disagreement, the old nobility and the new church acted in concert to destroy the Romish clergy, to annul the influence of France, and to weaken the royal authority. The Treaty of Edinburgh, and the Acts of Parliament passed in August, 1560, constituted Scotland a sort of Protestant republic, governed by nobles and ministers, and placed under the protectorate of England. The Lords of the Congregation did not hesitate to say: 'That in providing for the security and liberty of Scotland, the realm was more bounden to her Majesty (Queen Elizabeth) than to their own sovereign.'[4]

In the absence of the Queen, the Parliament appointed twenty-four of the most important members of the victorious party to administer justice and govern the kingdom.[5] Sir James Sandilands, of Calder, Prior of the Knights of St. John of Jerusalem, was sent to France to communicate to Mary Stuart and Francis II. the measures which had been taken, and to request their ratification;[6] but Mary Stuart and Francis II., both as sovereigns and as Catholics, could not give their sanction to a revolution which had changed the conditions of the monarchy and the religion of the country. The usurpation of the supreme authority by the nobility of Scotland, the conclusion of an alliance with a foreign power, the deposition of the Regent, the convocation of a Parliament without the concurrence and assent of the sovereign, the change effected in the national religion by public deliberation, and

---

[1] Spotswood's History of the Church of Scotland, pp. 154-160.
[2] Knox, vol. ii., pp. 128-129.   [3] Ibid., vol. ii., p. 89.
[4] MS. letter, State Paper Office, quoted in Tytler, vol. v., p. 131.
[5] Tytler, vol. v., p. 148.   [6] Knox, vol. ii., pp. 125-126.

the formation of a council of regency by an assembly, all irritated them to the last degree. They felt they were virtually, if not actually, dethroned. The Cardinal of Lorraine complained bitterly to the English ambassador, Throckmorton, of the support which Queen Elizabeth had given to such acts of rebellion.[1] 'I will tell you frankly,' he said; 'the Scots, the King's subjects, do perform no part of their duties; the King and Queen have the name of their sovereigns, and your mistress hath the effect and the obedience.[2] When Throckmorton requested Mary Stuart to ratify the Treaty of Edinburgh, she peremptorily refused to do so, and said with some warmth: 'My subjects in Scotland do their duty in nothing. I am their Queen, and so they call me, but they use me not so. They must be taught to know their duties.[3] Throckmorton then represented to her that if she did not accept the Treaty of Edinburgh she would give Queen Elizabeth reason to suspect her intentions and those of the King her husband, and would appear to retain her pretensions with regard to England, the arms of which she still continued to bear; but she dismissed him with a very unsatisfactory answer.[4]

Notwithstanding all her discontent, Mary Stuart found that she was not in a position to bring back her subjects to their former obedience by force. The French troops had evacuated Leith, and King Francis II. was too busily employed in subjugating the Huguenots and crushing the rising resistance of the Bourbons and their party, to take any vigorous measures with reference to Scotland. Her uncles, the Duke of Guise and the Cardinal of Lorraine, who governed in his name, thought that the chief point was to gain time, to allow the confederates to become divided amongst themselves, and meanwhile, to destroy all opposition in France. To this task they applied themselves with as much boldness as vigour. After having foiled the conspiracy of Amboise, and hanged its subordinate and ostensible leaders, they arrested the Prince of Condé, and prosecuted him as its mysterious and principal head; they also intimidated the King of Navarre, nullified the old Constable and his son, and threatened

---

[1] The court of France had already, on the 20th of April, 1560, addressed a *Protestation à la reine d'Angleterre et à son Conseil*, regarding the hostile proceedings of the English in Scotland; Queen Elizabeth, in reply, wrote a *Responsum ad protestationem*, &c. Both these documents are published in M. Teulet's collection of *Pièces et documents relatifs à l'histoire d'Ecosse*, vol i., pp. 429-436, and 436-459.

[2] MS. letter, State Paper Office, Throckmorton to Elizabeth, 17th November, 1560. Tytler, vol. v., p. 150.

[3] Tytler, vol. v., pp. 151-152.   [4] Ibid., vol. v., pp. 152-153.

the three brothers Chatillon. But their policy of violent compression in France, and adroit temporization in Scotland, was disconcerted by the death of Francis II., which happened on the 5th of December, 1560. Mary Stuart was left a widow; the Lorraine princes, her uncles, lost their authority; and, by the separation of the two crowns of Scotland and France, the connection of the interests of the two countries also ceased. With Charles IX. commenced another system of policy under the cautious direction of Catherine de Medici, who feared the Guises and did not like Mary Stuart; and who, anxious to avoid all appeal to force, strove to effect a compromise between the different parties and their leaders, at home; and abroad, to maintain friendly relations with foreign powers.

Thus, the marriage which had just been dissolved by death, had yielded Mary Stuart no advantage, and produced none but evil effects. In Scotland, it had weakened the monarchy by causing the absence of the royal authority. It had united the nobility, and given the predominance to their disorderly government. It had secured the triumph of the Protestant Reformation, and added to the evils which sprang from feudal turbulence those which could not fail to issue from a religious democracy, disposed to disobey their prince, under the pretext of obeying God. It had rendered the French alliance as odious as it had formerly been courted, and restored the English influence which had previously been so pertinaciously repulsed. When Mary Stuart became once more the Queen of Scotland only, she found her nobility accustomed to rebellion and in possession of the supreme power; her kingdom allied, against her wish, to a neighbouring, and long hostile state; and her people professing a different religion from her own. Habits, power, politics, creed—all wore a threatening aspect.

Left a widow at eighteen years of age, and after twelve years of residence in France, Mary Stuart felt all that death took from her by depriving her of her husband, and making her descend from the throne of France. She remained for some time plunged in the deepest affliction.[1] For several weeks she shut herself up

[1] She herself composed a poem upon her loss and affliction, the following stanzas, of which we extract from Brantôme:—

I.
'Fut-il un tel malheur
De dure destinée,
Ny si triste douleur
De dame fortunée,
Qui mon cœur et mon œil
Voit en bierre et cercueil

II.
'Qui en mon doux printemps
Et fleur de ma jeunesse,
Toutes les peines sens
D'une extrême tristesse,
Et en rien n'ay plaisir
Qu'en regret et desir.

in her room, and would admit no one but the Queen-mother, the King, his brothers, the King of Navarre, the Constable of Montmorency, and her uncles, the Princes of Lorraine.¹ As soon as she gave admittance to the foreign ambassadors, she had numerous offers of marriage, to which she would not listen, and the curious phases of which we shall presently point out. King Philip II., not having succeeded in his scheme of marrying Elizabeth himself, wished to obtain the hand of Mary Stuart for his son Don Carlos,² and thus to place Spain in that position which France had hitherto occupied with regard to Scotland. The Kings of Sweden³ and Denmark⁴ also aspired to her hand.

Elizabeth sent the Earl of Bedford to express her condolence with the widow of Francis II. This ambassador extraordinary arrived at Paris on the 3rd of February, and, after having discharged the formal duty devolved upon him by his mistress, he requested the Queen of Scotland to ratify the Treaty of Edin-

III.
' Pour mon mal estranger
Je ne m'arreste en place;
Mais j'ay beau changer
Si ma douleur j'efface,
Car mon pis et mon mieux
Sont les plus déserts lieux

IV.
' Si en quelque séjour,
Soit en bois ou en prée,
Soit sur l'aube du jour,
Ou soit sur la vesprée,
Sans cesse mon cœur sent
Le regret d'un absent.

V.
' Si parfois vers les cieux
Viens à dresser ma veüe,
Le doux traict de ces yeux
Je vois en une nüe;
Soudain je vois en l'eau
Comme dans un tombeau.

VI.
' Si je suis en repos,
Sommeillant sur ma couche,
J'oy qu'il me tient propos,
Je le sens qu'il me touche:
En labeur, en recoy,
Tousjours est prest de moy.'

¹ 'Immediately upon her husband's death, she changed her lodging, withdrew herself from all company, became so solitary and exempt of all worldliness, that she doth not to this day see daylight, and thus will continue out forty days. For the space of fifteen days after the death of her said husband, she admitted no man to come into her chamber, but the King, his brethren, the King of Navarre, the Constable, and her uncles.'—MS. letter, State Paper office, Throckmorton to the Council, 31st December, 1560. Tytler, vol. v., p. 158.

² This proposition came from the Cardinal of Lorraine himself, who opened the matter in these terms to the Spanish ambassador at Paris:—' El mismo Cardinal quexandose de la desgracia de su sobrina, y del poco remedio que tiene de hallar partido igual, me dixo claramente que no le avia sino era casandose con su alteza.' Chantonnay to Philip II., 28th December, 1560; Archives of Simancas, series B, file 12, No. 116.

³ Eric XIV., son of Gustavus Vasa, born in 1533, succeeded his father in 1560, and was dethroned in 1569.

⁴ Frederic II., born in 1534, ascended the throne in 1558.

burgh.¹ Mary expressed her desire to live with Elizabeth upon the best terms of neighbourhood and relationship. 'We are both,' she said to Bedford, 'in one isle, both of one language, both the nearest kinswomen that each other hath, and both Queens.'² But, after having given these reasons for maintaining a close friendship, she refused to sanction the Treaty of Edinburgh in the absence of her uncle the Cardinal of Lorraine, then away from the court, and on no account before she had consulted her nobility and Parliament. She graciously requested the portrait of Elizabeth, and wished she could have an interview with her, as it would lead to a more prompt and sure understanding than all these complicated negotiations could effect. Thus she eluded the ratification of the treaty, to which she was determined not to submit.³

All her thoughts now turned towards Scotland, where the news of the death of Francis II. had been received with unfeigned satisfaction. His death, by putting an end to the fears inspired by France, naturally divided parties once more. As the national interest of independence no longer existed, private interests resumed their sway. The Catholic party regained animation and courage. It held a secret meeting, at which the Archbishop of St. Andrews, the Bishops of Aberdeen, Murray, and Ross, the Earls of Athol, Huntly, Crawford, Sutherland, and Caithness, and several other noblemen, were present. They commissioned John Lesly, then Official of Aberdeen, and subsequently Bishop of Ross, to go and assure their young sovereign of their entire devotion to her person.⁴ Lesly found Mary Stuart, on the 14th of April, 1561, at Vitry, in Champagne. From Rheims, where he had spent part of the winter with her aunt, the Abbess of the Convent of St. Pierre-les-Dames, she proceeded to Lorraine. Lesly proposed to her, on behalf of the Catholics, to proceed at once to Scotland; to detain in France her brother James, who had been despatched to her by the insurrectionary Parliament, until after her return into her kingdom; and to disembark at Aberdeen, where she would find an army of twenty thousand men levied by her friends in the North of Scotland.⁵ Mary had the

¹ MS. instructions, State Paper Office, 20th January, 1561. Tytler, vol. v., pp. 167-169.
² MS. letter, State Paper Office, the Earl of Bedford and Sir Nicholas Throckmorton to the Privy Council, 26th February, 1561. Tytler, vol. v., p. 169.
³ Same despatch, in Tytler, vol. v., p. 172.
⁴ Keith, p. 159. Tytler, vol. v., p. 165.
⁵ De rebus gestis Scotorum, authore Joanne Leslæo episcopo Rossensi. London, 1725, vol. i., p. 226, *et seq.* Keith, p. 160.

wisdom to reject this proposition. Remembering that the leaders of this party had recently proved themselves either weak or seditious, she did not think that their devotion would be very zealous, their offer very sincere, or their fidelity very lasting. Besides, she was anxious not to appear exclusive, lest she should still further add to her weakness. She sought the assistance of every one. She had already directed Preston of Craigmillar, Ogilvy of Findlater, Lumsden of Blanern, and Lesly of Auchtermuchty, whom she had sent as her commissioners into Scotland, where they arrived, on the 20th of February, 1561, to convey to her subjects the assurances of her affection, the promise to pursue a conciliatory policy, and the announcement of her speedy return.[1] In order to restore the regular action of authority, she addressed a royal commission to the Duke of Chatelherault, the Earls of Argyle, Athol,[2] Huntly, and Bothwell, the Archbishop of St. Andrews, and Lord James Stuart, to convoke a legal Parliament.[3]

As soon as the Parliament met, Lord James was despatched to his sister. No envoy could have been selected better adapted than this nobleman to moderate Mary Stuart's displeasure, and induce her speedy return into her kingdom. He passed through England. Elizabeth and her ministers, with whom he had long been in constant communication, were not without fear lest the offers which the Court of France would be sure to make him should detach him from their party. He was the most important personage in Scotland, by reason of his royal descent, the position which he had taken in the affairs of the country, the influence which he exercised as the secular head of the reformed party, and the confidence with which he had inspired most of the nobility. Though still young, he had earned considerable distinction, both as a soldier and a politician. To the most undaunted courage he added the most consummate ability. Possessing great judgment, energy of character, and firmness of purpose; with less variableness and cunning than his astute and fickle countrymen; frank and blunt, though not incapable of dissimulation and falsehood, he was always guided by that resolute good sense which seldom fails to conduct a man quickly and safely to the object he has in view.

[1] These instructions, extracted from the archives of the French Foreign Office, are published in Prince Labanoff's collection, vol. i., pp. 85-88.
[2] John Stewart, fourth Earl of Athol,—a descendant of Alexander, *High Stewart* of Scotland, the common ancestor of the Stuart family,—succeeded to the earldom in 1542.
[3] MS. letter, State Paper Office, Randolph to Cecil, 26th February, 1561. Tytler, vol. v., p. 165.

The Prior of St. Andrews met the Queen, his sister, at St. Dizier, on the day after she had seen John Lesly, the Official of Aberdeen.[1] He endeavoured to render her favourable to the Congregation, and to an alliance with England. But Mary Stuart would not allow herself to be persuaded by the reasons which he adduced in favour of a course of policy calculated to strengthen her authority and insure her repose. She informed him of her intentions, declaring that she would not ratify the Treaty of Edinburgh, and that she would seek to dissolve the union between England and Scotland, which was very distasteful to her. She even endeavoured to gain over Lord James to her religion and plans, by offering him a cardinal's hat, and several rich benefices in France. But Lord James unhesitatingly refused all these advantages, and seemed to obtain his sister's confidence more thoroughly by this proof of his rectitude and disinterestedness. Mary promised to send him full powers to govern the kingdom during her absence; and merely desired him not to pass through England on his return to Scotland.[2]

Lord James would not consent to this. He continued so strongly attached to the alliance with Elizabeth, which constituted, in his opinion, the principal strength of his party, that he communicated what had passed between his sister and himself to the English ambassador, Throckmorton. This statesman, feeling how important it was that his Sovereign should retain the influence which she had acquired in Scotland, advised her to make sure of the most able and powerful men in the country by the annual distribution amongst them of 20,000*l*. sterling. 'There should be some special consideration had,' he wrote, 'of the Earl of Arran, because he is the second person of that realm; and, in like manner, of the Lord James, whose credit, love, and honesty, is comparable in my judgment to any man of that realm. . . . . I do well perceive the Lord James to a very honourable, sincere, and godly gentleman, and very much affected to your Majesty, upon whom you never bestowed good turn better than on him, in my opinion.'[3] The parsimonious Elizabeth thought she had sufficient hold upon him by the double bond of religious faith and political interest, and that it was unnecessary to add that of money. She received him very kindly when he came to London,

[1] Keith, p. 160.
[2] MS. letters, State Paper Office, Throckmorton to Elizabeth, 29th April and 1st May, 1568. Tytler, vol. v., pp. 174-179.
[3] MS. letter, State Paper Office, Throckmorton to Elizabeth, 29th April, 1561. Tytler, vol. v., p. 180.

but granted him nothing more than the inexpensive favour of a gracious reception.

Mary Stuart, finding that she could neither shake Lord James's fidelity to the reformed party, nor destroy his attachment to England, did not grant him the powers with which she had promised to invest him. Gilles de Noailles had been despatched to request the Scottish Parliament to break off the alliance they had lately concluded with England, and renew that which had so long been maintained with France. But Noailles failed of success in his mission; and the Scottish Parliament proved as immovable as the Prior of St. Andrews had been. They replied to Mary Stuart's envoy that the assistance afforded to Scotland by Queen Elizabeth had delivered the realm from Papal tyranny and French domination; and with this answer he was forced to content himself.[1] Mary Stuart, after having passed some time at Rheims and in Lorraine,[2] prepared to return into Scotland, taking with her an annual income of 60,000 livres as Queen Dowager of France.[3] She returned more from necessity than from choice. 'I have often seen her,' says Brantôme, 'dread this voyage as greatly as her death, and desire a hundred times rather to remain a simple dowager in France than to go and reign in her wild country.'[4] She requested Elizabeth to give her a safe-conduct through her dominions; and D'Oysel, who was to go before her into Scotland, was instructed to make this request.[5] But Elizabeth would not allow D'Oysel to pass through her dominions, and refused to grant Mary a safe-conduct.[6] 'Her Majesty,' wrote Cecil, 'would not disguise with her, but plainly would forbear to show her such pleasure until she should ratify it (the Treaty of Edinburgh), and that done, she should not only have free passage, but all helps and gratuities.'[7]

Mary Stuart was deeply wounded by this refusal. She displayed her feelings on the subject to the English Ambassador, Throckmorton, in words full of dignity and bitterness: 'There is nothing, Monsieur l'Ambassadeur, doth grieve me more,' she said, 'than that I did so forget myself as to require of the Queen,

---

[1] Keith, p. 161. Tytler, vol. v., pp. 183, 184.
[2] De Rebus gestis Scotorum, authore Joanne Leslæo, vol. i., p. 226.
[3] 'Avons, suyvant les conventions matrimoniales d'icelle nostre dicte sœur, résolu luy assigner son dict douaire, montant à la dicte somme de soixante mil livres tournois de revenu pour chacun an, sur le dict duché de Touraine, conté de Poictou, terres et seigneuries en dépendans.' Ordinance of Charles IX., 20th December, 1560, in Teulet, vol. i., p. 734.   [4] Brantôme, vol. v., p. 90.
[5] Keith, p. 169.   [6] Ibid., p. 171.   Tytler, vol. v., p. 186.
[7] MS. letter, Cecil to Sussex, 25th July, 1561. Quoted in Tytler, vol. v., p. 188.

your mistress, that favour which I had no need to ask.' Then, calling to mind her causes of complaint against Elizabeth, she added nobly, and with a somewhat threatening vehemence: ' But, Monsieur l'Ambassadeur, let your mistress think that it will be deemed very strange amongst all princes and countries that she should first animate my subjects against me, and now, being a widow, impeach my going into my own country. I ask of her nothing but friendship: I do not trouble her state, nor practise with her subjects. And yet I know there be in her realm some that be inclined enough to hear offers. I know also they be not of the same mind she is of, neither in religion, nor in other things. The Queen, your mistress, doth say that I am young and do lack experience. But I have age enough and experience to behave myself towards my friends and kinsfolks friendly and uprightly, and I trust my discretion shall not so fail me that my passion shall move me to use other language of her than is due to a Queen and my next kinswoman.'[1]

When, on the next day, the 21st of July, she had one more interview with Throckmorton before her departure, she addressed him in these beautiful words, marked by melancholy forebodings, which were not destined to be realized until a later period: ' I trust the wind will be so favourable as I shall not need to come on the coast of England, and if I do, then, Monsieur l'Ambassadeur, the Queen, your mistress, shall have me in her hands to do her will of me; and if she be so hard-hearted as to desire my end, she may then do her pleasure and make sacrifice of me. Peradventure that casualty might be better for me than to live; in this matter God's will be fulfilled.'[2]

After having passed a few days at St. Germain, with the royal family, she bade them farewell, and was accompanied as far as Calais by the Duke of Guise, the Cardinals of Lorraine and Guise, and a number of the Court. She embarked, on the 14th of August, with her three uncles, the Duke D'Aumale, the Great Prior, the Duke D'Elbeuf, M. de Damville, son of the Constable de Montmorency, and many other noblemen.[3] Brantôme, who was one of the gentlemen who followed her into Scotland, has left a touching narrative of her departure, some few sentences of which I will quote: ' The galley,' he says, ' having left port and

---

[1] MS. letter, Throckmorton to Elizabeth, 26th July, 1561. Quoted in Keith, pp. 172, 173.

[2] Ibid., p. 176.

[3] ' De cent ou six vingts gentilshommes que nous estions en ce voyage,' says Brantôme, vol. ii., p. 368.

a slight breeze having sprung up, we began to set sail. . . . She, with both arms resting on the poop of the galley near the helm, began to shed floods of tears, continually casting her beautiful eyes towards the port and the country she had left, and uttering these mournful words: Farewell, France! until night began to fall. She desired to go to bed without taking any food, and would not go down into her cabin, so her bed was prepared on the deck. She commanded the steersman, as soon as it was day, if he could still discern the coast of France, to wake her and not fear to call her; in which fortune favoured her, for the wind having ceased and recourse being had to the oars, very little progress was made during the night; so that when day appeared, the coast of France was still visible, and the steersman not having failed to perform the commands which she had given him, she sat up in her bed, and began again to look at France as long as she could, and then she redoubled her lamentations: Farewell, France! Farewell, France! I think I shall never see thee more!"[1]

But if she experienced sorrow at leaving her adopted country, her departure caused no less poignant regret, and Ronsard thus gracefully expresses the feelings of melancholy excited in his breast by the event:—

> 'Le jour que votre voile aux vents se recourba,
> Et de nos yeux pleurans les vostres déroba,
> Ce jour-là même voile emporta loin de France,
> Les Muses qui souloient y faire demourance.'[2]

Although she feared that she might be intercepted by the cruisers which Elizabeth had sent to sea, she arrived without accident in the Frith of Forth, after a passage of five days. A

[1] Brantôme, vol. v., pp. 92-94.
[2] The lines which follow are no less worthy of quotation:—

> 'Quand cet yvoire blanc qui enfle vostre sein,
> Quand vostre longue, gresle et délicate main,
> Quand vostre belle taille et vostre beau corsage
> Qui ressemble au portrait d'une céleste image,
> Quand vos sages propos, quand vostre douce voix
> Qui pourroit esmouvoir les rochers et les bois,
> Las, ne sont plus ici, quand tant de beautés rares,
> Dont les graces des cieux ne vous furent avares,
> Abandonnant la France, ont, d'un autre costé,
> L'agréable sujet de nos vers emporté,
> Comment pourroient chanter les bouches des poëtes,
> Quand par vostre départ les Muses sont muettes.
> Tout ce qui est de beau ne se garde longtemps,
> Les roses et les lys ne règnent qu'un printemps.
> Ainsi vostre beauté seulement apparue
> Quinze ans en nostre France, est soudain disparue,

thick fog which arose on the evening before her arrival, kept
from view the little fleet which was bringing her back to her
kingdom, and which had cast anchor at no great distance from
the shore. This fog cleared up on the morning of the 19th of
August, and Mary Stuart entered the harbour of Leith before she
was expected.[1] As soon as the news of her arrival became
known, the people flocked from all quarters to welcome her, and
the nobility hastened to conduct her to Edinburgh, to the palace
of her ancestors. This cordial reception touched, but did not
rejoice, her heart. She could not refrain from instituting a
mournful comparison between the poverty of the wild country to
which she had returned, after an absence of thirteen years, and
the magnificence of the Court in which the happy days of her
childhood and youth had been spent. A palfrey had been provided for her, but the noblemen and ladies of her retinue were
forced to be contented with small mountain ponies, 'such as they
were,' says Brantôme, 'and harnessed to match.' At sight of
them, he adds, 'the Queen began to weep, and to say that this
was not like the pomp, the splendour, the trappings, or the
superb horses of France.' She proceeded with this humble
cortége to Holyrood palace. During the evening, the citizens of
Edinburgh came beneath her windows to play on their three-
stringed violins, and to sing psalms, in demonstration of their joy
at her return.[2] The sound of their discordant music, and the
hymns of a creed which she deemed gloomy and heretical, added
to the melancholy impressions experienced by Mary Stuart on returning to a country where she felt she was a stranger, whose
manners she had not adopted, and whose faith she no longer
shared.

Comme on voit d'un éclair s'évanouir le trait,
Et d'elle n'a laissé sinon que le regret,
Sinon le déplaisir que me remet sans cesse,
Au cœur le souvenir d'une telle princesse.'
(RONSARD, Œuvres, vol. viii., pp. 6, 7.)

[1] Brantôme, vol. v., pp. 94-95. This fog was regarded as a bad sign by the
zealous Protestants. Knox says that the appearance of the heavens and the density
of the atmosphere showed 'what comfort was brought unto this country with her,
to wit, sorrow, dolour, darkness, and all impiety.' History of the Reformation,
vol. ii., p. 268.

[2] 'Et qui pis est, le soir, ainsi qu'elle se vouloit coucher, estant logée en bas, en
l'abbaye d'Islebourg, qui est certes un beau bastiment, et ne tient rien du pays,
vindrent sons sa fenêtre cinq ou six cents marauts de la ville lui donner l'aubade de
méchants violons et petits rebecz, dont il n'y en a faute en ce pays-là, et se mirent
à chanter des pseaumes, tant mal chantez et si mal accordez que rien plus!'
Brantôme, vol. v., p. 95 ; Knox, vol. i., pp. 269-270.

CHAPTER III.

FROM MARY'S RETURN INTO SCOTLAND TO HER MARRIAGE WITH DARNLEY.

Policy pursued by Mary Stuart.—Concessions to the Protestant party.—Lord James Stuart appointed Prime Minister.—Disgrace of the Hamiltons.—Rebellion of the Earl of Huntly.—Negotiations for the Queen's Second Marriage.—Her Rupture with Murray.—His Conspiracy.—Marriage of the Queen to Lord Darnley.

DIFFICULTIES of various kinds, and all of them of a very serious nature, beset the path of Mary Stuart in Scotland. How should she treat with triumphant Protestantism? How should she maintain in union and reduce to obedience her nobility, so long accustomed to division and revolt? How should she live in harmony with Queen Elizabeth, her powerful neighbour, and enemy at heart? And finally, how should she marry again without endangering her Crown, if she espoused a foreign prince, and disturbing the peace of her kingdom, if she bestowed her hand upon one of her own subjects? To steer clear of all these difficulties, she would have required a prudence beyond her years and contrary to her nature. She possessed finesse, but little circumspection; and though endowed with much ingenuity and tact, she was not capable of sustained action. Familiar and ready, graceful and enthusiastic, reposing unbounded confidence in all who pleased her, and abandoning herself with impetuosity to the ideas which momentarily influenced her, she had all the charms of a woman, without possessing in a sufficiently high degree the vigorous qualities necessary to a Queen.

Having been warned, however, of the dangers which awaited her, she acted at first with great discretion, under the prudent direction of Lord James Stuart and Lord Lethington. She appointed members of her Privy Council,[1] the Duke of Chatelherault, the Earls of Huntly, Argyle, Bothwell, Errol,[2] Marshal, Athol, Morton, Montrose,[3] and Glencairn, Lord James Stuart, and Lord John Erskine, together with the Treasurer of the Crown, the Secretary of State, the Clerk-register, and the Justice-clerk.[4] The Earl of Huntly still retained the dignity of Chan-

---
[1] This Act, dated September 6, 1561, is in Keith, p. 187.
[2] George, sixth Earl of Errol. [3] William, second Earl of Montrose.
[4] The Treasurer was Robert Richardson, Commendator of St. Mary Isle, and appointed to the former office in 1558. Lethington was Secretary of State. The

cellor, but she made Lord James Stuart her Prime Minister, and Lethington her Secretary of State.[1] These two Protestant leaders thus became the confidential advisers of a Catholic Queen. Apparently resolved to offer no opposition to the religious revolution which had taken place in her kingdom during her absence, she expected nothing less than toleration for herself. 'I mean,' she said to Throckmorton, a short time before she left France 'to constrain none of my subjects, but would wish that they were all as I am, and I trust they should have no support to constrain me.'[2]

But this toleration was not to be easily obtained from zealous secretaries who regarded the restoration of the mass as the reestablishment of idolatry. 'One mass,' said Knox, 'was more fearful to him than if ten thousand armed enemies were landed in any part of the realm.'[3] Accordingly, when, on the Sunday following Mary Stuart's arrival, mass was said in her private chapel, the Protestant party were moved almost to insurrection. The ministers threatened; the people murmured; and it was said on every hand, 'That idol shall not be suffered again to take place within this realm!'[4] The fanatical Master of Lindsay, clad in his coat of mail, and followed by a troop of men as exasperated as himself, rushed into the court-yard of Holyrood Palace, crying out that 'the idolater priest should die the death, according to God's law.'[5] Lord James Stuart, who had expected some tumult of this kind, dispersed the mob.[6] Resolved not to permit any infringement of his sister's religious freedom, he had taken up his post at the door of the chapel; and, opposing his authority and energy to their tumultuary fanaticism, he protected the Queen's chaplains, who performed the Catholic ceremonies without interruption, to the great scandal of Knox and others.

A short time after the occurrence of this scene, Knox wrote to his friend Calvin:—'The arrival of the Queen has disturbed the tranquillity of our affairs. She had scarcely been back three

---

Clerk-register was James Makgill, eldest son of Sir J. Makgill, Provost of Edinburgh, who had held that post since 1554. The Justice-clerk was Sir John Bellenden, who succeeded his father Thomas, in 1547. All the four were Protestants.

[1] Keith, pp. 188–189.
[2] Throckmorton to Elizabeth, 23rd June, 1561. Keith, p. 167.
[3] Knox, vol. ii., p. 276.
[4] Ibid., vol. ii., p. 270.
[5] Ibid., vol. ii., p. 270. This Patrick Lindsay of Byres, succeeded to his father's title in 1563.
[6] Ibid., vol. ii., p. 271. Tytler, vol. v., p. 195.

days, before the idol of the mass was again set up. Some prudent men of great authority endeavoured to prevent it, saying that their purified conscience could not suffer that that land should again be contaminated, which the Lord, by the efficacy of his Word, had purged from idolatry. But as the major part of those who adhere to our faith thought differently, impiety gained the victory, and is now acquiring fresh strength. Those who favoured it give as a reason for their indulgence, that all the ministers of the Lord are of opinion, and that you yourself declare, that it is not lawful for us to prevent the Queen from practising her religion. Although I contradict this rumour, which appears to me very false, it has taken such deep root in men's hearts, that it will be impossible for me to dislodge it, unless I learn from you whether the question has been actually submitted to your Church, and what was the answer of the brethren. I am always troubling you with such inquiries, but I have no one else into whose bosom I can pour my cares. I confess candidly, my father, that I have never until now felt how painful and difficult it is to combat hypocrisy when concealed under the mask of piety. I have never feared open enemies so greatly, but that, in the midst of my tribulations, I have hoped to gain the victory.'[1]

The discontent of Knox plainly revealed all that new species of intolerance, threatening indications of which were displayed to the Queen when she made her public entrance into Edinburgh. On the 2nd of September, the day appointed for that ceremony, Mary Stuart, after having dined at the Castle, proceeded towards the town under a canopy of violet-coloured velvet, and accompanied by the nobility and principal burgesses. A little child, six years of age, issued from a cloud as if he were descending from Heaven, and, having recited a copy of verses, presented her with the Keys of Edinburgh, a Bible, and a Book of Psalms. In order to recal to her memory the terrible punishments which, as the Scriptures inform us God inflicted upon idolators, among the pageants exhibited on the road were representations of the fate of

---

[1] This Latin letter from Knox to Calvin is dated October 24th. It belongs to M. Feuillet de Conches, and has recently been printed in M. Teulet's collection of *Pièces et documents relatifs à l'histoire d'Écosse*, vol. ii., pp. 12–14. After having declared to Calvin, 'Apertos hostes nunquam sic timui, quum in mediis ærumnis victoriam sperarem,' Knox concluded with these words :—'Salutat te Jacobus ille frater reginæ, maxime senex, qui solus inter eos qui aulam frequentant impietati se opponit ; ille tamen inter reliquos fascinatur in hoc quod veretur idolum illud violenter deturbare. Salutat te Ecclesia tota, et tuarum precun· subsidium flagitat. Dominus Jesu diu Ecclesiæ suæ incolumen servet. Amen.'

Korah, Dathan, and Abiram, swallowed up by the earth at the very moment when they were offering their sacrifice, and other spectacles of equally sinister signification. The people were with difficulty induced to refrain from exhibiting a most outrageous representation of a priest, burned upon the altar during the elevation of the host. Applauded as a Queen, but menaced as a Catholic, Mary, after having witnessed these various manifestations of popular delight and religious fanaticism, returned to Holyrood.[1]

The Queen, having succeeded, by her brother's firmness of conduct, in practising her worship in private, felt that it was necessary to assure her formidable Protestant subjects of the exclusive domination of their own faith. She accordingly made to them a number of concessions, which must have cost her dear. She declared in the Council and announced to the people by proclamation, that no alteration should be made in the established religion of the country, and that every act whether public or private, which tended to change its form, should be punished with death.[2] The regular authority of the Crown thus confirmed the decisions arrived at by the revolutionary authority of the Parliament. Mary next desired to see Knox, and, perhaps, hoped to mollify him, and attach him to herself. In an interview which she had with him,[3] she discussed the duties of the Christian subject. She pointed out to him, that, in his book against female government, he excited nations to rebel against their rulers; and she advised him to treat with greater charity those who differed from him in matters of religious belief. 'If, madame,' said Knox, 'to rebuke idolatry, and to persuade the people to worship God according to his Word, be to raise subjects against their princes, I cannot stand excused, for so have I acted; but, if the true knowledge of God, and his right worship, lead all good subjects (as they assuredly do) to obey the prince from their heart, then who can reprehend me?' He then professed his willingness to

[1] Wright's Queen Elizabeth and her Times, vol. i., p. 73; Chalmers' Life of Mary, Queen of Scots, 2nd edition, vol. i., p. 80; Keith, p. 189; Knox, vol. ii., pp. 287-288.

[2] This proclamation, extracted from the registers of the Privy Council, and dated August 25, 1561, is contained in Knox, vol. ii. pp. 272, 273. It contains this passage: 'Her Majestie ordains . . . . that nane of thame tak upoun hand privatly or oppinly to mak any alteratioun or innovatioun of the state of religioun, or attempt anything agains the same, quhilk her Majestie fand publicklie and universallie standing at her Majestie's arryvall in this her realme, under the pain of deyth.'

[3] 'The Quene spak with Johne Knox, and had lang resoning with him, none neing present, except the Lord James.' Knox, vol. ii. p. 277.

live in all contentment under her Majesty's government, so long as the blood of the saints was not shed; and he maintained, that, in religion, subjects were bound to follow, not the will of their prince, but the commands of their Creator. 'If,' said he, 'all men in the days of the Apostles should have been compelled to follow the religion of the Roman Emperors, where would have been the Christian faith?' The Queen, drawing a judicious distinction between conscientious dissent and rebellious insurrection, replied, 'But these men did not resist.' 'And yet,' answered Knox, 'they who obey not the commandment may virtually be said to resist.' 'Nay,' rejoined Mary, 'they did not resist with the sword.' 'That,' said Knox, 'was simply because they had not the power.' At this candid and bold declaration, that power conferred the right of insurrection, and that weakness was the only reason for submission to princes, Mary Stuart exclaimed in astonishment, 'What! do you maintain, that subjects, having power, may resist their princes?' The fanatical reformer, who considered that the state should be subordinate to religion, did not hesitate to adopt these consequences of his theory. 'Most assuredly, madam,' he replied, 'if princes exceed their bounds.' Then, comparing sovereigns who, in their blind zeal, would persecute the children of God, to a father who, struck with madness, should attempt to slay his own children, whose duty it would be to bind and disarm him, Knox continued, 'Therefore, to take the sword from them, to bind their hands, and to cast them into prison till they be brought to a more sober mind, is no disobedience against princes, but just obedience, because it agreeth with the word of God.' Mary was utterly amazed. A doctrine so subversive of all authority, which made subjects judges of the obedience which they owed to their rulers, and which authorized them to revolt at the instigation of their spiritual leaders, filled her with alarm. She pictured to herself the terrible future which was reserved for her, a Catholic Queen, in the midst of these haughty and insubordinate Protestants, with their stern and fanatical ministers. She had no strength to answer, for she felt reply was useless. She fell into a melancholy silence, and 'stood as it were amazed, for more than a quarter of an hour.'[1]

Lord James Stuart was the only other person present at this strange scene, when Knox presented himself before the young and amiable Queen, just as the Jewish prophets of old used to convey the admonitions of the Most High to the Kings of Judah and

---

[1] Knox, vol. ii., p. 282.

Israel. He endeavoured to calm the feelings and restore the courage of his sister, and Mary Stuart at length collected herself, and said, giving an ironical assent to the factious words of Knox, in order better to display their tendency, 'Well, then, I perceive that my subjects shall only obey you, and not me; they must do what they list and not what I command, whilst I must learn to be subject unto them, and not they to me.' Urged to this extremity, Knox changed his tone, and anxious to regain the ground he had lost, 'God forbid,' he replied ' that it should ever be so; far be it from me to command any, or to absolve subjects from their lawful obedience. My only desire is, that both princes and subjects should obey God, who has in his word enjoined Kings to be nursing-fathers, and Queens nursing-mothers to his Church.' Mary, who had no idea of becoming the protrectress of a religion which she detested, but was obliged to support, could no longer contain herself. She gave utterance to the feelings which she had hitherto repressed, and said, in anger, 'Yea, this is indeed true, but yours is not the Church that I will nourish. I will defend the Church of Rome, for I think it the true Church of God.'

At these words, Knox burst into furious indignation. He replied energetically to the Queen, that her will was no reason, and that her opinion respecting the Church of Rome could not change that harlot, as he called it, into the immaculate spouse of Christ. He then burst into the most violent invectives against that Church, and declared that it was full of errors, and polluted with vices. He offered to prove that its faith had more grievously degenerated than that of the Jewish Church, when they crucified Jesus Christ. The Queen, however, put an end to his vehement denunciations, and bade him farewell. He took his leave, praying God that 'she might be as blessed in the commonwealth of Scotland, as ever Deborah was in the commonwealth of Israel.'[1]

Knox's inconsiderate zeal incurred the censure of the political leaders of the Protestant party. Lethington even wrote to Cecil, ' You know the vehemency of Mr. Knox's spirit, which cannot be bridled, and yet doth sometimes utter such sentences as cannot easily be digested by a weak stomach. I could wish he would deal with her more gently, being a young princess unpersuaded. For this I am accounted too politic, but surely in her comporting with him she doth declare a wisdom far exceeding her age. God

[1] For a fuller account of this long interview, see Knox, vol. ii. pp. 277—286; or M'Crie's Life of Knox, vol. ii., pp. 31–39. Randolph also mentions it in a Letter to Cecil, on the 7th of September, 1561; Keith, p. 188.

grant her the assistance of his spirit."[1] Among the twelve Earls or Lords of whom Mary had composed her Privy Council, she had given the preponderance to the adherents of the reformed faith. In a General Assembly, called to determine the condition and means of existence of the Reformed Church, it was decided that a third part of the revenues of the ecclesiastical property which still remained in the hands of the prelates, or had been seized by the nobles, should be given to the Queen for the maintenance of preachers, the endowment of schools, the support of the poor, and the increase of the revenue of the Crown. Lord James Stuart, Lord Lethington, and the Earls of Argyle and Morton, were appointed to superintend the collection and distribution of this third. The Confession of Faith was retained as the rule of belief, but the Book of Discipline was rejected by the nobility, who, though willing to submit to the teaching of the ministers, would not accept their government.[2] The object of these early acts of Mary's administration was to effect a sort of compromise between the various interests which held sway in the country, and kept it always on the verge of civil war. The arrangement which prevailed at the return of Mary Stuart secured the religious domination of the reformed party, private liberty of conscience for the Queen, the distribution of authority in a mixed council, and the division of the ecclesiastical revenues, two-thirds of which were either retained by the Catholic clergy, or possessed by the nobility, and one-third devoted to the service of the new Church.

This arrangement was due in great measure to the increasing influence of Lord James Stuart, whom his sister created Earl of Mar on the occasion of his marriage with the daughter of the Earl Marshal, and invested with the most ample powers to reduce to submission the rebellious districts of the frontiers. He performered this task with singular energy and prompt success.[3] But the favour which he enjoyed did not fail to excite the jealousy of the principal members of the high aristocracy. The Gordons, who had remained Catholics, and the Hamiltons, who greatly regretted the power they had lost, were particularly discontented by it. The latter of these two families had been deprived of a great portion of their income by the changes which had recently taken place, and which the Romish clergy charged the Queen with having sanctioned. The Duke of Chatelherault and his

[1] MS. letter, State Paper Office, Lethington to Cecil, 25th October, 1561 Tytler, vol. v., pp. 199, 200.
[2] Tytler, vol. v., pp. 207, 209. Knox, vol. ii., pp. 295, 299.
[3] Tytler, vol. v., p. 211.

eldest son, the Earl of Arran, did not make their appearance at Court upon Mary Stuart's arrival.¹ They still held the fortress of Dumbarton, but they had lost all their influence, and a portion of the revenues of the Abbey of Arbroath had been taken from them. The Archbishop of St. Andrews, the duke's natural brother, was compelled to give up several of his benefices; Lord Claud Hamilton, his son, to renounce his claims to the Abbey of Paisley, of which he expected to be the future possessor; and the Abbot of Kilwinning and other Hamiltons, to resign themselves to the sacrifices imposed upon them by the General Assembly.² As for the Earl of Huntly, whose son, Alexander Gordon,³ had married a Hamilton, he united to the general causes of discontent felt by all the barons who were not in favour, the fear of being dispossessed of the earldom of Murray. He had long enjoyed this earldom, and was desirous not to lose it.⁴

It was seldom long before an union was effected among the discontented nobles in Scotland; but in this instance, their intrigues were not carried very far. The eldest son of the Duke of Chatelherault, the Earl of Arran, a man of rather weak intellect, was seized with a sudden attack of insanity. In his frenzy, he disclosed a plot which had been suggested to him by the Earl of Bothwell and the Abbot of Kilwinning, for invading the royal palace, seizing the person of the Queen, killing Lord James Stuart, and assuming the government of the kingdom.⁵ This conspiracy, thus discovered, was immediately frustrated. The Earl of Mar arrested the Earl of Bothwell (who made his escape soon after⁶) and the Abbot of Kilwinning. After having thus paralyzed the Hamiltons during the spring of 1562, he crushed the Gordons in the autumn.

The Gordons exercised as much authority in the Northern districts as the Hamiltons possessed in the West. Huntly⁷ had

---

¹ Chalmers' Life of Mary, Queen of Scots, vol. i., p. 81.
² They still possessed the Monastery of Failfurd, in Ayrshire, and the Abbey of Crossraguel, in the parish of Kirkoswald. Knox, vol. ii., pp. 167, 168, notes.
³ He had died in 1553. Knox, vol. ii., p. 360, note.
⁴ This earldom was held by James Stuart, a natural son of James IV., until his death in 1544, when it reverted to the Crown. On the 30th of January, 1562, the Queen promised it to her brother James, under her Privy Seal. Chalmers, vol. i., pp. 121, 122.
⁵ MS. letters, State Paper Office, Randolph to Cecil, 7th and 9th April, 1562. Tytler, vol. v., pp. 212, 213.   ⁶ Knox, vol. ii., pp. 346, 347.
⁷ George, fourth Earl of Huntly, had been appointed Lieutenant-General of the North in 1540, by James V., and had become Chancellor in 1547, on the death of Cardinal Beaton. One of his relatives was John Gordon, eleventh Earl of Sutherland, whom he induced to join in his rebellion.

plotted the death of the Earl of Mar and Secretary Lethington,[1] and designed to marry his second son, John Gordon, to the Queen.[2] The latter had already appeared in open rebellion. After having wounded Lord Oglivy in the streets of Edinburgh, in consequence of a private quarrel, he disregarded the orders of his Sovereign to repair to Stirling Castle. Having collected a band of a thousand horsemen, he set the royal power at defiance. The Earl of Huntly, his father, had fortified the Castles of Findlater, Auchendown, and Strathbogie:[3] and taking up his quarters in the mountains, he waited the arrival of Mary Stuart, who, after having visited the central parts of her kingdom during the previous year,[4] had determined to traverse its northern districts also. She accordingly proceeded thither at the head of a small army, under the command of the Earl of Mar. The Castle of Inverness being closed against her by the captain placed in command of it by the Gordons, she attacked it, compelled it to surrender, and ordered that its commander should be hanged.[5] During this royal progress, which was also a military expedition, she displayed great courage, and endured every fatigue with cheerfulness, traversing the rough country on horseback, crossing rivers, encamping on the open heath, and regretting 'that she was not a man, to know what life it was to lie all night in the fields, or to walk upon the causeway, with a jack and knapsack, a Glasgow buckler, and a broadsword.'[6] On her return to Aberdeen, she gave the earldom of Murray to her brother, and thus rendered a war with the Gordons inevitable. The Earl of Huntly at once advanced at the head of his troops as far as Corrichie, twelve miles from Aberdeen. But the royal army, led by the new Earl of Murray, in conjunction with the Earls of Athol and Morton, completely defeated him. He was left dead upon the battle-field, where his body remained unburied, like that of a criminal, and his defeat caused the temporary ruin of his house. Of his two surviving sons, John Gordon was condemned to be beheaded for rebellion, but his sentence was commuted into imprisonment in the fortress

---

[1] Tytler, vol. v., p. 225.

[2] MS. letters, State Paper Office, Randolph to Cecil, 23rd and 28th of October, and 2nd November, 1562. Tytler, vol. v., pp. 225, 226.

[3] MS. letter, State Paper Office, Randolph to Cecil, 2nd November, 1562. Tytler, vol. v., p. 224.

[4] During the month of September, 1561. Chalmers, vol. i., pp. 82-86. Diurnal of Occurrents, p. 69.

[5] Tytler, vol. v., p. 223.

[6] Letter from Randolph to Cecil, 18th September, 1562; in Chalmers, vol. i., p. 133.

of Dunbar,[1] and the other, Adam Gordon, was spared in consideration of his youth. This family, which was the second in the kingdom, and boasted that it could bring twenty thousand men into the field, lost its title, was deprived of its immense possessions, and fell into sudden insignificance. Lord James obtained from his sister, for his relative, the Earl of Morton,[2] the post of Chancellor of the kingdom, left vacant by the death of the Earl of Huntly. The disgrace of the Hamiltons and the ruin of the Gordons largely contributed to secure the triumph of Protestantism, whose political leader, Murray, now governed Scotland with as much authority as wisdom.

It was not, however, simply that she might reign more peacefully that Mary Stuart showed this deference to Murray and his party. She had other views, and her condescension covered great ambition. She aspired to be recognized by Queen Elizabeth as heir to the throne of England, and thought she would succeed in this more easily by the aid of the Protestants, as they belonged to the English party. Since the death of Francis II., she had ceased to bear the arms of England, and no longer declared herself the rival of Elizabeth. But, though renouncing the idea of deposing her, she aimed at becoming her successor. This was the object proposed to her by Lord James when she returned to Scotland, and towards which he had never ceased to direct her attention. Desirous to reconcile the affection which he owed to his sister with the zeal which he felt for his religion, Murray tried every means to establish a close friendship between the two Queens, in order that, at some future period, it might lead the two nations to live together under the same government and the same faith.

On the 6th of August, 1561, thirteen days before Mary Stuart disembarked at Leith, Murray wrote to Queen Elizabeth a letter which does equally great honour to his head and heart. It attests, on his part, perfect loyalty, profound judgment, and wise patriotism. Recommending the affectionate union of the two relations, and the unchangeable alliance of the two crowns, he addressed Elizabeth in language as judicious as it was kind: 'You are tender cousins, both Queens, in the flower of your ages, much resembling each other in excellent and goodly qualities, on

[1] He remained there until August, 1665, when he was relieved from his forfeiture by Mary, who had quarrelled with Murray, and became fifth Earl of Huntly. Knox, vol. ii., p. 360.

[2] James Douglas, fourth Earl of Morton, a principal Lord of the Congregation, and one of the cleverest politicians in Scotland. He played an important part in subsequent events, and was the fourth Regent during the minority of James VI.

whom God hath bestowed most liberally the gifts of nature and of fortune, whose sex will not permit that you should advance your glory by wars and bloodshed, but that the chief glory of both should stand in a peaceable reign.'[1] He then spoke of the title which had been assumed by his young sovereign when the two countries were at war, and expressed his regret that this circumstance should have led them to entertain a dangerous mistrust of each other. In order to change this subject of disagreement into a means of reconciliation, he suggested that, after Mary had fully acknowledged Elizabeth's present authority, her future rights should be as distinctly recognized: 'What inconvenience were it,' argued Lord James, 'if your Majesty's title did remain untouched, as well for yourself as the issue of your body, to provide that to the Queen, my Sovereign, her own place were reserved in the succession to the Crown of England, which your Majesty will pardon me if I take to be next, by the law of all nations, as she that is next in lawful descent of the right line of King Henry VII., your grandfather; and in the mean time this isle to be united in a perpetual friendship? The succession of realms cometh by God's appointment, according to his good pleasure, and no provision of man can alter that which He hath determined, but it must needs come to pass; yet is there appearance that without injury of any party, this accord might breed us great quietness.'[2]

This proposition caused Elizabeth no surprise. Immediately upon the death of Francis II., Lethington had opened the subject to Cecil, who had rather favoured than discouraged it.[3] Mary

[1] MS. letter, State Paper Office, Lord James Stuart to Queen Elizabeth, 6th August, 1561. Tytler, vol. v., p. 202.   [2] Tytler, vol. v., p. 203.
[3] Letter from Alvaro de la Quadra, Bishop of Aquila, and ambassador of Philip II. at London, dated 18th March, 1563. This letter was written immediately after a conversation which the Bishop of Aquila had had with Lethington, who had related to him all that had passed on this subject since the widowhood of Queen Mary Stuart. 'Ledington propuso a Sicel (Cecil) que para concertar las differencias y sospechas de las dos reinas, le parescia que seria bien que se procurasse que la d' Escoscia cediesse a esta todo el derecho que podia pretender a esta corona, con condicion que muriendo esta sin hijos, la de Escoscia sucediesse, y que esta declaracion fuesse hecha y approvada por los del regno desde luego. La qual cosa oyda por Sicel, dice este, que se puso muy pensativo y como atonito, pero que tornando sobre si, le dixo que el pensaria en aquello que le avia dicho, y le daria la repuesta. Passados dos otres dias, y viendo el Ledington que Sicel no le dezia nada, se partio, y llegado a la primera jornada de Londres dice que le alcanço un correo, con una carta de Sicel, en que le dezia que el avia pensado en lo que le avia propuesto para la concordia de las reynas sus amas, y que le avia pareçido muy bien, y mas que haviendo diestramente tentado el animo desta reyna sobre ello, la avia hallado es extremo bien inclinada al negocio.'

Stuart, informed at her return of what had taken place in the matter, had sent Lethington to London to carry on this important negotiation. She charged him at the same time to assure Elizabeth of her friendship, and to present her with several gifts, amongst which was a diamond cut in the form of a heart, as a testimony of her affection and esteem. The English Queen gave a very gracious reception to the envoy of Mary Stuart, whom she had already assured of her regard by means of her ambassador Thomas Randolph. But she was very indisposed to nominate her successor beforehand. The jealousy with which she guarded her authority would not allow her, during her whole lifetime, to appoint her heir. Without rejecting the proposals of the Queen of Scotland, she evaded compliance with them, and demanded, as a preliminary, that the Treaty of Edinburgh should be ratified. This request Mary Stuart persisted in refusing, for very good reasons. She stated that the treaty had been concluded with her husband rather than with herself, that its principal clauses had been carried into effect, that the French had evacuated Scotland, that the newly-constructed fortifications had been demolished, and that she had ceased to bear the arms and title of Queen of England and Ireland. She added that she could not absolutely renounce that title and those arms, as by so doing she would renounce her future rights. Finally she offered to submit the treaty to such a revision as should settle their reciprocal obligations, and conduce 'to the reasonable contentment of them both, to the common welfare of their kingdoms, and to the perpetual tranquillity of their subjects.'

The two Queens thus continued to pursue different ends; and, to terminate this conflict of pretensions, an interview was proposed as a means to dispel distrust, and to put an end to further disagreement. Accordingly, when Lethington returned to Edinburgh, on the 6th of July, 1562, with an affectionate letter from Elizabeth, who sent her portrait to Mary Stuart, declared her intention to maintain the friendly union of the two kingdoms, and offered her the agreeable prospect of a speedy meeting, she was transported with joy. With that vivacity of hope which was natural to her, and which neither age nor misfortune could ever quench, she felt the utmost confidence in both the interview and the happy results it would produce. 'I trust,' she said to Elizabeth's ambassador, 'by that time that we have spoken together, our hearts will be so eased, that the greatest grief that ever after shall be between us, will be when we shall take leave the one of the other. And let God be my witness, I honour her in my heart, and love her as my dear and natural sister.'[1] In her excessive joy, she spoke of Elizabeth with a mixture of tenderness and flattery which, though adapted to please the vanity of that princess, had no influence upon her policy.

The interview, appointed to take place at York, during the autumn of 1562, never occurred.[2] The civil wars of the Continent, in which Elizabeth took part, by the assistance she afforded to the Huguenots of France as she had formerly done to the Reformers of Scotland, gave her a pretext for postponing it until the summer of 1563. She despatched Sir Henry Sidney to inform Mary Stuart that she regretted she would not be able to meet her yet, and left her free to appoint the time of their interview between the 20th of May and the 31st of August in the following year.[3] Mary Stuart was disappointed and grieved by this delay, which was destined to be of frequent recurrence. She did not, however, continue less steadfast to the policy which she had adopted. Although strongly urged by her uncles, the Lorraine princes, to break with Elizabeth, who had furnished auxiliaries to the Prince of Condé, Admiral Coligny, and the Protestant nobles, she preserved a strict neutrality. Thus compelled to choose between her affections and her interests, her creed and her ambition, she interfered only to recommend peace. During the winter of 1563, she sent Lethington into England[4] to endeavour to effect a reconciliation between Elizabeth and the Guises, and to assert her rights if the Parliament should enter upon the question of the succession to the crown. Lethington was instructed to defend her right, as nearest heir to the crown of England, before that Assembly; and to entreat Elizabeth not to name any other than her, if the interests of her kingdom and the wishes of her subjects should compel her to regulate the succession.

But whilst pursuing these important plans, Mary Stuart abandoned herself to the amusements befitting her age and disposition in the Court of Scotland, which she animated by her taste and vivacity, and adorned by her grace and charms. She

[1] MS. letter, State Paper Office, Randolph to Cecil, 15th July, 1562. Tytler, vol. v., p. 219.
[2] Letter from Mary Stuart to Elizabeth, July 1562; in Keith, p. 221.
[3] Mary fixed the interview on any day between the 20th of August and the 20th of September, 1563, in some place situated between York and the river Trent. Letters Patent, dated Perth, 24th August, 1562. Labanoff, vol. i., pp. 150-156.
[4] Instructions given by Mary Stuart to William Maitland, laird of Lethington. Keith, p. 345; and Labanoff, vol. i., pp. 161-166.

had transferred thither the usages and pleasures of the Court of France. Surrounded by a number of young ladies belonging to some of the noblest families in the kingdom, she devoted her leisure hours to music and dancing, or sought relaxation from the cares of business in falconry, or the composition of French verses with those who were as fond of poetry as herself. The earnestness with which she engaged in these amusements, considered unholy and profane by the Presbyterian ministers, had exposed her to their severe reprehension.[1] Many times had Knox mounted his pulpit to inveigh against the prolonged festivities of that joyous court, destined ere long to become so desolate and sad; 'Princes,' said he, 'are more exercised in fiddling and flinging, than in reading or hearing of God's most blessed Word. Fiddlers and flatterers, who commonly corrupt the youth, are more precious in their eyes than men of wisdom and gravity, who, by wholesale admonition, might beat down in them some part of that vanity and pride, whereunto all are born, but in princes take deep root and strength by wicked education.'[2] Dancing was denounced as bitterly as music by this rigid censor, who did not fail to refer in his remarks upon it to the tragical history of Herodias and John the Baptist.

Unhappily for the amiable and light-hearted Mary, excessive familiarity exposed her at this time to indiscreet attacks. The respect due to the Queen was forgotten in the great liberty allowed by the woman. One Captain Hepburn ventured to behave towards her with brutal indelicacy, and escaped punishment only by flight.[3] His example did not, however, serve as a warning to the unfortunate Chastelard. He was a gentleman of Dauphiny, descended on his mother's side from the Chevalier Bayard,[4] highly accomplished, a good musician and an agreeable poet.[5] He formed one of the suite of M. de Damville, when that nobleman came into Scotland with Mary Stuart, of whom he was deeply enamoured. He had addressed verses to her, to which Mary had replied by others,[6] and he had allowed himself to fall under the influence of an imprudent passion. On his

[1] Knox, vol. ii., p. 330.   [2] Ibid., vol. ii., p. 333.   [3] Tytler, vol. v., p. 232.
[4] 'Il luy ressembloit de taille, car il l'avoit moyenne et très-belle, et maigreline, aussi qu'on disoit M. de Bayard l'avoit.' Brantôme, vol. v., p. 122.
[5] Il estoit gentilhomme très-accomply; et quant à l'âme, il l'avoit aussi très-belle, car il parloit très-bien, et mettoit par escrit des mieux, et mesme en rithme, aussi bien que gentilhomme de France, usant d'une poësie fort douce et gentille en cavalier.' Brantôme, ut sup.
[6] 'Et mesme luy faisoit response; et pour ce, luy faisoit bonne chère et l'entretenoit souvent.' Brantôme, vol. v., p. 123.

return to France, at the time of the first civil war, he had felt no disposition to march with Damville against his co-religionists, the Huguenots, or to join the Huguenots against his old master, Damville, and had consequently taken the opportunity to revisit Scotland. Mary received him very kindly, and Chastelard's passionate admiration was raised to the highest pitch by her conduct. If we are to believe the testimony of Knox, she encouraged his advances by behaviour unbecoming the decency of an honest woman. During all the winter of 1563, he was allowed more frequent access into her private cabinet than any one of her nobility. The Queen frequently leaned upon Chastelard's shoulder,[1] and these dangerous familiarities intoxicated him, and emboldened him to run every risk that he might satisfy his passion. One evening he concealed himself under the Queen's bed. He was discovered by Mary, who merely ordered him to quit the Court at once and for ever. Far from obeying her commands, he followed her secretly into Fife, and two days afterwards concealed himself again in her chamber. Mary again perceived him on entering the room ; uttering loud cries, she called for assistance. Her attendants hastened to her from every direction, and, in the first outburst of her indignation, she ordered Murray, who had hurried to her assistance, to poniard Chastelard on the spot. Murray calmed her excitement, and placed the unfortunate gentleman in arrest ; and two days afterwards he was sentenced to be beheaded. He walked to the scaffold, repeating his friend Ronsard's Hymn to Death,[2] in which occur the following lines, adapted at once to his situation and his sentiments :

'Le désir n'est rien que martire,
Content ne vit le désireux,
Et l'homme mort est bien heureux,
Heureux qui plus rien ne désire.'[3]

---

[1] 'Wise men would judge such fashions (viz. the Queen's dancing of the *purpose* with Chattelet) more like to the bordel than to the comeliness of honest women. In this dance, the Queen chose Chattelet, and Chattelet took the Queen. All this winter Chattelet was so familiar in the Queen's cabinet, early and late, that scarcely could any of the nobility have access unto her. The Queen would lie upon Chattelet's shoulder, and sometimes privily would steal a kiss of his neck ; and all this was honest enough, for it was the gentle entreatment of a stranger.' Knox, vol. ii., p. 368.

[2] 'Ne s'aidant,' says Brantôme, 'd'autre livre spirituel, ny de ministre, ny de confesseur.' Vol. v., p. 125.

[3] Ronsard's Odes, vol. ii., p. 540 (Paris, 1630). According to Knox, he died repentant : 'At the place of execution, when he saw that there was no remedy but death, he made a godly confession.' Knox, vol. ii., p. 369. Randolph also says, 'He died with repentance.' Tytler, vol. v., p. 232.

When he arrived at the place of execution, he raised his eyes to heaven and exclaimed, 'O cruelle dame!'[1]

This adventure created a great and unpleasant sensation. It furnished an additional reason why the Queen should avoid, by a new marriage, the dangers to which she was exposed by her beauty and widowhood. Besides, the necessity of giving an heir to the throne of Scotland compelled her to take this step, to which she was inclined by her youth and invited by her subjects; and her hand had long been sought by several European princes. This second marriage, the negotiation of which occupied four years, provoked the intervention of the greatest potentates. Philip II., Catherine de Medici, the Emperor Ferdinand, Elizabeth, the Kings of Sweden and Denmark, were all anxious either to consummate or prevent it. As it assumed extreme importance from the interests which it called into action, the plans which it developed, and the terrible consequences which it produced, it will be interesting to explain, at some length, and with the assistance of new documents, its curious phases and melancholy termination.

Francis II. had not been dead a month before several suitors aspired to the hand of his widow. Mary Stuart at once rejected the Kings of Denmark and Sweden, and her choice seemed to incline towards Don Carlos, the son of Philip II.[2] The Cardinal of Lorraine, her uncle, proposed this match to Chantonnay, the ambassador of his Catholic Majesty at the Court of France.[3] Such a project excited great alarm, and met with the opposition of both Elizabeth and Catherine de Medici, who were equally interested to prevent its execution. It would have been very dangerous to them both, if the heir of Spain, the Milanese, the

[1] Knox, vol. ii., p. 369. Brantôme says, that when he had finished reciting the Hymn to Death, 'il se tourna vers le lieu où il pensoit que la reyne fust, s'écria tout haut: "Adieu, la plus belle et la plus cruelle princesse du monde!" et puis, fort constamment tendant le col à l'exécuteur, se laissa défaire fort aisément.' Vol. v., p. 125.

[2] Don Carlos was born on the 12th of July, 1545. He was fifteen years and a half old when Francis II. died, and was nearly three years younger than Mary Stuart.

[3] 'El cardinal quexandose de la desgracia de su sobrina, y del poco remedio que tiene de hallar partido igual, me dixo claramente, que no le avia sino era casandose con su alteza. Yo no quise responderle sino que siendo ella tan hermoza y gentil princesa, no podia dexar de hallar marido conveniente a su grandeza. Por otra parte la reyna madre entiende este designo y tienece los por lo que ha siempre desseado casar a madama Margarita con el principe nuestro señor.' Chantonnay to Philip II., 28th December, 1560. Archives of Simancas, series B., file 12, No. 116.

Two Sicilies, the Netherlands, and the Franche-Comté, had married the Queen of Scotland, and heir presumptive to the Crown of England. Catherine de Medici, who was better able than Elizabeth to throw obstacles in the way of this marriage, instructed the Bishop of Limoges, her ambassador at Madrid, and her daughter Elizabeth, who had married Philip II. after the peace of Cateau-Cambresis, to use all their influence with the Catholic King against it. 'To avert this blow,' she wrote, 'I would blindly make any sacrifice in my power.'¹ She even gained the assistance of the Duke of Guise and the Cardinal of Lorraine, whose views she changed by her most politic reasons. She told them that, as their niece had claims to the kingdom of England, it might happen, if she married the Prince of Spain, that Scotland and England would be added to the already immense territories of the Catholic King, and she conjured them most urgently never to consent to a marriage which would expose the realm of France to greater dangers than it had ever before incurred.² The Duke and Cardinal promised her their support. They gave their word that they would act in strict conformity with her wishes, because, said they, they preferred the welfare of France to the advantage of their niece.³ To their credit be it spoken, they kept their promise. When Mary Stuart was about to leave France, she consulted the Duke of Guise respecting her future marriage. The Duke replied that he would give her no advice, because he could not give her that advice which was most pleasing to her, and he recommended her to make her own choice.⁴ But this choice, which continued to incline towards the Prince of Spain, was some time afterwards thwarted by the Cardinal of Lorraine, who, meeting the Emperor Ferdinand at Innspruck, negotiated with him, and without his niece's know-

¹ Catherine de Medici to the Bishop of Limoges, 3rd March, 1561. Paris's *Négociations sous François II.*, pp. 818, 819.

² 'La reyna madre habia entrada en gran sospecha del casamiento de su alteza por la pretensa de su reyna a este reyno, y llamado al duque de Guisa y al cardenal, pidiendo les con grandissima instancia, que en ninguna manera viniessen a este casamiento, porque seria el mayor daño e inconveniente y podria ser y venir al reyno de Francia ocupandose con la grandeza de V. M. estos dos reynos.' This was related by Lethington in April, 1565, to Guzman de Silva, ambassador of Philip II. at London, and transmitted by Silva to Philip II., in his despatch of the 26th April, 1565. Archives of Simancas, Inglaterra, fol. 818.

³ '.... y que ellos so lo habian prometido y dado palabra, de hacello assi, teniendo en mas el util de aquel reyno que el bien de su sobrina.' Ibid.

⁴ 'El duque le habia dicho que en materia de casamiento no le queria dar consejo, porque no le podia dar el que le convenia. que mirasse ella por lo que mejor le estaria.' Ibid.

ledge, a plan of marriage between her and the Archduke Charles, the Emperor's second son.[1] This plan could not fail to interfere with the other. It would inevitably inspire Philip II. with the fear of offending the Emperor, his uncle, by seeking to marry the Queen of Scotland to his own son, to the detriment of the Archduke, his cousin. This actually came to pass. As soon as he was informed of the new negotiation, Philip II. withdrew his claims.

Mary Stuart was greatly disappointed at this. The Archduke possessed neither power, nor army, nor money;[2] as a foreigner, he would be displeasing to the Scotch, and as a Catholic, he would have irritated the Protestant Church. Mary was therefore disposed to refuse him, because he would have compromised her, without bringing her any means of defence against the discontent and factious spirit of her subjects. Neither would she accept the Earl of Arran, whom the Queen of England wished her to marry,[3] nor the Dukes of Nemours and Ferrara,[4] who were proposed to her; for she considered these princes too weak and unimportant to wed with her. By a bold manœuvre, she renewed the negotiations for her marriage with Don Carlos, in spite of the opposition of her uncle, the Cardinal of Lorraine. She directed Secretary Lethington, while engaged in one of his numerous missions to London, to inform Philip II.'s Ambassador at the English Court, that she was resolved neither to marry a Protestant, nor to receive a Catholic from the hands of Queen Elizabeth;[5] that her position and interests would not allow her to accept the Archduke; and that if she were not united to the Prince of Spain, the only one of her suitors who entirely met her views, she had given orders to him (Lethington) to proceed to France, and propose a marriage with Charles IX., notwitn-

[1] 'Y que estando il mismo Ledington en este reyno (France) tuvo aviso que el de Lorena se veia con el emperador en Inspruch para tractar deste casamiento sin lo saber su reyna.' Ibid.

[2] 'Auquel elle ne trouvoit aucune commodité pour son royaulme, estant estranger, pauvre et fort esloigné, et le plus jeune des frères, et mal agréable à ses subjects, et sans auqune apparence de moyens ou force de luy aider au droict qu'elle prétendoit à la succession de ceste isle.' Fragment of a Memoir by Mary Stuart on her second marriage, in Labanoff, vol. i., pp. 296, 297 ; Letter from Mary Stuart to the Duchess of Arschot, 3rd January, 1565, in Labanoff, vol. i., p. 249.

[3] '.... obligarla a casar con el Conde de Aren hijo del duque de Chatelerau.' Quadra to Philip II., 18th March, 1563.

[4] Labanoff, vol. i., p. 215.

[5] '.... Que la reyna su ama jamas se casaria con Protestante, ni con Catholico, por mano de la reyna de Inglaterra.' Quadra to Philip II., 18th March, 1563.

standing their relationship and the difference of their ages. This last fear would, she thought, outweigh every other consideration in the mind of Philip II.

No sooner, accordingly, had this gloomy and unstable Prince received information of the interview between Lethington and Bishop Quadra, than he wrote to the latter that, as the marriage of the Queen of Scotland and the Prince Royal, his son, 'might be the means of remedying religious affairs in the kingdom of England, he had resolved to give it his sanction.'[1] He directed him to gain all the information he could with reference to the understanding which the Scottish Queen had with England, and to conduct these preliminaries of the marriage with the utmost secrecy, because the affair ought to be settled before it was made known,[2] lest it should provoke the opposition of both the French Court and the English monarch. He added that, by this means, they would be less likely to offend the Emperor, who was not aware of the real intentions of the Queen of Scotland, but relied entirely upon the proposals of the Cardinal of Lorraine. 'If I considered,' said he, 'that the Archduke's marriage was probable, and if I expected to derive the same advantage from it as from the marriage of the Prince my son, I would co-operate in it with the greatest pleasure, on account of the great affection which I feel for the Emperor my uncle, and for his children. The reasons which have decided me to negotiate my son's marriage are, the assurances you have given me, according to what you have heard from the lips of the ministers of the Queen of Scotland, of the little inclination which she feels for the other marriage, the little advantage which would result from it, and also the fear lest she should marry the King of France. I well remember the anxiety and disquietude which I felt whilst she was married to King Francis. If that King were still alive, we should doubtless be now at war with each other, because I should have been obliged to defend the Queen of England against the invasion of her kingdom, which had been resolved upon.'[3]

[1] 'Y asi viendo que efectuarse este casamiento podria ser principio de remediarsa las cosas de la religion en est reyno de Inglaterra, me he resuelto de admitir le platica.' Letter from Philip II. to Quadra, 15th June, 1563. Archives of Simancas, Negociado de Estado Inglaterra, fol. 816.

[2] 'Y haveis de encomendar en este negocio el secreto sobre todas las cosas que del se ayan de platicar, porque destar hecho este negocio primero que entendido.' Ibid.

[3] 'Si yo lo viese aparienza de hacerse (the marriage with Archduke Charles), yo que del se pudiese sacar el fruto, que al presente paresce que se podia sacar del casamiento del principe mi hijo, lo abrazaria y procuraria con mejor voluntad que

In obedience to these orders, Quadra sent Luis de Paz[1] to the Queen of Scotland to treat of her marriage with Don Carlos. He sent him through Ireland, in order that his visit might excite less suspicion. Luis de Paz had a conference with Lethington and Murray, in consequence of which he at once returned to London,[2] and Mary Stuart despatched her secretary Raullet to Brussels, to negotiate this marriage directly by the medium of her aunt the Duchess of Arschot, and of Cardinal Granvella.[3] At the same time Diego Perez, secretary of the Spanish embassy in England, proceeded for the same purpose into Aragon, where Philip II. then was.

These negotiations were not conducted so mysteriously that no rumour of them reached the ears of the Protestant ministers. These became alarmed at the proposed marriage of their Queen with a Catholic prince, and Knox, according to his custom, made it the subject of a public remonstrance. In an address to the Protestant nobility he warned them of the dangers which threatened them, and said, 'I hear of the Queen's marriage. Dukes, brethren to Emperors and Kings, strive all for the best gain. But this, my Lords, will I say,—note the day, and bear witness hereafter. Whenever the nobility of Scotland, who profess the Lord Jesus, consent that an infidel (and all Papists are infidels) shall be head to our Sovereign, ye do as far as in you lieth to banish Christ Jesus from this realm, and to bring God's vengeance on the country.'[4]

---

estotro, per el grande amor que al emperador mi tio y a sus hijos tengo. Lo que me ha movido a salir a este negocio y no esperar a que el emperador se acabase de desengañar en el, ha sido el advertimiento que vos me haveis dado de la poca gana que la reyna y sus ministros tienen al casamiento del archiduque, y mas particularmente el avisarme vos de que pretendian y procuraban tratar el casamiento del rey de Francia, acordandome del trabajo y inquietud en que me tubo el rey Francisco, siendo casado con osta reyna, que sé cierto si el viviera no pudieramos escusar de estar dias ha metidos en la guerra sobre defender yo a esa reyna queriendo la el invadir como lo tenia resuelto.' Ibid.

[1] 'Luis de Paz y Antonio de Guaras, che son como mercadores de quienes hazia el dicho obispo confianza.' Letter from Cardinal Granvella, published in Gachard's *Correspondance de Philippe II., sur les affaires des Pays-Bas*, vol. ii., p. 14. (Brussels, 1850.)

[2] Relacion que diò Diego Perez, secretario del Obispo Quadra. Mouzon, 4th October, 1563. Archives of Simancas, fol. 816.

[3] See Mary Stuart's Letters on this subject in Labanoff, vol. i., pp. 197-214; and also a very curious letter written by Cardinal Granvella to the new ambassador at London, Don Diego Guzman de Silva, dated 20th May, 1564, and printed in Gachard's Correspondance de Phillippe II., vol. ii., pp. 5-16.

[4] Knox's History of the Reformation, vol. ii., p. 385.

The Queen was very indignant at this language, and, notwithstanding the uselessness of her previous remonstrances, she summoned Knox again before her. She upbraided him with his ingratitude and temerity. She told him that she had used every effort to please and satisfy him, but that she had obtained no return of kindness from his untractable nature. She then burst out against him for having dared to discuss her marriage, with which he had nothing to do; and finally bade him beware of her vengeance. Knox replied that, in the pulpit, he was not master of himself, but must obey His commands who had ordered him 'to speak plain, and flatter no flesh;' that his vocation was neither to visit the courts of princes nor the chambers of ladies. 'I grant it so,' answered the Queen, but what have you to do with my marriage, or, what are you within the commonwealth?' 'A subject born within the same,' said the undaunted Reformer, 'and albeit, Madam, neither Baron, Lord, nor belted Earl, yet hath God made me, how abject soever in your eyes, a useful and profitable member. As such, it is my duty, as much as that of any one of the nobility, to forewarn the people of danger, and therefore, what I have said in public, I here repeat to your own face. Whenever the nobility of this realm shall so far forget themselves as to consent that you shall be subject to an unlawful husband, they do as much as in them lieth to renounce Christ, to banish the truth, betray the freedom of the realm, and, perchance, may be but cold friends to yourself.'[1] The Queen, no longer able to restrain her anger, commanded him to leave her presence. As he passed through the antechambers, in which were assembled a number of young ladies of the royal household, gaily dressed and talking merrily together, he apostrophized them with bitter irony. 'Ah! fair ladies,' he said, 'how pleasant were this life of yours, if it should ever abide, and then in the end we might pass to heaven with this gear! But, fie on that knave, Death, that will come whether ye will or not; and when he hath laid on the arrest, then foul worms will be busy with this flesh, be it never so fair and tender; and the silly soul, I fear, shall be so feeble, that it can neither carry with it gold, garnishing, targating, pearl, nor precious stones.'[2]

Knox had already quarrelled with Murray, who, he thought, looked with too much favour upon the plans of the Queen, his sister. He accused him of abandoning God in order to maintain himself in his authority and influence; but he assured him that

[1] Knox, vol. ii., pp. 387, 388.   [2] Ibid., vol. ii., p. 389.

all his ambitious condescension would not preserve him from a speedy downfall.¹ Murray, wounded by his remonstrances, kept at a distance from him. Their long-standing friendship grew cold, and for eighteen months they hardly exchanged a word. Lethington, on his return from England, also complained of the violence and distrust of the Reformer,² who had exposed his sovereign to suspicion and hostility, by spreading the report that she was about to marry the Prince of Spain. Knox, nevertheless, persisted in sounding the alarm, and wrote to Cecil, with whom he had long been in correspondence, that all was lost, and that out of the twelve members who formed the Queen's Council, nine were gained over to her side, and would support all her plans.³

But the plan which Mary had most at heart was never realized. Her marriage with Don Carlos, which had met with the strongest opposition in Scotland, and with hindrances of a different nature, but equal force, in England, France, and Austria, was broken off by the usual dilatoriness of the court of Spain, which allowed all these interests time to act and prevail. The Emperor Ferdinand so urgently besought Philip II. to use his good offices with the Queen of Scotland in favour of the Archduke, that Philip II. wrote on the 6th of August, 1564, to Diego de Guzman de Silva, who had succeeded Quadra as his ambassador at London:—' All these reasons oblige me to abandon the project as regards the Prince Royal. I am desirous neither to displease the Emperor, nor to interfere with the marriage of the Archduke Charles, whom I regard as my own son. I should be no less satisfied if the Queen of Scotland married him, than if she married the Prince, Don Carlos; and I shall do all in my power to bring this affair to a favourable conclusion.'⁴ He requested Silva to make known his relinquishment of the scheme, and to employ all his dexterity in favour of the Archduke. Independently of his natural irresolution, Philip II. was induced to abandon his suit by the character of Don Carlos himself. This

---

¹ Knox, vol. ii., pp. 382, 383.
² Ibid., vol. ii., pp. 390, 391. Tytler, vol. v., p. 243.
³ MS. letter, State Paper Office, John Knox to Cecil, 6th October, 1563. Tytler, vol. v., p. 244.
⁴ '.... Por esto y por otras causas que hay muy bastantes, cese de la platica de mi hijo, asi por no indignar al emperador, y al rey de Romanos mi hermano, como porque tengo al Archiduque Carlos en lugar de hijo, y no estimere menos que se concluya con el que con el principe, no dejare de hacer todo lo que en mi fuere para ayudar à la conclusion y buen suceso del negocio.' Philip II. to Guzman de Silva, Madrid, 6th August, 1564. Archives of Simancas, Inglaterra, fol. 817.

young man, whose ill-regulated mind was swayed by violent inclinations, and prone to extreme determinations, had injured his brain by a fall which had nearly cost him his life.[1] On the very same day on which Philip II. transmitted his definitive intentions to Silva, he wrote to Cardinal Granvella these remarkable words regarding the heir to his dominions, who, four years afterwards, met with so melancholy a fate:—' Considering the natural disposition of my son, and other tendencies which are manifest in him, it appears to me that I should not derive from this marriage those advantages which I hoped to gain; namely, the recovery of the kingdoms of Scotland and England to the Catholic religion, for which alone I would expose myself to all that might result therefrom.'[2]

Obliged to renounce Don Carlos, and unwilling to marry the Archduke, who, she said, ' was the husband least likely to advance her affairs both in Scotland and England,' Mary Stuart gave up all idea of espousing a Continental Prince. They were equally disqualified for her choice, some because of their religion, others because of their withdrawal; these on account of their great power, those on account of their unimportance; and all because they excited the repugnance of her subjects, and the opposition of the Queen, her neighbour. In this situation, what could she do? 'I resolved,' she says, 'to espouse some one from that island (England), to which both Protestan and Catholics strongly urged me, and loudly threatened never to suffer the contrary.'[3]

It was about this time that Elizabeth, still fearful that she would marry some foreign Prince, directed her ambassador Randolph to make a most curious proposition. She advised her to marry Lord Robert Dudley, her own favourite. Randolph at first hesitated to perform such a mission. Although Dudley was the son of the Duke of Northumberland, who had governed England with the greatest wisdom under Edward VI., after the fall of the Duke of Somerset, he was too far removed from the

[1] Philip II., when informing Quadra of this accident in his despatch of June 7, 1562, dated from Aranjuez, says, that the life of the Prince was exposed to danger by ' una herida que tuvo en la cabeza de una caida.' Archives of Simancas, Inglaterra, fol. 815.
[2] 'Considerada la disposicion de mi hijo y otras cosas que en ello se me representan, y parascerme que deste casamiento no se puedo sacar el fruto que yo esperava, que era reduzir al reyno de Escocia y al de Inglaterra a la religion Catholica, por la qual sola, y no por otra causa me pusiera a todo lo que pudiera venir.' Philip II. to Cardinal Granvella, 6th August, 1564; Archives of Simancas, fol 817.
[3] Labanoff, vol. i., p. 297.

throne seriously to aspire to the hand of a Queen, and it did not seem possible that Elizabeth could really intend to give her lover as a husband to her cousin.[1] However, upon receiving renewed orders from his sovereign, Randolph formally proposed the match to Mary Stuart. She considered the proposition offensive, and exclaimed indignantly, 'Now, think you, Master Randolph, that it will be honourable in me to imbase my state, and marry one of your mistress's subjects? Is this conformable to her promise to use me as her sister or daughter, to advise me to marry my Lord Robert; to ally myself with her own subject?'[2] Randolph intimated that Lord Robert Dudley would be rendered worthy of so exalted an alliance by the honours and preferments with which Queen Elizabeth intended to endow him. He thought he would thus tempt Mary by leading her to expect the succession to the throne of England as the price of this marriage. But Mary replied that even this prospect would not decide her, as Elizabeth herself might probably marry and have children. 'Where is my assurance in this,' said she; 'and what have I then gotten?' She consented, however, to speak on the subject to Murray, Lethington, and the Earl of Argyle. These noblemen would have been less opposed than Mary to this union if her right of succession to the throne of England had been recognized in consequence. They promised to use all their influence to decide their sovereign to the step, if Queen Elizabeth would declare her her heir, and by act of Parliament settle the crown of England upon the children that might spring from the marriage.[3]

But there soon appeared another suitor, half English and half Scotch, and occupying a much more favourable position than Lord Robert Dudley. The Earl of Lennox, a member of the house of Stuart, banished from Scotland for having embraced the cause of Henry VIII., had taken refuge in England, where he had married Lady Margaret Douglas, the daughter of the Earl of Angus and of Margaret Tudor, the widow of James IV. Of this marriage was born Lord Henry Darnley, who was thus closely connected with the two families which occupied the thrones of England and Scotland. He was at this time nineteen years of age. Ever since Mary Stuart's return into her kingdom, his mother had carefully kept up relations of friendship and kindred with her: and she now secretly proposed to her to take

[1] MS. letter, State Paper Office, Randolph to Cecil, 21st February, 1564. Tytler, vol. v., p. 245.
[2] MS. letter, State Paper Office, Randolph to Cecil, 30th March, 1564. Tytler vol. v., p. 247.   [3] Tytler, vol. v., p. 248.

him as her husband.¹ In order to dispose her in his favour, she reminded her that, like herself, he bore 'the surname of Stuart, so agreeable to the Scotch;'² that he professed the same religion as she did, and that he was, after her, the heir to the crown. In her embarrassment, Mary did not reject this overture, and authorized the Earl of Lennox to return into Scotland to resume the lands and honours of which he had been deprived since his forfeiture. But it was necessary for him to obtain Elizabeth's permission to leave England. Cecil inquired of Murray and Lethington whether Lennox's return would not produce evil results to the Protestant cause, and their party. Murray replied, on the 13th of July, 1564: 'Our foundation, thanks to God, is not so weak that we have cause to fear, if he had the greatest subject of this realm joined to him, seeing we have the favour of our Prince, and liberty of our conscience in such abundance as our hearts can wish. It will neither be he nor I, praised be God, can hinder or alter religion hereaway, and his coming or remaining in that cause will be to small purpose.'³ Elizabeth, after some tergiversation, gave Lennox permission to return to Scotland, and even recommended him by letter to Mary Stuart.⁴ She perceived the hidden purpose of this journey, and perhaps was not sorry, at the moment, that the son of the Earl of Lennox should aspire to the hand of the Queen, his cousin. Two suitors like Lord Robert Dudley and Lord Darnley were scarcely sufficient, in her opinion, to outweigh the continental rivals whom she still feared, and she doubtless expected she would easily be able to make each of these withdraw his pretensions at her will. She hoped thus to frustrate every project of marriage by her adroit manœuvres and opportune opposition, and to keep Mary Stuart in that state of singleness which she had voluntarily chosen for herself.

The Earl of Lennox arrived in Scotland on the 23rd of September, 1564.⁵ Mary Stuart received him with marked

¹ She had had this marriage in contemplation ever since 1561.
² 'Lors Madame de Lenox (comme tousjours despuis que je fus rentrée, par elle avvoit esté fayt) m'envoiay visiter, et par lettres et tokenes solisiter d'acsepter son filx, du sang d'Angleterre [et] d'Escosse, et le plus prosche après moy en sucsesion, Stevart de nom, pour tousjours entretenir ce surnom si agréable aux Escossois, de mesme religion que moy, et qui me respecteroit selon que l'honneur que je luy ferois en cela l'obligeoit. A cela insistoit le conte d'Athol, le Lord Lindsay, tous les Stevarts et les Catoliques.' Fragment of a Memoir by Mary Stuart on her second marriage, Labanoff, vol. i., p. 297.
³ MS. letter, State Paper Office, Murray to Cecil, 13th July, 1564. Tytler, vol v., p. 254. ⁴ Keith, p. 254.
⁵ Diurnal of Occurrents in Scotland, p. 77. Tytler, vol. v., p. 254.

favour, and immediately restored him to his former rank and possessions, to the great displeasure of the Hamiltons, his ancient enemies. She conferred with him upon the proposed marriage, which had been the chief cause of his return to his native country. But before taking any resolution, Mary was anxious to be informed more surely of Elizabeth's intentions with regard to her marriage, and to her eventual rights to the crown of England. This delicate mission was intrusted to James Melvil, whom she despatched to London forthwith, and who was also directed secretly to take measures with Lady Lennox to hasten Darnley's return to Scotland. An accomplished gentleman and skilful negotiator, James Melvil had spent his youth on the Continent, with the interests of which he was well acquainted, and could speak its principal languages. He had lived at the court of France, visited the courts of Germany, resided for nine years in the brilliant household of the Constable de Montmorency, been the confidential adviser of the Elector Palatine, and was held in high esteem by Elizabeth,[1] with whom he could not fail to succeed.

This Princess, as vain a woman as she was a politic Queen, really regarded him with singular favour. She caused him to dine with Lady Strafford, her principal confidante, in order that she might have more frequent opportunities of seeing and conferring with him. She played music and danced in his presence; dressed herself in the English, French, and Italian fashions, changing her costume several times a day in order to attract his attention and obtain his approbation; and even went so far as to ask him what colour of hair was reputed best, her own or that of the Queen of Scotland?[2] Melvil, like a wary courtier, replied that there was no one in England comparable to her, and no one in Scotland so beautiful as Mary Stuart. But Elizabeth would not be satisfied with this equivocal flattery, and Melvil at length told her that she had a fairer complexion than his Queen, that she played better upon the lute and virginals, and that she danced with greater stateliness.

Delighted at these trifling superiorities, she manifested an ardent desire to see Mary Stuart, affected extreme tenderness for her, and repeatedly kissed her portrait, which she took, in Melvil's presence, out of a cabinet where she kept a number of others. These outward demonstrations on her part were only a means of disguising

---

[1] Memoirs of Sir James Melvil, *passim*.

[2] 'Her hair,' says Melvil, 'was more reddish than yellow, curled in appearance naturally.' Memoirs, p. 50.

or exaggerating her feelings, and of serving her political plans. The artful Queen did not lose sight of those which occupied her attention at that time in Scotland. She inquired of Melvil if his Sovereign had instructed him to give an answer to the propositions she had received through Randolph, with reference to Lord Robert Dudley. Melvil having informed her that his mistress had no intention to enter into this marriage, Elizabeth appeared greatly displeased. 'Lord Robert,' she said, 'is my best friend; I love him as a brother, and I would myself have married him, had I ever minded to have taken a husband. But being determined to end my life in virginity, I wished that the Queen my sister might marry him, as meetest of all other with whom I could find it in my heart to declare my succession. For being matched with him, it would best remove out of my mind all fears and suspicions to be offended by any usurpation before my death; being assured that he is so loving and trusty, that he would never permit any such thing to be attempted during my time. And that the Queen, your mistress, may have the higher esteem of him, I will make him, in a few day, Earl of Leicester and Baron of Denbigh.'[1]

These dignities were actually conferred by Queen Elizabeth upon Lord Robert, with great solemnity, at Westminster. With her own hands she placed the earl's coronet upon the head of her favourite; and when the ceremony was concluded, she turned towards Melvil, and asked him what he thought of Lord Robert. Melvil replied, 'that as he was a worthy servant, so he was happy who had a Princess who could discern and reward good service.' 'Yet,' said she, pointing to Darnley, who, as nearest Prince of the blood, bore the sword of honour that day before her, and alluding to the presumed preference of Mary Stuart for him, 'yet you like better yonder long lad.' In order more effectually to deceive her with regard to the intentions of his mistress, Melvil replied, 'that no woman of spirit would make choice of such a man, who was more like a woman than a man, for he was handsome, beardless, and lady-faced.'[2]

Elizabeth frequently recurred to this subject, and assured Melvil that, if her sister the Queen of Scotland would marry according to her wish, the affair of her succession should be speedily concluded. She promised that, meanwhile, the ablest jurisconsults in the kingdom should be employed to examine into this important question. She reiterated her declaration, 'that it

[1] Melvil's Memoirs, p. 47. [2] Ibid., p. 48.

was her own resolution to remain till her death *a Virgin Queen*, and that nothing would compel her to change her mind, except the undutiful behaviour of the Queen her sister.' Melvil answered, that her resolution not to take a husband was in perfect accordance with the exalted nature of her sentiments, and that she was too high-spirited to think of sharing the sovereign authority with any one, and to run the risk of obtaining a master. When he took his leave, he says, 'she used all the means she could to oblige me to persuade the Queen, my mistress, of the great love she did bear unto her, and that she was fully minded to put away all jealousies and suspicions, and in times coming to entertain a stricter friendship than formerly.'[1]

After Leicester's elevation, Elizabeth appeared to be animated by a greater desire than ever that he should marry the Queen of Scotland. Randolph received the most formal instructions on this subject.[2] Leicester himself wrote to Mary Stuart several letters full of submission and flattery. Lethington and Murray, at a conference which they had with the Earl of Bedford at Berwick, renewed their promise to insure the success of the marriage, if an act of the English Parliament should settle the succession of England upon Mary Stuart.[3] The Queen herself, in spite of the repugnance which she had so proudly and decisively expressed, did not seem averse to the match upon this condition. At the beginning of 1565, having retired to St. Andrews for some time, to throw off the cares of State, and the restraints and formalities of her Court, she was followed thither by Randolph, whom she received with the greatest friendship and openness. She had thrown aside all pomp, and lived with a small train in a merchant's house in that city;[4] and she had some most lively conversation with Elizabeth's ambassador, both at table, where he was always seated by her side, and during her daily rides, in which he used to accompany her. She told him that she could defer her marriage no longer without incurring great inconvenience,

---

[1] For an account of Melvil's embassy to the English court, see his Memoirs, pp. 43-52.

[2] MS. Instructions, State Paper Office, Draft by Cecil, 7th October, 1564. Tytler, vol. v., p. 262.

[3] MS. letters, State Paper Office, Murray and Lethington to Cecil, 3rd and 24th December, 1564. Tytler, vol. v., p. 263.

[4] When Randolph ventured to speak of business, she said to him: 'I see now well that you are weary of this company and treatment. I sent for you to be merry, and to see how like a bourgeois wife I live, with my little troop, and you will interrupt our pastimes with your great and grave matters.' Randolph to Elizabeth, 5th February, 1565. Tytler, vol. v., p. 267.

and that she was disposed to follow the advice of his mistress. 'If,' she said, 'she will, as she hath said, use me as her natural-born sister or daughter, I will consider myself either the one or the other, as she please, and will show no less readiness to obey her and honour her than my mother or eldest sister. But if she will repute me always as her neighbour the Queen of Scots, how willing soever I be to live in amity, and to maintain peace, yet must she not look for that at my hands that otherwise I would, or she desireth.'[1] At the termination of this interview, when Leicester's name was mentioned, she said to Randolph, 'Marry! what I shall do lieth in your mistress's will, who shall wholly guide me and rule me.'[2] She thus appeared to make her determination depend on the recognition of her title of legal heir to the throne of England. Her queenly pride, however, might at last have led her to reject such a marriage, even upon this condition. Indeed, when Randolph asked her what she thought of Leicester, she replied, 'My mind towards him is such as it ought to be of a very nobleman, as I hear say by many; and such a one as the Queen, your mistress, my good sister, does so well like to be her husband, if he were not her subject, ought not to mislike me to be mine.'[3]

The negotiation had reached this point when Henry Darnley arrived in Scotland. Elizabeth had given him permission to join his father, the Earl of Lennox, under the pretext of assisting him in making some family arrangements. She was not ignorant of his pretensions, and perhaps she foresaw that he would thwart the marriage with Leicester, just as Leicester had put an end to the matrimonial negotiations of the continental Princes. It would appear that the real object of this crafty Princess was to prolong uncertainty, and keep all parties in suspense. Darnley met with a most affectionate reception from the Queen, his cousin.[4] He was a man of agreeable manners and distinguished appearance, and possessed, moreover, all the charms of youth. To these qualifications he united, when acting by the advice of his ambitious parents, considerable ability. With greater prudence than he displayed at a later period, he sought immediately

---

[1] Tytler, vol. v., p. 269.

[2] Mary found great fault with Elizabeth's irresolution on this subject. She says: 'How willing I am to follow her advice I have shown many times, and yet I can find in her no resolution or determination.' Tytler, vol. v., p. 269.

[3] Chalmers' Life of Mary, Queen of Scots, vol. i., pp. 190-197. Tytler, vol. v., p. 272.

[4] He arrived at Edinburgh on the 12th February, 1565. Tytler, vol. v., p. 272.

upon his arrival to gain the favour of Murray, by placing himself under his guidance. In the morning he went to hear Knox preach; in the evening he danced a galliard with the Queen;[1] and he thus manifested his desire to reassure the distrustful Church of Scotland, and to gain the good graces of the Court.

From this moment, the struggle began between the two candidates of the reformers and Catholics;—between Leicester, who was supported by Lethington and Murray—and Darnley, who was strongly sustained by the Earl of Athol, all the Scottish barons who had remained faithful to their ancient creed, and an Italian, named David Riccio, who had succeeded Raullet as the Queen's Secretary for French correspondence, and who had already gained great influence over her. Lethington, at this time, wrote to Cecil a number of letters full of the most politic considerations in favour of a marriage which he thought might be so useful to their common cause and their two countries, and besought him to obtain from Elizabeth that concession which alone was needed to insure its success. But Elizabeth complained that this was transforming the negotiation too much into a matter of bargain, and jocularly told Melvil, that Lethington, in his constant allusions to the succession, was, like a death-watch, ever ringing her knell in her ears.[2] Lethington replied that his mistress merely sought a probable reason to lay against the objections of foreign princes, that they might see that no vain or light conceit had moved her to yield to the Queen of England's request in her marriage. As for himself, giving way to an enthusiasm which was far from habitual in him, he reminded Cecil of the union of England and Scotland, which would be effectuated by this marriage, in language full of noble patriotism. 'Such a stroke of policy,' he remarked, 'would secure for us a more glorious memory, a more unfading gratitude in the ages to come, than belongs to those who did most valiantly serve King Edward the First in his conquest, or King Robert the Bruce in his recovery, of the country.'[3]

Murray, on his part, spared no efforts to persuade Elizabeth. He entreated Cecil to use his influence with her, in order that, recognizing the right of his sister to the Crown of England, she might hasten her marriage with Leicester. He told him that, unless that marriage took place, his ruin was inevitable; that the policy which, by his advice, had for four years been pursued

[1] Tytler, vol. v., p. 273.   [2] Tytler, vol. v., p. 275.
[3] MS. letter, State Paper Office, Lethington to Cecil, 7st February, 1565. Tytler, vol. v., p. 275.

towards England would infallibly be abandoned by his sister, who distrusted him the more because none of the hopes with which he had flattered her, and in view of which he had induced her to act, would have been realized; that the deference which she had manifested towards Queen Elizabeth would cease, and the good understanding with England be weakened; that she would resume her connection with her relations and the Catholic Princes of the Continent, whom she had hitherto discarded; that the new King would be mortally offended with him (Murray), because he had promoted the marriage of a rival, and sought to prevent his own; and that, finally, if the King were a Papist, it would be necessary either to obey him or be considered the ringleader of the disaffected, and thus expose the country to difficulties and miseries, from which it had been free for the last five years.[1]

These weighty reasons ought to have decided Elizabeth, whose determination Mary Stuart seemed to await in order that she might form her own. She had repeated to Randolph that the Queen of England might, if she pleased, exercise the greatest influence over her conduct. 'As to marriage,' she said, 'my husband must be such a one as she will give me.'[2] But Elizabeth, swayed by contending emotions, was urged by policy to yield Leicester to the Queen of Scotland, and by affection to keep him herself. Moreover she felt an invincible repugnance to appoint her successor. Thus Cecil wrote to Sir Thomas Smith: 'I see the Queen's Majesty very desirous to have my Lord of Leicester placed in this high degree to be the Scottish Queen's husband; but when it cometh to the conditions which are demanded, I see her then remiss of her earnestness.'[3]

It was, however, necessary to give an answer of some kind. Elizabeth had exhausted all her artifices and delays. Compelled at length to declare her resolution, she refused to recognize Mary's right to the succession until she were married. She directed Randolph to convey this message to her, and assure her at the same time that, if she accepted Leicester as a simple Earl, she might rely on the ulterior munificence of the Queen of England, and would have no cause to repent her confidence.[4] She well knew that Mary would disdainfully reject so disproportionate a marriage, now that its reward was no longer the Crown of England, and that its dishonour would not be counter-

---

[1] MS. letter, State Paper Office, Randolph to Cecil, 4th March, 1565. Tytler, vol. v., p. 274.   [2] Tytler, vol. v., p. 274.
[3] Cecil to Sir Thomas Smith, January, 1565; quoted in Wright's Queen Elizabeth and her Times, vol. i., p. 187.   [4] Keith, p. 270.

balanced by a corresponding advantage. Randolph performed the orders of his Sovereign. He communicated Elizabeth's refusal to Mary Stuart, who was deeply moved, and burst out into a passionate fit of weeping.[1] Thus deceived in the ambitious hopes she had so long entertained, what could the Queen of Scotland do? It only remained for her to turn towards Darnley. She suddenly fixed her choice upon him, and to this she was disposed as much by preference as by necessity. Darnley had pleased her exceedingly, and was not long in gaining her heart, which was as easily moved to affection as to disgust. Mary Stuart was not long able to conceal the passion with which he had inspired her, but quickly made it manifest to every eye. Darnley had fallen ill, and she never left him by day or by night, but watched over him as anxiously as if he had been already her husband.[2] The power of ardent love thus combined with the qualifications of birth and the exigencies of her position to render this marriage inevitable. It was, moreover, advocated by the Earls of Athol and Caithness,[3] Lord Robert Caithness, Lords Ruthven, Lindsay, and Hume,[4] those of the Douglas clan who were connected with the Lennox family by kindred or friendship, and all those noblemen who were secretly faithful to the Catholic religion. She recalled from France the profligate Earl of Bothwell,[5] that she might use him, if necessary, against Murray, whose personal enemy he was, and who had compelled him to live in exile on the Continent for several years: and she proposed to restore to favour the Earl of Huntly, whose family had been disgraced and crushed by Murray.

But this marriage, nevertheless, met with great hindrances, and caused much alarm. The Protestant party, and the Lords of the Congregation, opposed it as a step towards the restoration of Catholicism. The Duke of Chatelherault, and all the Hamiltons, who had long been the implacable adversaries of the

[1] MS. letter, State Paper Office, 17th March, 1565. Tytler, vol. v., p. 276.
[2] 'Elle use,' wrote Paul de Foix to Catherine de Medici on the 31st of March, 1565, 'de mêmes offices envers le fils du comte de Lenos que s'il estoit son mary, ayant, durant sa maladie, veillé en sa chambre une nuit toute entière, et se montrant soigneuse et ennuyée de sa maladye, parce qu'il a eu quelques jours fièvre assez fâcheuse, de laquelle il est maintenant délivré.' Nat. Lib. Paris, dep. St. Germain Harlay, No. 218. MS. letter, State Paper Office, Bedford to Cecil, 23rd April, 1565. Tytler, vol. v., p. 280.
[3] George, fourth Earl of Caithness, a descendant of the Norman family of Sinclair, which had settled in Scotland in the twelfth century. He married the daughter of the Earl of Montrose, and died in 1582.
[4] Alexander, fifth Lord Hume, died in 1575.   [5] Tytler, vol. v., p. 283.

Lennox family, perceived in it the future ruin of their house. Murray, who, in Darnley's opinion, possessed too much influence,[1] expected it would lead to his certain disgrace. And, finally, Queen Elizabeth was by it exposed to the speedy enmity of Scotland, whose King and Queen might obtain support from the Catholic princes of Europe, and excite against her the numerous body of her subjects who had continued attached to the ancient religion of the realm. The Earl of Lennox made no secret of these probable results; but had the imprudence to declare openly, that the King of Spain would be their friend, and that they could count on the support of the greatest part of England.[2]

Determined to marry Darnley in spite of these formidable opponents, Mary Stuart endeavoured to diminish their numbers and strength. She had easily gained the consent of the versatile Lethington to her marriage; and she now was anxious to make a convert of Murray, who was less accommodating, and had already withdrawn from the Court. She recalled him thither, and required him, unless he would incur her severe displeasure, to sign a paper containing his approval of her marriage, and promise to promote it by all means in his power. Murray refused to do so, and told her plainly that this marriage was too precipitate; that foreign princes would put a bad construction upon it; that the Queen of England would be offended by it; and that, moreover, considering above all things else the advantages which might accrue by the Queen's marriage to the true religion of Christ, he did not feel disposed to desire that she should unite herself to one who had hitherto proved himself rather its enemy than its friend.[3] Mary, irritated by this refusal, used every effort to make him yield; but her prayers and entreaties, her anger and menaces, were all in vain. She bitterly reproached Murray with his ingratitude, and put an end to the interview. She attributed to him the most ambitious intentions, and even insinuated that he aspired to become King of Scotland. 'I see clearly,' she said, ' whereabout he goes; he would set the crown upon his own head.'[4]

Murray partly justified his sister's suspicions by the hostility of his proceedings. He appeared in Edinburgh, at the head of five

[1] MS. letter, State Paper Office, Randolph to Cecil, 21st May, 1565. Tytler, vol. v., p. 281.
[2] Ibid., 3rd May, 1565. Tytler, vol. v., p. 288.
[3] Ibid., 8th May, 1565. Tytler, vol. v., pp. 291, 292.
[4] Ibid., 3rd May, 1565. Tytler, vol. v., p. 285.

or six thousand persons,[1] to procure the condemnation of the Earl of Bothwell, whom he accused of having plotted on several occasions against his life, and whom his sister had now recalled from banishment. He entered into a league with the Earl of Argyle and the Duke of Chatelherault, for mutual support and defence. When the ministers of the protestant Church assembled at Edinburgh, he concerted measures with them to protect their liberties against all aggression; and he applied to Queen Elizabeth, through Randolph, for that aid which she was quite disposed to afford him.[2]

This princess, in fact, had expressed her entire disapprobation of the proposed marriage with Darnley, which had been announced to her by the equivocating Lethington. Far from giving her consent to it, as she was requested to do, she had brought it before her Privy Council, who, on the 1st of May, 1565, unanimously declared it to be 'prejudicial to both Queens, and consequently dangerous to the weal of both countries.'[3] In her anger, forgetting the offers she had recently made in favour of Leicester, Elizabeth said to Paul de Foix, the French ambassador, 'that she should never had imagined that the Queen of Scotland would be so base of heart as to marry her own vassal, the son of the Earl of Lennox.'[4] At the same time, she directed Throckmorton to convey to Mary Stuart the opinion of the Privy Council of England, and to throw every possible hindrance in the way of the marriage. He was also to propose Leicester to her again, and if he were refused, to give her her choice of the Duke of Norfolk and the Earl of Arundel.'[5]

But when he arrived in Scotland, Mary Stuart had advanced so far that she could not retrace her steps. She had summoned a convention of her nobility at Stirling, and, on the 15th of May, had signified her intention of marrying Darnley, and the measure was sanctioned without a dissentient voice. On the same day she had created Darnley Lord of Ardmanach and Earl of Ross, and had connected with these titles large estates.[6] These decisive acts rendered Throckmorton's mission entirely useless. Elizabeth's envoy, however, communicated to Mary the remonstrance

[1] Tytler, vol. v., p. 283.   [2] Tytler, vol. v., pp. 286, 287.
[3] Keith, pp. 270-275.
[4] MS. despatch of Paul de Foix, 24th April, 1565. Nat. Lib. Paris, dep. Saint Germain Harlay, No. 218.
[5] 'Et si le mariage du fils de Lenos n'est conclud, incelluy empescher, en proposant à la royne d'Escosse des parts de la royne d'Angleterre, le choix de trois, qui sont: le duc de Norfolk, comtes d'Arundel et de Lecestre.' Despatch of Paul de Foix, *ut sup.*   [6] Keith, pp. 276-280.

of the Privy Council of England, and expressed the surprise felt by the Queen, his mistress, that the Earl of Lennox and Lord Darnley, her own subjects, had dared to engage without her consent, in an affair which concerned England as nearly as Scotland. Mary's reply to Throckmorton was both sarcastic and resolute. 'As to her good sister's great dislike to the match,' she observed, 'this was, indeed, a marvellous circumstance, since the selection was made in conformity to the Queen's wishes, as communicated by Mr. Randolph. She had rejected all foreign suitors, and had chosen an Englishman, descended from the blood royal of both kingdoms, and the first Prince of the blood in England; and one whom she believed would, for these reasons, be acceptable to the subjects of both realms.'[1] She, however, postponed the celebration of her marriage in the hope of propitiating her dangerous neighbour, and of avoiding a rupture with her. But this condescension was not enough for Elizabeth, who desired not the adjournment of the plan, but its entire abandonment, and in whose mind Mary Stuart's just reasons had no influence.

The English Queen, as passionate as she was crafty, now sent the Countess of Lennox to the Tower. She had long subjected her to strict surveillance in her own house, because she suspected her of intriguing with the leaders of the Papists in England.[2] She also sent a summons to the Earl of Lennox and Lord Darnley, commanding them on their allegiance, as English subjects, instantly to repair to her Court. When Randolph transmitted this order to them, Lennox refused to obey it, stating that his wife was kept prisoner in England, and that he should not venture to return thither until he were more assured of the favour of Queen Elizabeth. Darnley's refusal was less respectful, and more haughty. 'I do now,' said he, 'acknowledge no other duty or obedience but to the Queen here, whom I serve and honour; and seeing that the other, your mistress, is so envious of my good fortune, I doubt not but she may have need of me, as you shall know within a few days. Wherefore to return I intend not; I find myself very well where I am, and so purpose to keep me; and this shall be your answer.'[3] At the same time that she recalled Lennox and Darnley, Elizabeth directed Randolph to assure the Scottish Protestants of her support.[4]

[1] Throckmorton to Elizabeth, 21st May, 1565. Printed in Keith, p. 278.
[2] Tytler, vol. v., pp. 296-303.
[3] Randolph to Cecil, 22nd July, 1565. Keith, pp. 303, 304.
[4] Elizabeth to Randolph. 10th July, 1565. Keith, p. 296.

H

These now made a last effort to prevent the marriage. The General Assembly of the Church of Scotland, convoked by Knox and the Earl of Argyle, decided that the citizens of Edinburgh should be armed and organized, and that a supplication should be presented to the Queen, to request that the mass should be abolished, not only throughout the kingdom, but also in her own palace, and that it should be made obligatory upon all persons to attend the prayers and services of the established religion. The Earl of Glencairn and five Commissioners were deputed by the General Assembly to convey this supplication to the Queen, who promised faithfully to maintain their religion, but demanded for herself the same toleration which she granted to others.[1] She succeeded in quieting the Protestants; but failed to effect a reconciliation with Murray, who refused to appear at Perth, alleging that his life was in danger from Darnley and Lennox.[2] Murray, at this time, resorted to the extremest measures. In concert with the Duke of Chatelherault, the Earls of Argyle and Rothes, and Lord Boyd, he formed a plot to surprise the Queen and Darnley, as they rode from Perth to Callendar, a seat of Lord Livingston's. The conspirators intended either to kill Darnley, or deliver him up to the English, to imprison Mary Stuart in Lochleven, and to reinstate Murray at the head of the government.[3] But the Queen, having been informed of their traitorous intentions, left Perth precipitately with an escort of three hundred horse under the command of the Earl of Athol and Lord Ruthven, passed the defiles of Kinross, where she was to have been attacked, two hours before the Earl of Argyle had arrived there with his men, and reached Callendar House in safety.[4]

This criminal design excited the utmost indignation throughout the country, and left to its baffled projectors no resource but open revolt. This they adopted. Murray called the people and the *brethren* to arms, whilst Mary, on her side, summoned all the vassals of the Crown to meet her without delay at Edinburgh, in arms, and with the necessary provisions for a campaign. She prudently published a proclamation calculated to reassure the Protestant Church; and when at Callendar, she attended, for the first time in her life, the sermon of a Presbyterian minister, in order to prevent the religious party from joining the ambitious

---

[1] Spotswood, p. 190. Keith, p. 289.
[2] Randolph to Cecil, in Keith, p. 287. Tytler, vol. v. p. 305.
[3] Randolph to Cecil, 4th July, 1565; in Keith, p. 291.
[4] Tytler, vol. v., pp. 308, 309.

nobles.[1] Feeling how important it was to conclude her marriage in order to remove every inducement to opposition, she created Darnley Duke of Albany, on the 20th of July; and the Bishop of Dumblane having arrived from Rome on the 22nd, with a dispensation for the marriage, she appointed Sunday, the 29th of July, as the day on which the ceremony was to take place.

On the day previous, she conferred the title of King on Darnley, who was proclaimed during the evening at the Market-cross of Edinburgh by three heralds of the Crown.[2] On the next day, between five and six o'clock in the morning, they were married in the royal chapel of Holyrood. She appeared at this ceremony, the consequences of which were destined to be so melancholy, in deep mourning; and it was observed that she was habited in the dress of black velvet and the large white veil which she wore at the death of Francis II. After they had been united, according to the Catholic ritual, Darnley embraced the Queen, and left her at the foot of the altar to hear the mass alone,[3] being doubtless fearful that he would incur great suspicion by hearing it himself. He then induced Mary to renounce her widow's weeds, and assume a costume more suited to the happiness of the day. The banquet succeeded, at which according to feudal usage, they were both served by the most important nobles of the kingdom. The Queen's server was the Earl of Athol, Earl Morton was her carver, and the Earl of Crawford[4] her cupbearer; whilst the Earls of Eglinton,[5] Cassillis,[6] and Glencairn performed the same offices to the King. Money in abundance was scattered amongst the people, with cries of *Largesse!* and the remainder of the day was spent in dancing and festivity.[7] Darnley, now solemnly recognized as King, was intoxicated with pride, and Mary, thinking she had a long future of happiness before her, experienced all the delights of gratified affection. Elizabeth's ambassador thus wrote regarding them both, "His words be so proud that he seems a monarch of the world, and that it be yet not long

[1] Tytler, vol. v., p. 309.
[2] The Proclamation is printed in Keith, p. 306.
[3] Letter from Randolph to Leicester, Edinburgh, 31st July, 1565; in Robertson's History of Scotland, vol. i., Appendix 11.
[4] David, eighth Earl of Crawford.
[5] Hugh, third Earl of Eglinton, had continued a Catholic, and proved ever faithful to the cause of Mary Stuart, for whom he fought at Langside. He died in 1585.
[6] Gilbert, fourth Earl of Cassillis, long continued a Catholic, but became a Protestant in the summer of 1566, after having married Margaret Lyon, daughter of John, ninth Lord Glammis. Knox, vol. ii., p. 533.
[7] Randolph to Leicester, July 31st, 1565.

since we have seen and known the Lord Darnley. . . . All honour that may be attributed unto any man by a wife, he hath it wholly and fully. All praise that may be spoken of him, he lacketh not from herself. All dignities that she can endue him with, are already given and granted. No man pleaseth her that contenteth not him; and she hath given unto him her whole will to be ruled and guided as himself best liketh."[1]

This marriage put an end to the cordial union of the two Queens, which for four years had been based upon reciprocal hopes which, in both cases, had been deceived. Elizabeth had urged the ratification of the treaty of Edinburgh, but had failed to induce Mary to comply with her wish; and Mary had claimed the recognition of her right to the succession of England, but had not been able to obtain it from Elizabeth. With the animosity which thus arose between the two Queens, hostilities between the two kingdoms could not fail to recommence.

The faults, we must confess, were not on Mary's side, they must all be attributed to Elizabeth. This crafty, proud, mistrustful and imperious princess endeavoured to guide Mary without satisfying her requirements, and to isolate her from every one else without binding her strongly to herself. She was desirous that the Queen should not marry either a Continental Prince who would have rendered her too powerful, or an English subject who would have gained for her the succession to the throne of England, or a member of the Royal Houses of Tudor and Stuart who would have prepared the way for the union of the two Crowns; so she opposed Don Carlos, rejected the Archduke Charles, refused Leicester, and would have denied Darnley. She might have married her to any one she pleased, if she had consented to appoint her her heir. By not doing so, she condemned herself to a policy of vigilance, intrigue, rivalry, treachery, and conflict. To be incessantly framing plots in Scotland, and frequently foiling them in England; to foment civil war in the kingdom of her neighbour, and repress or prevent it in her own dominions—such was the course which she was forced to pursue from 1565 to 1586, a period of more than twenty years.

On the other hand, Mary Stuart beheld the course of her mournful destiny, which had been temporarily suspended, renewed by this reasonable but fatal marriage. She was compelled to break with her brother, the ambitious Earl of Murray, who had been her prudent counsellor ever since her return from France,

[1] Randolph to Leicester, July 31st, 1565.

and had secured for her the internal tranquillity of her kingdom, peace with England, the obedience of her turbulent nobility, and the confidence, or at least, the submission of the Presbyterian party. She was about to return to her old inclinations, to resume her connection with her uncles, the greatest of whom, Duke Francis of Guise, had been assassinated not long before,[1] to come to an understanding with the King of Spain and the Sovereign Pontiff, to favour the Catholics, alarm the Protestants, alienate the English, and finally, be wrecked upon the quicksands of her authority and reputation.

CHAPTER IV.

FROM MARY'S MARRIAGE WITH DARNLEY TO THE MURDER OF RICCIO.

Effect produced in England by Mary's Marriage—Negotiations for the Marriage of Elizabeth—Coolness between Elizabeth and Mary—Murray's Revolt, Defeat, and Flight into England—Influence of Riccio—Attempts to Restore Catholicism in Scotland—Darnley's Jealousy of Riccio—Conspiracy against Riccio—League between Darnley and Murray—Murder of Riccio—First Captivity of the Queen.

THE marriage of the Queen of Scotland caused the English Protestants great alarm. A short time before it took place, Elizabeth's Privy Council again declared it to be prejudicial to the interests of the reformed religion, and to the security of the kingdom. Cecil, the political leader of the Anglican party, displayed all its dangerous consequences in a memorial which he laid before Elizabeth. He stated, in the first place, that as the children born of this marriage would naturally be regarded as the heirs of both Crowns, 'a great number in this realm of England, not of the worst subjects, might be alienated in their minds from their natural duties to her Majesty, and favour all devices and practices that should tend to the advancement of the Queen of

---

[1] He was shot by Poltrot de Méré at the siege of Orleans, and died of his wound on the 24th of February, 1563. Mary Stuart deeply mourned his loss, although at that period she was less occupied with the interests of Catholicism than with her own rights to the succession of England. She wrote to Catherine de Medici, who had sent to condole with her: 'La démonstration qu'il vous a pleu me faire en dépeschant Du Croc pour me consoler de la perte si grande que j'ay faitte par la mort de feu monsieur le Duc de Guise, mon oncle, que aviez non seulement regret en la mort d'un si homme de bien et tant fidelle serviteur du Roy votre fils et de vous, mais aussi peine pour celle que j'en porte, me rend plus oblisgée à vous faire service qu'auqune autre qu'eussiez sçu faire en ma faveur. Labanoff. vol. vii., pp. 3, 4.

Scots;' and secondly, that the Papists would use this marriage, which alone offered them the means of restoring the Romish religion, 'to disturb the Estate of the Queen's Majesty, and the peace of the realm."¹ Reminding Elizabeth of the usurpation of the royal arms and title of England by the Queen of Scotland during her marriage with the Dauphin, he expressed his conviction that Mary Stuart would renew her pretensions, and impart new strength and vigour to the faction which supported them. 'And this faction,' added Cecil, 'except good heed were speedily given to it, would become so dangerous in this Court, both in hall and chamber, as the redress thereof would be almost desperate. And to this purpose it was to be remembered, how of late in perusing of the substance of the Justices of Peace in all the counties of the realm, scarcely a third part was found fully assured to be trusted in the matter of religion, upon which only string the Queen of Scots' title doth hang.'²

He proposed as means of avoiding these dangers: First, that Elizabeth's marriage should be no longer delayed; secondly, that measures should be taken to advance and fortify the profession of religion both in Scotland and in England; and thirdly, that a connection should be formed in Scotland with the party opposed to the marriage, and assistance given them from time to time.³ No measures could have been taken, or advice given, better calculated to secure the triumph of Protestantism. The Reform party was then particularly desirous to oppose the marriage of the Protestant Elizabeth to that of the Catholic Mary, and to consolidate the religious revolution effected by Henry VIII., by settling the throne of England upon an inheritor both of his lineage and his creed.

Elizabeth was then thirty years of age. Though not beautiful, she was of distinguished appearance and very vain. Her manners were alternately very unconstrained and very dignified, and she united the most familiar address to the most imposing majesty. Full of talent, passion, singularity, and grandeur, she governed her kingdom with a rare combination of prudence and vigour, but seemed entirely destitute of good sense in all matters relating to herself. What flattered her most, was to be asked in marriage; as such a proposal implied an admiration for her beauty and a taste for her person which she considered highly complimentary. In this respect she had no reason to be jealous of Mary Stuart. Philip II. had requested her hand very shortly after the death of

¹ Tytler, vol. v., p. 296.   ² Ibid., vol. v., p. 297.   ³ Ibid.

his second wife, Queen Mary. Most of the Princes who had aspired to the hand of the Queen of Scotland, had previously made offers to Elizabeth. Of this number were the King of Denmark, the King of Sweden, and the Archduke Charles, with the last of whom negotiations had long been pending, but had made very little progress. Among the Scotch, the Earl of Arran had been proposed;[1] and, among her own subjects, the Earl of Arundel had endeavoured to gain her affections,[2] and the Earl of Leicester had succeeded in doing so.[3]

Although she was accustomed to receive all sorts of propositions of marriage, one had been made to her which caused her no little surprise. Catherine de Medici, either because she was anxious to remove the Archduke Charles and prevent the Queen of England from contracting an alliance with the House of Austria, or because she was desirous to gain Elizabeth's political goodwill by flattering her vanity,—Catherine de Medici offered her Charles IX. as her husband. This strange proposal to unite a lad of fifteen with a woman of thirty, a Catholic with a Protestant, the King of France with the Queen of England, was mooted during the autumn of 1564. Catherine de Medici had just reached the conclusion of the first civil war, in which Elizabeth had assisted the Huguenots; and had regained Havre-de-Grâce, which the Huguenots had ceded to the English in return, and as a reward, for the succour they had received. The wily Italian, at the same time that she was about to secure the

---

[1] See Keith, pp. 54, 55, for the letter written on this subject by the Scottish lords, in 1560; and pp. 56, 57, for Elizabeth's answer.

[2] 'Dicenme que el conde de Arondel trae muy altos pensamientos . . . . . Todos creen que no se casara (Elizabeth) con estraugero, y no atinan a quien inclina, pero los mas dias sale grita de nuevo marido. Ya ha dexado al conde de Arondel, y dizen que se casara con hijo de Guillen Haubart (Howard).' The Count of Feria to Philip II., London, 14th December, 1558. Archives of Simancas, Inglaterra, fol. 811.

[3] 'Dizen que esta enamorada de milord Roberto.' The Connt of Feria to Philip II., 29th April, 1559. Archives of Simancas, Inglaterra, fol. 812. 'Era tan publica la voz de que Isabel tenia relaciones estrechisimas con Robert, que en una de las audiencias que dio ella al embajador Cuadra, trato de sincerarse manifestandole toda la disposicion de su camara y alcoba, persuadiendole que eran calumnias infundadas todos aquellos rumores. Robert por su parte hacia tambien oficios para ganar al embajador, y envió perros de caza y otros regalos a Felipe.' Apuntamientos para la historia del rey don Felipe Segundo de España por lo tocante a sus relaciones con la reyna Isabel de Inglaterra, desde el año 1558 hasta el de 1576, formadas con presencia de la correspondencia diplomatica original de dicha epoca, por Don Tomaz Gonzalez, p. 72; and Memorias de la Real Academia de la Historia, vol. vii., p. 284.

support of her son-in-law, Philip II., by the interview of Bayonne, was doubtless anxious to paralyze the dangerous ill-will of Elizabeth by an offer of marriage.

She instructed Paul de Foix, her Ambassador at London, formally to make the proposition to Elizabeth. 'I should desire,' she wrote to him, ' to cement our friendship by some closer bond, and I should feel myself the happiest mother in the world, if one of my children should transform my well-beloved sister into my very dear daughter.'[1] Paul de Foix requested an audience with Queen Elizabeth, which she appointed for the 14th of February, 1565, just at the time when Darnley arrived in Scotland to sue for the hand of Mary Stuart. He discharged his delicate mission with dexterity, and showed Elizabeth the despatch he had received from Catherine de Medici, in which she loaded her with praises, and declared that she would find in the young King Charles IX., 'enough, both of body and mind, to satisfy her desires.'[2] While reading this letter, Elizabeth frequently changed colour and countenance. She appeared pleased and confused, and told Paul de Foix in reply that the offer of such an honour would inspire her, during her whole life, with as much affection for the Queen-mother as if she really were her daughter. But she added that the Queen-mother was doubtless not well-informed about her age; that she was too old for so young a King; and that he would neglect her as the King of Spain had neglected her sister, the late Queen Mary. 'I would rather die,' she said, 'than see myself despised and forsaken.'

Nevertheless, at the entreaty of the French Ambassador, who represented in glowing colours the political and commercial advantages which would accrue from such an union, the negotiation was formally entered into, and continued for several months. The grave Cecil was called on to give his advice upon, or rather against, so singular a project of marriage, and Elizabeth also brought the matter before her principal nobles. During this period Catherine de Medici and Charles IX. displayed the most impatient anxiety for its settlement, as we are informed by Sir Thomas Smith,[*] who had succeeded Throckmorton as the English

---

[1] MS. despatch, Catherine de Medici to Paul de Foix, Nat. Lib. Paris, dep. St. Germain Harlay, No. 218. This despatch was dated January 24, 1565, as Paul de Foix himself informs us in his account of the negotiation with Elizabeth, contained in his despatch of the 18th February.

[2] MS. despatch, Paul de Foix to Catherine de Medeci, 18th February, 1565.

[*] MS. despatch from Smith, 15th April, 1565, State Paper Office.

Ambassador at the Court of France. Paul de Foix, on his side, strenuously endeavoured to weaken Cecil's strong objections, to gain over Elizabeth's most trusted advisers, and to overcome the repugnance of that Princess herself, whose vanity was flattered by a proposal from which her good sense revolted. This negotiation had not been long continued, before it became known to those Courts which were interested to prevent it. The marriage of the King of France to the Queen of England was as obnoxious to Spain as the recently-projected marriage of the Prince Royal of Spain to the Queen of Scotland would have been to France. We therefore find that Guzman de Silva, the Ambassador of Philip II., had an immediate interview on the subject with Elizabeth. His account of the conversation gives us an excellent picture of this vain, satirical, and clever princess.

'It is said,' began Silva, 'that your Majesty intends to marry the King of France.' Elizabeth slightly hung down her head and began to laugh: presently she added, 'I will make a confession to you, because we are now in Lent, and you are my friend. Propositions have been made for my marriage with my brother the Catholic King, with the King of France, and with the Kings of Sweden and Denmark.' 'And with the Archduke also,' interrupted Silva. 'You are right,' replied Elizabeth; 'your Prince Royal is the only one who has not been mentioned to me.' 'The reason of this is clear,' said Silva; 'the King, my master, must consider it certain that you do not intend to marry, because, when he offered you his hand, though he is the greatest Prince in Christendom, and, as your Majesty has yourself told me, you are under great obligations to him,—you did not accept him.' 'It does not appear so clear to me,' answered Elizabeth, 'for at that time, I thought much less about getting married. Even now, if I could appoint such a successor to my crown as I could wish, I promise you that I would not marry. I have never been much inclined to marriage. But my subjects urge me so strongly that I shall not be able to evade compliance, unless some other means are found, which it would be very difficult to do. A woman who does not marry is exposed to the scandal of everybody. It is supposed that she remains single on account of some physical imperfection, or else bad motives are attributed to her. It was said regarding me, for instance, that I did not marry because I was attached to the Earl of Leicester, and that I did not marry the Earl of Leicester because he had got a wife already. Now his wife is dead, and yet I do not marry him. But although we cannot restrain people's tongues, the truth prevails in the end and becomes universally acknowledged. God knows the thoughts of my heart, that they are very different from what they are supposed to be. But tell me, if this marriage with the King of France were to take place, what should you think of it?' 'That the road would be neither good, nor easy to travel. You would find very many rough places in it.' Elizabeth laughed and changed the subject.[1] A short time afterwards, she assured Silva that she did not intend to accept the propositions of the Court of France.

When the delay which she had required of Paul de Foix, in order to obtain the opinions of the most important personages in England on the matter, had expired, she gave him an audience on the 2nd of May, at which she prepared him for a refusal. At length, on the 12th of June, Paul de Foix was conducted to the Council-chamber at Westminster, to receive a definitive answer. There were present the Earl of Leicester, the Lord Chamberlain Howard, Cecil, Petre, and the Marquis of Northampton. The last-mentioned nobleman told him, in the name of his colleagues, 'That the principal difficulty in the way of the marriage of the King his sovereign and the Queen their mistress, was the inequality of their ages, and the prolonged and dangerous uncertainty with regard to an heir to the crown, as the youth of the King rendered it improbable that the Queen would have any children by him for several years.'[2] Paul de Foix then wrote to Catherine de Medici, that there was no hope. But he added that though he could not determine the Queen of England to marry the King of France, he would take care to prevent her from wedding the Archduke Charles, to propose whom an ambassador had been sent by the Emperor.

This ambassador, Adam Swetkowitz by name, was sent by the new Emperor Maximilian, to restore the insignia of the Order of the Garter which had been worn by his father Ferdinand I. He arrived in England on the 5th of May, and finding the attention of both the cabinet and nobility engrossed by the marriage of Elizabeth, he brought into prominent notice the pretensions of the Archduke Charles, whom the Queen of Scotland had already rejected. Cecil was not unfavourable to his suit, and he was moreover supported by the Duke of Norfolk and the Earl of

[1] Guzman de Silva to Philip II., London, March 24th, 1565. Archives of Simancas, fol. 818.
[2] Despatch from Paul de Foix, June 18th, 1565.

Sussex, who were Leicester's enemies. The affair seems to have been conducted with great seriousness. Cecil saw the imperial ambassador on several occasions, showed him the contract of marriage which had been signed ten years before by the Prince of Spain and Queen Mary, and informed him that, if the marriage now proposed took place, the following conditions would be enforced: that the religion of the country should not be changed; that the great offices of the kingdom should be bestowed on none but English; that England should not be involved in the wars of the Empire or of Spain; and that, if the Queen died childless, the Parliament should alone regulate all matters regarding the succession.[1]

Paul de Foix, feeling how injuriously this plan would affect the interests of the French Court, used the influence of the Earls of Pembroke, Shrewsbury, and Bedford, and particularly of Throckmorton and Leicester, to thwart it; and he himself besought Elizabeth not to do his sovereign the injury and the wrong of marrying the Archduke. In order more effectually to prevent the execution of this project, Paul de Foix, in obedience to the orders he had received from his court, strenuously urged upon Elizabeth the pretensions of Leicester, who still aspired to her hand. This ambitious favourite, the object of the ardent and continued affection of his sovereign, who had established him in her court, and given him apartments close by her own,[2] now sought the assistance of the King of France to promote his marriage with Elizabeth, just as earnestly as he had entreated that of the King of Spain during the early part of her reign.[3] In a conference which Paul de Foix had with her a short

[1] MS. despatch from Paul de Foix, at the end of July, 1565. Nat. Lib. Paris, dep. Saint Germain Harlay, No. 218.

[2] 'Le ha mandado la reyna dar un aposento en lo alto junto al suyo por ser mas sano que el que el tenia abajo' y esta contentissimo.' Despatch from Quadra to Philip II., April 12th, 1561. Archives of Simancas, Inglaterra, fol. 715.

[3] During a great entertainment which Lord Robert gave to Elizabeth on the 24th of June in the same year, the Queen, being alone with Bishop Quadra and Dudley, spoke to the Spanish ambassador regarding her marriage in a tone of pleasantry. Quadra gave Philip II. on account of this singular conversation, in his despatch of the 30th June, in the following words: 'Y se paso tan adelante en ellas (burlas) que llego milord Robert a dezirle que yo podia ser el ministro del acto del desposorio, si ella queria; y ella (que no le peseba de oyr aquello) decia que no sabia si yo entendia tanto Ingles. Yo les ayude a burlaz un rato, y al ultimo tornando à les veras les dije a entrambos qui si me creian ellos se eximirian de la tyrannia de estos sus consejeros, que se habian apoderado de la reyna y de todos sus negocios y restituirian al reyno la paz y union que ha menester con restituirle la religion, y despues podrian hacer las bodas que decian y ser yo ministro de ellas.' Archives of Simancas, Inglaterra, fol. 815.

time after she had refused Charles IX., and Mary Stuart had married Darnley, he advised her to take the Earl of Leicester as her husband, in order to insure the tranquillity of her kingdom, and the contentment of her subjects. He told her that she had had many years' experience of the Earl's affection, and that she would receive from him an obedience proportionate to the honour which she would confer upon him by raising him to so exalted a position; that, being an Englishman, he would never favour foreigners; that, not being powerful, she would never have occasion to fear him; that, moreover, she would not displease any of the princes, her neighbours, by showing preference for one to the rejection of all others; and that she would thus be sure to retain the friendship of all. Elizabeth answered, that she did not know yet whether she should marry at all; and that one of her own subjects, though not possessed of large resources, would acquire by his marriage ample power to execute any evil intentions he might entertain. She added, that she was determined, for this reason, never to confer upon her future husband either property, power, or influence, as her sole object in marrying would be to leave an heir to her throne; but, that, whenever she thought about marriage 'it seemed as if some one were tearing her heart out of her bosom.'[1] Paul de Foix repeatedly resumed this conversation. Without binding herself by any engagement, Elizabeth bestowed great praise upon Leicester, who daily made greater progress in her good favour and affection, and regarding whom she openly declared that she could not remain a single day without seeing him.[2]

Under these decisive circumstances, the confident favourite hoped to crown his good fortune by marriage. His enemies made overtures of friendship to him. The Earl of Sussex sought his society, and Cecil treated the Archduke with greater coolness. Leicester had an interview with the powerful Secretary for the purpose of explaining his plans, and seeking his assistance. He told him that he was desirous to inform him that he aspired to the hand of the Queen, and that he thought she was not likely to marry any one but himself; he therefore besought Cecil to abandon his other plans, and assured him that he would always take care that he should be not only maintained in his present dignity, but raised to a higher rank, to which he was entitled by

---

[1] MS. despatch, Paul de Foix to Catherine de Medici; London, August 22nd, 1565. Nat. Lib. Paris, dep. Saint Germain Harlay, No. 218.

[2] MS. despatch from Paul de Foix, September 27, 1565. Nat. Lib. Paris, dep. Saint Germain Harlay, No. 218.

the services which his rare prudence and skilful loyalty had rendered to the Queen and her realm. Cecil appeared moved by Leicester's representations; he expressed his gratitude for his offers of support, and like a crafty courtier, promised to devote himself to his interests.¹

Thus favoured in his ambitious designs by the support he obtained both at home and abroad, Leicester prevented Elizabeth's marriage with the Archduke, who required very unacceptable conditions, and discouraged the hopes of the Margravine of Baden, who came about this time to press the suit of the King of Sweden. Becoming more urgent in consequence of the failure of his competitors, Leicester requested the Queen, who, to all appearance, had engaged to marry him, to appoint a day for their union before the end of the year. She begged him to give her until Candlemas.²

But Candlemas arrived, and Leicester was as far from having consummated his marriage as were the King of Sweden, the Archduke Charles, and the King of France. Elizabeth was resolved not to share her authority with any one, and was desirous at the same time to keep on good terms with all. Calculating even in her irresolution, she declined all offers of marriage without giving any formal refusal. She thus discouraged Charles IX. by means of the Archduke, the Archduke and the King of Sweden by means of Leicester, and she now repressed the aspiring views of Leicester by suddenly bestowing such extraordinary favour upon the Earl of Ormonde, who had recently arrived from Ireland, that Leicester, in disgust, left the court and retired for some time to his own residence.³

As it was not probable that the succession to the crown of England would be settled by the Queen's marriage, it became necessary to determine the question by recognizing an heir to the throne. The Earl of Huntingdon and the Duke of Norfolk were suggested;⁴ and the members of Elizabeth's council devoted all their attention to the discussion of rival claims to this exalted dignity. But the Queen, notwithstanding all the representations made to her in favour of the step, was as determined

---

¹ MS. despatch from Paul de Foix, September 27, 1565. Nat. Lib. Paris, dep. Saint German Harlay, No. 218.
² MS. despatch of Paul de Foix, 19th December, 1565. Nat. Lib. Paris, dep. Saint Germain Harlay, No. 218.
³ MS. despatch, Paul de Foix to King Charles IX., 20th March, 1566. Ibid.
⁴ 'Il est mis quelques propos en avant pour faire déclarer aux prochains estats le comte d'Hontinton successeur de ce royaulme, et pour fortifier cette déclaration, nomme après lui à ladite déclaration le duc de Norfolk.'—Despatch of Paul de Foix, end of April, 1565. Ibid.

not appoint a successor, as she had previously been not to take a husband. By declining to give a Protestant heir to the Crown of England, she allowed the natural rights of the Catholic King and Queen of Scotland to subsist in all their force. She, at this time, even permitted her rival, Mary Stuart, to gain still greater advantage over her, by urging the discontented Scotch to revolt, without giving them such prompt and efficient aid as to prevent their defeat. This was entirely the fault of her indecision, and must not be attributed to any scruples of conscience. She used to say that her habitual slowness of determination had done her great injury, and that, although she knew that opportunity was bald and fleeting, she frequently failed to catch it in its flight.[1] Such a failure she experienced in this instance, and in many others.

Murray, a short time before his sister's marriage, had been summoned by her,[2] under pain of violating the duties of fidelity, to present himself at Court, in order to prove the criminal design which he and the Earl of Argyle had imputed to Darnley and the Earl of Lennox, by asserting that they intended to attempt their murder. He refused to comply with this summons, either because he seriously feared, as he said, some attempt against his life on the part of his adversaries, or because he had resolved to have recourse to arms, the only means which remained in his power. He now prepared to enter the field. In a manifesto, intended to rouse the nobility and people to rebellion, it was alleged that the Queen was violating the rights and infringing upon the liberties of the realm, by imposing upon them a king without the advice and consent of the Parliament,—a proceeding utterly at variance with the laws and usages of the country.[3] He wrote at the same time to the Earl of Bedford, to 'crave his comfort, as of one to whom God had granted to know the subtle devices of Satan against the innocent professors of the Gospel, to stir up the powers of the world against the same.'[4] Randolph, on his part, urged Elizabeth to assist Murray, unless she wished to see Protestantism and the English party in Scotland fall with him.[5] But the enterprising Mary, who had gathered round her person all her faithful barons, with their relatives and friends,[6] marched so rapidly against Murray that she compelled him to re-

[1] Despatch of Paul de Foix, 10th May, 1565.
[2] Keith, Appendix, p. 108. Letter from Randolph to Cecil, 21st July, 1565; in Keith, p. 304. [3] Keith, p. 308.
[4] Letter from Murray to Bedford, 22nd July, 1565; in Keith, p. 306.
[5] MS. letter, State Paper Office, Randolph to Elizabeth, 23rd July, 1565. Tytler, vol. v., p. 317. [6] Proclamation in Keith, Appendix, p. 107.

treat from Stirling to Glasgow, and from Glasgow into the territories of his ally, the Earl of Argyle. She at the same time replied with great energy to an English envoy, named Tamworth,[1] who had been sent by Elizabeth with a haughty message, and who, refusing to recognize Darnley as King, was waylaid on his return towards the frontier, and carried off prisoner to Hume Castle.[2] The Queen of England contented herself with sending a small sum of money and a large number of promises to the Duke of Chatelherault, the Earls of Murray, Argyle, Rothes, and Glencairn, and the Lords Boyd and Ochiltree,[3] who collected a force of about a thousand men, and marched upon Edinburgh.[4]

This city, the capital of the kingdom, was also the centre of Protestantism in Scotland. The insurgents thought that its citizens would rise as one man in their favour; but they met with a cool reception. None of the citizens joined them, and they were fired on by the cannon of the Castle.[5] Notwithstanding the tendency of the reformed doctrines to encourage civil insubordination, when there was any opposition between a man's duties to religion and his duties to the State,[6] notwithstanding the insurrectionary disposition of the Scottish nobles, Mary Stuart would have needed to commit many faults and be guilty of much imprudence, before a real revolt from her authority could have occurred. Astounded at the indifference of the people, and intimidated by their own weakness, the insurgent lords sent in all haste to request assistance from Cecil, who was Elizabeth's chief political adviser, and from the Earl of Bedford, who commanded the English forces on the frontier. They entreated that three thousand men might be sent to their aid, and that some ships of war might be directed to cruise in the Forth.[7]

But Mary, whose energetic activity was unintentionally

[1] See her Message in Keith, Appendix, p. 99, and Mary Stuart's Answer, ibid., p. 101.   [2] Tytler, vol. v., p. 320.
[3] Andrew, second Lord Stewart of Ochiltree in Ayrshire, succeeded to this title and barony in 1558. He was one of the first and most zealous supporters of the Protestant cause. Knox married his daughter.
[4] Randolph to Cecil, 31st August, 1565. Tytler, vol. v., p. 321.
[5] Tytler, vol. v., p. 321, according to MS. letters addressed to Cecil by Bedford from Berwick, and by Randolph from Edinburgh, on September 2, 1565. Knox, vol. ii., pp. 499-501.
[6] Knox himself states: 'There were divers bruits among the people, some alleging that the cause of this alteration was not for religion, but rather for hatred, envy of sudden promotion or dignity, or such worldly causes; but they that considered the progress of the matter, according as is heretofore declared, thought the principal cause to be only for religion.' Knox, vol. ii., p. 496.
[7] MS. State Paper Office, Instructions given to Robert Melvil, 10th September, 1565. Tytler, vol. v., p. 321.

seconded by Elizabeth's customary dilatoriness, did not leave them time to wait for these reinforcements. At the head of a feudal army of ten thousand men, she a second time marched resolutely against Murray and his supporters, whom she had declared rebels, and who fled precipitately from Edinburgh. She swept through the county of Fife, chastised the Laird of Grange and such other barons as had appeared to favour the insurgents, levied heavy fines upon Dundee and St. Andrews, and took Castle Campbell. She went through all these expeditions on horseback, with pistols at her saddle-bow, and pursued to Dumfries the defeated Earl of Murray, who had retreated with his little army towards the English frontier. In the keenness of her animosity, she declared to Randolph, who had accompanied her in her campaign, that she would rather peril her crown than lose her revenge.[1]

About this time she published a proclamation in which she unmasked the designs of Murray and his party. 'Certain rebels,' she said, 'the authors of this uproar lately raised up against us, have given the people to understand that the quarrel they have in hand is only religion, thinking with that cloke to cover their ungodly designs, and so to draw after them a large train of ignorant persons, easy to be seduced.' She then declared that, on the contrary, they were actuated only by ambition, and accused them of being as insatiable as they were ungrateful, since, although she had bestowed upon them all kinds of honours and benefits, they had rebelled against her. 'Their ambition,' she continued, 'could not be satisfied with heaping riches upon riches, and honour upon honour, unless they retain in their hands us, and our whole realm, to be led, used, and disposed at their pleasure. We must be forced to govern by counsel, such as it shall please them to appoint us—and what other thing is this, but to dissolve the whole policy, and (in a manner) to invert the very order of nature, to make the prince obey, and subjects command. The like was never demanded by any of our most noble progenitors heretofore, yea, not of Governors and Regents. When we ourselves were of less age, and at our first returning into this our realm, we had free choice of our Council at our pleasure, and now when we are at our full maturity, shall we be brought back to the state of pupils, and be put under tutory? This is the quarrel of religion they made you believe they had in hand; this is the quarrel for which they would have you hazard your lands, lives, and

[1] MS. letter, State Paper Office, Randolph to Cecil, 9th September, 1565. Tytler, vol. v., p. 322. Knox, vol. ii., pp. 502, 503.

goods, in the company of a certain number of rebels against your natural prince. To speak in good (plain) language, they would be Kings themselves, or at the least leaving to us the bare name and title, and take to themselves the credit and whole administration of the kingdom.' She concluded by promising her subjects the peaceable possession of their goods, and entire liberty of conscience, and demanded, in return, their loyal obedience, and continued fidelity.[1]

The insurgent nobles, feeling that they were lost unless prompt assistance were afforded them, transmitted to Robert Melvil, their envoy at the English Court, a paper entitled ' Informations to be given to the Queen's Majesty, in favour of the Church of Christ, now begun to be persecuted in the chief members of the same.'[2] In this document they attributed the persecution which they suffered to the influence of foreigners. They named, as the chief of these, David Riccio, whose usurpations Murray had endeavoured to oppose, and Darnley, who, the subject of another realm, had intruded himself into Scotland, and assumed, without their consent, the name and authority of King.[3] They ended by conjuring Elizabeth to sustain a cause which was, in reality, her own. But this artful and cautious Queen, who, on the 12th of September, had directed the Earl of Bedford to place both troops and money at their disposal,[4] countermanded the order three days afterwards,[5] on learning that the confederates were very weak and had suffered a defeat. She contented herself with informing them, through Cecil, that she was favourable to their cause, and moved by their distress.[6]

After the advantages which she had already obtained over the adversaries of her authority and her faith, Mary Stuart no longer concealed her predilections and projects. She had summoned to her Court Murray's implacable enemy, the young Earl of Bothwell,[7] whom she confirmed in his hereditary office of High Admiral of Scotland, and appointed Lieutenant of the west and middle marches.[8] She liberated from prison the son of the Earl of

[1] This proclamation, dated December 10th, 1565, is given in Knox, vol. ii., pp. 504-506.
[2] MS. State Paper Office, 22nd of September, 1565. Tytler, vol. v., p. 322.
[3] Tytler, vol. v., p. 323.
[4] Elizabeth to the Earl of Bedford, 12th September, 1565; in Robertson, vol. i., Appendix 13.   [5] Tytler, vol. v., p. 325.
[6] MS. State Paper Office, An Answer for Robert Melvil, October 1, 1565, entirely in Cecil's hand. Tytler, vol. v., p. 325.
[7] He arrived from France on the 17th of September, 1565. Diurnal of Occurrents in Scotland, p. 83.   [8] Knox, vol. ii., p. 509.

Huntly, and gave him a post near her person. She placed at the head of her Council the Catholic Earl of Athol, the declared enemy of the Earl of Argyle, and a man of great courage, but no judgment.[1] Under the guidance of the Italian, David Riccio, she began secret preparations for the restoration of the ancient faith. In concert with Darnley, she made applications to Philip II and the Pope for assistance in the struggle about to commence between herself and the Protestants, and grounded her application on the fact that Murray and the Protestant lords had sought aid from Elizabeth. She told the King of Spain that he was the natural protector of the Catholic religion, and that her husband and herself,—in view of the utter ruin which impended over those of the Scotch who had remained faithful to that religion, and in the fear of being themselves deprived of their crown as well as of *the rights which they claimed elsewhere*, unless they had the assistance of one of the great Princes of Christendom,—had not hesitated to have recourse to him. She despatched to him an English gentleman, formerly a servant of Queen Mary Tudor, and now one of Darnley's suite, to inform him of the state of her affairs, and besought him to send him back speedily in the interest of the Crown and the Church, 'for the maintenance of which,' she added, ''we will not spare either life or estate, being supported and advised by you.'[2] She also requested the aid of her brother-in-law, Charles IX.

The Courts of France and Spain had both approved of her marriage. They were extremely well satisfied with it, the one, because Mary had married neither Don Carlos nor the Archduke Charles, and the other, because she had not taken as her second husband a member of that powerful house, the influence of which was universally dreaded and opposed by Philip II. This monarch, the head of Catholicism in Europe, sent Mary Stuart twenty thousand crowns, and wrote to the Pope, who also sent her eight thousand, that it was not convenient for him at the moment to send her any other succour, as such a course would certainly be dangerous and could not possibly be useful. He added that they must not, however, renounce the idea of asserting, by armed force, the Queen of Scotland's right to the succession of England.[3] ' This project,' he said, ' concerns the cause of God which

[1] Paul de Foix to Catherine de Medici, 18th September, 1565.
[2] Letter from Mary Stuart to Philip II., 10th September, 1565 ; in Labanoff, vol. i., pp. 381, 382.
[3] Philip II. to Cardinal Pacheco, Segovia, 16th October, 1565 ; Archives of Simancas, fol. 818.

is mentioned by the Queen of Scotland, since it is evidently the only door by which religion can enter into the kingdom of England, for all others are now shut."[1]

Before receiving this slender and timid assistance, Mary had refused the mediation offered her, in the name of his court, by Castelnau de Mauvissière, the French ambassador. 'I would rather lose all,' she proudly said, 'than treat with my subjects.'[2] In her warlike ardour she a third time entered the field, on the 9th of October, to expel from her kingdom the remnant of the insurgent army which was posted at Dumfries. Accompanied by the Earls of Bothwell and Huntly, with an army of ten or twelve thousand men, she easily routed Murray and his faction, who fled for refuge to England on the 14th of October. Mary triumphed. The life of activity, enterprise and conflict, which she had lately led, intoxicated her. Victory was with her the beginning of vengeance. She not only intended to crush the rebel lords by causing them to be condemned as traitors, and depriving them of their dignities and possessions; her designs became every hour more bold and comprehensive. All her kingdom bowed before her. Out of twenty-one earls and twenty-eight barons, there were only five earls and three barons hostile to her, and they were now fugitives.[3] Considering herself sure of Scotland, feeling that she was supported by the orthodox party in England, and believing that she had the countenance of the Catholic powers of the Continent, she hoped to make Elizabeth herself repent that she had not recognized her as her heir, and that she had encouraged her subjects to revolt. She even allowed her intentions to creep out in her conversation. Some noblemen of her retinue having represented to her that she would fatigue herself by so much riding and by following her army during the inclement weather, she replied 'That she would never cease to continue in such fatigues, until she had led them to London.'[4]

She now assumed a haughty tone in her communications with Elizabeth. She wrote to her that she could not imagine that she

---

[1] 'Pues se entiende evidentamente ser aquella la puerta por donde a de entrar la religion en el reyno de Inglaterra, viendo por el presente cerradas todas las otras.' Ibid.

[2] Mary Stuart to the Archbishop of Glasgow, 1st October, 1565; in Labanoff, vol. i., p. 288.

[3] 'Sur vingt-un comtes qui sont audit royaulme d'Ecosse, et vingt-huit millords, il n'y a que cinq comtes et trois millords qui ne soient du cousté de la royne et prêts à faire ses commandements, encore que la plupart d'iceulx soient Protestants.' Paul de Foix to Catherine de Medici, 29th September, 1565.

[4] Paul de Foix to Catherine de Medici, 29th September, 1565.

would consent to assist rebels, and threatened, if she should make common cause with them, to denounce her conduct to all the foreign princes who were her allies.[1] Elizabeth was greatly embarrassed by this proceeding. She was also much perplexed by the ambassadors of France and Spain who, in the name of their masters, defended Mary Stuart's interests, and the common authority of all sovereigns. Moreover she was not without fears for the peace of her own realm, and had collected some bodies of troops on the Scottish border. In order to prevent any movement on the part of the English Catholics, she had summoned to London, under the pretext of asking their advice, but really because she believed several of them to be favourable to her rival, the Duke of Norfolk, the Marquis of Northampton, and the Earls of Arundel and Pembroke. The same suspicions had determined her to summon to court the Earls of Northumberland, Westmoreland, and Cumberland, who possessed estates on the confines of Scotland.[2]

After having taken these precautions, she felt anxious to calm Mary Stuart's haughty displeasure, and in so doing, manifested more humility and less irritability than she usually displayed. As deceit cost her nothing, she extricated herself from the false position in which she had placed herself, by one of those scenes of audacious trickery which were familiar to her. She appeared greatly incensed at Murray's conduct, and gave him a public order to return to Newcastle, whilst she authorized him by a secret message to present himself at her court. He came, accompanied by the Abbot of Kilwinning, one of the Hamilton family. Elizabeth received them in the presence of the French and Spanish ambassadors and the members of her council, in order that she might enact this odious comedy with more advantage to herself. When Murray entered her presence, he knelt down on one knee, and began to speak in Scotch. The Queen interrupted him and bade him speak in French, as he was acquainted with that language. Murray excused himself on account of his want of practice, and the difficulty he would feel at having to express himself in a language with which he was but slightly acquainted, and had nearly forgotten. The Queen replied that he remembered enough to speak it intelligibly, and at all events to understand it when spoken; and she then told him in French that she was astonished that they had dared, without permission, to

[1] Mary Stuart to Elizabeth, 8th October, 1565; in Labanoff, vol. i., pp. 293, 294.
[2] Letter from Paul de Foix, 29th September, 1565.

come before her.¹ 'Are you not branded as rebels to your sovereign?' she exclaimed. 'Have you not spurned her summons, and taken arms against her authority? I command you, on the faith of a gentleman, to declare the truth.'² Murray, in confusion, replied by repelling the charge of treason, declaring that he had been unable to go near his sovereign's court because she was surrounded by his enemies, and denying that he had ever plotted to seize her person. He finally declared that the Queen of England had not encouraged him to take arms.

Elizabeth begged the French ambassador to remember these words, and then, addressing Murray with anger and contempt, she added, 'It is well that you have told the truth; for neither did I, nor any one else in my name, ever encourage you in your unnatural rebellion against your sovereign; nor, to be mistress of a world, could I maintain any subject in disobedience to his prince; it might move God to punish me by a similar trouble in my own realm; but as for you two, ye are unworthy traitors, and I command you instantly to leave my presence.'³

After this shameless disavowal, Elizabeth, who thus ignominiously rejected the men whom she had excited to revolt, and discouraged the faction⁴ of which she might soon feel the need, made very friendly advances towards Mary Stuart. She directed Randolph, who not long before had been supplied by her with money for the use of the insurgent lords, to relate to the Queen of Scotland how she had received them, and what she had said to them. 'I could have wished,' she wrote with her own hand to Mary Stuart, in a letter in which she justified herself adroitly, as she thought, but, as we think, most basely, 'that your ears had been judges to hear both the honour and affection which I manifested towards you, to the complete disproof of what is stated that I

---
¹ 'El conde habiendo pusto una rodilla en terra, comenzo a hablar en escoces. La reyna incontinente le digo, que hablose en frances, pues sabia la lengua. El se excuso, diciendo que por el poco uso que habia tenido de habrarlo lo habia olvidado, y no podria en aquella lengua explicar su intento. Respondio de la reyna, que aunque el no la hablase expeditamente sabia que la entendia bien por lo cual en lo que ella le respondiese o preguntase, le queria hablar en frances y asi comenzo a decirle, que ella se maravillaba de que hubiese venido a sa presencia, sin licencia, habiendo sido declarado rebelde por la de Escocia.' Guzman de Silva to Philip II., 5th November, 1565. Archives of Simancas, Inglaterra, fol. 818.

² MS., State Paper Office, Copy of the Queen's Speech to the Earl of Murray, before the French ambassador, the Sieur de Mauvissière, and the Queen's Council, October 23, 1565. Tytler, vol. v., p. 327.

³ Tytler, vol. v., pp. 327, 328. Also, Melvil's Memoirs, p. 57.

⁴ 'All the contrary faction are discouraged, and think themselves utterly undone.' MS. letter, State Paper Office, Randolph to Cecil, 8th November, 1565. Tytler, vol. v., p. 328.

defended your rebel subjects against you; which will always be very far removed from my heart, it being too great an ignominy for a princess, I will not say, to do, but even to suffer.'¹

Mary Stuart had never before occupied so powerful a position. She possessed the obedience of her subjects, and commanded the respect of foreign powers. It now behoved her to employ all her skill in consolidating the power which she had obtained by her courage. If she had been merciful as she was victorious, if she had pardoned Murray and the other exiles, she would have gained their gratitude and fidelity. After the humiliation they had just experienced in England, they would have been only too glad to be able to return into Scotland, and, abandoning all connection with the treacherous Elizabeth, would have become devoted servants of the generous Mary. This princess would thus have dissolved the English party within her dominions, whilst she would have augmented the Scottish faction in the neighbouring kingdom. Nothing so effectually disarms enemies and gains partisans as a combination of strength and wisdom. Murray, lately, so haughty and obstinate in his resistance, humbly returned to his allegiance. He sent a valuable diamond ring to David Riccio, to bespeak the good offices of this all-powerful adviser of the Queen his sister, and promised him his friendship if he should restore him to her favour.² Murray shaped his conduct in accordance with the advice given to the Queen by James Melvil and Nicholas Throckmorton, who wished to incline her to the side of mercy. Melvil, whom she permitted freely to express his sentiments, told her at Edinburgh that she must pardon if she would reign peacefully; and the same advice was sent to her from England by Throckmorton, whose jealousy of Cecil had attached him to Mary's cause.³ They both urged her to be merciful, that she might promote both her power and her ambition—that she might rally all her subjects around her, leave Elizabeth no means of disturbing her kingdom, and dispose even the Protestants themselves to favour her rights in England.

But Mary was too passionate to be politic. She did not follow this prudent advice. She preferred to pursue her schemes of vengeance, and yielded to the suggestions of the court of France and the Cardinal of Lorraine, who had sent Rambouillet and Clernau into Scotland to convey to Darnley the order of St. Michael, and to inform Mary of the coalition of the Catholic Princes against the Protestant cause in Europe. Mary signed

---

¹ Elizabeth to Mary Stuart, 29th October, 1565; in Labanoff, vol. vii., p. 59.
² Melvil's Memoirs, p. 157.   ³ Ibid., pp. 141-144.

the league;¹ and, far from listening to Melvil's representations that persons should not be urged to extremity lest they should become dangerous, she angrily told him, 'I do not fear them. What would they dare, or what could they undertake?'² After having granted a conditional pardon only to the Duke of Chatelherault, the weakness of whose character rendered him not very formidable, and having separated the Hamiltons from the other exiles,³ she determined to crush Murray, Argyle, and the other companions of their rebellion, by procuring their condemnation as traitors at the next Parliament.

A short time before the meeting of this assembly, which she destined to further her revenge, and was desirous to associate in her plans in favour of the ancient Church, she sent the Bishop of Dumblane to assure the new Pope, Pius V., of her devoted obedience.⁴ She besought him to grant her both temporal and spiritual assistance, 'in order to change,' she wrote, 'the deplorable and unfortunate state of our kingdom. The moment is propitious, because our enemies are partly banished, and partly placed within our hands.... If God and your Holiness, whose cause we maintain, come to our aid, with such assistance we shall overcome all obstacles.'⁵ David Riccio, who was in the pay of the Pope,⁶ and was the principal agent of the Catholic party, strongly advised the Queen to act implacably towards the exiles, and to plunge into the perilous path of a religious restoration.

This young Italian, who had acquired so much importance in Scotland, and who was destined soon to meet with so tragical a fate, had come to Edinburgh during the month of December, 1562, at about twenty-eight years of age.⁷ He came thither as

¹ Tytler, vol. v., p. 331.   ² Melvil's Memoirs, p. 144.
³ The Abbot of Kilwinning returned to give up the castles of Hamilton and Draffen, and then left Scotland to join the Duke of Chatelherault on the Continent. Knox, vol. ii., p. 515, note 2.
⁴ Mary Stuart to Pope Pius V., 21st January, 1566; in Labanoff, vol. vii., pp. 8, 9.
⁵ 'Ut, auxiliis spiritualibus simul et temporalibus, miserum quidem adhuc et infelicem regni nostri statum juvet..... Eam spem a S. T. augendam et implendam fore certo nobis persuademus, cum jam hostes nostri partim exulent, partim in nostris manibus positi sint. Si Deus et S. T. nobis aderit (quorum causam agimus) murum his fretæ transgrediemur.' Mary Stuart to Pope Pius V., 21st January, 1566; in Labanoff, vol. vii., p. 10.
Melvil's Memoirs, p. 141.   Tytler, vol. v., p. 331.
⁷ 'Essendo nel 1562 andato monsignor de Moretto, ambasciatore alla regina di Scotia per l'illustrissimo et excellentissimo signor Duca di Savoia, menò per suo cameriere un M. David Riccio, Piemontese, huomo di 28 anni in circa, accorto, savio e virtuoso.' Despatch to the Duke of Tuscany, 8th October, 1566; in Labanoff, vol. vii., p. 86.

cameriere in the suite of the Savoy ambassador, the Count of Moretto. He was a man of great intelligence, and possessed a more cultivated mind than was usual among the rough retainers of the Scottish court; he was moreover an agreeable musician, and the Queen kept him as a *valet de chambre*, when the Count of Moretto returned to Piedmont. Mary Stuart was endowed with a great taste for music, and had organized a band to play on the violin, lute, and flute for her amusement; she had also three singers in her pay, with whom Riccio was sometimes joined, as he had a good bass voice.[1] Finding that he was fully qualified for some higher office than that of a valet, she appointed him her private secretary, in December 1564, on the dismissal of Raulet. 'He succeeded so well in this employment,' says the Tuscan ambassador in a despatch addressed to Duke Cosmo I., 'that the greater part of the affairs of this kingdom passed through his hands. He managed them with so much prudence, and brought them to so satisfactory a conclusion, that he was greatly beloved by her Majesty.'[2] It was he who had advised and effected her marriage with Darnley;[3] it was he whose views, in conformity with Mary's opinions, tended to draw closer the connection between the Queen of Scotland, the Pope, and the King of Spain; and thus to separate her from England, and effect a rupture with the Protestant party. He assumed great state in his dress, equipage, and establishment; and the extreme favour with which he was treated rendered him arrogant and presumptuous.[4] The relation in which he stood to the Queen, and the ascendancy which he had acquired over her were very injurious to Mary's reputation. Thus Elizabeth, speaking to the French ambassador about Murray's proscription, said, 'That it was all owing to an Italian named David, whom the Queen of Scotland loved and favoured, and granted more credit and authority than were authorized by her affairs and honour.'[5]

Darnley, after having for some time displayed considerable friendship for Riccio, at length quarrelled mortally with him. This ambitious and vain young man, destitute alike of gentleness and courage, possessing neither talents nor humility, and with a mind utterly unequal to his good fortune, had speedily repelled Mary Stuart's affection. Her susceptible heart had been deceived,

---

[1] Keith, p. 268.
[2] Despatch to the Duke of Tuscany; Labanoff, vol. vii., p. 87.
[3] Ibid., p. 88.   [4] Spotswood, p. 193.
[5] Despatch from Paul de Foix to Charles IX., 17th October, 1565. Nat. Lib. Paris.

and he neglected no efforts to lose the empire which he had momentarily assumed over it. He was strongly addicted to drinking,[1] spent part of his time in hunting and hawking,[2] and was of a haughty, surly, and imperious temper.[3] He had urged Mary Stuart to grant him the *crown matrimonial*,[4] by which was meant, an equal share in the sovereign authority, which she had promised him in the ardour of her early affection, and which had been possessed by her first husband, Francis II. But she had refused to grant his request, either because she considered him incapable of governing, or because she had ceased to love him. Darnley's faults made evident to her the dangers which the kingdom would incur, and in which she would herself be involved, if she conferred on him the exercise of the royal power. In less than six months after their marriage, Mary was disgusted with Darnley, and was as careful to shun his presence as she had previously been anxious to see him. A rupture between them was not far distant, and Darnley's discontent had prepared a grievous humiliation for Mary Stuart.

Frustrated in his ambition, and wounded in his affection, Darnley attributed the Queen's refusal and dislike to the influence of Riccio; and believed that the Italian Secretary was at once her counsellor and her lover. He even went so far as to assert that 'the villain David' had dishonoured his bed;[5] and he therefore determined to get rid of him. He first expressed his resolution to his cousin George Douglas, to whom he divulged his grief, and communicated his ardent desire for vengeance. He then sent his confidant to Lord Ruthven, one of the most zealous friends of his family, a bold and resolute man, to request his assistance in obtaining revenge, and executing his plans of aggrandisement. He intended, in short, to murder Riccio and seize the matrimonial crown by force.[6] Lord Ruthven, although he was at that time very ill, after some hesitation, joined in the conspiracy, which was also communicated to Lord Lindsay, and of which even Randolph was cog-

---

[1] 'All people say that Darnley is too much addicted to drinking.' The Queen having remonstrated with him on his conduct, he used such language and behaviour towards her, that 'she left the place with tears.' Drury to Cecil, Berwick, 16th February, 1565; in Keith, p. 329. [2] Keith, p. 328.
[3] 'Darnley is of an insolent, imperious temper, and thinks that he is never sufficiently honoured.' Randolph to Cecil, 24th January, 1566; in Keith, p. 329.
[4] Randolph to Cecil, in Keith, p. 329.
[5] Ruthven's Narrative in Keith, Appendix, p. 119; also MS. letter, State Paper Office, Ruthven and Morton to Cecil, 27th March, 1566. Tytler, vol. v., p. 333. [6] Ruthven's Narrative, in Keith, Appendix, p. 120.

nisant. Rather less than a month before its execution, Randolph wrote to Leicester on the 13th February, 1566: 'I know now for certain, that this Queen repenteth her marriage; that she hateth him (Darnley) and all his kin. I know that he knoweth himself that he hath a partaker in play and game with him. I know that there are practices in hand, contrived between the father and son to come by the crown against her will. I know that if that take effect which is intended, David, with the consent of the King, shall have his throat cut within these ten days. Many things grievouser and worse than these are brought to my ears; yea, of things intended against her own person, which, because I think better to keep secret than write to Mr. Secretary (Cecil), I speak not of them but now to your lordship.'[1]

The plot extended without being discovered. Ruthven, who was intimately connected with the banished lords, thought it necessary to obtain their co-operation. As it had previously been requisite that the friends of Mary Stuart and the party of Lennox should unite against Murray and his faction, so now it was found indispensable to effect a junction between the supporters of Lennox and Murray against Mary Stuart and the servants of her authority. The Lennox party alone could not have kept Murray and the other exiles in banishment, and have subjected the Queen to their will, by striking so insolent a blow at the possession of the throne itself. It was therefore determined to associate in the conspiracy those noblemen who had been so bitterly persecuted. The Earl of Morton, a near relation and particular friend of Murray, strongly attached to the Protestant faith, and in fear of being deprived of the office of Chancellor of the kingdom, as well as of certain Crown-lands which he had obtained, was chosen to conduct the enterprise. He performed his task with secrecy and skill. To obtain the concurrence of the principal ministers and most powerful barons of the reformed party: to bring back the exiles, and to restore to them the authority which they had lost; to secure the support of Elizabeth and her chief ministers, Cecil and Leicester; to murder Riccio; to dissolve the Parliament, about to be convoked for the purpose of legally consummating the ruin of the fugitive lords; to imprison the Queen; to confer the nominal sovereignty upon Darnley; to replace Murray at the head of the Government: such was the plan conceived by Morton, and adopted in Scotland by Lords Lindsay, Ruthven, and Lething-

[1] Tytler, vol. v., p. 334.

ton, by Knox and Craig, the two ministers of Edinburgh, Bellenden, the justice-clerk, Makgill, the clerk-register, and the lairds of Brunston, Calder, and Ormiston. The Earl of Lennox himself proceeded to England to communicate it to Murray, Rothes, Glencairn, Grange, and Ochiltree, the father-in-law of Knox, who readily embraced it, and agreed to repair to the frontier, so as to be ready to return to Edinburgh as soon as the plot had succeeded.[1]

Two solemn covenants were immediately drawn up, to bind the King, on the one hand, and the conspirators on the other, to the performance of those conditions which were thought to be for their mutual advantage. The first, which was signed by the King, Morton, and Ruthven, declared that the Queen's 'gentle and good nature' was abused by some wicked and ungodly persons, specially an Italian called David, and that the King had determined, with the assistance of certain of his nobility and others, to seize these enemies of the realm, and, if they resisted, ' to cut them off immediately, and to slay them wherever it happened.' He pledged himself, on the word of a Prince, to maintain and defend his associates in the enterprise, though carried into execution in presence of the Queen's Majesty, and within the precincts of the palace.[2] In the second covenant, the Earls of Murray, Argyle, Glencairn, and Rothes, the Lords Boyd and Ochiltree, and their 'complices,' promised to support Darnley in all his just quarrels, to be friends to his friends and enemies to his enemies, to give him the Crown matrimonial, to maintain the Protestant religion, and to put down its enemies. The King, on his side, engaged to pardon Murray and the banished lords, to stay all proceedings for their forfeiture, and to restore them to their lands and dignities.[3]

These covenants were submitted to Randolph's inspection, who sent a copy of them to Cecil. Randolph and the Earl of Bedford at the same time wrote from Berwick, on the 6th of March, to Elizabeth's Secretary of State, enjoining him to keep the secret most religiously, and to inform none but the Queen and Leicester of 'the great attempt then on the eve of being

[1] Tytler, vol. v., pp. 336, 337; and Proofs and Illustrations, No. 15, pp. 498-507.
[2] British Museum, Caligula, B. ix., fol. 212; Copy of the time endorsed by Randolph. Tytler, vol. v., pp. 337, 338.
[3] State Paper Office, copy by Randolph from the original:—' Conditions for the Earls to perform to their King,' and ' Conditions to be performed by the King of Scots to the Earls.' Endorsed in Cecil's hand, Primo Martii, 156⁵ (1566, as the year still ended at Easter). Tytler, vol. v., pp. 338, 339.

put in execution.' 'You have heard,' they said, 'of divers discords and jars between this Queen and her husband, partly for that she hath refused him the Crown matrimonial, partly for that he hath assured knowledge of such usage of herself, as altogether is intolerable to be borne, which, if it were not overwell known, we would both be very loth to think that it could be true. To take away this occasion of slander, he is himself determined to be at the apprehension and execution of him whom he is able manifestly to charge with the crime, and to have done him the most dishonour that can be to any man, much more being as he is.' They then go on to detail the arrangement entered into by the conspirators, and conclude their despatch with these words: 'If persuasions to cause the Queen to yield to these matters do no good, they purpose to proceed we know not in what sort. If she be able to make any power at home, she shall be withstood, and herself kept from all other counsel than her own nobility. If she seek any foreign support, the Queen's majesty, our Sovereign, shall be sought, and sued unto to accept his and their defence, with offers reasonable to her Majesty's contentment. These are the things which we thought and think to be of no small importance; and knowing them certainly intended, and concluded upon, thought it our duties to utter the same to you, Mr. Secretary, to make declaration thereof as shall seem best to your wisdom."¹

Elizabeth was thus duly informed of the plot, and offered no opposition to it. Neither Mary Stuart, thus shamefully betrayed, nor David Riccio, thus fatally menaced, had any suspicion of the conspiracy formed against the power and honour of the one, and against the life of the other, although this dark intrigue was known to so many persons. The Queen was not, however, ignorant of the deep aversion entertained by her nobility for her favourite secretary. In a paper² in which she expressed her opinions on this matter, she replied with cutting sarcasm to those nobles who, priding themselves upon the merits of their ancestors, and considering themselves, as they said, better instructed and more liberally educated than all other persons, desired to have the entire administration of the State in their own hands, under the pretext that they could devote to its service more honour and greater property than any one else. She found that in general, instead of being valiant and wise like their ancestors, they were sticklers for their family, careless of their honour, rash and

¹ MS. letter, State Paper Office, 6th March, 1566, Bedford and Randolph to Cecil. Tytler, vol. v., p. 340.
² Printed in Labanoff's Collection, vol. vii., pp. 297-299.

traitorous, loving only to command, and setting at nought the monarch and the laws. She asked herself whether, under these circumstances, it would be right to allow them to disregard or diminish the royal authority, and to respect none but their own; and she added: "If the Sovereign finds a man of low estate, poor in means, but generous in mind, faithful in heart, and well adapted to fill an office in his service, he will not dare to intrust him with any authority, because the nobles who already possess power are ever craving for more!"[1] She had therefore firmly resolved to support Riccio against them, as he was a man of low condition, but generous mind, and faithful heart.

Riccio, on his part, reckoning on the energetic support of the courageous Queen, was utterly devoid of fear. He had, however, been warned to be on his guard by an astrologer, named Damiot, whom he was in the habit of consulting. But the mysterious hints of this person, who bade him, it is said, beware of the bastard, (evidently alluding to George Douglas, the natural son of the Earl of Angus,) pointed, as he thought, to Murray.[2] But as Murray, then in banishment, had recently besought Riccio's influence to obtain his pardon, the too confident favourite derided this equivocal admonition. He took no precautions, and continued to live in imprudent familiarity with the Queen.[3]

Mary Stuart, having discovered that the English Ambassador had furnished Murray with a supply of money at the time of his rebellion, gave Randolph orders, on the 17th of February, to quit Scotland, and he had accordingly retired to Berwick. She had convoked her Parliament to ratify the condemnation of Murray and the banished lords. She opened it in person on the 7th of March, appointed the Lords of the Articles on the same day, and restored to the spiritual estate of the realm the place in Parliament which it had occupied before the occurrence of the change in the national religion, in order, as she states herself, 'to have done some good anent restoring the auld religion, and to have proceeded against our rebels according to their demerits.'[4] The act of forfeiture to be passed against the

[1] Printed in Labanoff's Collection, vol. vii., p. 299.
[2] Knox, History, vol. ii., pp. 521, 522. Spotswood, p. 194. Tytler, vol. v., p. 342.
[3] 'This David Rizio was so foolish, that not only had he drawn unto him the management of all affairs, the King being set aside, but also his equipage and train did surpass the King's; and at the Parliament that was to be, he was ordained to be Chancellor.' Knox, vol. ii., p. 521.
[4] Mary Stuart to the Archbishop of Glasgow, 2nd April, 1566; in Labanoff, vol. i., p. 343; and Keith. p. 330.

exiles was drawn up, and was to be voted on Tuesday, the 12th of March. But the conspirators did not delay so long, and chose Saturday, the 9th of March, for the execution of their plan, which was vigorously seconded by the Presbyterian ministers.

On the 3rd of March commenced the week of the great general fast of the Reformed Church, which had brought all the most zealous Protestants to Edinburgh. Knox and Craig, who were both privy to the conspiracy, chose subjects for sermons calculated to inflame the public mind, and prepare it for what was about to happen. The Bible abounded in startling examples of punishment. The death of Oreb and Zeeb, the defeat of the Benjamites, the history of Esther, and the execution of Haman, all impressed upon these alarmed and violent men the duty of inflicting swift and summary vengeance on the enemies of the people of God.[1] At this time the enemy of the people of God was the poor Italian secretary, who was detested as a foreigner, envied as a favourite, and feared as a Catholic ; and whom the nobles engaged in the conspiracy had resolved to sacrifice in the presence of the Queen herself.

On the Saturday evening, as it had been agreed, Morton, Ruthven, and Lindsay proceeded, with about two hundred armed men, to Darnley's apartments in Holyrood Palace, which were situated below those of Mary Stuart.[2] He had supped earlier than usual, and was quite ready to receive them. At eight o'clock he went up to the Queen's chamber by a secret staircase, followed at a short distance by Ruthven, George Douglas, Andrew Ker of Faudonside, and Patrick Bellenden ;[3] whilst Morton and Lindsay, with their men, occupied the court-yard, and seized the gates of the palace. Darnley was the first to enter the Queen's cabinet, a little room of about twelve feet square, where he found Mary Stuart at supper with her natural sister, the Countess of Argyle,[4] and attended by David Riccio, who had

[1] Tytler, vol. v., p. 343. See also his Historical Remarks on Knox's Implication in the Murder, Appendix, vol. v., pp. 498-507.

[2] 'Comparvero circa ducento homini bene armati alle camere del Re, il quale era appunto alloggiato sotto la camera stessa della Reina, or dissero queste medesime parole: "Sire, noi siamo qua pronti." Et senza dir altro, il Re, s'incaminò per una lumaga segreta verso la camera della Reina.' Memoir addressed to Cosmo I., Grand Duke of Tuscany, extracted from the Archives of the Medici, and published in Labanoff, vol. vii., pp. 63-80.

[3] Labanoff, vol. i., p. 333. Tytler, vol. v., p. 344. Ellis's Original Letters, first series, vol. ii., p. 213.

[4] Lady Jane Stuart, natural daughter of James V. and Elizabeth, the daughter of Lord John Carmichael. She married the Earl of Argyle in 1554, and was separated from him in 1564.

'his cappe upon his heade,'[1] the Commendator of Holyrood,[2] the Laird of Creich, Arthur Erskine,[3] and some others of her household. He took his seat behind the Queen, who turned towards him, and embraced him affectionately.[4]

A minute had scarcely elapsed before Ruthven, clad in complete armour, and pale and haggard with disease, broke into the room. He was followed almost immediately by George Douglas, Faudonside, and Patrick Bellenden, armed with daggers and pistols. This invasion of her private apartments, at such an hour and with such weapons, left Mary Stuart no doubt of the sinister design of the King and the conspirators. She demanded of Ruthven what was his business, and by whose permission he had ventured to enter her presence.[5] Ruthven replied, pointing to Riccio, 'Let it please your Majesty that yonder man David come forth of your privy-chamber, where he hath been over long.' 'What offence hath he done?' said the Queen. Ruthven answered, 'That he made a greater and more heinous offence to her Majesty's honour, the King her husband, the nobility and commonwealth.'[6] The Queen then said that if any one had any charge to bring against David, she would cite him before the Lords of Parliament, and she ordered Ruthven to retire under pain of treason.[7] Ruthven, however, paying no attention to her commands, approached Riccio to seize him. But he took refuge behind the Queen, crying out in his broken language, ' Madame, je suis mort! Giustizia, giustizia! Sauve ma vie, Madame, sauve ma vie!'[8] In his attempts to avoid the danger which threatened him, the table was thrown down upon the Queen, who

[1] Despatch of Bedford and Randolph to the Council, 27th March, 1567 ; in Wright's Elizabeth and her Times, vol. i., p. 227.
[2] Lord Robert Stuart, the natural son of James V. and Euphemia Elphinstone whom the King his father appointed Commendator of the Abbey of Holyrood. He joined the Reformers in 1560. In 1569, he exchanged his abbey for the temporalities of the bishopric of Orkney, which was made an earldom on the 28th of October, 1581. Knox, vol. i., p. 458, note 4.
[3] Erskine of Blackgrange, cousin-german of Lord John Erskine, and captain of the Queen's Guard. Knox, vol. ii., p. 288.
[4] 'El Re se poso dietro la sedia della Reina, la quale subito rivoltata si bacciorno insieme.' Memoir addressed to Cosmo I., Labanoff, vol. vii., p. 73.
[5] 'La Reina li disse chi lo facesse andare in quel luogo in quell' hora, et chi gliene haveva data licentia?' Labanoff, vol. vii., p. 73.
[6] Ruthven's Narrative in Keith, Appendix, p. 123.
[7] 'Also we commanded the Lord Ruthven, under the pain of treason, to avoyd him forth of our presence ; declaring we should exhibite the said David before the Lords of Parliament, to be punisht, if any sorte he had offended' Letter from Mary Stuart to the Archbishop of Glasgow, 2nd April, 1566 ; in Labanoff, vol. i., p. 344. [8] Labanoff, vol, vii., p. 74. Birrel's Diary, p. 5.

was six months gone with child, and who strove to defend him from the assassins, whose short swords and pistols were for a moment turned against herself.¹ Riccio had seized the pleats of her gown, and clung tightly to them. Darnley, however, loosed his hands; and whilst the rest were carrying off their victim, he held the Queen in his arms,² that she might make no farther efforts to save him.

Alarmed at the danger of her unfortunate servant, and not altogether without fear for herself,³ Mary implored the pity of the conspirators for Riccio,⁴ who, while he was being dragged away, reminded Darnley of the good services which he had rendered him.⁵ Darnley hypocritically assured the Queen that they would do him no harm.⁶ The poor and trembling Italian was dragged from her cabinet, and through her bedroom to the entrance of her presence chamber, which was close at hand.⁷ He found there most of the conspirators, waiting for their victim. Morton and Lindsay wished to keep him until the next day, and then to hang him;⁸ but George Douglas, more impatient than they,

---

¹ 'Notwithstanding Lord Ruthven perforce invadit him in our presence (he then for refuge took safeguard, having retired him behind our back), and with his complices cast down our table upon ourself, put violent hands on him, struck him over our shoulders with whinzeards, one part of them standing before our face with bended daggs.' Letter form Mary Stuart to the Archbishop of Glasgow, 2nd April, 1566; Labanoff, vol. i., p. 344.

² 'David took the Quene by the blyghtes (pleats) of her gowne, and put himself behynde the Quene, who wold gladly have savid him; but the King havinge loosed his hands, and holdinge her in his arms, &c.' Despatch from Bedford and Randolph to the Council, Ellis, vol. ii., p. 210. 'Il Re la prese, et 'abbraciò tenendola in modo che non si poteva muovere.' Despatch to the Grand Duke of Tuscany, 8th October, 1566; Labanoff, vol. vii., p. 93.

³ 'In doing whereof, we were not only struck with great dreadour, but also by sundrie considerations was most justly induced to take extream fear of our life.' Letter from Mary to the Archbishop of Glasgow; Labanoff, vol. i., p. 345.

⁴ 'La Regina gridava che non dovessino farli male por amor di lei.' Despatch to Cosmo I.; Labanoff, vol. vii., p. 93.

⁵ 'Dicendo anco al Re se voleva comportare che l'ammazzassino davanti li suoi ochi, sovvenendoli li buoni et fedeli serviti che gl' haveva fatto.' Labanoff, vol. vii., p. 93.

⁶ 'Lasciatelo andare, Madama, disse, che non le sara fatto alcun male.' Ibid.

⁷ He was not murdered in the Queen's cabinet and in her presence, as it has frequently been asserted. Testimonies are unanimous on this point. The Queen herself states the fact in her letter to the Archbishop of Glasgow: 'They most cruelly took him forth of our cabinet.' Labanoff, vol. i., p. 345. 'Presero David nel collo, per trascinarlo fuora del camerino.' Labanoff, vol. vii., p. 74. 'Fu preso davanti li suoi ochi, et menato fuora del gabinetto.' Despatch to Cosmo I., in Labanoff, vol. vii., p. 93. 'He was not slayne in the Queens presens, as was saide, but goinge downe the stayers owte of the chamber of presence.' Despatch of Randolph and Bedford, in Ellis, vol. ii., pp. 210, 211.

⁸ Ellis, vol. ii., p. 210.

struck him, while on the staircase, with the King's dagger, which he had got hold of, and called out that that was the royal blow.¹ The others immediately rushed upon him, nor did they think their work complete until the body was mangled with fifty-six wounds. His corpse was thrown out of window into the courtyard, and carried thence to the porter's lodge.²

On being informed of the completion of the murder, the Queen, full of sorrow and anger, gave utterance to her feelings with regard to Darnley. She reproached him with having authorized so cowardly an action, and with having inflicted such a disgrace upon her, who had taken him from his humble condition, and raised him to the throne; and she called him a traitor, and son of a traitor.³ Darnley, in his turn, reproached her with having avoided his company for several months, with having frequently refused to remain with him any longer than while David was present, and with having at last admitted Riccio to her society more often than himself. 'It is for this reason,' he added, ' for your honour and my own contentment, that I gave my consent that he should be taken away.'⁴ 'My lord,' replied Mary, 'all the offence that is done me, you have the wite thereof, for the which I shall be your wife no longer, nor lie with you any more, and shall never like well till I cause you to have as sorrowful a heart as I have at this present.'⁵ At this moment, Ruthven, faint from sickness, and reeking from the scene of blood, entered the room. He desired her Majesty's permission to sit down, and asked for a cup of wine. He then roughly told the Queen that they had put Riccio to death, because he was a disgrace to herself, and a curse to her kingdom; and because the pernicious influence which he exercised over her, had induced her to tyrannize over the nobility, to banish the exiled lords, to maintain close and blameworthy connections with foreign princes, in order that she might restore the ancient religion, and to admit into her council the Earls of Bothwell and Huntly, who were both of them traitors. Mary Stuart, thus humiliated, wept bitterly, and

---

¹ 'Fu uno che arditamente mise la mano all'estesso pugnale del Re . . . et diede un colpo a David, lasciendogli il pugnal nelle schiene, et dissegli esser quello il colpo del Re.' Memoir addressed to Cosmo I.; Labanoff, vol. vii., p. 74.

² Narrative of Morton and Ruthven, in Keith, Appendix, p. 126.

³ 'Allora voltatasi la Reina verso il Re gli disse: "Ha traditore, figliuolo di traditore, questa è la ricompensa che hai dato a colui che t'ha fatto tanto bene et honor cosi grande; questo é il reconoscimento che dai a me pet haverti inalzato a dignità cosi alta!"' Labanoff, vol. vii., p. 75. 'She blamed greatly her howsbonde that was the autor of so fowle an acte.' Ellis, vol. ii., p. 211.

⁴ Ellis, vol. ii., p. 211   ⁵ Ruthven's Narrative, in Keith, Appendix, p. 124.

answered him with bitter menaces. 'Well,' she said, 'it shall be dear blood to some of you.' Ruthven, whose rude energy was excited by the disease under which he sank in less than two months afterwards, added, 'God forbid! for the more your Grace shows yourself offended, the world will judge the worse.'[1] Deprived of a dear and devoted servant, wounded in her honour, and despoiled of her power, Mary Stuart was now a prisoner in the hands of her enemies.

The Earls of Huntly and Bothwell[2] having heard that Murray and Argyle were expected on the next day, and believing that they were in as much danger as Riccio, escaped out of one of the palace windows by means of a cord, which enabled them to descend into the fields. The Earl of Athol, the Lords Fleming and Livingston,[3] and Sir James Balfour, who were in Holyrood when the conspirators invaded the palace and Riccio was killed, also took to flight. On being informed of the tumult in the palace, the inhabitants of Edinburgh were greatly alarmed. The Provost of the city, at the information of Sir James Melvil,[4] had sounded the tocsin, and at the head of a body of armed citizens, had presented himself at the palace gates to inquire what was going on, and demanded to be admitted to the presence of the Queen. But the conspirators refused to admit him, and threatened, if she attempted to see and speak to them, to put the Queen to death, and throw her over the walls.[5] As the citizens insisted on an explanation, the King went out and informed them that the Queen was in safety, that no harm had happened to her, and that only the Italian Secretary had been put to death, because he had conspired with the Pope and the King of Spain to introduce foreign troops into the country to conquer it and restore the ancient religion.[6] Darnley then commanded them on their allegiance to go home.[7] His orders were instantly obeyed; and the Queen, hopeless of receiving any assistance, remained captive

---

[1] Ellis, vol. ii., p. 212.
[2] Letter from Mary Stuart to the Archbishop of Glasgow; in Labanoff, vol. i. pp. 345, 346. Ellis, vol. ii., p. 212.
[3] John, fifth Lord Fleming, hereditary Lord High Chamberlain of Scotland, succeeded to his title in 1558. William Livingston was fifth Lord of Callendar. Both remained constantly attached to the cause of the Queen.
[4] Melvil's Memoirs, p. 150.
[5] 'Who in our face declared, if we desired to have spoken them, they should cut us in collops and cast us over the walls.' Letter from Mary Stuart to the Archbishop of Glasgow; Labanoff, vol. i., p. 346.
[6] Despatch to Cosmo I.; in Labanoff, vol. vii., p. 94.
[7] Knox, vol. ii., p. 522. Labanoff, vol. i., p. 346.

in her room during the whole of this terrible night, and was not even allowed the company of her servants and gentlewomen.[1] She felt it was necessary to control her feelings, to dissimulate her intentions, and to divide her enemies, that she might first escape from their hands, and then take vengeance upon them. And this she did with patient artifice and well-planned hatred.

CHAPTER V.

FROM THE ASSASSINATION OF RICCIO TO MARY'S MARRIAGE WITH BOTHWELL.

Mary's Reconciliation with Darnley—Pardon of Murray and the other Exiles—Punishment of Riccio's Murderers—Birth of the Prince Royal of Scotland—Mary's Aversion to Darnley—Her attachment to Bothwell—Her Illness—Plots against Darnley's Life—His Alarm and Illness—Pardon of Riccio's Murderers—Murder of Darnley—Public Indignation—Trial and Acquittal of Bothwell—His Marriage with the Queen.

THE Queen's marriage with Darnley had once more involved Scotland in civil warfare; the assassination of Riccio plunged it in conspiracies and murders. The history of this distracted kingdom for several years, presents one unvarying scene of treason, violence, and intrigue. All persons took their part in these proceedings; the King, the Queen, and three Regents, were all mixed up with them at different periods, and to a greater or less extent. Assassination, imprisonment, and the scaffold were their lot. Such is the ordinary fate of persons of unbridled passions, or unregulated interests. They find their punishment where they had sought their satisfaction.

During the fearful night which followed Riccio's murder, Mary Stuart was plunged in the deepest affliction. She was a prisoner in her palace, which was closely guarded by Morton and the other conspirators. On the next day, Darnley spoke and acted as King. He pronounced the dissolution of the Parliament, and commanded its members, on pain of treason, to leave Edinburgh within three hours.[2] He also wrote, with his own hand, to enjoin the Provost of the city to keep a vigilant watch, and suffer none but Protestants to leave their houses. When he went into the Queen's chamber, he found her in a state of the most painful agitation. The tragic spectacle which she had witnessed, the threatening recollec-

[1] Labanoff, vol. i., p. 346.
[2] Keith, Appendix, p. 126. Labanoff, vol. i., p. 346.

tions which rang in her ears, the image of the terrible Ruthven, who seemed ready to strike her down, and the dark designs which she feared were entertained against her by a nobility accustomed not to respect their monarchs, had thrown her into a sort of delirium. At the sight of her anguish, pity revived affection in Darnley's heart. He obtained permission from the confederates that her gentlewomen should go to her assistance; but none of them, however, were allowed to pass 'muffled' from her chamber, lest the prisoner should escape under the disguise of one of them.[1] From that moment Mary Stuart, expecting deliverance from herself alone, employed all her address and all her dissimulation to obtain it.

When Murray, to meet whom she had despatched Sir James Melvil, arrived on Sunday evening with the other banished lords,[2] she summoned him at once to her presence. On seeing him she threw herself into his arms in an agony of tears, and exclaimed, 'Ah! my brother, if you had been here, you never would have suffered me to have been thus cruelly handled.'[3] Murray appeared moved. But, nevertheless, on the next day all the conspirators met together, and deliberated upon the course they intended to take. They seemed disposed to confer the matrimonial crown and the government of the kingdom on Darnley, to complete the establishment of Protestantism, and to confine the Queen in Stirling Castle until she had given her sanction to all their deeds.[4] This plan, which is attributed to them by Mary Stuart, and which they did not realize till the year following, was at this time foiled by the ability of the Queen and the weakness of Darnley.

During the numerous private interviews which Mary had with her husband, she represented to him the miserable position in which he would be placed with regard to the nobles if he permitted them to conquer her, and the danger to which he would be exposed by the princes, her allies, if he suffered any further alterations in the religious state of the realm.[5] She had no

[1] Ruthven's Narrative, in Keith, Appendix, pp. 126, 127.
[2] Ellis, vol. ii., p. 213. Labanoff, vol. i., p. 347.
[3] Melvil's Memoirs, p. 151.
[4] 'In their council they thought it most expedient we should be warded in our castle of Streviling, there to remain while we had approved in Parliament all their wicked interprizes, establisht their religion, and given to the King the crown matramoniall, and the haill government of our realme; or else, by all appearance, firmly purposed to have put us to death, or detained us in perpetual captivity.' Letter from Mary Stuart to the Archbishop of Glasgow, 2nd April, 1566. Labanoff, vol. i., p. 347. [5] Labanoff, vol. i., pp. 347, 348.

difficulty in gaining him over to her side. Darnley was vain and weak, with an ambitious mind, but a timorous heart. Notwithstanding the harsh and humiliating explanations which the husband and wife had lately interchanged, Darnley forgot the injury which he pretended had been done to his honour, and Mary passed over the outrage which had just been inflicted on her reputation, and the violence with which her authority had so recently been attacked. Abandoning his friends and their projects, Darnley consented to procure the Queen's escape, and to accompany her in her flight.

This escape could be effected only by deceiving the other conspirators. On Monday, therefore, Darnley announced to them that the Queen had been seized with fever, and was threatened with miscarriage, unless she were allowed a change of air. He assured them, at the same time, that she was ready to pardon all that they had done, to satisfy them personally of her forgiveness, and to sign such acts as they might judge necessary for their safety. The conspirators at first declared that this proposition was a mere artifice, and advised Darnley to be on his guard. But Darnley reiterated his perfect confidence in the Queen's good faith, and led Morton, Ruthven, and Murray into her presence. Mary told them that she had never desired to take away the life or lands of any of her nobility; and that, continuing to act as she had done ever since her return to Scotland, she would restore the exiles to favour, pardon the murderers of Riccio, and forget all that had occurred. She sent them away to draw up, for her signature, such articles as they might consider necessary for their security.[1] Then, taking Darnley by one hand, and Murray by the other, she walked with them for some time in a confiding and friendly manner.

Forced to yield to the wishes of the King, who was about to desert them, and to comply with the Queen's request, the conspirators drew up the act which was destined to provide for their security, and gave it to Darnley, who promised to obtain the Queen's signature. He also requested them to leave her under his guardianship alone, that she might appear free to act, and to give such orders as she might please; and assured them that he would answer for all that happened. On Monday evening, therefore, they left Holyrood Palace with their men, not, however, without giving the King to understand that they feared he was playing them false, and that they expected the Queen and

Ruthven's Narrative, in Keith, Appendix, p. 128.

himself would retire, either to the Castle of Edinburgh or Dunbar. 'And the Lord Ruthven protested that what bloodshed or mischief should ensue thereon, should fall upon the King's head and his posterity, and not upon theirs.'[1]

The suspicions of the conspirators were realized. At midnight, on the 11th of March, Mary Stuart, accompanied by Darnley and Arthur Erskine, her captain of the guard, secretly left Holyrood, mounted on fleet horses, and fled to Dunbar.[2] As soon as she had arrived there, she convoked her nobility to meet her in arms. On Tuesday morning, when the confederated lords discovered that she had escaped without signing the articles which she had promised them, they sent Lord Semple after her to demand the performance of her promise. But she made him wait for three days without an answer. Then, finding herself at the head of an army which had been collected for her by the Earls of Bothwell, Huntly, Athol, Marshal, and Caithness, the Archbishop of St. Andrews, and the Lords Hume and Yester, she abandoned all further disguise.[3] On the 16th of March she published a proclamation[4] against the rebels who had dared to shed blood in her palace, and to hold herself in captivity. Wisely bent on dividing her enemies, she effected a reconciliation with Murray, Argyle, Glencairn, and Rothes, on condition that they should not join the murderers of Riccio.[5] She pursued all these with implacable resentment. Morton, Ruthven, Lindsay, George Douglas, Andrew Ker of Faudonside, and sixty-five other lairds or gentlemen[6] were cited to appear before her to answer for their share in the crime; and she marched upon Edinburgh, where they still remained, but whence they fled to England on her approach. Mary Stuart returned into the city, where she had been outraged and made prisoner, with an earnest desire for vengeance, and full power to gratify her wish.

She ordered the Earl of Lennox never again to appear at her Court.[7] Lethington was deprived of his office of Secretary of State, and directed to retire to Inverness.[8] Joseph Riccio was

[1] Keith, pp. 128, 129.
[2] Keith, Appendix, p. 129. Labanoff, vol. i., p. 348. Ellis, vol. ii., p. 214.
[3] Ruthven's Narrative, in Keith, Appendix, p. 129. Labanoff, vol. i., pp. 348, 349. Wright, vol. i., p. 230. [4] Printed in Keith, Appendix, p. 130.
[5] Melvil's Memoirs, p. 66. Labanoff, vol. i., p. 348.
[6] Keith, Appendix, pp. 129-131. A list of their names will be found annexed to the despatch of Bedford and Randolph to the Council, in Wright, vol. i., p. 231; and Ellis, vol. ii., pp. 220-222.
[7] Wright, vol. i., p. 234. Ellis, vol. ii., p. 222.
[8] Ellis, vol. ii., pp. 216, 217. Melvil's Memoirs, p. 67.

appointed the Queen's Private Secretary in the place of his brother David,[1] to whose remains great honours were done.[2] The principal authors of the murder having taken flight, Mary ordered that several of the subaltern accomplices, who had guarded the gates of the palace during its perpetration, and who thought their obscurity would save them from punishment, should be seized and put to death.[3] In the violence of her animosity, she imprisoned the Laird of Drumlanrig and his son, the Provost of Glenkonden, who were not in Edinburgh at the time of Riccio's assassination, but who had refused to join a league formed for the purpose of discovering and punishing all those who had been concerned in the conspiracy.[4]

Darnley, on his part, had been obliged to disavow all connection with the plot in a public declaration which was proclaimed at Edinburgh on the 20th of March. He therein contradicted the calumnious reports by which wicked persons had dared to associate him in what he termed ' the late cruel murder committed in presence of the Queen's Majesty, and treasonable detaining of her Majesty's most noble person in captivity.' 'His Grace,' he added, ' for the removing of the evil opinion which the good subjects may be induced to conceive through such false reports and seditious rumours, hath, as well to the Queen's Majesty as in the presence of the Lords of Secret Council, plainly declared upon his honour, fidelity, and the word of a Prince, that he never knew of any part of the said treasonable conspiracy whereof he is slanderously and falsely accused, nor never counselled, commanded, consented, assisted, nor approved the same.' He confessed, however, that he had, without the Queen's knowledge, consented to the return of the Earls of Murray, Glencairn, and Rothes, and the other exiles from England.

This disavowal did not restore him to the favour of the Queen, to whom he even went so far as to denounce the Secretary Lethington, the Justice-clerk Bellenden, and the Clerk-register Makgill, as having been concerned in the conspiracy.[6] But his codnuct brought him nothing but dishonour, and completely ruined him in the opinion of his accomplices. They could not learn, without the utmost indignation, the breach of faith of which

[1] Keith, Appendix, p. 129.
[2] Laing's History of Scotland, 3rd edition, vol. i., p. 50, note 8.
[3] Keith, p. 334. Melvil's Memoirs, p. 67.
[4] Wright, vol. i., p. 233. Ellis, vol. ii., pp. 217-221-222.
[5] Ellis, vol. ii., p. 222.
[6] MS. letters, State Paper Office; Forster to Cecil, 16th May, and Randolph to Cecil, 13th May, 1566. Tytler, vol. v., p. 359.

he had been guilty. To have incited them to conspire for the defence of his honour, and the increase of his power, and then to separate from them and betray them to the vengeance of the Queen, appeared to them the basest treason. In revenge for his faithlessness, therefore, they communicated to Mary Stuart the two bonds[1] which he had signed, and by which it had been determined to confer on him the matrimonial crown, and to murder Riccio. The Queen had previously thought that, blinded for a moment by jealousy, he might have acted without due reflection. But now, informed of the whole extent of his criminality, she for ever withdrew from him her confidence, and regarded him with feelings of unmitigated disgust. He was evermore considered by her as an ungrateful husband, a perfidious conspirator, and a cowardly liar.

From this time forth she manifested an insurmountable aversion to him. Already, before her return to Edinburgh, she had displayed the real feelings which she entertained concerning him, although it was still her interest to dissimulate them. She often expressed her views to James Melvil, who had temporarily succeeded Lethington as Secretary of State. 'The Queen,' says Melvil, in his Memoirs, ' lamented unto me the King's folly, ingratitude, and misbehaviour; I excused the same the best I could, imputing it to his youth, which occasioned him to be easily led away by pernicious counsel, laying the blame upon George Douglas, and other bad counsellors; praying her Majesty, for many necessary considerations, to remove out of her mind any prejudice against him, seeing that she had chosen him herself against the opinion of many of her subjects. But I could perceive nothing from that day forth but great grudges that she entertained in her heart."[2] Mary's hatred of Darnley increased with her contempt. She withdrew him more than ever from any share in public business, which she conducted with the assistance of the Earls of Bothwell, Huntly, and Athol, and the Catholic Bishop of Ross, who possessed her entire confidence; and she condemned him to a life of isolation in the midst of her Court. Melvil, who beheld with grief and alarm the progress of her antipathy, vainly advised her to pardon her husband, and become reconciled with him; but his

---

[1] MS. letter, State Paper Office: Randolph to Cecil, 4th April, 1566. Tytler, vol. v., p. 352.

[2] Melvil's Memoirs, p. 66. Randolph informs us, 'The King is not loved by the Queen, on account of the said murder. The people hated him because he had broken his oath to the conspirators.' Letter from Randolph to Cecil, 4th April, 1566; in Robertson, Appendix 16.

interference was considered importunate and troublesome, and he was obliged to desist.¹ The Queen called him a traitor and flatterer, because he had given a spaniel to the neglected king,² and she forbade him to hold further converse with him. 'He went up and down all alone,' adds Melvil, ' seeing few durst bear him company.'³

Mary Stuart did not proceed to further extremes against Darnley, until her passion for another was added to her increasing repugnance to himself. The time of her confinement was now at hand. Rendered mistrustful by the plots which had been laid in so short an interval, with the intention of seizing her person in the defiles of Kinross, and of overthrowing her authority in the palace of Holyrood, she proceeded to Stirling Castle, that she might be brought to bed there in perfect safety. On the 19th of June, between nine and ten o'clock in the morning,⁴ she gave birth to that royal infant, of whom the Scottish nobles made use, thirteen months afterwards, to dispossess her of the throne, and who, after having reigned thirty-five years in Scotland under the title of James VI., succeeded Elizabeth on the English throne as James I. As soon as he was born, Melvil was despatched to inform the English Queen of the event, which so closely concerned both kingdoms, and to request her to act as godmother to the Prince of Scotland. Elizabeth was at Greenwich, giving a ball to her Court, when Cecil, the Secretary of State, and Mary Stuart's envoy, arrived. Cecil went up to her while she was dancing, and whispered the news into her ear. She was filled with sudden melancholy by the intelligence. Interrupting the dance, she sank dejectedly into an arm-chair, and said to the ladies who surrounded her, ' That the Queen of Scots was mother of a fair son, while she was but a barren stock.'⁵

But although Elizabeth sometimes gave impetuous flow to her feelings, no one was better skilled in subduing and disguising them. At the audience which she granted Melvil on the following day, she received him with a smiling countenance, and appeared rejoiced at the event, though it really caused her great grief, and gave her a successor in spite of all her wishes to the contrary. She thanked him for bringing her such good news, and 'gladly condescended to be a gossip to the Queen.'⁶ She

---

¹ Melvil's Memoirs, p. 67.
² Letter from the Earl of Bedford to Cecil, 3rd August, 1566; in Robertson, Appendix 17.
³ Melvil's Memoirs, p. 67. ⁴ Keith, p. 338. Melvil's Memoirs, p. 6ʒ.
⁵ Melvil's Memoirs, p. 70. ⁶ Ibid.

immediately sent Sir Henry Killegrew to congratulate the Queen of Scotland on her behalf, to assure her of her friendship, and to express her approbation of her conduct towards Riccio's murderers, whom she had nevertheless granted an asylum in her dominions.

The birth of the Prince of Scotland revived the question of the English succession. Melvil had received orders to renew his solicitations to Elizabeth on this subject. Mary Stuart skilfully effected a junction between Murray, Argyle, and Lethington[1] on the one hand, and Bothwell, Huntly, Athol, and the Bishop of Ross on the other; in the hope that they would have sufficient influence, the former on the Protestant party, and the latter on the Catholic party in England, to aid her in obtaining that which she had so ardently sought after for so many years. But at the same time that she was effecting a reconciliation between the principal personages of her realm, and was treating with favour the Lairds of Brunston, Ormiston, Hatton, and Calder, the leaders of the Presbyterian body[2]—the extreme Catholics thwarted her plans by recalling attention, at this moment, to her rights to Elizabeth's crown. A Scotchman, named Patrick Adamson, published at Paris a Latin Work in which he recognized Mary Stuart as Queen of England, and designated her son Prince of Scotland, England, and Ireland.[3]

Melvil's adroit suggestions led to no decisive result. Elizabeth, as usual, refused nothing, and promised as little. But the English Parliament ere long took up this important question. The Commons wished to settle it to the advantage of Protestantism, and consequently, to the detriment of Mary Stuart. In spite of all the repugnance of Elizabeth, who would not consent to appoint her successor, for fear of thereby weakening her authority, the two Houses met on the 2nd of October, and debated the question of the transmission of the crown, which they thought to render pacific by making it legal. The debate was continued for some time, until the Queen of England, in great irritation, resolved to put an end to it, and summoned the members of Parliament before her. She explained to them her egotistical, but prudent, policy in the most imperious language; and told them that several among them, during the reign of her sister, had offered her their

---

[1] On the 2nd of August, five months after the murder, Lethington was pardoned and admitted to the Queen's presence. Cecil's Abstract, p. 169.

[2] MS. letter, State Paper Office; Forster to Cecil, 19th September, 1566. Tytler, vol. v., p. 356.

[3] Letter from Elizabeth to Mary Stuart, 2nd December, 1566. Labanoff, vol. vii., pp. 99, 100.

assistance, if she were desirous to obtain the crown, and that persons would not be wanting,[1] under her own government, to disturb the general peace by similar intrigues, if she were to appoint her successor beforehand. 'I am your natural Queen,' she added in conclusion, 'and although you show yourselves so adverse to my will in this affair, I will not consent to its being carried further.'[2]

This injunction stopped the proceedings of the House of Lords; but had no such effect upon the Lower House, which continued the debate it had begun. Elizabeth was greatly irritated by this, and complained that the Commons were so strongly attached to their liberty that they forgot the submission which was due to their Prince. She sent them a positive order to cease all deliberation upon this subject, unless they would become guilty of disobedience to their sovereign.[3] To this command the Lower House yielded submission, although it considered that such an order was an infringement of its freedom of discussion.[4] Elizabeth, who had thus vigorously opposed the choice of a Protestant heir, repressed, with no less vehemence, the desires of the Catholic aspirant to the succession. She intimated to Mary Stuart her extreme displeasure at Patrick Adamson's temerity, and pressed her to disavow, by some public act, a book, which, she said, 'is so scandalous to you, so injurious to me, and so foolish in itself.'[5] She added that this publication would be sufficient to procure her condemnation 'as ungrateful to her who daily acted as her advocate against all her traducers.' 'You know, madam,' she continued, 'that there is nothing in the world which so much concerns my honour as that there should be no other Queen of England but myself.'[6]

---

[1] '... Entre los cuales havia havido algunos que, reinando su hermana, le ofrecian à ella ayuda y la querian mover á que quisiese procurar, en su vida, la corona; por lo cual se podia bien dare conoscer que nombrandose succesor no faltaria quien le andiese con semejantes platicas por turbar la paz comun.' Gusman de Silva to Philip II., 11th November, 1566. Archives of Simancas, Inglaterra, fol. 819.

[2] '... Si aunque soy vuestra reyna natural os mostrais tan contrarios à mi voluntad en este negocio, el cual non consentire que pase adelante.' Ibid.

[3] '... Y cuan afecionados estavan a su libertad sin mirar a la obediencia que devian a sus principes... Dixo me que les havia embíado un mandato, en que les ordeneva que no tratasen mas dello, so pena que incurririan en caso de los que contravienen al mandato y obediencia del principe et que todos havian obecido.' Gusman de Silva to Philip II., 11th November, 1566. Archives of Simancas, Inglaterra, fol. 819.

[4] Silva to Philip II., 13th November, 1566. Ibid., fol. 819.

[5] Letter from Elizabeth to Mary Stuart, 2nd December, 1566. Labanoff, vol. vii., p. 100.   [6] Ibid.

Notwithstanding Mary Stuart's ardent desire, the English succession remained in the same state of uncertainty as before. She still retained her claims, but had not succeeded in obtaining their recognition. She soon, however, compromised them, and, moreover, exposed herself to the loss of the crown of Scotland. After the birth of the Prince Royal, the misunderstanding increased between her husband and herself. A fatal passion, at this period, took possession of her heart. The object of this passion was the Earl of Bothwell, the most enterprising and dangerous man in Scotland. James Hepburn, fourth Earl of Bothwell, was then thirty years of age.[1] He had succeeded his father in 1556, was possessed of large property, and held important offices in the kingdom. By his marriage with Lady Jane Gordon,[2] he had become the brother-in-law of the Earl of Huntly, and had united one of the most powerful families of the South with the most powerful family of the North. He was distinguished for great bravery, consummate audacity,[3] boundless and unscrupulous ambition. Equally undisguised in his plans as in his vices,[4] he aspired first to gain the affection of the Queen, and afterwards to marry her. Although he was far from handsome,[5] his martial bearing, his taste for pleasure, the undaunted resolution of his character, his air of chivalrous devotion, and the easy and elegant continental manners beneath which he concealed the wild and extravagant passions of his country, charmed the imagination of the Queen, and gave Bothwell great influence over her. Mary Stuart sought to render Bothwell a faithful and useful servant; but she speedily found in him a lover and a master.

His progress in the royal favour,[6] towards the end of the sum-

[1] 'James, fourth Earl of Bothwell, was served heir to his father, 3rd November, 1556. The retour bears, that his father died five weeks or thereabouts preceding; therefore the date of his birth may be fixed to 1536 or 1537, as Queen Mary describes him as in his very youth at his first entry into this realm, immediately after the decease of his father.' Douglas's Peerage of Scotland, vol. i., p. 229.

[2] During the month of February, 1566, he had married Lady Jane Gordon, second daughter of George, fourth Earl of Huntly.

[3] When Bothwell returned from France to Scotland for the first time, Throckmorton wrote thus to Queen Elizabeth concerning him, on the 28th November, 1560: 'He is a glorious, rash, and hazardous young man; and therefore it were meet his adversaries should both have an eye to him, and also keep him short.' Hardwicke's State Papers, vol. i., p. 149.

[4] 'I assure you Bothwell is as naughty a man as liveth, and much given to the detestable vices.' Letter from Randolph to Cecil, 6th April, 1566; in Chalmers, vol. ii., p. 26.

[5] Brantôme, vol. v., p. 98.

[6] 'Bothwell is still in favour, and has a great hand in the management of

mer of 1566, was manifest to all. He arranged everything at his pleasure in the Court of Scotland, and was the sole director of his sovereign's will. The power which he wielded, and the reconciliation which had been effected between him, Huntly, Athol, Murray, Argyle, and Lethington, caused great alarm to the young King, whom Mary Stuart avoided and detested more and more. When he saw the Queen surrounded by men whom he considered were all his personal enemies, Darnley felt not merely offended, but believed that he was menaced. He turned towards the Catholic party in the hope of gaining their support ; wrote secretly to the Pope to denounce the Queen as lukewarm in the cause of religion ; and, in the excess of his fears, which were still premature, suspected that a plot had been formed against his life.[1] He even formed the idea of retiring to the Continent. He had a ship in readiness to convey him to France, and, towards the end of September, his father having come to see him at Stirling, he informed him of his intention. The Earl of Lennox immediately wrote to Mary Stuart, who was then at Edinburgh, to acquaint her with her husband's determination, and to report the failure of his attempts to change his purpose.[2]

On the 29th of September, the very same day that the Queen received the Earl of Lennox's letter, which led her to believe that Darnley had already sailed from Scotland, he arrived at Holyrood Palace.[3] The weakminded Prince formed plans, but never executed them ; after threatening a departure, he came to attempt a reconciliation. But the scene which occurred between the Queen and himself did not at all contribute to such a result. Mary at once assembled the members of her Council, and invited the French ambassador, Du Croc, to join them. In their presence she had an explanation with Darnley. She asked him plainly why he was desirous to leave Scotland, and what cause she had given him for wishing to take such a step? Darnley, who had come to seek an amicable meeting,[4] and who did not

---

affairs.' Bedford to Cecil, 9th August, 1566. ' Now the Earl of Bothwell's favour increased, which miscontented many.'. Melvil's Memoirs, p. 67. 'The Earl Bothwell, whom the Queen preferred above all others, after the decease of David Rizio.' Knox, vol. ii., p. 528.

[1] 'When his letters were intercepted, and his practices discovered, he accused the nobles of a plot against his life.' Tytler, vol. v., p. 356.

[2] Du Croc to Catherine de Medici, 17th October, 1566; in Labanoff, vol. i., p. 375. Letter from the Lords of the Council to the Archbishop of Glasgow, 8th October, 1566; in Keith, p. 348. [3] Labanoff, vol. i., p. 376. Keith, p. 348.

[4] ' Je vois bien qu'il ne sçait où il en est, il vouldroit que la reine le redemandast.' Du Croc, in Labanoff, vol. i., p. 377.

expect to be thus closely questioned, was struck dumb with amazement. He had, doubtless, no inclination to enter upon the discussion of his grievances, and, at the same time, of his wrongs. The Lords of the Council repeated the question, but he still remained silent. Du Croc then told him that his departure involved the Queen's honour as well as his own, and that the blame would fall upon her Majesty or himself, according as she had given him some good reason for the step, or he had undertaken it without due cause; he, therefore, earnestly entreated him to explain himself. Thus urged, Darnley at length avowed that the Queen had not given him any cause for his conduct. This was all that Mary Stuart wished; she had extracted from her husband a declaration which fully justified her behaviour, and freed her from all reproach regarding him, whether he left the country or remained in it; accordingly she said that 'she was satisfied.'[1]

After this interview, which had not answered Darnley's expectations, and in which neither party had acted with sincerity,—for the King had been unwilling to declare the causes of his discontent, and the Queen had shown no disposition to put an end to them,—they were on less amicable terms than ever. The melancholy and inconsiderate young man, who could neither endure his fate nor free himself from it, who had lost the affection of the Queen, awakened her resentment, and deserved her contempt by his vulgar tastes, his unfounded pretensions, his listless pride, his resultless plans, his odious participation in Riccio's murder, and his cowardly desertion of those whom he had induced to perpetrate it, coldly took leave of Mary, and returned to Stirling, after having told her, that she would not see him again, for a long while.[2] He wrote to her from thence that his motives for quitting Scotland were but too well-founded, and he based them upon the little confidence which she reposed in him, his deprivation of all authority, and the contempt and desertion which he experienced from the nobility, who had ceased to honour him when they perceived he was neglected by her Majesty.[3] No mention, however, was made in his letter of the fears which he had entertained for his life. He then continued his preparations for a departure

---

[1] Labanoff, vol. i., pp. 376, 377. Keith, p. 349.

[2] 'Sy est que, en ce desespoir, sans occasion comme il déclara, il s'en alla et dist adieu à la royne, sans la baiser, l'asseurant que sa Majesté ne le verroit de longtemps.' Du Croc, in Labanoff, vol. i., p. 377.

[3] Letter of the Lords of the Council to the Archbishop of Glasgow, 8th October, 1566; in Keith, p. 350.

which he was continually threatening,[1] but which, to his own and the Queen's misfortune, he never had the courage to carry into effect.

Far from offering any opposition to his departure, Mary Stuart proceeded about this time, and without inviting him to accompany her, towards the south-eastern frontier of her kingdom, which was disturbed by the quarrels of the insubordinate Borderers. The Armstrongs, Elliots, and Johnstones, three powerful families of Liddesdale, were then engaged in war with each other. On the 6th of October,[2] the Queen had sent thither the Earl of Bothwell, with the title of Lord Lieutenant, to repress these disorders, and restore tranquillity. On the 8th, she repaired in person to Jedburgh, to hold her assizes,[3] and to add the sanction of justice to that of armed force. On that same day,[4] Bothwell had, with great bravery, engaged in a personal conflict with John Elliot of Park, a notorious freebooter. In the scuffle Bothwell was severely wounded, and it was found necessary to convey him without loss of time to the neighbouring Castle of Hermitage. His illness furnished most conclusive proofs of Mary Stuart's attachment to him. 'Understanding the certain report of this accident,' says Crawford, 'the Queen was so highly grieved in heart, that she took no repose in body until she saw him.'[5]

The discharge of her judicial functions detained her at Jedburgh until the 15th of October; but no sooner was she at liberty than she took horse and hastened to the Castle where her favourite lieutenant was lying wounded. She was accompanied on her journey by Murray and some other nobles. Although Hermitage was eighteen miles distant from Edinburgh, she went and returned on the same day.[6] She spent an hour with Bothwell; and, notwithstanding the fatigues of the day, she sat up until late at night[7] writing to him whom she had just left. The prostration of strength which ensued, and, adds Crawford, 'the great distress of her mind for the Earl of Bothwell,'[8] threw her the next day, into a most dangerous illness. She fell into a

---

[1] Labanoff, vol. i., p. 377.   [2] Chalmers, vol. i., p. 294.
[3] 'On the 8th of October, the Queen went out of Edinburgh to Jedburgh to hold a *justice aire*.' Birrel's Diary; in Chalmers, vol. i., p. 295.
[4] On the same day Bothwell was wounded in the hand by Elliot of Park.' Ibid.
[5] Crawford's Memoirs, quoted in Keith, p. 352.
[6] Keith, p. 352.
[7] Letter from Lethington to the Archbishop of Glasgow, in Laing's History of Scotland, vol. ii., p. 74; and Sharon Turner's History of the Reigns of Edward the Sixth, Mary, and Elizabeth, 2nd edition, vol. iv., pp. 68-73.
[8] Crawford's Memoirs, in Keith, p. 352.

swoon, and remained for some hours at the point of death. The was then seized with a violent fever, and continued insensible for several days. When she had somewhat recovered from this apparently desperate state,[1] she thought her end was approaching, requested the nobles who were present to pray for her, confided her son to the guardianship of the Queen of England,[2] and sent to inform her husband of her precarious condition.[3] Bothwell, now convalescent,[4] had hastened to her with the other members of her Privy Council, and many of the most important nobles of the kingdom. Darnley did not arrive at Jedburgh until the 28th of October, two days after a favourable crisis had placed the Queen's life out of danger. Finding her so much recovered, he remained at Jedburgh only one night, and returned immediately to Glasgow.[5] This tardy and hurried visit, equally devoid of cordiality and solicitude, was not calculated to restore good feeling between the Queen and her husband.

Mary Stuart's recovery was slow, and she was unable to leave Jedburgh for Kelso until the 8th of of November. She travelled by short stages along the coast to Dunbar, and thence to Craigmillar Castle, about a league from Edinburgh, where she arrived on the 20th of November, and remained for nearly a fortnight.[6] She appeared careworn and melancholy, ready to sink under the weight of her trials and of the contradictory feelings which agitated her bosom. She still suffered from pains in her right side, and her liver also was disordered. 'The Queen is not at all well,' wrote the Ambassador Du Croc to the Archbishop of Glasgow. 'I do believe the principal part of her disease to consist of a deep grief and sorrow. Nor does it seem possible to make her forget the same. Still she repeats these words, "I could wish to be dead." '[7] Her feelings were too manifest to escape the notice of any round her, and the clear-sighted Lethington describes the true cause of her trouble when he says:

---

[1] See various letters to the Archbishop of Glasgow, in Keith, Appendix, pp. 133-135; and Laing, vol. ii., p. 73.

[2] Keith, pp. 352-354.

[3] Keith, Appendix, p. 133.

[4] 'My Lord Boythwell is heir, quha convalescis weill of his woundis.' Letter from the Bishop of Ross to the Archbishop of Glasgow, 27th October, 1566; in Keith, Appendix, p. 136.

[5] Chalmers, vol. i., p. 297. Sharon Turner, vol. iv., p. 68.

[6] Letter from Du Croc to the Archbishop of Glasgow, 2nd December, 1566; in Keith, Preface, p. vii. On the 18th, Mary was still at Dunbar, whence she wrote to Cecil and to the English Council. See Labanoff, vol. i., pp. 380-382.

[7] Keith, Preface, p. vii.

It is an heart-break for her, to think that he should be her husband, and how to be free of him she sees no outlet.'[1]

This knowledge of Mary Stuart's private feelings originated a number of fatal ideas in the minds of those who surrounded her. The members of her Privy Council, who were united by ties of kindred or friendship to Morton, Ruthven, Lindsay, and the other murderers of Riccio, hoped, if we are to believe an account which was prepared under the inspiration and in the interest of Mary Stuart, to obtain their pardon by pandering to the Queen's present passion, before which all past resentments dwindled into insignificance. The astute Lethington organized this plan with consummate skill and perversity. Scrupulous in nothing, suiting his policy to the circumstances in which he was placed, now assisting Darnley against Riccio, and now plotting with Bothwell against Darnley,—he negotiated the return of the exiles at the price of a divorce, and if necessary, of a murder. He communicated his plan to Bothwell, who joined in it with all the ardour of his headstrong ambition, and made it known to Argyle and Huntly, who promised their co-operation. According to the statement of the Queen's friends, he mentioned it also to Murray, who offered no opposition to the scheme. After having concerted the matter among themselves, the new confederates repaired to Mary Stuart.[2]

Lethington addressed her in their name. He reminded the Queen of the great and intolerable injuries that she had received from her husband, laying much stress upon the ingratitude which he had displayed towards her, and upon the offences of which he continued daily to be guilty. He then added that, if Her Majesty would be pleased to pardon the Earl of Morton and the Lords Ruthven and Lindsay, they, in concert with the rest of her nobility, would find means to separate her from her husband by a divorce, so that she would no longer be involved in disagreement

[1] Letter from Lethington to the Archbishop of Glasgow, 24th October, 1566; in Laing, vol. ii., p. 74.
[2] 'The Protestation of the Erles of Huntley and Argyll touching the murthour of the King of Scots,' in Keith, Appendix, pp. 136–138. This Protestation was sent either by the Queen, or in her name, to the Earls of Huntly and Argyle, ready drawn up for their signature. Laing says, 'During the subsequent conference at Westminster, (1568–69), she sent a Protestation touching the King's murder, to be signed again by Argyle and Huntly, and again returned.' Vol. i., p. 20. Murray utterly denies having taken the part which was attributed to him at Craigmillar. After having said that his enemies calumniated him in his absence, he adds, that during the month of November, at Craigmillar, nothing was proposed in his presence, 'tending to any unlawful or dishonourable end.' See his Answer to the aforesaid Protestation, in Keith, Appendix, p. 138.

L

with him. This proposition caused her no surprise. She at first gave her consent upon condition that the divorce should be legal, and should do no prejudice to the rights of her son.[1] But a divorce was not to be so easily obtained, since it would be necessary to allege as the reason for it their near relationship, in reference to which the Pope had granted them a dispensation, or to bring Darnley to trial for adultery, or else to prosecute him on a charge of treason.

These difficulties could not escape Mary's notice, and she knew that she would be exposed either to the delays of an uncertain negotiation, or to the scandal of a disgraceful trial. She accordingly affected scruples, and said that she would willingly retire into France and leave Darnley in Scotland until he acknowledged his faults. But Lethington replied to her that the nobles of her kingdom would not allow her to do so; and he even ventured, in mysterious terms, to inform her of their dark designs. 'Madam,' he said, 'soucy ye not, we are here of the principal of your Grace's nobility and Council, that shall find the means well to make your Majesty quit of him without prejudice of your son; and albeit that my Lord of Murray here present, be little less scrupulous for a Protestant than your Grace is for a Papist, I am assured he will look through his fingers thereto, and will behold our doings and say nothing to the same.'[2] The Queen understood the full meaning of this insinuation, and replied, that it was her pleasure nothing should be done 'by which any spot might be laid upon her honour;' but she displayed no great indignation at the idea, and contented herself with saying, 'Better permit the matter remain in the state it is, abiding till God in his goodness put remedy thereto.' Lethington took no heed of this slight opposition, and answered, 'Madam, let us to guide the business among us, and your Grace shall see nothing but good, and approved by Parliament.'[3]

Such was this extraordinary conference. It was followed, on the part of the promoters of the homicidal league, by an act which gave its full signification to their last overture. They swore, by a bond or agreement, to cut off the King as a young fool and tyrant, who was an enemy to the nobility, and had conducted himself in an intolerable manner to the Queen. 'They

---

[1] Keith, Appendix, p. 137.

[2] Anderson's Collections, relating to the History of Mary, Queen of Scotland, vol. iv., p. 192. Keith, Appendix, p. 138.

[3] Ibid.

also pledged themselves to stand by each other, and defend the deed as a measure of state. Sir James Balfour, a devoted partisan of Bothwell, drew up the bond, which was signed by Huntly, Lethington, Argyle, and himself, and placed in the hands of Bothwell.[1]

A month had not elapsed since the formation of this plot against the life of Darnley, when the baptism of his infant son took place at Stirling Castle. The Queen of England, who had consented to be his godmother, appointed the Countess of Argyle to act as her representative, and despatched Bedford with a font of gold,[2] to be used at the ceremony. It was performed on the 17th of December with much magnificence; and the Comte de Brienne, as well as the Ambassador Du Croc, attended on behalf of the King of France. Although the ceremony was performed according to the Roman Catholic ritual, by the Archbishop of St. Andrews,[3] its arrangement was committed to the Protestant Bothwell.[4] Darnley was not present, although he was then residing in Stirling Castle. At once irritated and ashamed, he had threatened two days before to leave the country. He remained, however, but shut himself up in his own apartments during the baptism and the festivities which succeeded. He requested an interview with the French ambassador, who refused to see him, because he was not upon good terms with the Queen. Du Croc himself tells us that he even went so far as to inform him, 'that as it would not be very proper for him to come to my lodgings, so he might know that there were two passages to it; and if he should enter by the one, I should be constrained to go out by the other.'[5]

What humiliation could have been greater than this? The King was contemned in the midst of the Court,—the father had no place at the baptism of his son. But this state of things, though intolerable to Darnley, was overwhelming to the Queen. Though she seemed to have thrown aside her sadness, and had momentarily recovered her natural amiability and grace while presiding over the festivities of the occasion, Mary soon relapsed into her former melancholy. She became pensive and mournful

[1] See the Laird of Ormiston's Confession, in Laing, vol, ii., pp. 321, 322. Tytler, vol. v., p. 368.
[2] Tytler, vol. v., p. 369.
[3] Letter from Du Croc to the Archbishop of Glasgow, 23rd December, 1566; in Keith, Preface, p. vii.
[4] MS. letter, State Paper Office, Sir John Foster to Cecil, 11th December, 1566. Tytler, vol. v., p. 369.
[5] Keith, Preface, p. vii.

as before. Du Croc was one day sent for by her, and he found her 'laid on a bed, weeping sore,' and complaining of a violent pain in her side. He augured most alarming results from the increasing hostility of the King and Queen. In a letter which he wrote to the Archbishop of Glasgow, a few days after the baptism, he says: 'I can't pretend to foretell how all may turn, but I will say that matters cannot subsist long as they are, without being accompanied with sundry bad consequences.'[1]

These consequences developed themselves with tragic rapidity. At the earnest entreaty of Lethington and Bothwell, Mary Stuart, laying aside her animosity against the principal murderers of Riccio, pardoned Morton, Ruthven, Lindsay, and seventy-six other exiles. She excepted, indeed, from this act of mercy, two marked delinquents, George Douglas and Andrew Ker of Faudonside, because the former had stabbed Riccio over the Queen's shoulder, and the latter had presented a pistol to her breast.[2] On being informed of the speedy return of those who had once been his most steady adherents, but were now his implacable enemies, Darnley was greatly terrified. He imagined that dark designs were intended against him, and in his alarm he abruptly left the Court and took up his residence with his father, the Earl of Lennox, at Glasgow. Shortly after his arrival there, he fell ill. Popular rumour, fully aware of the dangers to which he was exposed, though mistaken as to the cause of his indisposition, affirmed that he had been poisoned. The disease threw an eruption over his body, and proved to be the small-pox.[3]

Meanwhile the plot against his life was steadily pursued. Bothwell continued to seek and obtain new accomplices. He had already gained the concurrence of Lord Caithness, the Archbishop of St. Andrews, and the Laird of Ormiston; and, no sooner had Morton returned to Scotland, in the beginning of January, 1567,[4] than Bothwell used every endeavour to obtain the co-operation of a man of such great resolution and importance. He paid him a visit at Whittingham, the seat of Archibald Douglas, his near relation. He informed him of his projected enterprise, and pressed him to join the plot, adding that

[1] Keith, Preface, p. vii.
[2] MS. letter, State Paper Office, Bedford to Cecil, 9th January, 1567. Tytler, vol. v., p. 372.
[3] Ibid.
[4] Morton arrived at Berwick on the 10th January. MS. letter, State Paper Office, Morton to Cecil from Berwick, 10th January, 1567. Tytler, vol. v., p. 377.

the Queen had given her consent.[1] Morton was neither surprised nor disgusted by this proposition; he was well aware of, and shared in, the excitable, interested, and violent passions of the Scottish nobles. But the banishment which he had just suffered had rendered him more circumspect, and he replied that he would have nothing to do with the matter, unless they brought him 'the Queen's hand-writ for a warrant.' Bothwell determined to try a second interview, to which Lethington was admitted; but not having been able to extort from Morton anything more than this conditional promise, he returned to Edinburgh to endeavour to obtain the Queen's written consent. He failed in this attempt; and Lethington sent Archibald Douglas to inform Morton that the Queen 'would receive no speech of the matter appointed unto him.'[2] Had Bothwell gone too far in making unauthorized use of Mary's name? or did prudential motives alone induce Mary to refuse to give her sanction to the plot?

However this may be, she still retained feelings of distrust and animosity towards Darnley, whom she now accused of conspiring against her life. According to statements attributed to William Hiegate and William Walcar, two servants of the Archbishop of Glasgow, but which they denied when they were interrogated and confronted, the King had resolved to seize the person of the young Prince his son, to have him crowned without delay, and to govern in his name. Out of fear of this chimerical plot, the Queen removed the Prince Royal from Stirling to Edinburgh, on the 14th of January, 1567, so as to guard against any surprise.[3] The weak and impotent young man to whom this plot was attributed, possessed neither authority, adherents, nor character. He lived in the isolation and powerlessness of disgrace, and had been confined to his bed by his malady ever since the 5th of January. Mary nevertheless accused him of conspiracy, and after having mentioned his pretended designs in a letter which she wrote to the Archbishop of Glasgow, on the 20th of January, she added: 'His behaviour and thankfulness to us is equally well known to God and the world; especially our own indifferent subjects see it, and in their hearts, we doubt not,

[1] Morton's Confession, in Laing, vol. ii., pp. 354-362, Appendix. Letter from Archibald Douglas to Queen Mary, April, 1568; in Robertson, Appendix 47; and Laing, vol. ii., pp. 363-369, Appendix.
[2] Ibid.
[3] Deposition of Thomas Crawford, a gentleman in the service of the Earl of Lennox, MS. State Paper Office, endorsed by Cecil, but without date. Tytler, vol. v. p. 378. Labanoff, vol. vii., pp. 396, 397.

condemn the same. Always we perceive him occupied and busy enough to have inquisition of our doings; which, God willing, shall always be such as none shall have occasion to be offended with them, or to report of us any ways but honourably, however he, his father, and their fautors speak, which we know want no good will to make us have ado, if their power were equivalent to their minds. But God moderates their forces well enough, and takes the means of the execution of their pretences from them."[1]

On the day after she had expressed herself with such suspicious severity of Darnley, she set out for Glasgow, to lavish marks of the strongest affection upon him whom she judged so unfavourably, and detested so thoroughly. Darnley, who was still an invalid, was greatly surprised at this unexpected visit. He knew that Mary Stuart had recently spoken of him in very harsh terms, and he had received some vague warnings of the Craigmillar conspiracy. He did not conceal his apprehensions from the Queen, but told her that he had learned from the Laird of Minto, that she had refused to sign a paper which had been presented to her, authorizing his seizure, and, if he resisted, his assassination.[2] He added that he would never think that she, who was his own proper flesh, would do him any hurt; and then, with more vanity than confidence, he declared that if any others should intend to injure him, he would sell his life dear, unless they took him sleeping.[3] Mary in her turn reminded him of his intention to retire to the Continent, and of the project attributed to him by Hiegate and Walcar. He affirmed that he had never been serious in his threats of departure, and denied the second charge with vehemence. After having reproached him with his fears and suspicions, and evinced more gentleness and less aversion towards him than usual, Mary had no difficulty in regaining all her former influence over him.[4] At heart, Darnley had always been strongly attached to her; and his unrequited affection, and wounded pride,

---

[1] Tytler, vol. v., p. 373.

[2] Deposition of Crawford, to whom Darnley related this conversation between himself and the Queen, and who immediately wrote it down, and communicated it to Elizabeth's Commissioners at York, 9th December, 1568. Tytler, vol. v., p. 379.

[3] Tytler, vol. v., p. 379. This deposition conforms in this, as in many other points, to the first secret letter written by Mary Stuart, and found in the famous silver casket. See Anderson's Collections, vol. ii., p. 115; and Mémoires de l'Estat de la France sous Charles IX., vol. i., p. 160 (Midlbourgh, 1578).

[4] Mémoires de l'Estat de la France, vol. i., p. 163.

had been the the causes of his withdrawal from the Court. He professed sincere repentance for his errors, ascribed his faults to his youth and inexperience, and promised to act more prudently in future. He also expressed his extreme delight at seeing her once more by his side, and begged her never to leave him again.[1] Mary then proposed to convey him in a litter to Craigmillar, as soon as he was strong enough to travel; and he declared his readiness to accompany her, if she would consent that they should again live together as husband and wife. She promised that it should be as he had spoken, and gave him her hand; but added, that he must be thoroughly cleansed of his sickness first. She also requested that he would keep their reconciliation secret, lest it should give umbrage to some of the lords.[2]

This change of tone and conduct on Mary's part was very extraordinary. Had she passed, suddenly and sincerely, from feelings of aversion towards her husband, to tender solicitude for him—had her disgust changed into fondness? It is impossible to believe this when we consider that Darnley's murder, which was perpetrated a few days afterwards, caused her no grief, inspired her with no regret, called forth in her no desire for vengeance, and induced her to take no means for bringing the assassins to justice;—when we know that at the very moment when she appeared to have become reconciled to him, her criminal intimacy with Bothwell still continued,[3] and that she became shortly afterwards the wife of her husband's murderer. But then, how are we to explain this reconciliation? Must we believe that, blinded by passion, and obedient to the ferocious and ambitious will of her lover, Mary Stuart went to Glasgow to gain Darnley's confidence by manifesting an hypocritical interest in his condition, that she might bring him to Edinburgh, and place him in the hands of his enemies? Such perfidy appears incredible, and yet both moral probability and written evidence rise up against Mary Stuart with crushing force.

Bothwell had placed in her service, as valet, a Frenchman named Nicholas Hubert, who had been his own servant for very many years, and who was usually called Paris, from the place of his birth. This Paris, who was one of the agents employed by his old master in the execution of the plot against the King's life,

---

[1] Letters from Mary Stuart to Bothwell, in the Mémoires de l'Estat de la France, vol. i., p. 159. Mary Stuart's letters and sonnets are also printed in Anerson's Collections, vol. ii., pp. 115-159.
[2] Mémoires de l'Estat de la France, vol. i., pp. 159-162.
[3] Ibid., vol. i., p. 161.

accompanied the Queen from Edinburgh to Glasgow, when she paid Darnley her late visit.[1] Two days after her arrival, Mary Stuart sent him back to Bothwell with a letter which attests at once the affection which she felt for Bothwell, and the part which she took in his sinister designs. 'Being departed from the place where I left my heart,' she said, 'it is easy to be judged what was my countenance.' After having given him an account of her journey to Glasgow, and having described to him Darnley's fearful mistrust and affectionate demonstrations, as they are mentioned in the deposition of Thomas Crawford (a gentleman in the service of the Earl of Lennox, to whom Darnley communicated his interview with the Queen), she went on to say: 'I have never seen him better, or speak so humbly, and if I had not known from experience that his heart is as soft as wax and mine as hard as diamond, I should almost have taken pity on him. However, fear nothing.' She was nevertheless disgusted at the perfidy which her passion induced her to practise, and which she called her *hateful deliberation*. 'You constrain me to dissimulate,' she added, 'that I am horrified, seeing that you do not merely force me to play the part of a traitress; I pray you remember that, if desire to please you did not force me, I would rather die than commit these things; for my heart bleeds to do them. In brief, he will not come with me, unless upon this condition, that I shall promise to use in common with him a single table and the same bed as before, and that I shall not leave him so often, and that if I will do this, he will do all I wish, and will follow me.' Carried away by the violence of her love, she told Bothwell that she would obey him in all things; and begged him not to conceive a bad opinion of her; 'because,' she continued, 'you yourself are the occasion of it; I would never act against him, to gratify my own private revenge.' She did not conceal the object she had in view—an object which was attained two months after the murder of Darnley, by Bothwell's divorce from Lady Jane Gordon, and marriage to herself. In order to gain this end, she did not fear to expose her honour, to burden her conscience, to endanger her person, to forget her dignity, and to sacrifice, against her own inclination, the man who obstructed the gratification of her wishes. No wonder that she cried with remorse: 'God forgive me!'[2]

[1] Second deposition of Nicholas Hubert, named Paris, 10th August, 1569. British Museum, Caligula, B. i, fol. 318; quoted in Laing, vol. ii., p. 308; and Anderson's Collections, vol. ii., pp. 192-205.
[2] This letter from Mary Stuart to Bothwell is printed in Anderson's Collections

At the same time that he conveyed this letter to Bothwell, Paris was charged to deliver to him a purse containing three or four hundred crowns, and some bracelets which Mary Stuart had just completed for him.[1] The Queen also directed Paris to learn from Lethington and Bothwell, whether, on the King's return, he was to be lodged at Craigmillar or Kirk of Field, that he might have the benefit of good air, as it was not advisable that he should take up his residence at Holyrood Palace, lest the Prince Royal should catch the disease.[2] In reference to this matter Mary wrote to Bothwell, 'Let me know what you have determined to do touching you know what, that we may understand each other, and that nothing may be done otherwise.'[3] Paris fulfilled all the commissions with which he had been entrusted. He saw Bothwell and Lethington, who were both of opinion that it would be better to take the King to Kirk of Field. This was a large open space adjoining the gates of Edinburgh, and near an old Dominican convent of Black Friars. It was airy and pleasant, occupied by gardens and houses; among others, by the town residence of the Duke of Chatelherault, and by that of Robert Balfour, one of Bothwell's creatures, and a relative of Sir James Balfour, who had drawn up a bond for the murder.[4] Balfour's house, though less spacious, was more isolated than the Duke's, and the conspirators accordingly selected it as more convenient for the execution of their project.[5] Paris twice perceived Bothwell in conference with James Balfour, and was finally sent back with the following message: 'Return to the Queen, and recommend me very humbly to her grace, and tell her all will go well,

---

vol. ii., pp. 131-144, and in the Mémoires de l'Estat de la France, vol. i., pp. 158-164. Towards the end she says: 'Now seeing to obey you, my dear love, I spare neither honour, conscience, hazard, nor greatness whatsoever; take it, I pray you, in good part, and not after the interpretation of your false brother-in-law (the Earl of Huntly), to whom I pray you give no credit against the most faithful lover that ever you had, or ever shall have. See not her (Lady Jane Gordon) whose feigned tears should not be so much praised nor esteemed as the true and faithful travails which I sustain for to merit her place, for the obtaining of the which, against my natural [disposition], I betray them that may hinder me. God forgive me.'

[1] Second deposition of Nicolas Hubert, named Paris, in Anderson's Collections, vol. ii., p. 192, and Laing, vol. ii., p. 368; and also Mary Stuart's first letter to Bothwell, in the Mémoires de l'Estat de la France, vol. i., pp. 162, 163.

[2] Laing, vol. ii., p. 281. Anderson's Collections, vol. ii., p. 193.

[3] Mémoires de l'Estat de la France, vol. i., p. 161.

[4] 'Quhilk writing, as said Earl (Bothwell) shew unto me, was devysit be Sir James Balfour,' &c. Confession of the Laird of Ormiston, who was executed for Darnley's murder in 1573; in Laing, vol. ii., p. 294.

[5] Laing, vol. i., pp. 31, 32.

for Mr. James Balfour, and I have not slept the whole night, so we have set all things in order, and have got ready the house. And tell the Queen that I send to her this diamond by your hands, and that if I had my heart I would send it to her very willingly.'[1]

Darnley was soon well enough to travel in a litter. The Queen, whom he overwhelmed with caresses, but who was always attacked by a pain in her side whenever she entered his room,[2] announced their speedy departure to Bothwell. 'According to the commission which I have received,' she wrote, 'I shall bring the man with me on Monday.'[3] The original plan of conducting the King to Craigmillar had been abandoned, because he had evinced great repugnance for the place. But he had consented to remain at Kirk of Field until his health should be completely restored. Meanwhile, notwithstanding Mary's affectionate behaviour and his great fondness for her, Darnley's alarm was not entirely dispelled. 'I have fears enough,' he said to Thomas Crawford, 'but may God judge between us. I have her promise only to trust to, but I have put myself in her hands, and I shall go with her, though she should murder me.'[4] With these feelings he left Glasgow, and travelled to Kirk of Field by easy stages. Bothwell came to meet Mary and Darnley at a short distance from the capital; and on the 31st of January, the young King, still an invalid, and rendered melancholy by his fears, entered the fatal house, in which he was, ere long, to meet his death.

This house had formerly belonged to the prebendaries of the Kirk of Field, and was not at all adapted for the reception of a King and Queen. Small, confined, and ill-furnished, it consisted only of two stories, one of which contained a cellar and another room, and the other, a gallery which extended above the cellar, and a bed-chamber, which corresponded with the room on the ground-floor.[5] Nelson, Darnley's servant, when he arrived at Kirk of Field, was about to prepare the Duke of Chatelherault's house for the reception of his master. But the Queen prevented

---

[1] Paris's Second Deposition; in Anderson, vol. ii., pp. 194, 195.

[2] 'He puttis me in remembrance of all thyngis that may make me me beleve he luffis me. Summa ye will say that he makes love to me: of the quhilk I take sa greit plesure, that I entir nevir quhair he is, but incontinent I take the sickness of my sore side, I am sa troublit with it.' Mary's second letter to Bothwell; in Laing, vol. ii., p. 185.   [3] Ibid.

[4] Deposition of Thomas Crawford, MS. State Paper Office. Tytler, vol. v., p. 380.

[5] Laing, vol. ii., p. 18.

him, and directed him to Balfour's house,¹ whither the necessary furniture was conveyed, and which Bothwell had evidently chosen that he might carry out his murderous intentions with greater facility. Darnley was established on the first floor, where his three servants, Taylor, Nelson, and Edward Simons occupied the gallery, which served at once as a wardrobe and cabinet. The cellar on the ground-floor was transformed into a kitchen, and the Queen had a bed prepared for herself in the room immediately below that in which the King slept. She also directed that the door at the foot of the staircase, which communicated between the ground-floor and the upper rooms, should be removed.² Thus installed, though very uncomfortably, by Darnley's side, she passed several nights under the same roof with him. Her assiduity, her attention, and the manifold proofs which she gave him of her affection, were all well calculated to dispel his fears.

Whilst Mary Stuart seemed to have returned to her former affection for Darnley, Bothwell was occupied in making all due preparations for the murder. In addition to those accomplices of high rank, whose co-operation he had secured at Craigmillar, and on subsequent occasions, in order that he might carry out his design with impunity, he had procured a number of subaltern assistants to put it into execution. His chamberlain Dalgleish, his tailor Wilson, his porter Powrie, Laird James of Ormiston and his brother Robert, and two men-at-arms, Hay of Tallo and Hepburn of Bolton,³ whose courage and devotedness he had amply tested during his border warfare, were admitted into his confidence, and unhesitatingly became his instruments. He had

---

¹ 'It wes dewysit in Glasgow, that the King suld haif lyne first at Craigmyllare; bot becaus he had na will thairof, the purpois wes alterit and conclusioun takin that he suld ly besyde the Kirk of Field, at quhilk tyme this deponir belevit evir that he suld haif had the Duikis hous, thinking it to be the lugeing preparit for him; bot the contrare was then schawin to him be the Quene, quha convoyit him to the uthir hous, and at his cuming thairto the schalmir wes hung, and ane new bed of black figurat welwet standing thairin.' Evidence of Thomas Nelson, concerning the murder of King Henry Darnley; in Anderson, vol. iv., part 2, p. 165, and Laing, vol. ii., Appendix 25.

² Laing's History of Scotland, vol. i., pp. 31-33, and vol. ii., pp. 17-19. Laing's narrative is based upon the depositions of Nelson, Paris, and Hay of Tallo, and the letter written by the Scottish Council to the Queen-Mother of France, in reference to Darnley's death.

³ Examinations and depositions of George Dalgleish, William Powrie, the Laird of Ormiston, John Hay, and John Hepburn, before the Privy Council of Scotland; in Laing, vol. ii., Appendix, pp. 268-319; and Anderson's Collections, vol. ii., pp. 165-192.

false keys made,[1] by means of which easy access could be gained into Balfour's house; and he sent to Dunbar for a barrel of gunpowder,[2] which was to be placed underneath the King's apartment, and to destroy the house and its inmates by its explosion.

The assistance of the Frenchman Paris, whom he had placed in Mary Stuart's service, was indispensable to him for the purpose of ascertaining whether the false keys were exactly similar to those in use, and of placing the powder in the room occupied by the Queen below Darnley's bedchamber. But when he revealed his plan to Paris on Wednesday, the 5th of February, the poor man displayed great hesitation to serve him, fearing that he would thus insure his own destruction. In the narrative which he gave to his judges, two years after the murder, when he was captured and hanged for his complicity, he relates, in terms of striking simplicity, the conversation which he had with Bothwell, on being made acquainted with the terrible secret. 'On hearing him,' he says, 'my heart grew faint; I did not say a word, but cast down my eyes!' Bothwell, who was not pleased at his silence and consternation, looked at him with impatience, and asked him what he thought of the plan. 'Sir,' he replied, 'I think that what you tell me is a great thing.' 'What is your opinion of it?' reiterated Bothwell. 'Pardon me, sir, if I tell you my opinion according to my poor mind.' 'What! are you going to preach to me?' 'No, sir, you shall hear presently.' 'Well! say on.' Paris then reminded him of the trouble and misfortunes of his past life, and sought to dissuade him from this murder, which would destroy his present tranquillity, and endanger the extraordinary favour which he had attained. He concluded by telling him: 'Now, sir, if you undertake this thing, it will be the greatest trouble you ever had, above all others you have endured, for every one will cry out upon you, and you will be destroyed.' 'Well,' said Bothwell, 'have you done?' 'You will pardon me, sir,' answered Paris, 'if you please, if I have spoken to you according to my poor mind.' 'Fool that you are!' said Bothwell, 'do you think that I am doing this all alone by myself?' 'Sir,' said Paris, 'I do not know how you are going to do it, but I know well that it will be the greatest trouble that you ever had.' 'And how so?' said Bothwell; 'I have already with me Lethington, who is esteemed one of the most prudent men in this country, and who is the undertaker of all this; and I have also the Earl of Argyle, my brother Huntly, Morton,

---

[1] First deposition of Paris; in Laing, vol. ii., p. 275.
[2] Depositions of Hepburn, and John Hay; in Laing, vol. ii., pp. 253, 257.

Ruthven, and Lindsay. These three last will never fail me, for I have begged for their pardon, and I have the signatures of all those I have mentioned to you. We were desirous to do it the last time we were at Craigmillar; but you are a fool and poor of mind, unworthy to hear any thing of consequence.'[1]

Paris finally consented to do what Bothwell required. He was entirely in his power, and very probably was not so long in giving his promise as he would have us believe. He enabled Bothwell to compare the keys of the house with the false ones he had had made, and promised to introduce Hay of Tallo, Hepburn, and Ormiston, into the Queen's chamber, on the evening appointed for the execution of the murder, that they might deposit the powder there, whilst the Queen was with Darnley. Bothwell had forbidden Paris to place the Queen's bed immediately under that of the King, because he intended to have the powder strewed there. Paris did not attend to this, and when Mary Stuart came into the room in the evening, she herself ordered him to change the position of the bed.[2]

The night of Sunday, the 9th of February, was fixed for the execution of this horrible design. Mary Stuart's conduct, when the time for the murder drew near, is but too well calculated to confirm the accusations which result from the depositions of the witnesses, the confessions of the perpetrators, and her own letters. Nelson says that she caused a bed of new velvet to be removed from the King's apartment, and substituted an old one in its place.[3] Paris declares that she also removed from her own chamber a rich coverlet of fur,[4] which she was, doubtless, desirous

---

[1] First deposition of Paris; in Laing, vol. ii., pp. 271, 272.

[2] Paris thus relates this incident, which, if true, is of itself sufficient to place Mary's complicity beyond doubt: 'The Queen said to me, "Fool that you are, I will not have my bed in that place," and so made me remove it; by which words I perceived in my mind that she was aware of the plot. Thereupon I took the courage to say to her, "Madam, my Lord Bothwell has commanded me to take to him the keys of your chamber, because he intends to do something in it, namely, to blow up the King with gunpowder." "Do not talk about that, at this hour," said she, "but do what you please." Upon this, I did not venture to say anything more.' Second deposition of Paris; in Laing, vol. ii., p. 285.

[3] Nelson, who was found beneath the ruins of the house, relates in these terms the opening of the door which communicated between the Queen's chamber and that of the King, and the removal of the bed of new velvet: 'Sche (the Queen) causit tak doun the uttir dour that closit the passage towart baith the chalmeris . . . and sua ther wes nathing left to stope the passage into the saidis schalmeris, bot only the portell durris; as alsua sche causit tak doun the said new blak bed, sayand it wald be sulzeit with the bath, and in the place thairof sett upe ane auld purple bed.' Laing, vol. ii., p. 267.

[4] On the Saturday evening. First deposition of Paris; in Laing, vol. ii., p. 276.

not to leave there on the evening of the explosion. On the
Sunday, she came to spend the evening with the King, whom she
had assured that she would remain in Balfour's house during the
night.¹ Whilst she was talking familiarly² with him in the room
upstairs, the preparations for his death were actively going on
below. On the previous evening, Hepburn had brought the
barrel containing the powder into the nether hall of the lodging
occupied by Bothwell in Holyrood Abbey.³ Before evening, on
Sunday, Bothwell had assembled all his accomplices in that same
room, had concerted his plan with them, and had allotted to each
the part he was to perform in the nocturnal tragedy.⁴ At about
ten o'clock in the evening, the sacks of powder were carried,
across the gardens, by Wilson, Powrie, and Dalgleish, as far as
the foot of Blackfriars Wynd, where they were received by Hay
of Tallo, Hepburn, and Ormiston, and conveyed into Balfour's
house by the assistance of Paris.⁵ As soon as the powder had
been strewed in heaps over the floor of the room, just beneath the
King's bed, Ormiston went away, but Hepburn and Hay of
Tallo remained with their false keys in the Queen's bedchamber.⁶
When all was ready, Paris went up into the King's room, and the
Queen then recollected that she had promised to be present at a
masquerade, given in Holyrood Palace, in honour of the marriage
of her servant Bastian with Margaret Carwood, one of her
favourite women.⁷ She therefore took farewell of the King, left
the house with her suite, including Bothwell, and proceeded by

¹ She had already slept there twice, and, according to Nelson's deposition, had
promised the King that she would remain there on Sunday night also: ' The
chalmer quherin sche lay the saids tua nytis, and promist alsua to haif bidden thair
upoun the Sounday at nyt.' Laing, vol. ii., p. 276.
² ' Bot efter sche had tareit lang, and intertenit the King verey familalrlie, sche
tuk purpoise, and departit.' Ibid.
³ Powrie's second deposition; in Laing, vol. ii., p. 248.
⁴ Depositions of Powrie, Dalgleish, and Hay of Tallo; in Laing, vol. ii. pp. 243,
249, 252.
⁵ Depositions of Powrie, Hay of Tallo, and Hepburn of Bolton; in Laing, vol. ii.,
pp. 243, 253, 257.
⁶ Ibid.
⁷ ' Paris passes to the Kingis chalmer, quhair the King, the Quene, and the Erle
Bothwell and uthers were . . . and as the deponar believes, Paris shew the Erle
Bothwell that all things were in readiness, and syne sone yareftir, the Quene and
the lordis returnet to the abbay.' Deposition of Hay of Tallo; in Laing, vol. ii.,
p. 255. After what is said by Hay of Tallo, who remained concealed in the
Queen's chamber, read the statement of Nelson, who was in the King's room:
'Sche (the Queen) tuk purpoise (as it had bene on the sudden), and departit as
sche spak to gif the mask to Bastyane, quha that nyt wes mariet her servand.'
Nelson's deposition; in Laing, vol. ii., p. 267.

torchlight to Holyrood.[1] Darnley beheld her departure with grief and secret fear. The unhappy Prince, as though foreboding the mortal danger by which he was threatened, sought consolation in the Bible, and read the 55th Psalm,[2] which contained many passages adapted to his peculiar circumstances. After his devotion, he went to bed and fell asleep, Taylor, his young page, lying beside him in the same apartment.[3]

Bothwell remained for some time at the ball, but stole away about midnight to join his confederates. He changed his rich costume of black velvet and satin, for a dress of common stuff;[4] and left his apartments, followed by Dalgleish, Paris, Wilson, and Powrie. In the hope of attracting less attention, he went down the staircase which led from Holyrood into the Queen's garden, and directed his course towards the southern gate. The two sentinels on guard, seeing a party of men coming along this unusual path at so late an hour, challenged them: 'Who goes there?' 'Friends!' answered Powrie. 'Whose friends?' demanded one of the sentinels: 'Friends of Lord Bothwell!' was the answer.[5] On this they were allowed to proceed, and going up the Canongate, found that the Nether-bow gate, by which they intended to leave the city, was shut. Wilson immediately awoke John Galloway, the gate-keeper, calling to him to 'open the port to friends of Lord Bothwell.' Galloway, in surprise, inquired what they were doing out of their beds at that time of night.[6] They made no answer, but passed on. Both-

[1] 'The Quene's grace was gangand before yame with licht torches.' Powrie's deposition; Laing, vol. ii., p. 244.
[2] MS. letter, State Paper Office, Drury to Cecil, 18th April, 1567. Tytler, vol. v., p. 383.
[3] 'The Quene being departit towart Halyrud hous, the King within the space of ane hour past to bed, and in the chalmer with him lay wmquhill William Taylyour.' Nelson's deposition; in Laing, vol. ii., p. 268.
[4] 'Immediately tuk aff his claythes yat wer on, viz., a pair of blak velvet hoise, trussit with silver, and ane doublet of satin of the same maner, and put on ane other pair of black hoise and ane doublet of canwes, and tuk his side rideing cloak about him.' Powrie's deposition; in Laing, vol. ii., p. 244.
[5] 'As yai came by the gait of the Quene's south garden, the twa sentinellis yat stude at the zet yat gangis to the utter closs, speirit at yame, Quha is yat? and yai answerit, Frends. The sentinel speirit, Quhat friends? and yai answerit, My Lord Bothwell's friends.' Powrie's deposition; in Laing, vol. ii., p. 245. Dalgleish gives a similar account. Ibid., pp. 249, 250.
[6] 'Yai come up the Canongate, and to the neither bow, and findand the bow steikand, Pat Willson cryet to John Galloway, and desirit him to opin the port to friends of my Lord Bothwell, quha came and oppenit the port.' Powrie's deposition; in Laing, vol. ii., p. 245. Dalgleish gives the same account, and adds: 'Galloway came down to let yame in, and speirit at yame, Quhat did yow out of yair beds yat time of night.' Ibid., p. 250.

well intended to have taken up Ormiston as they passed; but the
Laird, though he had assisted in conveying the powder into the
King's house, had gone to bed and would not answer the summons, as he feared his participation in the murder might bring
him to the scaffold, which it actually did a few years after.[1]
Continuing his route as far as Blackfriars Wynd, Bothwell left
Powrie, Wilson, and Dalgleish at this point, and proceeded with
Paris alone to Kirk of Field, where he waited for Hepburn and
Hay of Tallo in Balfour's garden.[2]

It was at this moment, we have every reason to believe, that
the two murderers concealed within the house perpetrated their
crime. By the aid of their false keys they gained access into the
King's apartment. On hearing the noise, Darnley jumped out
of bed in his shirt and pelisse and endeavoured to escape. But
the assassins seized and strangled him. His page was put to
death in the same manner; and their bodies were carried into a
small orchard near at hand, where they were found on the next

[1] Laing, vol. ii., pp. 245-250.
[2] This version of Darnley's murder does not conform to the depositions of the
murderers, who were doubtless to make sure of Darnley's death by other means
than the uncertain effect of an explosion, and were perhaps afraid to admit that
they had laid hands on the person of the king; but we have based our narrative
on a despatch from the Pope's Nuncio to Cosmo I., which has been copied from
the archives of the Medici by Prince Labanoff. This despatch, moreover, is the
only document which explains how it was that the bodies of Darnley and his page,
Taylor, were found at such a distance from Balfour's house, and that they bore no
marks of injury by the explosion, or by the falling of the house. This despatch
is printed in Prince Labanoff's Collection, vol. vii., pp. 108, 109, and contains the
following passage: 'Quanto al particular della morte di quel Re, il detto signor di
Muretta ha ferma opinione che quel povero principe sentendo il rumore delle genti
che attorniavano la casa, et tentavano con le chiave false apprir gl'usci, volese
uscir per una porta che andava al giardino, in camiscia con la peliccia, per fugirre
il pericolo; et quivi fu affogato, et poi condotto fuori del giardino in un picolo
horto fuori della muraglia della terra et che poi con il fuoco ruinassero la casa per
amazzar il resto ch'era dentro; di che se non fa congiettura, perciochè il Re fut
trovato morto in camiscia con la peliccia a canto, et alcune donne che allogiavano
vicino al giardino, affermano d'haver udito gridar il Re: "Eh fratelli miei;
habiate pietà di me per amor di colui che hebbe misericordia de tutto il mondo?"'
This despatch was communicated to Mr. Tytler by Prince Labanoff, and the Scottish
historian has framed his narrative of Darnley's death in accordance with its statements; see Tytler, vol. v., pp. 383, 384. This was also the prevalent belief in
Scotland, as is proved by a proclamation published on the 20th June, 1567, in
which Bothwell is accused not only of having conspired against the life of the
King, but of having killed him with his own hands: 'Of the quhilk murder, he is
found not onlie to have bin the inventor and devyser, *but the executor with his
awin handis*, as his awin servantis, being in companie with him at that unworthy
deid, has testifiet.' Anderson's Collections, vol. i., p. 140 Buchanan and Laing
also hold this opinion.

morning, unscathed by fire or powder, the King covered by his shirt only, and the pelisse lying by his side. After the execution of this dark deed, Hepburn lighted the match which communicated with the gunpowder in the lower room, and the house was blown up, in order completely to obliterate all traces of the murder. Bothwell, Hepburn, Hay of Tallo, and the other bandits, went to a little distance to await the explosion, which occurred about a quarter of an hour afterwards, between two and three o'clock in the morning, with a fearful noise.[1] The confederates immediately ran back to Edinburgh as fast as they could; and Bothwell, having been prevented by his wounded arm from clambering over a breach in the ramparts of the city, was constrained, with most of his band, to return home through the Netherbow gate, and awake John Galloway once more. On reaching Holyrood Palace they were again challenged by the sentinels,[2] and suffered to pass on. Bothwell hurried to his apartments, drank some wine to calm his agitation, then hastened to bed.[3]

He had scarcely been half an hour in bed, when George Hacket, one of the servants of the palace, knocked loudly at his door and demanded admittance. The door was opened, and Hacket came in, but his terror was so great that he could not speak a word. Bothwell, with extreme coolness, asked him what was the matter. 'The King's house,' said Hacket, 'is blown up, and I trow the King is slain.' At these words Bothwell started up in well-feigned astonishment, and shouted, 'Treason!'[4] He then dressed himself, and having meanwhile been joined by the Earl of Huntly, the two noblemen went to communicate the intelligence to the Queen.[5]

Bothwell, with consummate audacity, soon repaired with a body of soldiers to the scene of his crime. The people of Edinburgh, who had been awakened by the explosion, had crowded to the Kirk of Field at daybreak. They gathered in multitudes around the ruins of the house, beneath which Nelson had been found alive,[6] and filled the orchard in which the bodies of the King and his page, Taylor, were lying. Bothwell dispersed the

[1] Laing, vol. ii., pp. 245, 250, 255, 258.
[2] Ibid., pp. 246, 251, 258.
[3] 'My Lord come into his ludgeing, and immediately callit for ane drink, and tuk off his cloathes incontinent, zeid to his bed.' Depositions of Powrie and Dalgleish; in Laing, vol. ii., pp. 246, 251.
[4] Depositions of Powrie and Dalgleish; in Laing, vol. ii., pp. 246, 251.
[5] Ibid.; and Hepburn's deposition, p. 259.
[6] Nelson's deposition; in Laing, vol. ii., p. 268.

horror-stricken crowd, and conveyed his two victims into a neighbouring house, without suffering any one to approach or examine them. But it had escaped the notice of none of the spectators that the bodies displayed no wounds, and had not been mutilated by the gunpowder; that the King's pelisse, which lay by his side, was not even scorched by the fire; and that the two corpses could not have been hurled to so great a distance by the explosion of the house without great external injury.[1] A few days afterwards Darnley was buried with great privacy in the chapel of Holyrood.[2]

What was the effect produced upon Mary Stuart by this terrible occurrence, which filled Edinburgh with indignation and mistrust? She appeared overwhelmed with sorrow, and fell into a state of silent dejection. She manifested none of that activity, anger, resolution, and courage which she had displayed after Riccio's murder: but shut herself up in her room, and would communicate with her most faithful servants by the medium of Bothwell alone.[3] Darnley's murderer was the only person admitted to her presence. Even were we not furnished with the most unquestionable proofs of her complicity by the confessions contained in her letters, the authenticity of which we have established elsewhere, as well as by the declarations made in presence of their judges and upon the scaffold, by the subaltern actors in this tragic drama, her conduct both before and after the murder would suffice to convince us that she was a party to the crime. Her journey to Glasgow, at a time when she was loudest in her expressions of distrust and hatred of Darnley; the marks of tenderness and hopes for reconciliation which she had displayed towards him, in order to induce him to come with her to Edinburgh; the selection of Balfour's house, which was convenient only for the commission of a crime, and wherein she consented to reside that he might not refuse to remain in it; the care with which, on the evening before the murder, she removed from it all the furniture of any value which it contained; the

[1] MS. Letter, State Paper Office, 11th February, 1567; enclosure by Drury to Cecil. Tytler, vol. v., p. 385.
[2] Chalmers, vol. ii., p. 556. Tytler, vol. v., p. 386.
[3] Melvil's Memoirs, p. 78; and Paris's second deposition. 'Le lundy matin (après le meurtre), entre neuf et dix heures, le dict Paris dict qu'il entre dans la chambre de la Royne, laquelle estoit bien close, et son lict là tendu de noyr en signe de deuil, et de la chandelle allumer dedans ycelle, là où Madame de Bryant luy donnoyt à desjeusner d'ung œuf frais, là où aussy Monsieur de Boduel arryve et parle à elle secrètement soubz courtine.' Second deposition of Paris; in Laing, vol. ii., pp. 287, 288.

conveyance of the powder and introduction of the two principal assassins into her own room, where neither the powder could have been strewn nor the murderers concealed without her connivance, as she might otherwise have come down stairs and discovered all; and finally, her departure from Balfour's house, where she had promised to pass the night, a few hours before Darnley was killed and the house blown into the air—prove only too conclusively that she was acquainted with the whole plot.

But if her conduct previous to the commission of the crime thus deeply criminates Mary Stuart, what must we think of her proceedings after its perpetration?[1] Her behaviour, both as a wife and a Queen, render her guilt all the more flagrant, because, far from avenging the husband upon whom she had so recently lavished her hypocritical caresses, she rewarded his murderer, and eventually married him. It will now be our task to unveil the sad picture of her errors and her punishment. Horror-struck as she appeared to be, Mary Stuart left the task of communicating this catastrophe to the French Court to her Privy Council, which was almost entirely composed of accomplices in the murder, and the secretary and guide of which was Lethington, one of its principal instigators. The despatch of the Council, addressed to Catherine de Medici, was intrusted to Clarnault,[2] who was at the same time the bearer of a letter from the Queen to the Archbishop of Glasgow. In this letter, which she wrote two days after the murder to her ambassador in France, Mary Stuart deplores 'that mischievous deed' which had struck terror throughout all Scotland, and says, 'the matter is horrible and so strange, as we believe the like was never heard of in any country.' She further declares that a lucky chance alone saved her from being a victim to the conspiracy, which was directed

---

[1] Paris gives the following account of the Queen's feelings on the subject, thirty hours after the murder:—' Mardi au matin elle se leue, et le dict Paris estant entré en sa chambre, la Royne luy demande: Paris, qu'as tu ? Helas ! ce dict-il, Madame, je voys que chascun me regarde de costé. Ne te chaille, ce dict-elle, je te feray bon vysage, et personne ne t'oseroyt dire mot. Cependant, elle ne le dict chose de consequence jusques à ce qu'elle voulloyt aller à Seton ; alors elle luy demandast de prendre une cassette où il y avoyt des corceletz d'escus que le thrésorier luy avoyt aporté de France, pour la porter à la chambre de Monsieur de Boduel, qui estoyt à cette heure-là logé dedans le pallays, au dessus de la chambre là où ce tenoyt le conseil ; et puis après luy commandast de prendre son coffre des bagues, et le faire porter au chasteau, et le delyvrer entre les mains du Sieur de Skirling, pour lors cappitaine soubz Monsieur de Boduel, chose qu'il feist; en apres elle voyant le dict Paris toute fasché, elle pressoyt souvent de faire service à Monsieur de Boduel.' Second deposition of Paris ; in Laing, vol. ii., p. 288.

[2] Labanoff, vol. ii., p. 2.

against herself as well as the King. 'By whom it has been done,' she adds, 'it appears not as yet; but the same being discovered by the diligence our Council has begun already to use, we hope to punish the same with such rigour as shall serve for example of this cruelty to all ages to come.'¹ After having thus endeavoured to conciliate the favourable opinion of the Court of France, she at length decided, on Wednesday, the 12th of February, to offer, by proclamation, two thousand pounds reward to any who would come forward with information regarding the perpetrators of the crime.² Scarcely was this made known, when public opinion gave utterance to its convictions, and a paper was fixed during the night on the door of the Tolbooth, or common prison, in which Bothwell, James Balfour, and David Chambers (another of Bothwell's intimates), were denounced as guilty of the King's slaughter. Voices, too, were heard in the streets of Edinburgh at dead of night, arraigning the same persons. A second placard charged the Queen's servants with the crime, and mentioned the names of Signor Francis, Bastian, John de Bourdeaux, and Joseph, David Riccio's brother.³ The Queen took no steps to secure the subaltern conspirators, and kept the greatest criminal of them all by her side.

Far from adopting any vigorous measures, she left Edinburgh, and removed to the residence of Lord Seton.⁴ Bothwell followed her thither, and remained with her, guarded by Captain Cullen, one of his most devoted adherents, and in the company of Huntly, Argyle, Lethington, and the Archbishop of St. Andrews, who had all approved of his plan for Darnley's assassination.⁵ Did Mary pass her time at Seton Castle in mourning and affliction? No: this is the account given of her residence there by Mr. Fraser Tytler, who is inclined, by hereditary feelings, to be very favourable to Mary, and who is the most recent, and in many respects the most trustworthy of the historians of Scotland:—'It did not escape attention,' he says, 'that scarce two weeks after her husband's death, whilst in the country and in the city all were still shocked at the late occurrences, and felt them as a stain on their national character, the Court at Seton was occupied in gay amusements. Mary and Bothwell would shoot

---

¹ Labanoff, vol. ii., pp. 3, 4.   ² Keith, p. 368.   ³ Tytler, vol. v., p. 387.
⁴ Seton Castle was the property of George, sixth Lord Seton, whose daughter had accompanied the Queen into France, and was one of the four Marys. He was descended from a Norman family, and remained constantly attached to the Queen and her cause.
⁵ MS. letter, State Paper Office; Drury to Cecil, 17th February, 1567. Tytler, vol. v., p. 386.

at the butts against Huntly and Seton; and, on one occasion, after winning the match, they forced these lords to pay the forfeit in the shape of a dinner at Tranent.'[1]

While engaged in these recreations, Mary Stuart was besieged by the accusing distrust of her people, and the bitter complaints of the Earl of Lennox. At Edinburgh, which had been disturbed, on the fatal night of the 9th of February, by the band which had left Holyrood Palace, reports were current which denounced by name the deviser of the assassination, and vaguely indicated his accomplices. A bill fastened on the Tron in the market-place declared that the smith who had furnished the false keys to the King's apartment would, on due security, come forward and point out his employers.[2] Two new placards were also hung up, on one of which were written the Queen's initials, M.R., with a hand holding a sword; and on the other Bothwell's initials with a mallet painted above, as having been the instrument with which the murder was committed.[3] The whole city was in a state of extreme agitation. The Presbyterian ministers preached with sombre vehemence, exhorting all men to fasting and prayer, and calling on God 'to reveal and revenge.'[4] The Queen was included in the suspicions of the populace, and the idea of her complicity daily gained ground. Bothwell became furious, and attempted to intimidate public opinion. Accompanied by fifty armed men, he rode into Edinburgh and publicly declared that if he knew who were the authors of the placard, he would 'wash his hands in their blood.' But, animated by suspicion as much as by anger, whenever he spoke to any one, of whose friendship he was not assured, he watched his movements with a jealous eye, and always kept his hand on the hilt of his dagger.[5]

The unhappy father of the murdered King, seeing that Mary Stuart remained inactive, conjured her, in the most pathetic language, to direct vigorous search to be made after the assassins. 'I am forced by nature and duty,' he wrote to her on the 20th of February, 'to beseech your Majesty most humbly, for God's cause, and the honour of your Majesty, and this your realm, that

[1] Tytler, vol. v., p. 390.
[2] MS. letter, State Paper Office; Drury to Cecil, 28th February, 1567. Tytler, vol. v., p. 389.
[3] Tytler, vol. v., p. 390.
[4] MS. letter, State Paper Office; Killigrew to Cecil, 8th March, 1567. Tytler, vol. v., p. 393.
[5] MS. letter, State Paper Office; Drury to Cecil, 28th February, 1567. Tytler, vol. v., p. 389.

your Highness would, with convenient diligence, assemble the whole nobility and estates of your Majesty's realm, and they, by your advice, to take such good order for the perfect trial of the matter, as I doubt not but, with the grace of Almighty God, his Holy Spirit shall so work upon the hearts of your Majesty and all your faithful subjects, as the bloody and cruel actors of this deed shall be manifestly known. And although I know I need not put your Majesty in remembrance thereof, the matter touching your Majesty so near as it does, yet I shall humbly desire your Majesty to bear with me in troubling your Highness therein, being the father of him that is gone.'[1]

On the following day, Mary wrote an affectionate but evasive answer to the Earl of Lennox. She informed him that she had already convoked her Parliament, before the receipt of his letter, and that its first business would be to inquire thoroughly into 'the King her husband's cruel slaughter.'[2] But the Parliament was not to meet until Easter; and, in the meanwhile, Joseph Riccio, Bastian, and Signor Francis, the Queen's Italian steward, whose names had been mentioned in one of the placards, took their departure from Scotland;[3] whilst Powrie and Wilson were sent by Bothwell to the Castle of Hermitage, close by the English border.[4] The Earl of Lennox, surmising the reasons of this long delay, renewed his entreaties on the 26th of February, and represented to the Queen that this was not an ordinary matter for discussion in Parliament, 'but of such weight and importance, which ought rather to be with all expedition and diligence sought out, and punished to the example of the whole world.' He therefore besought her to order the arrest of those persons who had been denounced in the placards.[5] She replied that the placards contradicted each other, and that she was at a loss on which to proceed: but, she said, 'if there be any names mentioned in them that you think worthy to suffer a trial, upon your advertisement we shall so proceed to the cognition-taking as may stand with the laws of this realm; and, being found culpable, shall see

---

[1] Keith, pp. 369, 370.   [2] Ibid., p. 370.
[3] They were accompanied by six other persons. MS. letter, State Paper Office; Drury to Cecil, 19th February, 1567. Tytler, vol. v., p. 388. On the 20th, Mary gave Signor Francis a pension of 400*l.* Scots, out of the revenues of the bishopric of Ross. Laing, vol. i., p. 50. She also gave a pension and the post or master of the wardrobe to the Prince her son, to Darnley's porter, a man named Durham, who had abandoned or betrayed his master on the day of his murder. Privy Seal Records, Book 36, fol. 15; quoted in Laing, vol. i., p. 33.
[4] Powrie's deposition; in Laing, vol. ii., p. 246.
[5] Keith, p. 371.

the punishment as vigorously executed, as the weight of the crime deserves.'¹

Whilst Lennox was thus loudly crying for justice, Elizabeth despatched a letter, by Sir Henry Killigrew, in which she hinted her suspicions of Mary's implication in the murder, and displayed the passionate hatred which she entertained against her, in the vehemence of her ill-concealed reproaches, and the feigned character of her hypocritical condolence. 'Madam,' she wrote, ' my ears have been so astonished, and my mind so grieved, and my heart so terrified at hearing the horrible sound of the abominable murder of your late husband and my deceased cousin, that I have even now no spirit to write about it; and although my natural feelings constrain me greatly to deplore his death, as he was so near a relation to me, nevertheless, boldly to tell you what I think, I cannot conceal from myself that I am more full of grief on your account than on his. O madam! I should not perform the part of a faithful cousin or an affectionate friend, if I studied rather to please your ears than to endeavour to preserve your honour; therefore I will not conceal from you what most persons say about the matter, namely, that you will look through your fingers at taking vengeance for this deed, and have no intention to touch those who have done you this kindness, as if the act would not have been perpetrated unless the murderers had received assurance of their impunity. Think of me, I beg you, who would not entertain such a thought in my heart for all the gold in the world.' She then went on to urge her, in the strongest terms, not to leave so great a crime unpunished. 'I exhort you,' she adds, ' I advise and beseech you to take this thing so much to heart, as not to fear to bring to judgment the nearest relation you have, and to let no persuasion hinder you from manifesting to the world that you are a noble Princess, and also a loyal wife.'² The same advice was given her by the Archbishop of Glasgow, her ambassador at the Court of France, where it was believed that she was the cause of her husband's death. He informed her, with courageous honesty, of the unfavourable opinion which was entertained in foreign countries of the miserable state of her kingdom, and the shameful conduct of her nobility. 'Yourself,' he added, 'is greatly and wrongously calumniated to be the motive principal of the whole;' and he conjured her to take a rigorous vengeance for the crime, observ-

---
¹ Letter from Mary Stuart to the Earl of Lennox; written from Seton, March 1, 1567; in Keith, p. 371.
² Labanoff, vol. vii., pp. 102, 103.

ing, 'that rather than it be not actually taken, it appears to me better, in this world, that you had lost life and all.'¹

A month had now elapsed since Darnley's assassination, and yet Mary had taken none of the steps required by the law of the land, and due to her own innocence. On the contrary, she had not left Bothwell for a moment. Instead of ordering his arrest, which had been demanded by the Earl of Lennox in a third letter,² she loaded him with new favours. She invested him with the command of the Castle of Edinburgh, which had previously been held by the Earl of Mar, governor of the Prince Royal; and soon after, she conferred upon him the Castle of Blackness, the Inch, and the Superiority of Leith.³ At length, however, the blunt, and somewhat offensive counsels of Elizabeth, the deep displeasure of her relatives in France, the energetic remonstrances of the Archbishop of Glasgow, and the reiterated entreaties of the Earl of Lennox, determined her to quit her dangerous and humiliating position. She resolved to screen herself by a show of justice, and shelter her favourite by a judicial acquittal. In a council held on the 28th of March, at which she presided, and which was attended by the Earls of Bothwell, Huntly, Argyle, and Caithness, and the Bishops of Ross and Galloway, it was decided that Bothwell should be brought to a public trial.⁴ Mary now became as anxious to hasten, as she had previously been to prevent, her favourite's impeachment. The Earl of Lennox received orders to appear at Edinburgh, on the 12th of April, to prefer and maintain his charges against Bothwell.⁵

Public notoriety alone denounced this great criminal. No one dared to bear witness against him, or had even been requested to do so. The smith who had manufactured the false keys to the King's apartments had not been provided with the security he claimed, in order to state what he knew. 'The suspected persons,' wrote the Earl of Lennox to the Queen on the 11th of April, 'continuing still at liberty, being great at Court, and about your Majesty's person, comforts and encourages them and theirs, and discourages all others that would give an evidence against them.' He therefore demanded that they should be placed in arrest, conformably to the usages of the realm, and that a delay should be granted sufficient for the collection of the necessary evidence; adding that, otherwise, a fair and just trial

¹ Keith, Preface, p. ix.   ² On the 17th March, 1567; Keith, p. 372.
³ Tytler, vol. v., p. 393.   Robertson, vol. ii., p. 334.
⁴ Laing, vol. i., p. 58.   ⁵ Tytler, vol. v., p. 394.

would be impossible.¹ Elizabeth, on her side, advised Mary Stuart to allow the father and friends of the deceased King time enough to obtain such evidence as might bring the guilt home to its authors. She warned her that a refusal would excite strong suspicions against her, and urged her to give the world occasion to declare her guiltless of so base a crime; for, otherwise, she would be shunned by all princes, and hated by all peoples; 'and rather than this should happen to you,' she says, in her nervous language, ' I would wish you an honourable burial more than a sullied life. I pray the Lord to inspire you to do what may most conduce to your own honour and the consolation of your friends.'²

Mary Stuart would yield neither to Lennox's just request, nor to Elizabeth's prudent advice. She consented that everything should be done according to the arrangement of Bothwell and his friends.³ On April 12th, the day appointed, the assize opened at the Tolbooth, before a jury of noblemen, Bothwell's peers and partisans.⁴ The tribunal was presided over by one of the fautors of the murder, the Earl of Argyle, then hereditary Lord High Justice, and guarded by two hundred hackbutters; while four thousand of Bothwell's armed adherents mustered in the streets and squares of Edinburgh.⁵ The law officers of the Crown were either bribed or intimidated into silence: no witnesses were summoned. The accuser, the Earl of Lennox, who was on his road to the city, surrounded by a large force of his friends, received orders not to enter Edinburgh with more than six in his company; and he, therefore, declined to come forward in person.⁶ The accused, the Earl of Bothwell, presented himself before the Court of Justice with a confident and careless air. Mounted on the late King's favourite horse,⁷ and surrounded by guards, he was escorted to the Tolbooth, with base obsequiousness, by a large number of gentlemen. As he passed before the Queen, who was standing, with Lady Lethington, at one of the windows of Holyrood Palace, he turned towards her, and she gave him a friendly greeting for a farewell.⁸ She expressed her sympathy

---

¹ Keith, pp. 374, 375.

² MS. letter, State Paper Office; Queen Elizabeth to Mary Stuart, 8th April, 1567. Robertson, vol. ii., Appendix 19.

³ Tytler, vol. v., p. 396. Anderson's Collections, vol. i., p. 50.

⁴ Their names are given in Keith, p. 377.

⁵ MS. letter, State Paper Office; Drury to Cecil, 15th April, 1567. Tytler, vol. v., p. 395, and Proofs and Illustrations, vol. v., No. 19.

⁶ MS. letters, State Paper Office; Forster and Drury to Cecil, 15th April, 1567. Tytler, vol. v., p. 397. Anderson, vol. ii., pp. 98, 107.

⁷ Tytler, vol. v., p. 398. ⁸ Ibid., p. 396.

with his position, even more publicly, by sending him, rather from impatience than anxiety, a token and message whilst he was before his judges.[1]

It was quite impossible for her to feel any uneasiness about the result of this judicial farce. The session of the Court of Justiciary was neither long nor uncertain. After the indictment, which inculpated Bothwell, but brought no direct charge against him, had been read, the Earl of Lennox was called upon to make good his accusation. Upon this a gentleman named Robert Cunningham stood forward, explained the reasons which had prevented the Earl his master from appearing in person, and declared that he was sent by him to reiterate the charge of murder against the Earl of Bothwell, but to request delay for the purpose of obtaining the necessary evidence. On this being refused, Cunningham protested against the validity of any sentence that should acquit 'persons notoriously known to be,' as he said, 'the murderers of the King, as my lord, my master, alleges.'[2] The Crown lawyers were silent, to the great disapprobation of the people; and Bothwell having pleaded not guilty, a unanimous verdict of acquittal was pronounced in the absence of all evidence.[3] He then had the audacity to challenge his accusers by a public cartel, and offered to maintain his innocence by arms, against any gentleman who should still brand him with the murder.[4]

After this scandalous and premeditated acquittal, Mary Stuart, adding new favours to those which she had so recently lavished upon Bothwell, gave him the lordship and castle of Dunbar, and extended his powers as High Admiral.[5] No one of the nobility had sufficient power, or seemed indeed to have any desire, to compete with him. Lennox took refuge in England;[6] Murray, who was the most powerful person in Scotland, had withdrawn from the Court some time before the King's assassination, and left Scotland for France three days before Bothwell's trial at the Tolbooth.[7] No one remained to check the Queen and her triumphant favourite. Accordingly when—two days after the trial—Parliament assembled, Mary selected him to bear the crown and

[1] MS. letters, State Paper Office; Drury to Cecil, April 19th, and April (undated), 1567. Tytler, vol. v., p. 398.
[2] His protest is given in Keith, p. 376.
[3] Keith, p. 377. Tytler, vol. v., p. 397. [4] Tytler, vol. v.. p. 397.
[5] MS. letter, State Paper Office; Drury to Cecil, 19th April, 1567. Tytler, vol. v., p. 400.
[6] Keith, p. 378, note.
[7] On the 9th April; Laing, vol. i., p. 59. MS. letter, State Paper Office; Drury to Cecil, 9th and 10th April, 1567. Tytler, vol. v., p. 400.

sceptre before her at its opening.¹ The three estates of Scotland ratified the sentence of the jury, had condemned and suppressed the placards which had been posted up in Edinburgh.² All Bothwell's partisans were rewarded for their connivance. Five of the jurors obtained confirmation of their respective grants from the crown.³ Huntly consented to the divorce of his sister from Bothwell, and the whole of his property, which had been under confiscation for several years, was restored to him.⁴ The Catholic Mary, blinded by her passion for the Protestant Bothwell, consented to abolish all laws affecting the lives of her subjects, on the score of their religion, and passed an act securing a provision to the poorer ministers.⁵ She thus hoped to gain the support of the nobility, and to conciliate the favour of the Presbyterian Church.

But the Presbyterian Church would not be bribed to alter its unfavourable judgment of her; and the people, seeing her daily become more intimate with Bothwell, ere long included her in the same condemnation as himself. Even the lowest classes entertained suspicions of her culpability; and the market-women, as she passed, would cry out, 'God preserve your Grace, if you are sackless (innocent) of the King's death.'⁶ Unfortunately for Mary Stuart, the cry of public conviction could not stem her passion.

Bothwell was not satisfied with impunity. The high favour of a subject, the transitory power of a lover, were not sufficient to content him. He had aimed higher when he slew the King. His object was to marry the Queen, and thus to raise himself to the throne by less unproductive and more audacious designs than those of the ambitious and unfortunate Darnley. Two obstacles opposed the execution of his plans, and these were his recent marriage to Lady Jane Gordon, and the life of the young Prince Royal. A divorce from Lady Gordon would remove the first of these hindrances; and he hoped that when he had married the Queen he would have her son at his mercy, and thus get rid of the second. Public opinion again proved correct, and believed that

---

¹ 'He was appointed on Monday, the second day after his trial, to carry the crown and sceptre at the opening of Parliament.' Laing, vol. i., p. 72. Keith, p. 378.   ² Keith, p. 380.
³ 'Crawford, Rothes, Caithness, Herries, Semple, Ogilvie of Boyne, obtained ratifications.' Records of Parliament, quoted in Laing, vol. i., p. 73, note.
⁴ Laing, vol. i. p. 74. Keith, pp. 379, 380.
⁵ Keith, p. 379. Tytler, vol. v., p. 399.
⁶ MS. letter, State Paper Office; Drury to Cecil, April, 1567. Tytler. vol. v., p. 398.

Bothwell, to secure the fruit of his first crime, would commit many others. 'The marriage of the Queen to Bothwell,' wrote Drury to Cecil, 'and the death of the Prince, is presently looked for.'[1]

This language is employed not only by the sagacious agent of Queen Elizabeth, but also by one of Mary Stuart's most faithful servants. 'The bruit began to rise,' says Sir James Melvil, 'that the Queen would marry the Earl of Bothwell. Whereat every good subject that loved the Queen's honour and the Prince's safety, had sore hearts; and thought her Majesty would be dishonoured, and the Prince in danger to be cut off by him that had slain his father.'[2] Few, however, ventured to dissuade the Queen from this step, as Bothwell's power and anger were held in universal dread. One gentleman, indeed, with more courage than the rest, Lord Herries,[3] travelled express to Edinburgh, threw himself at Mary's feet, and implored her not to marry the man who was considered by all her subjects to be the murderer of her husband, or she would compromise her honour, endanger her son's life, and ruin herself. The Queen appeared surprised, and told him, with her accustomed dissimulation, that she did not understand the meaning of the rumour, and 'that there was no such thing in her mind.' After having given her this salutary but useless advice, Herries hastened home by relays of horses which he had stationed along the road, in order to escape Bothwell's pursuit and revenge.[4]

Melvil was urged by similar feelings of loyalty to give the same advice, but his interference was very ill received by the Queen, who informed Bothwell of it. The prudent Lethington blamed Melvil for his dangerous candour. 'So soon,' said he, 'as the Earl Bothwell gets word, as I fear he will, he will not fail to slay you. I pray you retire with diligence.' 'It is a sore matter,' replied Melvil, ' to see that good Princess run to utter wreck, and nobody to forewarn her.' 'You have done more honestly than wisely,' said Lethington. He was not mistaken with regard to the danger which Melvil had just incurred. Bothwell declared that he would have his life, and Melvil was obliged to conceal himself for several days until the Queen had succeeded in allaying her lover's anger.[5]

[1] Tytler, vol. v., p. 519.   [2] Melvil's Memoirs, p. 78.
[3] Sir John Maxwell, second son of Robert, fourth Lord Maxwell, and head of a powerful family in the south of Scotland. He married Agnes, eldest daughter and co-heiress of William Herries of Terreigles, and took the title of Lord Herries, in right of his wife. He joined the Lords of the Congregation in 1559, and generally espoused the cause of the Queen.
[4] Melvil's Memoirs, p. 78.   [5] Ibid., p. 79.

Bothwell's imperious audacity was now manifested by a most extraordinary proceeding. He was determined to secure the consent of the leading nobility to his marriage with the Queen. Accordingly, on the evening of the 19th of April, the day on which the Parliament rose, he invited the Earls of Morton, Argyle, Huntly, Cassilis, Glencairn, Rothes, Sutherland, Caithness, and Eglinton, with Lords Boyd, Seton, Sinclair, Semple, Oliphant, Ogilvy, Ross Haccat, Carlile, Hume, Invermeith, and others, to supper in a tavern kept by a person named Ansley. During the entertainment a band of two hundred hackbutters surrounded the house and overawed its inmates. Bothwell then rose, told his guests that the Queen had consented to marry him, and produced, according to the testimony of some of the witnesses of this strange scene, her written warrant empowering him to propose the matter to her nobility. In the confusion which ensued, the Earl of Eglinton made his escape. The others, with disgraceful cowardice, affixed their signatures to a bond, in which they declared their conviction of Bothwell's innocence, promised to defend him against all traducers, and recommended ' this noble and mighty lord' as a suitable husband for the Queen, whose continuance in solitary widowhood was, they said, injurious to the interests of the commonwealth.[1] They further engaged to maintain Bothwell's pretensions to the Queen's hand with their lives and fortunes; and if they failed to perform their promise, to pass for men devoid of honour and loyalty, unworthy and infamous traitors. The Bishops of St. Andrews, Aberdeen, Dumblane, Brechin, Ross, Orkney, and others, signed this bond,[2] which constituted the shame of all those Scottish nobles who subscribed or submitted to it, and hastened the destruction of Mary Stuart, by encouraging her to pursue her fatal plan of marriage to Bothwell.

She was more passionately fond of him than ever, although his violent temper sometimes led him to act offensively towards her. He seemed to distrust her affection and fidelity; displayed his bad opinion with injurious brutality; and substituted his sister, Lady Coldingham, in the place of Lady Reres, her confidante.[3] The unfortunate Queen was compelled to write to him, with all the weakness and humility of love: ' I will take such (servants) as shall content you for their conditions. I beseech you that an opinion of another person be not hurtful in your mind to my constancy. Mistrust me but when I will put you out of doubt, and

---

[1] Tytler, vol. v., p. 401.   [2] Keith, pp. 382, 383.   [3] Tytler, vol. v., p. 520.

clear myself. Refuse it not, my dear life, and suffer me to make you some proof by my obedience, my faithfulness, constancy, and voluntary subjection.'[1] Bothwell was supreme at Court, and disposed of everything at his pleasure. Murray, the only man who, up to a certain point, could have resisted him, had left the country without waiting for his sister's marriage, which he foresaw, but could not prevent.

However incredible it may appear, this marriage had been decided upon by a contract signed by Mary Stuart herself on the 5th of April, seven days before Bothwell's acquittal.[2] It was prepared with mysterious precipitation. Bothwell could not openly claim, or the Queen voluntarily consent to, its fulfilment so soon after the death of Darnley, who had been murdered by the one only two months and a half before, and for whom the other would long have to wear mourning apparel. What was to be done? They determined that he should carry her off by force —a proceeding which would place Mary, in some measure, under the constraint of necessity, and would explain the resignation of the Queen, by the violence done to the woman. Here, again, she was unhappily Bothwell's accomplice, as we have abundant evidence to demonstrate. She agreed with him that he should meet her, with a force more numerous than her own retinue, as she was returning from a visit to the young Prince her son, at Stirling Castle, and that he should, with a show of violence, make himself master of her person and will. Bothwell at once departed to complete his preparations. During his absence, Mary wrote to him several letters which betray her anxiety, her jealousy,[3] her unchangeable resolution, and the impatience which she felt at the objections of Bothwell's own confidants. Huntly had been let into the secret, and endeavoured to dissuade the Queen from carrying out the plan. She immediately conceived great suspicion of him, and wrote to Bothwell: 'He preached unto me that it was a foolish enterprise, and that with mine honour I could never marry you, seeing that being married you did carry me away, and that his folks would not suffer it, and that the lords would unsay themselves, and would deny that they had said. I told him that, seeing I was come so far, if you did

---

[1] Fourth letter from Mary Stuart to Bothwell; in Laing, vol. ii., p. 194.
[2] This contract was found in the silver casket, with Mary's secret letters and sonnets to Bothwell.
[3] 'I would I were dead, for I see all goeth ill. You promised other manner of matter of your foreseeing, but absence hath power over you, who have two strings to your bow.' Mary's fifth letter to Bothwell; in Laing, vol. ii., p. 198.

not withdraw yourself of yourself, that no persuasion, nor death itself, should make me fail of my promise.'¹

In another letter she explains the part which she was to act in the abduction. 'As for the handling of myself,' she says, 'I heard it once well devised. Methinks that your services, and long friendship, having the good will of the lords, do well to deserve a pardon, if above the duty of a subject you advance yourself, not to constrain me, but to assure yourself of such place nigh unto me, that other admonitions, or foreign persuasions, may not let (hinder) me from consenting to that that you hope your service shall make you one day to attain; and to be short, to make yourself sure of the lords, and free to marry; and that you are constrained for your safety, and to be able to serve me faithfully, to use an humble request, joined to an importunate action.'² When the moment of execution arrived, difficulties arose on the part of those who were to form her escort. The Earl of Sutherland declared that he would rather die than suffer the Queen to be carried off whilst she was under his protection. The Earl of Huntly, filled with grief, and apprehensive of a conflict, was afraid of being accused of ingratitude towards the Queen, and of appearing to have betrayed her. 'I have thought good,' wrote Mary Stuart to Bothwell, 'to advertise you of the fear he hath that he should be charged and accused of treason, to the end that, without mistrusting him, you may be the more circumspect, and that you may have the more power; for we had yesterday more than three hundred horse of his and of Livingston's. For the honour of God, be accompanied rather with more than less; for that is the principal of my care.'³

Bothwell consequently augmented his forces. On Monday, the 21st of April, Mary Stuart went, as she had promised, to visit her son at Stirling Castle; but was not allowed to enter the royal apartments with more than two of her ladies, for the Earl of Mar, from some suspicion which he entertained, refused to admit the rest of her suite. She left Stirling three days afterwards, on Thursday the 24th, to return to Edinburgh; but when she reached Almond Bridge, six miles from the city, Bothwell met her, accompanied by six hundred horsemen. He took her

---

¹ Laing, vol. ii., pp. 196, 197.   ² Ibid., vol. ii., p. 200.
³ Ibid., vol. ii., p. 202.   A letter was written at the same time from Scotland to Cecil, informing him of all that was about to happen: Bothwell's divorce from Lady Gordon, and Mary Stuart's abduction. 'He is minded,' said the writer, 'to meet the Queen this day called Thursday, and to take her by the way and bring her to Dunbar. Judge you if it be with her will or no?' Tytler, vol. v., p. 404.

horse by the bridle, made himself master of her person without opposition, and conducted her to his Castle of Dunbar, which he had fully prepared for her reception. Lethington, Huntly, and Melvil were among the captives; and when Melvil remonstrated against such usage, he was informed by Captain Blacater that all had been done with the Queen's own consent.[1] Mary Stuart passed some time under the roof and in the public possession of Bothwell; but her abduction was only the prelude to her marriage. Bothwell hurried his divorce from Lady Jane Gordon through the Court of the Archbishop of St. Andrews, who obtained, as the price of his complaisance, the restoration of his consistorial rights; and also through the commissariat, or ecclesiastical court of the Presbyterians.[2] The two jurisdictions of the ancient and the modern Church gave their consent, one on behalf of the Catholic Jane Gordon, and the other on behalf of the Protestant Bothwell, and the sentence of divorce[3] was pronounced on the 3rd of May. On that day Mary returned from Dunbar to Edinburgh. As she entered the city, Bothwell respectfully took the Queen's horse by the bridle, and his soldiers cast away their spears, as if to prove that Mary Stuart was completely free, and that Bothwell was only her obedient and unarmed servant. The Queen, on her side, declared that she pardoned Bothwell, and announced her intention to marry him.[4]

Although this had long been expected, its announcement excited the greatest indignation. The Reformed Church received orders to publish the banns of marriage, but refused to do so. In the absence of Knox, who had left Scotland after Riccio's murder, Craig, one of the leading Presbyterian ministers, alleged as his excuse that the Queen had sent no written command, and stated the common report that she was held captive by Bothwell. Upon this, the Justice Clerk brought him a letter from the Queen, enjoining the publication of the banns, and contradicting the report of her captivity. Craig still resisted, and desired to be confronted with the parties, in presence of the Privy Council. There, with courageous vehemence, he laid to Bothwell's charge the dreadful crimes of which he was suspected, rape, adultery, and murder. Having thus exonerated his conscience, he did not deem himself justified in longer refusing to obey the injunctions he had received, but added from the pulpit, and in presence of the congregation, these words: 'I take heaven and earth to witness, that

---

[1] Melvil's Memoirs, p. 80.   [2] Tytler, vol. v., p. 406.
[3] Robertson, vol. ii., Appendix 20. Laing, vol. i., pp. 82, 83.
[4] Anderson, vol. ii., p. 276. Laing, vol. i., p. 84.

I abhor and detest this marriage, as odious and slanderous to the world, and I would exhort the faithful to pray earnestly that a union against all reason and good conscience, may yet be overruled by God, to the comfort of this unhappy realm.'[1]

The infatuated Mary was not aroused to the folly of her conduct by this universal reprobation; she braved every danger that she might satisfy her passion, and raise her favourite to her own rank. On the 12th of May, she came in person to the High Court at Edinburgh, and declared to the assembled magistrates and nobility of Scotland, that she was free, that she pardoned Bothwell the offence he had committed against her, in consideration of his subsequent good conduct, and that she meant to promote him to still higher honour.[2] On the same day, accordingly, she created him Duke of Orkney and Shetland, and placed the coronet on his head with her own hands.[3] Two days afterwards, she signed her contract of marriage with 'this noble and mighty lord,' in order that she might put an end to her solitary widowhood, and increase the number of her descendants. And, finally, on the 15th of May, at four o'clock in the morning, the marriage ceremony was peformed in Holyrood Palace according to the Catholic ritual, and afterwards after the rite of the Protestant Church, by the Bishop of Orkney, in presence of Craig.[4]

Few of the Scottish nobility were present at the disgusting ceremony,[5] which, three months after the King's assassination, united his widow in marriage to his murderer. The people received the intelligence with gloomy silence and sombre disapprobation. On the following morning, a paper was found on the palace gates, with the following verse:—

'Mense malas Maio nubere vulgus ait.'[6]

The ominous prognostics drawn from a union thus generally condemned by the public conscience, were destined too soon to be realized.

[1] MS. letter, State Paper Office; Drury to Cecil, 14th May, 1567. Tytler, vol. v., p. 412.
[2] Anderson, vol. i., p. 87. Tytler, vol. v., p. 413.
[3] MS. letter, State Paper Office; Drury to Cecil, 16th May, 1567. Tytler, vol. v., p. 413. [4] Ibid. [5] Tytler, vol. v., p. 413.
[6] Ovid. Fast., lib. v., l. 490. Keith, p. 386.

CHAPTER VI.

FROM MARY'S MARRIAGE WITH BOTHWELL TO HER FLIGHT INTO ENGLAND.

League of the nobility against Mary and Bothwell—Applications to Queen Elizabeth for assistance—Attack of Borthwick Castle—Mary's flight to Dunbar—Entry of the confederates into Edinburgh—Mary levies an army—Her defeat at Carberry Hill—Her separation from Bothwell—She yields to the confederates, is led captive to Edinburgh, and finally imprisoned in Lochleven—Government of the Lords of the Secret Council—Arrest and confessions of Bothwell's accomplices—Deposition of the Queen—Coronation of James VI.—Murray is appointed Regent—Conduct of Queen Elizabeth—Behaviour of Murray—Convocation of Parliament—Flight and fate of Bothwell—Mary escapes from Lochleven, and collects an army at Hamilton Castle—Battle of Langside—Defeat of the Queen's army—Her flight into England.

It was not long before Mary Stuart paid the penalty of her imprudent marriage. Even on her wedding day she had a violent quarrel with Bothwell. The French ambassador, Du Croc, who had refused to be present at the nuptials, wrote to Catherine de Medici and Charles IX.: 'Your Majesties could not do better than be very displeased with the marriage, for it is a very unfortunate one, and already is repented of. On Thursday (May 15th) her Majesty sent for me to inquire whether I had perceived any strangeness between her and her husband; which she wished to excuse to me, saying that, if I saw she was sorrowful, it was because she would not rejoice, as she says she never will again, and desires only death. Yesterday (May 16th) being both in a closet with the Earl of Bothwell, she called out aloud for some one to give her a knife that she might kill herself. Those who were in the adjoining room heard her. They think that unless God aids her, she will fall into despair.'[1] Melvil confirms this account of the speedy disagreement of the Queen and her new husband. 'The Queen,' he says, ' was so disdainfully handled, and with such reproachful language, that Arthur Erskine and I being present, heard her ask a knife to stick herself, " or else," said she, " I shall drown myself." '[2]

Bothwell displayed the most offensive suspicions of her conduct, and humiliated her by his coarse requirements. His real or affected jealousy made him forbid the Queen to indulge in those innocent familiarities which she was wont to use towards her friends.

[1] Labanoff, vol. vii., pp. 110, 111.   [2] Melvil's Memoirs, p. 80.

Doubtless afraid that she would as soon become disgusted with him as she had with Darnley, he tortured her heart in order to occupy it, and rendered her unhappy that he might prevent her from being inconstant. 'Ever since the day after her marriage,' wrote Du Croc to Catherine de Medici, 'she has passed her time in nothing but tears and lamentations, as he (Bothwell) will not give her liberty to look at any one, or allow any one to look at her, although he knows that she loves to take her pleasure, and pass her time agreeably as much any one.'[1]

Mary Stuart, though thus tormented by Bothwell, was still attached to him, and endeavoured to induce foreign Courts to recognize him as her husband. She accordingly despatched the Bishop of Dumblane to France and Rome, with an adroit apology for her new marriage. It had been rendered inevitable, she said, by the written and, so to speak, unanimous wish of the nobility of Scotland; and its reason, as well as its excuse, was to be found in the noble qualities and eminent services of Bothwell. Therefore, after having read the pressing request of the principal lords of her kingdom, and having heard Bothwell's explanations, she had pardoned the violence which his ardent love and the exigencies of his position had emboldened him to commit against her person The Bishop of Dumblane was to add that, as the factious turbulence of her rebellious nation, which would neither submit to the authority of a woman, nor suffer her to marry a foreign Prince, had compelled her to espouse one of her own subjects, she had been unable to find amongst them any one who could be compared

[1] In a letter from Du Croc to Catherine de Medici, dated Edinburgh, 17th June, 1567. In May, 1848, I published this despatch, which I extracted from vol. 218 of the Saint-Germain-Harlay MSS., in the National Library at Paris, and which has since been printed in Teulet's Pièces et Documents relatifs à l'histoire d'Ecosse, vol. ii., p. 170.—Some lines by Mary Stuart, found, together with her marriage contract and some letters, in the famous silver casket, give eloquent expression to her complaints in this respect:—

> 'Et vous doutez de ma ferme constance,
> O mon seul bien et ma seule espérance,
> Et ne vous puis asseurer de ma foy.
> Vous m'estimez légère que je voy.
> Et, si n'avez eu ma nulle asseurance,
> Et soupçonnez mon cœur sans apparence,
> Vous defiant à trop grand tort de moy.
> Vous ignorez l'amour que je vous porte,
> Vous soupçonnez qu'autre amour me transporte,
> Vous estimez mes paroles du vent,
> Vous dépeignez de cire mon, las, cœur,
> Vous me pensez femme sans jugement,
> Et tout cela augmente mon ardeur.'

to the Earl of Bothwell for the reputation of his family, his own merits, his wisdom, and his valour, and that she had, therefore, assented without repugnance to the desire of the three estates of her realm.[1] She despatched Robert Melvil to England with similar instructions. If the Queen of England considered it strange that she should have espoused the man who was suspected of having murdered her husband, and whose first wife was still living, Melvil had orders to remind her, in the first place, that the Earl of Bothwell had been acquitted by the justice of his country, and had moreover offered to maintain his innocence by arms; and in answer to the second objection, he was to say, that a legal divorce had rendered Bothwell perfectly free to marry again. Mary begged the Courts of France and England to excuse her if she had consented to a precipitate marriage, and requested them, now that it had become irrevocable, to extend to her husband that friendship which they had so long manifested towards herself.[2]

Bothwell, on his side, wrote a short and submissive letter to Charles IX.,[3] whilst he offered his services to Elizabeth in a bold and almost kingly tone. He protested against the bad opinion which that Queen appeared to entertain regarding him, and added: 'Men of greater birth might have been preferred to the high station I now occupy, but none could have been chosen more zealous for the preservation of your Majesty's friendship, of which you shall have experience at any time it may be your pleasure to employ me.'[4] Before seeking the assistance of those foreign powers which were most intimately connected with the affairs of Scotland, he had taken into his own hands all the authority of the kingdom, and had insured to himself the full exercise of royal power, by composing the Privy Council of his friends and partisans. He had introduced into that body the Archbishop of St. Andrews, the Lords Oliphant, Boyd, Herries, and Fleming, and the Bishops of Ross and Galloway; and he had appointed Master of Requests Hepburn, the parson of Auldhamstocks, who had conducted his divorce from Lady Gordon.[5]

Whilst Mary and Bothwell thought they were providing for their

[1] See the instructions given him by Mary Stuart, in Keith, pp. 388-392, and Anderson's Collections, vol. i., p. 89.
[2] These instructions, also, are printed in Keith, pp. 392-394, and Anderson's Collections, vol. i., pp. 102-107.
[3] Letter from Bothwell to Charles IX., 27th May, 1567; in Teulet's Pièces et Documents relatifs à l'histoire d'Ecosse, vol. ii., p. 156.
[4] MS. letter, State Paper Office, Bothwell to Elizabeth; 6th June, 1567. Tytler, vol. v., p. 418.
[5] Laing's History of Scotland, vol. i., p. 95.

safety by these precautions, severe trials and terrible punishments were in preparation for them elsewhere. A formidable confederation had been formed against Bothwell, and consequently against Mary Stuart. This league, which was long thought to have been subsequent to the marriage, existed before its consummation, as has been proved by the valuable correspondence recently extracted by Mr. Patrick Fraser Tytler from the English State Paper office.[1] Immediately after the famous supper at Ansley's tavern on the 19th of April, the principal nobles, whom Bothwell had forced to subscribe to his propositions, entered into a secret league to oppose him. Argyle, Athol, Morton, and Kirkaldy of Grange, feared that the Queen, being no longer the mistress of her actions, but carried away by her passion for Bothwell, would deliver up her son into his hands, and that he would get rid of him, as he had previously got rid of Darnley. The Laird of Grange, in their name, demanded Elizabeth's assistance against Bothwell, whose power would become irresistible when he had added the authority of the Crown to his own natural audacity. On the 20th of April, he wrote to this effect to the Earl of Bedford, and told him that the Queen had become so shamelessly enamoured of Bothwell, that she had been heard to say, in presence of several persons, 'She cared not to lose France, England, and her own country for him, and shall go with him to the world's end in a white petticoat, before she leave him.'[2]

Two days after Mary Stuart's abduction, the Laird of Grange wrote a second letter to Bedford. 'This Queen,' he said, 'will never cease, unto such time as she have wrecked all the honest men of this realm. She was minded to cause Bothwell ravish (seize) her, to the end that she may the sooner end the marriage whilk she promised before she caused Bothwell murder her husband. There is many that would revenge the murder, but they fear your mistress. I am so suited to for to enterprise the revenge, that I must either take it upon hand, or else I must leave the country, the which I am determined to do, if I can obtain licence. I pray your lordship let me know what your mistress will do, for if we will seek France, we may find favour at their hands.'[3] On the 8th of May, he wrote again in a still more precise and urgent manner to Bedford, and told him that most of

---

[1] These letters have been used by him in the preparation of his account of Queen Mary's reign, in his History of Scotland.

[2] MS. letter, State Paper Office, Grange to Bedford, 20th April, 1567. Tytler vol. v., p. 403.

[3] Ibid., 26th April, 1567. Tytler, vol. v., p. 405.

the nobility who, before the last Parliament and for fear of their lives, had subscribed to matters equally opposed to their honours and consciences, had since met together at Stirling, and entered into a league. 'The heads, that presently they agreed upon,' he continued, ' is, first, to seek the liberty of the Queen, who is ravished and detained by the Earl of Bothwell, who was the ravisher, and hath the strengths, munitions, and men of war at his commandment. The next head is, the preservation and keeping of the Prince. The third is, to pursue them that murdered the King. For the pursuit of these three heads, they have promised to bestow their lives, lands, and goods. And to that effect their lordships have desired me to write unto your lordship, to the end they might have your sovereign's aid and support for suppressing of the cruel murderer Bothwell, who, at the Queen's last being in Stirling, suborned certain to have poisoned the Prince; for that barbarous tyrant is not contented to have murdered the father, but he would also cut off the son, for fear that he hath to be punished hereafter. The names of the lords that convened in Stirling was the Earls of Argyle, Morton, Athol, and Mar. . . . . . There is to be joined with the four forenamed lords, the Earls of Glencairn, Cassillis, Eglinton, Montrose, Caithness; the Lords Boyd, Ochiltree, Ruthven, Drummond, Gray, Glammis, Innermeith, Lindsay, Hume, and Herries.' He added that the confederates had dispersed to raise troops in their respective districts.[1]

A striking proof of the general feeling which united the nobles against Bothwell is to be found in the fact that Robert Melvil, who possessed Mary Stuart's entire confidence, and who was sent by her shortly afterwards on a mission to Elizabeth, had joined the confederacy. In a letter which he wrote about the same time to Cecil, he demanded the assistance of England to set the Queen at liberty, and to punish the murderers of the King; and, as the Laird of Grange had done, he intimated that, if England refused her aid, France was ready to grant them succour. In fact, the Court of France, seeing that Mary Stuart multiplied the commission of degrading disorders and destructive errors, and fearing that Scotland might thereby fall under the dominion of England, had preferred to abandon the Queen rather than lose the kingdom. Charles IX. sent Villeroy to Du Croc, with secret instructions, from which we extract the following curious passage :—'The said Sieur de Villeroy will say,

[1] MS. letter, State Paper Office, Grange to Bedford, 8th May, 1567. Tytler, vol. v., pp. 407-409.

that his Majesty having made known to him the opinion which he entertains of the pitiable success of the affairs of the Queen of Scotland, seeing what has been written to him of her behaviour by the said Sieur du Croc, and the strange news which he has received from other quarters; and being also concerned that the enterprise of the said lords is secretly assisted and favoured by the English—whose charity would only entail their ruin—the King wishes the said Sieur du Croc to know, that the desire and principal intention of his Majesty is to keep the kingdom of Scotland in its attachment to himself, without permitting it, under the pretext of the many follies which are committed, to rebel and alienate itself from its attachment to himself, as it is certain it would do towards the said English, whom the said lords would seek as their protectors in this affair, if they saw they would have no assurance from the King."[1] It appears that Du Croc, in conformity with these instructions, offered the confederate lords a company of men-at-arms, and pensions to several noblemen and gentlemen.[2]

But the confederates preferred to have the support of Elizabeth, who hesitated what course to pursue in the matter, as she would have to choose between the interests of her tortuous policy, and her theories of royal prerogative. On the one hand she feared, by refusal, to compel the Scottish lords to an alliance with France; and on the other, she felt a great repugnance to countenance so dangerous a proceeding as the rebellion of a nation against its sovereign. She had been incensed by the letters of the Laird of Grange,[3] and had said that a subject was never justified in making known to the world the weaknesses and faults of his prince. She declared that the coronation of the Prince Royal during the lifetime of his mother would be sanctioned neither by herself, nor by any other monarch. She added, however, that to prevent him from being given up to the French by Bothwell, she would be disposed to assist the confederates, if they would place him in her hands. But as her actions rarely corresponded with her words, she gave them every encouragement, although she had not obtained from them what she required. That able and steadfast politician, Cecil, under-

---

[1] Instructions to M. de Villeroy, ambassador to Scotland. Harlay MSS., No. 218, Nat. Lib. Paris; published in Teulet's Pièces et Documents, &c., vol. ii., pp. 182-185.

[2] MS. letter, State Paper Office, Robert Melvil to Cecil, 7th May, 1567. Tytler, vol. v., p. 407.

[3] Upon this point a remarkable conversation took place between her and Randolph, in the palace garden. See Tytler, vol. v., pp. 410, 411.

took to make her feelings subordinate to her interests, and to lead her, slowly but surely, to adopt those resolutions which were least agreeable, but most advantageous. Robert Melvil, who was sent by Mary Stuart to inform her of her marriage, and who had joined the confederacy out of hatred for Bothwell, obtained an assurance not long afterwards, notwithstanding Elizabeth's monarchical scruples and high-flown sentiments, that the Queen of England would assist the lords in their honourable enterprise.[1]

The league of the nobility increased daily in numbers and importance. Lethington, having become suspected by Bothwell, who had attempted to kill him in the Queen's own chamber,[2] had taken refuge with his friend the Earl of Athol, with the intention of joining the confederates. Mary Stuart was not entirely ignorant of the designs of her enemies, who had all withdrawn from her Court. She did not seem to fear them, and treated their leaders with the utmost disdain. In allusion to their character and position, she observed sarcastically: 'Athol is but feeble; for Argyle, I know well how to stop his mouth; as for Morton, his boots are but new pulled off [alluding to his recent return from banishment] and still soiled, he shall be sent back to his own quarters.'[3] She discovered ere long that they were far more formidable than she imagined. Bothwell had quickly manifested the intentions attributed to him, by making an imperious demand for the Prince Royal. The Earl of Mar, when summoned with threats to deliver him up, replied that he would not consent to do so unless the young Prince were placed in Edinburgh Castle under the care of a governor without reproach, and on whose fidelity all could rely.[4] But instead of pursuing his attempts to gain possession of Darnley's son, Bothwell was now obliged to defend himself.

The Queen had left Edinburgh shortly after her marriage, as the citizens had not appeared very favourably disposed towards her, and had retired to Borthwick Castle, a seat of the Laird of Crookston's, about ten miles from the capital.[5] She had summoned her nobles to attend her with her feudal forces on an expedition against the borderers of Liddesdale;[6] but no one had responded to the summons, and Bothwell, who had been

---

[1] Tytler, vol. v., p. 438.   [2] Ibid., vol. v., p. 415.
[3] MS. letter, State Paper Office, Drury to Cecil, 20th May, 1567. Tytler, vol. v., p. 416.
[4] Melvil's Memoirs, p. 80.   [5] Tytler, vol. v., p. 420.
[6] This proclamation, dated May 28, is in Keith, p. 395.

appointed to command the army, had returned to the Queen at Borthwick very much disconcerted.¹ The confederates seized this opportunity, not only for refusing their obedience, but also for manifesting their insurrection. The Earls of Morton, Mar, Glencairn, and Montrose, and the Lords Hume, Lindsay, Ruthven, Sanquhar, Semple, Kirkaldy of Grange, Tullibardine, and Lochleven collected two thousand horsemen, and advanced towards Borthwick Castle.² Lord Hume was the first to arrive with eight hundred men. On the 10th of June he hoped to surprise Bothwell, who had been informed of his coming, and had made a precipitate escape. On the same evening the Queen, disguised in man's apparel, left the castle on horseback, joined Bothwell at a short distance from it, and rode with him to Dunbar, where they arrived at about three o'clock in the morning.³

Disappointed in their attempts against Borthwick, the confederates marched towards Edinburgh, where they arrived on the 11th of June. Their little army had meanwhile been increased, by reinforcements, to three thousand men. The people of Edinburgh declared in their favour. Accordingly the Earl of Huntly, Lord Claud Hamilton, the Archbishop of St. Andrews, the Abbot of Kilwinning, and the Bishop of Ross, who had been left in the city by the Queen, took refuge in the castle,⁴ which had been left by Bothwell under the command of James Balfour, who was now ready to join the confederates, and would not point his artillery against them. An hour after the confederates had entered Edinburgh, they published the following proclamation: 'That whereas the Queen's Majesty, being detained

¹ 'Mais lui (Bothwell) venu audit lieu ne trouva personnes ; porquoi so volant dépourveu de son entreprise, retorna trouver la royne à Borthik, où ils furent advertis, avant couché, qu'ils seroient assiégés audit lieu.' Narrative of Events from the 7th to the 15th June, 1567, by the Captain of Inchkeith, in Teulet's Pièces et Documents, vol. ii., pp. 159, 160. This Captain of Inchkeith, a small island opposite Leith, made this short campaign in the Queen's army.
² Keith, p. 398.
³ ' A dix heures au soir, la royne print habillementz de homme, et privément monté sur un courteau, estant à Borthik, et prent son chemin vers Donbar ; et avant avoir faict grand chemin, rencontre le duc son mari ; et s'en alèrent au château de Donbar ensemble, et arrivèrent à trois heures du matin, et fait tout le chemin en une selle d'homme.' Narrative of the Captain of Inchkeith, in Teulet, vol. ii., pp. 161, 162.—' Hir Maiestie in mennis claiths, butit, and spurit, departit that saming neicht of Borthwick to Dunbar, quhairof na man knew saif ma lord Duk and sum of his servants, quha met hir Maiestie a myll of Borthwick, and convoyit hir Hieness to Dunbar.' Letter from James Beton to his brother, the Archbishop of Glasgow, dated Edinburgh, 17th June, 1567 ; in Laing, vol. ii., p. 107. See also a letter from Du Crocto Charles IX, 17th June, 1567 ; in Teulet, vol. ii., p. 172. ⁴ Keith, p. 398, note.

in captivity, was neither able to govern her realm, nor try the murder of her husband, we of the nobility and council command all the subjects, specially the burghers of Edinburgh, to assist the said noblemen and council in delivering the Queen and preserving the Prince, and in trying and punishing the King's murderers. And we command the Lords of Session, commissaries, and all other judges, to sit and do justice according to the laws of this realm, notwithstanding any tumult that may arise in the time of this enterprise; with certification to all who shall be found acting contrary to these proceedings, that they shall be reputed as fautors of the said murder and punished as traitors.'[1] On the following day, being joined by Athol and Lethington, they ordered the Queen's lieges to be ready within three hours to march against the Earl of Bothwell, who, they said, 'having put violent hands on the Queen's person, having proceeded to a dishonest marriage with Her Majesty, and having already murdered the late King, was now attempting by his gathering together of forces to murder the young Prince also.'[2]

Bothwell, in truth, had lost no time. As soon as the Queen arrived at Dunbar she published a proclamation, in which the confederate lords were arraigned as traitors, and all her faithful subjects were summoned to her standard. An army of two thousand five hundred men having been gathered together in two days, Mary Stuart and Bothwell marched at once against the insurgents, lest delay should render them more powerful. They left Dunbar on Saturday, the 14th of June, and slept at Seton, whilst their troops passed the night at Preston.[3] On the following day they resumed their march, and on their arrival at Gladsmoor the Queen caused a proclamation to be read to her little army, to the effect, 'That a number of conspirators having discovered their latent malice, borne to her and the Duke of Orkney, her husband, after they had failed in apprehending their persons at Borthwick, had made a seditious proclamation to make the people believe that they did seek the revenge of the murder of the King, her late husband, and the relieving of herself out of bondage and captivity, pretending that the Duke her husband was minded to invade the Prince her son; all which were false and forged inventions, none having better cause to revenge the King's death than herself, if she could know the authors thereof. And for the Duke, her present husband, he had used all means to clear his innocence, the ordinary justice had absolved him, and

[1] Keith, pp. 398, 399. [2] Ibid., p. 399. [3] Ibid., p. 400.

the Estates of Parliament approved their proceedings, which they themselves that made the present insurrection, had likewise allowed. As, also, he had offered to maintain that quarrel against any gentleman on earth undefamed, than which nothing more could be required. And as to her alleged captivity, the contrary was known to the whole subjects, her marriage with him being publicly contracted and solemnized with their own consents, as their hand-writs could testify. Albeit to give their treason a fair show they made now a buckler of the Prince, her son, being an infant and in their hands; whereas their intention only was to overthrow her and her posterity that they might rule all things at their pleasure and without controlment.'¹ Finally, in order to encourage her troops to fidelity, and to increase the number of her adherents, she promised them, 'in recompense of their valorous service, the lands and possessions of the rebels, which should be distributed according to the merit of every man.'² Mounted on horseback, preceded by the royal standard of Scotland, and dressed in a red gown which reached only to her knees,³ the Queen, who had been joined by the Lords Seton, Yester, and Borthwick,⁴ led her army to Carberry Hill, six miles from Edinburgh, on the eastern side of which she intrenched herself.

The confederate nobles, having been informed of her march at midnight on Saturday, left Edinburgh between two and three o'clock on Sunday morning,⁵ with the intention of giving her battle. In place of the lion of Scotland,⁶ a banner was displayed, on which was painted the body of the murdered King, lying under a tree, with the young Prince kneeling beside it, and underneath the motto, '*Judge and avenge my cause, O Lord!*'⁷ The sight of this lugubrious banner had greatly moved the people of Edinburgh, and strongly excited the confederate

---

¹ Keith, p. 400.   ² Ibid.
³ Narrative of the Captain of Inchkeith, in Teulet, vol. ii., p. 162.
⁴ Tytler, vol. v., p. 422.
⁵ ' Les seigneurs estant advertis et craignant que la royne ou se duc se présentassent devant le château de cette ville, qui promettoit toujours de tenir bon si elle faisoyt gens, commencèrent à desloger dimanche à deux heures après minuit, pour aller combattre près de Seiton.' Letter from Du Croc to Charles IX., in Teulet, vol. ii., p. 173.—'Upon the morn, at twa hours of the morning, thair trumpet blew, and they for the maist pairt maid thame till thair horses.' Letter from James Beton to the Archbishop of Glasgow, in Laing, vol. ii., p. 109.
⁶ ' La royne en sa bandière portoyt un lion, qui sont les armes de ce royaume.' Du Croc to Charles IX., 17th June, 1567; in Teulet, vol. ii., p. 177.
⁷ Narrative of the Captain of Inchkeith, in Teulet, vol. ii., p. 164; and letter from Du Croc to Charles IX., 17th June, ibid., p. 177.

soldiers. The two armies were soon in presence of each other; that of the lords took up its position on the heights of Musselburgh, about a mile from the Queen's encampment.¹ Separated by a little brook, and both occupying positions difficult of access, they were nearly equal in point of numbers, but very different in spirit and quality. On the Queen's side scarcely any of the nobility were to be found,²—her servants wavered in their fidelity, and her soldiers were dispirited by the unpopularity of her cause; on the opposite side were the most powerful barons in the kingdom, with troops animated by enthusiastic ardour, burning to overthrow an ambitious upstart, and to punish a hateful murderer.

Whilst the two armies were lying opposite each other, the French ambassador, Du Croc, made an attempt at mediation in the name of the King, his master. He repaired first to the camp of the confederates. To his offers of reconciliation the lords replied that, in order to avoid bloodshed, they were ready, if the Queen would separate herself from 'the wretch who held her captive,'³ to acknowledge her sway, to serve her faithfully, and to continue her very obedient subjects; that, if Bothwell would come out between the armies, he would be met by some one from among their ranks who would maintain against him that he was the real murderer of the late King; and that if he required two, four, ten, or twelve opponents, they would be forthcoming. Du Croc expressed his repugnance to be the bearer of these two propositions. The first was an abandonment of Bothwell, to which the Queen, in his opinion, would never consent; and the second, a single combat, which she would never permit. But the lords firmly replied that nothing else could be done, and that they would rather be buried alive than suffer the truth regarding the death of the King to remain longer concealed.⁴

The French ambassador left them with but little hope, and, having been escorted to the outposts of the royal army, went in search of Mary Stuart. He found her sitting on a hillock, very resolute and animated. After having kissed hands, he tried to mollify her resentment against those who, though now opposed to her, had not ceased to be her subjects, and proclaimed them-

---
¹ Inchkeith's Narrative; in Teulet, vol. ii., p. 163.
² En nostre armée il n'y avoit ni comte, ni grand seigneur, n'est milord Ross, et milord Borthike.' The Captain of Inchkeith's Narrative; in Teulet, vol. ii., p. 166.
³ Letter from Du Croc to Charles IX., 17th June, 1567; in Teulet, vol. ii., p. 173.
⁴ Ibid. p. 174.

selves still her very humble and affectionate servants. Interrupting him at these words, she said vehemently: 'They show their affection very ill, by running counter to what they have signed, and by accusing the man whom they acquitted, and to whom they have married me.' She added, however, that if they returned to their duty, and begged her pardon, she was ready to receive them with open arms. At this moment Bothwell came up. 'Is it of me that they complain?' he said to Du Croc in a voice loud enough to be heard by his army. 'I have just been speaking to them,' replied Du Croc as loudly, 'and they have assured me that they are the Queen's very humble subjects and servants; and your mortal enemies,' he added in a lower tone, 'since you will know it.' 'What have I done to them?' answered Bothwell in the same tone, as if desirous to communicate his own assurance to those who heard him, and did not feel so bold as himself: 'I have never caused displeasure to a single one of them; on the contrary, I have sought to consult them all. What they are doing is out of envy for my greatness. Fortune is free to any who can receive her; and there is not a man among them who would not like to be in my place.' He then proposed, in order to prevent bloodshed, to fight between the two armies, although he had had the honour to espouse the Queen, any of his enemies who might leave their ranks, provided he were a gentleman. The Queen opposed this proposition, saying that she would not allow anything of the kind, and that his quarrel was hers also.[1]

During this conversation, the confederate army had put itself in motion, and passed the brook which separated it from the royal troops. Bothwell left Du Croc to place himself at the head of his men, and Du Croc, having taken leave of the Queen, returned to the confederates, for the purpose of making a last attempt. He promised Morton and Glencairn the pardon of their sovereign, on condition that they should return to their duty. 'We have not come here,' said Glencairn, 'to solicit pardon for ourselves, but rather to give it to those who have offended.' 'We are in arms,' added Morton, 'not against our Queen, but against the Duke of Orkney, the murderer of her husband. Let him be delivered up, or let her Majesty remove him from her company, and we shall yield her obedience.'[2]

[1] Letter from Du Croc to Charles IX., 17th June, 1567; in Teulet, vol. ii., pp. 175, 176.
[2] MS. letter, State Paper Office, Scrope to Cecil, Carlisle, 17th June, 1567; and Drury to Cecil, Berwick, 18th and 19th June, 1567. Tytler, vol. v., p. 423.

They then put on their casques, and refused to pay further attention to Du Croc, who thereupon returned to Edinburgh.[1]

In both armies, the men had dismounted to do battle, and left their horses behind, according to the custom of the country.⁴ As the confederates drew near, a cry arose among the royal troops that some means must be found to avoid a conflict.[2] The Duke was surprised, and the Queen alarmed, at this demonstration. It was immediately demanded that the Duke should decide the quarrel single-handed with a champion from the other side. Bothwell consented without hesitation; and the Queen, observing that her troops were falling away, could no longer refuse her permission. The Laird of Tullibardine accepted the defiance on behalf of the confederates, but was rejected by Mary Stuart, as not being of sufficiently high rank. Bothwell then singled out Morton, who prepared to fight him on foot, and with two-handed swords. Upon this, the intrepid Lindsay interfered, and contended that the honour belonged of right to him, as the servant of the murdered King. Morton yielded to his request, and armed him with the famous sword which had belonged to his renowned ancestor, Archibald Bell-the-Cat;[4] and Lindsay, kneeling down in presence of the whole army, prayed aloud to God that He would strengthen his arm, 'and that it would please His mercy to preserve the innocent, and His justice to vanquish the vicious murderer who had shed the blood of the King.'[5]

But before Bothwell could obtain from Mary Stuart—who feared to expose her husband to so dangerous a conflict—permission to enter the lists with the fanatical champion of the confederates, it became evident that desertion was spreading rapidly in the royal army. During all these parleys, the soldiers

[1] Letter from Du Croc to Charles IX., in Teulet, vol. ii., p. 177.—'De fachon que Monsieur du Croq ne pouvoit trouver fasson ne aulcun moyen d'accord. Ce voyant, nous lesse l'ung et l'autre, et s'en va à Lislebourg.' Inchkeith's Narrative, in Teulet, vol. ii., p. 163.

[2] Du Croc's letter of the 17th June. Teulet, vol. ii., p. 178.

[3] 'Et nous les voyons marcher, nous-mesmes les nostres en ordre de bataille; mais je trouvois les nostres qu'ils cherchoient plustot moyen d'appointement plustot que de combattre.' Narrative of the Captain of Inchkeith, in Teulet, vol. ii., p. 165.—' A la fin il se fit ung bruit dedans l'armée de la royne, qu'il valloit mieulx chercher quelque expédient; ce qui estonna grandement la royne et le duc, connoissant ce qu'il avoyt tousjours craint.' Du Croc to Charles IX., 17th June, 1567; in Teulet, vol. ii., p. 178.

[4] Tytler, vol. v., p. 424. Bell-the-Cat was the surname given to Archibald, Earl of Angus, who was the first to attack the favourites of James III., who were finally hanged upon the bridge of Lauder.

[5] Narrative of the Captain of Inchkeith; in Teulet, vol. ii., p. 164.

of both parties had mingled with each other, and the Queen's troops had lost courage. The Laird of Grange, taking advantage of the disorder which prevailed in the enemy's ranks, wheeled round Carberry Hill with a strong body of his men, so as to cut off all possibility of Bothwell's retreat upon Dunbar. At sight of this, the panic became general—nearly all the royal army disbanded, and the Queen and Bothwell were left with only sixty gentlemen, and the band of hackbutters.[1]

In this extremity the Queen, no longer able to fight, and deprived of almost every hope of escape, determined at least to save the man whom she loved, and sent the Laird of Ormiston to demand an interview with the Laird of Grange. Sir William Kirkaldy advanced towards her, and told her that the lords would return to their allegiance if the man who stood near her, and was guilty of the King's murder, were dismissed, and if she would consent to follow them to Edinburgh. The Queen then promised to leave the Duke, and surrender herself into the hands of the lords, if they would promise faithfully to perform their duty towards her. The confederates solemnly assured her that, on such conditions, they were ready to receive and obey her as their sovereign.[2] Then, Mary had a short private conversation with Bothwell on Carberry Hill, to induce him to withdraw. What passed between them at this last interview? They were observed to speak together with much agitation, and then to separate 'with great anguish and grief.'[3] 'At last,' says an eye-witness of the scene, 'the Duke asked the Queen whether she would keep the promise of fidelity which she had made to him. Of which she assured him, and gave him her hand upon it. Thereupon he mounted his horse, with a small company of about a dozen of his friends, and went off at a gallop, taking the road to Dunbar.'[4] Bothwell had seen Mary Stuart for the last time.

After this sacrifice, which she did not think was so great as it proved to be, Mary, full of sorrow and confidence, advanced towards the Laird of Grange, and said that she surrendered to him on the conditions he had specified in the name of the lords. She then gave him her hand, which he kissed respectfully, and, taking her horse by the bridle, he led her into the midst of the confederates, who received her with great deference and submission. 'My lords,' she said, 'I am come to you, not out of any

[1] MS. letter, State Paper Office, Scrope to Cecil, 17th June, 1567. Tytler, vol. v., pp. 424, 425. Keith, p. 401.
[2] Keith, p. 401. Tytler, vol. v., p. 425.
[3] Narrative of the Captain of Inchkeith; in Teulet, vol. ii., pp. 165, 166. [4] Ibid.

fear I had of my life, nor yet doubting of the victory, if matters had gone to the worst; but I abhor the shedding of Christian blood, especially of those that are my own subjects; and therefore I yield to you, and will be ruled hereafter by your counsels, trusting you will respect me as your born Princess and Queen.'[1] She thus made her first appearance among them as their sovereign, and was received by them on their knees. 'Here, madam,' said Morton, 'is the true place where your Grace should be, and here we are ready to defend and obey you as loyally as ever nobility of this realm did your progenitors.'[2] The lords, who complained more of Bothwell's power than of his crimes, being now satisfied with having vanquished and removed him, conducted themselves towards the Queen in a manner which quite accorded with her hopes and their own promises. The soldiers, less accommodating than their leaders, gave vent to their coarse fanaticism, and malignant reprobation, by bursting out into invectives against the Queen. The Laird of Grange, however, drew his sword, and compelled them to silence.[3]

But the behaviour of the nobles soon underwent a change, and their actions became, ere long, utterly at variance with their words. Whilst James Balfour, Bothwell's creature and accomplice, who had remained neutral during the struggle, declared in favour of the victorious confederates, after having had three hours' conference with Lethington in Edinburgh Castle[4]—the Hamiltons, faithful to Bothwell and the Queen, had collected in arms, and advanced in considerable force, to Lithlingow.[5] Mary Stuart, supposing that her will was still sovereign, and that she might continue to act as she pleased, was desirous to communicate with them. The lords refused to allow her to do so, fearing that she might contrive some means for renewing the war, and rejoining Bothwell. Their refusal made her aware of the imprudence of the resolution which she had taken, and she burst into reproaches

---

[1] Keith, p. 402.   [2] Tytler, vol. v., p. 426.   [3] Keith, p. 402.

[4] James Beaton, brother of the Archbishop of Glasgow, had conveyed the Queen's orders to Balfour in an interview which he had with him on Sunday morning, the same day that the encounter took place at Carberry Hill. This is his account:—'Betwix 5 and 6 hours (in the morning) I passit... to the Castell quhair, being arryvit, I doit my commission as was commanded me by the Queinis Majestie... I found the Captain very cauld in his answering to her Majestie's commandments.... That saming day my Lord Secretair (Lethington) cam to the Castell, at twa hours efter none, and spak with the Captain the space of three hours.' James Beaton to the Archbishop of Glasgow, 17th June, 1567; in Laing, vol. ii., pp. 109, 110.

[5] MS. letter, State Paper Office, Drury to Cecil, 18th June, 1567; in Tytler, vol. v., p. 426.

against the confederates, who, she said, had broken their promise, and treated her not as a Queen, but as a prisoner. In the excess of her anger, she called for Lindsay, and bade him give her his hand. He obeyed. 'By the hand,' said she, 'which is now in yours, I'll have your head for this.'[1] This imprudent threat, combined with her declaration to the Earls of Morton and Athol, that she would have them both hanged,[2] only served to aggravate her unfortunate position.

From this moment she was a captive in the hands of the confederate lords, who conducted her at once to Edinburgh. She entered the city at ten o'clock in the evening, preceded by the banner on which was painted the murdered King, and was received with yells and execrations by the populace.[3] At first she was taken to the Provost's house, and deprived of the company of her serving-women. Although she had eaten nothing for twenty-four hours, she refused to take any refreshment.[4] She was in despair. During the night, she frequently opened the window of her room, and cried aloud for help. The next morning, with pitiless barbarity, the soldiers held up before her window the banner representing the sad picture of her son crying for vengeance on the murderers of her husband. At this sight, she fell into an agony of despair and delirium, and rushed to the window like a maniac, partially clothed and with dishevelled hair, uttering loud cries, and imploring the people, for the love of God, to deliver her from the hands of her tyrants. 'No man,' says a narrator of this piteous spectacle, 'could look upon her, but she moved him to pity and compassion.'[5]

---

[1] Tytler, vol. v., p. 427.
[2] 'Le soir mesme elle commança à tancer au conte de Athol, et après encontre le conte de Morton.' Narrative of the Captain of Inchkeith; in Teulet, vol. ii., p. 166.—'Après qu'elle fut prise, en venant à Lisleboure, ne parla jamais que de les faire tous pendre et crucifier, et continue tousjours; ce qui augmente leur désespoir, car ils voient que, s'ils la mettent en liberté elle ira incontinent trouver le duc son mari, et ce sera à recommancer.' Du Croc to Catherine de Medici, 17th June, 1567; in Teulet, vol. ii., pp. 168, 169.
[3] Tytler, vol. v., p. 427. Keith, p. 402.
[4] Narrative of the Captain of Inchkeith; in Teulet, vol. ii., p. 166.
[5] 'Sche cam yesterday to ane windo of hir chalmer that lukkit ou the Hiegait, and cryit forth on the pepill quhow she was holden in prison, and keepit be her awin subjects quha had betrayit hir. Sche cam to the said windo sundrie tymes in sa miserable a stait, her hairs hingand about her loggs, and her breist, yea the maist pairt of all her bodie, fra the waist up, bair and discoverit, that na man could luk upon hir bot sche movit him to pitie and compassion.' James Beaton to the Archbishop of Glasgow, 17th June, 1567; in Laing, vol. ii., p. 114. Du Croc to Charles IX., 17th June, 1567; in Teulet, vol. ii., p. 179.

The lords, fearing that the changeful disposition of the people might effect a reaction in her favour, now endeavoured to calm the agitation of the unfortunate Queen, by leading her to hope that she would soon be set at liberty and restored to her palace of Holyrood. But their real intentions were of a very different nature. The unalterable attachment which Mary displayed for Bothwell had inspired them with no slight alarm.[1] According to Melvil, they had intercepted a letter which she had written to Bothwell, whom she still called her 'dear heart,' and entrusted to one of her guards, whom she had bribed to forward it to Dunbar. She told Bothwell, in this letter, that she would never forget or abandon him; and that, though forced momentarily to separate from him, in order to preserve him from the evils by which he was menaced, she besought him to take consolation, and keep well on his guard.[2] She manifested the ardour of her affection for Bothwell in a conversation which she had with Lethington on that same day. She bitterly reproached the lords for having separated her from her husband, 'with whom she would be happy to live and die,' and entreated them 'to put them both together into a ship, to send them whithersoever fortune might lead.'[3] Her unshaken passion for Bothwell, the certainty that she would join him, and recommence the war, as soon as she was set at liberty, and her threat 'to have them all hanged and crucified'[4] as soon as she had regained her power, rendered the lords merciless, by depriving them of all hope. They determined, therefore, to imprison and dethrone her.

At eight o'clock in the evening, they conducted her from the Provost's house to Holyrood Palace. She went thither on foot, between Athol and Morton, accompanied by the ladies Semple and Seton, and escorted by three hundred hackbutters.[5] The lords then assembled in council, and took their determination. In their order for the Queen's imprisonment, they related all that had

[1] Du Croc to Catherine de Medici, 17th June, 1567; in Teulet, vol. ii., pp. 168, 169.
[2] Melvil's Memoirs, p. 83.
[3] Du Croc to Catherine de Medici, 17th June, 1567; in Teulet, vol. ii., p. 170.
[4] Ibid.
[5] 'Le jour ensuyvant, à huit heures du soir, elle fut ramenée au château de Halirudes (Holyrood), conduicte de trois cens harquebouziers, le comte de Morton de l'ung cousté et le comte d'Atheul de l'aultre; et alla à pied, deux haquenées menées devant elle; et adonc estoit accompagnée de madamoyselle de Sempel et Seton, avecques quelques autres de la chambre, abillée d'une robe de nuict de couleur variable.' Narrative of the Captain of Inchkeith; in Teulet, vol. ii., p. 167. Du Croc to Charles IX., 17th June, 1567; Ibid., p. 179.

occurred since 'the shameful and horrible murder of the late King:' 'the ungodly and dishonourable marriage' of the Queen to the Earl of Bothwell, its principal author; the necessity that existed for the nobility to rise in arms to avenge this crime, save the life of the Prince Royal, prevent their own ruin, and avert the entire overthrow of the State; the voluntary surrender of the Queen at Carberry Hill; and the flight of Bothwell, without having given battle. They then went on to say that, 'after they had opened and declared unto her Highness her own estate and condition, and the miserable estate of this realm, with the danger that her dearest son the Prince stood in, requiring that she would suffer and command the said murder and authors thereof to be punished, they found in her Majesty such untowardness and repugnance thereto, that rather she appeared to fortify and maintain the said Earl Bothwell and his accomplices in the said wicked crimes, nor to suffer justice to pass forward; whereby, if her Highness should be left in that state, to follow her own inordinate passion, it would not fail to succeed to the final confusion and extermination of the whole realm. So that, after mature consultation, by common advice, it is thought convenient, concluded and decreed, that her Majesty's person be sequestered from all society of the said Earl Bothwell, and from all having of intelligence with him or any others, whereby he may have any comfort to escape due punishment for his demerits. And finding no place more meet or commodious for her Majesty to remain in, than the house and place of Lochleven, ordains, commands, and charges Patrick Lord Lindsay of the Byres, William Lord Ruthven, and William Douglas of Lochleven, to pass and convoy her Majesty to the said place of Lochleven, and the said lords to receive her therein, and there they and every one of them to keep her Majesty surely, within the said place, and in nowise to suffer her to pass forth of the same, or to have intelligence from any manner of persons, or yet to send advertisements or directions for intelligence with any living persons, except in their own presence and audience, or by the commandments and directions of the lords undersubscribing, or part of them representing the council at Edinburgh, or otherwise where they shall resort for the time, as they will answer to God, and upon their duty, to the commonweal of this country, keeping these presents for their warrant.'[1]

By virtue of this order, which was signed by Athol, Glencairn, Morton, Mar, Grahame, Sanquhar, Semple, and William Ochil-

[1] Order of Council for Queen Mary's imprisonment in Lochleven; in Laing, vol. ii., pp. 116-118.

tree, the unfortunate Mary, during the night of the 10th of June, was taken from the palace of her ancestors, mounted on a sorry hackney, and conducted to Lochleven Castle, by Lindsay and Ruthven,[1] men of savage manners, even in that age. This castle, by reason of its strong position and complete isolation, was exactly suited to the designs of the confederates. It stood in the midst of a lake, and was surrounded by water on every side half a mile in breadth. It belonged to William Douglas, half-brother of the Earl of Murray. The royal captive was to be kept there under the charge of her most implacable enemy, Margaret Erskine, mother of William Douglas, and formerly mistress of James V. She had once been beautiful, but had retained, in her old age, her proud and imperious spirit, and was wont to boast that the son whom she had borne to Mary Stuart's father was the rightful heir to the throne of Scotland. She was the daughter of Lord Erskine, and, in the licence of Scotch morals, claimed to have been the King's lawful wife. She, therefore, considered that Mary of Lorraine had robbed her of the heart of James V., and that Mary Stuart had dispossessed Murray of the rank and inheritance which were his due.[2] To the resentment aroused by wounded pride and disappointed ambition, she added the stern vehemence of intolerant piety. She was a zealous Presbyterian. Her daughter had married Lord Lindsay, and her son William was next heir to the Earl of Morton. Her character and creed united with her parentage and hatred to render her an inexorable jailor of the captive Queen.

The detention of a Queen by her subjects was an extraordinary circumstance, even in that age of civil wars and religious revolutions. Insurrection against authority had rarely been carried so far as the imprisonment of those who were considered its sacred depositaries. But notwithstanding its enormity, this bold deed aroused no strong disapprobation, or serious resistance, in Scotland. The unwise, passionate, and blameworthy conduct of Mary Stuart had deprived her of all devoted adherents. The murder of Darnley, and her marriage to Bothwell, had destroyed her reputation; and the unshaken attachment which she displayed to this proscribed murderer precluded the possibility of a recon-

[1] MS. Letter, State Paper Office, Drury to Cecil, 18th June, 1567; Tytler, vol. v., p. 428. 'Et bientost apiès, elle fut convoyée aut Petit-Liet (Leith) en grande compagnye, où on luy fait passer l'eau du Forthe, et après on la conduict en bonne compagnye jusques à Laucheleven; et là sont demeurés milord Lindesey et milord Reven, et plusieurs.' Narrative of the Captain of Inchkeith; in Teulet, vol. ii., p. 167. Du Croc to Catherine de Medici, 17th June, 1567; Ibid., p. 169.
[2] Keith, p. 403, note. Tytler, vol. v., p. 437.

ciliation with the confederate lords. Crushed by her victorious adversaries, her intimidated partisans took no vigorous steps for her defence. They met together at Dumbarton, ostensibly to concert measures for her deliverance;[1] but far from making any demonstration in her favour, they exhibited, as we shall presently see,[2] the utmost readiness to betray her. Thus deserted by her own subjects, what hopes had she of assistance from foreign powers?

Her cause, as a Queen, was the cause of every Prince. The imprisonment of a sovereign by her subjects presented a terrible example for the consideration of crowned heads; and it produced the same effect in every court of Europe. But nearer and more pressing interests soon diverted attention from this distant and abstract occurrence. Philip II. had not yet entered into such close relations with Mary Stuart as made that persecuted and dethroned Queen the religious client of his crown, and the political auxiliary of his ambition. Moreover, he was then busy in crushing the rising revolt of the Netherlands, whither he had sent the Duke of Alva with a large army, at a very great expense. Catherine de Medici and her son, Charles IX. were once more engaged in the civil wars of France. Even had they been willing, they could not have come to Mary Stuart's assistance. But they had little disposition to help her; for, although not callous to her misfortunes, they were offended by her inconsistency, and deterred by her vagaries. Queen Elizabeth only remained. The exalted ideas which that princess entertained with regard to the inviolability of royal prerogative could not but lead her to feel the utmost indignation at what she considered the sacrilegious audacity of the confederate lords. But, on the other hand, her mistrustful dislike of a Queen who had laid claims to her crown, and who still possessed the affection of her Catholic subjects, made her hesitate to restore to her throne the unfortunate sovereign whom she had largely contributed to overthrow. Thus she wavered undecidedly between her doctrines and her animosities, speaking sometimes as a monarch, but more frequently acting as a rival.

She despatched Robert Melvil, who had been accredited to her by Mary Stuart, but who had acted as the secret envoy of the confederates,[3] and consented to serve the tortuous policy of Elizabeth, to Scotland with a letter expressive of friendship and con-

[1] Tytler, vol. v., p. 433.
[2] See the proofs of this assertion, given in Tytler, vol. v., pp. 447-453.
[3] MS. letters, State Paper Office, quoted in Tytler, vol. v., pp. 417, 432, 437 440.

solation to the prisoner of Lochleven, and assurances of support to the rebel lords.[1] He arrived at Edinburgh on the 29th of June, twelve days after the imprisonment of Mary Stuart, whose danger had been augmented by a recent discovery. On the 20th of June, George Dalgleish, Bothwell's chamberlain, had been arrested with a casket which he was, doubtless, conveying to Dunbar, and which contained some private papers that furnished decided proofs of Mary's guilt. This casket was made of silver, overgilt with gold and surmounted with the cypher of Francis II., who had given it to Mary. Mary, in her turn, had given it to Bothwell, who had enclosed in it some letters which she had written to him in her own handwriting both before and after the murder of the King, some sonnets breathing the most passionate affection for him, and a contract of marriage which she had signed some time before the premeditated surprise at Almond Bridge.[2] Bothwell had, doubtless, preserved these papers as guarantees against the possible inconstancy of the Queen. He had left the casket in Edinburgh Castle, under the care of two of his accomplices, George Dalgleish and James Balfour. Either by chance, or by the perfidy of the odious Balfour,[3] who like many others,

[1] MS. letters, State Paper Office, Robert Melvil to Cecil, June and July, 1567. Tytler, vol. v., p. 440.

[2] 'Ane silver-box owergilt with gold, with all missive letteris, contractis or obligationis, for marriage-sonetis or luif-balletis, and all utheris letteris contenit thairin, send and past betwix the Quene our said Soverane Lordis moder, and James, sumtyme Erle Bothuile; quhilk box and haill pieces within the samyn were takin and fund with umquhill George Dalgleisch, servand to the Erle Bothuile, upon the xx day of June, the zeir of God, 1567 zeiris.' Discharge to my Lord Morton, given on the 16th of September, 1568, by Murray to Morton (who ever since the 22nd of June, 1567, had kept possession of the silver box), in presence of Lord Lindsay, the Bishop of Orkney, the Commendator of Dunfermline, the Commendator of Balmerinoch, Mr. Secretary Lethington, the Justice Clerk, and Master Henry Balnaves. See Keith, Appendix, p. 140. In a letter from Throckmorton to Queen Elizabeth, dated Edinburgh, 25th July, 1567, allusion is made to the discovery of these papers in the following terms: 'They mean to charge her with the murder of her husband, whereof they say they have as apparent proof against her as may be, as well *by testimony of her own hand-writing, which they have recovered*, as also by sufficient witnesses.' See Keith, p. 426.

[3] 'Bothwell sent a servant to Sir James Balfour to save a little silver cabinet which the Queen had given him. Sir James Balfour delivers the cabinet to the messenger, and under-hand giveth advice of it to the Lords. In this cabinet had Bothwell kept the letters of privacy he had from the Queen; thus he kept her letters to be an awe-bond upon her, in case her affections should change. By the taking of this cabinet, many particulars betwixt the Queen and Bothwell were clearly discovered. These letters were after printed; they were in French, with some sonnets of her own making.' Knox's History of the Reformation, vol. ii., p. 562.

had joined the confederacy under the pretext of punishing a crime to which he had been a party, Dalgleish had been seized, and the papers secured. Powrie, Bothwell's porter, met the same fate. When examined before a Court of Justice on the 23rd and 26th of June,[1] they had both confessed how the plot against the King's life had been contrived and executed. The depositions of these two servants of Bothwell had furnished a surer basis for the prosecution of that great criminal; and the Lords of the Secret Council commanded that he should be seized in his Castle of Dunbar, and conducted to Edinburgh to be punished as the murderer of the King.[2] But whilst the confessions of Powrie and Dalgleish placed Bothwell's culpability beyond doubt, the papers found in the silver casket furnished terrible weapons against the Queen to those who wished to accuse and destroy her. Such was the position of affairs when Robert Melvil rejoined the confederates.

Melvil, who had communicated to Elizabeth the intention of the Lords of the Secret Council to depose the Queen, announced to them that Elizabeth approved of their plan, and would sustain them in 'their honourable enterprise.'[3] He then proceeded to Lochleven. On the 1st of July, he delivered the letter of the English Queen to Mary Stuart, who was allowed to see him only in presence of Lindsay and Ruthven. Believing him still to be her faithful and devoted servant, Mary expressed her bitter regret that she was not permitted to converse with him in private.[4] Melvil's mission was rather suddenly followed by one of a very different nature, which Elizabeth had entrusted to Nicholas Throckmorton. This new envoy was charged to negotiate Mary Stuart's deliverance, and conditional restoration to authority. The wary Elizabeth doubtless perceived that she had acted in a manner too directly opposed to her views and interests. What she most urgently required was, that Scotland should remain in a state of disturbance and powerlessness. She ought not to desire either that the Queen should entirely recover her authority, or that the Lords, who now governed the kingdom in the name of their infant Prince, should gain a complete triumph. In the former case, the Queen of Scotland might again assert her

---

[1] Anderson's Collections, vol. ii., pp. 165-173. Laing, vol. ii., pp. 243-249.
[2] Proclamation of the 26th June, 1567; in Keith, p. 408.
[3] MS. letter, State Paper Office, Robert Melvil to Cecil, 1st July, 1567. Tytler, vol. v., p. 440.
[4] Hopetoun MSS., Robert Melvil's Declaration. Also MS. letter, State Paper Office, Sir J. Melvil to Drury, 8th July, 1567. Tytler, vol. v., p. 442.

claims to the English crown; and in the latter, the lords might do without English assistance. What, then, was her most advantageous policy? She proposed to place the Queen and the lords once more in a position of equality; doubtless in order that their conflicts might render her intervention continually indispensable in Scotland, and that their weakness might consolidate her own security in England.

Throckmorton was ordered to blame Mary Stuart for her marriage, and the lords for their rebellion. He was then to propose, as the basis of an arrangement between them, that the Queen should be divorced from Bothwell, and restored to liberty and power; that Bothwell and his accomplices should be punished; that the Castles of Dunbar and Dumbarton should be intrusted to the keeping of those nobles who were hostile to Bothwell; that a Parliament should be assembled, which should appoint the wardens of the marches, and the governors of Edinburgh, Stirling, Inchkeith, and the other strongholds of the kingdom; that a great council should be established, at which five or six of its members should always be present, without whose advice and consent the Queen should be unable to pass any act or make any appointment; and, finally, that a general amnesty should be proclaimed.[1] This proposition divided the government between the Queen and the high nobility. Elizabeth would thus have constituted disunion in Scotland, whither she would have been summoned, sometimes to support the Queen in virtue of her opinions about royal prerogative, and sometimes to sustain the high nobility in behalf of her political advantage.

But the victorious lords were not disposed to enter into her views upon the subject. Her ambassador, Throckmorton, perceived this as soon as he arrived in Scotland. In the fortalice of Fastcastle,[2] he had a conversation on this subject with Lethington, Sir James Melvil, and Lord Hume, who had all three come

---

[1] Instructions given on the 30th June, 1567, by the Queen of England to Sir Nicholas Throckmorton, her envoy into Scotland regarding the questions to be treated of with the Queen and the Lords; in Keith, pp. 411, 414. See also Proposals delivered to Sir Nicholas Throckmorton at his going into Scotland in July, 1567. Ibid., 416.

[2] 'Very little and very strong; a place fitter to lodge prisoners than folks of liberty.' Such is Throckmorton's description of this stronghold, which resembled most of the fortresses that were scattered over the Scottish territory. It belonged to Lord Hume, who came thither to receive Throckmorton, with Melvil and Lethington. Throckmorton to Cecil, from Fastcastle, 12th June, 1567; in Robertson, Appendix 21; and Tytler, vol. v., p. 443.

to meet him. The Scottish secretary explained to him the position and designs of the confederates. He loudly complained of the political inconstancy of the English Queen, who, he said, 'would leave them in the briars, if they ran her fortune,' and who now proposed to ruin them by demanding the liberation of Mary Stuart. On his entrance into Edinburgh, on the 12th of July, accompanied by the three above-named gentlemen and a numerous escort,[1] Throckmorton found that city in a state of strong excitement, which greatly increased three days afterwards, when the general assembly of the Church was held.

Knox had again made his appearance in his native land. Immediately after the assassination of Riccio, he had taken refuge in England; but he at once returned to Scotland on hearing of the imprisonment of the Queen.[2] He had offered the confederate lords the support of the Presbyterian party if they would adopt as laws of the kingdom those Acts of the Parliament of 1560, which Mary Stuart had refused to ratify. His proposition was accepted, and it was determined to abolish the last remains of Catholicism; to restore the patrimony of the Church to the Presbyterian clergy; to intrust to their care all universities, colleges, and schools for the instruction of youth, into which none should be admitted 'but after due trial, both of capacity and probity;' to give the Prince Royal a Protestant education; to pursue and punish the murderers of the King; and to make all future sovereigns of the country swear, before their coronation, 'to maintain the true religion now professed in the Kirk of Scotland, and suppress all things contrary to it.'[3] On these terms, a close connection was established between the heads of the Church and the leaders of the nobility. Knox denounced the royal prisoner with the most violent severity.[4] The pulpit became a place of accusation, from which Mary Stuart was publicly declared guilty of adultery and murder, and deserving of the most rigorous punishment. The Presbyterian ministers urged against her the moral equality of all Christians, and maintained that her sovereign rank did not give her the privilege

---

[1] Throckmorton to Elizabeth, Edinburgh, 14th July, 1567; in Robertson, Appendix 22.

[2] M'Crie's Life of Knox, vol. ii., p. 150; and Tytler, vol. i., p. 434.

[3] This agreement, in eight articles, was adopted and subscribed by a large number of the nobles. See Knox, vol. ii., pp. 563-565.

[4] 'This day being at Mr. Knox's sermon, who took a piece of the Scripture forth of the Books of the Kings, and did inveigh vehemently against the Queen, and persuaded extremities towards her by application of his texte.' Letter from Throckmorton to Elizabeth, Edinburgh, 19th July, 1567; in Keith, p. 422.

of impunity. In support of their doctrines, they quoted the examples which the Old Testament furnishes of the deposition of Kings, and took the Jewish democracy for their model, and the Bible for their law. Under the influence of their persuasions, the people became cruel and fanatical, and openly declared that 'their Queen had no more liberty nor privilege to commit murder or adultery, than any other private person, neither by God's laws nor by the laws of the realm,'[1] and that she ought to be punished with as much severity as any other malefactor. To those rigid moralists who, like Knox, disavowed the doctrine of royal inviolability, were added men like the celebrated Buchanan, who, taking their stand on precedents, in their own history, of similar severity exercised by subjects against their sovereigns, declared the right of revolt to be a part of the law of Scotland, and subordinated the power of the monarch to the will of the people.[2] A party of gloomy reasoners was thus formed, of men of strict morality and unbounded audacity, detesting the faith of the Queen, despising her conduct, revolting from her authority, and loudly demanding her judgment, her deposition, and even her death. The Assembly of the Presbyterian Church became the organ of their wishes, as Throckmorton informs us, by presenting a request that the murder of the late King might be severely punished, 'according to the laws of God, according to the practices of their own realm, and according to the laws which they call *jus gentium*, without respect of any person.'[3]

Fortunately for the Queen, the confederate lords were not all disposed to adopt such terrible resolutions. The most moderate of them desired that she should be divorced from Bothwell, and restored to the administration of the kingdom; this was the wish of Lethington and Melvil.[4] Others rather less indulgent, such as the Earls of Athol and Morton, wished to restore her to liberty without reinstating her in authority, and to compel her to retire to France, after she had abdicated the crown in favour of her son.[5] Lastly, there were some even more severe, who demanded

---

[1] Throckmorton to Elizabeth, Edinburgh, 18th July, 1567; in Robertson, Appendix 22, and Tytler, vol. v., p. 448.
[2] Buchanan *De Jure Regni*, in vol. i. of the folio edition of his Works.
[3] Throckmorton to Elizabeth, Edinburgh, 25th July, 1567; in Keith, p. 426.
[4] Throckmorton to Elizabeth, Edinburgh, 19th July, 1567; in Keith, p. 420.
[5] 'The next and second degree is, that the Queen shall abandon this realm, and remain either in France or in England, with assurance of the Prince where she remaineth, to perform the conditions ensuing; that is to say, to resign all government and regal authority to the Prince her son, and to appoint under his authority a council of the nobility and others to govern this realm, and she never to return

that she should be brought to trial, condemned for murder, publicly deposed, and detained in perpetual captivity.[1] Attempts were first made to induce her to consent to a divorce from Bothwell, which, by diminishing the fears, might possibly have modified the severity of the Lords of the Secret Council.

Robert Melvil was sent to Lochleven Castle on two occasions, the 8th and 15th of July, to endeavour to gain her consent to this step. Having received permission to speak to her in private, he conjured her, as she valued her crown, her safety, and her honour, and with the most urgent and affectionate entreaties, to abandon Bothwell and sanction his prosecution. But she peremptorily refused to do so. She told Melvil that she would rather renounce her throne than give up Bothwell—that she believed herself to be pregnant, and that she would never consent, by nullifying her marriage, to render her child illegitimate.[2] Notwithstanding the known desire of the Court of France, whose ambassador, Villeroi, had not been admitted to an audience of her; notwithstanding the salutary advice which had been sent her by Throckmorton, who had also been refused permission to see her; and notwithstanding the reiterated entreaties of Melvil, Mary Stuart continued immoveable in her attachment to Bothwell. She, however, stated her willingness to commit the government of the realm either to her brother, the Earl of Murray, or to a council composed of the principal nobles. She wrote a letter to this effect to the leaders of the confederates, beseeching them to transfer her to Stirling Castle, where she might have the comfort of seeing her son; and imploring them, if they would not obey her as their Queen, not to forget that she was the mother of their Prince, and the daughter of their King. Before Melvil took his leave, she produced a letter, and requested him to convey it to Bothwell. This he declined to do, upon which she threw it angrily into the fire.[3]

---

hither again, nor to molest or impeach the authority of her son, nor the government in his name. To this opinion I find the Earl of Athole and his followers only inclined; albeit the Earl of Morton doth not seem to impugn it.' Throckmorton to Elizabeth; Keith, p. 421.

[1] 'The third end and degree is, to prosecute justice against the Queen, to make her process, to condemn her, to crown the Prince, and to keep her in prison all the days of her life within this realm. To this opinion there doth lean, as far as I can understand, both the most part of the counsellors and a great many others.' Ibid.

[2] Hopetoun MSS., Robert Melvil's Declaration; Tytler, vol. v., p. 449. Throckmorton to Elizabeth, 18th July, 1567; in Robertson, Appendix 22.

[3] Tytler, vol. v., p. 450.

The Queen's obstinate determination not to desert Bothwell, alarmed and irritated the Lords of the Secret Council. They resolved to preclude the possibility of her doing them any future injury, by deposing her. This deposition was prepared under the form of a voluntary abdication, which would deprive her of power without degrading her. Three acts were accordingly drawn up for Mary Stuart's signature.[2] By the first, she renounced the government of the kingdom, declaring that it was a burden of which she was weary, and which she no longer had strength or will to bear; and authorized the immediate coronation of her son. The second and third conferred the regency on the Earl of Murray, during the minority of the young King; and appointed the Duke of Chatelherault, with the Earls of Lennox, Argyle, Morton, Athol, Glencairn, and Mar, regents of the kingdom till the return of Murray from France, with power to continue in that high office, if he refused it. In case Mary Stuart should refuse to sign these acts, the assembled lords had determined to prosecute and condemn her for these three crimes—'first, for breach and violation of their laws; secondly, for incontinency as well with the Earl Bothwell, as with others; and thirdly, for the murder of her husband, whereof, they say, they have as apparent proof against her as may be, as well by the testimony of her own handwriting, as also by sufficient witnesses.'[3]

On the morning of the 25th of July,[4] the ferocious Lindsay, and the insinuating Melvil, left Edinburgh on their way to Lochleven. One was the bearer of the three acts which were to strip her of her authority; the other was directed to warn the Queen of the dangers to which she would expose herself by refusing to sign them. Melvil saw her first, and told her all. That a public trial would be substituted for an abdication—that the hostility of the lords towards her would become implacable— that her defamation would be certain, and the loss of her crown

---

[1] 'She will not consent by any persuasion to abandon the Lord Bothwell for her husband, but avoweth constantly, that she will live with him; and saith that if it were put to her choice, to relinquish her crown and kingdom or the Lord Bothwell, she would leave her crown and kingdom to go as a simple damsel with him, and that she will never consent that he shall fare worse, or have more harm than herself.' Letter from Throckmorton to Elizabeth, 14th July, 1567; in Robertson, Appendix 22.
[2] These acts are in Keith, pp. 430-433.
[3] Throckmorton to Elizabeth, Edinburgh, 25th July, 1567; in Keith, p. 426.
[4] 'The Lord Lindsay departed this morning from this town to Lochleven,' says Throckmorton in his letter to Elizabeth on the 25th July; printed in Keith, p. 425; and yet the three above-mentioned acts are dated on the 24th of July only the day before. See Keith, pp. 431-433.

inevitable,—and that her life would probably be endangered—were some of the consequences which Melvil assured Mary Stuart would result from refusal; whilst he did not fail to insinuate, on the other hand, that any deed signed in captivity, and under fear of her life, would be invalid. He did not, however, succeed in convincing her. The royal prisoner found it a hard and humiliating thing thus to condemn and depose herself; and she passionately declared, that she would sooner renounce her life than her crown. But the dangers by which she was threatened had shaken her firmness of mind, and she passed from expressions of generous courage to demonstrations of timid depression. She was still wavering between submission and resistance, when Lindsay entered with the three acts of the Secret Council. He placed them silently before the Queen, and presented them for her signature. Mary Stuart, as if terrified by his presence, took the pen without uttering a single word; and with eyes filled with tears, and a trembling hand, put her name to the papers.[1] Lindsay then compelled Thomas Sinclair to affix the privy seal beside the royal signature, notwithstanding his protest that, as the Queen was in ward, her resignation was ineffectual.[2]

After having thus forced their sovereign to abdicate, the lords hastened to crown her son. They convoked all those who were willing to assist at his coronation, and to swear allegiance to him, to meet at Stirling on the 29th of July; and despatched Sir James Melvil to invite the Hamiltons and their adherents to be present at the solemnity.[3] These last now formed a powerful party. They had held a convention at Dumbarton, and had expressed their determination to set the Queen at liberty in a bond signed by the Archbishop of St. Andrews, the Earls of Argyle and Huntly, Lord Arbroath, the Bishops of Galloway and Ross, the Abbot of Kilwinning, the Lords Fleming, Herries, and Skirling, and Sir William Hamilton of Sanquhar.[4] No active measures, however, had followed this declaration, and they had done nothing to deliver the prisoner and prevent her deposition. They would not consent to sanction the coronation of her son by their presence, but they assured the confederates that they would offer no opposition, provided nothing was done to prejudice the title of the Duke of Chatelherault as next heir to the crown.[5]

[1] Spotswood, p. 211. Tytler, vol. v., p. 452.
[2] Blackwood's Magazine for October, 1817. Tytler, vol. v., p. 453.
[3] Melvil's Memoirs, p. 85.   [4] This bond is printed in Keith, p. 436.
[5] MS. letter, State Paper Office, Throckmorton to Elizabeth, 31st July, 1567, Stevenson's Selections, illustrating the reign of Mary, Queen of Scotland, p. 258. Tytler, vol. v., p. 453. Keith, pp. 485, 436.

The English ambassador peremptorily refused to proceed to Stirling.[1] He had been unable to see the Queen, and the prudent advice which he had transmitted to her, as well as the threatening admonitions which he had addressed to the Lords of the Secret Council, had failed to prevent the overthrow of her authority. Foreseeing the anger which his mistress would feel when she learned that her influence had been thus utterly contemned, and the royal prerogative thus audaciously violated, he held himself aloof, and awaited further orders from his Sovereign.

Elizabeth did not long delay to send them. On the 27th of July[2] she wrote to her ambassador in a strain of the greatest vehemence and indignation against the project which the lords entertained of deposing the Queen, and crowning the Prince Royal of Scotland. She declared that they had 'no warrant nor authority, by the law of God or man, to be as superiors, judges, or vindicators over their Prince and Sovereign. What warrant,' she added, 'have they in Scripture, being subjects, to depose their Prince; but contrary, and that with express words in St. Paul, who to the Romans, commanded them to obey *potestatibus supereminentioribus gladium gestantibus*, although it is well known that rulers in Rome were then infidels? Or what law find they written in any Christian monarchy, how and what sort subjects shall take and arrest the person of their Princes, commit and detain them in captivity, proceed against them by process and judgment, as we are well assured no such order is to be found in the whole civil law? And if they have no warrant by Scripture or Law, and yet can find out for their purpose some examples, as we hear by seditious ballads they put in print, they would pretend; we must justly account those examples to be unlawful, and acts of rebellion; and so, if the stories be well weighed, the success will prove them. You shall say that this may suffice to such as do pretend to be carried in their actions by authority either of religion or of justice. And as to others that for particular respect look only to their own surety, it were well done, before they proceeded any further, if they did well consider how to stay where they be, and to devise how to make surety of their doings already past, than to increase their peril by more dangerous doings to follow. We detest and abhor the murder committed upon our cousin their King, and mislike as much as any of them the marriage of the Queen our sister with Bothwell. But

---

[1] MS. letter, State Paper Office, Throckmorton to Elizabeth, 26th July, 1567 Stevenson's Selections, p. 251. Tytler, vol. v., p. 453.

[2] This letter is printed in Keith, pp. 428-430.

herein we dissent from them, that we think it not lawful nor tolerable for them, being by God's ordinance subjects, to call her, who also by God's ordinance is their superior and Prince, to answer to their accusations by way of force; for we do not think it consonant in nature the head should be subject to the foot.' Finally, Elizabeth charged Throckmorton to inform the Lords of the Secret Council, that 'if they shall determine anything to the deprivation of the Queen their sovereign lady of her royal estate, we are well assured of our own determination, and we have some just and probable cause to think the like of other Princes of Christendom, that we will make ourselves a plain party against them, to the revenge of their sovereign, and for example to all posterity."[1]

But these reasons and menaces neither persuaded nor intimidated the Scottish lords. They boldly carried out their designs, and, in company with many members of the Parliament, repaired to Stirling on the day appointed for the coronation.[2] The ceremony took place with great solemnity in the High Church of the city. In the procession, Athol bore the crown, Morton the sceptre, and Glencairn the sword, whilst Mar carried the infant Prince in his arms into the church. After the deeds of resignation by the Queen had been read, and Lindsay and Ruthven had sworn that Mary's demission was her own free act, Morton, laying his hand upon the Gospels, took the oaths on behalf of the new monarch, James VI. The Bishop of Orkney then crowned the baby-king, the lords swore allegiance, placing their hands on his head, and Knox inaugurated his stormy reign by a sermon.[3] This revolution, which had been entirely accomplished by a few of the nobility, whose supremacy it insured during the long minority of a sovereign only thirteen months old, met with the hearty concurrence of the people, who manifested their joy by bonfires, dances, and illuminations.[4] It encountered no opposition in any part of the kingdom, which the leaders of the confederates continued to govern, until the return of Murray, who had been informed without delay of his appointment as Regent of Scotland.

[1] Keith, pp. 428, 429.
[2] The names of the nobles present at the ceremony are given in 'An Authentick Account of the whole progress of the King's Coronation,' printed at length in Keith, pp. 437-439, from the registers of the Privy Council.
[3] Keith, p. 438. Throckmorton to Elizabeth, 31st July, 1567; in Stevenson's Selections, p. 257. Calderwood's MS. History, p. 684; quoted in Tytler, vol. v., p. 454.
[4] Throckmorton to Elizabeth, 31st July, 1567; Tytler, vol. v., p. 454.

Murray, who had spent the last four months in France, had been successively informed of the pretended abdication of Mary Stuart, her disgraceful marriage, her speedy defeat, her harsh captivity, and the rapid succession of her follies and misfortunes. He had been touched with compassion for her, and had not yet lost all feelings of fidelity towards her. Thus, notwithstanding the care which the confederate lords had taken to write to him, in order to gain him to their cause, he had disapproved of their violent proceedings, and had sent Elphinstone to remonstrate severely with them for having imprisoned the Queen.[1] On being informed not long afterwards of the deposition of his sister, the coronation of his nephew, and his own elevation to the Regency, he had set out for Scotland with views still favourable to the captive Queen. He had, however, declined to give any pledge to the Court of France, which had offered him high bribes, and appointed M. de Ligneroles to accompany him and watch his proceedings. The avowed object of this envoy was to carry a message from Charles IX. to the Lords of the Secret Council, and to advocate the interests of Mary Stuart, and the maintenance of the alliance between the two countries.[2] Murray's feelings underwent a change upon his journey. He met Elphinstone[3] coming back from Scotland, where the confederate lords, in order to justify their conduct, had endeavoured to convince him of the Queen's culpability by means of the papers found in the silver casket. Elphinstone assured Murray that he had seen and read a letter from the Queen to Bothwell, which proved that she was privy to her husband's murder.[4]

Either from ambition, or from more exact information upon the state of Scotland, Murray was less ardent for his sister's liberation when he arrived at London. Elizabeth, who took great interest in Mary's position on this occasion, did not act wisely towards him. Irritated by the blow which had been struck at the sovereign

[1] Tytler, vol. v., pp. 445, 461.
[2] MS. letters, State Paper Office, Morris to Cecil, 2nd and 16th July, 1567; Stevenson's Collections, p. 243. Tytler, vol. v., p. 462.
[3] Tytler, vol. v., p. 463.
[4] 'Mostró sentir mucho que la junta de Edimburg hubiese preso á la Reyna, pero que á el siempre la habia parecido mal lo de Bodwel ; que el sabia de cierto de una carta, toda de mano de la Reyna Maria de mas de tres pliegos, escrita á Bodwel, en que le apresuraba á poner en obra lo que tenian concertado sobre la muerte del Rey, dandole algun bebedizo, ó en todo apuro, quemando la casa, que aunque él no habia visto la carta, lo sabia per persona que la habia leido.' Gonzalez, Apuntamientos, in the Memorias de la Real Academia, vol. vii., p. 323. Throckmorton to Cecil, 2nd August, 1567, in Stevenson's Collections, p. 263.

authority in Scotland, she haughtily expressed her determination to restore Mary Stuart to her throne, and to punish the audacious subjects who had deposed her.[1] Murray was offended at the menacing and dictatorial tone which Elizabeth had employed, with so little success, in her communications with the Scottish lords by means of Throckmorton. Far from being thereby useful to the unfortunate prisoner, she had only added to the dangers of her position; and it would seem that she was destined to injure her even by her efforts to do her service. In fact, the confederates who had dethroned Mary Stuart had not entirely renounced the idea of bringing her to trial. With monstrous treason and sanguinary calculation, the Hamiltons had proposed that she should be put to death, as the only certain method of reconciling all parties. By getting rid of the Queen, who might otherwise marry again and have many children, the Hamiltons hoped to reach the throne, from which they would then be separated only by a weakly infant. The Archbishop of St. Andrews, the Abbot of Kilwinning, and the Earl of Huntly accordingly offered to make an agreement with the confederate lords upon these terms. The Comptroller Murray of Tullibardine, and Secretary Lethington, both informed Throckmorton of this horrible negotiation. Indeed, when Elizabeth's ambassador mentioned the threatening designs of his mistress, Lethington said to him: 'My Lord Ambassador, I assure you, if you should use this speech unto them (the confederates) which you do unto me, all the world could not save the Queen's life three days to an end.'[2]

Such was the imminent danger to which Mary Stuart was exposed when Murray, after having left London very dissatisfied with Elizabeth, arrived in Scotland on the 11th of August. His return and future policy were the objects of universal expectation. At Berwick he was met by two envoys from the lords of the confederacy, Sir James Makgill, the Clerk-register, and Sir James Melvil. The first was the representative of the fanatical section among them, and was to entreat him, in the name of Glencairn, Morton, Lindsay, Ruthven, and the Presbyterians, to act inexorably towards the Queen, and not allow himself to be influenced by her misfortunes. The second, who shared the more moderate

---

[1] MS. letter, State Paper Office, Bedford to Cecil, 10th August, 1567, after his interview with Murray at Berwick. Tytler, vol. v., p. 463.
[2] MS. letter, State Paper Office, Throckmorton to Elizabeth, 9th August, 1567; Tytler, vol. v., p. 458. From this previously unpublished despatch, Mr. Tytler has constructed the very full account of this negotiation which will be found in his History, vol. v., pp. 456-459.

P

sentiments of Athol, Mar, Lethington, Tullibardine, and Grange, who had joined the league in order to overthrow Bothwell, and save the Prince Royal, had been deputed by them to urge him to adopt no extreme measures, but, whilst keeping the Queen in captivity until her liberation could produce no dangerous results, to treat her mercifully and respectfully.[1] Murray listened to them both, but refused to give any pledge. He even appeared to have no desire to become Regent.[2] Pursuing his journey, he crossed the Scottish frontier, where he was met by a troop of four hundred gentlemen.[3] He entered Edinburgh, surrounded by the nobility, and amid manifestations of the delight and enthusiasm of the citizens. For two days he remained uncertain, questioning everybody, examining into the charges brought against the Queen, and observing that public opinion regarding her wore a threatening aspect. Before accepting the office which had been conferred on him, he requested that he might see her, in order to learn from her own lips whether it were true that her abdication had been voluntary, and would not vitiate his title to the Regency. In spite of their fears about the result of the interview which was to determine his answer, the lords were obliged to consent ;[4] and on the morning of the 15th of August he proceeded to Lochleven with Morton, Athol, and Lindsay.[5]

Prudent in his ambition, Murray was desirous to receive the power offered him by the confederates, from the hands of her whom the confederates had robbed of her crown. He had taken no part in the recent occurrences, and if the Queen conferred the supreme authority upon him, he hoped to be able to administer the government of Scotland without difficulty, as he had obtained it without revolt. He secured his object with cruel craftiness. On seeing him enter her prison, Mary thought that her brother had come to be her friend and protector. She burst into a flood of tears, and passionately complained of the unjust treatment she had experienced. Murray listened to her in silence, and neither commiserated nor consoled her. The suppliant Mary then said, turning towards Athol and Morton : 'My lords, you have had experience of my severity, and of the end of it; I pray you also let me find that you have learned by me to make an end of yours, or, at least, that you can make it final.'[6] But they were as taci

---

[1] Melvil's Memoirs, p. 87. Tytler, vol. v., p. 464.
[2] Keith, p. 443. Melvil's Memoirs, p. 87.
[3] Tytler, vol. v., p. 464.   [4] Ibid., p. 466.
[5] Throckmorton to Elizabeth, 20th August, 1567 ; Keith, p. 445.
[6] Ibid., p. 446.

turn and gloomy as Murray. Alarmed at a visit that seemed to confirm the sinister reports which had been spread concerning her, Mary took her brother aside before supper, anxiously questioned him as to the intentions of the lords, and in vain endeavoured to fathom his own projects; but for two hours Murray continued silent and impenetrable. When the bitter meal had passed away, Mary again desired to converse with her brother, 'and everybody being retired, they conferred together until one of the clock after midnight.'¹ In this second interview Murray threw off his premeditated reserve, and spoke to the Queen with terrible frankness and inexorable severity. He told her what he thought of herself and her misgovernment, pitilessly reminded her of her improprieties of conduct, and laid before her, one by one, all the actions which, he said, had violated her conscience, sullied her honour, and compromised her safety. The unhappy Queen was plunged into despair by this terrible accusation, and she lost all courage. 'Sometimes,' says Throckmorton, in his narrative of this painful scene, 'she wept bitterly; sometimes she acknowledged her unadvisedness and misgovernment; some things she did confess plainly; some things she did excuse; some things she did extenuate.'² After having crushed her with the weight of these dreadful recollections, Murray left his sister in an agony of fear; she thought that her fate was sealed, and that she must expect nothing but from God's mercy. In this state of mind she passed the remainder of the night.

The next morning she sent for her brother, and Murray once more entered her room. Perceiving the impression he had made, he assumed a milder mood, changed his tone, threw in some words of consolation, and assured her that he desired to save her life, and, if possible, to preserve her honour. 'But,' he added, 'it is not in my power only; the lords and others have interest in the matter. Notwithstanding, Madam, I will declare to you which be the occasions that may put you in jeopardy. For your peril, these be they:—your own practices to disturb the quiet of your realm and the reign of your son; to enterprise to escape from where you are, to put yourself at liberty; to animate any of your subjects to troubles or disobedience; the Queen of England or the French King to molest this realm, either with their war, or with war intestine, by your procurement or otherwise; and your own persisting in this inordinate affection with the Earl Bothwell.'³

At these words, Mary, who had remained under the dreadful

Throckmorton to Elizabeth, 20th August, 1567; in Keith, p. 445.
Keith, p. 445. ³ Ibid., p. 446.

impressions of the previous night, discerned a gleam of hope. She threw herself into her brother's arms, and expressed her satisfaction at his assurance that he would protect her life, and the hopes he allowed her to entertain that her honour would be saved. In order to arrive more surely at this desired result, she conjured him not to refuse the Regency, ' for by this means,' she said, ' my son shall be preserved, my realm well governed, and I in safety.'[1] Murray hesitated; and alleged reasons, the sincerity of which we cannot suspect, against undertaking so arduous a task. Always hurried away by irresistible impulses, Mary only entreated him the more urgently to sacrifice his own repugnance to the welfare of his sister. She suggested that he should make himself master of all the forts in the kingdom, requested him to take her jewels and other valuables into his custody, and offered to give to his Regency the support of her letters and the authority of her name. Murray at length assented, appearing to accept with resignation what he doubtless most ardently coveted. Before leaving his sister he enjoined the Lords Lindsay, Ruthven, and Lochleven, ' to treat the Queen with gentleness, with liberty, and with all other good usage.' He then bade her farewell, ' and then began another fit of weeping, which being appeased, she embraced him very lovingly, kissed him, and sent her blessing unto the Prince her son by him.'[2]

On this, as on so many other occasions, Mary Stuart yielded to one of those rapid momentary impressions which so frequently guided her conduct, and set at nought the dictates of prudence. At Lochleven she displayed the same character as at the Kirk of Field, Almond Bridge, Carberry Hill, and shortly afterwards at Carlisle, always yielding to invincible passions or deceptive opinions. After having been terrified into signing her deed of abdication, she had been surprised into giving her consent to it. This consent, which she ere long repented, had been obtained from her by the cold and astute Murray, whilst her troubled heart was passing from intense alarm to buoyant hope.

Assured of her important approbation, Murray proceeded to Stirling to visit the infant monarch, in whose name he was to govern, and returned to Edinburgh on the 19th of August.[3] Three days after he was declared Regent in the Council-chamber at the Tolbooth. Laying his hand upon the Gospels, like a true sectary and ardent supporter of the liberties of the realm, he took the following oath : ' I, James, Earl of Murray, Lord Abernethy, promise faithfully, in the presence of the Eternal, my God,

[1] Keith, p. 445.   [2] Ibid., p. 446.   [3] Ibid.

that I, during the whole course of my life, will serve the same Eternal, my God, to the uttermost of my power, according as He requires in His most holy word, revealed and contained in the New and Old Testaments; and, according to the same word, will maintain the true religion of Jesus Christ, the preaching of His holy word, and due and right administration of His sacraments, now received and practised within this realm; and also will abolish and withstand all false religion contrary to the same; and will rule the people committed to my charge and regiment during the minority and less-age of the King, my sovereign, according to the will and command of God revealed in his aforesaid word, and according to the loveable laws and constitutions received in this realm, noways repugnant to the said word of the Eternal, my God; and will procure to my uttermost, to the Kirk of God and all Christian people, true and perfect peace, in all time coming. The rights and rents, with all just privileges of the Crown of Scotland, I will preserve and keep inviolate; neither will I transfer nor alienate the same. I will forbid and repress in all estates and degrees, reif, oppression, and all kind of wrong. In all judgments I will command and procure that justice and equity be kept to all creatures without exception, as He be merciful to me and you, that is the lord and father of all mercies; and out of this realm of Scotland, and empire thereof, I will be careful to root out all heretics and enemies to the true worship of God, that shall be convicted by the true Kirk of God of the aforesaid crimes. And these things above-written I faithfully affirm by this my solemn oath.'[1] The seventy-third psalm was then sung,[2] and Murray was proclaimed Regent at the Market Cross, amid the acclamations of the people.[3]

The revolution which had dethroned Mary Stuart, and transferred the government to other hands, had now reached its consummation. Most of the dissident nobility submitted to the new ruler. The Earls of Rothes and Crawford, the Masters of Menteith and Errol, the Lords Drummond, Ogilvy, Oliphant, Somerville, Borthwick, and Yester, assured the Regent of their obedience and fidelity; and the Lords Fleming, Boyd, and Livingstone ere long followed their example.[4] The Hamiltons attempted no resistance, although Elizabeth had given them every encouragement to do so.[5] Murray encountered as little opposi-

[1] Anderson, vol. ii., pp. 252, 253. Keith, p. 453.
[2] 'Après il mist la main sur la Bible, puis fut chanté le 73ᵉ psaume.' Teulet, vol. ii., p. 194. [3] Keith, p. 454.
[4] Throckmorton to Elizabeth, 20th August, 1567; in Keith, p. 447.
[5] Elizabeth to Throckmorton, 29th August, 1567; in Keith, pp. 451, 452.

tion abroad as at home. The Court of France, pre-occupied with its own difficulties, and wearied by the faults of Mary Stuart, was unwilling to break with the new government, for fear of throwing Scotland entirely into the arms of England. Accordingly M. de Ligneroles, in some measure abandoning the Queen, assured the confederates that he not been sent to do them any injury, and that France was the ally not of any particular Prince, but of the established government in Scotland.¹ He departed without even complaining that he had not been allowed to visit the Queen, and authorized to confer with the Hamiltons.²

As for Elizabeth, although greatly irritated at the changes effected by the lords, and accepted by Murray, in spite of her admonitions to the contrary, she had neither means nor reasons for restoring Mary to her throne, and overthrowing the Regent. This was perfectly understood by the confederates. They took no notice of her anger, and when the English ambassador, Throckmorton, left Scotland after the proclamation of the Regent, he had a last interview with Murray and Lethington. He found them both full of resolution, and ready for resistance. 'If there be no remedy,' said Lethington, ' but that the Queen your Sovereign will make war, and nourish war against us, we can but be sorry for it, and do the best we may. But, to put you out of doubt, we had rather endure the fortune thereof, and suffer the sequel, than to put the Queen to liberty now in this mood that she is in, being resolved to retain Bothwell and to fortify him, to hazard the life of her son, to put the realm in peril, and to forfeit all these noblemen. You must think, my lord ambassador, your wars are not unknown to us; you will burn our borders, and we will do the like to yours; and whensoever you invade us, we are sure France will aid us.' Then, to show his resentment of the imperious tone which Elizabeth had assumed towards them, he finished by telling Throckmorton: ' Much strange language has been used, but it is enough to reply that we are another Prince's subjects, and know not the Queen's majesty to be our sovereign.' Murray was more brief, but quite as peremptory. He told Elizabeth's ambassador, who had attempted to separate his cause from that of the confederates, by reminding him that he was a stranger to what they had done: ' Though I were not here at the doings past, yet surely I must allow of them ; and seeing the Queen and they have laid upon me the charge of the Regency, (a burden which I would gladly have eschewed,) I do mean to ware my

¹ Melvil's Memoirs, p. 87. Keith, p. 443.
² Throckmorton to Elizabeth, 20th August, 1567; in Keith, p. 444.

life in defence of their action, and will either reduce all men to obedience in the King's name, or it shall cost me my life.'[1]

The intention which he thus proudly declared, was carried into effect by him with great vigour. Like a true disciple of Knox, well versed in the narratives of the Bible, ' he went stoutly to work,' says Throckmorton, ' resolved to imitate those who had led the people of Israel.'[2] The Lairds of Grange and Tullibardine were instantly despatched by the Privy Council in pursuit of Bothwell, who had been outlawed by proclamation on the 26th of June, and had fled to Orkney.[3] Murray's next care was to secure to himself all the fortresses in the kingdom.[4] Balfour delivered the Castle of Edinburgh into his hands. But this infamous accomplice of Bothwell's crimes would not give up the keys of the fortress until he had received the sum of five thousand pounds, and an assurance of impunity; and had stipulated that an annuity should be given to his son, and the Priory of Pittenweem to himself.[5] Murray, who had soon gained possession of Dunbar, Inchkeith, and other strongholds,[6] determined to commit the guard of Edinburgh Castle to Laird Kirkaldy of Grange[7] who was then in pursuit of Bothwell. The bold Kirkaldy had sworn to capture this public enemy, and very nearly succeeded in doing so. Of the three or four vessels which Bothwell had equipped, and with which he attempted to maintain a footing in the Orkney and Shetland Isles, two fell into the hands of the Laird of Grange, who was in hot pursuit of the one commanded by Bothwell himself, when his own ship, one of the largest in the Scottish navy, struck upon a sand-bank.[8] Bothwell succeeded in making his escape; and leaving a locality where he was no longer safe, sailed into the Northern Ocean, and was driven by a tempest to the coast of Norway. Here he fell in with a Danish man-of-war, and not being able to produce his papers, was arrested as a pirate, and taken to Denmark. Frederic II., who then occupied the throne of that country, would not give him up either to Murray

---

[1] Keith, p. 449.
[2] Throckmorton to Cecil, 20th August, 1567; in Stevenson's Selections, p. 282; and Tytler, vol. vi., p. 20.
[3] Anderson's Collections, vol. i., pp. 139-145. Keith, p. 442. Tytler, vol. vi., p. 20.
[4] Tytler, vol. vi., p. 21.
[5] Keith, p. 455. MS. letter, State Paper Office, Throckmorton to Cecil, 26th August, 1567; Tytler, vol. vi., p. 21.
[6] Keith, pp. 456, 459.   [7] Ibid., p. 455.
[8] Labanoff, vol. ii., p. 59. Robertson, vol. ii., p. 233. MS. letter, State Paper Office, Murray to Cecil, 11th September, 1567; Tytler, vol. vi., p. 23.

or Elizabeth, but imprisoned him in the castle of Malmoe. His captivity was an expiation of nine years, which he passed in the dread of being surrendered to the governments of Scotland or England, which were unceasingly demanding his extradition, and in the despair of interminable solitude.[1]

Several of his subaltern accomplices were, however, brought to punishment. In addition to Powrie and Dalgleish, Hay of Tallo, and Hepburn of Bolton, the chief actors in the crime at Kirk of Field, had been arrested.[2] They all confessed their guilt, and were condemned to death. On the scaffold they acknowledged the justice of their punishment, and Hepburn of Bolton addressed the people. 'Let no man,' he said, 'do evil by the counsel of great men, or their masters, thinking they will save them; for surely I thought, on that night that the deed was done, that although it might become known, no man durst have said it was evilly done, seeing the handwritings of those who approved it, and the Queen's consent thereto.'[3]

But those to whom Hepburn thus alluded were too powerful to be punished. The bond which they had signed, and which constituted the evidence of their guilt, had been left by Bothwell in the custody of Sir James Balfour, who had committed it to the flames.[4] Neither Lethington, Huntly, Argyle and Balfour, who had signed their concurrence in the crime; nor the Archbishop of St. Andrews, who had verbally consented to its perpetration; nor Morton, who had been informed of the intentions of the conspirators, although he had not joined in their league, were brought to trial before the justice of their country, which was inexorable or inactive, according to the rank and position of the culprit. The Regent did not dare to act with severity towards them. They had raised him to power, and his tenure was still so insecure that a new revolution would easily have overthrown him. He was therefore obliged to bestow favours, instead of punishment, upon several of their number. Argyle remained Lord Justice-

[1] See a small quarto volume of 31 pages and an appendix, entitled *Les Affaires du Conte de Boduel, l'an* 1568, printed in 1829, by the Bannatyne Club at Edinburgh, from the original in the Royal Collection at Drottningholm, in Sweden.
[2] These four men were executed on the 3rd of January, 1568. Keith, p. 467.
[3] Anderson's Collections, vol. ii., p. 160.
[4] 'The writings which did comprehend the names and consents of the chief for the murdering of the King, is turned into ashes, the same not unknown to the Queen; and the same that concerns her part kept to be shown, which offends her. MS. Letter, State Paper Office, Drury to Cecil, 28th November, 1567; Tytler vol. vi., p. 30.

General, Huntly continued a member of the Privy Council, Lethington was appointed Sheriff of Lothian, and Morton was promised the Lord High-Admiralship of Scotland, vacant by the forfeiture of Bothwell.[1]

In this land of violence, treason, inconsistency, and political iniquity, the Regent was determined at least to enforce the observance of the common laws of the realm, and to maintain the safety of the state with strenuous vigour. 'He took great pains,' says Melvil, 'to steal secret roads upon the thieves on the borders, tending much to the quieting thereof: he likewise held justice-ayres in the in-country.'[2] The Parliament, which he had convoked for the 15th of December, was extremely numerous. Four bishops, fourteen abbots, twelve earls, sixteen lords and eldest sons of lords, and twenty-seven commissioners of burghs were present.[3] This Parliament enacted religious uniformity, by ratifying the Confession of Faith of 1560, and sanctioning the entire abolition of Catholicism; it resumed from the laymen a third of that ecclesiastical property which they had seized, and applied it to the support of ministers and schools belonging to the Reformed Church;[4] it recognized the legal elevation of the young King to the throne of Scotland,[5] sanctioned the appointment of the Regent,[6] and keenly debated the course to be pursued with regard to the Queen—some wishing to bring her at once to trial, while others desired merely to retain her in captivity.[7] The more moderate party gained the victory; but, in order to justify the confederate lords for having taken arms, imprisoned, and dethroned their sovereign, the Parliament passed an act, by the terms of which Mary Stuart was seriously criminated. It contains the following clause: 'That the cause, and all things depending thereon, were in the Queen's own default, in so far as by divers her privy letters, written wholely with her own hand, and sent by her to James, sometime Earl of Bothwell, chief executor of the said horrible murder, as well before the committing thereof, as thereafter; and by her ungodly and dishonourable proceeding to a pretended marriage with him, suddenly and immediately thereafter, it is most certain that she was privy to it and part of the afore-named murder of the King her lawful husband, committed by the said James, sometime Earl of Bothwell, his complices and partakers.'[8]

[1] MS. letter, State Paper Office, Drury to Cecil, 4th January, 1568; Tytler, vol. vi., p. 34.   [2] Melvil's Memoirs, p. 90.   [3] Keith, pp. 465, 466.
[4] Spotswood, p. 214. Tytler, vol. vi., pp. 26-28.
[5] See the Act of Parliament, in Anderson, vol. ii., p. 206.   [6] Ibid., p. 215.
[7] Tytler, vol. v., p. 28.   [8] Anderson's Collections, vol. ii., pp. 221, 222.

This harsh expression of opinion, tantamount to a condemnation, rendered Mary Stuart's captivity more stringent, although by Murray's orders she was treated with respect and consideration. She was more closely watched, lest she should write to request the assistance of any foreign power, or should devise a plan for her escape with her friends in Scotland. She was able to write only while her keepers were at their meals or asleep, for the daughters of the castellan slept with her.[1] But all these precautions proved insufficient. Her beauty, grace, and misfortunes exercised an irresistible influence upon all around her. One of Margaret Erskine's sons, George Douglas, a half-brother of the Regent, became smitten by her beauty and touched by her afflictions. Soon he fell deeply in love with his seductive prisoner, who did not check his hopes,[2] and he resolved to deliver her. On one occasion, eluding the vigilance of his mother, he conducted Mary Stuart from the castle in the garb of a laundress, who was in the the habit of bringing her clothes to Lochleven.[3] In this disguise the captive passed all the gates undiscovered. She had entered the boat which was to convey her to the other side of the lake, where George Douglas, Semple, and Beton awaited her arrival.[4] She thought her escape was now certain; but, when they were about half way across, one of the boatmen, not suspecting who she was, came near her, and jocularly attempted to raise her veil. Mary hastily raised her hand to prevent him from seeing her face, and the boatman, on seeing her beautiful white hand, at once guessed that it was the Queen he had on board.[5] Thus discovered, Mary put a bold face on the matter, and commanded the boatmen, on pain of death, to carry her to the other side; but

---

[1] 'Je suis guestée de si près, que je n'ay loisir que durant leur diner, ou quand ils dorment, que je me reslesve: car leurs filles couschent avecques moy.' Mary Stuart to Catherine de Medici, Lochleven, 1st May, 1568; Labanoff, vol. ii., p. 69.—'Je n'ai ni papier ni temps pour écrire davantage, sinon prier le Roi, la Reine, et mes oncles de brûler mes lettres: car si l'on sait que j'ai écrit, il coûtera la vie à beaucoup et mettra la mienne à hasard, et me fera garder plus étroitement.' Mary Stuart to the Archbishop of Glasgow, Lochleven, 31st March, 1568; Labanoff, vol. ii., p. 66.

[2] Letter from Drury to Cecil, 3rd April, 1568; in Keith, p. 469.

[3] 'There cometh in to her the landress early as other times before she was wonted, and the Queen putteth on her the weed of the landress, and so with the furdel of cloaths and her muffler upon her face, passeth out.' Keith, p. 470.

[4] Ibid.

[5] 'After some space, one of them that rowed said merrily: "Let us see what manner of dame this is," and therewith offered to pull down her muffler, which to defend she put up her hands, which they spied to be very fair and white, wherewith they entered into suspicion whom she was.' Ibid.

they, fearing the severity of the Laird of Lochleven more than the threats of a deposed princess, took her back to the castle.

After this unsuccessful attempt on the 25th of March, George Douglas was sent from the Castle, but he did not, however, leave the neighbourhood of the lake.[1] The prisoner, now almost hopeless of regaining that liberty which she had so nearly attained, passed the end of March and the whole of April in all the anguish and discomfort of captivity. She sought aid on every hand, and wrote to Catherine de Medici:—' I have with great difficulty despatched the bearer of this to inform you of my misery, and entreat you to have pity upon me.'[2] On the 1st of May, she addressed Queen Elizabeth in terms of the most earnest supplication, assuring her that if she would come to her assistance, she would never have a more affectionate relation in the world. ' You may also consider,' she added ' the importance of the example practised against me.' In conclusion, she called upon God to preserve the English Queen from all misfortune, and to grant herself the patience of which she stood in need.[3] On the same day she wrote to invoke the support of Catherine de Medici and Charles IX., telling them: ' Unless you deliver me by force, I shall never leave this place.'[4]

But while she deemed herself thus irrevocably doomed to imprisonment for life, the hour of her deliverance was close at hand. George Douglas devoted himself to her cause with all the ardour and ingenuity of a lover, and busied himself with plans for her escape. Remaining in the immediate vicinity of Lochleven, he kept up constant communication with the castle, by means of one of his mother's pages, called Little Douglas. In concert with this page, who was only sixteen years old, he made his preparations for the Queen's escape; and he arranged that Lord Seton and the Hamiltons should be in readiness to receive her as soon as she had left the castle. Sunday, the 2nd of May, was the day appointed for the execution of this second flight, which, as it was better contrived than the first, had a more successful issue. All the household took their meals together at Lochleven, and whilst they were at table, the doors of the fortress were all closed, and the keys placed on the table, beside the castellan. At the evening meal on the day appointed,[5] Little

[1] Keith, p. 471. Tytler, vol. vi., p. 36.
[2] Mary Stuart to Catherine de Medici, Lochleven, 31st March, 1568; in Labanoff, vol. ii., p. 64.
[3] Mary Stuart to Queen Elizabeth, 1st May, 1568; Ibid., p. 68.
[4] Mary Stuart to Catherine de Medici, 1st May, 1568; Ibid., p. 69.
[5] Mary escaped from Lochleven at nine o'clock on Sunday evening, according to the account given two days afterwards to Villiers de Beaumont, the French ambas-

Douglas, in placing a plate before the laird, contrived to drop his napkin over the keys of the castle, and carried them off unperceived. He immediately hastened to inform the Queen of what he had done, and she at once joined him, in the dress of one of her serving-women. They got out of the castle without difficulty, and the young page locked the gate behind them, to prevent pursuit. They then threw themselves into a little boat, unmoored it with all speed, and rowed across the lake. On reaching the shore, Mary, springing out with the lightness of recovered freedom, was received first by George Douglas, and almost instantly after by Lord Seton and his friends, who had remained concealed in a neighbouring village.[1] Once more in possession of her liberty, and hopeful that she would soon regain her power, she sprang lightly and joyously on horseback, and rode off at full speed towards the west. She galloped on till she came to Niddry Castle, Lord Seton's residence in West Lothian. Here she took a few hours' rest, and then pursued her journey to the strong fortress of Hamilton, where she was received by the Archbishop of St. Andrews, and Lord Claud Hamilton, the latter of whom had met her on the road with fifty horse.[2]

On arriving at this place of safety, she issued an appeal to all her partisans. She despatched Hepburn of Riccarton, one of Bothwell's servants, to Dunbar, with the hope that the castle would be delivered to her, and commanded him to proceed afterwards to Denmark and inform his master that she was again at liberty, and would doubtless soon recover her lost authority.[3] At the same time that her first thoughts were turned towards him from whom she had been separated by adverse circumstances, but whom she had never ceased to love, Mary Stuart despatched John Beton,[4] brother of the Archbishop of Glasgow, into France

---

sador, by John Beton, who was a party to her escape, and who was sent immediately by Mary into France to request assistance. 'Elle se sauva Dimanche, à neuf heures du soir, comme vous le dira le sieur de Béthon, présent porteur.' M. de Beaumont to Charles IX., 5th May, 1568; in Teulet, vol. ii., p. 203, note.

[1] 'Modo che la Regina di Scotia ha usato per liberarsi dalla prigione.' This narrative, annexed to a despatch addressed, on the 21st May, 1568, by Petrucci, the Tuscan ambassador at Paris, to his master, the Grand Duke, Cosmo I., was derived from information supplied by John Beton, on his arrival at the French Court. It was extracted from the Medicean Archives at Florence by Prince Labanoff, and will be found in his Collection, vol. vii., pp. 135-138.

[2] Tytler, vol. vi., p. 37.

[3] MS. Memoir towards Riccartoun, State Paper Office; Tytler, vol. vi., p. 37.

[4] Keith, pp. 472, 473.

to request assistance in the struggle which was now about to recommence, but which she did not expect would reach so speedy a termination

The news of her escape flew rapidly through the kingdom, and was received with joy by a large portion of her nobility. All those who had stood by her on former occasions, all those who had forgotten her errors in their compassion for her misfortunes, and all those who had been offended by Murray's stern and haughty administration, crowded round her with devoted offers of homage and support. The greater number of the nobility declared in her favour. Before many days had elapsed, nine earls, nine bishops, eighteen lords, twelve abbots and priors, and nearly a hundred barons, had signed a league to restore her to her throne.[1] She now assembled her Council, revoked her abdication as having been extorted by the imminent fear of death, and declared all the acts, by which Murray had become Regent, treasonable and of none effect. The Earls of Argyle, Cassillis, Eglinton, and Rothes; the Lords Somerville, Yester, Livingstone, Herries, Fleming, Ross, Borthwick, and many other barons of power and note, joined the Hamiltons and Setons with their vassals, and Mary soon found herself at the head of an army of six thousand men,[2] determined to defend her person and restore her authority. The French ambassador, Villiers de Beaumont, who had just been sent into Scotland by Charles IX.,[3] repaired to her camp, saying that he recognized in her the real sovereign of the country. Queen Elizabeth, on her part, sent Dr. Leighton to congratulate her on her deliverance, and to offer to compel her subjects to obedience, if she would place her affairs in her hands, and abstain from calling in any foreign aid.[4]

Mary was not overwhelmed by this return of fortune. She preferred an accommodation to a conflict with her adversaries, for she was fully aware that a victory, by force of arms, was not only uncertain, but might be dangerous. If conquered, she would fall again into the formidable hands of the Regent; if victorious, she would remain at the mercy of the Hamiltons, who

---

[1] This bond, signed on the 8th May, is printed in Keith, pp. 475-477, with the names of those who subscribed it.   [2] Keith, p. 472.

[3] He arrived at Edinburgh on the 22nd April, 1568, and gave letters from Charles IX. to several Scottish lords, ' Que j'ay trouvés,' he says, ' fort affectionnés à son service, et (à celui) de la Royne sa sœur, leur prisonniere, leur naturelle princesse.'   M. de Beaumont to the Queen Mother, 4th May, 1568; in Teulet, vol. ii., p. 203.

[4] MS., State Paper Office, ' Instructions for Mr. Thomas Leighton, sent into Scotland;' Tytler, vol. vi., p. 40.

intended to marry her to one of their family, and to govern in her name.¹ She therefore judged it more prudent, if possible, to effect a reconciliation between the two parties, and by counterbalancing one by the other, to avoid being subject to either. She therefore sent to Murray to propose an amicable arrangement, to be negotiated by the French ambassador and the two brothers, Robert and James Melvil, the former of whom had joined the Queen, whilst the latter remained with the Regent.²

Murray was at Glasgow, alone, with no other escort than his personal suite, and engaged in holding a Court of Justice, when his sister escaped from Lochleven, and arrived at Hamilton Castle, not eight miles from the place where he was. Any other man would have left the city, in fear of being attacked and surprised by forces so far superior to his own. This he was urgently requested to do, but he absolutely refused;³ feeling that his retreat from Glasgow would be a mark of fear, and would act as a signal for all his followers to desert him. He therefore remained at his post with unflinching courage. He requested time to reflect upon Mary Stuart's overtures,⁴ in order that he might collect his troops and fight a battle which should settle the question between himself and his sister, between the lords of the King's party and those who adhered to the Queen. Under these difficult circumstances, he displayed that rapid decision and clearness of judgment which mark a great man. He hastily summoned his friends to the standard of the young King. His resolution gave courage to those who would have wavered if he had been inactive or undecided, and most of the old confederate barons, and the soldiers of the Presbyterian towns, rapidly joined him. Dunbar remained faithful to him;⁵ Edinburgh furnished him with four hundred hackbutters; and Glasgow armed in his cause.⁶ The Earl of Mar despatched reinforcements and cannon from Stirling;⁷ the valiant Alexander Hume brought him six hundred lances from the Merse country; the energetic Morton, the ardent Glencairn, and the veteran Kirkaldy speedily arrived with their vassals, and, in ten days after the escape of the Queen, the Regent found himself at the head of an army of four thousand resolute

---

¹ Keith, p. 478.
² Letter from Drury to Cecil, 7th May, 1568; in Keith, p. 474.
³ Tytler, vol. vi., p. 38.
⁴ Letter from Drury to Cecil, 7th May, 1568; in Keith, p. 474.
⁵ Tytler, vol. vi., p. 39.
⁶ Letter from Drury to Cecil, 7th May, 1568; in Keith, p. 475.
⁷ Letter from Drury to Throckmorton, 9th May, 1568; in Teulet, vol. ii., pp. 208, 209.

men. He therefore proposed to attack the Queen's army without delay, before she received the reinforcements which the Earl o Huntly and Lord Ogilvy were bringing from the northern districts of the kingdom.

But if Murray had good reasons for wishing to fight, it was equally the Queen's interest to refuse a battle. If she could only gain time, her success was certain. Either from distrust or prudence, she was anxious to retire to the impregnable fortress of Dumbarton,[1] which was not far from Glasgow, and whose governor, Lord Fleming, was one of her staunchest adherents.[3] But the Hamiltons, finding themselves the strongest party, were determined to fight. They confidently expected a victory, and hoped, by the same blow, to crush their ancient enemy, the Regent, and to secure their own ascendancy over the Queen and government. So far, however, Mary's influence prevailed, that they consented to march from Hamilton to Dumbarton, and to accept a battle if the enemy should attack them on their march. This was the worst course they could have pursued, for it exposed them to the chance of having to fight whilst in retreat, which is always very dangerous, as it is then impossible to select either opportunity or position. Mary Stuart had fatal experience of this, on the 13th of May, eleven days after her escape from Lochleven.

Her army, which lay on the left bank of the Clyde, had to pass to the south of Glasgow, on its way to Dumbarton. In order to guard this road, the Regent sent a strong body of his troops to occupy an advantageous position on that side of the river. In accordance with the advice of the experienced Laird of Grange, he occupied the heights of Langside with the main body of his forces, and posted an ambush of hackbutters in a lane through which the Queen's army would have to pass before it could reach the hill. In this defile, which was intersected with hedges, and studded with houses and plantations, the Queen's cavalry, though infinitely more numerous than those of the Regent, would not be able to act to advantage, whilst her infantry would be exposed to inevitable defeat. Accordingly when the Hamiltons, at the head of the vanguard, two thousand strong, attempted to carry the lane, a close and deadly fire from the ambushed hackbutters threw them into confusion. They then pressed forward

---

[1] MS., State Paper Office, Advertisements of the Conflict in Scotland, 16th May, 1568. Tytler, vol. vi., p. 39.
[2] Keith, pp. 475-477. Tytler, vol. vi., p. 40.
[3] Robertson, vol. ii., p. 243. Tytler, vol. vi., p. 40.

up the steep of the hill, and reached the top, exhausted by the ascent and harassed by the enemy's fire. Here they were met by the Regent's fresh troops, who gave them a warm reception. A desperate combat ensued, and the pikemen on both sides especially distinguished themselves by their intrepidity. But, in three quarters of an hour, the able manœuvres of the Laird of Grange, who hastened with reinforcements to every weak point, the cool courage of Morton, the dashing bravery of Hume, and a decisive movement on the part of Murray, who charged the Queen's wavering troops with his own main battle, had gained a complete victory. Only three hundred men of the Queen's army were left dead on the battle-field of Langside, for the Regent would not allow the fugitives to be slaughtered after the victory. Ten pieces of brass cannon were taken, and many prisoners of note.[1]

Fortune had once more declared against Mary Stuart. The unfortunate Queen, stationed on an eminence,[2] had watched with breathless eagerness the vicissitudes of the battle which was to decide her fate. She had beheld the march, the attack, the disorder, and the defeat of her army. She had seen her last hopes fall together with her last defenders. After Carberry Hill, she still retained the strong party of the Hamiltons; after Langside, no adherents were left to her. It only remained for her to fly; and she fled in a state of the deepest consternation. Descending in all haste from the hill on which she had been the unhappy witness of this irremediable disaster, she mounted on horseback, and followed by a few servants, rode at full speed in the direction of Dumfries; nor did she draw bridle until she had ridden sixty miles towards the south. On arriving at Dundrennan Abbey, near the Solway Frith, she would be able either to embark for France, or take refuge in England. Of these two courses, the former was the most safe, and the latter the most easy. Relying on the marks of interest which Elizabeth had shown for her whilst she was in captivity, and trusting to the offers of friendship which that Queen had renewed to her since her escape, she resolved to place herself under her protection. Lord Herries, who accompanied her, wrote in her name to Lowther, the deputy-governor

[1] Keith quotes three different accounts of the battle of Langside, by Crawfurd, Melvil and Calderwood; pp. 477-480. Tytler also quotes, from a manuscript in the State Paper Office, a narrative of the battle, under the title of 'Advertisements of the Conflict in Scotland;' vol. vi., pp. 469-472. See further, Teulet, vol. ii., pp. 215, 216.

[2] 'When the Queen, who stood on an eminence to view the armies, perceived that her friends had lost the day, she lost courage, which she had never done before.' Keith, p. 481. Tytler, vol. vi., p. 43.

of Carlisle, desiring to know whether his royal mistress might come safely to that city;[1] but without waiting for an answer, without obtaining any pledge of security from Elizabeth, the inconsiderate fugitive, with lamentable precipitation, crossed the Solway Frith, on the 16th of May, in a fisherman's boat, and landed at Workington, on the coast of Cumberland. To escape from Murray she placed herself at the mercy of Elizabeth. She believed herself sure of an asylum in England; she was destined to find only a prison.

CHAPTER VII.

FROM MARY STUART'S ARRIVAL IN ENGLAND TO THE RETURN OF MURRAY TO SCOTLAND.

Arrival of Mary Stuart on the English frontier—Her detention at Carlisle—Plans of Elizabeth—Mission of Middlemore—His propositions are rejected by Mary Stuart—Her appeal to the Princes of the Continent—She accepts the arbitration of Elizabeth—Suspension of hostilities in Scotland—Conference at York—Position, character, and wishes of the Duke of Norfolk—His secret negotiations with Lethington and Murray—Transfer of the Conference from York to Westminster—Accusation of Mary Stuart—Her defence—Rupture of the Conference—Murray returns to Scotland.

THE resolution which Mary Stuart had taken, to seek refuge in Elizabeth's dominions, was destined to produce the most fatal results. She might easily have withdrawn to France, or remained for some time without danger in the south of Scotland, until she had negotiated a retreat into some place of safety.[2] It would even have been better for her to have fallen into the hands of her revolted subjects; for although they would have again imprisoned her, they would not have put her to death. Indeed, as no one could govern them for any lengthened period,—as their restless disposition, uncertain character, and changing interests, quickly destroyed their obedience, and transferred the exercise of the supreme authority from one hand to another,—it is very

[1] Anderson, vol. iv., pp. 2, 3. Letter from Mary Stuart to Queen Elizabeth, Workington, 17th May, 1568; in Labanoff, vol. ii., pp. 73-77.
[2] Lord Herries thus expresses himself on this subject in a letter which he addressed to Mary Stuart, on the 28th June, 1568, and which M. Teulet has printed from the original in the National Library at Paris : ' Devant que sa Mageste partoit d'Escosse, je lui offrey, à peine de perdre ma teste et tout ce que j'ay au monde, qu'elle demourroit seurement au païs où elle estoit l'espace de quarente jours, et après, selon son bon plaisir, qu'elle pourroyt prendre la voye de France ou de Dumbarton. Car lors, il n'y avoit ennemys plus près de soixante milles. Teulet, vol. ii., p. 234.

probable that they would ere long have released her from captivity and restored her to her throne. A very different fate, however, awaited her in England.

Before she crossed the Solway Frith, she wrote to Elizabeth from Dundrennan Abbey to request an asylum. Her letter runs thus: 'My very dear sister, without giving you a narrative of all my misfortunes, since they must be known to you already, I will tell you that those of my subjects whom I have most benefitted, and who were under the greatest obligations to me, after having revolted against me, kept me in prison, and treated me with the utmost indignity, have at last entirely driven me from my kingdom, and reduced me to such a condition that, after God, I have no hope in any one but you.'[1] No sooner had she arrived at Workington than, on the 17th of May, she addressed to her a longer and most touching letter, to crave her generous assistance against the rebellious Scotch, who had violated the royal prerogative in her person. After giving an account of their persevering aggressions and her final defeat, she went on to say: 'God, in his infinite goodness, has preserved me, for I found refuge with Lord Herries, with whom and some other lords I am come into your country, being assured that, on learning their cruelty and how they have treated me, you will, according to your kind disposition and the trust that I place in you, not only receive me for the preservation of my life, but aid and assist me in my just quarrel, and summon other princes to do the like. It is my earnest request that your Majesty will send for me as soon as possible, for my condition is pitiable, not to say for a Queen, but even for a simple gentlewoman. I have no other dress than that in which I escaped from the field; my first day's ride was sixty miles across the country, and I have not since dared to travel except by night; as I hope to prove to you, if it pleases you to take pity on my extreme misfortune.'[2]

The Queen of England, far from acceding to Mary Stuart's request, soon dispelled all her hopes. On learning that her former rival had fallen into her hands, she was somewhat at a loss what course to pursue. Should she take her back to Scotland in triumph? should she simply grant her hospitality in England? or should she permit her freely to retire to France? These three courses were open to her, and seemed to be in conformity either

---

[1] Labanoff, vol. ii., pp. 71, 72.

[2] She concluded this letter by presenting 'her humble recommendations,' and signed herself 'your very faithful and affectionate good sister and escaped prisoner.' Labanoff, vol. ii., pp. 76, 77.

to the feelings which she had displayed towards Mary Stuart as
a relative, or to the obligations which she owed to her as a
Queen. But in her opinion, all these three courses were fraught
with danger. She feared that if Mary Stuart regained her throne,
she would make some arrangement with the Court of Rome and
the Catholic Princes of the Continent, for the purpose of overthrowing the Protestant party in Scotland, and would then resume
her pretensions to the crown of England. In the second place,
if she remained at liberty in England, she might become a permanent cause of agitation, a centre for the intrigues and plots of the
numerous and powerful body of English Catholics, who, considering her to be their legitimate sovereign, would enter readily
into any scheme she might propose, and would probably revolt in
her favour. Lastly, if she retired into France, she might, in
concert with her uncles and their allies, prepare a military expe
dition for the subjugation of Scotland, which would compel
Elizabeth to maintain the authority of the Regent and defend the
interests of Protestantism in that country, and would expose her
to the formidable consequences of another conflict. Her own
experience had led her to believe that positions were stronger
than promises, and the necessities of policy superior to the sentiments of gratitude; and she could not conceive it possible that
Mary Stuart could become her devoted friend and affectionate
kinswoman, as she had promised.[1] She therefore listened only to
the dictates of State-policy, which had been her sole guide for
nearly forty years; and she resolved to keep in her hands the
imprudent Queen who had thrown herself upon her generosity.
By so doing, she hoped to be able to insure her preponderance in
Scotland and to consolidate her strength in England.

But under what pretext could she detain within her realm a
princess who was her relative and equal, who had done her no
wrong, and over whom she had no jurisdiction? Such a pretext
she quickly discovered. Mary Stuart was at first conducted with
all the honour due to her rank from Workington to Cockermouth,
and from Cockermouth to Carlisle. There she was strictly
watched, in obedience to a warrant sent by Elizabeth to the
Sheriffs and Justices of the Peace of Cumberland, ordering them
to take all necessary measures to prevent her escape.[2] At the
same time Lady Scrope, sister to the Duke of Norfolk, was sent
to wait upon her; Sir William Drury was directed to send fifty

[1] Letter from Mary Stuart to Elizabeth, 28th May, 1568. Labanoff, vol. ii.,
p. 81. Anderson, vol. iv., p. 46.
[2] Tytler, vol. vi., p. 45.

soldiers from Berwick to Carlisle;[1] and Lord Scrope, the warden of that part of the border, and Sir Francis Knollys, the Vice-Chamberlain, were despatched to that city with secret instructions to guard the Queen of Scotland as closely as though she were already a prisoner. They were also to convey to her letters of condolence from Elizabeth; and to inform her that their mistress sympathized greatly with her misfortunes, but could not receive her until she had proved her innocence of her husband's murder.[2] The necessity for this preliminary justification was the means that Elizabeth had devised for keeping her from her presence, and detaining her in her dominions.

On the 29th of May, Lord Scrope and Sir Francis Knollys were admitted into Mary Stuart's presence, and delivered their message. When they had informed her of the hypocritical regret and offensive refusal of their mistress, Mary Stuart, with tears in her eyes, sorrowfully complained that the answer of the Queen her sister was so little in conformity with her expectations. She indignantly protested against the imputations that had been cast upon her, and said that her unworthy subjects had misrepresented her conduct that they might the more easily overthrow her authority. She pressingly renewed her request that the Queen her sister would either aid her to vanquish their rebellion, or permit her to go to the Continent to invoke the assistance of her relatives and allies, who would not refuse either to receive or succour her. The dignity of her attitude, the eloquence of her language, the keenness of her judgment, and the courage she displayed under her reverses, made a deep impression upon Elizabeth's envoys.[3] Struck by those amiable and brilliant qualities for which she was so remarkable, they depicted her, in their letters to their mistress, as a woman of singularly resolute character, ready to recommence the struggle on the very day after she had suffered a defeat.[4]

After her conference with Lord Scrope and Sir Francis Knollys, Mary Stuart despatched Lords Fleming and Herries to

[1] Letter from Bochetel de la Forest to Charles IX., London, 22nd May, 1568. Teulet, vol. ii., p. 220.

[2] Anderson, vol. iv., pp. 53, 54. Lord Scrope and Knollys to the Queen, Carlisle, 29th May, 1568.

[3] 'We fownd hyr in hyr answers to have an eloquent tonge and a discreet hedd; and it seemethe by hyr doyngs that she hath stowte courage and liberalle harte adjoyned therunto.' Anderson, vol. iv., pp. 53, 54. Lord Scrope and Knollys to the Queen, Carlisle, 29th May, 1568.

[4] Knollys gives a very curious description of her in his letter to Cecil, on the 11th June, 1568. Anderson, vol. iv., pp. 71. 72.

London, to endeavour to raise a loan upon the security of her income as Queen Dowager of France.[1] The money thus obtained would have served to maintain her partisans in Scotland, whom Murray had pursued with determined severity ever since the battle of Langside. Dumbarton Castle still held out for her. The southern districts of the kingdom were still strongly attached to her cause, and the northern parts had suffered very little from the war, as their military contingents had arrived too late to take any part in the battle. Mary therefore despatched from Carlisle a warrant to the Earl of Huntly, authorizing him to reorganize her party.[2] Herries and Fleming were intrusted with a letter to Elizabeth, begging her to come to her assistance, as she was bound to do by the ties of neighbourhood and relationship, by the promises of friendship, and by the duties of royalty. In this letter she expressed her ardent desire 'to be admitted, with all diligence and without ceremony, to an interview with her, that she might make known her wrongs, and vindicate herself from the false aspersions which had been cast upon her by her ungrateful subjects.'[3] If Elizabeth would not consent either to receive her at her Court or to assist her in Scotland, she requested permission to leave her dominions, and seek the aid of some other monarch. Lord Fleming was to proceed to France on her behalf. Mary Stuart sent by him most touching and politic letters to Charles IX., Catherine de Medici, and the Cardinal of Lorraine.[4] In these letters she besought the French Court to deliver her from her unfortunate position by sending two thousand infantry to the relief of Dumbarton; by furnishing the money and accoutrements necessary for the equipment and maintenance of five hundred horse-soldiers; by sending artillery and ammunition to enable her to recover the other fortresses of Scotland; and by bestowing the order of St. Michael on two or three of those noblemen who had especially distinguished themselves by their valour and devotion to her cause, in order to encourage the others, and confirm them in their fidelity.[5]

Elizabeth yielded to none of Mary Stuart's requests; but, according to her custom, she did not give an open and decided refusal. She deceived Mary Stuart, that she might not render her desperate. She therefore adroitly seized upon the offer

[1] Instructions to Lord Fleming; Labanoff, vol. ii., pp. 86-90.
[2] Labanoff, vol. ii., pp. 94, 95.
[3] Letter from Mary Stuart to Elizabeth, 28th May, 1568. Labanoff, vol. ii. p. 80.
[4] Labanoff, vol. ii., pp. 78, 86, 91.   [5] Ibid., pp. 87, 88.

which that too confiding Princess had made to exculpate herself before her, and interpreted it as an acknowledgment of her jurisdiction. The Regent Murray also seemed inclined to accept her judgment in the matter. On learning that the fugitive Queen was at Carlisle, he had sent to Elizabeth to express his readiness to prove before her Mary's culpability, and the justice of her deposition. He even consented, it is said, to enter himself prisoner in the Tower of London, if he did not furnish the most ample evidence of her guilt.[1] This proposal of both parties to vindicate themselves before Elizabeth was turned to her own advantage by that artful Queen. Changing an offer of explanation into a pledge of defence, she resolved to constrain Mary to prove her innocence of Darnley's murder, which was charged upon her by Murray, and Murray to clear himself from the accusation of rebellion which was brought against him by Mary. She affected, however, that her only object in accepting the office of arbitrator between them, was to obtain an opportunity of reconciling them to each other.

After having made the two envoys of the Queen of Scotland wait for some time, she admitted them to an audience.[2] They earnestly besought her to embrace the cause of their mistress, and she displayed great willingness to do so. 'But,' she added, 'her subjects have disseminated throughout the world a scandalous and disgraceful report, of which she is well aware; her honour and mine require that the matter should be looked into—not that I should constitute myself her judge, but that I should inquire of her accusers what cause they have to speak thus of her, and by what right they have seized her person, her crown, her fortresses, and all her property, in doing which they cannot be excusable.' 'But, madam,' said Lord Herries, 'if it should appear to be otherwise, which God forbid?' 'Even then,' she replied, 'I would not fail to arrange with her subjects, in the best and most careful manner possible, so as to secure her honour and provide for their safety.'[3] When, however, Herries requested that his mistress might be allowed to withdraw to the Continent, or, at all events, to return to Scotland in the little boat which had brought her over to England, Elizabeth absolutely refused. 'As for the passage of my good sister into

[1] MS. letters, State Paper Office, Drury to Cecil, 22nd May and 17th June. 1568. Tytler, vol. vi., p. 47.
[2] Letter from Bochetel de la Forest to Charles IX., 28th June, 1568. Teulet, vol. ii., p. 226.
[3] Lord Herries to Mary Stuart, 28th June, 1568. Teulet, vol. ii., p. 237.

France,' she said, 'I will not prove myself so imprudent as to permit it, and be thus held in low esteem among other Princes. When she was there before, the King her husband assumed for her the title and arms belonging to my crown, though I was then alive; and I will not place myself again in such embarrassing circumstances. . . . As for her return into Scotland in the humble conveyance which you have mentioned, since she has come into my country, it would be neither to her honour nor to mine for her to go back; and besides, it would not be to her advantage to do so.'¹ She therefore persisted in adhering to the plan which she had formed, and promised to act on Mary Stuart's behalf with an earnestness of friendship which she was far from feeling.²

As she was especially afraid of the intervention of France in the affairs of Scotland, she would not allow Lord Fleming to proceed to the court of Charles IX.³ She had already despatched Mr. Middlemore to announce to Mary Stuart and to Murray her intention to arbitrate between them. Middlemore was to demand a suspension of hostilities in Scotland,⁴ where the victorious Regent, at the head of an army of six thousand men, was engaged in crushing his enemies, and imposing upon all obedience to the young King.⁵ Elizabeth was not satisfied with doing this service only to Mary's party. In order to inspire that princess with greater confidence, she wrote a severe letter to Murray, in which she declared that she was both surprised and shocked at the acts to which he was indebted for his elevation, and by which the Queen of Scotland had been deprived of her throne. 'All these things,' she wrote, 'cannot but sound very strange in the ears of us, being a Prince Sovereign, having dominions and sub-

---

¹ Lord Herries to Mary Stuart, 28th June, 1568; Teulet, vol. ii., p. 238. She expressed herself in the same language to the Spanish ambassador, Don Gusman de Silva, who wrote thus to Philip II.: 'Porque dexarla yr a Francia no la haria en ninguna manera; y tornár a su reino sola, haviendose metido en sus manos, seria gran dishonor suyo y deste reino, haviendose venido a soccorrer a el; y que tenerla con libertad en este reino, por las pretensas que tenia a la corona, era peligroso, porque saliendo algunas veces, como lo haria, podia satisfazer al pueblo de las cosas passadas y ganarle.' MS. despatch from Gusman de Silva to Philip II., 3rd July, 1568. Archives of Simancas, Inglaterra, fol. 820.
² Bochetel de la Forest wrote to Catherine de Medici on the 24th June, that this conduct was only 'subterfuges et delayemens.' Teulet, vol. ii., p. 230.
³ 'Quant à Flemmyng, ceste Royne luy a denyé tout à plat son passeport.' Bochelet de la Forest to Charles IX., 19th June, 1568. Teulet, vol. ii. p. 228.
⁴ 'Some privat instructions to Mr. Midlemore.' Anderson, vol. iv., p. 67.
⁵ Letter from Knollys to Cecil, 12th June, 1568. Anderson, vol. iv., p. 77. Tytler, vol. vi., p. 46.

jects committed to our power, as she had. For remedy whereof she requireth our aid, as her next cousin and neighbour; and for justification of her whole cause, is content to commit the hearing and ordering of the same simply to us. We have thought good and necessary, not only to impart thus much unto you, wherewith she chargeth you, and others joined with you, but also to require and advise you utterly to forbear from all manner of hostility and persecution against all such as have lately taken part with the said Queen, and to suspend all manner of actions and proceedings against them, both by law and arms, and to impart unto us plainly and sufficiently all that which shall be meet to inform us of the truth for your defence in such weighty crimes and causes as the said Queen hath already or shall hereafter object against you, contrary to the duty of natural born subjects; so that we, being duly informed on all parts, may, by the assistance of God's grace, direct our actions and orders principally to his glory, and next to the conservation of our own honour in the sight of all other princes, and finally to the maintenance and increase of peace and concord betwixt both these two realms."[1]

Middlemore arrived at Carlisle on the 13th of June, and was admitted to an audience of the Queen of Scotland on the following morning, in presence of Lord Scrope and Vice-Chamberlain Knollys. He told her, in rather harsh language, that the Queen his mistress, out of regard for her own reputation, could not grant her a personal interview until she had proved she was innocent of her husband's murder. Mary complained bitterly of this insult, and demanded if she were a prisoner. Middlemore replied that she was not; but dissuaded her from seeking an interview with the Queen of England, on the ground that her enemies, who already suspected Elizabeth's partiality towards her, would thereby be induced to reject her judgment. 'If it could please you,' he added, 'to forbear until some good trial be made of your innocency, then you would see with what love, with what heart, and with what joy her majesty would both receive you and embrace you, yea, and do everything for you that you could desire.'[2]

At these words, *judgment* and *trial*, Mary's spirit rose. 'I have no other judge but God,' she exclaimed; 'neither can any take upon themselves to judge of me. Of my own free will,

[1] Letter from Elizabeth to Murray, 8th June, 1568. Anderson, vol. iv., pp. 68-70.
[2] Letter from Middlemore to Cecil, 14th June, 1568. Anderson, vol. v., pp. 81-87.

indeed, and according to the good trust I reposed in the Queen my sister, I offered to make her the judge of my cause. But how can that be, when she will not suffer me to come to her?'[1] In spite of all Middlemore's efforts to re-assure her by communicating to her Elizabeth's letter to Murray, and affirming that the trial would assuredly end in the discomfiture of her enemies, and her own restoration to honour and authority, Mary demanded either to be admitted to an interview with Elizabeth, or to be promptly supplied with assistance, or to be permitted to go elsewhere to obtain means for returning into her kingdom, and punishing her rebellious subjects.[2]

On the same day, whilst still agitated by her conversation with Middlemore, she wrote a pathetic and spirited letter to Elizabeth. She was astonished, she said, that the Queen of England refused to see her, on the ground that such a step would tend to her dishonour. 'Alas! madam,' she continued, 'when did you ever hear that a Prince was blamed for listening in person to the complaints of those who aver that they are falsely accused?' She then indignantly protested against the insulting proposal that she should enter into a controversy with her subjects. 'Remove from your mind, madam,' she exclaimed, 'the idea that I came here for the preservation of my life (for neither the world nor the whole of Scotland have rejected me), but I came to regain my honour, and to request aid to chastise my false accusers; not to reply to them as though they were my equals, but to accuse them before you, whom I chose in preference to all other princes, as being my nearest relative, and staunch friend: doing you, as I supposed, an honour in naming you the restorer of a Queen, who expected to receive this benefit at your hands. I find, however, to my great regret, that you have put another interpretation on what I have done.' She then besought Elizabeth not to do her a greater wrong than had been done her even by her enemies, and concluded with these words: 'I neither can nor will reply to their false accusations, and justify myself as a defendant against my own subjects. They and I, madam, are in no respect on an equality, and even were I to be kept prisoner here, I would rather die than submit to this indignity.'[3]

If Mary Stuart had maintained this haughty bearing, and per-

[1] Letter from Middlemore to Cecil, 14th June, 1568; Anderson, vol. iv., p. 87.
[2] Ibid., p. 88.
[3] Letter from Mary Stuart to Queen Elizabeth, 13th June, 1568. Labanoff, vol. ii., pp. 96-100.

sisted in this determined refusal, Elizabeth would have been unable to bring her to trial, and would have found it very difficult to detain her in captivity. All the Princes of Europe manifested a lively interest in the fate of a princess, whose cause was the cause of royalty itself.[1] Charles IX., and Philip II., to both of whom the unfortunate Mary had addressed her complaints and entreaties, were, however, unable to give her any immediate assistance. The former had only just emerged from the second civil war, and was on the point of engaging in a third, destined to be longer and more violent than those which had preceded it. The latter was fully occupied in repressing the insurrection which the excesses of his governors and the bigotry of his religious zeal had excited in the Netherlands, and in opposing the Moors who had been driven to revolt in the mountains of Granada, by the severity of his home administration. But they had both interceded with Elizabeth on behalf of Mary Stuart. Philip II. sent special instructions to his ambassador, Gusman de Silva, on the subject;[2] and Montmorin, the envoy of Charles IX., after having strongly recommended Mary Stuart to Elizabeth's favour in the name of the King and Queen-mother of France,[3] paid her a visit at Carlisle.[4] In that fortress he found the former Queen of France, and the fugitive Queen of Scotland, reduced to the condition of a prisoner. 'The room which she occupies,' he stated, on his return from Carlisle, 'is gloomy, being lighted only by one casement, latticed with iron bars. You go to it through three other rooms, which are guarded and occupied by hackbutters. In the last of these, which forms the antechamber to the Queen's apartment, resides Lord Scrope, the governor of the border districts. The Queen has only three' of her women with her. Her servants and domestics sleep out of the castle. The doors are not opened until ten o'clock in the morning. The

[1] Catherine de Medici wrote to Elizabeth on the 26th May, 1568, to say that her son and herself were fully assured that Mary Stuart would receive ' toute l'ayde, faveur, secours, et amitié que une princesse, affligée comme elle est, doibt espérer de vous, et que vous demeurerez en la mesme opinyon en laquelle vous avez esté, qui est qu'il fault que les princes se secourent les ungs les aultres pour chastier et punier les subjects que se eslèvent contre eulx, et sont rebelles à leurs souverains, et d'autant que cecy nous touche à tous, et que nous debvions embrasser le faict et protection de cette Royne desolée et affligée, pour la remectre en sa liberté et en l'auctorité que Dieu luy a donné, et laquelle de droict et equité luy appartient, et non à aultre.' Anderson, vol. iv., p. 45.
[2] Gonzalez, Apuntamientos, p. 83.
[3] Catherine de Medici to Elizabeth, 26th May, 1567. Anderson, vol. iv., p. 44.
[4] Letter from Bochetel de la Forest to Charles IX., 19th July, 1568. Teulet, vol. ii., pp. 226, 229.

Queen is allowed to go as far as the church in the town, but she is always accompanied by a hundred hackbutters. She requested Scrope to send her a priest to say mass; but he answered that there were no priests in England."[1]

Mary Stuart was thus deceived in her confidence, thwarted in her intentions, threatened in her honour, subjected to personal restraint, and denied the free exercise of her religion. Montmorin left England without having obtained anything more than empty promises from Elizabeth. Then, giving up all hope of assistance from the Queen of England,[2] Mary turned her entreaties to the Princes of the Continent.[3] She issued a manifesto summoning them to her defence;[4] and in a letter to her uncle, the Cardinal of Lorraine, she drew a lamentable picture of her own distressing position, and the misfortunes of those of her subjects who still remained faithful to her. 'I entreat you,' she says, 'to have pity on the honour of your poor niece, and to procure for me the support I need. Meanwhile, I beseech you to send me some money; for I have none wherewith to buy either food or clothing. The Queen of England has sent me a little linen, and supplies me with one dish. The rest I have borrowed, but I can get no more. You will share in this disgrace. God is subjecting me to a hard

[1] This is the description given by Gusman de Silva, from information supplied him by Montmorin, of Mary Stuart's residence and treatment at Carlisle, in the postscript to his despatch to Philip II., dated 27th June, 1568. 'Dice que esta en una pieza oscura, porque no tiene sino una ventanilla, peña con fuerte reja de hierro ... y que tiene la Reina en su compañia tres solas mugeres de las suyas, y que hay dos ò tres piezas antes de adonde esta, y en todas hay guarda de arcabuzeros; y en la pieza que esta antes de la Reyna esta milord Scroop, que es el gobernador de aquella frontera à la parte de Carlel, y quo la entran à servir à la mesa algunos de sus criados Escoceses, pero que duermen fuera del castillo y salen temprano à la tarde, y el castillo no se abre hasta las diez del dio; y que la dejan salir hasta la yglesia del lugar para que pueda hacer algun ejercicio, pero van con ella cien arcabuzeros; no va á hora que se hacen sus officios y que hay pedido un sacerdote à Scroop, y ha le respendido que no le hay en Inglaterra.' Archives of Simancas, Estado Inglaterra, fol. 820.

[2] When Montmorin returned to London, Mary wrote thus to Elizabeth on the 21st June: 'Il faut que je supplie et le Roy de France et celui d'Espagne, si n'i voulés avoir respect, d'avoir esguard á ma juste querelle, et me remettent en mon lieu.' Labanoff, vol. iii., p. 110.

[3] On the 21st of June she wrote to Gusman de Silva, and on the 11th July to Philip II., two letters which may be found by historical students on reference to the originals in the Archives of Simancas, Inglaterra, fol. 820. Her letters to Charles IX. and Catherine de Medici are in Labanoff, vol. ii., pp. 112, 128."

[4] A French copy of this manifesto will be found in Teulet, vol. ii., pp. 241–252; and an Italian translation of the same, taken from the Archives of the Medici at Florence, is printed in Labanoff, vol. vii., pp. 313–328.

trial; nevertheless, rest assured that I shall die a Catholic. God will quickly remove me from these miseries, for I have suffered insults, calumnies, imprisonment, hunger, cold, heat; flight, without knowing whither to go, for ninety-two miles across the country without stopping or dismounting, and then being obliged to sleep on the hard ground, and drink sour milk, and eat oatmeal without bread; and at last I am come into this country, where, as a reward, I am nothing better than a prisoner; and meanwhile the houses of my servants are pulled down, and I cannot assist them, and my servants themselves are hanged, and I cannot recompense them."[1]

Her pathetic appeals to the Catholic powers of the Continent produced only unproductive tokens of interest in her fate.[2] Even had not the Kings of France and Spain been utterly unable at that time to engage in any foreign expedition, they would have hesitated to assist her, through fear of each other, and particularly of Elizabeth, whom they were obliged to humour lest she should openly protect the insurgent Netherlanders and the French Calvinists. Mary Stuart, therefore, speedily found herself obliged to submit to the will of the Queen of England. The Regent of Scotland had already acknowledged her jurisdiction. On receiving at Dumfries the imperious message which she had sent him by Middlemore, Murray had expressed his readiness to appear before Elizabeth to defend himself, and accuse his sister.[3] He had sus-

[1] Letter from Mary Stuart to the Cardinal of Lorraine, 21st June, 1568. Labanoff, vol. ii., pp. 117, 118.

[2] In the letter in which she implores the assistance of all monarchs, she says: 'Sa Majesté s'est mise en Angleterre où ... elle attendoit secours et faveur de la Royne dudict pays; mais à ceste heure, elle n'y voit apparence sinon que de ce costé là elle est frustrée de ce qu'elle en espéroit ... parquoy se trouvant en telle affliction elle prie et exhorte tous les princes Chrestiens, par cest amour qu'ilz portent à nostre Seigneur Jésus-Christ, duquel ils tiennent leurs noms et leurs estats, et par la révérence qu'ils ont à sa saincte Eglise, et finalement par l'affection et desir qu'ils ont à la conservation d'eux et de leur postérité, vouloir aider ceste pauvre dame oppressee si cruellement par la desloyauté et trahison de si malheureux et inicques subjectz, à celle fin que ce détestable et horrible exemple ne demeure impugny, ainz que par là les aultres subjectz appreignent qu'attempter contre leurs souverains, c'est la commune querelle des princes, pour estre contre toutes bonnes lois et coutumes. Autrement par la tolérance de telle présomption, il n'y a doute que plusieurs ne veulent imiter ceux-ci en cest endroict, comme ils ont desjà faict en aultres choses, et que l'insolence des aultres ne passe ceste-cy, s'il est possible.' Teulet, vol. ii., p. 252.

[3] MS. letter, State Paper Office; Murray to Cecil, 22nd June, 1568. Tytler, vol. vi., p. 53. Murray's Answer to Middlemore, 22nd June, 1568; in Goodall's Examination of the letters said to be written by Mary, Queen of Scots, to James, Earl of Bothwell, vol. ii., p. 75 (Edinburgh, 1754).

pended hostilities against Mary's partisans,[1] but this did not prevent him from obtaining from Parliament declarations of forfeiture against the most able and active of his opponents. Among these were the Archbishop of St. Andrews, Lord Claud Hamilton, and the Bishop of Ross.[2]

But how was Mary Stuart's resistance to be overcome? Elizabeth, fearful that she might escape, had already given orders that the Scotch should not be allowed that freedom of access to the royal prisoner, which had at first been granted them. By thus rendering her isolation more complete, she hoped to increase her weakness. The Privy Council of England, when consulted on the subject, acted in strict conformity to her wishes. They decided unanimously that Queen Mary should be removed from the frontier to some place in the interior of the kingdom. They maintained, moreover, that in virtue of the ancient feudal superiority of the crown of England over that of Scotland—a superiority which had frequently been asserted by the one, and as frequently denied by the other—Queen Mary might be brought to trial; that the wish which she had expressed to be restored to her throne before her innocence had been proved, or else permitted to withdraw to France before she had been tried, was equally opposed to the honour and safety of Elizabeth; but that, after her cause and justification had been thoroughly examined, she should be taken back to her kingdom and restored to her authority.[3]

First of all, however, it was determined to transfer her to a safer place. Under the pretext of bringing her nearer to Elizabeth, Sir George Bowes, on the 13th of July, came with a strong escort, and conducted her, in spite of her remonstrances, from Carlisle to Bolton.[4] Here were renewed, with greater success Elizabeth's persevering endeavours to induce Mary Stuart, whose powers of resistance were weakened by discouragement, to acknowledge her jurisdiction. Lord Herries, gained over by false promises, repaired to Bolton and informed the Queen his mistress, that Elizabeth desired to examine into her affairs, not as a judge,

---

[1] MS. letter, State Paper Office; Drury to Cecil, 17th June, 1568. Tytler, vol. vi., p. 52.   [2] Anderson, vol. iv., pp. 125, 126.

[3] 'A memoriall of the consultation of the Privy Council of England, touching the Quene of Scotts, June 20, 1568.' Present: the Lord Keeper (Bacon), the Duke of Norfolk, the Marquis of Northampton, the Lord Steward (Earl of Pembroke), the Earls of Arundel, Bedford, and Leicester, the Lord Admiral (Clinton), the Lord Chamberlain (Howard), Mr. Secretary (Cecil), Mr. Sadler and Mr. Mildmay. Anderson, vol. iv., pp. 102-106.

[4] Bolton was a castle belonging to Lord Scrope, in Yorkshire. Labanoff, vol. ii., p. 138.

but as her dear cousin and friend, with the intention of restoring her to her throne, even by force of arms, if she proved her innocence; and of making arrangements, without war or disturbance, between her and her subjects, if the latter should adduce satisfactory reasons for their conduct towards her. To this promise, Elizabeth annexed as conditions, that Mary should renounce all claim to the crown of England during the life of the present Queen or her issue; that she should forsake the league with France, and, abandoning the mass, receive the Common Prayer after the form of England.[1]

After two months of negotiation, Mary Stuart allowed herself to be convinced, and yielded. She consented that a conference should be held, at which her differences with her subjects should be submitted to the decision of Commissioners appointed by Elizabeth, with the sole object of putting an end to those differences, and without any prejudice to her rights as a Queen, to her honour as a woman, or to her claims as heir to the crown of England.[2] Whilst Elizabeth was giving all these assurances to the captive Queen, she suggested hopes of a very different nature to the Regent Murray. 'Whereas we hear say,' she wrote, 'that certain reports are made in sundry parts of Scotland, that whatsoever should fall out now upon the hearing of the Queen of Scots' cause, in any proof to convince or acquit the said Queen concerning the horrible murder of her late husband our cousin, we have determined to restore her to her kingdom and government, we do so much mislike hereof, as we cannot endure the same to receive any credit; and therefore we have thought good to assure you, that the same is untruly devised by the authors to our dishonour. For as we have been always certified from our said sister, both by her letters and messages, that she is by no means guilty or participant of that murder, (which we wish to be true,)

---

[1] Letter from Knollys to Cecil, 28th July, 1568. Anderson, vol. iv., p. 109-114.

[2] In a letter which she wrote to Elizabeth on the 28th of July, 1568, she explained her change of resolution on this subject, by the formal promises of Elizabeth. 'Toutesfoyes, sur votre parolle, il n'est rien que je n'entreprisse, car je ne doubtay jamays de votre honneur et royalle fidélitay, ayns seray contante, selon quo milord Heris m'a requis de votre part, que deus, quels qu'il vous plaira, viennent, m'assurant que sçaurés bien choisir gens de qualitay pour si importante charge. Cela faict, Mora ou Morton, ou tous deux, comme prinsipaulx, à qui le soubtien de cette cause est attribué contre moy, pourront venir comme désirés, pour prandre aveques eulx tel ordre que bon vous semblera; m'usant moy comme leur Royne, sellon la promesse de milord Heris en votre nom, sans préjudisier à mon honneur, couronne, estast ou droyt, que je puisse avoir comme plus prosche de votre sang.' Labanoff, vol. ii., pp. 140, 141; and Haynes's Collection of State Papers, p. 468 (London, 1740).

so surely if she should be found justly to be guilty thereof, as hath been reported of her, (whereof we would be very sorry,) then, indeed, it should behove us to consider otherwise of her cause than to satisfy her desire in restitution of her to the government of that kingdom. And so we would have you and all others think, that should be disposed to conceive honourably of us and our actions."[1] Thus Elizabeth induced Mary Stuart to acknowledge her jurisdiction, by promising to restore her to her throne if she would accept an arbitration which could do her no injury; and persuaded Murray to yield to her authority by giving him hopes that he would be confirmed in the Regency, if he adduced evidence to prove his sister's guilt, and to justify her detention in captivity.

A conference having thus been agreed on by both parties, hostilities were suspended in Scotland until Elizabeth had attempted her proffered mediation.[2] Mary Stuart herself enjoined the Earls of Argyle and Huntly—who had held a convention at Largs, on the 28th of July, with a large number of the Scottish nobility,[3] and were preparing to recommence the war—to lay down their arms.[4] She chose for her Commissioners to the conference, which was appointed to be held at York, Lesley, the Bishop of Ross, Lords Herries, Boyd, and Livingston, Sir John Gordon of Lochinvar, and Sir James Cockburn of Skirling.[5] The Regent was summoned to appear in person, and he repaired to York, accompanied by the Earl of Morton, the Protestant Bishop of Orkney, Lord Lindsay, and Robert Pitcairn, the Commendator of Dunfermline.[6] To them he added as assistants, the celebrated Dr. George Buchanan, Sir James Makgill the Clerk-register, and Mr. Secretary Lethington, whom he already suspected of a return to his attachment to the Queen's cause, and dreaded to leave behind him.[7] Queen Elizabeth directed the Duke of Norfolk, the Earl of Sussex, and Sir Ralph Sadler to appear on her part.[8] The first of these was Earl-Marshal of the kingdom, and the most

[1] Letter from Elizabeth to Murray, 20th September, 1568. Robertson, Appendix 28. [2] Tytler, vol. vi., p. 57.
[3] The confederates, among whom were the Archbishop of St. Andrews, the Earls of Huntly, Argyle, Crawford, Errol, Rothes, Cassillis, Eglinton, and Caithness, the Bishop of Ross, the Lords Fleming, Sanquhar, Ogilvy, Boyd, Oliphant, Drummond, Borthwick, Maxwell, Somerville, Forbes, and Yester, wrote a letter to Elizabeth on the same day, in favour of their Queen. This letter is printed in Anderson, vol. iv., pp. 120-124. They also wrote to the Duke of Alva to request his assistance. Tytler, vol. vi., p. 54.
[4] Tytler, vol. vi., p. 56. [5] Anderson, vol. iv., part 2, pp. 33, 34
[6] Their commission was drawn up in the name of the young King. Anderson, vol. iv., part 2, p. 35.
[7] Tytler, vol. vi., p. 57. [8] Anderson, vol. iv., part 2, pp. 3-7.

powerful noble in England; the second held the military command of the northern districts, and was President of the Council at York; and the third was Chancellor of the Duchy of Lancaster, a member of the Privy Council, and a statesman who had long been employed in affairs of an important and delicate nature. All three were strongly attached to the Protestant cause, and appeared to be devoted in their fidelity to their sovereign.

Mary Stuart had taken this important resolution without consulting the Bishop of Ross. When this able and attached servant joined her at Bolton, on the 18th of September, he expressed his sorrow that she had agreed to such a conference.[1] He pointed out to his imprudent sovereign that if she brought any accusation against Murray and his friends, they 'would undoubtedly utter all they could for their defence, although it were to her dishonour, and that of the realm,' and he maintained that it would have been far better to have attempted an amicable arrangement. But Mary was now full of hope. She believed that Elizabeth was sincere in her professions of friendship; and that the Duke of Norfolk would be favourable to her cause.[2] Lady Scrope, the duke's sister, had assured her he would do all in his power to help her, and had made the first overtures of that mysterious and fatal project, which was to constitute the duke her advocate, that he might afterwards become her husband.[3] Mary Stuart accordingly flattered herself with the belief that the Duke of Norfolk would have no difficulty in influencing the Earl of Sussex; that Sir Ralph Sadler would not venture to oppose their united opinion; and that the presence at York of the Earl of Northumberland and the leading Catholics of northern England,[4] would produce a most favourable effect upon the progress and issue of the Conference.

[1] 'The Examinacyon of the Bishop of Rosse, at the Toure, the sext of November, 1751;' in Murdin's Collection of State Papers, p. 52.
[2] 'To this the Quene replyed, that there was no suche danger in the mater as I supposed, for she trusted I wold find the juges favorable, principalie the Duke of Norfolke, who was first in commission, and douted not bot Therle Sussex wold be rewled by him, as his tender freind; and Sir Rauph Sadler wold not ganestand thair advyses.' Murdin, p. 52.
[3] By a message from the Duke to his sister, Lady Scrope, Mary Stuart 'onderstude of the Duke's good-will toward her, and the bruict was ellis spread abrod of a mariage betuix the Duke and her.' Ibid.
[4] 'And besydis this, she had mony good freindis in the cuntrey that did favor her and steik to her, such as Therle Northumberland and his lady (be whom she had many intelligences and messages), the Nortounes, Marconwele, and otheris . . . who wold all be with the Duke at York, and wold persuade him to favor her cause.' Ibid.

She received, however, a communication well adapted to dispel her illusions. Lethington, whose complicity in the murder of the King she had frequently asserted,[1] still retained for her considerable affection, not altogether irrespective of his own personal interests. He was anxious to prevent a discussion which might ruin and dishonour the Queen, as well as place himself in a very embarrassing position. He had procured copies of the letters which had been found in the silver casket, and which Murray intended to produce at York in proof of the murder. These copies he sent to the captive Queen by Robert Melvil; and charged him to ask her in what manner she would wish him to prove his attachment to her, when at the Conference.[2] Mary, after having carefully examined these letters, did not dispute their authenticity.[3] In reply, she requested Lethington to use his efforts 'to stay the rigorous accusations of Murray,' to confer with the Bishop of Ross, who possessed her entire confidence, and to labour with the Duke of Norfolk in her favour.[4] Lethington's conduct at York was in strict conformity with Mary Stuart's wish. The able Scottish secretary undertook to frustrate the plan of the astute Queen of England.

In this attempt he was seconded by the Duke of Norfolk, whose ambition led him to entertain the same views. The head of the noble family of Howard, which was no less illustrious by the grandeur of its misfortunes than the splendour of its achievements, he had inherited the power of his forefathers, and was destined to share in their calamities. Several of his ancestors had met with a tragical fate, through having become formidable opponents of their sovereigns. His grandfather, Thomas Howard, the third Duke of Norfolk, had continued at the head of the Catholic party in England, although he was the uncle of Anne Boleyn and Catherine Howard, two of those short-lived Queens whom the Protestant Revolution had raised to the throne of England. In the latter years of his reign, the suspicious and

---

[1] Letter from Middlemore to Cecil, 14th June, 1568; in Anderson, vol. iv., p. 90. [2] Murdin, p. 52.

[3] 'Mary, after having carefully examined these letters, which were only the translations from the original French into the Scottish language, sent her answer to Lethington. It is worthy of note, that it contained no assertion as to the forgery or interpolation of these letters, now, as it appears, communicated to her for the first time.' Tytler, vol. vi., pp. 58, 59.

[4] 'To this she answered be Robert Melvill, that she wished hym to stay these rigorous accusations; and becaus he was wele acquented with the Duke of Norfolke, desyred him to travell with the Duke in her favers; and that he wold confer with the Bishop of Rosse.' Murdin, pp. 52, 53.

R

tyrannical Henry VIII. had imprisoned him together with his son, the Earl of Surrey. The earl was beheaded a few days before the death of Henry VIII. The aged Duke of Norfolk, though saved from the block, remained a prisoner during the whole of the reign of Edward VI., and did not recover his liberty until the accession of Mary Tudor. Then by actively promoting the restoration of the ancient faith of the country, by declaring himself in favour of the marriage of the daughter of Catherine of Arragon to Philip II., and by advising a close alliance between England and Spain, he had attained the highest pitch of favour, and had died in the exercise of immense power.

Sprung from this ardent supporter of the old religion of the country, the heir of one of its noblest martyrs, and having himself, nothwithstanding his youth, suffered for some time the distrust of royalty, and shared in the perilous disgrace of his family, Thomas Howard, the fourth Duke of Norfolk, was the object of the hereditary devotion of the Catholics, who suspected him of being secretly attached to their faith, and was regarded with respect by the Protestants, in whose doctrines he had been brought up, and whose worship he outwardly practised. On her accession to the throne, Elizabeth had given him a seat in her Privy Council. No one had a better standing at Court, or wielded a more extensive influence throughout the kingdom. He possessed immense wealth, was related to the most illustrious families, held several counties at the disposal of himself and his friends, and could command the services not only of the entire body of Catholics, but of a large number of Protestants. Though scarcely thirty-two years of age, he was now for the third time a widower; and he gradually allowed the most ambitious and dangerous thoughts to take possession of his mind. Noble, affable, and generous; with a restless, but vacillating mind; not possessing firmness of character in proportion to his ambition; able to prepare with mystery what he was not capable of exercising with resolution; he was about to form a plan with a boldness which he never possessed in action, and to engage in an enterprise which was destined to effect his ruin.

The Duke of Norfolk repaired to York, with feelings very favourable to the Scottish Queen. He acted as President of the Conference, which opened on the 4th of October, and at which the Regent appeared with his colleagues, whilst Mary Stuart was represented by her commissioners. For the purpose of gaining time, or in conformity with the directions of the Privy Council and the wishes of Elizabeth, the duke commenced the proceedings by asserting the ancient feudal supremacy which England had in former times claimed over Scotland.[1] This reference to a pretension which had long been abandoned, and which had only been revived by the formation of a tribunal before which the Queen and the Regent of Scotland had consented to explain their conduct and discuss their rights, filled Murray with confusion, and he maintained an angry silence. But the Secretary, Lethington, was not equally taciturn. With that presence of mind which never failed him under any circumstances, and which ever supplied him with decisive reasons and dignified language when the interests and honour of his country were concerned, he coolly replied that, 'when the Scottish monarchs received back again the territory they had formerly possessed in England, it would be time to talk of homage. This recognition of supremacy,' he added, ' had always been conditional and limited on the part of Scotland, which had remained entirely independent as regarded its own territory, and in this respect had been more free than England, which until lately had paid Peter's pence to the Pope.'[2] After this haughty and conclusive answer, the Duke of Norfolk did not press his demand, and the matter fell to the ground.

Anxious to avoid the melancholy exposure which he foresaw would result from this Conference, the Duke of Norfolk endeavoured to effect a reconciliation between Murray and his sister. He had an interview with Lethington on the subject, in which he expressed his surprise that a man of his sagacity should have taken part in the accusation of his sovereign. 'Is England,' he asked, 'judge over the Princes of Scotland? How could we find it in our hearts to dishonour the mother of our future King? or how could we answer afterwards for what we had done, seeing that, by bringing his mother's honesty in question, we jeopardize his right to the crown of England? It had been rather the duty of you his subjects,' he continued, 'to cover her imperfections if she had any, leaving her punishment unto God, who is the only judge over Princes.'[3] These opinions exactly harmonized with the views entertained by Lethington, who readily undertook to communicate with the Regent on the subject, and to arrange a secret interview between Murray and Norfolk.

The interview took place at night, in the gallery of the house in which the Duke resided.[4] Norfolk unfolded Elizabeth's policy to Murray, and told him, that by accusing Queen Mary before

[1] Melvil's Memoirs, p. 94.   [2] Ibid.   [3] Ibid.
[4] Letter from Murray to Lord Burleigh; Robertson, Appendix 33.

her commissioners, he would endanger the dearest interests of Scotland. He assurred him that the Queen his mistress would never consent to regulate the English succession; that she cared less about the difficulties which might arise after her death in consequence of the uncertainty of the succession, than about the embarrassment which might accrue to herself from the appointment of her successor during her lifetime. Under these circumstances, he said, the crown of England would inevitably devolve upon the Queen of Scotland, unless her opponents were so imprudent as to weaken her claims and compromise the right of her posterity, by bringing an accusation against her.[1] Such an act of imprudence, he reminded the Regent, might turn to the advantage, in Scotland, of his enemies the Hamiltons, and prove detrimental to the Stuarts, who were his blood-relations and from whom he had reason to expect better treatment and greater advantages. In conclusion, he begged him to 'consider what inconveniences the Queen's defamation in the matters laid to her charge might breed to her posterity;' and suggested that the best plan would be for Mary to ratify her abdication in favour of her son, whilst Murray, on his part, should suppress the letters on which he based his accusation.[2]

This conversation made a deep impression upon Murray. He replied, however, that the letters could not be suppressed, as several persons had seen them, and they had been communicated to the Scottish Parliament. The Queen, moreover, would derive no benefit from their suppression, whilst he would incur the ignominious reproach of having preferred a charge which he was unable to substantiate. He would not consent to destroy the letters, but the Duke dissuaded him from using them. 'You are grievously deceived,' said Norfolk, 'if you imagine the Queen of England will ever pronounce sentence in this cause. Do you not see that no answers have been returned to the questions which, upon this point, were addressed by you to us, and forwarded to the Queen? Nay, you can easily put the matter to a more certain proof. Request an assurance, under the Queen's hand, that when you accuse your sovereign and bring forward your proofs, she will pronounce sentence. If you get it, act as you please—if it is not given, rest assured that my information is true, and take occasion thereupon to stay from further proceedings.'[3]

Murray acted in conformity with the Duke of Norfolk's advice,

[1] Melvil, p. 95.   [2] Robertson, Appendix 33.   [3] Melvil's Memoirs, p. 95

which he communicated to Lethington and Sir James Melvil, but to none of the other Scottish commissioners.[1] He resolved to justify himself, without really attacking the Queen his sister. On the 8th of October, Mary Stuart's commissioners—who, on the previous evening, had presented a written protest, in which they asserted the rights and independence of the Queen their mistress,[2] laid before the Conference a statement of the recent occurrences in Scotland, and inveighed, in clear and energetic language, against the rebellion of the lords, and the excesses they had committed in combatting, imprisoning, and deposing their sovereign; in substituting an illegal Regency instead of the regular authority of the crown; and in constraining the Queen, whom they had defeated and put to flight, to seek refuge in England.[3] Finally, they expressed their confident hope that, by the mediation of Elizabeth, the Queen of Scotland might be speedily restored to the peaceable enjoyment of her throne and kingdom.[4]

Instead of assuming an aggressive position, as it was expected he would, Murray took merely a defensive attitude. The odious marriage of the Queen to Bothwell, the danger to which the Prince Royal was thereby exposed, the necessity of defending him by force, and of subjecting his mother to a temporary imprisonment, with Mary's voluntary resignation of the crown, and consent to the Regency which had been established during the minority of her son: these were the reasons alleged by him in explanation of the conduct of the lords, and in justification of his own assumption of authority. Not a syllable was added which, directly or indirectly, charged Mary Stuart with complicity in the murder of her husband.[5] Her commissioners, whose task was greatly simplified by this proceeding, replied that the marriage with Bothwell had been forced upon the Queen by the lords themselves, who had recommended Bothwell, after his acquittal, as a suitable husband for her. Murray, to the great

---

[1] 'The Regent took very well with this advice of the Duke's and kept it secret from all his company, save Secretary Lidingtoun and me.' Melvil's Memoirs, p. 95.   [2] Anderson, vol. iv., part 2, p. 49.
[3] Letter from the English Commissioners to Elizabeth, 9th October, 1568, in Anderson, vol. iv., part 2, pp. 42, 43; and Bishop Leslie's Negotiations, in Anderson, vol. iii., pp. 15, 16.
[4] Goodall, vol. ii., pp. 123, 126. Tytler, vol. vi., p. 60.
[5] Bishop Leslie's Negotiations, in Anderson, vol. iii., pp. 16-18. Goodall, vol. ii., pp. 144, 149. Despatch from Lamothe Fénelon to Charles IX., 29th November, 1568; in Purton Cooper's *Recueil des Dépêches, &c., des Ambassadeurs de France en Angleterre et en Ecosse, pendant le XVIe Siècle*, vol. i., pp. 17, 18.

surprise and extreme discontent of his party, made no answer, and declined saying another word upon the subject.[1]

The silence of the Regent gave an unexpected turn to the contest, and completely changed the position of the Queen of Scotland with reference to the Queen of England. Elizabeth had now no reason for excluding Mary Stuart from her presence, and detaining her in captivity. Murray, however, had not thoroughly determined not to employ the terrible means which he had it in his power to use. In compliance with the advice of Norfolk, he had applied both to Queen Elizabeth and to Queen Mary, to compel the one to explain herself, and the other to effect a compromise. In a private conference which he had had with the English commissioners, he had explained to them his scruples about accusing the mother of his sovereign of having been a party to the murder of her husband, and had asked them whether the Queen of England, in case he should prove her guilt, would pronounce Mary Stuart's condemnation, support the government of the young King, approve of the conduct he had himself pursued, and maintain him in possession of the Regency.[2] On the other hand, he secretly despatched Robert Melvil to Bolton, to propose to his sister to avoid the accusation with which she was threatened, by ratifying her abdication of the crown, and consenting to reside in England, under the protection of Elizabeth, and with an income suitable to her royal dignity.[3]

In order to prove that he was fully competent to strike the blow he had hitherto withheld, he instructed Lethington, Makgill, and Buchanan *privately* to exhibit to the English commissioners the papers contained in the silver casket.[4] After having carefully perused them, Elizabeth's commissioners wrote to that Princess that the matter appeared to them as manifest as it was detestable, and that if the letters ascribed to the Scottish Queen really were in her handwriting, they afforded conclusive proof of her culpability.[5] The Duke of Norfolk feared that this letter would be

[1] Tytler, vol. vi., p. 62.
[2] 'Articles proposed by the Earl of Murray to the Commissioners of the Queen of England at York.' Anderson, vol. iv., part 2, pp. 55, 56.
[3] Hopetoun MSS. Declaration of Robert Melvil; also MS. letter, State Paper Office, Knollys to Cecil, 25th October, 1568; and Tytler, vol. vi., p. 66.
[4] 'A letter to Queen Elizabeth from her Commissioners at York, the 11th of October, 1568;' in Anderson, vol. iv., part 2, p. 58.
[5] 'Afterwards,' say the Commissioners in their letter to Elizabeth on the 11th of October, 'they (the Scotch) showed unto us one horrible and long letter of her own hand, as they saye, contayning foule matteir, and abominable . . . with diverse fond ballades of her own hand. The said letters and ballades do discover

productive of disastrous consequences to Mary Stuart. He saw the Bishop of Ross, and told him that the Queen of Scotland would be dishonoured for ever if these letters were produced.¹ 'If they were once published,' he added, 'her Majesty the Queen of England would be advised by those who love not your mistress, to send ambassadors to all other Christian Princes, to make the same known to them, that they might make no further suit for her deliverance; and perhaps her person might be subjected to severer treatment.' He therefore advised him to consult with Lethington as to the best means of averting this danger. The Bishop of Ross replied that, in Lethington's opinion, Mary Stuart ought to ratify her abdication—by doing which she would no more prejudice her rights at York than she had done at Lochleven, since she was just as much a prisoner in England as she had been in Scotland. 'Within six months,' he continued, 'she will be honourably restored to her country, and then she may revoke all she has done.' 'However that may be,' answered the Duke, 'our best plan is to get quit of present infamy and slander, and let time work the rest.'² Lesly, after having conferred with Norfolk and Lethington on the subject, proceeded to Bolton on the 13th of October, to advise Queen Mary to accept the offer which Robert Melvil had made her on behalf of the Regent. Mary consented, after some little hesitation; and it seemed probable that this dangerous contest would be concluded by an arrangement which would confirm the authority of the Regent, and preserve the honour of the Queen.³

---

such inordinate love betweene her and Bothaille, her loothsomeness and abhorringe of her husband that was murdered, in such sorte as everie good and godlie man cannot but detest and abhorre the same.' After giving a summary of the principal points contained in these letters, they go on to say: 'We have noted to your Majestie the cheife and speciall points of the said letters, to the intent it may please your Majestie to consider of them, and so to judge whether the same be sufficient to convince her of the detestable crime of the murder of her husband, which, in our opinions and consciences, if the said letters be written with her own hand, is verie hard to be avoided.' Anderson, vol. iv., part 2, pp. 62, 63. This letter was written on the 11th of October, and is signed by Norfolk, Sussex, and Sadler. On the same day the Duke of Norfolk wrote another letter, which he addressed to the Earls of Pembroke and Leicester, and Secretary Cecil. In it he says: 'Yff the facte schall be thowghte as detestable and manefeste to you, as for owght we cane perceave ytt semethe here to us, then condynge jugement with open demonstratyon to the holle world, maye dyrectlye appeare. Yff here Majestie schall not allowe off thys, then make suche a composycion as in so broken a cawse may be.' Anderson, vol. iv., part 2, pp. 77, 78.

¹ Examination of the Bishop of Ross. Murdin, p. 53. ² Murdin, p. 53.
³ Hopetoun MSS., Declaration of Robert Melvil. MS. letter, State Paper Office, Knollys to Cecil, 25th October, 1568. Tytler, vol. vi., p. 66.

But Elizabeth was not to be so easily defeated. Rumours of the mysterious negotiations which were being carried on at York had reached her ears, and Murray's unexpected behaviour had doubtless inspired her with still further apprehensions. She therefore suddenly transferred the Conference to Westminster. The reasons which she alleged had prompted her to take this step, were the necessity that existed of examining more closely into so delicate a matter, and the desire that she felt to bring it to a speedy termination.[1] When she saw the Duke of Norfolk, she told him 'she had heard somewhat of his intention to marry the Scottish Queen, though she could not believe it.' The Duke 'did with great oaths deny it,' and added: 'Why should I seek to marry so wicked a woman, such a notorious adulteress and murderer? I love to sleep upon a safe pillow. By your Majesty's favour, I count myself as good a Prince at home in my bowling-alley at Norwich, as she is though she were on the throne of Scotland. Besides, knowing as I do, that she pretendeth a title to the present possession of your Majesty's crown, if I were about to marry her, your Majesty might justly charge me with seeking to take your own crown from your head.'[2] Reassured by these declarations, Elizabeth gave Mary's commissioners reason to hope for the speedy restoration of their mistress by a suitable arrangement with her subjects. At the same time, however, she pursued a different course with regard to Murray, informed him that she was fully aware of the intrigues in which he had engaged, and threatened to invest the Duke of Chatelherault with the Regency of Scotland, if he refused to pursue his accusation against his sister.[3]

Murray was placed in a difficult position by this threat; and to increase his embarrassment, Mary Stuart now refused to ratify the abdication, to which she had at first consented.[4] Thus placed between Mary's refusal and Elizabeth's menace, it was equally dangerous for him to speak or to be silent. By following Norfolk's advice, he would lose the favour of Elizabeth, and by yielding to Elizabeth's desire, he would incur the opposition of Norfolk. In this dilemma, he resolved on taking a middle course, and drew up his accusation of Mary with the determination not to lay it before the new Conference, unless the Queen of

---

[1] Correspondence of Lamothe Fénelon, vol. i., p. 18.
[2] 'A sommary of the matters wherewith the Duke of Norfolk was charged at his arraynment, 1572;' in Murdin, pp. 179, 180. Haynes, p. 574.
[3] Tytler, vol. vi., p. 67.
[4] Hopetoun MS., Robert Melvil's Declaration. Tytler, vol. vi., p. 67.

England gave him those assurances which he had demanded while at York.¹ Mary Stuart, on her side, resolved to parry the accusation by forbidding her commissioners to reply to it. She enjoined them never to allow her adversaries to act otherwise than as defendants, and even proposed a reconciliation with them. Being desirous, she wrote, to act towards her subjects with the affection of a mother, she had no wish to prosecute them before a foreign tribunal, as so rigorous a proceeding was calculated only to impede the restoration of an affectionate and friendly understanding between them. She therefore authorized her commissioners to extend her clemency to her disobedient subjects, in presence of Elizabeth, and to promise them an accommodation, the terms of which should do no prejudice either to her honour, her title, or her authority, which she had no idea of submitting to any Prince in the world. If matters took a different turn, she ordered her representatives immediately to break up the negotiation.²

The Conference began at Westminster on the 25th of November. To her three former commissioners Elizabeth had added Lord Chancellor Bacon, the Earls of Arundel and Leicester, the Lord Admiral Clinton, and Mr. Secretary Cecil.³ After Mary's commissioners had read a protest in conformity to the recent instructions they had received from their sovereign,⁴ the Lord Chancellor, who acted as President of the Conference, informed Murray that the defence he had made at York was considered inconclusive; and with a view to encourage the Regent to speak more openly, he added: 'Her Majesty principally wisheth that, upon the hearing of this great cause, the honour and estate of the Queen of Scots may be preserved, and found sincerely sound, whole, and firm; but if she shall be justly proved and found guilty of the murder of her husband, which were much to be lamented, she shall either be delivered into your hands, upon good and sufficient sureties and assurances for the safety of her life and good usage of her; or else she shall continue to be kept in England, in such sort as neither the Prince her son, nor you, the Earl of Murray, shall be in any danger by her liberty. And for the time to come, her Majesty will maintain the authority of the said Prince to be King, and

---

¹ Tytler, vol. vi., p. 68.
² Labanoff, vol. ii., pp. 229-231.
³ 'The Journal or first session of the Commissioners upon the 25th day of November, 1568.' Anderson, vol. iv., part 2, p. 101.
⁴ Anderson, vol. iv., part 2, pp. 103, 104.

the government of the realm by you, the Earl of Murray, according to the laws of Scotland."¹

Somewhat reassured by this declaration, Murray spoke. He said that it had long been repugnant to his feelings to make public acts of a nature calculated to sully the honour of the mother of his sovereign in the eyes of strangers; but that he was now compelled by necessity to defend himself, and that all blame must rest upon those who had forced him to drag into light the proofs which he had hitherto concealed.² However, as the verbal declarations which had been given in Elizabeth's name did not satisfy him, as he knew that Princess would readily disavow them, Murray required an assurance under the English Queen's hand, that she would pronounce a judgment, before he gave in his accusation. To this Cecil replied, that he had ample assurance already; and it ill became him to suspect or doubt the words of their royal mistress. 'Where,' he added, 'is your accusation?' 'It is here,' answered John Wood, the Regent's secretary, plucking it from his bosom, 'and here it must remain till we see the Queen's handwrit.'³ As he spoke, the Bishop of Orkney — who was dissatisfied with the Regent's vacillating policy, and who agreed with Morton, Lindsay, the Abbot of Dunfermline, and Buchanan, in wishing to push matters to extremities—stepped up to Wood, snatched the paper from his hands, and running to the table, placed it before the English commissioners. Wood remained, for an instant, motionless from real or feigned astonishment; but quickly recovering himself, he sprang after the bishop. He was, however, too late to stop him, and was obliged to resume his seat amid the ill-suppressed laughter of many present.⁴ This scene of violence and buffoonery formed the fitting introduction to the defamation of a Queen by her own subjects, before the subjects of another sovereign.

In his accusation, Murray stated that as Bothwell was the author of Darnley's murder, so the Queen, his wife, had persuaded him to commit it; that she was not only in the foreknowledge of the same, but a maintainer of the assassins, as she

¹ Goodall, vol. ii., pp. 201, 202. Anderson, vol. iv., part 2, pp. 109-113.
² Protestation by the Earle of Murray and his colleagues, when they exhibited their accusation against Queen Mary.' Anderson, vol. iv., part 2, pp. 115-118.
³ Melvil's Memoirs, pp. 96, 97.
⁴ Sir James Melvil, who was present, formally accuses him of having made an arrangement with Cecil and the Commissioners of the young King, who were adverse to Mary. Memoirs, p. 96.

had shown by thwarting the course of justice, and by marrying the chief executor of that foul crime.[1] To give additional force to this solemn denunciation of Mary's culpability, the father of the murdered King added his demand for vengeance. The Earl of Lennox presented himself before the English commissioners, and in the most pathetic language accused Queen Mary of having conspired the death of his son, declared that until that moment he had not expected to obtain justice, except at the hand of God, but that he now laid his case in full confidence before their lordships, whom her Majesty the Queen of England, whose natural-born subject his son was, had authorized to hear this cause.[2]

Elizabeth had now attained her object: Mary Stuart laboured under a most terrible accusation. Her deputies were thrown into great consternation, and deliberated for two days, upon the course they ought to pursue.[3] Before breaking up the Conference, in conformity to the latest instructions they had received from their sovereign, they repelled the imputations which had been cast upon her in contempt of all divine laws and human obligations; and bitterly complained that so unlawful and unexpected a proceeding had been allowed in England. 'My lords,' they wrote to the English commissioners, 'we are heartily sorry to hear that our countrymen intend to colour their most unjust, ungrateful, and shameful doings against their natural sovereign, liege lady, and mistress, who hath been so beneficial to them. Her Grace hath made them, from mean men, earls and lords; and now without any evil deserving on her part, in either deed or word, to any of them, she is thus recompensed with calumnious and false reports, and slandered to her reproach in this great matter, whereof they that now pretend herewith to excuse their treason were the first inventors—having written with their own hands that devilish bond, the conspiracy for the slaughter of that innocent young gentleman, Henry Stuart, late spouse of our sovereign, and presented her in marriage to their wicked confederate James, Earl Bothwell, as was made manifest before ten thousand people in Edinburgh.'[4]

After protesting against what 'these rebels and calumniators

[1] 'The Accusation against Queen Mary.' Anderson, vol. iv., part 2, pp. 119-121.
[2] 'The Journal or third session of the Commissioners, 29th November, 1568.' Anderson, vol. iv., part 2, pp. 121, 122.
[3] Laing's History of Scotland, vol. i., p. 155.
[4] A letter from the Commissioners of the Queen of Scots to the Commissioners of the Queen of England, 1st December, 1568.' Anderson, vol. iv, part 2, pp. 129, 130.

had done in Scotland,' Mary's commissioners affirmed that their usurpation was not assented to by an eighth part of the kingdom, and pointed out the consequences that might ensue to other Princes from granting impunity to this example of successful revolt and disloyal accusation. 'If this in them be tolerated,' they wrote, 'what Prince lives upon the face of the earth whose ambitious subjects may not invent some slander, to deprive them of their supreme authority during their lifetime? Your wisdoms well understand how far their doings exceed the bounds permitted to subjects in the holy and sacred Scriptures, and violate the loyal duty which they owe to their native Princes.'[1] They attributed the insurrection of Murray's party in Scotland, not to any desire to punish the murderers of the King, but to their ambition to govern the kingdom; and in conclusion, they repeated that their mistress, whose ancestors had been independent monarchs, and who was herself an independent Princess, could not be judged by any living authority, as the Queen of England herself had admitted.

Their next step was to demand an immediate audience of Elizabeth.[2] When admitted to her presence, they complained in strong terms of the manner in which the proceedings had been conducted. They reminded her of her promise that in the absence of their royal mistress, nothing should be done which might affect her honour and authority; complained that, in violation of this promise, her subjects had been encouraged to load her with the most atrocious imputations; reiterated their demand that she should, in common justice, be allowed to appear in person and plead her own cause; and meanwhile besought that her accusers might be arrested.[3] This bold demand perplexed Elizabeth, but she extricated herself from the dilemna with her usual astuteness. After declaring that she had never believed the Queen of Scots guilty of the murder of her husband, she went on to say, that as the Regent and his colleagues had brought this accusation against her in their own defence, it would be unjust not to give them an opportunity to prove their allegations. She had, therefore, resolved to send for them, and to demand their proofs; after which she would willingly hear their mistress in her own justification.[4] The partiality of this proceeding, which transformed those who were accused of rebellion into the accusers of a murder, filled Mary's commissioners with indignation. They remonstrated against a further hearing being granted to Murray, and ended by

[1] Anderson, vol. iv., part 2, p. 130.   [2] Goodall, vol. ii., pp. 209-213.
[3] Ibid., vol. ii., pp. 213-219. Correspondence of Lamothe Fénelon, 10th December, 1568, vol. i., pp. 38, 39.   [4] Goodall, vol. ii., p. 221.

solemnly protesting that nothing that might be done hereafter had their consent, or should in any way prejudice the rights of their sovereign.¹

Their indignation, however, was only assumed as a cloak for their alarm; and whilst they were most bitterly inveighing against the Regent, they sent to him to propose a compromise. In order to prevent the production of those formidable documents, which Elizabeth's perfidious animosity so ardently desired, they suggested that he should become reconciled to his sister, who would, doubtless, restore him to her favour, and give him and his adherents every pledge that they might require.² But this was only a reconciliation, whilst Murray and the lords of his party demanded an abdication. Elizabeth, moreover, declared that a Queen who laboured under so grave a charge, ought not to compromise the matter, but to defend herself. With Machiavelian subtlety, she affirmed that the defendants, having indulged in such odious recriminations in order to justify their own acts, were bound to prove what they had advanced, on pain of being treated as defamers of their sovereign, as well as rebels against her authority.³

Mary's danger had now become imminent. Under the pretext of defending himself, Murray was to produce the evidence on which he rested his accusation, at the next meeting of the Conference. Mary's commissioners, finding they would be unable to save their mistress by an amicable arrangement, determined to try legal means. On the 6th of December, when the Regent was summoned before the English commissioners, the Bishop of Ross and his associates demanded admission. They complained that all the promises of friendship, as well as all the rules of justice, had been violated, and declared that since the Queen of England was determined to receive from the Regent the proofs of his injurious allegations against their sovereign, before she was heard in her own defence, they were compelled to dissolve the Conference. They then delivered a written protest, in which they rejected, as null and void, everything that might be done hereafter to the prejudice of the honour or royal dignity of Mary Stuart.⁴ Cecil declined to receive this protest, on the ground that it misinterpreted the answer of Queen Elizabeth; but the Scottish deputies withdrew, repeating that they would neither treat nor appear again.⁵

¹ Goodall, vol. ii., p. 223.
² The Journal of the Privy Council of England, 4th December, 1568. Anderson, vol. iv., part 2, p. 135.   ³ Goodall, vol. ii., p. 224.
⁴ Anderson, vol. iv., part 2, p. 145.   ⁵ Ibid., p. 146.

Notwithstanding their withdrawal, the English commissioners summoned Murray and his friends before them. Like faithful executors of Elizabeth's tortuous policy, they stated that 'the Queen's Majesty thought it very strange that they, being native subjects of the Queen of Scots, should accuse her of so horrible a crime, hateful both to God and man,—a crime against law and nature, which, if their accusation were true, would render her infamous in the sight of all Princes in the world. Her Majesty, therefore, had willed her commissioners to tell them that, although in this deed they had forgotten their duties of allegiance towards their sovereign, she did not mean to forget the love of a good sister, a good neighbour, and a good friend of the Queen of Scots.'[1] The apparent interest which their language displayed only concealed the most premeditated perfidy, for the English commissioners at once summoned the Regent to defend himself, by proving the truth of his accusation.

By this subterfuge Murray was induced to bring forward documents in support of his charge. He successively produced the Book of Articles drawn up for the instruction of the Scottish Council, and containing the examinations of Dalgleish, Powrie, Hepburn, and Hay of Tallo, which proved that Bothwell was the chief author of Darnley's murder; the letters and sonnets in Mary Stuart's handwriting, which had been found in the silver casket, and which proved her foreknowledge of the murder, as well as her consent to the abduction which had led to her marriage with Bothwell; the depositions of Nelson and Crawford, which confirmed the authenticity of the letters, by the similarity of certain facts related in both; and the speeches made upon the scaffold by Hepburn and Hay of Tallo, which added to Mary's written confessions the oral declaration of one of Bothwell's most resolute accomplices.[2] All these documents, either originals or certified copies, were laid before the English commissioners, to assist whose inquiries Elizabeth had deputed the Earls of Northumberland and Westmoreland (both of whom were Papist peers), and the Earls of Shrewsbury, Worcester, Huntingdon, and Warwick.[3]

Elizabeth's intention plainly was to ruin her rival in the opinion of these noblemen, who were the most influential personages in England. On the 14th of December they met at Hampton Court, to enter into a solemn examination of the documents which had

[1] Anderson, vol. iv., part 2, pp. 146, 147.
[2] Ibid., pp. 150-154, 165-169, and 173. Goodall, vol. ii., pp. 141, and 257-259. [3] Ibid., vol. iv., part 2, p. 170.

been laid before them. Several authentic letters, which Mary had written to Elizabeth at various times, were compared with those now attributed to her, which so deeply implicated her in Darnley's murder.[1] After a careful comparison of the handwriting and orthography of the two sets of letters, the Privy Council declared that they could discover no difference between them.[2]

This verification, though irregular in form, was crushing in its effect. The Bishop of Ross and Lord Boyd had endeavoured to avoid it by renewing their protest against the progress of the Conference, and pronouncing its dissolution a second time.[3] With persevering industry they had continued their demand that the Queen of England should allow the Queen of Scotland to speak for herself. But the Privy Council approved of all Elizabeth's proceedings, and decided: 'That as the crimes wherewith the Queen of Scots had been by common fame burdened are made more apparent by many vehement allegations and presumptions upon things now produced, the Queen's Majesty cannot, without manifest blemish of her own honour, agree to have the said Queen come into her presence until the said horrible crimes may be, by some just and reasonable answer, avoided and removed from her.'[4]

Supported by this decision of her Privy Council and chief nobility, Elizabeth more peremptorily refused to grant Mary Stuart the interview which her commissioners continued hopelessly to solicit. She informed them, at the same time, that the documents given in evidence by Murray should be communicated to their mistress, if she would consent to give a direct answer to them, either by means of her commissioners at Westminster, or by send-

[1] 'It was thought mete that the originall lettres and wrytyngs exhibited by the Regent, as the Quene of Scotts' lettres and wrytyngs, shuld also be shewed, and conference thereof made in their sight, with the lettres of the said Quene hertofore wrytten with hir own hand, and sent to the Quene's Majesty; wherby may be serched and examyned what difference is betwyxt the same.' Goodall, vol. ii., p. 252. Laing, vol. i., p. 169.

[2] 'There were produced sundry lettres written in French, supposed to be written by the Quene of Scott's owne hand to the Erle Bothwell, and these being redd were duly conferred and compared for the manner of writing and fashion of orthography, with sundry other lettres long since hertofore written and sent by the said Quene of Scotts to the Quene's Majesty; in collation wherof no difference was found.' The Journals of the Proceedings of the Lords of the Privy Council of England, with some of the chief of the nobility, at Hampton Court, the 14th and 15th days of December, 1568. Anderson, vol. iv., part 2, pp. 172, 173.

[3] Anderson, vol. iv., part 2, pp. 157-163.

[4] Ibid., pp. 177, 178. Goodall, vol. ii., p. 269.

ing some confidential person to court with her defence, or by permitting her to send some confidential nobleman to Bolton to receive her justification. A rejection of these three means of defence, they were told, on the ground that Queen Mary could gain no access to Queen Elizabeth, would seriously injure that Princess in the eyes of the world, which would never consider the refusal of an interview a sufficient reason for silently enduring such imputations.[1] A few days afterwards, Elizabeth wrote a letter to Mary herself, in which, after blaming her deputies for breaking up the Conference without replying to Murray's charge, she hypocritically says: 'We have long been very sorry for your mishaps and great troubles, but we find our sorrows now doubled in beholding such things as are produced to prove yourself the cause of all the same. And our grief therein is also increased, in that we did not think at any time to have seen or heard matters of so great appearance and moment to charge and condemn you; nevertheless, both in friendship, nature, and justice, we are moved to cover these matters, and stay our judgment, and not to gather any sense thereof to your prejudice, before we hear of your direct answer thereunto.' She therefore urged her to send this answer, which had become absolutely necessary, by one of the three methods she had mentioned to her commissioners.[2]

Mary declined this insidious request. She would not condescend to appear as the accused party. Adroit and courageous, sometimes perplexed, but never cast down, she now displayed all the resources of her mind and all the energy of her character. After having tried every means to prevent the publication of the documents which criminated her; after having had recourse to the skilful manœuvres of Lethington, and the prudent counsels of Norfolk; after having once offered to abdicate, and frequently to forgive, even when she was most grievously offended—she now stood up with all the dignity of a Queen, and proved herself as bold as she had previously appeared accommodating. Instead of defending herself, she attacked Murray.

On the 19th of December, she wrote to her commissioners: 'Forasmuch as the Earl of Murray and his adherents, our rebellious subjects, have added unto their pretended excuses, produced by them for colouring of their horrible crimes and offences committed against us, their sovereign lady and mistress, the charge that, "as the Earl of Bothwell was the principal executor of the

[1] Goodall, vol. ii., pp. 257, 260, 263, 264.
[2] Letter from Elizabeth to Mary, 21st December, 1568. Anderson, vol. iv., part 2, pp. 183, 184.

murder committed on the person of Harry Stuart our late husband, so we knew, counselled, devised, persuaded, and commanded the said murder,"—they have falsely, traitorously, and wickedly lied; maliciously imputing unto us a crime of which themselves were authors and inventors, and some of them even executors.' Repelling the charge of having impeded the proceedings of justice against Darnley's murderers, and of having given her consent beforehand to her marriage with Bothwell, she alluded, with consummate ability and eloquence, to the danger to which the lords declared that she had exposed her son: 'That calumny,' she pathetically observed, 'should suffice for proof of all the rest. The natural love of a mother towards her bairn confounds them; but in the malice and impiety of their hearts, they judge others by their own affection.'[1]

She maintained, in the next place, that having determined to revolt and obtain possession of her authority, and being desirous to gain the people to their side by plausible pretexts, they had feigned a wish to deliver her from the hands of Bothwell who had carried her off with their consent, to avenge the death of her husband whom they had murdered, and to preserve the life of her son, who was under the care of one of their confederates, the Earl of Mar. Their actions, she added, had not corresponded to their declarations, and had plainly proved that their sole object was to make themselves masters of her person, and to usurp her power. In conclusion, she referred to all they had done from the murder of Riccio until that time; and she protested at once against the abdication which she had been compelled to sign, and the imputations which they had dared to cast upon her.[2]

Mary Stuart thus justified herself by recrimination. The lords, who had attacked, imprisoned, and dethroned her—who had forced her to fly, and had even pursued her into a foreign land—deserved her reproaches to a very great extent. Members of the Scottish nobility, turbulent, factious, and brutal; without fidelity, honour, or conscience; passing carelessly from one conspiracy to another; now rising in favour of the Queen, and now against her; confederated on one day with Murray, on the next with Lennox, and on the next with Bothwell; killing Riccio and abandoning Darnley; proscribing Bothwell after having given him every encouragement, and allowing him to escape after having risen in arms to capture him—they now pretended anxiety to avenge a crime

---

[1] Letter from Mary Stuart to the Bishop of Ross, Lord Herries, and the Abbot of Kilwinning, 19th December, 1568. Labanoff, vol. ii., pp. 257-259.
[2] Labanoff, vol. ii., pp. 259, 260.

which many of them had either advised, or foreknown, or allowed. Murray was an ambitious man, who was ready to sacrifice to his own elevation, the power, the liberty, and the reputation of his sister. He had consented to Riccio's assassination, and though not an accomplice in Darnley's murder, it is doubtful whether he was entirely ignorant of it. Morton had directed the commission of the first of these crimes, and had deliberated with Bothwell upon the second. Lethington had been connected with both. None were entirely innocent. Neither the orthodox zeal of Mary Stuart, nor the Presbyterian austerity of Murray, Morton, and Lethington, had made them turn aside from the most blameworthy actions, or the most hateful plots. In this age of violence, creeds were less powerful than customs, and though religion exercised much influence over the minds of men, it had very little effect upon their conduct. Thus we meet with the passions which distinguished that age and country, in the Queen as well as in her subjects. These passions were in both cases accompanied by disorders, concealed by falsehood, satisfied by acts of criminal boldness, and followed by severe chastisement. As neither party had been exempt from their influence, so neither was allowed to go unpunished.

Mary Stuart's commissioners, in obedience to the orders they had received from their mistress, accused the Regent and his partisans of having been the authors of the murder which they now denounced.[1] They had already requested copies of the letters attributed to their sovereign; and the Bishop of Ross had attempted to invalidate their authority. In a long memorial,[2] he had maintained that they could not be admitted as a means of evidence, that the comparison of the handwritings was fallacious, and that such documents were insufficient to constitute legal proof. He did not, however, sustain with great vigour the accusation which had been brought against Murray and his adherents, in answer to that which they had preferred against the Queen. On hearing of this unexpected attack, the fiery Lindsay had sent a challenge to Herries,[3] and on the 11th of January, Murray summoned his sister's commissioners before the English Council, to adduce evidence in support of their charge.[4] Mary's deputies, thus called upon, read the vague recriminations which had been sent to them from Bolton, declared that of themselves they knew

[1] Goodall, vol. ii., pp. 271, 272. Laing, vol. i., p. 178. Tytler, vol. vi., p. 77.
[2] Ibid., vol. ii., p. 392. Laing, vol. i., p. 178. Haynes, pp. 495, 496.
[3] Ibid., vol. ii., p. 272. Laing, vol. i., p. 178.
[4] Ibid., vol. ii., p. 307. Laing, vol. i., pp. 185, 186.

nothing, and simply alluded to the statements which Bothwell's accomplices had made regarding Morton and Lethington. They further stated that, as they had come to defend the honour of their mistress, they merely obeyed her will by constituting themselves accusers of others, in her name and by her instructions.[1]

An accusation thus evidently subsidiary to the main cause, and so difficult of proof in the case of Mary's principal adversary, who offered to go to Bolton and deny the charge in presence of his sister,[2] could not be carried very far. Mary's abdication was once more suggested. Elizabeth directed Vice-Chamberlain Knollys to propose it to her again, as the only means of bringing matters to a final arrangement.[3] Lethington also had recently expressed the same views,[4] and the commissioners of the Queen of Scots had concurred in his opinion. But the evil was done; the defamation was made public. By renouncing her crown, Mary Stuart would have confessed her own culpability. She, therefore, did not hesistate for a moment. If, before the opening of the Conference at York, she had for a short time been willing to sacrifice her authority to her honour, she was not so after the irrevocable Conference at Westminster. She told her commissioners that by yielding to her adversaries all that they demanded, she would appear ' to have been her own judge and to have condemned herself;' that the 'reports which had been spread regarding her,' would be thereby confirmed, and she would be 'held in abhorrence by all the people of this isle.'[5] After having pointed out to them the various dangerous consequences which such an act on her part would produce, she added that she would not thus destroy her reputation, break off her alliances, and even expose her life. 'I pray you therefore,' she wrote, 'do not speak to me again about abdication, for I am deliberately resolved rather to die than resign my crown; and the last words that I shall utter in my life shall be the words of a Queen of Scotland.'[6]

An abdication having been thus irrevocably refused, and the Conference dissolved, all was at an end. These long and painful

[1] Goodall, vol. ii., pp. 308, 309. Anderson, vol. iii., p. 34. Laing, vol. i., pp. 185, 186.
[2] Goodall, vol. i., p. 309.
[3] Goodall, vol. ii., pp. 279, 300. Tytler, vol. vi., p. 76.
[4] Anderson, vol. iv., part 2, pp. 140-144.
[5] Declaration presented by Mary Stuart's Commissioners to the Conference, on the 9th January, 1569. Labanoff, vol. ii., pp. 274-277.
[6] Labanoff, vol. ii., p. 274.

debates could not be continued. Elizabeth had neither the means to dispossess Mary, nor the right to condemn her. But she had succeeded in defaming her, and had obtained a pretext for keeping her in captivity. The Regent, anxious to return to Scotland,[1] where the insecurity of his authority rendered his presence necessary, requested and obtained permission to do so.[2] On the 10th of January, he appeared before the Privy Council of England, which expressed its entire approval of his conduct, and gave him leave to depart, saying 'that nothing had been as yet adduced against him and his adherents, that might impair their honour or allegiance.'[3] To this declaration, says Mary Stuart's commissioners, the following clause was added, by way of compensation: 'On the other hand, nothing had been sufficiently proven or shown by them against the Queen their sovereign, whereby the Queen of England should conceive any evil opinion of her good sister.'[4]

Notwithstanding this declaration, which was utterly at variance with Elizabeth's subsequent conduct,[5] she continued to press the charge of murder on her unfortunate prisoner. Mary Stuart had, on several occasions, requested copies of the letters which had been brought in evidence against her.[6] Elizabeth refused to send them until Mary promised to justify herself. This Mary would consent to do only in presence of Elizabeth and the ambassadors of the various foreign Princes. An endless contest thus began: Elizabeth made the transmission of the letters depend on a promise which Mary Stuart would not make, and Mary Stuart offered to defend herself on conditions which Elizabeth had invariably refused to accept.[7] This lasted during the whole of January, and neither party manifested any intention to yield. The commissioners of the Queen of Scots again demanded that she might be permitted freely to leave England, as Murray and just done. But their demands were vain. They then concluded this lengthy negotiation by entering their protest against anything that might be done to the prejudice of their mistress during her captivity.[8] This done, they joined Mary Stuart, who had been removed from the custody of Lord Scrope, the Duke of Norfolk's brother-in-law, and conducted on the 26th January

[1] Tytler, vol. vi., p. 78. Laing, vol. i., p. 184.   [2] Goodall, vol. ii., p. 309.
[3] Mary's Register, in Goodall, vol. ii., p. 305.   [4] Ibid.
[5] See the 'Answer to the Queen of Scots' Commissioners,' dated 13th January, 1568; in Laing, vol. i., pp. 189, 190.
[6] Labanoff, vol. ii., pp. 263, 273. Goodall, vol. ii., p. 310.
[7] Laing, vol. i., pp. 189, 190. Goodall, vol. ii., p. 310. Tytler, vol. vi., p. 81.
[8] Goodall, vol. ii., pp. 310, 313. Tytler, vol. vi., p 81.

from Bolton to Tutbury. On her arrival at Tutbury, on the 3rd of February, she had been placed under the surveillance of the Earl of Shrewsbury.[1] Four days after she had reached this fortress, which was farther than Bolton from the Scottish frontier, the Bishop of Ross, Lord Herries, and her other commissioners arrived to present her with the register they had prepared of the Conferences at York and Westminster, and to receive her approval of their conduct.[2] Thus ended this disastrous inquiry, which Mary Stuart ought not to have accepted under any form, which did not entail any decision to her dishonour, but which, by permitting her defamation, furnished a pretext for her imprisonment.

By thus adding the climax to his sister's misfortunes Murray had placed himself in a most dangerous position. The Duke of Norfolk was incensed against him. He could not pardon him for having broken at Westminster the pledges which he had given at York, and thus placed new difficulties in the way of his marriage with the Queen of Scotland. The Earls of Northumberland and Westmoreland were also furiously indignant, and wished to punish Murray for having accused the Catholic heir to the Crown of England of adultery and homicide. These devoted partisans of Mary Stuart proposed to have the Regent waylaid and slain before he crossed the border on his return home.[3] Murray was aware of their intention; and after he had taken his leave of Queen Elizabeth, he remained for several weeks in London without daring to commence his journey.[4]

In order to avoid the fate with which he was threatened, he had recourse to stratagem. Throckmorton, whose hatred of Cecil, interest of Mary, and friendship for the Regent, led him to desire the restoration of peace in Scotland, and the union of the two kingdoms into one, arranged an interview between Murray and the Duke of Norfolk.[5] In this interview, Murray displayed the deepest contrition for what had passed, and declared that he had been compelled by Elizabeth's manœuvres to act against his sister. He further affirmed that he had only engaged in this painful affair in order to preserve his young Sovereign, and expressed his hope that God would touch the heart of the Queen of Scotland, that she might repent of her past conduct, and renounce the impious and illegitimate marriage which she had con-

---

[1] Labanoff, vol. ii., pp. 279, 280, 286, 296. [2] Ibid., vol. ii., pp. 296, 297.
[3] Examination of the Bishop of Ross; in Murdin, pp. 46, 51, 54. Melvil's Memoirs, p. 99.
[4] Letter from Murray, in Robertson's History of Scotland, Appendix 33.
[5] Melvil's Memoirs, p. 98.

tracted. If his sister, he adroitly added, should then espouse an honourable and pious person, well affectioned to the true religion, and if that person were the Duke himself, he would be truly thankful, and would give his sister, who had never ceased to be dear to him, as strong proofs of his attachment and good-will towards her as he had ever been able to afford at other periods of his life. These promises, though more politic than sincere, appeased the Duke of Norfolk. With the credulity of desire, he admitted the Regent's explanations and trusted to his promises. He considered him to be more capable than any other person of facilitating his union with Mary Stuart. 'Earl of Murray,' said he, 'thou hast Norfolk's life in thy hands.'[1] He sent the strictest injunctions to his adherents not to molest him in any way on his road home, and the Regent returned fearlessly and without danger to Scotland, where he arrived towards the end of January, 1569.[2]

As for Mary Stuart, she remained a prisoner in England. Elizabeth not only did not assist her against her subjects, as she had offered to do, but she did not even restore her to liberty, of which she never had any right to deprive her. Regardless of the rules of justice, the rights of hospitality, and the prerogatives of royalty, she had not scrupled to imprison a suppliant, and to bring a Queen to trial. She had shown no respect either to the trust of the fugitive, the claims of relationship, the affliction of the woman, or the honour of the Sovereign. Mary Stuart, in her turn, had now no reason to act considerately towards Elizabeth. She had been perfidiously arrested, remorselessly defamed, and iniquitously imprisoned. She might now try all means to regain her liberty; and these means she did not fail to exert.

[1] Robertson, Appendix 33. Anderson, vol. iii., pp. 36-39.
[2] Melvil's Memoirs, p. 99. Lesly's Negotiations, in Anderson, vol. iii., pp. 40, 41. Tytler, vol. vi., p. 87.

CHAPTER VIII.

FROM MURRAY'S RETURN TO SCOTLAND TO THE EXECUTION OF
THE DUKE OF NORFOLK.

Mary's efforts to restore her party in Scotland—Murray's activity and energy—
Proposed Marriage of Mary to the Duke of Norfolk—Negotiations on the subject
—League of the Nobility against Cecil—He joins Norfolk's party—Secret intrigues of Norfolk in Scotland—Convention at Perth—Alarm and anger of
Elizabeth—Norfolk and his Friends retire to their Estates—Arrest of Norfolk—
Catholic Insurrection in the North of England—Defeat of the Insurgents—
Assassination of Murray—Insurrection of Mary Stuart's party in Scotland—
Invasion of the English Border—The Earl of Lennox appointed Regent—Negotiations for Mary's Liberation; they are broken off—Conspiracy of Mary Stuart
and the Duke of Norfolk—Mission of Ridolfi—Discovery of the Conspiracy in
England—Trial and Condemnation of Norfolk—His Execution and Mary's
distress.

MARY STUART, though a prisoner, was far from inactive.
Without giving up her negotiations with Murray and Elizabeth,
she interested France in her favour, armed Scotland in her cause,
roused the North of England to battle for her deliverance,
animated the Catholics to a religious conflict, excited the Spaniards to an invasion of the island; in a word, she had recourse at
various times to the most opposite means, for the purpose of
punishing those subjects who had driven her from her throne,
and that Queen who had reduced her to captivity.

She had never ceased to maintain the closest communications
with her partisans in Scotland; and she had always been careful
to encourage their hopes. In the west of her kingdom, the
fortress of Dumbarton, situated on an almost inaccessible rock
jutting out into the sea, still held out for her. In the north, the
Earls of Argyle, Huntly, and Crawford, and Lord Ogilvy, had
remained faithful to her, and kept that part of the country true
to its allegiance. In the south, the warlike border clans, the
Scotts, Kers, and Maxwells, were anxiously waiting an opportunity to serve her. The Hamiltons, notwithstanding their
defeat at Langside, still had considerable forces at their disposal.
Mary Stuart, who was incessantly entreating the Court of France
to send her soldiers, artillerymen, arms, and ammunition, had
written to her adherents to hold themselves in readiness to
recommence the contest.[1] In order to add fresh motives to those

[1] Mary Stuart to the Commendator of Arbroath and other lords, December,
1568; Labanoff, vol. ii., p. 248.

which already led them to hate the Regent and distrust Elizabeth, she had informed them that the rebel lords intended to deliver the Prince her son, and the three fortresses of Edinburgh, Stirling, and Dumbarton (after they had besieged and captured this last), into the hands of the Queen of England, who, on her side, had promised to appoint the young Prince her successor, and if he died, to recognize Murray as King of Scotland.[1] In reliance upon this imaginary arrangement, which Mary Stuart was compelled, by Elizabeth's complaint, to disavow in England[2] after having asserted it in Scotland, the faithful lords published a vehement proclamation, and made an appeal to arms.[3] The Duke of Chatelherault, accompanied by Lord Herries, appeared in their midst as the Queen's lieutenant, in conjunction with the Earls of Huntly and Argyle.[4] Mary had, moreover, flattered the Duke by calling him her adoptive father. Her adherents fortified their houses, mustered their partisans, and treated the Regent as a rebel and usurper.[5]

Murray was not in so strong a position on his return as he had been at his departure; but, like a resolute man, he allowed his enemies no time either to deliberate or to act. His party was still zealous and numerous. He was supported by the inhabitants of the towns, the Presbyterian clergy, and the most determined and sagacious of the nobility. He also possessed the public authority, which always insures the advantage in civil contests to those who are able to use it opportunely and with vigour. He held a Convention of the nobility, clergy, and commissaries of the burghs at Stirling,[6] and having obtained from them their

[1] Labanoff, vol. ii., pp. 250, 251.
[2] She wrote to Elizabeth, who had loaded her with reproaches for this false statement, and demanded that she should disavow it:—' Je n'en ay nulle connoissance, et n'écrivis jamais de si vaines phantésies quant je les eusse soupçonnées; parquoy s'il vous plaist enquérir, vous n'y trouverez rien ni de mon commandement, ni de ma mayn, ni lettres.' Mary Stuart to Elizabeth, 27th January, 1569, Labanoff, vol. ii., p. 289. See also the despatch of Lamothe Fénelon to Charles IX., 30th January, 1569; vol. i., pp. 161, 162; and the letter from Mary Stuart to Cecil, 28th January, 1569; vol. ii., pp. 292, 293. Robertson, Appendix 31; Letter from Elizabeth to Knollys on the 22nd January, and from Knollys to Elizabeth on the 28th January, 1569.
[3] Lord Hunsdon to Cecil, 15th January, 1569; Haynes, p. 503.
[4] Labanoff, vol. ii., p. 268.   [5] Tytler, vol. vi., p. 87.
[6] This Convention met on the 12th of February, 1569. The document is in Anderson, vol. iv., part 2, p. 196. It is signed by the Regent, the Earls of Athol, Morton, Mar, Glencairn, Menteith, and Buchan; the Masters of Grahame, Marshall, and Errol; the Bishop of Orkney; the Commendators of Dunfermline, Balmerino, Dryburgh, Cambuskenneth, Coldinghame, and Whithorne; the Lords Lindsay, Glammis, Saltoun, Innermeith, Cathcart, and Ochiltree; the Secretary

approbation of his conduct, and a ratification of his proceedings in England, he ordered an immediate muster of his troops, and marched against the Queen's adherents before they could concentrate their forces. Directing his course westward, he surprised the Duke of Chatelherault and Lord Herries, and compelled them to enter into an accommodation. In a conference which they had with him at Glasgow, on the 13th of March, 1569, these two servants of the Queen concluded a provisional treaty of peace between the two parties which then divided Scotland. They consented to acknowledge the young King, on condition that all who had been forfeited for their obedience to the Queen, should be restored. It was agreed, further, that a Committee selected from the nobles on both sides, and including the Earls of Argyle and Huntly, should meet at Edinburgh on the 10th of April, to deliberate upon a general and definitive pacification of the kingdom.[1] Meanwhile, they all went to pay their homage to the young King at Stirling. The Archbishop of St. Andrews, the Earl of Cassillis, and Lord Herries remained as hostages in the hands of the Regent, who, on his part, liberated the prisoners taken at the battle of Langside.[2]

Murray did not, however, disband his troops. He took advantage of the truce made at Glasgow to proceed to the southern frontier and crush the Borderers. Issuing with new strength from this double expedition, he returned in triumph to Edinburgh, in time to attend the Convention of the nobles. Huntly and Argyle had refused to take part in this assembly, and had rejected the provisional arrangement made at Glasgow, which they not unreasonably considered most disastrous to the cause of Mary Stuart. Alarmed at the threatened dissolution of her party, and the general recognition of her son, the captive Queen had written to the Duke of Chatelherault and Lord Herries to express her surprise and dissatisfaction at the course they had adopted.[3] Her letters had reached them on the evening before the day on which the assembly began. Both were much affected by her

---

Lethington, the Treasurer Richardson, the Comptroller Tullibardine, the Clerk-register and Justice-clerk, and the deputies of the burghs of Edinburgh, Stirling, Dundee, Peebles, Glasgow, Cupar, St. Andrews, Perth, and Haddington.
[1] MS. letter, State Paper Office, Murray to Sir John Forster, 15th March, 1569 ; Tytler, vol. vi., p. 88. The Convention of the 13th March is in the Correspondence of Lamothe Fénelon, vol. i., pp. 300-302.
[2] Tytler, vol. vi., pp. 88, 89.
[3] Despatch from Lamothe Fénelon to Charles IX., 6th May, 1569. Correspondence, vol. i., p. 369. The Earl of Huntly had written to Mary Stuart to complain of the conduct of the Duke of Chatelherault. Ibid., vol. i., p. 379.

reproaches; the Duke wept all night long, and Lord Herries fell ill.[1] They both resolved to revoke their acknowledgment of the King's authority. Accordingly, when the Regent desired them to sign a recognition of the sovereignty of James VI., they remonstrated, and declared that the conditions of an accommodation ought first to be discussed. The most essential of these conditions, they said, was the restoration of the Queen. Murray vouchsafed no answer to their remonstrance, but ordered his guards instantly to apprehend them; and they were led as prisoners to the Castle of Edinburgh, and placed in the custody of Kirkaldy of Grange.[2] This act of violence enraged, but intimidated, Mary's party.

The Regent was not content with this outrage. After arresting the old chieftain of the west, and the most enterprising baron of the south, he marched his veteran and confident troops against the two earls who were in arms in the north. Alarmed, however, by the late scenes in the capital, they did not venture to oppose him. Argyle quickly effected a reconciliation with his old friend, the Regent. Huntly, and the other northern lords, knowing that defeat would be followed by entire forfeiture of their possessions, also submitted. On the 10th of May, they met at St. Andrews, subscribed their adherence to the government of James VI., surrendered their artillery to the Regent, and delivered hostages for their future good behaviour.[3] To secure his advantage, Murray led his army into the north, where the clans had invariably remained faithful to the Queen, his sister. He ravaged their territory, took their castles, carried off their arms, and levied heavy fines on all who had risen in Mary's favour.[4] In a few months he had crushed all resistance, and reduced to submission the whole country from Inverness to Dumfries, and from Dunbar to Glasgow. He then convoked an Assembly of the Estates of the realm, to meet at Perth, on the 25th of July, 1569.

But whilst Mary Stuart's hopes were thus overthrown in Scotland, her position in England was improving. A powerful

[1] 'Le duc de Chatellerault fut meu de si grand repentance qu'il ne cessa toute la nuicte de pleurer, et millord Herriz tumba malade, et tant ces deux que les aultres principaux du party de ladicte dame ne vollurent le lendemain rien accorder.' Tytler, vol. i., p. 379.
[2] Tytler, vol. vi., p. 90.
[3] MS. letter, State Paper Office, Lord Hunsdon to Cecil, 19th May, 1569; Tytler, vol. vi., p. 91. Spotswood, p. 229.
[4] MS letter, State Paper Office, Murray to Cecil, 7th July, 1569; Tytler, vol. vi., p. 91.

party had been formed in the latter country to promote her marriage with the Duke of Norfolk,[1] whose ambition had led him to renew a project which fear had forced him to disavow after the Conference at York. Supported by Lethington, and feeling certain of Murray's consent, he had, since the termination of the Conferences at Westminster and Hampton Court, secretly gained the concurrence of the principal members of the English nobility, and even of a large number of the Privy Council. This project, of which Elizabeth was kept entirely ignorant, met with great encouragement in the public interest which it inspired. The succession to the crown, which that Princess had hitherto refused to regulate, occasioned general apprehension. The people remembered with terror the dynastic wars of the two houses of York and Lancaster, which had desolated England for nearly half a century; and felt naturally desirous to prevent the recurrence of a similar struggle between the various claimants who aspired to the inheritance of a Queen whose frequent illnesses rendered it probable that she would not live much longer. The marriage of the most powerful nobleman in England to the nearest relation of Elizabeth and the most direct descendant of Henry VII.—the union of the Catholic Mary with the Protestant Norfolk—seemed a fortunate and most desirable combination.

The numerous adherents of the ancient religion entertained the hope that under Mary's sway their faith would be restored, or at least tolerated; and the Protestants believed that they had every guarantee for the maintenance of the Established Church, in the religious zeal which they supposed Norfolk to possess. The Earl of Arundel, a member of the Privy Council, and in rank inferior only to the Duke of Norfolk; the Earl of Pembroke, Master of the Queen's Household, and possessed of great influence in Wales; the Earls of Westmoreland and Northumberland; Lord Lumley, the son-in-law of the Earl of Arundel; and other peers, more or less openly Catholics, gave the scheme their full concurrence. The Earls of Cumberland, Bedford, Sussex, and Derby, when consulted by Norfolk upon the subject offered no opposition. Leicester himself earnestly promoted it,[2] either from anxiety to secure a supporter if he lost Elizabeth, whose favour had excited against him much envy and hostility,[3] or from a desire to know all that was going on, that he might better serve the Queen his

[1] Despatch of Lamothe Fénelon, 27th July, 1569; vol. ii., p. 126.
[2] Lesly's Negotiations, in Anderson, vol. iii., pp. 55, 62. Throckmorton to Lethington, 20th July, 1569; in Robertson, Appendix 32.
[3] Despatch from Lamothe Fénelon, 27th July, 1569, vol. ii., pp. 123, 124.

mistress when it became necessary. In addition to the co-operation of the more powerful nobles, the Duke of Norfolk reckoned on the assistance of the country gentlemen. He also consulted the ambassadors of France and Spain,[1] with whom he maintained a close and mysterious connection, and who assured him of the assent of their respective sovereigns.[2] The chief members of this league trusted in the end to procure the consent of their own sovereign, or, in case of refusal, to obtain her sanction by force.[3]

In the first place, however, it was necessary to secure the concurrence of that vigilant minister who directed her administration. Cecil had rendered Elizabeth the universal protectress of Protestantism, by inducing her to pension the Lutheran Princes in Germany, to support the Lords of the Congregation in Scotland, to encourage the armed Huguenots in France, and secretly to aid the religious insurgents in the Netherlands. He had already placed her in a position of extreme difficulty with regard to Philip II. Some Genoese merchants who were conveying, in Basque and Galician ships, a large sum of money for the payment of the troops of the Duke of Alva, had sought shelter in an English port from the pursuit of pirates. Elizabeth seized their vessels, under the pretext that they had arrived in her dominions without either authorization or passport. The money which they had on board was confiscated, notwithstanding the Duke of Alva's demands for its restitution. In reprisal, the haughty Spaniard seized a number of English merchants and their goods, by virtue of a measure which Philip II. applied to Elizabeth's subjects throughout his dominions. Elizabeth, on her side, pursued the same course towards all the subjects of Philip II. who were settled as traders in England; and this violent interruption of commerce between the two countries was speedily followed by the arrest of the ambassadors of the two sovereigns—Dr. John Mann at Madrid, and Don Gueraldo d'Espès, who had succeeded Guzman de Silva, at London.[4] Though already involved in a contest with France, with which country commercial relations had also been suspended, in consequence of the support she had given to the revolted Huguenots, Elizabeth was now on the eve of a war with Spain. Cecil urged her to commence hostilities without delay.[5]

---

[1] Despatch from Lamothe Fénelon, 27th July, 1569, vol. ii., p. 127.
[2] Lesly's Negotiations, in Anderson, vol. iii., p. 63.
[3] Despatch from Lamothe Fénelon, 27th July, 1569, vol. ii., pp. 126, 127.
[4] The Spanish ambassador was arrested at his residence, on the 8th of January 1569, by Secretary Cecil and Admiral Clinton. Gonzalez, Apuntamientos, p. 88.
[5] Despatch of Lamothe Fénelon, 21st June, 1569, vol. ii., p. 51.

By his advice, the ports of England had been fortified, arms and ammunition had been collected, vessels equipped, and troops levied ;[1] and the two most formidable Catholic Powers of the Continent had been affronted.

This course of policy was becoming dangerous. The heads of the nobility did not conceal their apprehensions from the Queen, but openly attacked the adventurous minister who had given such advice.[2] Elizabeth had her moments of uncertainty and timidity; and at this period she was not without fears regarding her own position. The inhabitants of the sea-ports and other towns suffered greatly from the cessation of trade, and manifested extreme displeasure at her conduct. The oppressed Catholics were quite ready to revolt in favour of the Catholic granddaughter of Henry VII., then a prisoner in their midst. At Rome, Pope Pius V. was taking measures to dethrone her as an obstinate heretic. Mary Stuart had denounced her to Philip II., as being desirous to poison her.[3] The Catholic nobles, and several leading members of the Privy Council had paid clandestine visits to the Spanish ambassador, and had assured him that an invasion of the country would inevitably be successful.[4] Moreover, such an invasion might easily be effected, as the Duke of Alva had just reduced the Netherlands to obedience, and had no other immediate use for the greater part of his army. Finally, the Catholic party, menacing in England, and triumphant in Flanders, was victorious in France, where the Duke of Anjou and the Marshal de Tavannes had just gained the battle of Jarnac over Admiral Coligny and the Prince of Condé, leaving the latter dead on the field.

Matters were in this state, when the Duke of Norfolk, the Earl of Arundel, and several other members of Elizabeth's Privy Council, rose in opposition to the measures proposed by Cecil.[5] For a short time they destroyed his credit with the Queen, and Elizabeth seemed to have rejected her minister's policy. Cecil

[1] Despatch of Lamothe Fénelon, 21st June, 1569, vol. ii., pp. 48-51.
[2] Correspondence of Lamothe Fénelon, vol. ii., p. 51.
[3] 'Por estos dias supo el mismo embajador (Don Gueraldo D'Espès, Knight of the order of Calatrava, who had succeeded Don Gusman de Silva as the ambassador of Philip II. in London, in September, 1568), por avisos de la Reina Maria y participò al Rey Felipe que habia cerca de su persona sugetos pagados por Isabel para darle veneno.'—Gonzalez, Apuntamientos, pp. 87, 96.
[4] 'El duque de Norfolk, y el conde de Arundel, y el conde de Northumberland aseguraban á cada paso á Espès que si el Rey Felipe emprendia una invasion en Inglaterra, seria seguro el exito seguir el desafecto de la mayor parte de las clases y personas al gobierno de Isabel.'—Don Tomas Gonzalez, Apuntamientos, p. 90.
[5] Despatch of Lamothe Fénelon, 21st June, 1569, vol. ii., pp. 51-53. Gonzalez, Apuntamientos, p. 91.

himself, whom his adversaries were desirous to humiliate, yielded in order to avert his impending fall.¹ He regained the good graces of the Duke of Norfolk by appearing to devote himself to his interests.²

The Duke gained his point. Elizabeth, isolated in the midst of her Council, and no longer possessing Leicester's unwavering fidelity and Cecil's entire confidence, began to negotiate. By means of Robert Ridolfi, the head of the company of Florentine merchants in London, and a secret agent of the Pope, she entered into communication with the Spanish ambassador, with a view to settle, by a pacific arrangement, the differences which had arisen between herself and Philip II.³ She also listened to the remonstrances of the French ambassador, Lamothe Fénelon, in favour of Mary Stuart, which became more urgent in proportion as they received greater attention.

Mary was still a prisoner, and her captivity was rendered far more painful by the overthrow of her party in Scotland. She had written to Elizabeth to complain, in the most energetic terms, of the violent proceedings of Murray, who, notwithstanding the pledges Elizabeth had given, was employing armed force against all who remained faithful to their Queen. She requested the Queen of England, 'without any further trifling,' to declare formally whether she intended to restore her to her country or not. 'Any other answer,' she added in a resolute and threatening tone, ' I cannot but take to be a refusal, which would cause me, to my great regret, to accept any other aid that it might please God to send me.'⁴

This was what Elizabeth feared, and what she was particularly anxious to avoid in the difficult circumstances in which she was then placed. Accordingly, in May, 1569, she recognized the Bishop of Ross as Mary Stuart's ambassador,⁵ and opened a negotiation on the basis suggested by this plenipotentiary of her captive. The Bishop of Ross proposed the following articles to

¹ 'Cecil ... previno el golpe, manifestose muy humano con Norfolk, Arundel, y otros grandes y caballeros Católicos, y procuró tambien captar la benevolencia del embajador español.' Apuntamientos, p. 91.

² 'Et cependant luy (Cecil) ayant pris grand peur de ce qu'on luy vouloit ainsy imputer tout le mal de ceste guerre, tant odieuse à tout ce royaulme, a heu recours au duc de Norfolc, et luy a requis sa protection, avec promesse de suyvre doresnavant son party, et de se porter en toutes choses pour son certain et tout déclairé serviteur.' Despatch of Lamothe Fénelon, 21st June, 1569; vol. ii., p. 53.

³ Correspondence of Lamothe Fénelon, vol. ii., pp. 55, 56.

⁴ Mary Stuart to Elizabeth, 26th April, 1569; Labanoff, vol. ii. p. 333.

⁵ Lesly's Negotiations, in Anderson, vol. iii., p. 46.

the Queen and Council of England : First, the Queen of Scotland shall not disturb the Queen of England nor the legitimate heirs of her body, with regard to their title to the crown of England and Ireland, provided that, in their default, it be fully reserved to the Queen of Scotland and her heirs. If this be granted, the treaty made at Edinburgh in July, 1560, shall be ratified. Secondly, a treaty of alliance and friendship shall be made between the two kingdoms, by the advice of the Estates of both countries, in order better to secure their future union. Thirdly, the two preceding clauses, sealed with the seals of both princes, and confirmed by their oath, shall be rendered still more inviolable by receiving the sanction of the Parliaments of both countries; and if further assurance be required, the Queen of Scotland will procure the Kings of France and Spain to act as her sureties that she will keep the promises she has made. Fourthly, in order to please the Queen of England, and by her desire, the Queen of Scotland will extend her clemency to all those of her subjects who have offended her, provided that they will return to their allegiance, deliver to her the Prince her son, restore to her the fortresses of her kingdom and her jewels which they have seized, and will conduct themselves in future as faithful subjects. Fifthly, those who plotted and executed the murder of Lord Darnley, her late husband, shall be punished without delay, in accordance with the laws of the kingdom. Sixthly, in order to reassure the Scottish nobility with regard to the return of the Earl of Bothwell, the Queen promises never again to receive him into her kingdom, but, by the advice of her nobles, to obtain a divorce from him, that he may be deprived of all claims upon her for the future. Seventhly, after the adoption of these articles, the Queen of Scotland shall be conveyed, with an honourable escort from the Queen of England, back to her kingdom, where the Estates in Parliament assembled shall restore her to possession of her crown; and all acts and statutes contrary to her authority shall be annulled and destroyed as if they had never existed.[1]

These propositions were carefully discussed by the Privy Council of England. The commissioners whom Elizabeth appointed to treat with the Bishop of Ross, were the more disposed to admit his proposals, as John Wood, the Regent's secretary, assured them that from letters he had recently received, the Regent would joyfully resign the government of Scotland, of which he was already weary.[2] They required, moreover, that

---

[1] Lesly's Negotiations, in Anderson, vol. iii., pp. 46-49.   [2] Ibid., p. 49

the league between England and Scotland should be a perpetual alliance, both offensive and defensive; that Mary Stuart should not only become reconciled to those who had taken arms against her, but that she should receive them into favour; that she should maintain the Protestant religion in Scotland; and that she should give assurance that she had not yielded to the Duke of Anjou her title to the crown of England.[1] Whilst this negotiation was proceeding openly, the projected marriage of Mary to the Duke of Norfolk was being arranged, unknown to Elizabeth, by many of the leading members of her Privy Council.

The Earls of Arundel, Pembroke, and Leicester, and Lord Lumley, sent a gentleman named Candish to Wingfield, to propose to Mary Stuart the articles which were to constitute the basis of the treaty. They had, however, added another to the following effect: 'Because it was feared that the Queen of Scotland might marry some foreign prince, whereby the religion of the country might be altered, and the good estate of both realms endangered, it is therefore desirable that she should accept some nobleman of England in marriage, specially the Duke of Norfolk, who is first of the nobility of that realm, and most fit of all others.'[2] Mr. Candish also delivered to her, on behalf of the noblemen who had sent him, a very affectionate letter, written by Leicester himself.[3] Mary Stuart gave immediate assent to all the conditions imposed on her restoration. The only article to which she demurred was the offensive and defensive alliance between England and Scotland. On this point, she requested time to consult the Court of France,[4] being unwilling to lose her dowry and deprive herself of an ancient ally, before she was sure of having obtained a new one.

As to her marriage with the Duke of Norfolk, she expressed her willingness to conclude it at once, in order to conciliate the favour of the English nobles. She had already commenced a secret correspondence with the Duke, and had written to him several letters full of tenderness and confidence. 'I have no other matters in head,' she wrote, 'than those you have in hand.'[5] In her reply to Candish, however, she feigned some hesitation, and said 'that she had been so vexed by her marriages in times past, that she had no thought of any such matter,

---

[1] Lesly's Negotiations, in Anderson, vol. iii., p. 50.
[2] Anderson, vol. iii., pp. 50-52.
[3] Camden, vol. i., p. 186.   [4] Anderson, vol. iii., p. 53.
[5] Mary Stuart to the Duke of Norfolk, 11th May, 1569. Labanoff, vol. ii., p. 345.

but rather was minded to live a solitary life all her days; yet, nevertheless,' she added, 'all other things being agreed and concluded to her honourable satisfaction, she was content to use the advice of the Queen and nobility of England in her marriage, and specially in favour of the Duke of Norfolk, whom she liked before all others, because he was well reported of and loved by the nobility and estates of his country.'[1]

She despatched Lord Boyd to London with her answer on these points, and directed James Borthwick to go to France to obtain a declaration that she had never ceded her rights to the crown of England to the Duke of Anjou. This declaration was obtained without very great difficulty;[2] for the eventual cession of the 4th of April, 1558, had been made to the King of France himself, upon conditions which no longer existed. Lord Boyd, after having conferred with Elizabeth and the principal members of her Council, returned to Scotland with the propositions of the Queen and nobility of England. He called at Wingfield on his way, and delivered to Mary Stuart some very favourable letters from Elizabeth and several dignitaries of her Court.[3] The captive Princess thought she had now nearly reached the end of her trials, and charged Lord Boyd with her messages to the Regent and Estates of Scotland.

Lord Boyd proceeded at once to Murray, on whose conduct depended Mary's restoration and marriage to Norfolk. He met him at Inverness,[4] on his return from his northern expedition, at a time when complete victory had greatly consolidated his dominion. He gave him a letter from the Duke of Norfolk, reminding him of his promise with regard to the marriage of the Queen his sister. 'I have proceeded so far therein,' said Norfolk, 'that I can neither with conscience revoke what I have done, nor with honour proceed further until you shall remove all such stumbling-blocks as are hindrances to our more apparent proceedings. When these obstacles are removed,' he continued, 'the rest shall follow to your contentment and comfort. Wherefore, my very earnest request to you, my good lord, now is, that you will proceed herein with such promptitude that the enemies to this good purpose of uniting this land into one kingdom in

---

[1] Anderson, vol. iii., pp. 53, 54.
[2] Charles IX. on the 10th July, and the Duke of Anjou on the 17th July, furnished the two declarations required. See Lamothe Fénelon's Correspondence, vol. ii., pp. 431, 452. Borthwick brought them to England, and laid them before Elizabeth in August, 1569. Lamothe Fénelon, vol. ii., p. 178.
[3] Anderson, vol. iii., p. 55.   [4] Ibid., p 70

T

time coming, and of maintaining God's true religion, may not have opportunity, through delay, to hinder our determination."[1] Throckmorton, who had so frequently been sent on embassies into Scotland, recommended this plan no less strenuously to his friend Lethington, and urged him to use all his ability to insure its success, as it was the most fortunate thing that could happen to the two kingdoms. He assured him that the Duke of Norfolk, the Earls of Arundel, Pembroke, Leicester, Bedford, and Shrewsbury, indeed, all the English nobility, and Secretary Cecil himself, had given their consent to the project. 'It hath been hitherto concealed from Queen Elizabeth,' he added, 'that you, as the fittest minister, might propound it to her, on behalf of the Regent and nobility of Scotland.'[2]

Lethington was ardently desirous that this marriage should take place, as he saw that it would lead to present concord, and to the future union of the kingdoms of England and Scotland. It was not to be expected that Murray would entertain the same views, notwithstanding the offers he had made to Norfolk just before he left London. The restoration of his sister would have deprived him of the supreme authority, the possession of which he valued more highly than he cared to acknowledge; and it would finally have compromised not only his safety but his religion. He was too prudent in his ambition, and too zealous in his sectarian feelings, to consent to the marriage, still less to promote it. Nevertheless, with his usual dissimulation, he manifested no opposition to the wishes of Mary Stuart and the Duke of Norfolk, but referred Lord Boyd to the General Assembly of the Estates of the realm, which he had summoned to meet at Perth on the 26th of July.[3] In public, he appeared faithful to the promises he had made in England, but in secret he persuaded the partisans of the young King and the jealous friends of the Presbyterian cause to reject so dangerous a proposition.[4]

The Convention, on which Mary Stuart's fate seemed to depend, met at Perth on the day appointed. It contained more adversaries than friends to the restoration of the deposed Queen, and listened with no great favour to the somewhat equivocal propositions made by the insincere Elizabeth upon the subject. These propositions were three in number. The Queen of

---

[1] Letter from Norfolk to Murray, 1st July, 1569: in Haynes, p. 520.
[2] Sir Nicholas Throckmorton to Lord Lethington, 20th July, 1569. Robertson, Appendix 32.
[3] Anderson, vol. iii., p. 70.   [4] Ibid., p. 71.

England advised the Estates of Scotland either to restore Mary Stuart to the full exercise of her authority, or to associate her with her son in the government of the country, or to receive her simply as a private person, and assign her an income suitable to her rank. By leaving them free to choose between these various projects, she encouraged them to reject all. Elizabeth did not display this impartial condescension to the wishes of others when she seriously desired to secure the triumph of her own. The Convention at Perth, therefore, taking advantage of the independence allowed them by a princess ordinarily less scrupulous, unhesitatingly rejected the first two propositions, and declared that Mary Stuart's unconditional restoration to the throne, or even her participation in the royal authority, was dangerous and impossible.[1] The third plan remained, which proposed that Mary Stuart should return to Scotland, to live in privacy, without any power, but in a condition suitable to her former dignity. She would, by this arrangement, cease to be a sovereign and a prisoner. Although the Convention perceived that inconvenience and danger might arise to an infant monarch and an envied Regent by admitting into the kingdom a Queen who had so long governed the country, and was still upheld by so powerful a party, this arrangement was not at once rejected.[2]

Then ensued an examination of the request that Mary Stuart had made to the Convention to annul her marriage with Bothwell, in order that she might contract another. She hoped to be able to associate the Scottish Parliament in the scheme adopted by the English nobility, and to facilitate that marriage with the Duke of Norfolk from which she hoped to gain her deliverance and restoration. The debate on this request was extremely violent, and both parties gave vent to the passions which animated them. Lethington expressed his entire approval of the rupture of a marriage which had been so disastrous, and maintained that the Queen's divorce might be pronounced without either detriment to the King, or danger to the Established Church. James Makgill, the secretary of the Convention, combatted this opinion with all the hatred of an implacable enemy, and all the fanaticism of a zealous Presbyterian. Mary Stuart had written to the Estates of Scotland as though she were still their Queen. Makgill was indignant at this, and said that they recognized no other sovereign but the young King. He also

[1] MS. letter, State Paper Office, Lord Hunsdon to Cecil, Berwick, August 5th, 1569. Tytler, vol. vi., p. 97.
[2] Tytler, vol. vi., p. 96.

reproached Mary with having addressed the Archbishop of St. Andrews as the head of the Church, whereas he was a rebel and a heretic. He declared that, by discussing such claims, the Convention would admit their justice, and render itself guilty of treason against the State, and blasphemy against the Church.[1]

Notwithstanding the resistance of Lethington, who sarcastically expressed his surprise that those who had recently been so furious in their opposition to this marriage, should now refuse to annul it, the personal interests of the victorious party, the inexorable passions of the Presbyterian sect, and the secret intrigues of the ambitious Regent, gained the victory in the Convention at Perth. After most tumultuous debates, the assembly broke up without even having admitted the possibility of Mary Stuart's residence in Scotland in a private condition, or having sanctioned her divorce from Bothwell.[2] Murray announced this intelligence to Elizabeth in a letter, in which he says, 'that he could not listen to the restoration of the deposed Queen without offending his conscience, prejudicing the little King his master, and injuring the welfare of the country.' He added that 'he thought he had so firmly established the young King, as to be able to defend him by force.'[3]

The result of the Perth Convention neither disappointed nor surprised Elizabeth; but it cruelly deceived the hopes of Mary Stuart. No longer able to reckon on Scotland, where her partisans were either imprisoned or crushed, and her adversaries obstinately refused to become reconciled to her, the captive Queen had now no other resource than the resolute intervention of the English nobility, and the firm support of those of the Catholic Powers of the Continent with whom she was in correspondence. The Duke of Norfolk had for some time kept open house,[4] in order to gain the favour of the people, and accustom them, by the frequent display of his magnificence, to the approaching increase of his grandeur. 'The affairs of the Queen of Scotland,' wrote Lamothe Fénelon to Catherine de Medici, 'are obtaining great strength by means of the Duke of Norfolk, who proposes to marry her . . . . and even if the Queen of England should not approve of the scheme, they will

---

[1] Tytler, vol. vi., p. 97.   [2] Ibid.
[3] Lamothe Fénelon's Correspondence, vol. ii., p. 154.
[4] 'The Duke . . . was the more incouraged to sett forward his purpose, by publique enterteinment of the nobilitie and councell, in keepinge open house, and usinge all honest familiaritie with gentlemen for obteyninge of universall goodwill therto.' Anderson, vol. iii., p. 64.

nevertheless carry it out, so far are matters already advanced .... and if she does not speedily resolve to procure the liberation and restoration of the Queen of Scotland, they will force her to do so against her will."[1] But would the Duke of Norfolk, who had requested the Court of France to send five or six hundred hackbutters, with ammunition, to the relief of Dumbarton, and who had also implored the assistance of the Court of Spain, dare openly to pursue the object towards the attainmen* of which he had hitherto proceeded by secret means? He and his adherents had hoped to gain Elizabeth's consent, by inducing the principal personages of England and Scotland to join in their request. Now that they had lost the support of the Scotch, would they venture single-handed either to persuade or compel the Queen of England into acquiescence, as some of them had boasted that they would? By so doing, they would presume too much upon their own strength, and utterly misjudge that haughty, jealous, and violent Princess, who never followed any advice that was opposed to her interests, and who would certainly not have suffered any infraction of her authority.

The plans of Mary Stuart and the Duke of Norfolk could not have been communicated, either in England or Scotland, to so many persons of different positions and opinions, without coming to the knowledge of Elizabeth. She had heard a report of the projected marriage of the Duke to that Queen who had so often claimed to be recognized as her heir. She had observed that her own Council was favourably inclined towards her rival, whose presence had revived the Catholic party in England, and was about to become a source of embarrassment and danger to hei self. She therefore declared to Lamothe Fénelon, who continued to urge her, in the name of his sovereign, to restore Mary Stuart to her throne, that Mary Stuart should not be restored, and that she had deserved her imprisonment by her crimes. 'I am aware,' she said to the French ambassador, ' of all the intrigues that have been carried on since she entered this kingdom. Princes have large ears, which hear far and near. She has attempted to move the interior of this realm against me, by means of some of my subjects, who promise her great things; but they are persons who conceive mountains, and bring forth only mole-hills. They thought I was so foolish that I should not perceive their doings."[2]

In her apprehensive suspicion, she set about the discovery of

[1] Despatch of Lamothe Fénelon, 27th July, 1569; vol. ii., pp. 126-128.
[2] Ibid., 1st September, 1569; vol. ii., pp. 211, 212.

an intrigue which it was so much her interest to unveil and prevent. Ere long she discovered all. Leicester, in fearful penitence, revealed to her the whole secret of the negotiation.¹ She then questioned the Regent of Scotland as to the part he had taken in the matter, and Murray delivered up the whole of his secret correspondence with Norfolk.² Before she had obtained this full information, and while she was still influenced merely by suspicion, she had advised the Duke of Norfolk, in menacing allusion to the words he had himself employed on his return from York, to beware on what pillow he leant his head.³ She then signified to him her absolute will with regard to a marriage which offended her pride and thwarted her policy, forbade him to think any more about it, and ordered him to have nothing more to do with the Queen of Scotland, on pain of forfeiting his allegiance. The mysterious intrigues of the nobility, and the conspiracy that had been formed among her own councillors in favour of her rival, threw her into one of those furious paroxysms of rage, which made all tremble before the formidable daughter of Henry VIII.

The Duke of Norfolk, notwithstanding the injunctions of his Sovereign, did not renounce the idea of marrying Mary Stuart. Nothing now remained but for him to place himself at the head of his partisans in the provinces, and revolt against Elizabeth. Influenced partly by fear and partly by ambition, he left Court suddenly, on the 23rd of September, and withdrew into Norfolk. The Earls of Arundel and Pembroke, and Lord Lumley, followed his example.⁴ They retired to their estates, whilst their friends, the Earls of Northumberland and Westmoreland, were ready to rise in the northern counties. Now was the time for executing a portion of the plan which had been for some time entertained by all these important personages. They had even gone so far as to contemplate changing the religion of the country,⁵ which would entail the downfall of Elizabeth, and the elevation of Mary.

¹ Camden, vol. i., p. 188. Lamothe Fénelon's Correspondence, vol. ii., p. 272. Anderson, vol. iii., pp. 79, 80. ² Haynes, pp. 521-523, 525.
³ Sharpe's Memorials of the Rebellion of 1569, p. xiii., note. Camden, vol i., p. 188. ⁴ Anderson, vol. iii., pp. 72, 73.
⁵ See Lamothe Fénelon's Correspondence, vol. i., pp. 258-262, under date March 13th, 1569. 'Mémoire pour communiquer a la Royne (Catherine de Medici), prenant promesse d'elle qu'elle n'en parlera à personne du monde.' This memoir begins thus: 'Le Sʳ Roberto Ridolfy, Florentin, ayant receu charge et commandement de la propre personne du Pape, de tretter de la restitution et restablissement de la religion Catholique en Angleterre avec les seigneurs Catholiques du pays, il s'est principallement adressé au comte d'Arondel et à milhord Lumley, auxquels auparavant il avoit eu affaire pour quelquer sommes qu'il leur

The Spanish ambassador, Don Gueraldo d'Espès, had already, in the name of his sovereign, given six thousand crowns to the Duke of Norfolk, the Earl of Arundel and Lord Lumley,[1] and ten thousand crowns to Mary Stuart,[2] who frequently sent messengers to the Duke of Alva, with a view to interest him in her cause, and persuade him to undertake her defence.[3] Pope Pius V. had strongly recommended the unfortunate captive to the leader of the Spanish troops in the Netherlands, where he appeared to have completely quelled the insurrection, and had written to him on the subject in the following terms: 'We conjure thy nobleness, and we beseech thee with our whole soul not to forget to restore to liberty our dear daughter in Jesus Christ, the Queen of Scotland, and again to establish her, if possible, in her kingdom. Thy nobleness could not undertake anything more agreeable and more useful to Almighty God, than the deliverance of this Queen, who has deserved well of the Catholic faith, and who is oppressed by the power of her heretical enemies.'[4]

---

avoit presteés.' He adds, that though well disposed, they did not dare to undertake anything 'si le duc de Norfolk ne se mettoit de la partie, lequel a esté tres difficile á gaigner; mais enfin s'estant layssé persuader, il prend, à ceste heure, plus à cueur la matière que ne faisoient les deux aultres. Son influence s'est étendue sur les Comtes de Derby, de Shrewsbury, de Pembroke, de Northumberland, et de plusiers aultres qui ont dit qu'ils seroient prêts de le suyvre.' The plan is indicated as it was followed out, though not executed with sufficient vigour. They intended to overthrow Cecil, or get Elizabeth to disgrace him, to gain Leicester without informing him of the proposed change of religion, and to expel the new men from the Council, 'affin que, ayant le gouvernement en leurs mains, ils puissent, peu après, de leur seule authorité et sans contredict, bien conduyre le faict de ladicto religion Catholique . . . Ils ont espéré que pour la différence de ce qu'ils sont des plus nobles et des plus puyssans du pays, et bien aymés du peuple, au regard des aultres, qui sont presque touts gens noveaulx mal appuyés . . . qu'ils conduyront sans grand payne, au poinct qu'ils desirent, leur entreprinse.'

[1] 'La embajada de España prestó al mismo duque (de Norfolk) al conde de Arundell à lord Lumile seis mil escudos.' Gonzalez, Apuntamientos, p. 93.

[2] 'La Reina de Escocia el veinto de agosto, escribe al embajador Espés agraciendole la remesa que le habia hecho de una lettra de cambio de diez mil escudos, y le dice que el portador Hamilton le dará menuda cuenta del estado de sus negocios.' Ibid.

[3] Mission of Lord Seton and John Hamilton to Brussels; Labanoff, vol. ii., p. 358. Mission of Raullet, 13th June, 1569, 'amply informed,' says Mary to the Duke of Alva, 'of my intentions;' Labanoff, vol. ii., p. 359. Mission of George Douglas on the 8th of July, 1569; Labanoff, vol. ii., pp. 362, 363.

[4] In the brief which Pope Pius V. wrote, on the 3rd of November, to the Duke of Alva, after the flight from court of the leading nobles of England, and eleven days before the Catholics of the North took arms, he said: 'Agnovimus Catholicos in regno Angliæ adversus hæreticos atque adeo contra eam, quæ se pro Anglia gerit, sess commovisse.' He exhorted him, therefore, to seize the opportunity for restoring the Catholic religion in England. Annals of Baronius, continued by Becchetti,

Circumstances were certainly favourable to an aggression against Elizabeth. If all those who had reason to complain of her conduct, or who detested her sway, had agreed to attack her in concert;[1] if the nobles, who had just retired from her Court, had boldly thrown themselves into the provinces, where they possessed great influence, and had joined the Catholics who were disposed to rise in arms to defend the exercise of their worship; if the Duke of Alva, transporting into England a portion of those troops which he no longer needed, and which he was disbanding in the Netherlands, had lent the military assistance of the King his master to the political malcontents and oppressed religionists of that country, both Elizabeth and Protestantism would have run equal danger.

Elizabeth appreciated the perilous position in which she was placed, and at once took the measures best adapted to her preservation. Mary Stuart was at Wingfield, under the somewhat lenient guardianship of the Earl of Shrewsbury, who threw no obstacles in the way of her secret correspondence and negotiations. Elizabeth had her transferred immediately to the less accessible Castle of Tutbury,[2] where she was placed under the stricter surveillance of the Earl of Huntingdon, who, as the rival aspirant to the English crown, did not regard her with very friendly feelings.[3] Frustrated in her expectations, and trembling for her life,[4] the captive Queen, though her followers had been driven away and her servants searched, nevertheless found means to despatch four of her adherents to the Duke of Norfolk, the Bishop of Ross, and the French ambassador Lamothe Fénelon. 'I beseech you,' she wrote to the last of these, 'encourage and advise my friends to be on their guard, and to act for me now or never.'[5] At this decisive moment, notwithstanding the perils which threatened her, and caring more for her plans than for her dangers, she told the Duke of Norfolk to act bravely, without troubling himself about her life, as God would keep her in safety.[6]

On his arrival in Norfolk, the Duke had surrounded himself with

[1] The civil administration of Elizabeth had created considerable dissatisfaction amongst the ancient nobility.' Sharpe's Memorials of the Rebellion, p. x.
[2] On the 21st September, 1569. Labanoff, vol. ii., p. 379.
[3] Haynes, pp. 525, 526. Labanoff, vol. ii., p. 379.
[4] Mary Stuart to Lamothe Fénelon, 25th September, 1569. Labanoff, vol. ii., p. 381.   [5] Ibid.
[6] 'La Reina de Escocia le escribió instándole á que obrara valerosamente, y que no triviera cuidado por la vida de ella, pues Dios la guardaria.' Gonzalez, Apuntamientos, p. 94.

Catholics.[1] From his house at Kenninghall he despatched messengers to the Earls of Northumberland and Westmoreland, who were much more determined than himself.[2] But, at the same time, he wrote a most humble and obsequious letter to Elizabeth, alleging that grief at her displeasure was the only cause of his retirement, and asseverating that he had never entertained any thought contrary to her crown and dignity.[3] Elizabeth, rejecting his explanations and assurances, commanded him to return to London within four days, on pain of treason; and sent summonses to the Earls of Arundel and Pembroke, and Lord Lumley, to appear in their places at the Privy Council without delay or excuse.[4] She further directed that the forces necessary for the maintenance of the public peace [5] should be raised in those counties which had been thrown into a state of excitement by the news that the Duke of Norfolk had withdrawn from Court.

Like a disobedient subject, Norfolk refused to return to London, on the ground that he was kept at home by an attack of fever;[6] and, like a timid conspirator, he did not dare to raise the standard of revolt, though he had received certain promises of assistance. His refusal irritated the Queen, and his hesitation dispirited his partisans. At length, discouraged by the coolness which his own irresolution had occasioned,—intimidated by the imperious messages of Elizabeth, who had directed him to travel to London in a litter if his fever prevented him from coming on horseback, and who had sent down some of her guards that, acting in concert with the sheriffs, they might arrest him in the midst of his estates if he refused to obey,[7]—and relying upon the written assurance of Cecil that 'the effects of the Queen's anger would not exceed words,'[8] he determined to return to Court. In order that he might not be compromised by an inopportune insurrection of the northern counties, he despatched a faithful messenger to beseech his brother-in-law, the Earl of Westmoreland, not to stir, as any revolt would expose him to certain death.[9] On his arrival in

[1] Haynes, p. 538. Gonzalez, Apuntamientos, p. 94.
[2] 'Cantrell (a servant of the Duke of Norfolk) brought a letter to me (the Earl of Northumberland) from the Duke, the effect whereof was, for so much as he had bene moovid by soondry noblemen and his frends, he thought it appertaynid him not to enter into yt without the advise and consent of his deare frends: amongst which he accompted me one, and thereunto, I aunswered by woord of mouthe, he should fynd my liking therein, as he should find of other noblemen.' Sharpe's Memorials of the Rebellion, Appendix, p. 195.
[3] Haynes, pp. 528, 529. [4] Ibid., pp. 529, 530. [5] Ibid., pp. 531, 532.
[6] Ibid., p. 532. [7] Ibid., pp. 533, 539. [8] Ibid., p. 533.
[9] The name of this messenger was Havers. He arrived at Topcliff, the seat of the Earl of Northumberland, whilst the northern conspirators were assembled

London he was committed to the Tower,[1] whilst his friends, the Earls of Pembroke and Arundel, and Lord Lumley, who had not delayed to yield obedience, and who were considered less compromised and less dangerous, were arrested, guarded, and interrogated in their own houses.[2]

The timidity, surrender, and imprisonment of the Duke of Norfolk and his principal adherents diminished the chances of the success of an insurrection, but did not prevent its outbreak. When the Duke retired from Court[3] an extraordinary degree of excitement had been aroused in the northern counties,[4] where resided the two Catholic heads of the ancient and powerful families of Percy and Neville. The rashest hopes had been entertained by the numerous class who still remained attached to the interdicted religion. In addition to the Earls of Northumberland and Westmoreland, who possessed great strength and considerable popularity in those parts, the powerful families of Dacre, Norton, Markenfield, and Tempest, were all disposed to take up arms. Meetings of the leaders of the malcontents were held in the castles of Topcliff and Brancepath, the princely residences of the Earls of Northumberland and Westmoreland.[5] These secret conclaves were attended by Leonard Dacre of Gisland, who alone was able to raise a small army, by old Richard Norton and his three sons, Thomas Markenfield of Markenfield, Robert and Michael Tempest, Captain John Swinburn, Plumpton of Plumpton, Varison of Haselwood, Andrew Oglethorpe, and Christopher Danby. Their object was to obtain the deliverance of Mary Stuart and the restoration of the Catholic religion. While these dangerous deliberations were in progress, the Earl of Sussex, who held the chief command in the north, alarmed at the excitement which prevailed, and in obedience to the orders of the Queen, summoned the Earls of Northumberland and Westmoreland to meet him at York, and interrogated them regarding their intentions.[6] They succeeded in laying his fears to rest, and were allowed to depart in liberty.

---

there. Seeing the Earl of Westmoreland in the park, 'he required him, for all the brotherly love that is betwixt them, that he woold not sturre; for if he did, the said Duke was then in danger of losing of his hed.' Sharpe's Memorials of the Rebellion, Appendix, pp. 195, 196.

[1] Haynes, p. 540.   [2] Ibid., pp. 534-536.
[3] Confession of the Earl of Northumberland, Sharpe's Memorials of the Rebellion, Appendix, p. 201.   [4] Sharpe's Memorials, pp. 8, 9.
[5] Ibid., pp. 192, 196, 201, 202. The book abounds with curious details regarding the rebellion and the families engaged in it.
[6] Sharpe's Memorials of the Rebellion, Appendix, p. 291.

They were on the point of abandoning their designs when they heard of the pusillanimous return of the Duke of Norfolk to London, and his subsequent imprisonment in the Tower. The Spanish ambassador[1] and the Bishop of Ross[2] had both, as well as the Duke, sent to request them to postpone their insurrection. Even the Catholic doctors whom they had consulted on the question whether it was permitted, by the laws of God, to take arms against a Prince, were divided in opinion. Some thought that it was unlawful, until the Queen had been excommunicated by the head of the Church; while others maintained that it might legally be done, as the Queen had already excommunicated herself, by refusing to receive the ambassador of the Pope.[3] Amid these uncertainties, they were impelled to action by the ardent passions which animated them, and by the fear of being arrested in their turn. When again invited by the Earl of Sussex to meet him at York, and summoned to Court by express order of Elizabeth, they refused to obey.[4] They had no other alternative but to leave the country or take arms. 'Our peril,' said old Richard Norton, 'is so great, and our action so just, that we must, of force, either enter into the matter, and take such fortune as God shall send, or else we must seek to depart out of the realm. It would be a marvellous blot and discredit to us, thus to depart, and to leave this godly enterprise.'[5] The Earl of Northumberland left Topcliff, where he feared he might be surprised, and, on his arrival at Brancepath, the insurrection was determined on.[6]

After having written to Pope Pius V., the Spanish ambassador, and the Duke of Alva, to request their assistance, and to advise that a port should be seized, on the eastern coast of England, where it would be easy to disembark troops;[7] after having solicited the support of the Earls of Cumberland and Derby, and Lord Wharton,[8] who they knew were powerful in those counties, and whom they supposed favourable to their project, they left Brancepath on the 14th of November, at the head of five hundred

[1] Confession of the Earl of Northumberland, ibid., p. 195.
[2] The Bishop of Ross said to Wilkinson, the Earl of Northumberland's messenger; 'In good faithe, my lord cannot be holpen; for the factors are taken away and comytted to prison.' Ibid., p. 364.
[3] Sharpe's Memorials of the Rebellion, Appendix, p. 204.
[4] Haynes, p. 552. Sharpe's Memorial's, pp. 27, 292-294.
[5] Sharpe's Memorials of the Rebellion, p. 196.
[6] Ibid., pp. 199, 200.
[7] Murdin, p. 42. 'Wilkinson was the principal person sent from the Earls to the Spanish ambassador, with letters directed to the Duke of Alva, to give the rebels aid, so as a port might be taken.' Sharpe's Memorials, p. 363.
[8] Sharpe's Memorials, pp. 198, 210, 211.

horsemen,[1] and marched towards Durham. The insurrection was entirely Catholic. They had painted Jesus Christ on the cross, with his five bleeding wounds, upon a banner borne by old Norton, who was inspired by the most religious enthusiasm.[2] The people of Durham opened their gates, and joined the rebels. Thus made masters of the town, the insurgents proceeded to the Cathedral, burned the Bible, destroyed the Book of Common Prayer, broke in pieces the Protestant Communion-table, and restored the old form of worship.[3]

Without openly declaring against Elizabeth, whose authority they did not entirely renounce,[4] but would infallibly have been dethroned[5] if they had gained the victory, the two earls announced in their proclamations that they were desirous to obtain the recognition of Mary Stuart's right to the English succession, and to restore the ancient religion of the country.[6] They declared that the Duke of Norfolk, the Earls of Arundel and Pembroke, and Lord Lumley, whom they intended to liberate from prison, as well as the Catholic heir to the throne,[7] were on their side, and they seemed to have taken up arms principally against Cecil and the new men, whom they accused of having misled the Queen and endangered the State. 'Forasmuch,' they proclaimed, 'as divers disordered and evil-disposed persons about the Queen's Majesty have, by their subtle and crafty dealing to advance themselves, overcome in this our realm the true and Catholic religion towards God; and by the same abused the Queen, and disordered the realm; and now, lastly, seek and procure the destruction of the nobility; we therefore have gathered ourselves together to resist by force, and the rather by the help of God and you, good people; and to see redress of these things amiss, with restoring of all ancient customs and liberties to God's Church, and this noble realm; lest, if we should not do it ourselves, we might be reformed by strangers, to the great hazard of the state of this our country.'[8] Their appeal was heard, and they were soon at the head of a little army of

---

[1] Sharpe's Memorials, pp. 37, 322.
[2] Strype's Annals of the Reformation, vol. i., part 2, p. 323.
[3] Sharpe's Memorials of the Rebellion, pp. 36, 37.
[4] See their proclamations in Strype, vol. i., part 2, pp. 313, 314.
[5] 'I doe not remember, I harde it opened or moved at any man's hands to proclaime her (Mary Stuart) Quene of England.' Confession of the Earl of Northumberland, Sharpe's Memorials, Appendix, p. 193.
[6] Strype, vol. i., part 2, p. 314.
[7] Sharpe's Memorials, pp. 193, 202, &c.
[8] Strype, vol. i., part 2, p. 313.

one thousand cavalry, tolerably well equipped, and five or six thousand infantry.[1]

There was no force capable of resisting them in the north, where they were joined by Sir Egremont Ratcliffe, the Earl of Sussex's brother.[2] The Earl himself remained faithful to the Queen, and prepared to defend York against all attacks.[3] The three Wardens of the Eastern, Middle, and Western Marches, Lord Hunsdon, Sir John Forster, and Lord Scrope, occupied Berwick, Newcastle, and Carlisle with their troops.[4] The two insurgent Earls, meeting with no one to oppose them in open field, successively took possession of Richmond, Allerton, and Ripon. Christopher Neville was sent to secure and fortify Hartlepool, as that port was favourably situated, on a little peninsula between the Tyne and the Tees, for the reception of the supplies which the Duke of Alva would, doubtless, not fail to send them, when he was informed of their insurrection.[5] Meanwhile they continued their march towards the south, and passed, unopposed, through all the unwalled towns.

By the perfidy of her conduct towards Mary Stuart, Elizabeth had exposed herself to the troubles which now, after eleven years of tranquillity, agitated her kingdom and menaced her authority. By detaining so dangerous a prisoner in England, she had herself furnished the Catholics and other disaffected persons with a reason for revolt, and hopes of success in so doing. But though she had provoked the danger, she did not allow herself to be cast down thereby. Never did she display so much energy as in critical conjunctures. In addition to the noblemen already named, she had arrested Throckmorton, the Bishop of Ross, and the Florentine Ridolfi, all of whom she suspected of having joined in the plans of the Duke of Norfolk.[6] One of the most enterprising generals of the Duke of Alva, Ciapino Vitelli, had arrived in England, for the purpose of settling the commercial disputes which had arisen between Elizabeth and Philip II. Fearing that he had come with other intentions, she ordered him to leave his military escort at Dover, and he was obliged to come with a retinue of only five men to London, where he was closely watched.[7]

[1] Strype, vol. i., part 2, p. 315; and Sharpe's Memorials, pp. 65, 66, 71.
[2] Sharpe's Memorials, p. 71.   [3] Ibid., pp. 76, 77.
[4] Ibid., p. 77.   [5] Ibid., pp. 79, 80.
[6] Gonzalez, Apuntamientos, p. 95. Haynes, pp. 541, 544. Labanoff, vol. ii., pp. 386, 387.
[7] Ibid., pp. 95, 96. Labanoff, vol. ii., pp. 386, 387.

In order that Mary Stuart might not be liberated by the insurgents, whose zeal would have been encouraged and whose chances of success would have been increased by her presence, Elizabeth directed that she should be transferred immediately from Tutbury to Coventry, a strong town in Warwickshire,[1] where she would be beyond the reach of a surprise. It even appears that her keepers had orders to put her to death if the insurrection were successful.[2] To prevent the rebels from receiving any aid from abroad, Elizabeth ordered seven of her largest men-of-war to cruise between the coasts of England and the Netherlands.[3] She declared the Earls of Northumberland and Westmoreland rebels and traitors,[4] wrote with her own hand to all those whose fidelity and devotion she wished to confirm or increase, and ordered Sir Ralph Sadler and Lord Hunsdon to unite their forces to those of the Earl of Sussex, whom she directed to collect all the northern contingents, and prepare to take the field.[5] At the same time she appointed lieutenants to raise forces in the various counties,[6] and ordered the rapid formation of two armies in the southern counties, one under the Earl of Warwick, the other under Admiral Clinton, who were to march in all haste towards York and assist the Earl of Sussex in quelling the rebellion.[7]

Whilst Elizabeth was taking these active measures, the Earls of Northumberland and Westmoreland remained masters of the country which they had overrun, but did not make much further progress. The southernmost point which they reached was Boroughbridge. Then, instead of marching forward, either because they despaired of being able to raise the midland counties,

---

[1] Labanoff, vol. ii., p. 395.

[2] 'Remember, how upon a less cause, how effectually all the Council of England once dealt with her Majesty for justice to be done upon that person (Mary Stuart), for being suspected and infamed to be consenting with Northumberland and Westmoreland in the rebellion. You know the great seal of England was sent then, and thought just and meet, upon the sudden, for her execution.'—Letter from Leicester, 10th October, 1585; Tytler, vol. vi., p. 472.

[3] 'Et parcequ'on a raporté que le Duc d'Alve avoit quatre ou cinq milles hommes de pied ou de cheval en Zélande desjà toutz pretz à s'embarquer, avec artillerie, rouages, munitions et tout aultre équipage de guerre, ladicte dame a ordonné mettre, encores promptement quatre de ses grand navyres en mer, avec les trois qui y sont, pour tenir le Pas de Callais.'—Lamothe Fénelon's Correspondence, vol. ii., pp. 401, 402.

[4] Sharpe's Memorials, p. 77. Lamothe Fénelon, vol. ii., pp. 372-374.

[5] Ibid., pp. 55, 67, 68. Haynes, pp. 553, 555.

[6] Haynes, pp. 559, 560, 562.

[7] Ibid., pp. 560-567. Lamothe Fénelon's Correspondence, vol. ii., p. 401.

or because they were desirous to remain in the north until they received reinforcements from Pius V. and Philip II., they retraced their steps.[1] Finding themselves unable to gain an entrance into any of the large towns which had remained faithful to the Queen, they laid siege to Barnard Castle, which was occupied by Sir George Bowes.[2] They spent twelve days in the attack of this small fortress, which Sir George Bowes defended valiantly until failure of provisions and the mutiny of his soldiers forced him to surrender on the 12th of December.[3] This was the last success obtained by the insurgents.

Two days after the surrender of Barnard Castle, the Earl of Sussex, at the head of about twelve hundred cavalry and four thousand foot soldiers, advanced against them, ready to give battle if they would accept it.[4] The Earl of Warwick and Admiral Clinton were coming by forced marches from the south, with about twelve thousand men, and were daily expected at Boroughbridge.[5] Pressed on the north by Sir John Forster, who was marching from Newcastle, on the east by Sussex, with an army equal to their own, and on the south by Warwick and Clinton with forces vastly superior in number, the leaders of the rebellion, hopeless of victory, assembled their adherents in Durham on the 16th of December, recommended each man to provide for his own safety, disbanded the infantry, and proceeded to Hexham at the head of their cavalry. Thence, after having evacuated Hartlepool, they crossed the Tyne and took refuge in Scotland.[6] The Earl of Westmoreland, Sir Egremont Ratcliffe, Norton, Markenfield, Swinburn, and Tempest found an asylum among the hospitable clans of Scott, Ker, Hume, and Johnstone.[7] The Earl of Northumberland, less fortunate, fell into the hands of a border freebooter, named Hecky Armstrong, who kept him captive for a short time in his tower of Harlaw, and then was bribed to surrender him to Murray, who imprisoned him at Lochleven.[8]

Thus terminated this insurrection, which might have been fraught with disastrous results to Elizabeth, if it had been more wisely conceived and more boldly executed. The union of the nobility and the Catholics should have been more complete; and these two parties, resting upon the name and rights of Mary

---

[1] Sharpe's Memorials, pp. 65, 66.   [2] Ibid., pp. 18-20, 91.
[3] Ibid., pp. 95-98.   [4] Ibid., pp. 78, 102, 103.   [5] Ibid., p. 108.
[6] Ibid., pp-104, 109.   Lamothe Fénelon's Correspondence, vol. ii., p. 426.
[7] Ibid., pp. 148-150, 295.   Tytler, vol. vi., p. 105.
[8] Tytler, vol. vi., pp. 105, 108.   Sharpe's Memorials, pp. 118, 323.

Stuart, avowed by Norfolk, and supported by the Duke of Alva, should have declared their intentions with greater resolution, and acted with greater harmony, if they really wished to endanger the throne of the Protestant Queen. But the timidity of the Duke of Norfolk; the lukewarmness of the Duke of Alva, who, by excessive prudence, allowed a most favourable opportunity for advancing the interests of his religion, and of his master, to escape; and the irresolution of the Catholics themselves, who wavered between their religious belief and their political fidelity, rendered the rebellion of the northern earls most rash, by making it partial, and condemning it to be powerless. This rebellion did infinite injury to the cause of the ancient faith and the captive Queen, in those districts where Catholicism and Mary Stuart possessed the greatest number of partisans. The Percys, Nevilles, Nortons, Markenfields, and Tempests, left the country that they might escape proscription. The flight of these great families, and the terror with which the people were inspired by most sanguinary executions,—more than three hundred persons having been put to death by martial law in the bishopric of Durham alone,[1]—wonderfully diminished the strength and blighted the hopes of Elizabeth's opponents in those parts.

The Catholic insurrection in the north of England had filled the Regent of Scotland with the greatest alarm. His power depended upon Elizabeth's triumph. He, therefore, offered to march to the assistance of the Queen, his protectress and ally, with a large body of Scottish troops, which he summoned to meet at Peebles on the 20th of December;[2] but his aid was rendered unnecessary by the suppression of the revolt. Murray's conduct had become more violent in proportion as his power increased. By refusing to promote, at the Perth Convention, the plan for his sister's marriage to the Duke of Norfolk, and the pacification of the kingdom, he had lost the support of those who had promoted the marriage and desired the restoration of peace. Lethington was at the head of this party. As he mistrusted the Regent, who, on his part, held him in great suspicion, he had placed himself under the protection of his constant friend, the Earl of Athol.[3] Murray was alarmed at his intrigues, and resolved to get rid of him. He craftily invited him to attend the meetings of the Council, of which he still continued Secretary, and to

[1] Sharpe's Memorials, pp. 123, 124, 133, 144.
[2] MS. letter, State Paper Office, Murray to Cecil, 22nd November, 1569; MS. copy, State Paper Office, the Regent's Proclamation, Edinburgh, 18th December, 1569; Tytler, vol. vi., p. 108.   [3] Tytler, vol. vi., p. 101.

discharge the duties of his office; and when Lethington was in presence of Morton, Mar, Glencairn, Lindsay, and the other lords who continued faithfully attached to the cause of the young King, Captain Crawford presented himself on behalf of the Earl of Lennox, to accuse him and Sir James Balfour of having been accomplices in Darnley's murder.[1] He was at once arrested, and taken prisoner to the house of one of the Regent's servants. But he did not remain long in captivity. Kirkaldy of Grange released him from confinement and took him to Edinburgh Castle, where he gave him an asylum until the 22nd of November, the day appointed for his trial.[2] On that day, the friends of the Scottish Secretary appeared in arms; Lord Hume occupied the streets of Edinburgh with a large body of cavalry,[3] while the Laird of Grange commanded the whole town from his citadel. Lethington's condemnation was thus rendered as impossible as his imprisonment had been futile; and Murray ordered the proceedings to be adjourned,[4] in order to prevent an acquittal, which would have been a triumph to Lethington, and a mortification to himself.

His rupture with so able and popular a man did him great injury throughout the kingdom; it added to the hatred which was already felt for him, and detached from his interests several of those who had powerfully contributed to his elevation after Carberry Hill, and decided his victory at Langside. Among these were Kirkaldy of Grange and Alexander Hume. Murray was accused of perfidy towards Mary Stuart, treason against Norfolk, violence against Chatelherault, disloyalty and ingratitude towards Lethington, and servility towards Elizabeth. Although the Presbyterian Church zealously supported him as its useful head, and the townspeople were favourable to him because of his vigorous administration of the laws, and the strict observance of justice which he universally enforced, the majority of the nobility detested him and desired his downfall.

In order to strengthen his tottering authority, Murray applied to Elizabeth for assistance, both in money and military stores.[5] He requested, moreover, that Mary Stuart should be sent back to Scotland, where he promised that her life should run no

---

[1] MS. letter, State Paper Office, Lord Hunsdon to Cecil, 7th September, 1569. Diurnal of Occurrents, pp. 147, 148; Tytler, vol. vi., p. 101.
[2] Tytler, vol. vi., pp. 102, 103.
[3] Ibid., p. 107.   [4] Ibid.
[5] MS. State Paper Office. A Note of the principal matters in Nicholas Elphinstone's instructions; Tytler, vol. vi., p. 112.

U

danger,[1] and that her deliverance should be rendered much more difficult than it was in England. He successively despatched the Abbot of Dunfermline and Nicholas Elphinstone to remind Elizabeth of all the troubles that Mary Stuart had already caused in her court and kingdom, to point out to her the risks she would run by keeping her within her dominions, and to declare to her that, surrounded as he was in Scotland by difficulties and enemies, he would soon be unable to maintain the common cause any longer, if the person, whose practices daily threatened the safety of both kingdoms, were not placed in his hands.[2] In return for Mary's surrender, he had the baseness to offer to give up to Elizabeth the unfortunate Earl of Northumberland, then a prisoner in Scotland.[3] The extradition of their late sovereign was formally demanded of the English Queen by the Earls of Murray, Morton, Mar, and Glencairn, the Masters of Montrose and Marshall, and the Lords Lindsay, Ruthven, and Temple,[4] while Cecil was earnestly solicited to support their demand by Knox, who wrote, he said, 'with his one foot in the grave.'[5] She would perhaps have acceded to their request, had not a sinister event put an end to the negotiation.

James Hamilton, of Bothwell-Haugh, had sworn a deadly hatred to the Regent. Taken prisoner at the battle of Langside, he had recovered his liberty by the arrangement made at Glasgow on the 13th of March, 1569, by the Regent and the Duke of Chatelherault. But he had been stripped of all his property. Confiscation, which ruined the vanquished to enrich the victors, was the least baneful effect of these civil wars; and this unpleasant consequence of defeat would probably have been submitted to with resignation by Bothwell-Haugh, if it had not been iniquitously extended over his wife, who ought not to have shared in his punishment, as she had not participated in his offence. She possessed the small estate of Woodhouselee. on the river Esk; and this had been taken from her, and given to Bellenden, one of the most devoted, but most insatiate, of the Regent's creatures. The injustice of this robbery was increased by the cruelty with which it was perpetrated. In the midst of a winter's night, the unfortunate wife of Bothwell-Haugh was driven by Bellenden from

---

[1] 'She should live her natural life, without any sinister means taken to shorten the same.'—MS. State Paper Office, copy of the 'Instrument;' Tytler, vol. vi., p. 105.
[2] Ibid.   [3] Ibid., p. 111.   [4] Ibid., p. 109.
[5] MS. letter, State Paper Office, John Knox to Cecil, 2nd January, 1569; Tytler, vol. vi., p. 110.

the humble abode to which she had retired, and left to wander half-clothed in a wood till morning. When morning came, she was furiously mad; despair had turned her brain.[1] From that day, an implacable thirst for vengeance took possession of the heart of Bothwell-Haugh. He resolved to slay the Regent, to whom he attributed the desolation of his household. Several times he attempted to effect his purpose, but without success. His hatred, encouraged by the Hamiltons, eagerly sought an opportunity for punishing the author of his ruin, and laying low the oppressor of his party. This opportunity ere long presented itself.

The Regent was on his way from Stirling to Edinburgh, and intended to pass through Linlithgow. In the High-street of this last-named town, the Archbishop of St. Andrews, uncle of Bothwell-Haugh, possessed a house in front of which Murray and his cavalcade would necessarily pass. This house was placed at the disposal of Bothwell-Haugh, who made every preparation for the unfailing performance of the act of vengeance which he had concerted with the Hamiltons. He took his station in a small room, or wooden gallery, which commanded a full view of the street. To prevent his heavy footsteps being heard, for he was booted and spurred, he placed a feather-bed on the floor; to secure against any chance observation of his shadow, which, had the sun broke out, might have caught the eye, he hung up a black cloth on the opposite wall; and, having barricaded the door in front, he had a swift horse ready saddled in the stable at the back. Even here his preparations did not stop; for, observing that the gate in the wall which enclosed the garden was too low to admit a man on horseback, he removed the lintel stone, and, returning to his chamber, cut, in the wooden panel immediately below the lattice window where he watched, a hole just sufficient to admit the barrel of his caliver. Having taken these precautions, he loaded the piece with four bullets, and calmly awaited his victim.[2]

Murray had spent the night in a house in the neighbourhood. Rumours had reached him of the danger by which he was threatened. One of his friends had even persuaded him to avoid the High-street, and pass round by the back of the town.[3] But the crowd, pressing round him, rendered it impossible for him to do

[1] MS. Calderwood, Ayscough, 4735, pp. 746, 747; Tytler, vol. vi., p. 113.
[2] Historie of King James the Sext, p. 46. Tytler, vol. vi., p. 114.
[3] MS. letter, State Paper Office, Lord Hunsdon to Cecil, 26th January, 1570. Tytler, vol. vi., p. 114.

so; and he rode onwards through Linlithgow, with calm courage, amidst the acclamations of the populace. He proceeded at a slow pace along the High-street till he reached the Archbishop's house. He was thus exposed to the fire of the assassin, who, taking deliberate aim, discharged his caliver. The Regent, shot right through the lower part of his body, fell mortally wounded.[1] At this sight, the crowd rushed towards the house from whence the shot had been fired. But whilst they were endeavouring to break down the door, Bothwell-Haugh, escaping at the back, had mounted his horse and fled at full speed in the direction of Hamilton Castle. Here he was received in triumph by Lord Claude Hamilton, Lord Arbroath, and the Archbishop of St. Andrews, who welcomed him as the deliverer of their party.[2]

Murray expired on the same day, the 23rd of January, 1570, in a state of noble calmness and fervent piety.[3] His death caused immense joy to all Mary Stuart's partisans in Scotland,[4] and gave unmixed satisfaction to all the Catholic Princes of Europe.[5] In the opinion of the friends of the captive Queen, Murray had been an ungrateful subject, an inhuman brother, and an odious rebel; in the opinion of the Kings of Europe, he had been a triumphant adversary of legitimate authority. In him had fallen the able chief of the Scottish Protestants, the resolute head of the young King's government, and the useful ally of Elizabeth. He possessed great qualities, a valiant heart, a lofty and determined mind, an energetic character, an honest and stern disposition; but, nevertheless, he had been sometimes violent and sometimes treacherous, and had displayed haughtiness or humility, according as the necessities of his cause or the interests of his greatness required. He had acted as an ambitious sectary. To maintain his faith, he had made himself master of the State. In the exer-

[1] MS. letter, State Paper Office, Hunsdon to Cecil, 24th and 26th January, 1570; Tytler, vol. vi., p. 115.
[2] MS. letter, State Paper Office, Hunsdon to Elizabeth, 30th January, 1570; and Information anent the punishment of the Regent's murder; Tytler, vol. vi., p. 115.   [3] Spottiswood, p. 233.
[4] MS. letter, State Paper Office, Hunsdon to Cecil, 30th January, 1570; Tytler, vol. vi., p. 120. Mary Stuart herself was pleased, and gave a pension to Bothwell-Haugh. 'Ce que Bothwellhac a faict,' she wrote, 'a esté sans mon commandement; de quoy je luy sçay aussi bon gre et meilleur qui si j'eusse esté du conseil. J'attends les mémoires qui me doivent estre envoyez de la recepte de mon douaire, pour faire mon estat, où je n'oublieray la pension dudict Bothwellhac.' Mary Stuart to the Archbishop of Glasgow, 28th August, 1571; Labanoff, vol. iii., p. 334.
[5] MS. letters, State Paper Office, French Correspondence, Norris to Cecil, Angers, 17th and 25th February, 1570; Tytler, vol. vi., p. 120.

cise of the supreme power, he had displayed the most unflagging vigilance, and enforced the observance of the strictest regularity; and the people, who beheld impartial justice and unprecedented order introduced into the kingdom under his administration, bestowed on him the title of the Good Regent, which he has ever since retained. Conforming his private conduct to his religious creed, he had given his residence the aspect of a church rather than of a court, and had thus acquired the confidence as well as the affection of the Presbyterian body. But the interests of religion had overcome in him the feeling of nationality, and in his relations with Elizabeth he had shown himself a Protestant rather than a Scotchman. Educated among troubles, he had grown accustomed to deeds of violence. He had consented to the murder of Riccio, and had not acted with severity towards all those concerned in the assassination of Darnley. An author of the civil war, he had ended by becoming its victim; an accomplice in one murder and tolerator of another, he had himself perished by the hand of an assassin. The means which men employ for their elevation are frequently those by which they fall. Thus is the hidden justice of Providence revealed in the ordinary course of events!

The death of Murray inspired the Queen's despondent party with renewed hope. Though it had just been vanquished in England, it suddenly resumed activity in Scotland. The Hamiltons took arms.[1] Lethington, who had found no difficulty in obtaining his acquittal of the charge brought against him by the late Regent,[2] speedily joined them with the Laird of Grange. The Duke of Chatelherault and Lord Herries regained their liberty. The partisans of the captive Queen, now numbering a large majority of the nobles, advised by the most sagacious politician, and supported by the most experienced captain in the country, were soon predominant in Scotland. They seized Edinburgh, and appeared on the point of restoring Mary Stuart, whose authority they again acknowledged and proclaimed. At the same time that fortune thus once more declared in Mary Stuart's favour in her native country, her rival found herself menaced by a renewal of those dangers, in her own dominions, which she had only succeeded in averting not long before. Pope Pius V., doubtless regretting that he had not previously supported the insurgent English Catholics by the aid of his spiritual weapons, fulminated a sentence of excommunication and deposition against

[1] Tytler, vol. vi., p. 120.
[2] Diurnal of Occurrents, p. 158; Tytler, vol. vi., pp. 124, 125.

Elizabeth on the 25th of February, 1570.[1] The Lairds of Buccleugh and Fernyhirst, chiefs of the powerful border clans of Scott and Ker, in company with the Earl of Westmoreland, broke into England,[2] where Leonard Dacre of Gilsland, who had been unable to take part in the preceding rebellion, had again raised the standard of insurrection, and placed himself in a few days, at the head of an army of three thousand men.[3]

Elizabeth now believed she was in great danger. The successive victories which the French Catholics had gained over the Huguenots—who had been defeated at Moncontour and Jarnac, had lost St. Jean d'Angely, and failed in their attempt upon Poitiers,—led her to fear that French troops would be sent into Scotland. She was no less apprehensive that the Duke of Alva, who was daily strengthening his position in the Netherlands, and constructing citadels to prevent any further revolt on the part of the enemies of his sovereign, would make a descent upon England. The murder of the Regent had caused her as much sorrow as it had occasioned joy to Mary Stuart. On receiving the intelligence, she had shut herself up in her room, and said with tears that she had lost the best and most useful friend she possessed in the world.[4] But she did not rest satisfied with barren expressions of regret. Dacre's outbreak was overcome by the combined forces of Lord Hunsdon and Sir John Forster, who attacked the fierce insurgent on the banks of the little river Gelt, in Cumberland, and defeated him, after a sanguinary battle. Dacre followed the example of the Earls of Northumberland and Westmoreland, and fled across the border into Scotland.[5]

It was especially important to Elizabeth not to lose the influence which she had taken so much pains to acquire in Mary's dominions. If Scotland escaped from her, she might next be deprived of England. Deposed by the Pope, whose bull was soon afterwards fixed on the door of the Bishop of London's residence;[6] threatened by France and Spain; fearing the strength of the English Catholics, who had already revolted twice within a few months, in a single district; and aware of the ambitious discontent of her nobility, she felt that her throne would be insecure if

---

[1] Becchetti, vol. xii., pp. 105, 107.   [2] Tytler, vol. vi., p. 120.
[3] Lingard's History of England, vol. viii., p. 53. MS. letters, State Paper Office, Hunsdon to Elizabeth, 20th and 27th February, 1570; Tytler, vol. vi., p. 126.
[4] 'Pour l'ayder, disait-elle, à se maintenir et conserver en repos.' Lamothe Fénelon's Correspondence, vol. iii., p. 54.
[5] Camden, vol. i., p. 197. Lingard, vol. viii., p. 53. Sadler, vol. ii., p. 140.
[6] On the 15th of May. Lingard, vol. viii., p. 56. Camden, pp. 211, 213.

Mary Stuart were restored to the possession of her crown. Cecil, himself deeply alarmed, advised his sovereign to take those measures which were best adapted to prevent the destruction of the English party in Scotland.[1] This party, though sustained by most of the towns, and supported by the Presbyterian Church, had few adherents among the nobility. These were the Earls of Morton, Mar, Glencairn, and Buchan, and Lords Glammis, Ruthven, Lindsay, Cathcart, Methven, Ochiltree, and Saltoun.[2] The Queen's party possessed by far the most numerous and most powerful supporters. The Duke of Chatelherault, the Earls of Huntly, Argyle, Athol, Errol, Crawford, Marshall, Caithness, Cassillis, Eglinton, and Sutherland, and the Lords Herries, Lethington, Grange, Hume, Seton, Ogilvy, Ross, Borthwick, Oliphant, Yester, Fleming, Boyd, Somerville, Innermeith, Forbes, and Gray,[3] were all ready to secure her triumph by force of arms. If these two parties had been left to themselves, the Queen's adherents would easily have overcome those of the King, who had already been driven out of the capital of the kingdom.

Elizabeth, therefore, interfered to prevent them from gaining a complete victory, and proceeding to the restoration of Mary Stuart, which appeared imminent, and was regarded by her with the utmost apprehension. The incursions made by the Scots and Kers upon the English border, and the asylum which had been given in Scotland to the English rebels after both insurrections, furnished her with a natural pretext for intervention. Three days after the death of Murray, she had despatched Sir Thomas Randolph, an accomplished master in political intrigue, to Scotland, to oppose a reconciliation of the two parties.[4] Early in the spring, she ordered the Earl of Sussex and Lord Scrope to invade Scotland on the east and west. They accordingly ravaged the country of Buccleugh, Fernyhirst, Hume, Maxwell, and Herries, destroyed fifty castles, ravaged three hundred villages, set fire to a large number of granges,[5] and struck terror into the Queen's partisans. To follow up this severity, the Earl of Lennox was sent into Scotland by Elizabeth, to direct the party of the King, his grandson, in Murray's place. Escorted by the

[1] MS. letter, State Paper Office, entirely in Cecil's hand. Tytler, vol. vi., p. 122.
[2] MS. copy, State Paper Office, Instructions given by the Lords of Scotland to the Commendator of Dunfermline, 1st May, 1570; Tytler, vol. vi., p. 128.
[3] Tytler, vol. vi., p. 127.   [4] Ibid., p. 122. Melvil's Memoirs, p. 80.
[5] Spottiswood, p. 178. Tytler, vol. vi., pp. 132, 133. Lesly's Negotiations, in Anderson, vol. iii., pp. 89, 90.

old bands of Berwick, under the command of Sir William Drury,[1] he joined Morton, regained possession of Edinburgh, and marched to the relief of Glasgow, which was then besieged by the Hamiltons. The ravages which Sussex and Scrope had committed in the southern districts, were renewed by Lennox and Drury in the centre of Scotland, and they commenced a pitiless devastation of Clydesdale and Linlithgowshire, razing the castles of the Queen's adherents.[2]

These odious expeditions, which continued throughout the summer of 1570, plunged Scotland into desolation and anarchy. Without giving the victory to the King's party, which recovered Edinburgh and did not lose Glasgow, they effectually prevented the Queen's friends from completing their triumph. The two factions, now nearly equal in strength, counterbalanced each other. Two governments were called into existence; that of the King, which was recognized by most of the burghs and a few of the nobility; and that of the Queen, which owned the obedience of the most powerful barons, and extended over the greater part of the kingdom. The Earl of Lennox, who was elected Regent, at Elizabeth's instigation, on the 12th of July, 1570,[3] directed the first administration; the Duke of Chatelherault, and the Earls of Huntly and Argyle, who had been invested with Mary Stuart's authority, were at the head of the second.

When Elizabeth had thus restored and reconstituted the young King's party, she withdrew her troops from Scotland.[4] By allowing them to remain longer in that country, she would have provoked the military intervention of the French King, who had already sent M. de Verac to the relief of Dumbarton,[5] with letters of encouragement and ample promises of succour to Mary's friends. Charles IX. would soon be in a position to give effectual assistance to his sister-in-law. The third civil war was nearly at an end, and those negotiations had already been commenced, which finally led to the peace of St. Germain, concluded between the Catholics and Protestants, on the 15th of August, 1570. Under these circumstances, Elizabeth thought it best to yield to the representations of the French ambassador.[6] She evacuated Scotland, restored the Bishop of Ross to liberty,[7] and resumed

[1] Diurnal of Occurrents, p. 176. Tytler, vol. vii., p. 133.
[2] Murdin, p. 769. Diurnal of Occurrents, p. 177. Tytler, vol. vi., pp. 133, 134. [3] Spottiswood, p. 241. Tytler, vol. vi., p. 141.
[4] MS. draft by Cecil, State Paper Office, Queen to the Lords of Scotland, 31st May, 1570; Tytler, vol. vi., p. 135. [5] Tytler, vol. vi., p. 131.
[6] Lesly's Negotiations, in Anderson, vol. iii., p. 91.
[7] Ibid., p. 89. Labanoff, vol. iii., p. 53.

the treaty with Mary Stuart which had been discussed before the Convention at Perth during the summer of 1569.

Cecil and Mildmay, two members of the English Privy Council, were sent to discuss the conditions of an accommodation at Chatsworth,[1] in Derbyshire, where Mary had resided since the end of May, 1570, and whither the Bishop of Ross repaired before them, to lay the matter before his mistress, and to assist her by his advice.[2] The nature of the demands made in the name of Elizabeth, and the political character of the persons entrusted with the negotiation, seemed to indicate that the English Queen was now in earnest. Whilst Mary Stuart's restoration was being discussed at Chatsworth, Elizabeth had concluded a treaty between the opposing parties in Scotland, which lasted from September, 1570, until April, 1571, and was destined to lead to a general pacification.[3]

Mary Stuart hopefully accepted the new overtures which were made to her. She consented to give Elizabeth every assurance that did not compromise her own dignity. She acquiesced in the Treaty of Edinburgh, and renounced all right to the crown of England during the lifetime of Elizabeth and her legitimate descendants, if she had any. She did not reject the formation of an offensive and defensive alliance between England and Scotland, provided its object were definite and limited. She promised to hold no communications with the subjects of the Queen, her neighbour, without her consent. While refusing, from motives of humanity and honour, to give up the Earl of Northumberland and the other English rebels who had taken refuge in Scotland, she pledged her word to send them out of her dominions within a given time. Before she was restored to liberty, she undertook to place the Prince, her son, as a hostage in the hands of Elizabeth, to be brought up in England until he was fifteen years old; and finally, she promised not to marry again without Elizabeth's consent.

As six hostages, chosen from among the Scottish nobility, were required moreover, in order to insure the execution of the treaty, Mary Stuart demanded that the number should be reduced to four; that the Duke of Chatelherault, the Earls of Huntly, Argyle, and Athol, and Lords Fleming and Seton, as well as the wardens of the borders, should be excepted; and that the earls and lords, or the eldest sons of earls and lords who might be chosen, should be allowed to return to Scotland to attend to their affairs, on providing substitutes of their own rank. She consented

---

[1] Labanoff, vol. iii., p. 87. Anderson, vol. iii., p. 99.
[2] Lesly's Negotiations, in Anderson, vol. iii., p. 95.
[3] Lesly's Negotiations, pp. 95, 96. Tytler, vol. vi., p. 144.

to have this treaty confirmed by the Parliament of the realm, and if she violated it, either by attacking Elizabeth or assisting her enemies, to be deprived not only of her rights to the throne of England, but also of her possession of the crown of Scotland, which would then pass immediately to her son.[1] After a discussion, sustained on her part with dignity and skilfulness, all the principal points were agreed on; and the poor prisoner, wearied of her captivity, and a victim to mental anguish and bodily infirmities,[2] which had fallen upon her notwithstanding her comparative youth, thought she had now reached the crisis which was to restore her to freedom and sovereignty.

Full of hope and joy, she wrote a most affectionate letter to Elizabeth. 'No scruple now remains,' she said, 'to prevent our sincere and reciprocal friendship, which I desire beyond that of any other Prince, in proof of which I consent to place in your hands the dearest jewel and only comfort which God has given me in this world, my only and beloved son, whose education, though desired by many, is entrusted to you, to be preferred both by him and by me to all others.' She further declared that she valued Elizabeth's goodwill more than that of any other person, and that she would willingly give the pledges required of her, adding: 'My intention is sincere to observe the conditions agreed on between us, and I am resolved henceforward, in order to end my unfortunate voyage, to cast my anchor in the port of your natural goodness towards me. Having recourse, instead of any other surety, to the merit of my humble submission and obedience, which I offer you as though I had the honour to be your daughter (as I have to be your sister and next cousin); and yielding to none in desire to obey and honour you in future, may it please you to accept me as entirely yours.'[3]

Believing in the sincerity of this negotiation, she sent to the Kings of France and Spain copies of the articles which had been proposed to her, and which she had subscribed,[4] and she announced to Pope Pius V. that she had been compelled by necessity to submit. She alleged as her excuse the disordered state of Scotland, the lamentable evils by which she was overwhelmed, the incessant dangers which assailed her, and the shameful manner in which she had been abandoned by those who ought to have assisted her. 'I call God to witness,' she bitterly wrote, 'to whom all is

[1] See the articles of this negotiation in Labanoff, vol. iii., pp. 88-115; and Anderson, vol. iii., pp. 101-108.
[2] Lesly's Negotiations, in Anderson, vol. iii., p. 111.
[3] Labanoff, vol. iii., pp. 107, 108.
[4] Lesly's Negotiations, Anderson, vol. iii., p. 109.

known! He knows with what floods of miseries I have constantly had to contend until this day! And whilst this furious and continually-increasing tempest lasted, those who promised to come to my assistance, forgetting their promises, brought me no aid. I no longer expect they will bring me any, unless perchance the minds of these men may be more disposed to uphold my cause when circumstances render it more difficult to insure its triumph.' She expressed her resolution to conclude a peace with Elizabeth on the disadvantageous conditions which were offered her; but she assured the Sovereign Pontiff that she would never fail to discharge the duties of conscience or the laws of honour; and that her son should receive a Catholic education in England, whither she found herself compelled to send him as a hostage.[1]

The treaty, though terminated in some sort at Chatsworth, was to be finally concluded in London. The contending parties in Scotland were both summoned to send Commissioners to confer with Elizabeth upon the restoration of the captive Queen, and the close alliance of the two kingdoms. The Bishop of Galloway and Lord Livingstone, the deputies of Mary's adherents, hastened to join the Bishop of Ross in London.[2] But the Earl of Morton, the Abbot of Dunfermline, and Sir James Makgill, who were chosen to represent the contrary faction, were a long while in coming. Four months had elapsed since Mildmay and Cecil left Chatsworth; two months had passed since the Bishop of Galloway and Lord Livingstone arrived in London; but Morton, Makgill, and Pitcairn had not made their appearance.[3] When at last they arrived, the treaty was already gravely compromised. The Duke of Alva disapproved of its tenor;[4] and Charles IX. was unfavourable to the two clauses most essential to Elizabeth, namely, the rupture of the ancient league between Scotland and France, and the education of the Prince Royal in England.[5] But even on these conditions, Elizabeth, who had throughout been insincere,[6]

[1] This letter, dated 31st October, 1570, is in Bzovius, p. 710.
[2] Lesly's Negotiations, in Anderson, vol. iii., p. 111.
[3] Ibid., p. 125. Letter from Mary Stuart to the Earl of Sussex; Labanoff, vol. iii., pp. 197-199.
[4] The Duke of Alva 'hath declared openly, he is of opinion that if the former appointment has effect, it shall be to my destruction and ruin.'—Memoir addressed by Mary Stuart to the Bishop of Ross, 8th February, 1571; in Labanoff, vol. iii., p. 182.
[5] Letter from Mary Stuart to Lamothe Fénelon, 31st March, 1571; Labanoff, vol. iii., pp. 262, 263. Lesly's Negotiations, in Anderson, vol. iii., p. 121. Lamothe Fénelon's Correspondence, vol. iv., pp. 3, 6, 7.
[6] See Cecil's letters to Walsingham, 24th March and 7th April, 1571. Digges, pp. 67, 68.

was not disposed to liberate Mary Stuart. She multiplied difficulties, and added new demands to those she had originally made.[1] Morton, Pitcairn, and Makgill seconded her artifices by their behaviour. They declared that they had no power to receive Mary Stuart into Scotland, or to give up to Elizabeth the person of their infant Sovereign, and that they were only authorized to treat of the amity of the two kingdoms.[2] Under this base pretext, Elizabeth put an end to the Conference which she had commenced when France was emerging from the third civil war; which she had protracted as long as she had reason to fear that Charles IX. and Philip II. would unite to restore Mary Stuart; but which she broke off as soon as propositions for her own marriage to the Duke of Anjou had relieved her from all apprehensions with regard to the policy of the French Court.[3]

Mary Stuart's hopes were thus once more deceived.[4] During the two years and a half which she had been a prisoner in England, she had sought to obtain her deliverance and restoration by the exertions of her party in Scotland, by her marriage with the head of the English nobility, by the insurrection of Elizabeth's Catholic subjects, by the union of the Scottish lords, sustained by the Court of France, after Murray's death, and finally, by an accommodation with her fortunate and powerful rival. All attempts had, however, failed. The Scotch who were faithful to her cause had been overcome by Murray in 1569, and weakened by Elizabeth in 1570; her marriage with the Duke of Norfolk had met with but little favour in Scotland, and had been positively prohibited in England; the English Catholics had twice revolted, and had been twice defeated; the accommodation negotiated at Chatsworth, with so many concessions on her part, had been rejected; and France had not only failed to support her, but seemed likely to renounce her ancient league with Scotland, to form a new alliance with England. What course was left for Mary to pursue? King Philip II. was

[1] Mary Stuart to Lamothe Fénelon, 31st March, 1571. Labanoff, vol. iii., pp. 203, 263, 264. Tytler, vol. vi., p. 143.
[2] Anderson, vol. iii., pp. 125, 127, 130, 131, 133. Lamothe Fénelon's Correspondence, vol. iv., p. 4.
[3] Lamothe Fénelon's Correspondence, vols. iii. and iv., *passim*.
[4] On the 4th March, 1571, she wrote to the Archbishop of Glasgow: 'Ce sont témoignages que l'intention de ceste royne est autre que sa parole, et qu'il ne faut que je m'attende à aucun traicté.' Labanoff, vol. iii., pp. 204, 205. On the 20th of March, she stated in a memorial which she drew up for the Duke of Alva: 'Quant au traité de la royne d'Angleterre et de moy, il en est advenu comme j'ay tousjours espéré; c'est rien qui vaille.' Ibid., p. 220.

her last resource. She had recourse to him, and prompted him to a Spanish invasion, combined with an English insurrection.

In order to determine Philip II. to make an armed descent upon the kingdom of England, it was necessary to promise him powerful assistance, and to assure him that the Duke of Norfolk would embrace Catholicism, and revolt against Elizabeth. The slow and circumspect King of Spain had hitherto been deterred from engaging in the enterprise by representations of the risk by which it would be attended. The Duke of Alva had for more than a year maintained that the invasion of England was beset by the greatest difficulties; that it would be attended by enormous expense; that it would meet with the opposition of both France and Germany, the first of which would interfere from political jealousy, and the second from religious interest; and that it was to be feared that these two countries would either excite a new insurrection in the Spanish provinces, or would seize upon them as soon as he withdrew his troops.[1] These

[1] At the time when Pius V. wrote to the Duke of Alva, on the 3rd of November, 1569, to recommend to his notice the Queen of Scots and the Catholic party in England, he said to Don Juan de Zuñiga, the Spanish ambassador at Rome: 'Y lo que a el agora le parese seria que se (the Duke of Alva) ayudase de alguno de la misma nacion que fuese Catolico con dineros y con gente, paraque le alzase con el reyno, y si para tener mas parte pudiese ayudar el casarse con la Reina de Escocia que lo hiciese, que Su Santidad la daria la investidura como reyno que esta en feudo de la Iglesia.' Don Juan de Zuñiga to Philip II., Rome, 3rd November, 1569. Archives of Simancas, Roma, fol. 911.

The Duke of Alva thus replied to this invitation from the Pope. 'Acuerdo me aver dicho a Carlos de Evoli quando de su parte me hablo en esta materia, la facilidad con que el Rey nuestro señor podria hacer esta empresa, si el Rey de Francia le dejare, y remitiendo a Su Beatitud el tentarla, pero con el recato y tiento que en materia de tal calidad combenia, ó á los menos mudar el govierno en persona Catolica obediente a esa santa sede. Agora dijo lo mismo con a segurar á Su Beatitud que la hora que Su Magestad lo intentase ternia en contraria al Rey de Francia y a los de Alemanes, el Rey por estorvar la grandeza de Su Magestad y los otros por divertirle de la empresa, y por resistir tan duros adversarios, y Su Santidad vee si combiene ser muy ayudado hallandose tan atras du su patrimonio, por haver hecho tan excesivos gastos en allanar lo de aqui, en los socorros que ha hecho al Rey Cristianissimo y al Emperador, y los que agora hace en pacificar lo de Granada, que con haverse sacado aqui lo que ha sacado, se halla su Magestad sin un real, y me cuestan las banderas de gente que agora licencio 800,000 ducados y a los que tengo en Francia debo mas de 200,000. No embargante todo lo dicho, he dado quenta a Su Magestad.' He added, 'No veo en las cosas del Norte sobre que hacer fundamento, ni el de Norfolc hizo mas de descubrir su voluntad y venirse ameter en la prision donde queda agora mas estrecho que antes.' The Duke of Alva to Don Juan de Zuñiga, Brussels, 5th December, 1569. Archives of Simancas, Roma, fol. 913.

reasons had their force; and Philip II. was struck by them.[1] Nevertheless, he had for a moment been on the point of declaring in favour of the Earls of Northumberland and Westmoreland, when he was informed of the insurrection in the north of England. From Cordova, where he was holding the Cortes of Castile, he had despatched to them a trusty messenger, George Quempe, with letters of encouragement and promises of prompt assistance, which he ordered the Duke of Alva to send them, if they kept the field.[2] Their rapid defeat had prevented him from sustaining them; and it was now indispensable, in order to induce him to fit out an expedition, to prove to him that its accomplishment would be easy, and its success certain, by reason of the support which the Duke of Norfolk would obtain among the nobles, and in the counties of England, which would rise in arms, as soon as the Spanish fleet appeared, and the soldiers of Philip II. had disembarked.

Mary Stuart had maintained constant and affectionate communications with the Duke of Norfolk during his imprisonment in the Tower. She had sent him her portrait,[3] and, although they had never seen each other, their letters breathed the most passionate love.[4] These letters were written in cypher; and were sent through the hands of the Bishop of Ross, whose secretary, John Cuthbert, decyphered them for Mary, whilst Banister

[1] In April, 1569, Philip II. had refused to make war upon Elizabeth. He had written to the Cardinal de Guise: 'Que de manera ninguna se declarasse la guerra, y que le convenia aquietar de todo punto sus estados, y runatar la victoria que acababa de conseguir contra sus rebeldes, limitando sus oficios en favor de Maria de Escocia, a solicitar de Isabel por todos medios su libertad, que era lo mismo que el hacia.' Gonzalez, Apuntamientos, p. 90.

[2] 'Estando Felipe Segundo en Cordoba, en vista de las noticias recebidas de Inglaterra, se inclinó a favorecer las rebeliones de aquel reyno y de Escocia, a cuyo efecto se determinó á Jorge Quempe, caballero principal, con despachos para los condes y otras personas de importancia, animándoles á continuar en su proyecto y promitiendoles con toda seguridad socorros de todos clases, prontos y eficaces, para acreditar á los condes que el Rey se decidia a soccorrerlos de todas maneras, llevata cartas para el Duque de Alba con ordenes al intento.' Ibid., p. 98.

[3] 'His Grace delyvered to me, a lyttle tablett of golde, wherein was sett the Quene of Scott's picture.' Banister's Declaration; in Murdin, p. 136.

[4] 'And most certen yt is, that those lettres tended all togeather to matters of love.' Banister's Declaration and Submission; in Murdin, p. 138. Some of the letters written by Mary Stuart to the Duke of Norfolk while he was in the Tower, will be found in Prince Labanoff's Collection, vol. iii., pp. 11, 19, 31, 35, 36, 47, 61. She addressed him as, 'myne own good constant lord,' and subscribed herself 'Your own faithful to death.' Sometimes even, the Duke of Norfolk manifested symptoms of jealousy. 'Aboute that tyme,' says Banister, 'thear was halfe a jalowsie of my lord's parte, towchinge the Quene of Scott's faithefullnesse towardes him.' Banister's Declaration and Submission; in Murdin, p. 138.

decyphered them for the Duke, whose servant he was.[1] They were carefully kept from the knowledge of Elizabeth, who believed that all private communications and common intentions had ceased between the two prisoners. Some time after the death of Murray, when her hopes revived in Scotland, Mary Stuart wrote to the Duke of Norfolk: 'If you mind not to shrink at the matter, I will die and live with you. Your fortune shall be mine; therefore let me know, in all things, your mind.'[2] At the time when the negotiation with Mary Stuart, which had been commenced in London, was transferred to Chatsworth, the plague found its way from the City into the Tower, and Elizabeth gave Norfolk permission to leave his prison.[3] Though not restored entirely to liberty, he was allowed to reside in his own house, under a slight guard.[4] But before he was released from the State-prison, she required him to give a solemn promise that he would have no more communications with the Queen of Scotland, and would abandon all pretensions to her hand. The Duke gave a written promise to this effect, and sealed it with his arms.[5] Notwithstanding the terrible penalties to which he exposed himself by violating this engagement, for he had consented, in that case, to be considered and treated as a traitor, he continued, by means of the Bishop of Ross, his secret correspondence with Mary Stuart, who, in the most ardent or most sorrowful language, raised his soul to ambition or to devotion, said she was entirely his, and besought him, with irresistible endearments, to give himself entirely to her.[6]

When she perceived that the negotiation which was pending between herself and Elizabeth was insincere, and would lead to no definite conclusion, and that she must enter again into the necessary but dangerous course of conspiracy, she drew the Duke of Norfolk along with her. The Bishop of Ross originated a plan for a new conspiracy, which the Florentine Ridolfi was to make known to the Duke of Alva, Pope Pius V., and Philip II. Ridolfi was not only a rich Florentine banker, a relative of the

---

[1] Murdin, p. 138.
[2] Mary Stuart to the Duke of Norfolk, 19th March, 1570; in Labanoff, vol. iii., pp. 31, 32.
[3] Lesly's Negotiations; in Anderson, vol. iii., p. 97.   [4] Ibid., p. 98.
[5] The Duke 'did give his hand and obligatioun to the Quene of England, written and subscribed with his hand, and sealed with his scale, before his departinge forth of the Toure, obliginge him, under paine of his allegiance, that he shall never medle in that marriage with the Quene of Scotland.' Lesly's Negotiations; in Anderson, vol. iii., p. 98.
[6] Labanoff, vol. iii., pp. 11, 19, 31, 35, 36, 47, 61.

Medici family, and director of the company of Italian merchants in London; he was also the secret correspondent of the Sovereign Pontiff, and the influential creditor of most of the English nobility, whose full confidence he possessed, and whom he endeavoured to alienate, as far as he could, from the cause of Elizabeth and of Protestantism. He was imprisoned for some months after the Catholic insurrection in the North, in which he was suspected of participation, but had regained his liberty on giving surety in the sum of one thousand pounds. He believed that the time had now come for delivering the Queen of Scots, by the assistance of the Pope and of Philip II., of marrying her to the Duke of Norfolk, who had become a convert to Catholicism, and of restoring the ancient religion in the two kingdoms of the island of Britain. The Bishop of Ross and himself had secret communications and conferences with the Duke of Norfolk on this subject.[1] Very minute instructions were drawn up in the name of the Queen and Duke, to be laid before Pius V. and Philip II. by Ridolfi.[2] The Duke refused to sign Ridolfi's powers, on account of the danger to which he would be exposed if they were discovered; but after having read them, he readily approved them, and signified his approbation to Don Gueraldo d'Espès, the Spanish ambassador.[3]

On the 20th of March, a few days before Ridolfi left London, Mary Stuart sent John Hamilton with a letter to the Duke of Alva, whom she addressed as 'the faithful councillor of the King of Spain, the defender and refuge of the Catholic Church.'[4] She 'besought him to furnish her with prompt assistance, which is very necessary,' she said, 'for the cause of God, for myself, and for my friends.'[5] Resuming her pretensions to the crown of England, she announced that she would speedily communicate her 'private plans'[6] to the Duke of Alva, with whom she

[1] Barker's answers to the last declaration; in Murdin, p. 103. The Examination of W. Barker; Ibid., p. 111. The Examination of the Bishop of Ross; Ibid., pp. 24, 25. Lesly's Negotiations, in Anderson, vol. iii., p. 159.

[2] An Italian copy of these instructions, extracted from the secret Archives of the Vatican, is printed in the third volume of Prince Labanoff's Collection. That part of them which concerns Mary Stuart will be found in pp. 221-233; and that which relates to the Duke of Norfolk in pp. 234-249. A portion of them will also be found in Spanish in pp. 215-219 of the Apuntamientos of Don Tomas Gonzalez, who extracted them from the Archives of Simancas. They are confirmed by the confession of the Bishop of Ross. Murdin, p. 19.

[3] Examination of the Bishop of Ross. Murdin, pp. 25, 26.

[4] Memoir given by Mary Stuart to John Hamilton, on the 20th March, for the Duke of Alva; Labanoff, vol. iii., p. 216.

[5] Ibid., p. 220. [6] Ibid., p. 218.

desired to treat 'not on her own part alone,' but also in order to lay 'all this island' under perpetual obligations ' to his master the King of Spain, and to himself, as the faithful executor of his commands.'[1]

Four days afterwards, Ridolfi set out for the Continent with the instructions of both Mary and Norfolk. We learn from these instructions that the Duke requested six thousand arquebusiers, four thousand arquebuses, two thousand corslets or cuirasses, twenty-five pieces of artillery, and a supply of ammunition and money. He desired that, if possible, ten thousand men should be sent, in order that four thousand might be employed in creating a diversion in Ireland. He promised, on his side, to furnish twenty thousand infantry and three thousand cavalry, to seize the Queen of England and all the members of her Council, to deliver the Queen of Scotland from her captivity, and to place her upon the throne as soon as the kingdom had been brought back to its religious allegiance to the Sovereign Pontiff.[2] In order to inspire greater confidence in the success of the enterprise, Ridolfi was to mention all those who would either promote the scheme or who would not oppose it. Annexed to his instructions was a list of the leading English nobles, with their sentiments marked opposite to their names: and, according to this list, an immense majority were either favourable to a change in the government or pledged to engage in the conspiracy.[3] Mary Stuart, who either believed in this statement or affected to believe in it, in order to secure the aid of Philip II., announced that the Duke of Norfolk was ready to place himself at the head of the nobility and to take arms. She offered to send her son into Spain, that he might receive a thoroughly Catholic education; and expressed her deep regret that Bothwell's violence had forced her into a marriage which she had sought to have annulled ever since her passion for him had abated.[4] She promised that the Roman Catholic religion should be restored, and directed Ridolfi to express orally the most secret object of his mission. 'And as

---

[1] Memoir given by Mary Stuart to John Hamilton, on the 20th March, for the Duke of Alva; Labanoff, vol. iii., pp. 218, 219.

[2] These instructions are printed in Labanoff, vol. iii., pp. 234-249.

[3] This list will be found in Prince Labanoff's Collection, vol. iii., pp. 251-253. Of two marquises, one was favourable, and the other neutral; of 18 earls, 10 were favourable, 3 hostile, and 5 neutral; of 3 viscounts, one was favourable, one hostile, and one neutral; of 40 lords, 28 were favourable, 10 neutral, and 2 hostile. Thus, of 63 English nobles, 40 were favourable, 17 neutral, and only 6 hostile.

[4] Secret instructions given by Mary Stuart to Ridolfi. Labanoff, vol. iii., pp. 221-233.

this,' she wrote, ' concerns the public interest of Christendom and of the Catholic King in particular, we ought not, by negligence or delay, to allow so certain an enterprise to fail. Ridolfi will add, by word of mouth, all that has been said to him by the Duke and by the Bishop of Ross.'[1] The Court of France had just concluded a peace with the Protestants, and was negotiating the marriage of the Duke of Anjou to Queen Elizabeth; Mary Stuart therefore regarded it with great mistrust, and charged Ridolfi to hold no communications with Catherine de Medici and Charles IX., on his way through Paris.

On his arrival at Brussels, Ridolfi had an audience of the Duke of Alva,[2] to whom he detailed the plan, the resources and the requirements of the conspirators who had deputed him to the Pope and Philip II. The Duke was as keen-sighted in his views as a politician, as he was unscrupulous in his actions as a general. He did not appear to place much confidence in the Florentine envoy, whom he called a great chatterbox (*parlanchin*) ;[3] or to repose much faith in his enterprise, which he considered too rash. On the 7th of May, 1571, he wrote a letter more than twenty pages in length to Philip II. on the subject.[4] In this long and curious despatch, hitherto unpublished, but of great importance as an historical document, the Duke of Alva, after having informed the King his master, of all that Ridolfi had proposed to him on the part of the Queen of Scotland and the Duke of Norfolk, for the deliverance of Mary Stuart, the restoration of Catholicism, the deposition of Elizabeth, and the capture of the Tower of London, added that the Duke of Norfolk announced that he could await in arms the arrival of the succour requested in his instructions, for forty days in his own county, which lay directly opposite Holland, and where it would be easy to disembark troops in July or August. The Duke of Alva enjoined Ridolfi to maintain the most absolute silence on the subject during his journey through France, if he had any regard for the lives of the Queen of Scotland and the Duke of Norfolk, who would inevitably be ruined by any indiscretion on his part. He wrote at

[1] Examination of the Bishop of Ross; Murdin, p. 25. Examination of W. Barker; Ibid., p, 110. Bailly's Letter; Ibid., pp. 16, 17.
[2] 'E per tanto che tocca dell'interesse publico di tutta la Christianita, e particularmente del Re Catolico, non si debbe trascurare, e lasciar perdere per tolleranza o troppo lunga dilatione tale sicura impresa, che al presente si offerisce, aggiungendo il Ridolfi in questo proposito, di bocca, quello che per il Duca e il Vescovo di Rosche gli é stato detto.' Labanoff, vol. iii., p. 22.
[3] Gonzalez, Apuntamientos, p. 111.
[4] In the Archives of Simancas, Inglaterra, fol. 823.

the same time to Don Juan de Zuñiga, the Spanish ambassador at the Papal Court, to inform him of Ridolfi's speedy arrival at Rome, and to request him to acquaint his Holiness of all the difficulties attaching to the enterprise, lest his zeal should lead him to embrace it with too much ardour.

As regarded the enterprise itself, the Duke of Alva wrote thus to Philip II.:—' Considering the pity and interest with which the unworthy treatment of the Queen of Scotland and her adherents cannot fail to inspire your Majesty; considering the obligation under which you are placed by God, to obtain, by all means in your power, the triumphant restoration of Catholicism in those islands; considering, moreover, the injuries which the Queen of England does in so many ways, and on so many sides, to your Majesty and your subjects, without any hopes of being on better terms with her, as regards religion and neighbourhood, as long as she reigns; it appears to me that the plan of the Queen of Scotland and the Duke of Norfolk, if it could be properly carried out, would be the best method of remedying the evil.'[1]

But although he approved of the enterprise, he maintained that it ought not to be commenced with the open assistance of the Catholic King. In that case, so many persons would be employed in the matter that it would be impossible to keep the secret, and 'if the secret were not kept,' he added, ' the enterprise would fall to the ground; the lives of both the Queen of Scotland and the Duke of Norfolk would be endangered; the Queen of England would find the opportunity, which she has sought so long, for getting rid of her and her partisans; the hopes of the Catholic religion would be crushed for ever, and the whole would recoil upon your Majesty.'[2] . . . . Wherefore, no one can think of advising your Majesty to furnish the assistance sought of you, under the form in which it is requested. But if the Queen of England should die, *either a natural death or any other death*,[3] or if her person should be seized without your Majesty's concurrence, then I should perceive no further difficulty. The proposals between the Queen of England and the Duke of Anjou would cease, the French would be less fearful that your Majesty

[1] 'Y que pudiendose effectuar este designo de la Reina de Escocia y del Duque de Norfolch, seria el mas apparente camino para el remedio de todo o de gran parte.' Archives of Simancas, Inglaterra, fol. 823.

[2] 'Y todo redundare contra Vuestra Magestad.' Archives of Simancas, Inglaterra, fol. 823.

[3] 'Y asci me paresce que en tel caso de la muerte de la Reina de Inglaterra, natural o de otra manera, o que ella estuviesse en poder del dicho Duque de Norfolch.' Ibid.

should seek to become master of England, the Germans would look upon you with less distrust, since you would have no other object but to sustain the Queen of Scotland against the rival claimants of the crown of England. In that case it would be easy to reduce them to reason before other Princes could interfere, as we could profit by the convenience of the Duke of Norfolk's county, where we could disembark the six thousand men he requires, not within the forty days during which he could maintain himself unassisted, but within thirty or even twenty-five days.' The Duke of Alva insisted that in case either of the natural death, the assassination, or the capture of Elizabeth, Philip II. should seize the opportunity for attaining the object he had in view, the restoration of the Catholic faith in the British Isles, and thus securing the future tranquillity of his own dominions. He concluded his despatch in these words: 'Your Majesty may then answer them that, if any of the three cases above mentioned occur, you will assist them from the Netherlands with the six thousand men they desire. For myself, Sire, I look upon this as so convenient, so honourable, and so easy for your Majesty, that if one of the three cases happens, I shall not hesitate to act without waiting for new directions from your Majesty, considering that such is your intention; and I shall do so, unless you order the contrary.'[1]

This despatch was forwarded from Brussels on the 7th of May, and reached Madrid on the 22nd. Philip II. adding his own distrust to the fears and counsels of the Duke of Alva, wrote thus, on the 20th of June, to Don Gueraldo d'Espès, his ambassador at London: 'Robert Ridolfi has not yet arrived here. If the mission with which he is intrusted were divulged, it would be death to the Queen of Scotland and the Duke of Norfolk, as we may consider it certain that, on learning their plans, the Queen of England would take the opportunity of executing her wicked intentions with some show of justice. Keep, therefore, on your guard; proceed with fitting caution; maintain a good understanding with the Duke of Alva, and act according to his orders.'[2]

A few days after, Ridolfi arrived at Madrid, on his way from

---

[1] 'A mi juicio tengo, yo por tan loable, y honroso a Vuestra Magestad, y tan facil a executar, que cuando de improviso yò tuviesse nuevas que uno de los tres casos havia acontescido estuviessen en pie, no me paresce, que yo devria poner dubda en executarlo, sin esperar otra comodidad o mandamiento de Vuestra Magestad.'

[2] Archives of Simancas, Inglaterra, fol. 823.

Rome, where the Pope had ardently adopted his plans. On the 28th of June,[1] he was admitted to an audience of Philip II. and presented to him, in addition to his credentials from Mary Stuart and the Duke of Norfolk, the following letter from the Sovereign Pontiff, Pius V. :—' Our dear son, Robert Ridolfi, by the help of God, will lay before your Majesty, certain things which interest not a little the honour of Almighty God, and the advantage of the Christian commonwealth. We require and beseech your Majesty to grant him, on this account and without hesitation, your most entire confidence, and we conjure you especially by your fervent piety towards God to take to heart the matters on which he will treat with your Majesty, and to furnish him with all the means which you may judge most suitable for the execution of his plans. Meanwhile we beseech your Majesty to do this, submitting the affair to the judgment and prudence of your Majesty, and from the bottom of our heart praying our Redeemer, in his mercy, to grant success to that which is projected for his honour and glory.'[2]

On the 7th of July, Ridolfi was questioned at the Escurial, regarding the enterprise which he had come to propose, by the Duke of Feria, whom Philip II. had deputed to hear his statements. His answers were written down in the handwriting of Zayas, the Secretary of State.[3] It was proposed to murder Queen Elizabeth. Ridolfi said that the blow would not be struck at London, because that city was the stronghold of heresy; but while she was travelling, and that a person named James Graffs[4] had undertaken the office. On the same day, the Council of State commenced its deliberations upon the proposed assassination of Elizabeth and conquest of England.[5] The subject of the discussion was, whether it behoved the King of Spain to agree with the conspirators, ' to kill or capture the Queen of England,'[6] in order to prevent her from marrying the Duke of Anjou and

[1] According to Gonzalez, he did not arrive at Madrid until the 3rd of July; Apuntamientos, p. 112. But from a letter from the Catholic King to his ambassador Espès, dated San Lorenzo, 13th July, we learn that he had an audience of Philip II. on the 28th June. Archives of Simancas, fol. 823.
[2] This Latin letter is in the Archives of Simancas, Inglaterra, fol. 822.
[3] 'MS. minuta de lo que respondió Ridolfi à las particularidas que le pregunto el Duque de Feria en San Geronimo, á 7 de Julio.' Archives of Simancas, Inglaterra, fol. 823.
[4] This name must be incorrect, as it is mentioned in no other place.
[5] 'Lo que se platico en consejo sobre las cosas de Inglaterra. En Madrid, Sabado, 7 de Julio, 1571.' In the handwriting of Zayas, Archives of Simancas, Inglaterra, fol. 823. [6] ' Matar o prender la Reina.' Ibid.

putting to death the Queen of Scotland; whether the blow should be struck while she was travelling, or, which would be easier still, when she was at the country-house of one of the conspirators, who had surrounded her with persons on whom they could depend; and whether they ought not to be assisted in case they carried out their intentions, which they would not do without the orders of the Catholic King. The Councillors of State severally gave their opinion, which were committed to writing, and have been preserved to this day. The Duke of Feria spoke first. 'Under present circumstances,' he said, 'the affair is embarrassing, but the Catholic King must not postpone it. The Queen of Scotland is *the true heir*[1] to the realm of England, and she will rightly discharge the duties of religion and friendship towards us. If we allow her to be crushed, we entail destruction on all those who are devoted to her. The proximity of the Duke of Alva greatly facilitates the matter, and not an instant must be lost if we intend to engage in the enterprise.' Don Hernando de Toledo, Grand Prior of Castile, who spoke next, said that Ciapino Vitelli was the proper man to accomplish the undertaking under the direction of the Duke of Alva, and that, in Vitelli's opinion, the months of September and October were favourable for the execution of such a plan. Ruy Gomez de Silva, Prince of Eboli, thought that a letter should at once be written to the Duke of Alva, that he might obtain the funds necessary for the enterprise. Doctor Martin Velasco was less inclined than his colleagues to engage in the attempt. He said that it was supposed that the Queen would be captured, and that her death would end the matter; but it was to be feared that communications made to powerful persons might be dangerous; that it was better to urge them to action, without giving any pledge to Ridolfi; not to write to them, but to send them money, and to promise indirectly that they should receive further assistance at the proper time. The Inquisitor General, the Cardinal Archbishop of Seville, maintained that the Duke of Alva possessed all the means for securing the success of such an enterprise, and that, with a view to its execution, the sum of two hundred thousand crowns should be placed in his hands, with an intimation that he should proceed in conformity with the declaration made by the Pope in his bull. The Cardinal added that Ciapino Vitelli had offered to go in person, with a dozen or fifteen resolute men, to seize the Queen of England in one of her

---

[1] 'La verdadera successora.' Archives of Simancas, Inglaterra, fol. 823.

pleasure-houses; and that he would present himself before her, under the pretext of demanding justice.

The Duke of Feria opposed the idea suggested by the Inquisitor General, that they should act in England in the Pope's name; and maintained that they should found their intervention on the claims of the Queen of Scotland to the succession to the crown of that kingdom. He did not, moreover, think it would be easy for a dozen men to capture Queen Elizabeth; and in this opinion he was supported by the Grand Prior of Castile, who further declared that a conquest by armed force presented the greatest possible difficulties, and that the Duke of Alva had not means to undertake it. As for Ruy Gomez, with his usual address, he threw the execution and the responsibility of the enterprise upon the Duke of Alva, saying that he thought it very arduous, although the Pope's Nuncio represented it as very easy to the Catholic King.

Philip II. replied to the Nuncio that he would willingly undertake it, but that it must be carried out with so much promptitude and with such powerful resources, that neighbouring princes would not have time to interfere. He insinuated that the Pope should supply the money which would be required. On the 13th of July, just about this time, he wrote to his ambassador at London: 'I am busily occupied with the affair of Ridolfi, and intend to act according to what is fitting and I am able to do.[1] I shall resolve the question very promptly and with great good will; but as it might happen that, by knowing this, the oppressed Catholics in England, moved by sentiments of hatred and a desire for vengeance, and desirous to obtain their object without the least delay, might declare themselves before the proper time and take arms unseasonably, you must enjoin them to do nothing until the affair is fully ripe and everything is properly arranged.'[2] He also announced to Don Gueraldo d'Espès that, by his directions, Ridolfi had written to express his wishes and intentions to the Queen of Scotland, the Duke of Norfolk, and the Bishop of Ross.

The King of Spain, who alone was powerful enough to liberate

[1] 'Quedo tractando dello conamino de hazer ceranto corweuga y se prudesse, de muy briena gana y lo resolvare muy en breve.' Archives of Simancas, Inglaterra, fol. 823.

[2] 'Se quisiessen arojar antès de trempo y declararse y tomar las armas sin sazon, hos haveis de advertir que en ninguna manera lo hagan, ni se muevan, hasta que las cosas esten maduras y despuestas como conviene.' Archives of Simancas, Inglaterra, fol. 823.

Mary Stuart, long remained, according to his custom, in that state of uncertainty into which he was constantly cast by the hesitation of his mind, and the irresolution of his character. His fears were in direct contravention of his desires. He wished, but did not dare, to engage in this enterprise. Among his counsellors, the most ardent urged him to undertake it, and the most prudent dissuaded him from it. He had only just subjugated the rebellious Moriscoes in the south-east of Spain. The greater part of his forces were employed in the Mediterranean against the Turks, and in the Netherlands against the religious insurgents, whose wavering allegiance the Duke of Alva was endeavouring to confirm. He was afraid of commencing an open war against Elizabeth, which might probably not succeed in England, and would then become fatal in the Netherlands. After several months of tergiversation, he determined to leave the matter entirely to the decision of the Duke of Alva, to whom he wrote thus, on the 14th of September: 'Perceiving that you think firmly and resolutely that it is not advisable to proceed in this matter, unless the confederates show themselves in force, and considering the careful attention you have given to the subject, I am led to leave it in your hands in order that, after examining into all points, you may act as you may consider advantageous to the service of God and of ourselves, and I feel assured that you will direct this great enterprise with all the zeal, solicitude, and prudence which it requires.'[1]

Whilst these deliberations were pending in Spain, the boldest of the confederates urged the Duke of Norfolk to declare himself in England. Elizabeth, after having suspended for five years the tenure of parliaments, whose increasing indocility had irritated and disturbed her, had at length convoked one, which met at the very time when the conspiracy was in progress on the Continent. This parliament was to pass terrible laws against all persons who should call in question the rights of the Queen of England upon any ground, whether political or religious. Thus, it was made treason in any individual to claim a right to the crown during the Queen's life; or to affirm that any person was the heir of the Queen, except the same were 'the natural issue of her body;' or to deny that the descent and inheritance of the crown was determinable by the statutes made in parliament; or to invalidate the Queen's royal authority under the pretext that she was a heretic and schismatic.[2] When the parliament met,

[1] Gonzalez, Apuntamientos, p. 208.
[2] Camden, vol. ii., p. 241. Lingard, vol. viii., pp. 69, 70.

and before it had taken these conservative measures in favour of Elizabeth, and in opposition not only to the Pope's recent bull, but also to Mary Stuart's constantly manifested desires, the Bishop of Ross thought the presence of the principal nobility in London afforded the Duke of Norfolk a good opportunity for declaring himself with success. He had received from Brussels, by Ridolfi, news which the Florentine conspirator had represented as favourable,[1] and he urged the Duke of Norfolk to anticipate and hasten the despatch of assistance from Spain by taking advantage of the presence of so many noblemen in London to place himself at their head, take possession of the Tower, which was at once the arsenal and citadel of the country, and seize the person of the Queen herself. Norfolk was too timid to venture so much. At best he would only consent to take arms when the presence of a foreign army should encourage him to do so.[2] Thus, whilst the Spaniards made their invasion of England depend upon the insurrection of the conspirators or the death of Elizabeth, the timorous leader of the conspirators would not revolt until the Spaniards appeared. This was conspiring for his own destruction and not for the triumph of his cause. It was impossible,—with so much dilatoriness on the Continent, so much hesitation in the island, and so much correspondence and inaction on the part of the conspirators,—to prevent all from being discovered and frustrated by the suspicious and vigilant government of Elizabeth.

Shortly after Ridolfi's arrival at Brussels, Cecil, whom Elizabeth had just created Lord Burghley,[3] had already gained a clue to the conspiracy. About the 10th of April, a Fleming named Charles Bailly, whom the Bishop of Ross had employed at Brussels, to print a book written in defence of the honour and rights of the Queen of Scotland, was arrested at Dover. Knowing that he possessed the Bishop's entire confidence, Ridolfi had informed him of the object of his mission, and had employed him to write in cypher the five despatches which he sent to Mary Stuart, the Bishop of Ross, the Duke of Norfolk, Lord Lumley, the son-in-law of the Earl of Arundel, and Don Gueraldo d'Espès, upon the result of his interview with the Duke of Alva. These letters, which contained the whole secret of the conspiracy, had been seized with the rest of Bailly's luggage on his arrival in

[1] Lesly's Negotiations, in Anderson, vol. iii., pp. 162, 163. Murdin, pp. 16, 17, 25, 110.
[2] Ibid., vol. iii., pp. 209-213. Answer of the Bishop of Ross, Murdin, pp. 42, 43.
[3] Camden, pp. 223, 224.

England.¹ The packet containing them was placed in the care of Lord Cobham, governor of the Cinque Ports, who, either from carelessness or complicity, allowed the Bishop of Ross to substitute in their place another packet of the same form, and containing letters of an innoxious description.² Bailly was nevertheless sent to the Marshalsea prison, where he commenced a correspondence with the Bishop of Ross, which fell into Burghley's hands, and informed Elizabeth's minister that Ridolfi's real letters had reached their destination in safety.³ Bailly was then sent to the Tower, and disclosed on the rack all that he knew about the conspiracy. By Burghley's order, the Bishop was arrested and his papers searched, but no documents of any importance were discovered. When interrogated by four lords of the Council, the Bishop refused to reply, declaring that 'he was answerable for his actions to no one but the Queen his mistress.'⁵ Thus reduced once more to captivity, he was left under the surveillance of two of the Queen's gentlemen, in the custody of the Bishop of Ely, who kept him from the middle of May until the middle of August in his house in Holborn,⁶ and then took him into his diocese. Burghley was thus made aware of the existence of a conspiracy;⁷ but he was incapable of proving it, and could not further trace its progress.

The vigilance of this formidable minister was thus strongly awakened, when a new imprudence enabled him, some months afterwards, to discover the entire plot. War had recommenced in Scotland, with more violence than ever, between the adherents of Mary Stuart and those of James VI. On the 2nd of April, 1571, the day after the expiration of the truce, during which both parties had suspended hostilities, the Earl of Lennox had gained possession of Dumbarton Castle by surprise.⁸ The Archbishop of St. Andrews, whom he detested as the enemy of his house, and accused of complicity in the murder of the King, his son, and his friend, the late Regent, was among the prisoners. The implacable Lennox brought him to trial at once, and he

---

¹ Lesly's Negotiations, in Anderson, vol. iii., pp. 163, 164.
² Ibid., p. 164.
³ See the letters of Bailly to the Bishop of Ross in Murdin, pp. 2, 3, 5, 6, 7.
⁴ Lesly's Negotiations, in Anderson, vol. iii., pp. 164, 165.
⁵ Ibid., pp. 165, 166.   ⁶ Ibid., p. 167.
⁷ In the month of May, he said to Lamothe Fénelon : ' Elle (la Reine d'Ecosse) a mené de très-mauvaises pratiques par Ridolfi avec le Duc d'Albe, et avec les rebelles Anglais qui sont en Flandres pour exciter une nouvelle rebellion dans ce royaulme.'   Lamothe Fénelon's Correspondence, vol. iv., p. 119.
⁸ Tytler, vol. vi., pp. 151-153.

was ignominiously hanged.[1] This act of cruelty and contempt towards one of the heads of the Hamilton clan, and the former Primate of the kingdom, led, ere long, to terrible reprisals upon the new Regent, and rendered the war merciless in its vengeance. On both sides, Parliaments were convoked to condemn their adversaries for treason. The lords of the Queen's party met at Edinburgh—the command of which had been given by Kirkaldy of Grange to Ker of Fernyhirst, a fierce and powerful Border chief[2]—and proscribed, by a sentence of forfeiture, the Earls of Lennox, Morton, and Mar, the Lords Lindsay, Hay, Cathcart, Ochiltree, and Glammis, the Bishop of Orkney, the Clerk-register Makgill, and nearly two hundred persons of the King's faction.[3] The Lords who adhered to James VI. met, on their side, in greater numbers, at Stirling, whither Morton had succeeded in bringing Argyle, Montrose, Cassilis, and Eglinton,[4] and pronounced the doom of treason upon the Duke of Chatelherault, the Earl of Huntly, Lethington, Kirkaldy of Grange, Lord Claude Hamilton, the Commendator of Arbroath, Sir James Balfour, Robert Melvil, and many others.[5]

Elizabeth supported the King's party by military expeditions, whilst the Kings of France and Spain forwarded subsidies of money to the Queen's adherents. The latter had great need of pecuniary assistance, to enable them to remain in arms, and defend the citadel of Edinburgh. It was a sum of money, intrusted by the French ambassador to Barker, one of the secretaries of the Duke of Norfolk, to be sent with some letters in cypher to Mary Stuart's partisans in Scotland, which led to the discovery of the whole plot. Higford, another of the Duke's secretaries, and Bannister, his steward, undertook, with their master's permission, to transmit to Lord Herries both the money and the letters; but the agent to whose care they committed them proved unfaithful, and placed them instead in the hands of Burghley.[6] All three were immediately arrested as guilty of criminal communications with the Queen's enemies, and interrogated regarding all the proceedings of the Duke their master.

[1] MS. letter, State Paper Office, Lord Herries to Lord Scrope, 10th April, 1571; also MS. letter, State Paper Office, Lennox to Burghley, 14th May, 1571. Tytler, vol. ii., p. 153.
[2] Diurnal of Occurrents, p. 226. Tytler, vol. vi., p. 157.
[3] Tytler, vol. vi., p. 158. Diurnal of Occurrents, pp. 236, 242, 243.
[4] Tytler, vol. vi., p. 160.
[5] Diurnal of Occurrents, p. 245. Tytler, vol. vi., p. 159.
[6] Lesly's Negotiations, in Anderson, vol. iii., pp. 169-171. See also the examinations and confessions of Barker, Higford, and Bannister, in Murdin, pp. 67-146.

Higford, on being taken to the Tower of London, was not satisfied with telling the secret to Elizabeth's government.¹ He indicated the places in Howard House where were concealed the cypher which the Duke used in his correspondence with Mary Stuart, the papers relative to Ridolfi's mission, and nineteen letters which the Duke had received from the Queen of Scotland and the Bishop of Ross.² The contents of these documents, which Higford had been ordered to burn, but which he had perfidiously preserved, were confirmed by the statements of Barker, who had been the principal intermediary between Norfolk, Lesly, and Ridolfi. Old and feeble, Barker was alarmed at the sight of the instruments of torture, and told all that he knew.³ Bannister was equally communicative; and the Bishop of Ross was transferred from Ely to London, and interrogated in his turn.⁴ He refused at first to reply, pleading the privilege of an ambassador; but the Crown lawyers having declared that an ambassador convicted of having taken part in a conspiracy against the State or Sovereign to whom he was accredited, lost all right to the privileges of his office, Burghley commanded him to answer, unless he wished to be put to the torture and executed, like a simple subject of the Queen of England. The terror which he felt at this threat, and the knowledge which he had of the confessions of Higford, Barker, and Bannister, determined him to speak.⁵ He related, without any reservation, all that had passed between the Queen of Scotland and the Duke of Norfolk, from the Conference at York until Ridolfi's mission to the Continent.⁶ His deposition completed the ruin of the Duke of Norfolk.

This nobleman, who had rather sanctioned than directed the plot in which he had engaged, and whose downfall was occasioned as much by his timidity as his ambition, was not accused of high treason. On being once more conducted to the Tower, he fell into a state of great depression.⁷ At first he denied everything; but when he learned that the conspiracy had been divulged by his

¹ Lesly's Negotiations, in Anderson, vol. iii., p. 172.
² Ibid., p. 173. ³ Ibid., pp. 173, 174.
⁴ Ibid., pp. 188, 189. ⁵ Ibid., pp. 189-200.
⁶ Examination of the Bishop of Ross, Murdin, pp. 20-32, 35-38, and 46-54.
⁷ 'About five of the clock, or somewhat afore, we conveyed the Duke from his howse to the Tower, without eny difficultie. He semith now very humble, and shewith as though he will come to open all.' Letter from Sir Ralph Sadler, Sir Thomas Smith, and Mr. Wylson to Lord Burghley, 7th September, 1571. Murdin, p. 148. 'He semyd very myche abasshed; and fallyng on his knees, protesting that he did it but to your Majestie, he confessed his undutifull and folish doengs, requyring mercy and pardon at your Highnes's hands.' Letter from the same to Elizabeth, 7th September, 1571. Murdin, p. 149.

own servants and by the Bishop of Ross, he cried out: ' I am betrayed !'[1] He then resolved to do what would compromise him the least.[2] He wrote most suppliant and submissive letters to Elizabeth, acknowledged the grave offences which he had committed against her, and implored her merciful pardon.[3]

But Elizabeth, influenced by the alarmed and fanatical party of the religious reformers, proposed to make a great and terrible example. The repeated rebellion of the Catholics in the north, the audacious publication of the sentence of deposition fulminated against her by the Roman Pontiff, the persevering proposal to marry the head of the English nobility to her rival claimant of the throne of England, and the application made to the King of Spain to combine a foreign invasion with a new insurrection in the island, had excited her fears and severity to the last degree. Don Gueraldo d'Espès was ordered to leave her dominions immediately.[4] Lord Lumley, Lord Cobham and his brother Thomas, the Earl of Southampton, Sir Henry Percy, Sir Thomas Stanley, Sir Thomas Gerard, Rowiston, Lowder, Powell, one of the Queen's band of Pensioners, were arrested, as well as all those who were compromised by the letters which had been seized or the confessions which had been obtained;[5] and the trial of the Duke of Norfolk was determined upon. When the preliminaries of this important trial were sufficiently advanced, the Lord Mayor and Aldermen of London were summoned to Westminster. The proofs of the Duke's culpability were then shown to them, and they were requested to communicate them at Guildhall to the principal inhabitants of the city,[6] in order to prepare the people for his judgment and condemnation.

These preparations having been made, Elizabeth cited the Duke of Norfolk to appear, on the 14th of January, 1572, before a jury of twenty-seven peers. The Court was held in Westminster Hall, and was presided over by the Earl of Shrewsbury, who had been appointed Lord High Steward on the occasion.[7] The Duke appeared before his judges with all the dignity of his rank,[9] and displayed greater firmness of mind than he had previously manifested. He was accused of having conspired to deprive the Queen of her crown, and consequently, of life ; of having sought to marry Mary Stuart (whom he had termed an adulteress and murderess),

[1] Lesly's Negotiations, in Anderson, vol. iii., p. 178.
[2] Murdin, pp. 157-164. [3] Ibid., p. 153.
[4] Gonzalez, Apuntamientos, pp. 119, 120.
[5] Lesly's Negotiations, in Anderson, vol. iii., p. 176. [6] Ibid., p. 189.
[7] Howell's State Trials, vol. i., p. 957. [8] Ibid., p. 959.

out of ambition that he might use the claims she possessed to procure his own accession to the throne of England; of having aided the Queen's enemies in Scotland; and of having plotted on the Continent with the Pope and the King of Spain to change the religion and overthrow the government of England.¹ His answer to these charges was skilful and plausible. Admitting all that he could not disprove, he confessed that he had been aware of matters which he ought not to have known, but to which he had never been willing to consent.² Although he repudiated indignantly all thought of treason against the Queen, and alleged his inaction as a proof of his innocence, he was unanimously found guilty by his peers, and, on the 16th of January, condemned to be hanged, drawn, and quartered.³ On hearing his sentence, he protested that he should die as faithful to his Queen as any man living; then, turning to his judges, he said with emotion: 'My lords, seeing you have put me out of your company, I trust shortly to be in better company. I will not desire any of you all to make any petition for my life: I will not desire to live: I am at a point. Only I beseech you, my lords, to be humble suitors to the Queen's Majesty for my poor orphan children, that it will please her Majesty to be good to them, and to take order for the payment of my debts, and some consideration of my poor servants.'⁴

On his return to the Tower, he wrote to the Queen a letter expressive of the deepest affliction and the most heartfelt repentance, recommending to her generosity his children, 'who,' he said, 'now they have neither father nor mother, will find but few friends.'⁵ He did not cease to deplore the connection which he had formed with the Queen of Scotland, and, in bitter truthfulness, he remarked, 'that nothing that anybody goeth about for her, nor that she doeth for herself, prospereth.'⁶

---

¹ These were the principal points of the accusation. See the *Indictment* in Howell's State Trials, vol. i., pp. 959-965. See also the Speech of the Queen's Serjeant, Ibid., pp. 988-992; and the Speech of the Attorney-General, pp. 1000-1006.

² Howell's State Trials, vol. i., pp. 1007-1013, and 1033-1034. Lesly's Negotiations, in Anderson, vol. iii., p. 186.

³ Howell's State Trials, vol. i., p. 1031.   ⁴ Ibid., p. 1032.

⁵ Thomas Howard, late Duke of Norfolk, to the Queen's Majesty, 21st January. Murdin, pp. 166, 167.

⁶ 'He sayeth verye ernestly, with vowe to God, that yf he were offered to have that woman in marydg, to chuse of that or death, he had rather take this death that now he is going to, a hundred parts; and he takes his Savyour to wytnes of this. He sayeth that nothing that anybody goeth aboute for her prospareth, nor that els she doth herselfe; and also that she is openly defamed.' Letter from Henry Skipwith to Lord Burghley, 16th February, 1572. Murdin, pp. 171, 172.

Whilst she was thus ignominiously disavowed by the Duke of Norfolk, the unhappy and fated Princess was plunged in deep grief at Sheffield. Ever since the discovery of her last plans, she had been confined in two of the chambers of the castle. Deprived of all communication with her officers, and served only by a few of her women, she complained that she was 'robbed of air and exercise,'[1] and prohibited from receiving news from her relatives and subjects, as well as from writing to them herself.[2] Her health, already much impaired, grew worse and worse. The trial of the Duke of Norfolk caused her the greatest anxiety. She did not leave her chamber for a whole week,[3] during his trial, and when she was informed of his condemnation she burst into a flood of tears.[4] Elizabeth, who for some time had ceased to answer her letters, now broke silence, and, with threatening severity, reproached her with her disordered passions, her blind errors, and her continual plots. She accused her of having seduced the Duke of Norfolk from his fidelity, and of having behaved with shameless ingratitude to herself, who, she said, had saved her from the pursuit of her subjects, and from an ignominious death. Mary Stuart, opposing her real grievances to Elizabeth's pretended benefits, reminded her that she had sustained with armed force the insurrection of Scotland under the Regency of her mother; that she had endeavoured to prevent her from returning into her kingdom after the death of Francis II., her first husband; that she had constantly received or assisted her rebellious subjects; and that, lastly, she had repaid her confidence by keeping her in imprisonment.[5] Without avowing the designs she had entertained, and which she said were merely applications for assistance to reduce the whole of Scotland to obedience, she did not conceal the fact that, on finding herself deceived in her last negotiation, 'she determined to allow herself to be fed with hopes no longer.'[6] God, she said, had granted her patience to endure affliction, and would if necessary give her courage to face

---

[1] Letter from Mary Stuart to Lamothe Fénelon, 18th November, 1571; Labanoff, vol. iv., p. 2.   [2] Ibid., pp. 18, 19.

[3] 'All the last weke this Quene did not ones loke out of her chamber, hering that the Duke stode upon his arraignement and tryall.' Letter from Sir Ralph Sadler to Lord Burghley, Sheffield, 21st January, 1572. Ellis's Original Letters, vol. ii., p. 331.

[4] 'For the which this Queen wept very bitterly, so that my lady (the Countess of Shrewsbury) founde her to be all wept and mourning.' Ellis's Original Letters, vol. ii., p. 330.

[5] Memoir from Mary Stuart to Queen Elizabeth, Sheffield, 14th February 1572; in Labanoff, vol. iv., pp. 17-41.   [6] Ibid., pp. 31, 32.

death.¹ As regarded the Duke of Norfolk, she declared she had never thought of taking him for her husband, except by the request of the Council of England.² She added, ' that she should think herself worthy to be universally reputed ungrateful, and of bad natural disposition, if she did not employ all the means which God had left her in this world to mitigate the anger of the Queen of England against the Duke of Norfolk and the other nobles who had got into trouble by bearing her some good-will, and if she did not supplicate her good sister to grant them her peace, or at least to prevent them suffering any pain on her account.'³

But the prayers of Mary Stuart could not avail to save the life of the Duke of Norfolk. Elizabeth had several times signed and revoked the order for his execution. Her first warrant was issued on Saturday, the 8th of February, a few days after the Duke's condemnation. But on Sunday night, before the day fixed for the punishment of the unfortunate nobleman, Elizabeth, who was too much disturbed to sleep, sent for Burghley and commanded him to postpone the execution.⁴ Burghley reluctantly obeyed. 'Sometimes,' he wrote to Walsingham, giving an account of Elizabeth's agitation, ' when her Majesty speaketh of her danger, she concludeth that justice should be done; at other times, when she speaketh of his nearness of blood, and superiority in honour, she stayeth. God's will be fulfilled, and aid her Majesty to do herself good.'⁵ Elizabeth was incessantly urged, from the pulpit and by her council, to take this cruel resolution. Allowing herself to be persuaded that the interests of both Church and Crown required the Duke's execution,⁶ she signed a new warrant on the 9th of April,⁷ and again revoked it at two o'clock in the morning.'⁸ The inexorable Burghley then induced the Parliament to interfere to conquer Elizabeth's humane irresolution or artful scrupulosity. The House of Commons, in which the fanatical Puritans formed the dominant party, resolved that the life

---

[1] Memoir from Mary Stuart to Queen Elizabeth, Sheffield, 14th February, 1572; in Labanoff, vol. iv., p. 36.
[2] Ibid., vol. iv., pp. 33, 34.   [3] Ibid., pp. 39, 40.
[4] 'Suddenly on Sunday, late in the night, the Queen's Majesty sent for me, and entered into a great misliking that the Duke should die the next day, and said she would have a new warrant made that night to the sheriffs, to forbear until they should hear further.' Burghley to Walsingham, 11th February, 1572; in Digges, p. 166.
[5] Digges, pp. 165, 166.
[6] Lingard, vol. viii., chap. 2.
[7] This warrant is printed in Murdin, pp. 177, 178.
[8] Lingard, vol. viii., chap. 2.

of the Duke was incompatible with the safety of the Queen;[1] they even ventured to demand the death of Mary Stuart, and said that the axe must be laid 'at the root of the evil.'[2] Elizabeth replied that she could not put to death the bird, which, to escape the pursuit of the hawk, had fled to her feet for protection.[3] She sacrificed the Duke of Norfolk, that she might atone for her irresolution respecting Mary Stuart. On the 31st of May she signed a third warrant, and this time it was not revoked.

On the 2nd of June, at about 8 o'clock in the morning, the Duke of Norfolk was conducted to the scaffold upon Tower Hill.[4] In his last moments he displayed a noble simplicity and intrepid firmness. He made a long speech to the people, in which he confessed that he was not entirely innocent, but asserted that he was only partially guilty. He declared himself a true Protestant, and attributed the doubts which had arisen regarding his religious opinions, to his having had Popish friends and servants. He thanked the Queen for the generous intentions which she had manifested towards his children, and recommended her to the affection, as well as to the obedience, of her subjects. 'They that have factions,' he said, recurring to his own case, 'let them beware they be given over betimes. Seek not to breviate God's doings, lest God prevent yours.'[5] After this speech, which moved the people to compassion, the Duke of Norfolk tranquilly 'made his prayers to God,' laid his head on the block, 'refusing to have any handkerchief before his eyes,' and died with greater courage than he had displayed in his conspiracy.[6]

His death completed the destruction of Mary Stuart's party in England. That unfortunate princess, whose cause entailed ruin on all who embraced it, thus beheld the successive failure of all the various means attempted for her deliverance and restoration. The insurrection of 1569, which the Duke of Norfolk and the other disaffected nobles might have joined, had they dared to do so, had brought about the defeat and discouragement of the Catholics. The conspiracy of the Duke of Norfolk, to which the King of Spain had not lent seasonable assistance, disconcerted, by its frustration, the ambitious hopes of the nobility. After the repression of revolt in the North, no other Catholic insurrection

---

[1] D'Ewes's Journal of all the Parliaments during the reign of Queen Elizabeth, pp. 206, 214, 220. Lingard, vol. viii., chap. 2.
[2] Lingard, vol. viii., p. 90.　　　　[3] Ibid.
[4] Howell's State Trials, vol. i., p. 1032.
[5] Ibid., pp. 1033, 1034.　　　[6] Ibid., pp. 1034, 1035.

took place: after the decapitation of the Duke of Norfolk, no other great aristocratic conspiracy was formed. Protestantism ruled with terrible laws throughout the whole of England; and the new men, headed by Burghley, henceforth ruled supreme in the councils of Elizabeth.

CHAPTER IX.

FROM THE EXECUTION OF THE DUKE OF NORFOLK TILL THE FORMATION OF THE PROTESTANT LEAGUE.

Alliance between England and France—State of parties in Scotland—Assassination of Lennox—The Earl of Mar appointed Regent—Massacre of St. Bartholomew —Its effects on Elizabeth's policy—Killegrew is sent into Scotland—Death of Mar and Knox—Morton appointed Regent—Treaty of Perth—Resistance of the Castilians—Capture of Edinburgh Castle—Death of Lethington—Execution of Grange—Position of Mary Stuart—Morton resigns the Regency—Destruction of the house of Hamilton—Esmé Stewart arrives in Scotland, and becomes the King's favourite—Judgment and execution of Morton—Catholic conspiracy for Mary Stuart's restoration—Raid of Ruthven—Flight of Lennox—Deliverance of James VI.—Fears of Elizabeth—Her negotiations with Mary Stuart—Projected expedition against England—Elizabeth's rupture with the King of Spain—Formation of a Protestant league to protect the life of Elizabeth—Mary Stuart offers to join it—Leicester is sent to the Netherlands with an army—League to oppose a Catholic invasion of Great Britain.

ELIZABETH, after having repressed the Catholic insurrection in the northern districts of her kingdom, and frustrated the conspiracy of Mary Stuart and the Duke of Norfolk with Philip II. and the Pope, had turned her attention to the prevention of those dangers by which she might still be threatened. Her prudent and industrious policy had succeeded in separating the two great Catholic powers of the Continent, and forming an alliance with one of them against the other. Taking advantage of the third peace, which was concluded in France during the month of August, 1570, she had negotiated a treaty of defensive alliance with Charles IX., in pursuance of a proposal for her marriage to the Duke of Anjou. This proposal was not at all of a serious nature; it was one of the means which her policy and vanity most willingly employed to make others desire her friendship and seek her hand, by offering to share with her a crown which she had determined to wear alone to the end of her life. But such was not the character of a treaty of alliance which presented reciprocal advantages to both Courts.[1] By this treaty, Elizabeth

See, for this proposition of marriage and alliance, the Diplomatic Correspondence of Lamothe Fénelon, vols. ii., iii., iv., and vii.

obtained, in some sort, an assurance that Mary Stuart would be left in her hands, whilst she abstained from fomenting religious disturbances in the dominions of the most Christian king who had now become her ally. This treaty, which secured to Elizabeth the assistance of France in the event of a Catholic invasion, and which seemed likely to preserve France from another civil war, by depriving the Huguenots of the support of England, was signed at Blois, on the 29th of April, 1572, between Sir Thomas Smith and Sir Francis Walsingham, who acted as Elizabeth's plenipotentiaries, and the Marshal de Montmorency, Biragne, the Keeper of the Seals, the Bishop of Limoges, Sebastien de l'Aubespine, and Paul de Foix, as representatives of Charles IX.[1]

Free from apprehension in this quarter, the Queen of England acted with no less ability and success with regard to Scotland. Mary Stuart's party was still very strong in that country. Since the renewal of hostilities between the Queen's partisans and those of the King, and since they had mutually proscribed each other in the Parliaments of Edinburgh and Stirling, the Earl of Lennox had met with the same fate as his predecessor, the Earl of Murray. On the morning of the 4th of September, 1571, he was surprised at Stirling by a troop which Kirkaldy of Grange had sent from Edinburgh, and which had unexpectedly entered the city under the command of the Earl of Huntly, Lord Claude Hamilton, the Laird of Buccleugh, and Ker of Fernyhirst. Lennox was pitilessly shot, in revenge for the violent and ignominious death which he had inflicted upon the Archbishop of St. Andrews. For a moment, all the principal lords of the King's party, who were then at Stirling, had been made prisoners. They were indebted for their escape to the dispersion of the Scots and Kers, who disbanded to pillage the town, and thus gave the inhabitants time to take arms, while the garrison of the castle, rushing into the streets, rescued their leaders, and drove out their too avaricious enemies. On the very next day, the nobles of the King's party appointed, as successor to the Earl of Lennox, the Earl of Mar, who was thus raised from the post of Governor of the King to the Regency of Scotland.[2]

Notwithstanding the capture of Dumbarton, and the assistance which they had on several occasions received from Elizabeth, the King's adherents were unable to overcome the Queen's partisans. These still remained in possession of the castle and city of Edinburgh, and occupied moreover the strong fortresses of Niddry,

[1] Dumont's Corps Diplomatique, vol. v., pp. 211-215.
[2] Tytler, vol. vi., pp. 159-163.

Livingstone, and Blackness. Adam Gordon of Auchendown, the brother of the Earl of Huntly, had rendered their cause victorious in the North, while Ker of Fernyhirst and Lord Herries in the South, and the Hamiltons in the West, were equally successful.[1] Matters were in this state, when Elizabeth, finding it impossible to crush, determined to disarm them. The treaty of Blois had given her peace with the Court of France, and she now negotiated a truce between the two opposing factions in Scotland. Her envoy, Sir William Drury, and the French ambassador Du Croc, induced them to sign this truce on the 30th of July, 1572;[2] with an express stipulation that, as soon as might be, the nobility and estates of the realm should assemble to deliberate upon a general peace.

In return for the services which she had rendered to the cause of the young King, Elizabeth obtained the extradition of the unfortunate Earl of Northumberland, who was beheaded at York on the 25th of August. But at the very moment when this Princess believed that she was in complete security, the terrible news of the massacre of St. Bartholomew arrived. A cry of terror and indignant rage arose throughout her dominions;[3] and, animated by alarm as much as by anger, she assembled her Council to deliberate upon the course which she ought to pursue.[4] She refused for several days to give an audience to the French ambassador, Lamothe Fénelon, who had come to Oxford to justify the massacre, by attributing it to the discovery of a conspiracy among the Protestants. When at length she admitted him to her presence, she was accompanied by the Lords of her Council, and the principal ladies of her Court, all dressed in mourning apparel. He was received in silence; the stillness of the grave, as he himself described it, seemed to reign in the apartments. As he passed through the crowd, the courtiers, fixing their eyes on the ground, refused to notice his greeting; and he advanced towards the Queen, who received him with a mournful and severe countenance.[5] She did not conceal from the ambassador of Charles IX. either the horror which she felt at the event, or her doubts of the truth of the explanations which he gave, or her fears of the consequences which might ensue. She expressed to Lamothe Fénelon her sorrowful surprise and distrustful reprobation of the conduct of the King his master; and, to the assurances

[1] Tytler, vol. vi., pp. 164, 165, 169.   [2] Ibid., p. 170.
[3] Lamothe Fénelon's Correspondence, vol. iv., pp. 116, 121.
[4] Ibid., vol. v., p. 122.
[5] Ibid. Carte's History of England, vol. iii., p. 522.

of friendship which he renewed to her on behalf of Charles IX., she replied, ' that she greatly feared that those who had led that Prince to abandon his natural subjects, would also lead him to abandon a foreign Queen like herself.'[1]

She believed, in fact, that she was betrayed by the Court of France; and Protestantism appeared to her to be threatened throughout the whole world by a vast conspiracy, the signal for which had been given by the Paris massacre, which she believed had been premeditated.[2] She accordingly made preparations to defend herself; renewed her alliances in Germany, whither she sent to prepare levies of troops; fortified Portsmouth, Dover, and the Isle of Wight; armed ten large ships of war to cruise in the Channel and guard the English coast: favoured the resistance of La Rochelle, the last bulwark of Protestantism in France; redoubled the severity of her surveillance over her Catholic subjects; and conceived the most sinister designs regarding that formidable prisoner, who was the hope of the Catholic party in both England and Scotland.[3]

After the discovery of the Duke of Norfolk's conspiracy, Elizabeth had formally declared that she would not be able to live in peace for a single hour if Mary Stuart were restored to her throne, and that she had therefore resolved to detain her henceforward in captivity. A slanderous book, written by Buchanan,[4] and containing Mary's secret letters to Bothwell, had been widely diffused. Protestant theologians had endeavoured to prove from the Bible that her execution would be just; and jurisconsults had proved from the ancient imperial code that it would be lawful.[5] Hatred and fanaticism had been carried so far, that the two Houses of Parliament wished to proceed against her by Bill of Attainder. Elizabeth forbade it; but notwithstanding her prohibition, Parliament determined at least to pass a law, formally excluding Mary Stuart from the succession to the crown of England. In order to defend her captive from this persecution, Elizabeth was compelled to prorogue the Parliament.[6] She had contented herself with intimidating her prisoner by a species of accusation which was not carried further than a menace.

[1] Lamothe Fénelon's Correspondence, vol. v., p. 126.   [2] Ibid., pp. 192, 207.
[3] Ibid., pp. 132, 136, 148, 153-156, 162, 175, 176, 198, 202, 210, 223, 224.
[4] ' Ane detectioun of the doingis of Marie, Quene of Scottis, twiching the murder of her husband, etc., translated out of the Latine, quhilk was written be M. G. B. Lanctandrois, be Robert Leckprevik, 1572.'
[5] Lingard, vol. viii., p. 91.
[6] Ibid., pp. 91, 92.   D'Ewes's Journals, pp. 200, 207, 224.   Digges, pp. 203, 319.

Lord Delawarr, Sir Ralph Sadler, and Thomas Bromley, were sent to Sheffield to interrogate the Scottish Queen, as a criminal, upon thirteen articles which were charged against her. The answers which she gave were more prudent than sincere. She affirmed that she had entertained no intentions of hostility to Elizabeth in consenting to marry the Duke of Norfolk; and that she had only contemplated the deliverance of Scotland by the mission of Ridolfi, and her relations with Pius V. and Philip II.[1] Elizabeth, who could not admit Mary Stuart's explanations, had at the time abandoned the idea of bringing her to a public trial; but after the massacre of St. Bartholomew, she embraced a more dark and secret expedient for getting rid of that unfortunate Princess.

This plan, conceived with hypocritical cruelty by Elizabeth, Burghley, and Leicester, was intended to be executed, not in England, but in Scotland, where its conduct was entrusted to one of the most skilful and trustworthy agents of the English Queen. Sir Henry Killegrew, Burghley's brother-in-law, set out for Scotland on the 7th of September, 1572,[2] with two missions— one public and the other secret.[3] By the first he was charged to effect, in the interest of endangered Protestantism, a reconciliation between Lethington, Kirkaldy of Grange, and the Earls of Mar and Morton; and by the second, to concert with the Earls of Mar and Morton a plan for putting Mary Stuart to death. This last mission was given him by Elizabeth herself, in presence of Leicester and Burghley, who were her only confidants in the matter. According to his instructions, which were written in Burghley's own hand, he was to explain to Elizabeth's two allies, that their common safety required that Mary Stuart should be put to death, and that, though she might easily be executed in England, it was thought better that she should be sent to Scotland and delivered to her enemies, 'to proceed with her by way of justice.' Killegrew was enjoined to employ all his address to induce the Regent and Morton to claim the prisoner, without appearing to have been urged to do so by Elizabeth, who was anxious to reap the advantage of this sanguinary transaction, without incurring its odium and disgrace.

Killegrew found Scotland in a state of the greatest excitement

[1] See Prince Labanoff's Collection, vol. iv., pp. 47-54.
[2] Lamothe Fénelon's Correspondence, vol. v., p. 121.
[3] For the history of this negotiation see Tytler, vol. vi., pp. 174-188. Mr. Tytler has traced its progress from the original documents contained in the State Paper Office.

at the massacre of St. Bartholomew.[1] The aged Reformer, John Knox, who had taken refuge at St. Andrews since the occupation of Edinburgh by the Queen's partisans, had returned to the capital after the signature of the truce in July. Though half paralysed by an attack of apoplexy, and so feeble that he could scarcely stand alone, he still mounted his pulpit, where, overwhelmed with grief and animated by indignation, he recovered his former energy of expression, to hold up to public execration the murderers of his brethren the Protestants of France.[2] Aided by his disciples, the Presbyterian ministers, he contributed powerfully to increase the unpopularity of the ancient alliance with France. Killegrew took advantage of this feeling to promote both his public and his secret mission. He had no difficulty in persuading Morton to consent to Mary Stuart's death; but the Regent Mar received his overtures more coldly. As matters were not brought to so speedy a conclusion as was desired in England, Burghley and Leicester wrote in covert language to Killegrew, on the 29th of September, in order to stimulate him to increased exertions. 'We earnestly require you,' they said, 'to employ all your labours to procure that it may be both earnestly and speedily followed there, and yet also secretly, as the cause requireth; and when we think of the matter, as daily, yea hourly, we have cause to do, we see not but the same reasons that may move us to desire that it take effect, ought also to move them, and in some part the more, considering both their private sureties, their common estate, and the continuance of the religion; all which three points are in more danger for them to uphold than for us. The cause thereof we doubt not but you can enlarge to them, if you see that they do not sufficiently foresee them. We suspend all our actions only upon this, and therefore you can do no greater service than to use speed.'[3]

By the aid of Knox, Killegrew excited the people against the Catholics and against France.[4] At the same time he had frequent conferences with Mar and Morton upon what he called 'the great matter.' The two Earls finally consented to give hostages in pledge of their determination to 'despatch the matter,' or, in other words, to put Mary Stuart to death, within four hours after she had been delivered into their hands,[5] and to rid Elizabeth of her

---

[1] Tytler, vol. vi., p. 176. Lamothe Fénelon, vol. v., p. 183.
[2] Tytler, vol. vi., p. 179.
[3] MS. letter, British Museum, Caligula, C. iii., fol. 394. Tytler, vol. vi., pp. 177, 171. [4] Ibid., p. 179.
[5] 'I am also told, that the hostages have been talked of, and that they shall be

rival, on these conditions: That the Queen of England should take their young King under her protection; that his rights should not be invalidated by any sentence which might be passed upon his mother, and that they should be maintained by a declaration of the English Parliament; that a defensive alliance should be established between the two kingdoms; that the Earls of Huntingdon, Bedford, or Essex, should be present at Mary's execution with two or three thousand men, and should afterwards assist the troops of the young King to reduce the citadel of Edinburgh; and finally, that that fortress should be placed in the Regent's hands, and that England should pay all the arrears due to the Scottish troops.[1]

These conditions appeared exorbitant to Killegrew, unacceptable to Burghley, too costly and too compromising for the narrow parsimony and hypocritical cruelty of Elizabeth.[2] She was anxious to put Mary Stuart to death, but she did not wish to take the murderers into her pay, or to appear as their instigatress or accomplice. The high price which the two Scottish Earls demanded for shedding the blood of their former sovereign, and the sudden death of the Regent Mar, who expired at Stirling, on the 28th of October, temporarily suspended this odious negotiation, which was not, however, entirely abandoned until 1574.[3] On learning the failure of their plan, Burghley, full of apprehensions and devoid of scruple, wrote to Leicester a letter in covert, but significant language; insinuating that the Queen, with whom Leicester was then staying, must get rid of Mary Stuart in England, as she could not send her to die in Scotland. 'If her Majesty,' he said, 'will continue her delays, for providing for her own surety by just means given to her by God, she and we all shall vainly call upon God when the calamity shall fall upon us. God send her Majesty strength of spirit to preserve God's cause, her own life, and the lives of millions of good subjects, all which are most manifestly in danger, and that only by her delays; and so, consequently, she shall be the cause of the overthrow of a noble crown and realm.'[4]

Elizabeth was afraid to follow this advice. Though she would

---

delivered to our men upon the fields, and the matter despatched within four hours, so as they shall not need to tarry long in our hands.' MS. letter, British Museum, Caligula, C. iii., fol. 375. Killegrew to Burghley and Leicester, 9th October, 1572. Tytler, vol. vi., p. 183.
[1] Tytler, vol. vi., p. 186. [2] Ibid., pp. 186, 187. [3] Ibid., pp. 186-188.
[4] MS. letter, British Museum; Caligula, C. iii., fol. 386. Burghley to Leicester, 3rd November, 1572. Tytler, vol. vi., pp. 187, 188.

not put Mary Stuart to death, she deprived her of those partisans whom she still retained in Scotland, by either weakening their attachment or crushing their resistance. On the 24th of November, 1572, Morton succeeded Mar in the title and authority of Regent. On the very day on which he obtained this dignity, which he had so long coveted, the celebrated Reformer, John Knox, died. This vehement and inflexible man, who, by his doctrines and actions, had contributed so powerfully to the political and religious revolutions in Scotland,—infirm in body,[1] but retaining all the vigour of his intellect and energy of his mind— expired at the age of sixty-seven, regretted by the Presbyterian Church which he had founded; beloved by burghers, whom he had rendered more pious, educated, and active than they had previously been; and respected by the nobility, who were partly indebted to him for the government of the State. He did not live to witness the final and speedy triumph of his party, but he foresaw it.[2] This triumph it was reserved for Morton to effect. More devoted than his predecessor Mar had been to the maintenance of Protestantism and the political views of England, Morton placed at the service of this double, and yet identical, cause, talents of no ordinary kind, a most energetic character, the power vested in him by the Regency, and the influence which he himself possessed as head of the Douglas family.

Seconded by Killegrew, who persuaded Elizabeth to grant him subsidies and promise him troops,[3] he renewed the negotiations which his predecessor had commenced with the principal nobles who still remained faithful to the Queen. Since the death of the Regent Murray, Mary Stuart's party had been composed not only of those who, like the Hamiltons and Gordons, had constantly supported her, but also of many deserters from the King's party, like Kirkaldy of Grange, Lord Lethington, and Lord Hume. Morton proposed to make a separate accommodation with each of these factions, fearing that if he treated with the whole party at the same time, he would place himself at their discretion, and be continually exposed to new insurrections. Hoping that he would be able more easily to detach from the Queen's cause those who had most recently joined her, and who seemed bound, by recent recollections, to respect the authority of the King whom they had placed upon the throne, Morton

---

[1] M'Crie's Life of Knox, vol. ii., pp. 226-234.
[2] See, *infra*, his message to Kirkaldy of Grange, written a short time before his death; and M'Crie, vol. ii., pp. 223, 224.
[3] Tytler, vol. vi., p. 193.

addressed himself, in the first instance, to Lethington and Kirkaldy of Grange. Confident in the strength of the citadel of Edinburgh, which they believed secure against the attacks of the Scotch, and daily expecting to receive the reinforcements which the Court of France had promised to send them if they held out until Easter of 1573,[1] Lethington and Kirkaldy would not accept the partial offers of Morton, whose sincerity they greatly mistrusted. They demanded that the pacification should embrace all the Queen's partisans, and that Kirkaldy of Grange should retain the command of the citadel of Edinburgh for six months after the conclusion of the amnesty.[2] They would thus obtain time to await the arrival of the troops from France, then occupied in the siege of La Rochelle, and would reserve to themselves the means of recommencing the conflict with greater resources for maintaining it. Such an arrangement could not be satisfactory to Morton. Renouncing the idea of gaining over the *Castilians*, as they were called, from their occupancy of Edinburgh Castle, he turned towards the Hamiltons and Gordons.

These powerful clans, after having fought unsuccessfully for five years in favour of the Queen, were beginning to grow weary of their efforts, and to feel their inutility. Elizabeth's decided intervention had greatly discouraged them, and they therefore manifested a disposition to treat with the Regent, at Killegrew's mediation. It was secretly resolved, between themselves and Morton, that no prosecution should be instituted against any concerned in the murder of Darnley and his father, the Regent Lennox,[3] as both the contracting parties were more or less implicated in these crimes. After this assurance had been given and received, with a view to facilitate a reconciliation, the conditions of a definitive accommodation were discussed at Perth, between the Regent's commissioners on the one hand, and the Earl of Huntly and Lord Arbroath, son of the Duke of Chatelherault, on the other. By the efforts and with the assistance of Killegrew, it was determined that the Queen's partisans should, by a formal declaration, give their approval to the reformed religion, as then established, submit to the government of the King and the Regency of Morton, and recognize as illegal all that had been done in opposition to the King's government since the coronation of James VI. at Stirling; in return for these concessions, they were to be restored to their possessions and honours, and all acts were to be annulled which had been passed

[1] Digges, p. 314.   [2] Melvil's Memoirs, pp. 118, 119.
[3] MS. letter, State Paper Office, 26th January, 1573. Tytler, vol. vi., p. 198.

against the Queen's partisans, who should obtain a complete amnesty.[1] The accommodation of the Hamiltons and Gordons, in which the Earl of Huntly included his gallant brother, Sir Adam Gordon, was followed by the submission of Lords Gray and Oliphant, the Sheriff of Ayr, and the Lairds of Buccleugh and Johnston.[2] On the 23rd of February, 1573, the Regent signed the articles of the pacification of Perth,[3] which disarmed and destroyed the Queen's party in Scotland.

Mary Stuart's adherents now possessed only the citadel of Edinburgh. 'Now,' wrote Killegrew to Burghley, 'there remaineth but the Castle to make the King universally obeyed, and this realm united.'[4] He supposed that the Castilians, abandoned by all their former friends, would cease to prolong a resistance which had become perfectly useless: and he expected that Kirkaldy of Grange would be more willing to enter into an accommodation, as Blackness Castle had just been betrayed to Morton by the wife of its commander, Sir James Kirkaldy, Grange's brother.[5] But this valiant captain, who had now become obstinate in his fidelity to his Queen, refused every offer of reconciliation. He even resisted the entreaties and religious menaces of his old friend Knox, who a short time before his death, sent him a message by Lindsay, the minister of Perth. 'Go,' he said, 'to yonder man in the Castle, whom you know I have loved so dearly, and tell him that I have sent you yet once more to warn him, in the name of God, to leave that evil cause. Neither the craggy rock in which he miserably confides, nor the carnal prudence of that man (Lethington) whom he esteems a demigod, nor the assistance of strangers, shall preserve him, but he shall be disgracefully dragged from his nest to punishment, and hung on a gallows against the face of the sun, unless he speedily amend his life and flee to the mercy of God.'[6] The imminent approach of danger had no more effect than the sombre message of Knox upon the Laird's resolution. With Lethington, Hume, Robert Melvil, and Pittarrow, defended by a garrison of less than two hundred soldiers,[7] but confident in the impregnable strength of the citadel, he expected to be able to hold out until

---

[1] Robertson, book 6.   [2] Tytler, vol. vi., p. 202.

[3] MS. letter, State Paper Office; Killegrew to Burghley, 23rd February, 1573. Tytler, vol. vi., p. 202. 'God so blessed this treaty, as this day, being the 23rd aforenoon, the Articles of Accord and Pacification were signed.'

[4] MS. letter, State Paper Office; Killegrew to Burghley, 18th February, 1573 Tytler, vol. vi., p. 201.

[5] Tytler, vol. vi., p. 201.   [6] M'Crie's Life of Knox, vol. ii., pp. 223, 224.

[7] Robertson, book 6. Crawford's Memoirs, p. 265.

the arrival of the reinforcements which had been promised from France.

These reinforcements, so long desired and so essentially necessary, never arrived.[1] Elizabeth, on the other hand, by advice of Killegrew, resolved to place at Morton's disposal those means which Scotland could not furnish for destroying this last bulwark of an almost desperate cause. Two skilful engineers, whom she appointed to examine the Castle, reported that if the place were regularly attacked, it might be taken in twenty days.[2] Its siege was accordingly determined upon, and Sir William Drury, the Governor of Berwick, was chosen to command the enterprise. Drury left Berwick, with a troop of five hundred hackbutters, a hundred and forty pikemen, and a battering train. He disembarked at Leith, and marched to Edinburgh, where he arrived on the 25th of April, and was joined by seven hundred soldiers of the Regent.[3] While this little army was preparing to besiege the citadel, a Parliament met, which confirmed the league with England, restored Huntly and Balfour to their estates and honours, in conformity with the treaty of Perth, and pronounced a sentence of treason and forfeiture against the Castilians.

A summons of surrender was then sent to Grange in the name of the Regent and of the English general, but he declared, in reply, that he would hold the castle till he was buried in its ruins. The artillery of the besiegers was thereupon posted on the principal spots which commanded the walls; and on the 17th of May, the batteries began to play. Their fire was directed against the principal bastion of the citadel, named David's Tower. The guns of the garrison were soon silenced, and after six days' uninterrupted cannonading, the southern wall of David's Tower fell with a great crash, in the afternoon of the 23rd of May. On the next day the Wallace Tower was beaten down; and on the 26th, the outer defences of the citadel were occupied, with little resistance, by the besiegers, who now made preparations for a general assault.[4]

But the besieged were not in a position to sustain another attack. Their ammunition was exhausted; their soldiers, deprived of water, were nearly all ill; and they had hardly forty men fit for active service. The Laird of Grange saw that further

---

[1] MS. letter, State Paper Office; Lethington and Grange to the Earl of Huntly, 23rd February, 1573. Tytler, vol. vi., p. 202. Verac, who was bringing them relief, was driven by a storm into Scarborough, and detained in England. Tytler, vol. vi., p. 201.

[2] Tytler, vol. vi., p. 193.   [3] Ibid., p. 204.   [4] Ibid., p. 207.

resistance was impossible; and on the evening of the 26th, he presented himself upon the ramparts, with a white rod in his hand, and obtained an armistice of two days, preparatory to the surrender of the castle. His requests were, to have surety for the lives and goods of the garrison, to have license for Lord Hume and Lethington to retire into England, and himself to be allowed to remain unmolested in his own country.[1]

These conditions were refused by the Regent. His principal adversaries were on the point of falling into his hands, and he was determined not to allow them to escape. As to the soldiers of the garrison, he said, he was ready, if they came out singly and without arms, to permit them to go where they pleased; but nine of their leaders, including Kirkaldy, Lethington, Hume, and Robert Melvil, must submit to have their fate determined by the Queen of England, according to the treaty already made between her Majesty and the King of Scotland.[2] This stern reply made it evident that they would receive no quarter. Perceiving the fate which was reserved for them, they broke off the conference, and declared their resolution to die with arms in their hands. But their soldiers refused to support them in their desperate resistance. They began to mutiny, and threatened to hang Lethington over the walls, if, within six hours, he did not persuade the Laird of Grange to surrender the citadel.[3] The valorous Laird, reduced to this cruel extremity, threatened with death by his enemies, and with desertion by his soldiers, adopted an expedient, by Lethington's advice, which left him at least a ray of hope. On the night of the 29th he secretly admitted two English companies within the walls, and placed himself and his companions in the hands of Drury, declaring that they were the prisoners of Queen Elizabeth, and not of the Regent Morton.[4]

Morton, however, was not thus to be baulked of his prey. He was anxious to rid himself of the two men whose ability and valour he most feared. In order to secure greater obedience and less opposition to his future government, he wrote to Burghley,[5] to demand that the prisoners might be given up to him to be punished as the chief authors of the troubles and misfortunes of Scotland. Killegrew, who had not the same reasons

[1] Tytler, vol. vi., p. 207.
[2] Copy of the time, State Paper Office; the Regent's Answer to the Castilians, 28th May, 1573. Tytler, vol. vi., pp. 207, 208.
[3] MS. letter, State Paper Office; Killegrew to Burghley, 20th June, 1573. Tytler, vol. vi., p. 208. [4] Tytler, vol. vi., p. 208.
[5] MS. letter, State Paper Office; Morton to Burghley, 31st May, 1573; Tytler, vol. vi., p. 209.

to hate and fear them, was ungenerous enough to support Morton's request. Lethington and Grange, on their part, wrote to Burghley to remind him of their ancient friendship, and to invoke the compassion, mercy, and provident interest of Elizabeth. 'We trust her Majesty,' they wrote, 'will not put us out of her hands to make any others, especially our mortal enemy, our masters. If it will please her Majesty to extend her most gracious clemency towards us, she may be as assured to have us as perpetually at her devotion as any of this nation; yea, as any subject of her own, for now with honour we may oblige ourselves to her Majesty farther than before we might, and her Majesty's benefit will bind us perpetually. In the case we are in, we must confess we are of small value. Yet may her Majesty put us in case, that perhaps hereafter we will be able to serve her Majesty's turn. Your Lordship knoweth already what our request is. We pray your Lordship to further it. There was never time wherein your Lordship's friendship might stand us in such stead. As we have oftentimes heretofore tasted thereof, so we humbly pray you let it not inlack us now in time of this our great misery, when we have more need than ever we had. If, by your Lordship's mediation, her Majesty conserve us, your Lordship shall have us perpetually bound to do you service. When we are in her Majesty's hands, she may make us what pleaseth her.'[1]

This touching letter, written the day after the surrender of the Castle to Drury, shook Elizabeth's resolution for a moment. Was she inspired by feelings of generous pity; or did she merely consider whether it would be more advantageous to her policy to preserve the lives of two men of so much influence and ability, than to sacrifice them to Morton? Whatever was the motive of her hesitation, she first required to be informed 'of the quality and quantity of the prisoners' offences.'[2] But Morton and Killegrew so strongly advised their execution, that she yielded, and barbarously commanded them to be delivered up to the Regent, to be dealt with as he pleased. This, as she must have known, was equivalent to signing their death warrant. Before, however, her cruel decision arrived in Scotland, Lethington died in prison. His death, whether natural or voluntary,[3]

[1] MS. letter, British Museum; Caligula, C. iv., fol. 86. Lethington and Grange to Burghley, 1st June, 1753. Tytler, vol. vi., pp. 209, 210.
[2] Tytler, vol. vi., p. 210.
[3] 'Lidingtoun dyed at Leith, after the old Roman fashion as was said, to prevent his coming to the shambles with the rest.' Melvil's Memoirs, p. 122.

saved him from the ignominious execution to which his chivalrous companion, Kirkaldy of Grange, was condemned by Morton's ruthless vengeance. In vain did Grange's friends attempt to bribe the avaricious Regent, and to calm his apprehensions. A hundred gentlemen, friends and kinsmen of the noble and gallant Laird, offered, for his pardon, to become perpetual servants to the house of Angus and Morton, in ' bond of manrent,' and to pay two thousand pounds to the Regent, besides an annuity of three thousand merks. Morton was inexorable;[1] he was determined to intimidate all who might hereafter be tempted to resist his authority, and he would not allow himself to be moved by any entreaties, or bribed by any offers. On the 3rd of August, the Laird of Grange and his brother, Sir James Kirkaldy, were ignominiously executed at the Cross of Edinburgh. He died with unflinching courage, and expressed on the scaffold the humble penitence of a true Christian for his sins, and the unshaken attachment of a faithful subject to his captive Sovereign.[2] With Lethington and Kirkaldy of Grange expired the last hopes of Mary Stuart in Scotland.

Their death threw their unfortunate Queen into a state of deep sorrow and depression.[3] She had not suspected the danger she had incurred by Killegrew's mysterious mission, although the Massacre of St. Bartholomew had exposed her to new severities. For five months she was kept a close prisoner in her apartments, and forbidden to write.[4] Her captivity was somewhat alleviated after the capture of Edinburgh Castle had entailed the total destruction of her party. The unhappy prisoner now lost courage. The English Catholics who had undertaken her deliverance in 1569 and 1570, were either dispersed or intimidated; the Duke of Norfolk, who had conspired on her behalf, was dead; the Scotch, who had remained faithful in their allegiance to her for five years, had been compelled to acknowledge her son as their King, and to submit to the powerful domination of the Regent

---

[1] Tytler, vol. vi., p. 211.
[2] MS. letter, State Paper Office; Killegrew to Burghley, 3rd August, 1573. Tytler, vol. vi., p. 212.
[3] Letter from Mary Stuart to Elizabeth, 20th February, 1574; to the Archbishop of Glasgow and the Cardinal of Lorraine, 29th March, 1574. Labanoff, vol. iv., pp. 113, 125.
[4] In Prince Labanoff's Collection, I find no letter written during the months of September, October, and November, 1572. There are only two dated in December: one on the 1st, to the Cardinal of Lorraine, the other on the 24th, to Burghley and Leicester. During the first eight months of 1573, I find four letters only, addressed to Lamothe Fénelon, the Duke de Nevers, and Burghley.

Morton; the King of Spain continually promised, but never acted, and was, at bottom, less disposed to succour her than to disturb Elizabeth by plots and insurrections; and the King of France, at variance with his Protestant subjects, and distrusting his Catholic lieges, had deserted her to conciliate the favour of her formidable and triumphant rival.

Under these circumstances, with no supporters at home, and hopeless of assistance from abroad, she changed her tone and conduct, and endeavoured to pacify Elizabeth by submission. The liberty which she had been unable to obtain by force, she now strove to gain by fair means. Her high spirit had been at first offended by the silence of Queen Elizabeth, who returned no answer to the numerous letters which she had written to her.[1] She now, however, subdued her feelings of irritation and pride, and assumed a tone of patient resignation; and the Queen, who had been so haughty in her bearing, so eloquent in her complaints, so bold and daring in her projects, became a gentle, calm, and humble prisoner. She avoided everything likely to give umbrage to Elizabeth;[2] and limited her correspondence, which had reference chiefly to matters connected with her dowry in France. In return, she obtained permission to walk in the park and gardens of Sheffield. The dampness of her prison walls had brought on an attack of rheumatism in the arms,[3] which frequently prevented her from writing, and added greatly to the unpleasantness of a liver-complaint, from which she had long suffered, and which had been greatly aggravated by her misfortunes. She therefore requested and obtained permission to go, from time to time, to the baths at Buxton,[4] in the vicinity of Sheffield.

In order to lessen the *ennui* of her tedious captivity, which was no longer occupied in the formation of plots in England, Scotland, and the Continent, in the construction and renewal of the cyphers necessary for her secret correspondence, in the dictation of letters to her Scottish secretary, Curle, or her French secretary, Raullet, or in procuring and employing skilful and trusty agents,

[1] 'Voyant le peu de compte que de tout ce temps passé vous avez faict de moy, de mes lettres, ministres, remonstrances et humbles requestes, jusques à desdaygner de m'en fayre response de vous mesmes ou par les vostres, en me traistant de pis en pis, j'avoys conclu de ne plus vous ennuier ny me rompre la teste en vain, résolue souffrir ce qu'il plairoit à Dieu m'envoyer par vos mains.'—Letter from Mary Stuart to Elizabeth, 25th December, 1571. Labanoff, vol. iv., p. 10.
[2] Labanoff, vol. iv., p. 112.
[3] She called it a catarrh. See her letter of 30th April, 1572. Labanoff, vol. iv., p. 44.
[4] All her changes of residence are mentioned by Labanoff.

she spent her time in needlework, and in attending to her dogs and birds. 'My lord of Glasgow,' she wrote to her ambassador in France, 'I beg you to obtain for me some turtle-doves and Barbary fowls, that I may try to bring them up in this country. I should take pleasure in feeding them in their cages, as I do all the little birds I can find. These are the only pastimes of a prisoner.'[1] On another occasion, she asked him to get her some little dogs. 'If my uncle, the Cardinal of Guise,' she wrote, 'has gone to Lyons, I am sure that he will send me a couple of pretty little dogs, and you will buy me as many more; for besides reading and working, I find pleasure only in the little animals that I can get.'[2]

She also directed her attendants to buy for her some silk, satin, and ribands, that she might, with her own hands, prepare little specimens of needlework, which she offered to Elizabeth, through the French ambassador, Lamothe Fénelon. Having learned that the Queen had accepted them, she wrote to her: 'Madam, my good sister, since it has pleased you to receive so graciously from Monsieur de Lamothe the little things that I took the liberty to send you by him, I cannot refrain from expressing to you how happy I shall feel, when it pleases you to allow me to endeavour by all means to regain some part of your favour, to do which I greatly desire you to have the goodness to aid me by informing me of the matters in which I can please and obey you.'[3]

So anxiously desirous was she to conciliate Elizabeth that she wrote to the Archbishop of Glasgow to send her from France anything that he thought suitable for a present to the English Queen. 'If my uncle, the Cardinal,' she wrote, 'would send me something pretty, such as a pair of bracelets, or a mirror, I would give it to the Queen. If you see anything new, please buy it for me; and if my uncle would contrive some suitable device between her and me, these little attentions would make her more graciously inclined to me than anything else.'[4]

As her presents were well received, she was highly delighted, and proposed to send others. 'I feel the greatest satisfaction,' she wrote to Lamothe Fénelon, 'at the news you give me, that it has pleased the Queen, my good sister, to accept my tablets: for I desire nothing so much as to be able always to please her, in the least as well as in the most important affairs, and I do this

---

[1] Labanoff, vol. iv., p. 183.
[2] 'Il me les fauldroit envoyer en des paniers, bien chaudement.' Labanoff vol. iv., pp. 223-229.
[3] Ibid., pp. 171, 172.   [4] Ibid., pp. 213, 214.

in the hope of recovering her favour in the first place, and then I do not doubt of her goodness in all the rest. I am desirous to make her a head-dress as soon as I can, but I have so few women to assist me in delicate needlework, that I have not been able to get it ready yet. If you think some articles of network would please her better than anything else, I will make them. Meanwhile, I beg you to get for me some gold lace, ornamented with silver spangles, the best and most delicate that you can, and to send me six yards of it, and twenty yards of double lace, or else narrow good lace.'[1]

Such was the abject condition to which poor Mary Stuart was reduced. This haughty princess, who not long before had kept the whole realm in agitation by her plots, now busied herself in her person with making articles of dress[2] for that Queen who was detaining her in captivity, in contempt of the law of nations and the dignity of sovereign rank. She also sought to gain the favour of Elizabeth's principal advisers; and begged the princes of her family to send presents and compliments to Leicester, who appeared to be well-disposed towards her.[3] She wrote friendly letters to Burghley,[4] who had met her at Buxton. She even flattered the restless Walsingham, who had been made a Secretary of State on Burghley's promotion to the office of Lord Treasurer. To use her own expressive language, she feared 'the turbulent imaginations' of this minister, who was now entrusted with the surveillance of the different parties which existed in the kingdom. She therefore wrote to the French ambassador: 'You will promise him from me that never in my life will I do anything against the Queen his mistress, and that on this condition, if he will be my friend, I will consent, though this is the contrary of what I have always feared of him until the present time.'[5]

The accession of Henry III. to the throne of France, after the death of Charles IX., slightly revived Mary Stuart's hopes. As Duke of Anjou, Henry had been the head of the Catholic party in France, and had acquired a reputation for ability and firmness which he did not long retain after he became a King.

---

[1] Letter of 14th September, 1574. Labanoff, vol. iv., pp. 222, 223.
[2] She wrote to Lamothe Fénelon, in reference to the 'accoustrement de réseuil,' which she had sent to Elizabeth: 'Et le jour qu'elle me fera cette faveur de le porter, je vous prie luy baiser très humblement les mains pour moy; de qouy je vous seray obligée, combien que je ne puisse avoir ce bien de la voir moy-mesme aussy bien que vous.' Letter of 13th December, 1574. Labanoff, vol. iv., p. 240.
[3] Labanoff, vol. iv., pp. 77, 190, 205.
[4] Labanoff, vol. iv., pp. 78, 104. 'Burleigh écrit fort honnestement de moy ... Burleigh même est en discrédit.' Ibid., pp. 199, 201. [5] Ibid., p. 240.

Of her three brothers-in-law, he was the one on whose sympathy Mary Stuart chiefly reckoned.[1] For a short time she entertained the belief that he would undertake her defence with greater vigour than Charles IX. had done. She besought him not to recognize her son as King of Scotland, and not to address him by that title. She desired him to form a secret league with her 'to aid her to recover her rights,'[2] and above all things, not to renew the treaty concluded between Charles IX. and Elizabeth, in April, 1572. 'If the King deserts me,' she wrote, 'and forms an alliance with her (meaning Elizabeth), he will barter away my life, and strengthen his enemies and mine.'[3]

But she lost at this time her principal ally at the Court of France, the Cardinal of Lorraine, that one of all her relatives to whom she was most tenderly attached, and in whom she reposed the greatest confidence. His death caused her the most poignant grief, which she expressed to the Archbishop of Glasgow, in these touching words: 'God be praised that he sends me no affliction which hitherto he has not given me grace to bear. Although at first, I could neither restrain nor prevent these eyes from weeping, yet nevertheless, the long continuance of my adversity has taught me to hope for consolation for all misfortunes in a better life. Alas! I am a prisoner, and God has taken from me that one of his creatures whom I loved best. What more shall I say? He has deprivd me at one blow of my father and my uncle; I shall follow him, when it pleases God, with less regret.'[4]

At the same time that she thus lost the support of the Cardinal of Lorraine at the Court of France, the hopes which she had rested upon Henry III. were all dissipated. This Prince possessed good talents, but knew not how to employ them aright; though full of courage he was devoid of character, and, by his mother's direction, he continued that undecided course of policy which had troubled and ensanguined the whole reign of

---

[1] At the period of his arrival from Poland, she wrote to the Archbishop of Glasgow: 'Ils sont bien surpris de la venue du roy, et craignent la guerre; toutes fois, ils se font fort d'estre recherchés dudit sieur mon bon frére. Ils m'ont eu plus grande jalousie que jamais pour le soubçon que vous sçavez qu'il y a longtemps qu'ils prindrent que j'avoys faict transport de mondroict au roy d'á présent, et aussy ils disent que j'aime trop ceux de Guise, et ils savent bien que de tous mes beaux-frères j'ay tousjours aultant espéré de celluy-cy que d'autres, et pour n'en mentir poinct, il est vray, pour la bonne vollenté qu'il m'a tousjours porté, d'enfance, j'espère qu'il ne l'aura point changée, je ne le mériteray point aussi.' Labanoff, vol. iv. pp. 191, 192.

[2] Ibid., pp. 244, 245.   [3] Ibid., vol. iv., p. 252.   [4] Ibid., p. 267.

Charles IX. This policy of compromising matters with parties, and acting with duplicity towards individuals—though mixed up with negotiations and wars, leading to acts of weakness from which it was possible to escape only by deception or excess, and necessitating alternately unlimited concessions and feeble resistance—was unfortunately too well suited to the situation of the kingdom, the spirit of the age, and the predilections of Catherine de Medici. Not having succeeded, by the exercise of the royal authority, in making the Catholics tolerate Protestantism, or converting the Protestants back to Catholicism, the adroit but changeful Catherine discontented both parties in their turn; and at last drove the King of Navarre and the Protestants to seek the aid of Elizabeth, and the Guises and the Catholics to look for support to Philip II.

Obedient to his mother's counsels, Henry III. sent M. de la Chatre to London in the spring of 1575, as his ambassador extraordinary, to renew the treaty of alliance which had been concluded in April, 1572. When Mary Stuart perceived that the new King intended to follow in his brother's footsteps, and had fallen completely under the influence of the Queen-mother, who regarded her with dislike, she expected nothing further from him, and turned again to Philip II. She resumed her secret negotiations with the Spanish Catholic party, and renewed her communications with the Pope by means of the Bishop of Ross, whom she had accredited to the Court of Rome, as soon as he was restored to liberty by Elizabeth, in the month of December, 1573. The papal chair was now occupied by Gregory XIII., who, in pursuance of the plans of his predecessor Pius V., kept Ireland for a long time in insurrection, and urged Philip II. to restore Catholicism in England, by sending thither an expedition under the command of Don John of Austria. He proposed that Mary Stuart should marry this young Prince, to whom the zealous Catholics of England and Scotland had turned their attention in 1571, in preference to the Duke of Norfolk, and who, after having vanquished the Moors in Spain, had conquered the Turks in the Mediterranean sea. His Holiness doubted not that the hero of Lepanto and of Tunis 'would marvellously serve this enterprise by his valour, and by the success which constantly attended his arms.'[1] This double project of marriage and inva-

---

[1] 'Servir bene a quelle impresa per il valore et per la felicità che porta seco . . . Essendo egli desiderato da Catholici Inglesi per loro Re, mediante i matrimonio con la Regina di Scotia, como hora di questo tratato la M^ta Vra, é prenamente informata.' Letter from the Pope's Nuncio to Philip II., 10th January, 1574. Archives of Simancas, Roma, fol. 924.

sion, which was rejected by Philip II. when first brought before him in 1574,[1] was renewed in 1577, when Don John was appointed Governor of the Netherlands, instead of the Grand Commander de Requesens, whose system of conciliation had succeeded no better than the system of compression adopted by the Duke of Alva. Don John, the close friend of the Duke of Guise, wrote to the King his brother, with equal ambition and foresight, that the submission of the Netherlands could be obtained only by the conquest of England.[2]

Philip II., however, displayed no inclination to embark in this enterprise. He was anxious not to remove his forces from Flanders and the coast of Africa, where they were then stationed. He would not suffer himself to be tempted by the offer which Mary Stuart made to place her son in his hands,[3] and which was somewhat difficult of realization, although she continually recurred to it. Nor was this the only offer which she made. After having proposed to place her son, as a hostage of Catholicism, in the hands of Philip II., Mary Stuart went so far as to contemplate his disinheritance by the transfer of all her rights to the powerful defender of her religion in Europe. Her frequent attacks of illness, the dangers which beset her captivity, and the consequences which might result from her plots, led her to project a will containing the following clause, which, though doubtless very Catholic, is certainly very unmaternal, and quite as unmonarchical. 'In order,' she says, 'not to contravene the glory, honour, and preservation of the Catholic, Apostolic, and Roman Church, in which I wish to live and die, if the Prince of Scotland, my son, shall be brought back to its creed in spite of the bad education he has received, to my great regret, in the heresy of Calvin among my rebellious subjects, I leave him the sole and only heir of my kingdom of Scotland, and of the right which I justly claim to the crown of England and its dependent countries; but if, on the other hand, my said son continues to live in the said heresy, I yield and transfer and present all my rights in England and elsewhere . . to the Catholic King or any of his relations whom he may please, with the advice and consent of his Holiness; and I do this, not only because I perceive him to be

---

[1] A debate took place in the Council of State on the Nuncio's proposition of the 4th February, 1574. ' Para consultar à V. M., sobre los negocios que el nuncio de Su Santidad le habló ultimamente de lo que paresce al consejo.' Archives of Simancas. Ibid. [2] Labanoff, vol. iv., p. 9.
[3] Letter from Mary Stuart to the Archbishop of Glasgow, 20th January, 1577. Labanoff, vol. iv., p. 345.

now the only true supporter of the Catholic religion, but also out of gratitude for the many favours which I and my friends, recommended by me, have received from him in my greatest necessity, and furthermore, out of respect to the rights which he may himself possess to the said kingdoms and countries, I beseech him, in return, to make alliance with the house of Lorraine, and, if possible, with that of Guise, in memory of the race from which I am sprung on my mother's side."[1]

In this will, which was written in February, 1577, Mary Stuart considered merely the interest of the cause of Catholicism, and contemplated only its triumph. A Queen, pursuing the same course as was adopted in France at a later period by the democratic faction of the League, did not hesitate to subordinate the possession of a crown to orthodoxy in matters of faith. But even this was destined to do her no service. She beshrewed herself, at this period, without attempting anything, and without being able to accomplish anything. In England no one had declared in her favour since the death of the Duke of Norfolk. In Scotland, Morton exercised for eight years an authority which, though temporarily overthrown in 1578, did not even allow a thought to be turned towards Mary Stuart. On the Continent, the somewhat vague plans of this indefatigable Princess met with serious obstacles in the formal desertion of Henry III., who declared that he preferred the friendship of the Queen of England to the freedom of the Queen of Scots[2]—in the circumspect inactivity of Philip II., who was preparing to occupy Portugal with a military force, and seize on its inheritance—in the death of Don John of Austria, which occurred before the subjugation of the Netherlands—and lastly, in the impotence of her cousin, the Duke of Guise, who was not in a position to attempt anything in her favour without the support of either France or Spain.

It was not until 1581, after the final overthrow of Morton, that Mary Stuart resumed her conflict with Elizabeth. Morton held the Regency for a longer period than all his three predecessors together. For five years he preserved peace in Scotland; no new parties were formed, and no old disputes revived. During this uninterrupted peace the country prospered, and reaped the fruits of the Protestant revolution and of the public tranquillity. The industry of the towns was developed, their maritime trade extended, the welfare of the population increased, and the happy change in the aspect of Scotland excited the surprise, and almost

[1] Labanoff, vol. iv., pp. 354, 355.
[2] MS. letter, State Paper Office; Annas Paulet to Elizabeth, 19th February, 1578.

the envy of Elizabeth's ambassadors.[1] But it was contrary to the spirit as well as to the habits of the Scottish nobility to remain for any length of time in repose and subordination. They soon grew weary of their obedience to Morton, whose insatiable avarice and haughty sway greatly facilitated the success of their new schemes.

A confederation for Morton's overthrow was formed, under the guidance of Alexander Erskine, the King's governor, and George Buchanan, one of his tutors. This confederation, which was joined by many of the principal members of the old parties—including the Earls of Athol, Argyle, Montrose, and Glencairn, the Chancellor Glammis, the Abbot of Dunfermline, the Comptroller Tullibardine, and the Lords Lindsay, Ruthven, Ogilvy, and Herries—deprived Morton of the Regency, in March, 1578, and conferred upon James VI., who was not yet thirteen years of age, the exercise of the royal authority, and appointed a council of members of their body, to aid him in administering the affairs of the kingdom.[2] Morton appeared resigned to his fate; and, after having proclaimed the direct government of the King at Edinburgh, he retired quietly to his Castle of Dalkeith. Apparently renouncing all thoughts of ambition, he gave himself up to the peaceful occupations of private life; but in his retirement he secretly devised the ruin of those who had occasioned his own downfal.

In less than two months after his resignation, this skilful and enterprising man had raised himself once more to power, with the most consummate ability and the most complete success. Seconded by his ally, the Earl of Mar, son of the former Regent of that name, and supported by the Douglas family, he regained possession of Stirling Castle and of the person of the young King.[3] Abandoning the idea of restoring the Regency, he convoked Parliament to meet at Stirling Castle, in July, under his eye and influence, and appointed a Council to conduct the administration of affairs under the nominal sovereignty of James VI. The chief place in this new council was allotted to Morton. Thus again invested with the royal power, though under another form, he either treated with his enemies or crushed them. Argyle, Lindsay and Montrose were admitted into the Privy Council. The Catholic Earl of Athol died suddenly, after leaving a banquet given by Morton.[4] The Hamilton family, so

---

[1] Murdin, pp. 282, 285. Tytler, vol. vi., p. 216.
[2] Tytler, vol. vi., pp. 235-242.
[3] Ibid., p. 246.   [4] Ibid., p. 259.

powerful by their possessions and nearness to the throne, were crushed. In order to conciliate the favour of the King, who had inherited the hatred of the Lennox clan for the Hamiltons, Morton resolved to destroy them. The old Duke of Chatelherault had died some years before;[1] his three sons were either taken prisoners or compelled to expatriate themselves. The eldest, the Earl of Arran, who had long been insane, was taken in Draffen Castle with his mother, and detained in captivity. The second, Lord Arbroath, took refuge in Flanders; and the third, Lord Claude Hamilton, threw himself upon the compassion of Elizabeth. After having overthrown this formidable house, which was proscribed as guilty of the murder of the two Regents, Murray and Lennox, and whose lands and titles were bestowed on others, Morton appeared to be firmly established by the submissive docility of the King, by the open support of England, and by the timorous obedience of Scotland.

Nevertheless a revolution of a most formidable nature was in preparation against him. It was the work of two young Scotchmen, who, having just arrived from the Continent, insinuated themselves into the confidence of James VI. and became his favourites. Esmé Stewart, commonly called M. d'Aubigny, a youth of prepossessing exterior, graceful manners, and elegant accomplishments, left the Court of France, where he had received his education, and appeared in the Court of Scotland, on the 8th of September, 1579,[2] with a secret mission from the Duke of Guise. He was a Catholic, and had come to fill the Earl of Athol's place as head of that party, which had remained faithful to the ancient religion of the country, and devoted to the hereditary line of its kings. James VI., whose cousin he was,[3] received him with marked favour, manifested a great liking for his society, appointed him his Chamberlain, and finally created him Earl of Lennox. His sudden elevation alarmed both Morton and Elizabeth. They suspected the projects of Lennox, who was attacked as a Catholic by the zealous Presbyterians, and accused by the English party of plotting to lay hands on the King, hurry him to Dumbarton, and thence transport him to France.[4] This suspicion was not altogether unfounded, for

[1] He died on the 22nd January, 1575. Camden, p. 301.
[2] Tytler, vol. vi., p. 261, from the letters of the English ambassadors, Sir R. Bowes, and Captain Arrington.
[3] His father, John Stewart, was brother of Matthew Stewart, the grandfather of James VI. He possessed by inheritance the estate of D'Aubigny, which Charles VII. had given to one of his ancestors. Camden, vol. ii., p. 331.
[4] Tytler, vol. vi., p. 268.

Mary Stuart, during the years 1579 and 1580,[1] was incessantly devising plans for getting her son out of Scotland. But she had as yet formed no connexion with D'Aubigny; and it was to Spain, and not to France, that she wished to convey the young King.

Elizabeth, by Morton's advice, sent Sir Robert Bowes into Scotland in order to counterbalance the influence of the agent of the Guises by promising James VI. the succession to the throne of England, if he remained attached to the English cause. But so distant a prospect had no influence, in the mind of the juvenile Monarch, over the enthusiastic admiration and affection with which he regarded his new favourite. Lennox retained all his influence. He calmed the apprehensions of the Presbyterian ministers by professing Protestantism, and ascribed the credit of his conversion to his young master, who, educated by Buchanan in the subtle dialectics of the time, was already a practised controversialist. He thus flattered the theological vanity of the Prince, who conferred on his hopeful convert the command of Dumbarton Castle. The possession of this fortress was necessary to Lennox to facilitate the accomplishment of his mission; but it was, first of all, essential to overthrow Morton.

This he resolved to do; and he was seconded in the undertaking by another Scotchman of greater ability and boldness than himself—James Stewart, second son of Lord Ochiltree, who, after having served as a soldier of fortune in the wars of the Continent, had returned to Scotland, where he held the post of Captain of the Royal Guard. He was held in great favour by the King and possessed the confidence of Lennox. In concert with the powerful confederation of nobles who were opposed to Morton, Captain James Stewart accused the ex-Regent of complicity in Darnley's murder, and had him arrested in the midst of the Council, and in presence of the King. This bold act was attended with complete success. It presaged the impending ruin of the English party in Scotland. Elizabeth was greatly concerned at it; and spared no exertion to save Morton. Her efforts were, however, unavailing; neither her menacing injunctions, nor the manœuvres of the great agitator Randolph, whom she despatched expressly to Edinburgh, nor the collection, under Lord Hunsdon, of an English army, ready at a moment's notice to cross the frontier and invade Scotland, were able to preserve this last leader of the old civil wars, this accomplice in several

---

[1] See the letters in Prince Labanoff's Collection.

murders, from the dreadful fate suffered by Riccio, Darnley, Murray, Lennox, Lethington, and Kirkaldy of Grange,—a fate which neither Bothwell nor Mary Stuart were destined to escape, as one of them had already died in a Danish fortress, and the other was doomed to captivity until her tragical end.

Morton was arrested on the 31st of December, 1580, and condemned, on the 2nd of June, 1581, to be beheaded, as guilty of having been implicated in the plot against the life of the King's father. He confessed that he was aware of the existence of the plot, but had not taken part in it, neither had he dared to reveal it, because all, he said, was done with the consent and under the direction of the Queen. He died with the stern courage of a Presbyterian, and the indomitable pride of a Douglas. His party was overthrown, most of his relatives and friends were condemned to various punishments, or compelled to fly the country; and King James, now freed entirely from his yoke, bestowed on his principal adversary, D'Aubigny, the title of Duke of Lennox, created his accuser Earl of Arran, conferred the Earldom of Morton on the Catholic Maxwell, granted the Earldom of Orkney to the Earl of March, and raised Lord Ruthven to the rank of Earl of Gowrie.[1]

Morton's death gave great satisfaction to Mary Stuart.[2] On learning it, she experienced the delight of consummated vengeance, and conceived hopes of a better fortune. She had now entered into correspondence with Lennox, whom she had at first distrusted. After having long refused to give her son the title of King, and having induced the Catholic powers of the Continent to do the same, she admitted a new project of *association* in the Crown, by which it was proposed that James should resign the Crown to his mother, under the condition, that she should retransmit it to him, and retire from all the active duties of the government. Mary Stuart gave the Duke of Guise full powers to negotiate and conclude this royal transaction.[3] But in addition to this plan, which no one had any interest in keeping concealed, there was another of an entirely secret nature, which parties have vaguely suspected, and historians imperfectly understood. This plan, prepared by the Jesuits, approved by the Pope, concerted with Lennox, assented to by the King of Scotland, possessing the ardent support of the House of Lorraine, and assured of the military assistance of the King of Spain, aimed at the restoration of the Catholic religion in Scotland, and the deli-

---

[1] Tytler, vol. vi., pp. 280-299. [2] Labanoff, vol. v., pp. 264, 265.
[3] Ibid., pp. 185-187.

verance of Mary Stuart from her prison, that she might be reinstated upon her throne.

The conspiracy of 1570 was thus renewed under another form. The Catholic party, since the last defeat which it had met with in England, the cruel losses which it had suffered, and the severe laws which had been passed against it, had striven to reorganize its forces and reanimate its vigour in that country by a mysterious, but active and persevering propagande. Two seminaries of English priests had been founded for this purpose on the Continent: one by Dr. William Allen, formerly principal of St. Mary's Hall, at Oxford, who had settled first at Douai, and afterwards at Rheims, in 1575; the other by Gregory XIII., who had endowed an institution of this nature, in 1579, with the buildings and revenues of two hospitals at Rome, destined for travellers of the English nation. Allen had gathered around him a hundred and fifty priests, educated a large number of scholars in the firmest adherence to the principles of Catholicism, and sent into England already about a hundred missionaries, who went secretly from house to house preaching the doctrines and practising the worship of the Romish faith, in spite of the rigorous penalties prescribed by law against such proceedings. Several of them had been discovered and condemned to death.[1]

The religious order recently instituted for the protection of Romanism in those countries where it was still retained, and its restoration in those in which it had been abolished—the conquering society of Jesuits—could not remain unconnected with this great movement. Their general had despatched two of their number, Robert Parsons and Edmund Campian, to England, and for a whole year they had traversed the country without falling into the hands of Elizabeth, although that Queen, aware of their presence in her dominions, had threatened to inflict the most terrible punishments upon all who should venture to give them shelter. At length, Campian was taken and condemned, with some other Catholic priests, for having violated the laws and conspired against the Queen. After having been put to the torture by a government which was rendered suspicious by its care for its own safety, and made cruel by the customs of the age, he was inhumanly put to death with several of his companions.[2]

Parsons was more fortunate, and escaped the vigilance of his pursuers. After having visited England and Scotland, he re-

---

[1] Lingard, vol. viii., p. 140.
[2] Camden, vol. ii., pp. 349, 379. Lingard, vol. viii., p. 148.

turned to Flanders, with a pretty accurate knowledge of the religious state of those two countries. The company to which he belonged was devoted to the aggrandisement of the pontifical authority, favourable to the ambitious views of the King of Spain, connected by strong ties to the Catholic house of Guise, and interested in the deliverance of Mary Stuart; it therefore entered with extreme ardour into the plot framed for the restoration of the captive Queen and the ancient Church. As early as the end of 1580,[1] before the death of Morton, the General of the Jesuits, the King of Spain, and D'Aubigny had entertained this idea. Prevented from actively intervening in England by the necessity he was under of defending the kingdom of Portugal against the attacks of the pretender, Don Antonio de Crato, and of opposing, in the Netherlands, the united forces of the Prince of Orange and the Duke of Alençon, who had been accepted as defender of Belgium, and was soon to be appointed Duke of Brabant, Philip II. merely offered to support D'Aubigny by granting James VI. subsidies equal in amount to the revenues of the crown of Scotland.[2] In a chapter of the order of Jesuits held at Rome, during the spring of 1581,[3] after Morton's arrest, the affairs of Scotland were discussed with increasing interest. The Scottish Jesuit William Creighton, and the English Jesuit Holt, were sent to consult with Lennox upon the best means of executing this enterprise in favour of the imprisoned Queen and the proscribed religion.

Furnished with letters of credence from the Archbishop of Glasgow at Paris, and from the Spanish ambassador, Don Bernardino de Mendoza, at London, they saw Lennox, and concerted their plans with him.[4] On the 7th of March, 1582,

[1] See Labanoff, vol. vii., pp. 152–161, for several important documents on this subject, viz.: a letter from the Archbishop of Glasgow to the General of the Jesuits, dated 14th October, 1580; a letter from the General of the Jesuits to the Archbishop of Glasgow, dated 8th November, 1580; and a letter from the Grand Master of the Order of Malta, presented by the Grand Commander of St. Giles.

[2] He desired, moreover, that they should not attempt to invade England until they had strongly established themselves in Ireland. The General of the Jesuits announced to the Archbishop of Glasgow that the Pope was resolved to complete so holy a work, which he called 'the sacred expedition:' he was also of opinion that they should first take possession of Ireland, whither the Knights of Malta would proceed, in accordance with a treaty made with the Grand Master, which would have made this militia of all Christendom against the infidels, an army of Catholicism against the heretics. Labanoff, vol. vii., p. 157.

[3] Despatch from J. B. de Tassis to Philip II., 18th May, 1582. Archives of Simancas, Francia, Series B., fol. 53, No. 80, in the National Archives.

[4] Archives of Simancas, Francia, B. 53, No. 81.

Lennox gave Creighton the following letter from Jean Baptiste de Tassis, Philip the Second's ambassador at Paris:—' Your King and the Pope, according to what I am told by the Jesuit Creighton, appear to desire to make use of me, in the design which they have conceived, for restoring the Catholic religion and delivering the Queen of Scots. Being persuaded that this enterprise is intended to promote the welfare and safety of the said Queen of Scots, and the King her son, to whom the crown will be preserved by the consent of the Queen his mother, I am ready to employ my life and possessions in the undertaking.'[1] He gave him, at the same time, a paper regarding the method of executing the enterprise, and announced his intention of going to France to levy the troops necessary to insure its success.

On their arrival at Paris with their documents, the Jesuits Creighton and Holt had a secret interview with Tassis, at whose house the Duke of Guise, the Archbishop of Glasgow, and Dr. Allen, met to discuss the project. Tassis asked Creighton if the King of France should be informed of the plan. 'By no means,' answered the Jesuit, 'for the scheme would be thwarted by being immediately communicated to the Queen of England.'[2] Several secret conferences were held from the middle to the end of May, 1582, either at the Spanish Embassy, or at the house of the Archbishop of Glasgow; and it was determined, that the expedition against England should not be effected by the King of Spain, but in the name of the Pope alone, in order to avoid giving umbrage to the King of France, and to prevent his acting against them. Philip II. was to furnish the Pope with money to levy the necessary troops, who were to be placed under the command of the Duke of Guise, who was very ardent in the matter.[3]

---

[1] 'Vuestro Rey, con el Papa, paraceme que dessean servirse de mi en el disegno que traen entre manos para la restauracion de la religion Catholica y la libertad de la Reyna de Escocia, segun que el dicho Criton me ha referido, y creyendo que esta empresa se haze por el bien y la conservacion de la dicha Reyna de Escocia y del Rey su hijo, y que a ese le sera sustentada y mantenida su corona con consentimiento de la Reyna su madre, estoy aparesado de emplear mi vida y hazienda para la execucion de la dicha empresa.' Copia de carta en Frances, que Mos. de Olivi (D'Aubigny), duque de Lenos, ha escripto a Don J. B. de Tassis, de Dalreith (Dalkeith), en Escocia, a vii de Março, 1582, descifrada. Archives of Simancas, Francia, B. 53, No. 81.

[2] 'En ninguna manera, porque entendian que por ally se perderia el negocio . . . estava claro que luego la de Inglaterra sabria el disegno.' Archives of Simancas, Francia, B. 53, No. 80.

[3] 'Hercules (this was the *nom-de-guerre* assumed by the Duke of Guise in his correspondence with Spain) muestra un extremo de emplearse á esta empresa.' Archives of Simancas, Francia, B. 53, No. 84.

On the same day that he wrote to Tassis, the Duke of Lennox addressed to Mary Stuart a letter filled with expressions of the most enthusiastic devotion. He offered to consecrate himself to the work of her deliverance, to the restoration of Catholicism, and to the assertion of her rights in Great Britain by means of an army of 15,000 men, which he was going to form on the Continent by the aid of the Pope and the King of Spain. He added, that he would soon overrun England with this army, and besought her to be of good courage, for she would find servants determined to risk their lives for her.[1]

Mary Stuart communicated Lennox's letter to Mendoza, and wrote to the latter, on the 6th and 8th of April, a very long and extremely curious despatch on the projected enterprise.[2] She told him that, to ensure its success, two points must be considered— the armed assistance which would be given by the Pope and the Catholic King, and the concurrence of Scotland itself in the scheme. She begged that the succour promised from abroad might be exactly stipulated and effectively furnished, 'so as not to deceive the Earl of Lennox and his party;' and she undertook to make the necessary arrangements in the kingdom itself. 'I will negotiate,' she said, 'with all diligence to strengthen and increase my party in Scotland, and will appoint the ports and harbours necessary for the reception of the said foreign aid.'

She recommended her friends, however, to conduct their secret arrangements with extreme prudence, and not to compromise her in any way. 'My life is in danger,' she wrote, 'and so is the entire state of my son, if they should be discovered; besides that, it is not my intention in any way to allow it to be proved that the said negotiations were carried on under my name; and if necessity requires that I should intervene, I have other means at hand, much more convenient, which I have determined to employ.'

Mendoza replied to Mary Stuart, that the Catholic King and his Holiness the Pope would, he was sure, equip a fleet equal to that which had been promised, and furnish an army of even greater magnitude, at any time when there was a possibility of attaining so inestimable an object; but that in the present state of affairs, they must avoid giving umbrage to the French by so

---

[1] This letter is in the Archives of Simancas, Inglaterra, fol. 836, annexed to the long despatch from Mary Stuart, which we quote, *infra*.

[2] This MS. despatch is in fol. 836 of the English Negotiations in the Spanish Archives of Simancas, under the title of ' Copia de carta descifrada de la Reyna de Escocia á Don Bernardino de Mendoza, quien la remite á S. M^{ad} en Carta de 2o Abril, y de la que el duque de Lenos escrivió à la Reyna.'

considerable an armament, lest, fearing to lose their influence in Scotland or England, they should unite themselves more closely than ever to Queen Elizabeth and the heretics.[1] Mendoza, in 1582, gave as little encouragement to the Catholic plot of Lennox and the Jesuits, as the Duke of Alva had given, in 1570, to that of Ridolfi and the Duke of Norfolk. The ecclesiastic who had come, under the disguise of a dentist, and on foot, to bring him letters from Mary Stuart, was despatched by him to the Duke of Lennox, with letters concealed in a mirror.[2] In these letters, he gave great praise to Lennox, reminded him of the glory and greatness which a person like himself might hope to gain from such an enterprise, intentionally omitted to speak of the 15,000 men promised by Creighton, and urged him to carry into effect the plan of the *association* of Mary and James in the crown, in order that all the Catholics and all the friends of the Queen of Scots, satisfied with this arrangement, might be ready, at the common invitation of the mother and son, to flock to his standard, and to sacrifice their property, their lives and their families in the cause.[3] Instead of urging a continental intervention, Mendoza simply advised an Anglo-Scottish attack. He wrote to the same effect to Dr. Allen; and it was with this object that he urged Father Parsons to proceed to Scotland with the money which had been furnished him by Rome and Madrid, and that he represented to the Archbishop of Glasgow how useful his return and residence in his country would be in such a conjuncture.[4] Mendoza informed the Catholic King of his views and proceedings with regard to the enterprise projected by the Jesuits, in his despatch of the 26th of April, which was not calculated to dispose Philip II. to support it.

While waiting for all these different wills to come to an agreement upon the means and time of action, Lennox had proceeded along the bold but dangerous course upon which he had entered:

[1] His answer is given in detail in his despatch to the Catholic King, dated 26th April, 1582. Archives of Simancas, Inglaterra, fol. 836.

[2] 'Justamente respondi al de Lenos con palabras generales con el despecho de la Reyna de Escocia, el cual llevo el mismo clerigo, que le truxo, que fue a pie por mas seguridad y en figura de sacamuelos como vino, y con un espexo que yo hice, dentro del cual van las cartas, de manera que no hay imaginar, persona que las le lleva.' Archives of Simancas, Inglaterra, fol. 836.

[3] 'Que conviene que los Escoceses procedan debaxo desta color, con la cual prendaran à los Catholicos de aqui y afecionados de la de Escocia, que segun ser voz como demanda de madre y hijo, y con esto estar asegurados que unanimes han de procurar por yrles en ello haciendas, vidas, hijos y sucesion de sus casas antes la aunstad de V. M. qua no la de Francia.' Ibid.

[4] Archives of Simancas, Inglaterra, fol. 836.

he was determined to overthrow every obstacle to the accomplishment of his designs. Before declaring himself a Catholic, he raised up the Episcopal Church, which had been re-established in 1571 for the benefit of the Protestant nobility,[1] and to which his young master was favourable. He had at the same time declared war against the Presbyterian Church, the obstinate fanaticism and formidable power of which he did not rightly appreciate. He met with inflexible resistance from the ministers. These bold men denounced from the pulpit the projects of Lennox and Arran, which the sagacity of fear, or the warnings of Elizabeth, had enabled them rightly to estimate. They loudly inveighed against the arrival of Signor Paul, the master stabler of the Duke of Guise, and one of the murderous authors of the massacre of St Bartholomew, who brought a present of horses to the young King, and who was suspected of being a secret messenger of the Popish conspiracy. They excommunicated Robert Montgomery, who had been reinstated in the bishopric of Glasgow, by the influence, and to serve the purposes, of Lennox. Carrying even to the feet of the King their complaints and apprehensions, in the free language, and with the intrepid attitude of their sect, they manifested their readiness to refuse obedience to the mandates of the Crown if they clashed with the superior obligations of the conscience towards God. The boldest among them, John Durie, the minister of Edinburgh, was exiled, and a severe contest began between Lennox and Scottish Protestantism. The all-powerful favourite struck, but could not intimidate, the Calvinist Church. Not only did he commence hostilities against the religious leaders of the burghers, but he extended his attacks to

---

[1] This re-establishment was of a more political than religious nature. Its object was, as death removed the old Catholic titulars of the bishoprics, to whom the temporalities of their sees and their seats in Parliament had been left by law, to retain their revenues and privileges in the hands of the Protestant ministers. The new bishops, chosen from among the Protestant ministers, gave up the greater part of their temporalities to the lay lords, who were their patrons, and their religious jurisdiction was subordinate to the General Assembly of the Calvinistic Church. This innovation, which tended to the profit of the nobles, and the maintenance of the political influence of the State, was introduced by Morton's avarice, in August, 1571. The archbishopric of St. Andrew's, left vacant by the execution of Archbishop Hamilton, was placed at the Regent's disposal. He had appointed John Douglas, Rector of the University of St. Andrew's, who had ceded to him the greater part of the episcopal revenues. This example had been followed, and several bishops were appointed in this manner. These were called *Tulchan bishops*, from the stuffed calfskins used to make the cows yield their milk more willingly. These bishops served to milk the Church. See M'Crie's Life of Knox, vol. ii. pp. 198–203. Tytler, vol. vi. pp. 199, 200, and 233, 234.

the political chiefs of the nobility, who were endeavouring to restore the English party in Scotland, which had sunk into impotence since the death of Morton, the flight of the Earl of Angus, the dispersion of the Douglas family, and the disfavour of the Erskines. The young Earls of Gowrie and Mar were at the head of this new movement, and had been joined by the Earls of Glencairn, Montrose, Eglinton, and Rothes, Lords Lindsay and Boyd, and several others. The inconstant Argyle had also promised his co-operation: and Elizabeth's government gave them every encouragement to proceed in their design.[1]

The English Queen had neglected no means of averting the dangers by which she was threatened by the triumph of the Hispano-French party on the most Catholic frontier of her kingdom. She had enjoyed thirteen years of almost entire security on this side, under the Regents Murray, Lennox, Mar, and Morton, all the four of whom had been attached to the maintenance of Protestantism and the preservation of the alliance with England. During this period her sole occupation had been to guard against the attacks to which she might be exposed upon the Continent, and these she had adroitly escaped by separating France from Spain. She had kept the first of these powers in check by the negotiation of treaties of peace, and by successive proposals of marriage to the three sons of Catherine de Medici; and she had paralysed the second, by opposing manœuvres to manœuvres, and diverting Philip's troops from England by giving constant support to the insurgents in the Netherlands. The fall of Morton and elevation of D'Aubigny had altered her position. She had vainly sought to save her old ally by declaring that Mary Stuart's life should answer for his safety. Indeed, after Morton's execution, she was on the point, partly from anger, and partly from policy, of getting rid of her prisoner by a condemnation, the expediency and advantages of which were discussed by her Council.[2] But she did not venture to carry out her wishes, and turned her attention to other plans.

In order to extricate herself from the difficult position in which she believed herself placed, and to resist the hostilities which she apprehended, she carefully fomented disunion between the Courts of France and Spain; encouraged to the highest pitch the ambition of the Duke of Alençon, and openly facilitated his establishment in the Netherlands, where the insurgents had chosen him to be their leader. She granted him large sums of

[1] Tytler, vol. vi., p. 317.
[2] Lingard, vol. viii., pp. 158, 159. Chalmers, vol. i., p. 383.

money to aid his undertakings, and allowed Lord Howard, the Earls of Leicester and Hunsdon, and many others of her nobility, to accompany him in English ships of war. In order to attach him more strongly to her interests, and to gain over Catherine de Medici, his mother, by the attractions of the throne of England, she carried the negotiation of her marriage to the Duke of Alençon much further than she had allowed her propositions of the same nature to the Duke of Anjou, in 1571, and to Charles IX, in 1565, to proceed. The conditions were agreed upon, the promises signed, and the presents exchanged. The Duke of Alençon saw Elizabeth on several occasions; she seemed pleased with his appearance, and, both in presence of her court and in their private interviews, she gave him proofs of the most ardent affection, and assurances of the most inflexible determination. All, however, was only a pretence of marriage, assumed for the purpose of effecting a rupture between the two great Catholic Courts of the Continent. Nor were these the only means employed by Elizabeth against the King of Spain; at the same time that she supported the Duke of Alençon in Flanders, she combined with Catherine de Medici in assisting Antonio de Crato to regain Portugal from Philip II., the rival claimant of the throne of that country.

Scotland was also the object of her surveillance and intrigues. She despatched Nicholas Arrington, a distinguished officer of the garrison of Berwick, to promote dissension between the Duke of Lennox and the Earl of Arran; but the two favourites had continued friends. Being then desirous to ascertain the secret intentions and thwart the hopes of Mary Stuart, she had sent Mr. Beal, the Secretary of the Council, and brother-in-law of Walsingham, to confer with the imprisoned Queen. He was entrusted with one of those deceptive negotiations which Elizabeth's policy so frequently employed to revive the patience of her prisoner, and lead her to abandon all other plans.[1] Mary Stuart did not conceal from him the plan for the association of herself and her son in the crown of Scotland, but she gave him no clue to the Catholic project, still pursued by the Duke of Guise, the King of Spain, the Pope, and the Duke of Lennox. But Elizabeth's government was already informed of its existence by means of intercepted letters. All that Mary Stuart gained from this negotiation, which was soon suspended without being entirely broken off, was a little more liberty, and a few new indulgences in her confinement.

[1] Labanoff, vol. v., pp. 274–293. Tytler, vol. vi., p. 350.

The English ambassador in Scotland, Sir Robert Bowes, unfolded to the Protestant lords and ministers the plan for associating Mary Stuart in the crown; and hinted that such a scheme would endanger their religion as well as their personal safety. They accordingly formed, by one of those bonds so customary in Scotland, a league for the overthrow of Lennox, the rejection of the Queen, and the maintenance of the Reformed religion. The Earls of Gowrie, Mar, Glencairn, Rothes, Argyle, Eglinton, and Montrose, Lords Lindsay and Boyd, the Master of Glammis, the Ministers Lawson, Lindsay, Hay, Leneton, Polwait, and Andrew Melvil, the leading spirits in the Presbyterian Church, entered into this confederation.[1]

It was evident that the conflict must soon commence. Lennox, proceeding with greater boldness than precaution in the course on which he had entered, contemplated the arrest of the confederated lords, and the banishment of the ministers and their accomplices, as having conspired against the authority of the King. But before he was able to effect his intention, the confederates were informed of his design by Sir Robert Bowes, who had learned it by some means, and had been directed by Walsingham to communicate it to his friends.[2] Bowes urged them to act at once, or they would be lost; they understood his meaning, and hastened their proceedings. The young King was enjoying the pastime of the chase in the neighbourhood of Perth, separated from Lennox, who was at Dalkeith, and from Arran, who was at Kenneil. The confederates embraced this opportunity for seizing his person, and removing him from his two favourites. The Earl of Gowrie invited him to his castle at Ruthven; and no sooner had he taken up his residence there, suspecting no such disloyal treason, than Mar, Lindsay, and Glammis collected a thousand men with all speed, surrounded the castle, disarmed the royal guards, and arrested the King himself. Notwithstanding his tears and entreaties, they kept him prisoner, and conveyed him to the strong fortress of Stirling. Arran hastened to his assistance, but he arrived too late to be of service. He was himself seized, and placed in close confinement. Lennox threw himself into Edinburgh, but was unable to maintain his position. He then retired to Dumbarton, and shortly afterwards withdrew into France, where he died not long after his arrival.[3]

Thus James VI., in 1582, fell into dpeendence upon the English party, just as Mary Stuart had fallen, in 1568. This

[1] Tytler, vol. vi., p. 317.   [2] Ibid. pp. 319, 320.
[3] Ibid., pp. 324–326.

unfortunate Princess, on learning that her son was a prisoner
and that Scotland was under the influence of her enemies, lost
once more both the means and the hope of obtaining deliverance.
Her sorrow was equalled only by Elizabeth's satisfaction. She
wrote to her fortunate rival a letter, which is remarkable for the
eloquent bitterness of her complaints, and the noble entreaties of
her despair.¹ In this letter she retraced the history of her connection with Elizabeth, and reminded her how her advances had
been met by acts of enmity, how the solemn promises which had
been made to her had been violated with mysterious perfidy,
how her reputation had been tarnished, her kingdom urged to
insurrection, her crown overthrown, her person held captive, her
health destroyed, and her son rendered the object of the same factious violence and oppressive treatment to which she had herself
fallen a victim. 'I cannot, Madam,' she exclaimed, 'suffer it any
longer; and, dying, I must discover the authors of my death.
The vilest criminals who are in your prisons, born under your
allegiance, are heard in their own justification, and their accusers
and accusation are always made known unto them. Why has
not the same order been observed with regard to me, a Sovereign
Queen, your nearest relation, and legitimate heir? I think
that that last-named quality has been hitherto the principal
reason on behalf of my enemies, and the cause of all their
calumnies, that, by keeping us two at variance, they may slip in
between us their own unjust pretensions. But, alas! they have
now little reason and less need to torment me further on this
account; for I protest to you on my honour that I now expect no
other kingdom than the kingdom of God, for the which I am
prepared, as the best end of all my past afflictions and adversities.'

With touching urgency she besought Elizabeth's favour on
behalf of her son, whose liberty was lost and safety menaced by
the machinations of her enemies; and she begged Elizabeth to
release her from captivity before she died. 'I entreat you,'
she wrote, 'for the honour of the grievous passion of our
Saviour and Redeemer, Jesus Christ—I beseech you once more
to permit me to withdraw out of this kingdom to some place of
rest, to seek some solace for my poor body, so worn out with
continual grief, and, with liberty of my conscience, to prepare
my soul for God, who daily summons me. Your imprisonment
of me without any right or just foundation has already destroyed
my body . . my soul only remains, which it is in your power to

---

¹ See Labanoff, vol. v., pp. 318–338.

captivate. Give me this contentment before I die, that, seeing all things well set at rest between us, my soul, delivered from my body, may not be constrained to pour out its complaints before God, for the wrong which you have suffered to be done me here below; but, on the contrary, in peace and concord with you, departing from this captivity, it may proceed to him, whom I beseech to inspire you with kind thoughts regarding my very just and more than reasonable complaints and grievances.'

Her entreaties were, however, as unsuccessful as her plots. Condemned to remain a prisoner, the unfortunate Queen justified herself without being believed, supplicated without being heard, and conspired without attaining her object. Her last plan, which had just been frustrated by a *coup-de-main*, was chimerical. That she might be associated with her son in the throne of Scotland, it was necessary that she should be set at liberty, either by the consent of Elizabeth, or by the employment of armed force. Elizabeth was now less disposed than ever to restore her to freedom, and the want of concord between France and Spain, whose rivalry daily became more virulent, rendered an invasion for her deliverance almost impracticable. Mary Stuart was reduced to dependence upon the feeble assistance of an infant King and his two inconsiderate favourites, who were incapable of reinstating upon the throne a Princess who had been unable to maintain herself in possession of it, and of rescuing from destruction a religion which it was found impossible to retain during the time of her dominion. The authors of this plan were therefore stopped upon the very threshold, before they could attempt anything for the restoration of the discarded religion and the dethroned Queen. An act of favour had raised them to power, a bold stroke overthrew them.

Revolutions multiplied in Scotland after the occurrence of the Raid of Ruthven. The King was utterly powerless to prevent them. He was hardly fifteen years of age. Precocious in mind and feeble in character, he resembled Mary Stuart in his intelligence, and Darnley in his pusillanimity. He had early acquired an extensive range of knowledge from his two learned preceptors, George Buchanan and Peter Young. At seven years of age he was able to translate the Bible extempore from Latin into French, and from French into English.[1] He had become a

---

[1] MS. letter, State Paper Office, Killegrew to Walsingham, 31st June, 1574; Tytler, vol. vi., pp. 221, 222.

practised theologian and a subtle reasoner. But he was irremediably weak, and his weakness was accompanied by precocious dissimulation. Even the troubles in which his youth was passed had shaken instead of strengthening his mind. Without authority or will of his own, addicted to fleeting fondness for temporary favourites, he was incapable of punishing, and frequently even of regretting. He did not love his mother, did not detest Elizabeth, and might, with equal facility, have been led to regard either with affection or aversion. Condemned by his position as well as by his character to be subject to foreign influence, attracted by the gold of Philip II., stimulated by the zeal of the Duke of Guise, affected by the entreaties of Mary Stuart, and overwhelmed by the intrigues of Elizabeth, he entered alternately into Catholic conspiracies and Protestant plots without seriously attaching himself to any party, or connecting himself in a lasting manner with any individual.

Meanwhile the captivity of the young monarch in the hands of the Gowrie faction, had not led to the abandonment of the project for invading England, restoring Catholicism, and liberating Mary Stuart. The Duke of Guise, who was to conduct the scheme in concert with Philip II. and the Pope, and by aid of their money, suddenly changed the direction of his designs. Instead of commencing his operations in Scotland, he determined at once to invade England. He was induced to take this step after the death of the Duke of Lennox and the return of Méneville, whom he had sent with a secret mission to Edinburgh, whither this confidant of his plots had accompanied Lamothe Fénelon, when he went to inform James VI. that his mother associated him with herself in the crown, and consented that he should receive the name, and exercise the authority of King.

'Hercules' (the Duke of Guise), wrote J. B. de Tassis to the King of Spain on the 4th of May, 1583, 'since the change which has occurred in the affairs of Scotland, has turned his eyes towards the Catholics of England, to see whether he might not commence his enterprise in that country. He has brought matters into so forward a state, that he thinks he will soon be able to put his plans into execution. He has resolved to march in person against the Queen of England, and he is confident of being sustained by his Holiness and by your Majesty. In order to engage in the enterprise with sufficient means, and to issue from it with success, he is desirous that his Holiness and your Majesty should, as soon as possible, place in his hands a hundred thousand crowns, that he may use them when it becomes needful."[1]

The Duke of Guise had a secret conference with the Spanish ambassador, on the subject, at the house of the Papal nuncio. He considered that the Catholic party in England was so powerful and so well prepared for action, that it would not be necessary to defer the expedition to a later period than the month of September. He said that, in order to prevent the King of France from feeling jealous, the expedition must not appear to be under the direction of the King of Spain, who would simply furnish arms and create a diversion in Ireland, whilst he, at the head of four thousand men, with his brother, the Duke of Mayenne, and his ally, the Duke of Bavaria (whom the Bishop of Ross, in 1578,[2] had gained over to the cause of Mary Stuart), with German troops and a band of English exiles from the Netherlands, would throw themselves on different points of England, where Dr. Allen had assured them a general insurrection would take place. Notwithstanding the inconveniences and dangers which would ensue from delay, Tassis proved that it would be impossible to do anything before the winter. The expedition was consequently deferred until the next year.[3]

Shortly afterwards, the Duke of Guise learned that the King of Scotland, according to a secret arrangement with Méneville, had cleverly regained his freedom by the aid of the Earls of Huntly, Crawford, Argyle, and Marshall, had thrown himself into the Castle of St. Andrew's, and had escaped from the yoke of the English faction. This occurred on the 27th of June, 1583. The young Prince had then recalled the Earl of Arran, and resumed the plans which had been suggested to him by the Duke of Lennox in favour of Mary Stuart. On the 19th of August he wrote to the Duke of Guise: 'The great affection and friendship which you do not cease to manifest to the Queen, my mother and liege lady, as well as to myself, which I have learned from your letters, and from those of the 13th August, in which my mother told me of the extreme confidence which she places in you, whose advice and counsels she desires me to

---

[1] 'Y de manera que pueda salir con lo que se pretende lessea que luego se provean aqui entra Su Sant^d y V. Mag^d cien mil escudosque esten à la mano, para que à la misma hora que sea menester, aya con que acudir à la necessitad.' Archives of Simancas, Francia, B. 54, No. 93.

[2] Intercepted despatches of the Bishop of Ross, September, 1578. British Museum, Caligula, C. v., fols. 104, 105, 106.

[3] Archives of Simancas, Francia, B. 54, No. 502.

follow, induce me to accept the overtures which have been made to me on your behalf. All that you have planned for the liberation of my mother and for the furtherance of our claims appears to me very good, and the means prepared seem to be suitable, provided that matters are adroitly conducted.' He begged him, in conclusion, to send into Scotland either Méneville or D'Entraigues, both of whom were his servants and agents.

On the 22nd of August, the Duke of Guise despatched Richard Melino to Rome, to inform the Pope of the progress of the enterprise and to request his assistance. In the instructions which he gave Melino, he explained the plan of the expedition, enumerated the forces which would be required to accomplish it, and stated the assistance which had been promised in England, and the names of those who would co-operate with him in that country. 'The Queen of Scots,' he said, 'having written, and the principal nobles of that kingdom having given information that everything is in a forward state of readiness, especially on the Scottish frontier, where the Spanish fleet is to disembark, it has been decided that it will be sufficient for his Catholic Majesty to supply four thousand soldiers, if he cannot find means to embark a greater number. But it is indispensable that this fleet should bring money enough to maintain an army of ten thousand men for some months, and also cuirasses, pikes, and arquebuses, sufficient to arm five thousand. As the preparations and dispositions of that kingdom are subject to great changes, and as the secret of affairs which pass through so many hands runs the risk of being discovered if any delay takes place; and further, as the King of Scotland has written that, unless he receives prompt assistance, it will be difficult for him to maintain himself in the liberty which he has miraculously regained (as he promised M. de Méneville that he would), being hard pressed by the Queen of England, who neglects no means of restoring her faction in Scotland: His Holiness will be besought, in the name of the Duke of Guise and of all the Catholics of this kingdom, liberally to grant a supply of money, which is the only thing we now need, and to furnish, for once, a sum proportionate to the greatness of the enterprise, and to rely upon the Duke of Guise for having it executed as soon as possible, and, if practicable, even this year."[1]

[1] 'Todo bien considerado, y aviendo escrito la reyna de Escocia y dado aviso los principales señores de aquel reyno que las cosas estan muy bien dispuestas principalmente ácia los confines de Escocia donde deve decender la armada de España, tandem se ha hecho resolucion que bastara que el rey catholico embiara armada de

He informed Gregory XIII. that the invading army would embark in Flanders, whence also reinforcements might afterwards be sent; and that it would descend upon the northern coast of England, where the Catholics would receive it joyfully. 'These,' he added, 'are so numerous, that in a few days twenty thousand of them will join the invading army on horseback, viz.: towards the Scottish frontier, three thousand from the Earl of Morton, and three thousand from the Baron of Fernyhirst, four thousand from Baron Dacre, a thousand from the Earl of Westmoreland, three thousand from the Earl of Northumberland, a thousand from the Earl of Cumberland, and two thousand from Baron Vorton (Wharton) and the new Bishop of Durham; all these lords are in the neighbourhood of Scotland, and of the port wherein the Spanish fleet will anchor. There are many others in the interior of the kingdom, such as the Earls of Rutland, Biethosburie (sic), Worcester, Aernden (sic), and Viscount Montague, who favour the enterprise; to facilitate the success of which his Holiness will be furthermore besought to renew the bull of Pius V. against the Queen of England, to declare that he has charged the Catholic King and the Duke of Guise to enforce it, to grant indulgences to all who engage in the expedition, and to appoint Dr. Allen, as Bishop of Durham, to act as his nuncio."[1]

Six days afterwards, the Duke of Guise secretly despatched into England, under the assumed name of Mopo, a refugee named Charles Paget, who, together with a Welshman named Thomas Morgan, was entrusted with the management of Mary Stuart's dower in France, and had taken a part in all the con-

---

quatro mil buenos soldados, si Su Mag[ad] no tubiere modo de embiar mayor armada. Pero es necessario que la dicha armada se trayga dinero para pagar diez mil soldados de aquellos partes por algunos meses, y coseletes, picas, ercabuzes, para armar cinco mil soldados de aquel reyno, y siendo las preparaciones y la disposicion de aquel reyno subjectas á muchas mutaciones, y aviendo aun peligro del secreto si las cosas van á la larga, passando estos negocios por tantos manos, y aviendo frescamente recebido nueva del rey de Escocia que si no es ayudado no podra mantener se en la libertad en la qual casi milagrosamente se ha puesto estas dias passadas segun havia prometido á Mons. de Meneville, haciendo la reyna de Inglaterra lo que puede por favorescer sa faccion en Escocia, sera supplicado Su Santidad en nombre de Hercules y de todos los catholicos de aquel reyno, pues que las cosas estan reduzidas en tal termino, que no es menester otra cosa que dinero, Su Santidad se digne de alargarse se un poco, y dar por una vez una suma de dineros proporcionada á la grandeza, dela impressa, y dexar todo el negocio al rey catholico y a Hercules para que esta empressa, se execute quanto antès, y si es possible este ano.' MS. Instruccion para Roma por los negocios de Inglaterra y Escocia... dada á 22 de agosto, 1583. Archives of Simancas, Francia, B. 54, No. 115.

[1] Archives of Simancas, Francia, B. 54, No. 115.

spiracies in her favour. Paget's mission was to the oppressed Catholics, to whom he was instructed to deliver this message:— 'Assure them, upon the faith and honour of Hercules (the Duke of Guise), that the enterprise has no other object than the establishment of the Catholic religion in England, and the peaceable restitution of the Crown of England to the Queen of Scotland, to whom that crown of right belongs.[1] As soon as this is done, all foreigners shall leave the kingdom, and if any refuse to do so, Hercules promises to join his forces to those of the inhabitants of the country in order to drive them out.'[2]

The Pope entered with ardour into a project which the Court of Rome had long desired to see accomplished, and pressed Philip II. to join in the enterprise without delay. Philip replied, by the mouth of the Count D'Olivares, his ambassador to the Holy See, that he would like nothing better; but that nothing was ready yet, and that the cold and dampness of England in the winter season would not allow of the encampment of an army.[3] Moreover, he assured Gregory XIII. that he intended immediately to transport to Flanders the soldiers who had returned from the conquest of the island of Terceira, in order to send four thousand of them into England, where the necessary arrangements had been made for a combined attack. And, as if the enterprise could not fail to succeed, he added, "that when once Elizabeth was overthrown, the whole island should be subjected to one Sovereign,[4] and that Sovereign should be a Catholic. For this purpose it was advisable that the young King should be converted from his errors by conferences with religious doctors; and that his mother should marry again; that fear of a rival heir to the crown of England might induce him to return to the bosom of the Church; or that, if he persisted in his heresy, God might remedy his wickedness by granting a Catholic successor to the Queen."[5] As he was the only person who could pay the

[1] 'Que por establescimiento de la fê y religiou Catholica en Inglaterra que para poner la Reyna de Escocia pacifica de la corona de Inglaterra, la qual de derecho le pertenezce.' Archives of Simancas, Francia, B. 54, No. 116.
[2] Instruccion para Inglaterra de 28 de Agosto de 1583. Ibid.
[3] 'Nota de Su Mag^d remitida al conde de Olivares en respuesta á la propuesta de Su Santidad sobre la empresa de Inglaterra.' Archives de Simancas, Roma, fol. 944. [4] 'Un señor de toda la isla.' Ibid.
[5] 'Serra tambien de mirar si se habian de poner los ojos en casar á la Reyna su madre y con quien, para que en este torcedor y nuedo de otro heredero hiciesse reducir al hijo por ne ser excluydo de la sucession de Inglaterra, o que cuando in aun esto bastasse, fuesse Dios servido remediarlo con dar sucesion Catholica de la Reyna.' Archives of Simancas, Roma, fol. 944.

expenses of the enterprise, Philip II. had placed a sum of money at the disposal of the conspirators, to enable them to commence their preparations.[1]

But this project, like those which had preceded it, was discovered. The vigilance of Elizabeth's ministers exceeded the activity of Philip's government. Every means that, on the one side, was called into play to destroy Protestantism in England was employed, on the other side, to render more irretrievable the ruin of Catholicism in that country. Opposing stratagem to stratagem, intrigue to intrigue, covert attack to projected invasion, and espionage to conspiracy, Elizabeth once more negotiated with Mary Stuart to deceive her into expectations of liberty, which were destined never to be realised; sent the artful Walsingham on a mission to James VI., to endeavour to bring over that young and feeble monarch to her interests; concerted with the Earls of Angus, Mar, and Gowrie, and the other fugitive Scottish lords, an expedition into Scotland to overthrow by armed force the recently-restored influence of the Earl of Arran; supported the insurgents in the United Provinces, by means of the Duke of Alençon, and sent Drake to ravage the settlements in the West Indies, in order to effect useful diversions in Philip II.'s own dominions; and finally, gained information by means of her agents, of the most secret designs of the Catholics against her. Walsingham had spies in every quarter. He had bought Cherelles,[2] the Secretary of the French ambassador, Castelnau de Mauvissière; gained Archibald Douglas, whom James VI. had accredited to Elizabeth, and who possessed Mary Stuart's confidence; and corrupted William Fowler, formerly a servant of the Countess Margaret of Lennox, and whose fidelity the distrustful captive already suspected.[3] By these men, Mary Stuart's correspondence and other secrets were made known to Elizabeth's minister.

It was by means of his spies, that—independently of a conspiracy against Elizabeth's person, attributed to two gentlemen named Arden and Somerville, and a priest named Hall, who were

---

[1] On the 24th of September in the previous year, he had ordered Tassis to give the Duke of Guise 10,000 crowns for distribution. Archives of Simancas, B.L., 66, No. 52.—On the 24th of January, 1583, he had directed him to pay 10,000 crowns to Lennox, who was then alive, and making arrangements for the deliverance of his master, James VI. Ibid., B. 54, No. 190.—Finally, about this time, had paid 20,000 crowns to the Duke of Guise, and 11,000 to the Archbishop of Glasgow, 'to be employed,' he said, 'in certain affairs which it is not convenient here particularly to mention.' Ibid., B. 54, Nos. 43, 45.

[2] Labanoff, vol. vi., pp. 19–27.   [3] Ibid., pp. 21, 22.

condemned to death in consequence—Walsingham became aware, towards the end of 1583, of the existence of the great Catholic plot for the invasion of England. He learned that Paget had come into the kingdom under an assumed name, that he had had interviews with the leading Catholics, and that he had concerted his plans with Sir Francis Throckmorton, son of John Throckmorton, the Chief Justice of Chester, who had been recently deprived of his office, by Leicester's influence. Walsingham had Sir Francis Throckmorton arrested immediately. He also placed Henry Percy, the new Earl of Northumberland, and his son, under restraint; cited the Earl of Arundel, with his wife, his uncle, and his brother, before the Privy Council; whilst Lord Paget and Charles Arundel, alarmed at this discovery, fled to the Continent. Sir Francis Throckmorton was put to the torture three times, but would make no avowal; the fourth time, however, he confessed all, declared that he had indicated the English ports where the invaders might land, and had given a list of the principal Catholics who were likely to join in the enterprise, and mentioned as those who had conceived the plan, and were entrusted with its execution, Philip II., the Ambassador Mendoza, and the Duke of Guise. Notwithstanding his subsequent disavowals, which he reiterated even upon the scaffold, Throckmorton suffered the punishment of a traitor.[1]

Elizabeth resolved to get rid of the Spanish envoy, whose residence in her dominions, and whose ambassadorial privileges, only aided him to conspire with greater security and boldness. Her diplomatic rupture with Philip II. occurred four years before she began open war with him. On the 18th of January, 1584, Mendoza was summoned to the house of the Chancellor of England, where he was met by Leicester, the Lord Chamberlain Howard, Hunsdon, and Walsingham.[2] The last of these addressed him in Italian, and told him 'that her Majesty the Queen was very ill-satisfied with him, because he had sought to disturb the kingdom; had put himself into communication with the Queen of Scotland, from whom he had received letters; had sought, in concert with the Duke of Guise, to deliver her from prison; and had even conspired with Sir Francis Throckmorton, with one of his brothers who had come from France, and with the Earl of Northumberland. Wherefore it was her Majesty's

---

[1] Camden, vol. ii., pp. 410–416. Lingard, vol. viii., p. 168.
[2] MS. despatch of Bernardino de Mendoza to the Catholic King, 24th January, 1584. Archives of Simancas, Inglaterra, fol. 839.

will that he should quit her kingdom within fifteen days."¹ Nothing disconcerted, Mendoza replied that these were idle dreams, that he could never have advised the Queen of Scots to do things which would have led to her ruin; that a man like himself did not treat of important affairs with an inconstant and imprudent young fellow like Throckmorton; that he had never spoken to the Earl of Northumberland, and that his actions had been very different from those which the English Queen and her Ministers had directed against the dominions of the King, his master. After having enumerated these acts of hostility, he added, that as it was not his custom to remain where he was regarded with displeasure, he would leave England after he had sent a courier with despatches to the Catholic King upon this subject.²

Elizabeth's Ministers then rose from their seats, and informed him that he must leave the country without delay, or he would expose himself to chastisement from the Queen.³ Mendoza proudly answered: 'That it belonged neither to the Queen of England nor to any other person in the world to judge of his conduct, for which he had to account to the King his master alone; that none of them, under existing circumstances, should dare to proceed further, unless it were sword in hand; that he laughed at the idea of the Queen's venturing to chastise him; that he would depart with great pleasure as soon as she sent him his passports; and that, though she had not been pleased with him as a minister of peace, he would endeavour to give her satisfaction as a minister of war.'⁴

The haughty Spaniard left them with these words, and took his departure from England on the 29th of January. On his arrival at Madrid, he explained all the affairs of Scotland to Philip II., who expressed complete satisfaction at his conduct,⁵

---

¹ 'A cuya causa era la voluntad de la Reyna, que dentro de 15 dias me partrese resolutamente de su reyno.' Archives of Simancas, Inglaterra, fol. 839.
² Ibid.
³ 'Replicaron levantandose de las sellas, que no, sino que haria de partirme luego . . . la Reyna no mamdase castigarme.' Ibid.
⁴ 'Que me encendió la colera diciendo que la Reyna no tenia de tratar dello ni ninguno del mundo, per ser solo V. Mag^d. á quien havia de dar cuenta; por lo cual no pasase adelante ninguno dellos en la materia sino fuese con la espada en la mano; que lo del castigarme la Reyna, era risa para mi, y excesivo contento el partirme al momento que me enviase pasaporte. . . . Pues no le havia dada satisfaccion siendo ministro del paz, me esforzana de aqui adelante para que la triviese de me en la guerra.' Ibid.
⁵ 'Y la respuesta que los distes, la qual fue la que convenia y me ha parescido muy bien, y que os haveis governado en la salida con le misma cordura y pecho que

and immediately placed twelve thousand crowns in the hands of Tassis, to be employed as Mary Stuart might direct. Philip II. soon made use again of so bold and stirring an ambassador, by sending him to the place where he could be most serviceable to his designs upon England and France.[1] After the death of the Duke of Alençon, which occurred at Chateau-Thierry, on the 10th of June, 1584, he sent him to express his condolence to Henry III., and Catherine de Medici,[2] and he soon afterwards accredited him to the French Court in the place of Tassis, who was appointed Inspector-General of the Army in Flanders. From Paris, where he excited the Guises and inspired the League, Mendoza's hatred and intrigues pursued Queen Elizabeth, who found in him an enemy as ardent as he was indefatigable.

At the same time that she expelled Mendoza, and frustrated the plot of Philip II. and the Duke of Guise, Elizabeth endeavoured to overthrow Mary Stuart's party in Scotland, by the aid of the exiled lords, who left their retreats to head an insurrection. The Earl of Gowrie repaired to Dundee. The Earls of Angus and Mar and the Master of Glammis entered Stirling, on the 22nd of April, with five hundred horse. But James VI. and the Earl of Arran gained information of their proceedings, and marched against them with an army of twelve thousand men. Gowrie was captured and beheaded. Angus, Mar, Glammis, and their adherents fled to England, and were declared guilty of high treason; while Arran, now more powerful than ever, governed both the King and the kingdom of Scotland with undisputed sway.[3]

Both parties had just been equally unsuccessful. The Catholic invasion of England had been discovered before it assumed a definite form; and the Protestant invasion of Scotland had been checked as soon as it was undertaken. Elizabeth then appeared disposed to enter upon another course of policy, in order to avoid the dangers by which she was threatened by the continued captivity of Mary Stuart and the implacable enmity of Arran. These dangers might become more serious in England, as she was deprived of the services of the Duke of Alençon, who died

---

en todo lo de mas que se offrescio durante vuestra estada en aquel reyno, de que quedo yo de vos con entera satisfacion y do vuestros buenos servicios de los quales mandare tener la quento y memoria que es razon.' Archives of Simancas, Francia, A. 56, No. 19.

[1] Archives of Simancas, Francia, Letter of the 1st May, A. 56, No 6.
[2] Archives of Simancas, Francia, A. 56, No. 17.
[3] Camden, vol. ii., p. 416. Tytler, vol. vi., pp. 376–386.

at Chateau-Thierry, on the 10th of June, 1584, and of the Prince of Orange, who was assassinated at Delft, on the 10th of July, by a fanatical emissary of the Jesuits. Delivered almost simultaneously from the leader of the ten Catholic provinces, and the Stadtholder of the seven Protestant provinces, Philip II., assisted by the military skill of the Prince of Parma, seemed about to regain possession of all the Netherlands, from whence he would easily be able to invade England. Elizabeth, under these alarming circumstances, momentarily entertained the idea of depriving the Catholic King of Mary Stuart's assistance and Arran's cooperation, by treating with them herself. In doing this she would have found no difficulty. Arran was too ambitious not to consent to anything that would strengthen his authority, and Mary Stuart was so weary of her confinement that her only desire was to regain her liberty.

In pursuance of a remarkable interview which took place at Foulden Kirk, near Berwick,[1] between the favourite of James VI., and the Earl of Hunsdon, an attempt was made to bring Scotland into closer alliance with England, and to reconcile Mary Stuart with Elizabeth by renewing the negotiations which had previously been suspended. The young Master of Gray was accredited to London as James the Sixth's ambassador, with this double mission. Concealing a most treacherous heart beneath a pleasing exterior, this young nobleman shared with Arran the affection of the King.[2] He was a Catholic, and had been brought up at the Court of France, treated as an intimate friend by the Guises, and admitted to the confidence of the Archbishop of Glasgow; he was acquainted with all Mary Stuart's plans, and had always professed the deepest attachment to that unhappy princess. The captive Queen, therefore, who sent her French Secretary Nau,[3] to London about this time, to treat of the conditions of her liberation,[4] thought she could rely upon the devoted service of the Master of Gray.[5] She seemed to have abandoned all her ambitious views. Her health was destroyed, her patience worn out, and her imagination clouded with melancholy. She had suffered much in her captivity. Outrageous reports had been spread abroad concerning her by the wife of the Earl of Shrewsbury, in whose custody she had so long been left by Elizabeth. The Countess of Shrewsbury had declared that she

[1] Tytler, vol. vi., p. 403.   [2] Ibid., pp. 408, 409.
[3] He had succeeded Raullet, who died in 1574. He had previously been secretary to the Cardinal of Lorraine.   [4] Labanoff, vol. vi., p. 57.
[5] Ibid., p. 28. Instructions by Mary Stuart to the Master of Gray, p. 48.

had formed a criminal intimacy with her husband, and was pregnant by him.

. Deeply wounded by this calumny,[1] which the Countess was compelled to retract,[2] the indignant princess complained of it with the most scornful bitterness. In order to cast suspicion on the Countess of Shrewsbury, she communicated to Elizabeth the dishonouring avowals which the Countess had made to her regarding the amours of the Queen of England. She thus avenged herself, with premeditated passion, upon both her enemies, by denouncing the one and wounding the pride of the other. 'I call my God to witness,' wrote Mary Stuart to Queen Elizabeth, 'that the Countess of Shrewsbury had told me what follows about you, nearly in the same words . . . first, that one man (the Earl of Leicester), to whom she said that you had promised marriage in presence of one of the ladies of your bed-chamber, had lain with you an infinite number of times, with all the license and privacy that can be used between husband and wife . . . that your marriage could not be accomplished, and that you would never lose your liberty to make love and have your pleasure always with new lovers; regretting, she said, that you did not content yourself with Master Hatton, and another of this kingdom; but that you had engaged your honour with a foreigner named Sumer, going to meet him by night in a lady's chamber, where you kissed him, and used divers dishonest privacies with him; . . . and that you had disported yourself with the same dissoluteness with the Duke D'Alençon, his master, who came to you one night to the door of your bedchamber, where you met him with only your shift and nightgown upon you, and that afterwards you allowed him to come in, and that he lay with you for three hours.'[3] This singular letter,—in which Mary related to Elizabeth all that the Countess of Shrewsbury had told her of the English Queen's excessive passion for the Vice-Chamberlain Hatton; of the extravagance of her vanity, which seemed to lead her to believe the fulsome compliment paid her, 'that it was impossible to look her full in the face, because her countenance shone like the sun;'[4] of the violence of her anger against the ladies of her suite, one of whom had had 'her finger broken,' and another had received, while serving her at table, 'a great cut from a knife upon her hand;'[5] and lastly, of a disgusting infirmity in her leg in consequence of an open

---

[1] Labanoff, vol. vi., pp. 37, 43.   [2] Ibid., p. 69.   [3] Ibid., pp. 51, 52.
[4] Ibid., p. 53.   [5] Ibid., p. 54.

wound ;[1]—this singular letter, very unlike to conciliate Elizabeth's good-will, probably never reached the hands of that Queen.[2]

The negotiation for the deliverance of the Scottish Queen, nevertheless, proceeded at London between Secretary Nau and the English ministers. In a paper presented to the latter by Nau, the conditions of her liberty were regulated nearly in the same manner as they had been at Wingfield in 1569, and at Chatsworth in 1570. It was added, that Mary Stuart should disavow the bull by which the Pope had deprived Elizabeth of her crown, in her favour; should have no communications with the subjects of that Queen to excite them to civil war under any religious or political pretext; should not sustain those who had already been guilty of rebellion, and convicted of treason; should not unite with foreign princes to disturb England, but, on the contrary, should defend that country with all her forces if it were attacked from abroad; should form an offensive and defensive alliance with Elizabeth; should give hostages for her conduct after leaving England; should make no religious innovations in Scotland, but merely demand liberty of worship for herself and her domestics; should grant a general amnesty for all the injuries which she had received; should obtain the pardon of the Scottish exiles if they consented to submit; and should arrange the marriage of the King her son, by the advice and with the consent of her good sister, the Queen of England.[3]

Whilst this negotiation was pending, Elizabeth had become more fully aware of the plots which had been formed against her in Europe. The Jesuit Creighton, and a Scottish priest named Abdy, had been captured by a Danish corsair, and delivered up to Walsingham. Their papers, which they had hastened to destroy, but the fragments of which had been put together again, and the confessions of Creighton when put to the torture, had fully revealed the projects of the Catholic party on the Continent, just as the avowals of Francis Throckmorton had made known the dispositions of the English Catholics. Protestant opinion was strongly excited; and the enemies of Elizabeth and of the reformed faith, whoever they might be, had been threatened with formidable reprisals. An association had been formed

---

[1] Labanoff, vol. vi., p. 55.
[2] Prince Labanoff, who saw the original of this letter among the Cecil papers, which places its authenticity beyond question, plausibly conjectures that Burghley never communicated it to Elizabeth.
[3] Labanoff, vol. vi., pp. 58-65. Articles presented by Nau on behalf of Mary Stuart.

2 B

throughout the kingdom, the members of which pledged themselves to pursue to the death not only all who should attempt the life of the Queen, but even the person in whose favour the attempt was made.¹

Meanwhile the English Parliament met, and, in the same spirit, passed two bills against Mary Stuart and the Catholics. The first of these bills, in case of the violent death of the Queen, deprived Mary Stuart and her descendants of all right to the succession of the crown, and authorised the associators to pursue to the death any person who had been pronounced privy to the treason, by a court of twenty-four commissioners. The second enacted the penalties of high treason against any English Catholic priest, ordained by the Bishop of Rome, who was found in the realm after the expiration of forty days; attainted with felony all persons who should receive or assist him; punished with fine and imprisonment, at the Queen's pleasure, all who knew of his being in the kingdom, and did not denounce him within twelve days; ordered that all students in Catholic seminaries abroad, who did not return to England within six months after proclamation to that effect, should be punished as traitors; that parents sending their children abroad without licence, should forfeit for every such offence one hundred pounds; and that children so sent to seminaries should be disabled from inheriting the property of their parents.

These measures alarmed the Queen of Scots, who saw in them the prelude to her death-warrant. On the 25th of August, 1584, she had passed from the custody of the Earl of Shrewsbury to that of Sir Ralph Sadler and Lord Somers, and had been transferred from Sheffield to Wingfield Castle. When the act of association was communicated to her, she proposed to affix her name to it, which was declined; but she alone signed an analogous declaration. Having learned that the Master of Gray was beginning to dissever her interests from those of her son, she wrote to him to take care what he was about, or he would throw doubt upon the kingly title which her son held from her, and that she intended ' to leave him all the government, only reserving to herself the authority due to a mother, as her misfortunes and cares had made her lose all taste for the rest.'² At this time, she desired nothing but repose. On the 5th of January, 1585, she wrote to the Archbishop of Glasgow, to say that she wished

¹ Camden, vol. ii., p. 418.   Lingard, vol. viii., p. 172.
² Labanoff, vol. vi., p. 71.

to leave to her son 'the administration of the estate and affairs of the country of Scotland.'[1] Peace for Elizabeth, power for James VI., and liberty for herself—these were, at this time, the last wishes of the much-deceived prisoner.

She was, alas! again deceived. A few days afterwards, the negotiations ceased, her moderate hopes vanished, the Master of Gray betrayed her, her son abandoned her, and the Queen of England transferred her from Wingfield to the gloomy fortress of Tutbury. What was the cause of this sudden change, and of this, as it proved, irretrievable rupture? The discovery of a new conspiracy against the life of Elizabeth, and the union of the Catholic Continent against the Protestant cause. A Welshman named William Parry, a secret agent of Walsingham, and who had visited the English and Scotch refugees in Italy and France, solicited another of Walsingham's agents, named Neville, to assassinate Elizabeth. Was Parry anxious to ruin Neville, and gain a reward by denouncing him; or did he really intend to use him to murder the Queen of England, as he pretended to have been urged to do so by Pope Gregory XIII., the nuncio Raggazoni, and Cardinal Corno, the Roman Secretary of State, to whom he had been introduced by that indefatigable conspirator, his countryman Thomas Morgan? It is difficult to explain this matter. Although Parry pleaded his equivocal services, he suffered the terrible punishment of traitors, and was disembowelled while still alive. Alarmed at this succession of plots,[2] and dreading the fate which the Prince of Orange had recently met with, Elizabeth looked with more anxious eyes upon the designs of the Catholic party against her person, crown, and cause, and felt that it had become necessary to act against them with greater vigour and foresight. The moment had, moreover, become a crisis in her history.

The death of the Duke of Alençon had caused Catholicism to pass into a new phase in France, and had led the way for the triumph of religion over royalty. Until that time, the presumptive heir to the crown had been a Catholic. Now, for the first time, the two principles upon which the possession of the old French royalty had, from its origin, rested—the political principle of male primogeniture, and the religious principle of Catholic orthodoxy,—did not combine in the same person, as the King of Navarre was heir to the throne by birth, and a Calvinist in

---

[1] Labanoff, vol. vi., pp. 78, 79, 82, 83.
[2] She demanded the extradition of Morgan from Henry III., but Henry would only consent to imprison him in the Bastille.

creed. In the conflict which inevitably arose between the two principles, the rule of faith prevailed over the rule of politics. The ardent Catholics, led by the princes of the House of Lorraine, and stimulated and subsidized by Philip II., reversed the order of primogeniture, and recognized the Cardinal of Bourbon as the successor of Henry III. The League was formed. The Duke of Guise and the Cardinal of Bourbon secretly confederated with the King of Spain, who granted them three hundred thousand gold crowns,[1] raised the standard of civil war at Rheims, and compelled Henry III., by the treaty of Nemours, to revoke his edict of toleration, and to commence a war of extermination against the Protestants. At the same time, the new Pope, Sixtus V., excommunicated the King of Navarre and the Prince of Candé. The Pope, the King of Spain, the Duke of Savoy, ond the French Leaguers, who had been joined by Henry III., agreed to attack Geneva, which was the centre of Protestantism, to subjugate the Calvinists of the Netherlands, and to annihilate the Huguenots of France; while they entertained more seriously than ever the idea of making use of Mary Stuart against the Presbyterians and Anglicans of Great Britain.

Whilst Philip II. thus proved himself the active and threatening head of Catholicism, Elizabeth did not hesitate to unite the forces and direct the resistance of Protestantism in Europe. On the 10th of August, 1585, she formed a treaty of alliance with the Netherlands, and engaged to furnish the States-General with six thousand men, under the command of Leicester. She formed a still closer connection with the King of Navarre; and overthrew the dominion of Arran in Scotland by the aid of the Earls of Angus and Mar, and of Lord Arbroath, the head of the Hamilton family, who, reconciled to the King by her good offices, and supported by her money, returned to Scotland at the head of eight thousand men, and easily made themselves the masters of the kingdom, and the councillors of the King.[2] This revolution, in consequence of which all the banished Presbyterian ministers returned to Scotland, restored Protestantism in that country in all its force, and prepared the way for the treaty of offensive and defensive alliance, which was signed, on the 1st of April, 1586, between James VI. and Elizabeth, to join their forces to repel all attempts to invade the island. At the same time that she thus provided for the defence of the Protestant cause in the Nether-

[1] The receipt, signed by the Cardinals of Bourbon and Guise, and by the Duke, in the Archives of Simancas, Francia, B. 66, No 39.
[2] Tytler, vol. vi., pp. 441–453.

lands, France, England, and Scotland, Elizabeth placed Mary Stuart under stricter surveillance. Her ministers went even further than this. They considered that the life of this formidable prisoner, whom the Catholics still aspired to make their queen, was incompatible with the safety of their own sovereign; and they regarded her pretensions to the British crown as dangerous to the safety of the kingdom, and subversive of the true religion: they therefore anxiously sought means to get rid of her.

CHAPTER X.

FROM THE FORMATION OF THE PROTESTANT LEAGUE TO THE FRUSTRATION OF BABINGTON'S CONSPIRACY.

Severity of Mary Stuart's treatment—Her complaints against her son—Her residence at Tutbury and Chartley—New schemes of the Catholic party on the Continent—Projected assassination of Elizabeth—Babington enters into the conspiracy—Mary Stuart's ignorance of the plan for Elizabeth's murder—Walsingham's efforts to involve Mary Stuart—Proceedings of Philip II.—Letters of Babington to Mary—They are communicated to Walsingham—Arrest of Babington and his friends—Mary is transferred to Texall—Trial and execution of Babington and his accomplices—Mary Stuart's death is resolved upon.

AFTER the discovery of all these conspiracies, Mary Stuart was subjected to harsher captivity by the alarmed and irritated government of Elizabeth. Removed from the gentle and kindly guardianship of the Earl of Shrewsbury, with whom she had spent nearly fifteen years, she was placed under the somewhat severe surveillance of Sir Ralph Sadler and Somers, and transferred, in midwinter, on the 13th of January, 1585, from Wingfield to Tutbury Castle, a ruinous and desolate place. She was domiciled here less conveniently than in any of the residences in which her long captivity had hitherto been spent. There was no stable in connection with the castle, and the sixteen horses which constituted her stud, were left behind at Sheffield.[1] 'Without them,' she wrote to Burghley, 'I am more a prisoner than ever.'[2] Her legs were so enfeebled by rheumatism and inactivity, that she was unable to take the least walking exercise in the open air.[3] Tutbury was situated in Staffordshire, on an

---

[1] Labanoff, vol. vi., pp. 91, 99, 104, 116.   [2] Ibid., vol. vi., p. 91.
[3] Ibid., vol. vi., pp. 91, 93. 'Sans cela je ne puis aller à pied, cinquante pas ensemble.' Letter to Mauvissière, 6th September. ' J'aye enfin perdu les jambes et la force et santé du reste du corps." Pp. 221, 222.

eminence, in the midst of an extensive plain; it was exposed on all sides to the winds; its walls were full of cracks and crevices; it was damp, cold, unhealthy, and ill-furnished;[1] and was by no means a fit residence for herself and her servants, now considerably reduced in number.[2]

She was, therefore, continually ill.[3] To the inconveniences of the place were added the severities of captivity, when, at the beginning of May, 1585, she passed from the custody of Sadler and Somers to that of Amias Paulet. This man had for some time been the English ambassador at Paris. He was a rigid Puritan, attached to Leicester, and devoted to Elizabeth; he detested the Catholics, and was incapable of showing the least condescension or commiseration for his prisoner. Mary Stuart was not allowed to walk out, unless he could accompany her, with an escort of eighteen men, fully armed.[4] He would not even suffer her to send the least alms to the poor of the village which lay beneath the castle, and Mary Stuart bitterly deplored her hard fate in being refused this Christian consolation; 'there being,' she wrote, 'no criminal so poor, vile, and abject, to whom she should ever be, by any law, denied.'[5] A report having been spread that she had attempted to escape, Paulet wrote to assure the Lord Treasurer of her safe custody, in these terrible words: 'Mary cannot escape without great negligence on my part. If I should be violently attacked, I will be so assured, by the grace of God, that she shall die before me."[6]

Under so inflexible a keeper, Mary was unable to maintain any secret correspondence. All the despatches in cypher which were addressed to her from France remained in the hands of Henry the Third's ambassador, Castelnau de Mauvissière, and after his departure, in those of his successor, L'Aubespine de Chateauneuf, who arrived in London towards the end of August, 1585. She was more unhappy than ever as a prisoner, utterly devoid of hope as a Queen, and in a state of poignant grief as a mother. Her son, under the influence of the Master of Gray, had, about this period, refused to acquiesce in the act of association, which her secretary,

[1] Labanoff, vol. vi., pp. 90, 166, 181. [2] Ibid., p. 93. [3] Ibid., pp. 198, 237.
[4] 'Je ne serois point marrie de changer d'hoste, car celui-cy est un des plus bizarres et farousches que j'ay jamais cogneu, et, en un mot, plus propre pour une geole de criminels que pour la garde d'une de mon rang et qualité. Mary Stuart to Chateauneuf, 13th July, 1586. Labanoff, vol. vi., pp. 369, 370.
[5] Labanoff, vol. vi., pp. 172, 173.
[6] MS. letter, State Paper Office, Sir Amias Paulet to Lord Burghley, 12th June 1585. Labanoff, vol. vi., p. 176.

Nau, had gone to London to negotiate, and was instructed subsequently to bind Scotland to England by a treaty of alliance. His conduct had filled her with violent anger and great discouragement. Her letters abound with indignant expressions and threats against the behaviour of her son, whom she called unnatural, ungrateful, disobedient, and ill-governed.[1] 'I will disown him as my son,' she said, 'and will give him my curse, disinheriting him not only of what he now holds, but also of all to which he may lay claim, through me, elsewhere.'[2] She desired that the Scotch would treat him as they had been induced to treat her, and that foreigners would invade his dominions, which she would willingly grant to them. 'I do not doubt,' she added, 'that in Christendom I shall be able to find plenty of heirs with nails strong enough to hold what I will put into their hands; and afterwards they may do with my body what they wish; the shortest road will be the most agreeable to me.'[3]

She declared, moreover, that she wished to come to an understanding with her son, only that she might regularly transfer to him the government of Scotland, without even desiring to set foot again in her former kingdom.[4] She simply requested emancipation from the 'servitude' in which she had been so long detained, and permission to leave the island where she had suffered so much, after having abandoned all her rights to the throne.[5] She expressed her willingness to accept any conditions, in order 'to give her afflicted soul and body some repose' before her death, which she knew was at hand.[6] But she clearly perceived that her enemies would restore her to liberty at no price, and she remarked, with equal perspicacity and grief, 'The old excuses of bygone times are alleged for my detention; now a change in Scotland, now a disturbance in France, now the discovery of a conspiracy in this country, and, in fine, the least innovation that may occur in any part of Christendom; so that it is likely I shall be liberated, as children say, when all the world is at peace and quietness. May God in his omnipotence be my aid and protection; and may he in his justice judge my cause between me and my enemies, as I hope he will do sooner or later.'[7] After a

---

[1] Labanoff, vol. vi. pp. 125, 126, 131.
[2] Mary Stuart to Elizabeth, 23rd May, 1585. Labanoff, vol. vi. p. 137.
[3] Ibid., p. 136.   [4] Ibid., p. 144.   [5] Ibid., pp. 133, 134.   [6] Ibid., p. 162.
[7] Ibid., pp. 182, 183. It was probably at this time that she composed these mournful lines:—

'Que suis-je, hélas! et de quoy sert ma vie?
Je ne suis fors qu'un corps privé de cueur,

year's residence at Tutbury, she was removed, towards the end of December, 1585, to Chartley in Staffordshire, where, though more conveniently accommodated, she was no less strictly watched.

But though she was now unable to conspire, her party was more active than ever in conspiracies on her behalf. Plots naturally multiplied amidst the extraordinary circumstances under which the two great causes of Protestantism and Catholicism in Europe were striving for the sway in France, the Netherlands, England, and Scotland. The English refugees, desirous to return to their native land, and the proscribed priests, anxious to effect the religious conquest of the country, thought the opportunity was favourable for dethroning Elizabeth and restoring Mary Stuart. Philip II., who had them all in his pay—for he gave two thousand golden crowns every year to Dr. Allen, the rector of the Seminary at Reims,[1] a hundred crowns per month to the Earl of Westmoreland,[2] a similar sum to Lord Paget,[3] eighty crowns to Charles Arundel,[4] other pensions to Charles Paget and Thomas Throckmorton,[5] and forty crowns per month to Morgan,[6] even during his confinement in the Bastille—encouraged their designs against Elizabeth, whilst he resumed with the Duke of Guise their former project of an expedition against England. The assassination of the Queen was now to be combined with the invasion of her kingdom.

The first man who undertook to commit this crime was an English Catholic, named John Savage, who had served as an officer

---

Un ombre vain, un objet de malheur,
Qui n'a plus rien que de mourir envie.
Plus ne portez, o ennemis, d'auvie
A qui n'a plus l'esprit à la grandeur !
La consommé d'excessive doulleur ;
Votre ire en brief se voirra assouvie ;
Et vous amys, qui m'avez tenu chère,
Souvenez-vous que sans heur, sans santay,
Je ne sçaurois auqun bon œuvre fayre,
Souhatez donc fin de calamitay ;
Et que sa bas estant assez punie,
J'aye ma part en la joye infinie.'

These lines, in Mary Stuart's handwriting, were found among her papers during her captivity, and deposited in the State Paper Office. They were inserted by Mr. Malcolm Laing, in the Appendix to the second volume of his History of Scotland. [1] Archives of Simancas, B. 66, No. 15. [2] Ibid., A. 56, No. 56.
[3] Ibid. [4] Ibid., B. 57, No. 309.
[5] Ibid., A. 56, No. 56; and B. 56, No. 57.
[6] Ibid. F. 53, No. 56, and A. 56, No. 53/77.

in the Spanish army under the Prince of Parma.[1] Happening to pass through Reims, he visited his fellow-countrymen and co-religionists of the Seminary; and mentioned his services in the presence of a priest named Hodgson and Dr. William Gifford. Gifford insinuated to him that he might render their cause a much greater service by killing the English Queen. Savage at first alleged sundry scruples, and objected the difficulties which lay in the way of the accomplishment of such a design. Gifford combated his scruples, saying that the death of an heretical Princess who was excommunicated by the Pope as an enemy to religion, would be a legitimate and meritorious act, and that he could do nothing which would be more useful to his country, or more likely to smooth his path to heaven. Other doctors of the Seminary urged the same considerations upon him; and at the end of three weeks Savage was persuaded and undertook to assassinate the Queen. It was agreed that he should strike her with his poniard, or shoot her with his pistol, either when she was going to her chapel through a gallery in which Savage would station himself, or when she was walking in her garden, or when she was taking the air accompanied by her women only.[2] Savage, whose promise was made known to Charles Paget and to Morgan, repaired to England in order to execute his design.

About the same time another plot of the same nature was formed. A priest named John Ballard, after having traversed England in every direction, under different disguises, for five or six years, and having confirmed the Catholics in the principles of their faith, and in their hatred of Elizabeth, returned to France in Lent, 1586.[3] He had had a conference with Charles Paget, Morgan, and Mendoza, regarding the invasion of England, and the means of delivering the Queen of Scots. At this conference Charles Paget had maintained that no enterprise could succeed so long as Elizabeth was alive.[4] Ballard, aware of Savage's intention, returned to England under the name of Captain Fortescue to devise means for attaining the object to which the Catholic party so ardently aspired. He arrived in London on the 22nd of May, and, four or five days after, he met a young gentleman named Anthony Babington,[5] of Dethick, in Derbyshire.

Babington was of good family, possessed a handsome fortune, and was endowed with considerable intelligence and a good edu-

---

[1] Howell's State Trials, vol. i., p. 1130. [2] Ibid., pp. 1130, 1131.
[3] Carte, vol. iii., p. 600. [4] Hardwicke's State Papers, vol. i., pp. 225, 226.
[5] Ibid., p. 226.

cation. He was strongly attached to the Romish faith,[1] and was intimately connected with the most dashing young men in London and the counties.[2] Four years previously, when at Paris, Babington had made the acquaintance of Thomas Morgan, who introduced him to the Archbishop of Glasgow; and he had allowed himself to be gained over to the cause of the Queen of Scots,[3] and had become her devoted partisan and chivalrous servant. After his return to London he had acted for two years as the intermediary for the correspondence of Mary Stuart, the Archbishop of Glasgow, Paget, and Morgan.[4] But since Mary's removal from the custody of the Earl of Shrewsbury, the correspondence had been broken off, and Babington's communications with the refugees at Paris, and with the prisoner at Tutbury and Chartley, had ceased. When Ballard met him he was in a state of great despondency, quite ready to leave England, and to retire to some Catholic country on the Continent for the remainder of his life.[5]

The emissary of the conspirators had no difficulty in rekindling Babington's devotion to Mary Stuart. He held, however, the same opinion as Charles Paget, and considered an invasion impracticable during Elizabeth's lifetime. Ballard then informed him that the Queen's assassination would precede the invasion of the kingdom, and he entered enthusiastically into the enterprise. But he declared that it was too important to be confided to a single person, and proposed to associate with Savage five of his friends.[6] These were Patrick Barnwell, sprung from a noble family in Ireland; John Charnock, of Lancashire; Edward Abington, whose father had been treasurer of the palace; Charles Tilney, one of the Queen's gentlemen-pensioners, whom Ballard had recently converted to the Romish faith; and Chidioc Tichbourne, whose devoted friendship led him to engage in all Babington's plans.[7] Several other friends of Babington, such as Edward, the brother of Lord Windsor; Thomas Salisbury, of an excellent family in Derbyshire; Robert Gage, of Surrey;

---

[1] Camden, vol. ii., p. 474. Carte, vol. iii., p. 600. Mendoza thus mentions him to Philip II.: 'Babington, moço muy Catolico de grande espiritu y de buena casa.' Archives of Simancas, B. 57, No. 66.
[2] Howell's State Trials, vol. i., p. 1157.
[3] Hardwicke's State Papers, vol. i., p. 227.   [4] Ibid.
[5] Letter from Babington to Mary Stuart, 6th July, 1586. Nat. Lib., Paris, MSS., Supp. French, $^{30}_{10}$, p. 68.
[6] Hardwicke's State Papers, vol. i., pp. 227–229. Camden, vol. ii., p. 475. Carte, vol. iii., p. 600.   [7] Camden, vol ii., p. 477.

John Travers, of Lancashire; John Thomas, the son of an officer of the late Queen Mary's wardrobe; and Henry Donne, entered into the conspiracy,[1] and met frequently, either at St. Giles's, near London, or in London itself, to make arrangements for its execution.[2]

None of their intrigues were unknown to Walsingham. That active and artful Minister fixed his eyes incessantly upon the Catholic party, and carefully watched all their movements. He had not merely gained over several of Mary's former confidants; he was not satisfied with having bribed Cherelles, the secretary of the French embassy, to furnish him with the cyphers and secret correspondence of the captive Queen, but he had organized a most extensive system of espionage. He had surrounded the principal conspirators with agents, who revealed to him all their actions; but whose apparent zeal for the cause of Catholicism and of Mary Stuart placed them above suspicion. Some of his spies belonged to families labouring under the severest persecution; and several members of the Seminary at Reims were in his pay. One of his agents, named Maud, had never left Ballard in all his journeys; and another, named Poley, who had frequently brought letters from the Continent, had insinuated himself into Babington's confidence, and regularly attended the meetings of the conspirators.[3] To this formidable network of espionage, Walsingham added the art of intercepting correspondence without giving the least grounds for suspicion. He kept two men for this especial service; one of them, Arthur Gregory, was an adept in opening letters, and the other, Phelipps, was equally skilful in decyphering them.[4]

By the aid of these miserable instruments he prepared the death of Mary Stuart. In common with Elizabeth's chief ministers, and the alarmed supporters of the reformed faith, he considered that the life of the Catholic Queen was fraught with continual danger to the Protestant Sovereign. But if, as was held by both Burghley and himself, Mary Stuart could not be kept a prisoner without peril, it was equally impossible to destroy her without a motive. State policy was not a sufficient excuse; there must be an appearance of justice in her condemnation. In order to obtain this end, Walsingham laboured to involve the

---

[1] Camden, vol. ii., pp. 476, 477. Carte, vol. iii., p. 601.
[2] Howell's State Trials, vol. i., pp. 1132–1135.
[3] Carte, vol. iii., p. 601. Babington, in a letter to Nau regarding Poley, said: 'Je suis forte privé avec lui.' Nat. Lib., Paris, MSS. Supp. French, No. $\frac{3003}{10}$, p. 68.   [4] Tytler, vol. vi., p. 23.

unfortunate prisoner in the plots which had been framed for her release. His principal instrument in communicating them to her, and gaining her sanction to them was a young Catholic priest, belonging to a noble family in Staffordshire. The name of this perverse and perfidious young man was Gilbert Gifford. His father was a prisoner in London on account of his religious opinions; and Gilbert himself had left England at the age of twelve, had been brought up in France by the Jesuits, and had been admitted into holy orders at the Seminary of Reims. Possessing the entire confidence of his masters, well acquainted with the languages of the different foreign countries which he had visited,[2] and affecting the most untiring devotion to the cause of Mary Stuart, he offered himself as an active, intelligent, and trustworthy intermediary between the refugees on the Continent and the English Catholics; and he proposed to renew the interrupted correspondence of the royal captive with her agents at Paris, Madrid, Rome, Brussels, and London. He had no difficulty in gaining the confidence of Morgan, Charles Paget, and the Archbishop of Glasgow. His youth[3] and religion led them to believe in his sincerity; and it was difficult to suppose that beneath his outward affectation of zealous devotedness, the most horrible treachery lay concealed.

His first connection with Morgan and Paget at Paris commenced during the summer of 1585,[4] eight months before the conspiracy was formed, and more than a year before it was discovered. During the months of June and July, Morgan mentioned Gifford and Poley, in his letters to Mary Stuart, as two servants on whose fidelity she might safely depend. Gilbert Gifford did not proceed to England until the end of December.[5] A correspondence was to be carried on with him under the assumed names of Pietro, Barnaby, and Nicholas Cornelius;[6] but whilst he took these precautions, for the purpose, as it were, of deceiving the vigilance of the English, he was an inmate in the house of Phelipps, the chief of Walsingham's secret agents.[7] He waited upon the French ambassador, Chateauneuf, with letters

[1] Labanoff, vol. vi., p. 213. See also the Memoir of the French ambassador Chateauneuf upon Babington's conspiracy. Ibid., pp. 274–293.
[2] Chateauneuf's Memoir, in Labanoff, vol. vi., p. 279.
[3] 'Il était fort jeune, et n'avait quasi point de barbe.' Labanoff, vol. vi., p. 282. [4] Ibid., p. 213.
[5] Chateauneuf's Memoir, in Labanoff, vol. vi., p. 281.
[6] Ibid., p. 282, and *passim* in the letters of Morgan and Mary Stuart, in 1586; also Tytler, vol. viii., p. 23. [7] Labanoff, vol. vi., p. 282.

from Paget, Morgan, and the Archbishop of Glasgow,[1] and told him that he had been sent to England by the servants of the Queen of Scots, in order to convey to her some secret despatches, which he would probably succeed in doing, as the castle in which the Queen was confined was in the neighbourhood of his father's house. He added, that after he had thus informed her of what was going on in France, means might be concerted with her for her deliverance from captivity. Chateauneuf received him rather coldly, fearing that he might be a spy, and advised him, if he really was what he assumed to be, he must be on his guard against discovery and imprisonment.[2]

Gifford spent the whole of January in making acquaintance with the Catholic party in London. He corresponded with Morgan, informing him of the progress of his intrigues by means of the French embassy, whither also Morgan's answers were forwarded to the address of Nicholas Cornelius.[3] After Mary Stuart's transference to Chartley, close by the house of Gifford's father, he applied to Chateauneuf for a letter to the Queen of Scots. Chateauneuf, still distrustful, gave him one of very little importance, which he wrote in cypher, as though it were of the highest interest. To his great surprise, on the 1st of March, 1586, Gilbert Gifford returned from Staffordshire, with Mary Stuart's answer, in an entirely new cypher, which she requested him to use in future for their secret correspondence; she enclosed a packet of letters to be transmitted to the Archbishop of Glasgow; and begged Chateauneuf to place entire confidence in Gifford, who would, henceforward, distribute her letters and orders to her partisans in England, and her servants on the Continent.

Mary Stuart thus entered upon the fatal course to which she had been prompted with so much perfidy. A few weeks before, she was much more circumspect; for, on the 17th of January, when answering one of Morgan's letters which Amias Paulet had allowed to reach her hands, she had said: 'I pray you continue to keep yourself from meddling in anything that may redound to your hurt, and increase the suspicion already conceived of you in these parts. At present I will not write more, as I fear the danger of sudden discovery. My keeper has settled such an exact and rigorous order in all places where any of my people can go, that it is very strange if they receive or deliver anything which he is not able to know very soon after.'[4] Alas! that she

[1] Labanoff, vol. vi., p. 279.   [2] Ibid., pp. 281, 282.   [3] Ibid., p. 282.
[4] Ibid., p. 254.

did not continue in this prudent resolution! As soon as she perceived a possibility of resuming her correspondence and renewing her plots, an ardent longing for liberty filled her mind, and she unhesitatingly followed the deceptive glimmering of hope which was offered to her by her enemies, in order that they might at last bring her to the scaffold.

But how did Gilbert Gifford succeed in making her believe that the letters which he had transmitted to her, had reached her unknown to Sir Amias Paulet, whose surveillance was so strict, who guarded Chartley Castle day and night with fifty armed men, who escorted her in her walks by eighteen soldiers, and who allowed none of her servants to go out unaccompanied and unwatched?[1] This was his method of operation.

Gifford never entered the castle, and did not once see Mary Stuart, for fear of incurring suspicion by obtaining too much facility. But he appears to have bribed the brewer, who supplied Mary's household with beer. The beer was brought weekly in a barrel, in which Gifford placed a small wooden box containing the packets of letters. Mary Stuart's butler took out the box and gave it to her secretary, Nau, who returned it to him with the Queen's answers to be replaced in the empty barrel which the carter took back to the brewer,[2] who went by the name of the 'honest man,' in their secret correspondence.[3] Some Catholic gentlemen of the neighbourhood, according to the explanation given by Gifford to Chateauneuf, received the packets of letters from the brewer, and forwarded them to the embassy by trusty messengers, under various disguises. Such was the arrangement by which Gifford satisfied Mary Stuart, and which he conducted in concert with Amias Paulet and Walsingham. The former took no notice of what entered or left the castle; and the other, to whom the despatches were communicated before they were taken to the embassy, or placed in the box, had them decyphered by Phelipps, and sealed up again by Gregory; they were then forwarded at once to the persons to whom they were addressed,[4] and no one suspected that they had been either intercepted or copied.

Mary Stuart was at first unaware of the plot against Elizabeth's life. Morgan seemed particularly careful to keep it from her

[1] Labanoff, vol. vi., p. 300.
[2] Chateauneuf's Memoir, Labanoff, vol. vi., pp. 284, 285.
[3] MS. letter, State Paper Office; Paulet to Walsingham, 29th June, 1586. Tytler, vol. vi., p. 40, note.
[4] Chateauneuf's Memoirs, Labanoff, vol. vi., pp. 284, 285.

knowledge. He had forbidden Ballard to seek to communicate with her. At the same time, he had informed her that an agent of that name was in England, labouring in her cause. 'He followeth some matters of consequence there,' he wrote, 'the issue whereof is uncertain. As long as these labours of his be in hand, it is not for your Majesty's service to hold any entelligence with him at all.' In order, however, to give Mary an inkling of Ballard's business, he added: 'The affairs that he and others have in hand, which tend to do good, I pray God may come to pass, and so shall your Majesty be relieved by the power of God.'[1] Unable, however, to maintain throughout the silence which he felt was so necessary for his mistress's safety, and which the confident pride of the conspirators rendered it so difficult to observe, he went further in a letter which he wrote, on the 24th of June, to her secretary Curle. In indiscreet allusion to those murderous intentions which he did not fear to place under the protection of God, he wrote thus from his confinement in the Bastille: 'I am not unoccupied, although I be in prison, to think of her Majesty's state, and yours that endure with her, to your honours; and there be many means in hand to remove the beast that troubleth all the world.'[2]

However, as soon as she thought she could safely correspond with her old friends and the Princes her allies, Mary Stuart resumed the projects, which she had so long entertained, of a Catholic revolution in Scotland, and a Spanish invasion of England. She had felt vehemently irritated with her son, ever since she had learned that a Protestant league had been concluded between him and Queen Elizabeth; and she resolved to transfer her rights to the kingdom of England, to the great champion of Catholicism in Europe. She communicated her intentions to Don Bernardino de Mendoza, in these terms: 'Considering the obstinate perseverance of my son in heresy (which, I assure you, I have wept over and lamented day and night, more than my own calamities), and foreseeing the great injury which would arise to the Catholic Church, if he came into the succession of this kingdom, I have deliberately determined, in case my son does not embrace the Catholic religion before my death, (as I must tell you, I have little hope of his doing so, so long as he remains in Scotland,) to yield and bestow my right to the succession of this crown, by will, to the King your master, on con

---

[1] Morgan to the Queen of Scots, Murdin, p. 527.
[2] MS. letter, State Paper Office; Morgan to Curle, decypher by Phelipps, 24th June (4th July, new style). Tytler, vol. vi., p. 33.

dition that he will henceforward take me entirely under his protection, as well as the estate and affairs of this country.' She added that she acted thus in obedience to the mandates of her conscience, and in order to obtain the restoration of the Catholic religion in the island, by the aid of that Prince who was most zealous and most able to re-establish it. 'I feel myself,' she said, ' more obliged to respect in this the welfare of the universal Church, than the aggrandisement of my own posterity. I beseech you that this may be kept very secret, for if it were revealed it would lead in France to the loss of my dowry, in Scotland to a complete rupture with my son, and in this country to my total ruin and destruction.'[1]

On the same day, the 20th of May she wrote a very remarkable letter to Charles Paget, regarding the means of attaining the double object which she pursued both in Scotland and England. She requested him to apply to the King of Spain, through his brother Lord Paget, who was then at Madrid, and through the ambassador Mendoza, to execute the enterprise which alone could release her from captivity, and save the Catholic religion from total annihilation in that island. In order to ensure its success, she proposed to associate Scotland in the league, either by persuading her son to enter into her views, or, if her son would not consent, by forming a confederacy of the principal Catholic lords to act in concert with the King of Spain. In the latter case, she offered to place her son in the hands of Philip II., or of the Pope, and to appoint Lord Claude Hamilton Regent of Scotland, assisted by a council composed of the leading nobility, without whose advice no matters of importance should be undertaken. Lord Claude, to whom Paget was to write on her behalf, should be the Lieutenant-General of her son, who should be instructed on the Continent in the principles of the Catholic religion, in order that he might accede to the throne after she was dead, and above all, that he might obtain salvation, ' which,' added Mary, 'I desire more than to see him monarch of all Europe. A thousand regrets and apprehensions would remain in my heart, if I should die, to leave behind me a tyrant and persecutor of the Catholic Church.'[2] Paget was further directed to communicate all her intentions to Lord Claude Hamilton, to whom she herself wrote soon afterwards.[3]

The Scottish nobles who continued attached to the ancient religion and the captive Queen, had already anticipated Mary's

[1] Labanoff, vol. vi., p. 311.   [2] Ibid., vol. vi., pp. 313–321.
[3] Labanoff, vol. vi., p. 371.

wishes. Some of them ventured to make an open profession of Catholicism. The Earl of Morton, head of the Maxwell family, and one of the most powerful barons of the Southern frontier, had had mass celebrated in the church of Lincluden. The Jesuits, Parsons and Holt, with other fathers of that enterprising order, were with the Earl of Huntly. These two noblemen, with the Earl of Argyle, Lord Crawford, and a number of the Highland chieftains, had formed a league with Lord Claude Hamilton to deliver the Queen of Scots, rescue her son from Elizabeth's dominion, and restore the Catholic form of worship in the country. Lord Claude, who had recently returned from Paris to Edinburgh, with secret instructions from the Duke of Guise, was the moving spirit of this confederacy, which communicated with Philip II. by means of the Lorraine prince. Robert Bruce was despatched to the Spanish King with letters[1] from Claude Hamilton, Huntly, and Morton, in which they announced to him that they were stronger than their adversaries in Scotland, but that they had need of his assistance against the intervention of the Queen of England. They called Philip II. 'the pillar of the Christian commonwealth,'[2] and said that they had recourse to him in full confidence of being able to restore the Catholic faith in the kingdom. 'In addition to the immortal glory,' they added, 'which your Majesty will obtain from the enterprise, and the singular good service which you will render to God, you will acquire, by joining your forces to ours, the advantage of shattering the power of the Queen of England.'[3]

Robert Bruce proceeded through France to Spain. He received a very pressing letter to the King of Spain from the Duke of Guise. 'Sire,' wrote the chieftain of the League to Philip II., 'after all the different schemes that I have conducted and sought out, for a long while, and with much pains, for the establishment of the Catholic religion in Scotland, God has granted me the grace of having induced and drawn over the greatest and principal men of the country to the good and holy resolution which I have always esteemed very necessary for surmounting the English factions, which have retarded our proceedings to this

---

[1] These letters are three in number, and are written in Latin. Archives of Simancas, B. 57, Nos. 359, 360, 362.

[2] 'Totius republicæ Christianæ columen.' Letter of Claude Hamilton, No. 360.

[3] 'Id vero V. Majestati, præter immortalem nominis sui gloriam, ac singulare numinis obsequium, emolumentum accedet, quod facile conjunctis copiis ita Angliæ Reginæ vires domi frangemus.' Letter of the Earl of Huntly. Archives of Simancas, B. 57, No. 362.

hour.' He assured the King that Lord Claude Hamilton, and the Earls of Argyle and Morton, with whom he had been in treaty, had two-thirds of Scotland at their disposal. But to attack the dominant party in the country, and to resist the forces of the neighbouring kingdom, appeared to him, he added, ' too difficult an enterprise without the support and assistance of your Majesty, whom we have with one accord, chosen to be the protector and maintainer of so noble and praiseworthy an enterprise.' He felt all the more interest in this enterprise, he continued, because it would advance the designs of Philip II. upon England— 'designs,' he said, 'which I could wish to be so fortunate as to be able to lend my feeble aid, and to engage in their promotion with a pike like a common soldier.'¹ The Duke besought Philip to supply the confederates with men and money, which they needed, and requested Mendoza² at the same time to support the demand of the Scottish chiefs, by using the influence with the King his master on their behalf.³

Mendoza, who was thus informed of all that was going on in England and Scotland, had long been aware of the project for Elizabeth's assassination. He had been privy to it when as yet there were only four persons engaged in its execution; and on the 12th of May, he wrote a short despatch to Philip II., in which he said: 'I am informed from England that four men of mark, who have the privilege of entering the royal palace, have resolved to kill the Queen; that they have all four bound themselves, by oath, to do it either by poison or by steel;⁴ that they

¹ Archives of Simancas, B. 57, No. 356.
² Letter from the Duke of Guise to Don Bernardino de Mendoza, 16th July, 1587. Archives of Simancas, B. 57, No. 237.
³ All the projects formed by the Scottish nobles who were opposed to England, in concert with the Duke of Guise and Philip II., were unknown to Henry III. Since the year 1567, France had ceased to maintain an ordinary ambassador in Scotland. Several agents had been sent thither at various times, to discharge temporary missions, such as Ligneroles, Poigny, Verac, Mondreville, Lamothe Fénelon, and Méneville. Some documents regarding these missions will be found in M. Teulet's second volume. In October, 1585, Henry III. decided on appointing the Baron d'Esnéval, Vidame of Normandy and son-in-law of the Secretary of State, Pinart, to be his ambassador to the Court of James VI. He was desirous to maintain the old alliance between Scotland and France, and to prevent the close connection which was speedily established between Scotland and England. The Baron d'Esnéval,—whose correspondence has been published by M. Teulet, vol. ii., pp. 727-788, to whom it was communicated as well as to myself by the learned and obliging M. Cheruel,—was not aware of the projects of Philip the Second's partisans in Scotland, and did not prevent the alliance of James VI. with Elizabeth. He returned home, in September, 1586, without having done anything.
⁴ 'De acabar a la Reyna, y a la fur averse acordado y juramentado todos. . . . de hagello y que sena con veneno o yerro.'

will inform me of the time appointed for its execution, that I may write to your Majesty to beg you to succour them when the deed is done: and that they will not communicate their plan to any man but myself, to whom they are under so many obligations, and in whom they place the greatest confidence.'¹ Mendoza, who had also instructed the Catholic King of Mary Stuart's intention to transfer to him her rights to the Crown of England, if her son continued a Protestant,² transmitted to him, on the 23rd of July, a letter from the Duke of Guise, with the articles by which the Scottish Lords declared themselves ready to act as soon as they were supplied with a hundred and fifty thousand crowns, which sum they would need in order to enter upon the campaign.³

Meanwhile, the Catholic conspiracy pursued its course in England. Babington and his friends had multiplied their councils; they had met a great many times in the environs of London, during the months of June and July, for the purpose of allotting to each man his share in the execution of their plan. In addition to the six who had undertaken to assassinate Elizabeth, others were appointed to raise the provinces in insurrection, and others to proceed to Chartley to liberate Mary Stuart.⁴ Babington, who generally resided at Lichfield, in the neighbourhood of Chartley, now paid more frequent and prolonged visits to London. He paid many visits to Walsingham, to whom he had offered his services as a spy, in the rash hope of being able to overreach the intrigues of the wily secretary, and of diverting suspicion from himself.⁵ He thus placed himself in the hand which was about to seize and crush him. The conspiracy, however, which had hitherto been confined to conversations, fraught with more danger to the conspirators than to Elizabeth,⁶ had made decided progress. Mary Stuart had imprudently been mixed up with it. Morgan, doubtless, at the instigation of Gilbert Gifford, whose visits to France were frequent at this period, had begged her to encourage Babington's zeal, by writing him a letter in very general terms, a draft of which he took the trouble to send her from the Bastille.⁷ In this letter which Mary Stuart despatched on the 25th of June, to the inconsiderate leader of the conspirators, whom she called 'her great friend,' she thanked him for the affection which he had never ceased to manifest for her, and charged him to forward by

---

¹ Archives of Simancas, B. 57, No. 310.   ² Ibid., B. 57, No. 239.
³ Ibid., B. 57, No. 235.   ⁴ Howell's State Trials, vol. i., pp. 1132-1135.
⁵ Tytler, vol. vii., p. 42.   ⁶ Howell, vol. i., pp. 1132-1135.
⁷ Labanoff, vol. vi., p. 344, note 3. Murdin, p. 513.

Gifford[1] any packets which might arrive from France. The letter was inclosed in one to this traitor, to whom her secretary Curle wrote: 'Her Majesty prayeth you to send it so secretly as you can to Master Anthony Babington.'[2]

This fatal letter, though perfectly innocent in its language, renewed the connection of the prisoner with Babington, and eventually placed her at the mercy of Walsingham. Indeed, as soon as Babington had received it, he wrote a long despatch in cypher, in which he related in passionate terms, to the Queen of Scots, 'his very dear Sovereign,' as he called her, all that had been done on her behalf since Ballard's arrival. He told her that he was engaged in a plan for her deliverance, in conformity with the wishes manifested by the Christian Princes, her allies. He explained to her his intentions, and enumerated all the means of the conspiracy for invading England and getting rid of Elizabeth. He requested Mary Stuart, whom he pledged himself to serve until death, to appoint persons to act as her lieutenants, and raise the populace in Wales, and in the counties of Lancashire, Derby, and Stafford. 'Myself in person,' he added, 'with ten gentlemen and a hundred others of our company and suite, will undertake the deliverance of your royal person from the hands of your enemies. As regards getting rid of the usurper, from subjection to whom we are absolved by the act of excommunication issued against her, there are six gentlemen of quality, all of them my intimate friends, who, for the love they bear to the Catholic cause and to your Majesty's service, will undertake the tragic execution. It remains now, that, according to their infinite desert and your Majesty's goodness, their heroic enterprise should be honourably recompensed in themselves, if they escape with their lives, or in their posterity, if they fall: and that I may give them this assurance by your Majesty's authority.'[3]

This terrible letter, written on the 6th of July, was placed by Gifford in the hands of Walsingham, on the same day. As Babington proposed to await Mary's answer at Lichfield, the cautious secretary feared that the delay which would be caused by sending the letters to London to be decyphered, might give the alarm to the conspirators, and thwart his own machinations; he therefore resolved to send Phelipps down to Chartley to inter-

---

[1] Labanoff, vol. vi., pp. 345, 346.
[2] MS. letter, State Paper Office; Tytler, vol. vii., p. 37.
[3] Copy of the time, Nat. Lib. Paris, MSS. Supp. French, No. $\frac{3993}{10}$, p. 68. Hardwicke's State Papers, p. 223.

cept and decypher the letters on the spot. Phelipps left London on the 7th of July.[1] He had with him Babington's long letter to Mary, which was to be delivered to her by the brewer, and to produce such fatal results. The poor prisoner, thus surrounded with snares, received it on the 12th of July, and was pleased with its contents, according to Paulet, who watched all her movements, and wrote to Walsingham on the 14th of July, in these terms: 'The packet sent by Mr. Phelipps has been thankfully received, with such answer given by writing as the shortness of the time would allow, and a promise made to answer more at length at the return of the honest man.'[2] On the same day, Phelipps, who had already decyphered a despatch from Mary to the French ambassador, Chateauneuf, and intercepted two of her letters, out of cypher, to Lord Claude Hamilton, and Courcelles, the *chargé d'affaires*,[3] sent copies of the three letters to Walsingham, with a note, in which he said: 'We attend her very heart in the next.'[4]

Whilst this odious agent of the most perverse machinations was discharging his vile duties under the roof of the unfortunate Princess he was labouring to ruin, he did not conceal himself from her sight, but met her with smiles and politeness. 'She did ride about in her coach yesterday,' he wrote to Walsingham, a few days after his arrival at Chartley. 'I had a smiling countenance, but I thought of the verse—

"Cum tibi dicit Ave—sicut ab hoste Cave."[5]

The distrustful Mary remarked the presence of this new guest at Chartley; she thought he was one of the old spies of Burghley and Walsingham, and supposed that he had been sent to assist Paulet, who was usually ill.[6] She even imagined that Phelipps had been proposed to her, as a fit agent for her secret service, by Morgan, who was a most hot-headed conspirator, and showed little discernment in the choice of his accomplices. She drew the following picture of Phelipps in a letter which she wrote to Morgan on the subject: 'He is of low stature, slender every way, dark, yellow-haired on the head, and clear yellow-bearded, pitted in the face with small-pox, short-sighted, and as it appears, about thirty years of age.'[7] The sight of this repulsive and artful personage inspired her with disgust; and she believed his

---

[1] Tytler, vol. vii., p. 43. [2] Ibid., p. 46. [3] Ibid., p. 45. [4] Ibid.
[5] MS. letter, State Paper Office, 14th July, 1586. Tytler, vol. vii., p. 45.
[6] Labanoff, vol. vi., pp. 419, 423. [7] Ibid., p. 423.

presence at Chartley to be fraught with danger to herself, which it was utterly out of her power to avert.

Still believing that her means of communication were safe, and her plots undiscovered, Mary wrote an answer to Babington on the 17th (new style, 27th) of July. She praised the zeal manifested by himself and his friends, and applauded their enterprise. She entered fully into the details of the intended invasion, enumerated the naval and military forces which would be required to carry it into effect; and added, if we are to believe the accusation subsequently brought against her by Elizabeth's government, that it would be necessary also to consider 'by what means the six gentlemen deliberated to proceed, and in what manner she should be assisted in making her escape.'[1]

She particularly enforced the necessity of maintaining a constant communication with Bernardino de Mendoza, and recommended them to attempt nothing until they had made every arrangement, at home and abroad, for the insurrection of the Catholics, and the invasion of the Spaniards. According to her accusers, she then went on to say: 'Affairs being thus prepared, then shall it be time to set the six gentlemen to work; taking order, upon the accomplishing of their design, I may suddenly be transported out of the place, and that all your forces, in the same time, be on the field to meet me, whilst we wait the arrival of help from abroad, which must then be hastened with all diligence. Nor for that there can be no certain day appointed of the accomplishing of the said gentlemen's designment,—to the end that others may be in readiness to take me from hence, I would that the said gentlemen had always about them, or, at the least, at court, four stout men furnished with good and speedy horses, for, so soon as the said design shall be executed, to come with all diligence, to advertise thereof those that shall be appointed for my transporting; to the end that, immediately thereafter, they may be at the place of my abode, before that my keeper can have advice of the execution of the said design, or at least before he can fortify himself within the house, or carry me out of the same. It were necessary to despatch two or three of the said advertisers by divers ways, to the end that if one be staid, the other may come through; and at the same instant, were it also needful, to essay to cut off the post's ordinary ways.'[2]

'If I remain here,' she continued, 'there is for my escape

[1] Labanoff, vol. vi., pp. 386, 387.   [2] Ibid., pp. 389, 390.

but one of these three means following to be looked to. The first, that at one certain day, appointed, in my walking abroad on horseback on the moors, betwixt this and Stafford, where ordinarily you know very few people do pass, a fifty or threescore horsemen, well horsed and armed, come to take me there; as they may easily, my keeper having with him ordinarily but eighteen or twenty horsemen. The second mean is to come at midnight, or soon after, to set fire in the barns and stables, which you know are near to the house; and whilst that my guardian's servants shall rush forth to the fire, your company (having every one a mark whereby they may know one another under night) might surprise the house, where I hope, with the few servants I have about me, I were able to give you correspondence. And the third: some that bring carts hither, ordinarily coming early in the morning; their carts might be so prepared, and with such cart-leaders, that being cast in the midst of the great gate, the cart might fall down or overwhelm, and that thereupon you might come suddenly with your followers to make yourself master of the house and carry me away.'[1] On the same day, Mary Stuart wrote to Charles Paget, the Archbishop of Glasgow, Thomas Morgan, and Bernardino de Mendoza, her regular correspondents at Paris, and to Sir Francis Englefield, her agent at Madrid,[2] to point out the opportunity for an invasion, to hasten its preparation, and to concert its execution simultaneously with the insurrection in England.

When he had seized Mary's letter to Babington, as well as all those which that unfortunate Princess had addressed to the conspirators on the Continent, Phelipps felt a sinister satisfaction. He rejoiced to see the noble prey, which had been pursued with so much ardour and dissimulation by his master Walsingham, entangled at length in his invisible nets. After having announced this impatiently-desired result to Elizabeth's secretary, he went on to say: 'I hope for your Honour's speedy resolution touching her apprehension or otherwise, that I may dispose of myself accordingly. I wish it may please God to inspire her Majesty with the heroical courage that were meet for the avenge of God's cause, and the security of herself and this State.'[3] The Puritanical Amias Paulet wrote, on his side, to Walsingham with fanciful delight: 'God has blessed my efforts, giving me the

[1] Labanoff, vol. vi., pp. 393, 394.
[2] See her letters in Labanoff, vol. vi., pp. 399-435.
[3] MS. letter, State Paper Office, Phelipps to Walsingham, 19th (new style, 29th) July; Tytler, vol. vii., p. 48.

reward of true and faithful service. I trust that the Queen and her grave Councillors will make their profit of the merciful providence of God towards her Highness and England.'[1] The ardent Calvinist Paulet entertained no more suspicions than the abject politician Phelipps, regarding the abominable iniquity to which he had been a party. State policy and the interests of religion concealed from the imperfect vision of both, all the hatefulness and dishonour of dragging into the snare of a conspiracy a poor captive who would never have fallen into it without their assistance. Believing that he had now obtained sufficient evidence to destroy the unhappy Queen, Walsingham yielded to the request of Phelipps, and a few days afterwards, on the 22nd of July, recalled him to London.[2]

Whilst Phelipps was returning to London, Gifford was on his way to Paris, having been charged by the English Catholics with the express mission to learn from Mendoza, whether they might rely upon the armed assistance of Philip II., as soon as Elizabeth's assassination had taken place.[3] The Spanish ambassador had a long conference with Walsingham's spy, who unfolded to him the whole conspiracy; informed him of the religious condition of England by communicating to him a very curious document setting forth the respective strength of either party, county by county; and gave him a list of the principal personages who, he said, were attached to the cause of Mary Stuart, to the restoration of Catholicism, and to the service of Philip II. This list contained thirty-nine names, amongst which were those of the son of the Duke of Norfolk; the Earl of Arundel and his two brothers, Thomas and William Howard; the young Earl of Northumberland, whose father had died a violent death in prison a year before; Lord Dacre, Lord Strange, the son of the Earl of Derby, Colonel Sir William Stanley, Lord Montague, Lord Compton, and Lord Morley.[4] Mendoza sent their names to Philip II., and told that Prince that he had given Gifford such a reception as his mission deserved, and that, in order to encourage the confederates, he had sent to them, by two different ways, two letters, one in Italian, and the other in Latin, 'stimulating them to an enterprise worthy both of their Catholic minds and of the ancient valour of the English, and assuring them that, if they succeeded in killing the Queen, they should certainly be

[1] MS. letter, State Paper Office; Amias Paulet to Walsingham, 20th (new style, 30th) July; Tytler, vol. vii., p. 49.
[2] Tytler, vol. vii., p. 55. [3] Archives of Simancas, B. 57, No. 74.
[4] Ibid., No. 69.

assisted by your Majesty with the reinforcement which they request from the Netherlands. I have promised them this,' he continued, 'as they requested me, upon my faith and word of honour, and I have urged them to hasten the execution of their enterprise by reasons which are likely to decide them so to do.'¹ Mendoza advised the confederates, as soon as they had made away with the Queen, to seize or kill Cecil, Walsingham, and Hunsdon; and requested them to imprison Don Antonio de Crato, who was then in England, and whose claims upon Portugal were still matter of apprehension to Philip II.²

The Spanish King had already received, with feelings of pride and satisfaction, the intelligence that Mary Stuart intended to nominate him her heir to the kingdom of England. 'The Queen,' he wrote to Mendoza on the 18th of July, 'has thereby gained great credit with me, and has increased the good-will which I have always felt for her affairs.'³ He praised her for having subordinated her love for her son to the service of God and of Christendom.⁴ He charged Mendoza to tell her this, adding, that he was delighted to take her under his protection, in order to replace her, by the help of God, in her proper position. His hopes were increased, and his determination strengthened, when he had learned from Mendoza's letters all the details of the Catholic conspiracy. He approved of the answer which his ambassador had given to Gifford. 'Considering,' he said, 'the importance of the event, if God, who has now taken her cause in hand, wills that it should succeed, you have done well to receive this gentleman favourably, and to urge him, as well as those who have sent him, to carry on their enterprise.'⁵

After having advised Mendoza to take precautions in order to avoid the discovery of a secret, which, he said, among many, did not last long, and was ill-kept, he added : 'While reading the

---

¹ 'Los he escrito dos cartas por diferentes vias, una en Italiano y otra en Latin, animandolos á la empresa como digna de animos tan Catolicos y del antiguo valor Inglès, y que se effetuando el matar á la Reyna tendran el assistencia que pidieren de los Payses Baxos y seguridad de ser socorridos de V. Mag^d, lo qual yo los prometra como ellos me pidian sobre mi fee y palabra, animandolos al presurar la execucion con algunas razones que los forçava a ello.' Archives of Simancas, B. 57, No. 73.

² Archives of Simancas, B. 57, No. 73.

³ 'Ha ganado gran credito con migo, y hecho me crecer la buena voluntad, que si siempre tuveá, suscansas.' Archives of Simancas, A. 56, No. ⁉

⁴ 'Que pospone el amor que se pudiera temer que la enganasse de su hijo al servicio d N. S^r., y bien publico de la Cristianidad, y particular de aquel reyno.' Ibid.   ⁵ Ibid., No. ⁉

names of the confederates, I remember some of them and the father of others. By the aid of such persons, the affair seems to me to be well-grounded; and for the service of God, the liberation of the Catholics, and the good of this realm, I am determined to support them. I have, therefore, ordered that the necessary succour shall be immediately prepared, both by way of Flanders and by way of Spain. It is true, that, as our success mainly depends upon our secresy and diligence, the troops will be got ready with little noise, and will not be so considerable as to prevent them from promptly leaving Spain and Flanders, as soon as we hear that the principal execution which Babington and his friends have undertaken, has occurred in England.' Philip II. instructed Mendoza to give the confederates the most positive assurance that they should receive timely assistance, and desired him to send Gifford to tell them that the safety of the Catholics in England depended upon the secresy of the enterprise, and the secresy of the enterprise upon the promptitude of its accomplishment."

On the same day, in another despatch written in triplicate[2] on account of its importance, Philip II. forwarded to his ambassador at Paris two letters for the Prince of Parma, Governor of the Netherlands. One of these letters directed Parma to make preparations; the other commanded him to act. Mendoza was to despatch the first at once, and to keep the other by him, until he knew that Babington had accomplished his project. 'In that case,' wrote Philip, 'send it at once to the Prince, that he may set sail with the reinforcements, without waiting any fresh orders from me, as this second letter, as you will perceive, is very precise upon this point.'[3]

But the time had already passed. The multiplicity of his affairs, the distance of his dominions, the extent of his distrust, and the slowness of his determinations, always made Philip II.

[1] 'No dexare de ayudarlos y assi desde luego mando que se apreste y aperciba el socorro necessario tanto por la via de Flandes como por la de aca de España, verdad es que por consistir todo el efecto en el secreto y averse de preparar esto con el menos ruydo que se pueda non sera el aparato tan grande. . . . Porque no dañe mas acudir a se con la mayor presteza que se pueda, por la una parte y la otra, en sabiendo que se ha hecho en Inglaterra la principal execucion de que Bavington y sus amigos se han encargado.' Archives of Simancas, A. 56, No. $\tfrac{49}{59}$.

[2] Upon this despatch, the following words are written in Philip's own handwriting: 'Todo se ha dicho de duplicar y aun de triplicar por le que importa.' Ibid. A. 26, No. $\tfrac{51}{53}$.

[3] Archives of Simancas. These two despatches from Philip II. to Mendoza, bear date of 5th September.

interfere too late. As soon as Walsingham possessed written proofs of the conspiracy, and the means of pursuing all those whom his patient and artful machinations had involved in the plot, from the royal captive, of whom the English government was desirous to get rid, down to her obscurest servant, he determined to put a stop to further proceedings. Elizabeth, whom he informed of the plans in existence for her own assassination and the invasion of her realm, was terribly alarmed,[1] and ordered that the conspirators should at once be arrested, that her life might be no longer exposed to continual peril. Maud then denounced Ballard, whose confidant and companion he had long been.[2] But, by Walsingham's directions, he denounced him at first only as a refractory priest,[3] in order to avoid giving the alarm to the other conspirators, and to prevent Mary Stuart from destroying all her papers at Chartley. Elizabeth's minister, therefore, ordered his secretary, Milles, to arrest Ballard simply for having infringed the laws of the kingdom. This was, however, not an easy task. Ballard took the utmost precautions, and incessantly changed his disguises and residences.[4] Before his pursuers had succeeded in capturing him, Babington had been informed of Maud's treachery.[5] He had not repaired to Lichfield as he had promised Mary Stuart that he would; and it was not until the 29th of July, ten days after it was written, that the letter of the Queen of Scots reached him in London, where he had remained to confer with the other confederates. He had promised the secret messenger who had brought it to him to have his answer ready on the 2nd of August. But Maud's treason made him leave London precipitately; he rode away from the metropolis, and no one knew what direction he had taken.[6] The unhappy man was in a state of inexpressible consternation. The greatest uncertainty and the most lively fear agitated his mind. Should he fly or return? This was the question which he anxiously put to himself, not knowing how far Maud's revelations had extended. By flight, he compromised the conspiracy, and renounced Mary's deliverance, if Walsingham did not know all; by return, he was lost, if the plot had been betrayed.

A gleam of hope brought him back to London, and he had the

[1] Tytler, vol. vii. p. 57. [2] Labanoff, vol. vi., p. 436. Tytler, vol. vii., p. 56.
[3] Tytler, vol. vii., p. 58.
[4] MS. letter, State Paper Office, Milles to Walsingham, 4th August. Tytler, vol. vii. p. 56.
[5] Copy of the time, Nat. Lib., Paris. MSS., Suppl. Fran., No. $\frac{3923}{48}$, p. 63.
[6] Tytler, vol. vii., pp. 56, 57.

boldness to pay a visit to Walsingham.[1] The deceitful minister, all whose springs were not yet in working order, received him with his ordinary serenity, and allowed him to depart in freedom. But he directed several of his agents to follow him and keep watch over him.[2] Babington, somewhat reassured, wrote to Mary on the 3rd of August to inform her of this perilous occurrence, and to say that he hoped, nevertheless, still to be able to remedy all. He besought her to believe in the fortunate issue of their design. 'My Sovereign,' he said, 'for the love of God, who has held you in his safe keeping, and for our common welfare, do not give way to discouragement. It is the cause of God, of the Church, and of your Majesty; it is an enterprise honourable before God and man. We have vowed it, and we will carry it into effect, or it shall cost us our lives.'[3] But Ballard was arrested on the next day, the 4th of August, and Babington feared that he would be put to the torture, and would discover all. He paid a visit to Savage, and asked him what was to be done. 'Nothing,' answered Savage, 'but to kill the Queen immediately.' 'Very well,' said Babington, 'then go to court to-morrow and strike the blow.' Savage objected that his court-dress was not yet ready, and Babington gave him his ring and all the money he had with him, that he might obtain one the same day.[4] Thinking that the disclosures which must have been made, and the alarm which had doubtless been given, would prevent Savage from appearing at Court, he resolved to go thither himself with the other confederates, and to perpetrate the deed. His courage, however, failed him, and during the night of the 5th of August he fled from London, followed by his distracted companions, and concealed himself in St. John's Wood. They were all discovered ere long, and conducted to the Tower.[5]

When Walsingham had Ballard, Babington, Savage, and the other conspirators in his power, he did not hesitate to treat Mary Stuart as their accomplice. This Princess did not know that the plot had been discovered, and had not received Babington's last letter, which might have awakened her fears upon the subject. She was in a state of the most perfect security. On the 8th of August, Amias Paulet proposed to her a hunting party in the neighbouring park of Tixall; and she accepted the proposition with delight. For some time the warm weather, and perhaps,

---

[1] Tytler, vol. vii., p. 57.   [2] Ibid., p. 57.
[3] Nat. Lib., Paris, MSS. Suppl. Fran, No. $\frac{3993}{10}$, p. 63.
[4] Confession of John Savage, in Howell, vol. i., p. 1130.
[5] Tytler, vol. vii., p. 61.

also, the buoyancy of hope, had improved her health. This hunting party was only a plan agreed upon beforehand between William Waad, who had been sent to Chartley by Walsingham, and Amias Paulet, for transferring her unexpectedly to another residence, separating her from her secretaries before she had arranged any plans with them, and seizing all her papers.[1]

On the way from Chartley to Tixall, Sir Thomas Gorges suddenly presented himself before her, and told her that Babington's plot was discovered, and that he had orders for her removal to Tixall Castle. On hearing this unexpected news, she remained silent for a moment. Then, regaining her presence of mind, and anger taking the place of surprise, she burst out into violent reproaches, and asked the servants of her retinue whether they would allow their mistress to be thus carried away, without striking a blow in her defence? Nau and Curle, who accompanied her, were seized and sent to London, each under a separate escort. The unfortunate Queen, sensible of her melancholy situation and her impotence, resigned herself to her fate, and allowed nerself to be conducted to Tixall Castle, which belonged to Sir Walter Ashton.[2] She remained there for seventeen days, shut up in a small room, far from all her servants, deprived even of her chaplain, with no means for writing, and waited upon entirely by strangers. During her absence from Chartley, Waad and Paulet opened her desks, seized her papers, her jewel-cases, and her money, and transmitted them to Elizabeth. The English Queen received them with transports of joy, and wrote to Paulet, thanking him for his useful services and his prudent conduct, and saying that she felt the deepest gratitude for his fidelity, which merited, and transcended, all recompense.[3]

On the 25th of August, when her apartments at Chartley had been ransacked with the most minute exactness, Mary Stuart was taken back thither. As she left Tixall, under the escort of Paulet and a hundred and forty mounted gentlemen of the neighbourhood, some poor people crowded round her to ask alms. 'I have nothing to give,' she said, with tears. 'All has been taken from me; I am a beggar as well as you.' She then turned towards Sir Walter Ashton, the owner of the castle, and the other gentlemen, and said to them: 'Good gentlemen, I am not

---

[1] Waad, a member of the Privy Council, had posted down from London on the 3rd of August, and had had a secret conference with Paulet in the fields to arrange this arrest. Tytler, vol. vii., p. 59, 60.

[2] State Paper Office, Sir Amias Paulet's postils to Mr. W. Waad's memorial; Tytler, vol. vii., p. 60.   [3] Strype, vol. iii., part i., p. 525.

witting of anything intended against the Queen.' When, on her arrival at Chartley, she found that her desks had been opened, her papers seized, her coffers ransacked and even her jewel-boxes carried off, she was unable to restrain her indignation, and gave utterance to bitter complaints against Elizabeth. 'There are two things,' she cried, 'which the Queen of England can never take from me—the blood royal which gives me a right to the succession of England, and the attachment which makes my heart beat for the religion of my fathers.'¹

Proceedings were commenced, without loss of time, against the conspirators who had projected the death of the Queen, and provoked the invasion of the realm. Elizabeth did not yet venture to include in their number the Queen of Scotland, whose letter to Babington had not been found in its original draft, as had been hoped. Moreover, Elizabeth, who lived in terror, feared that, if Mary Stuart were brought to trial, a desperate attempt would be made against her own life.² The charge of treason was, therefore preferred in the first instance, against Babington, Ballard, Savage, and their accomplices only. Overwhelmed by the mass of evidence brought against them, they all pleaded guilty, and were condemned to suffer the terrible punishment awarded to the crime of high treason.³ In order to terrify those who might be tempted to follow their example, none of the tortures prescribed by the ferocity of English law were spared them. On the 20th of September, Babington, Savage, Ballard, Barnwell, Tilney, Abington and Tichbourne, were taken to St. Giles's-in-the-Fields, where they had held their meetings, and drawn and quartered in the presence of a large number of people, who looked upon the scene with disgust and horror.⁴ On the following day, it was found necessary to shorten and mitigate the punishment of the seven prisoners who remained.⁵

By pleading guilty, Babington had acknowledged the authenticity of his correspondence with Mary Stuart, and although only copies of the letter which he had written to her and of that which he had received from her were produced, he had furnished a formal certification of their contents, and affixed his signature to each page.⁶ Tichbourne had also confessed that he had assisted

¹ MS. letter, State Paper Office, Paulet to Walsingham, 27th August, 1586; Tytler, vol. vii., pp. 3, 64.
² MS. letter, Burghley to Sir Christopher Hatton, 12th September; Tytler, vol. vii., p. 62.
³ Howell's State Trials, vol. i., pp. 1127–1162.   ⁴ Ibid., pp. 1156–1158.
⁵ These were Salisbury, Donne, Jones, Charnock, Gage, Travers, and Bellamy. Ibid.. pp. 1158–1162.   ⁶ Hardwicke, vol. i., pp. 227, 228.

Babington to decypher the long letter from the Scottish Queen; and Ballard and Donne admitted that copies of it had been communicated to them.[1] Nevertheless, this letter was not written in Mary Stuart's handwriting. Even her secretaries, Nau and Curle, had not at first confirmed its exactness. These two individuals had been placed in custody in Walsingham's house.[2] Knowing that they might be involved in the punishment of their mistress, if they acted as witnesses against her, as they would thus prove themselves to have been her accomplices, they at first maintained a silence which must doubtless be ascribed as much to fear as to fidelity. This was understood by both Burghley[3] and Walsingham,[4] who advised that their cause should be separated from that of the Queen whom they had served, and said that they would never be induced to betray her until they were satisfied about the consequences of their revelations.

Nau and Curle were, therefore, placed between the threat of torture if they continued silent, and the prospect of liberty if they consented to speak. These two feeble servants then broke the loyal and salutary silence which they had hitherto observed. They explained the method of Mary Stuart's procedure in her secret correspondence. Shut up in her closet with them, she dictated to Nau the principal points of her despatches, which Nau then reduced to a proper shape, and submitted to the Queen for correction. They were then given to Curle, who translated them into cypher and sent them off.[5] Nau declared that the letter to Babington, a great part of which was written in his mistress's handwriting, had been given to him by her, and had been cyphered by Curle.[6] These first revelations were considered insufficient, and more explicit information was required from Mary's secretary, who, in mortal fear of being sent to the Tower,[7] where prisoners were questioned on the rack, soon proceeded a little further. He avowed that his mistress had entered fully

[1] Hardwicke, vol i., p. 228.
[2] Letter from L'Aubespine de Chateauneuf to Henry III., 3rd September, 1586. MSS., Nat. Lib., Paris, No 9513. Mesmes, Lettres Originales d'Etat, vol. iii., fol. 337. Life of Thomas Egerton, vol. i., p. 330.
[3] MS. letter, Burghley to Sir Christopher Hatton, 4th September, 1586. Tytler, vol. vii., p. 66.
[4] MS. letter, State Paper Office, Walsingham to Phelipps, 4th September, 1586. Tytler, vol. vii., p. 66.
[5] MS., Confession of Nau, State Paper Office, 5th September. Tytler, vol. vii., p. 67. Hardwicke, vol. i., pp. 234, 235. [6] Ibid.
[7] Burghley to Walsingham 8th September, in Ellis's Original Letters, vol. iii., p. 5.

into the plot for the invasion of England; but that, having been merely informed of the plot against Elizabeth's life, she had not sought further details about it, and had not considered it her duty to denounce it.[1] Finally, at his last examination, on the 21st of September, after the terrible execution of the fourteen conspirators, he became even more communicative; he said that Curle had decyphered Babington's letter, and that he had himself written, at his mistress's dictation, the principal points of her answer to Babington, referring to the forces which the conspirators could collect, the places where those forces should be assembled, the intervention of the six gentlemen to assassinate Elizabeth, the means by which Mary was to be released from prison, and lastly, the well-mounted horsemen whom the six gentlemen were to keep near them, to give immediate information of the perpetration of their project to those who were to deliver the Scottish Queen.[2] A note in his handwriting had, moreover, been seized among Nau's papers at Chartley, containing a summary of the letters of Babington and Mary, in which the word 'blow' occurred, which Nau declared had reference to the plan for Elizabeth's assassination.[3] Curle made similar depositions, adding, that the Queen had ordered him to burn the English copy of the letters addressed to Babington, to whom he had entreated her not to write.[4]

The confessions of Mary Stuart's two secretaries, and the note in Nau's handwriting, served to confirm the declarations of Babington and his accomplices. Elizabeth hoped she would thus be enabled to bring to trial the unfortunate Queen, whom she had detained in captivity for nineteen years. But would she venture to do so? Would she dare to cite a sovereign Princess before a tribunal of her own subjects, and thus to infringe the royal prerogative? After having so odiously violated the law of nations by depriving Mary Stuart of her liberty from motives of state interest, would she go so far as to offend in a still graver manner against the hitherto respected privileges of crowns, by depriving her of life in order better to provide for her own safety? Would she not recoil before the fear of incurring the indignation of all Kings, and of adding to the formidable enmity of that powerful monarch whom all the Catholics of Europe acknow-

[1] MS., Declaration of Nau, State Paper Office, 10th September. Tytler, vol. vii., p. 69.
[2] MS., Declaration, State Paper Office, 21st September, 1586. Tytler, vol. vi., p. 68. Hardwicke, vol. i., p. 236. [3] Ibid., vol. i., p. 235.
[4] Ibid., vol. i., pp. 237, 250.

ledged as their head, the almost inevitable hostility of her near neighbours and useful allies, the Kings of France and Scotland, by putting to death the sister-in-law of the one and the mother of the other? Notwithstanding these reasons and fears, Elizabeth persevered in her intentions with unprecedented boldness and hypocrisy. She determined to procure the trial, condemnation, and death of a Queen whose subjects she had raised in revolt, whose confidence she had deceived, whose offers she had rejected, whose son she had alienated, on whom she had conferred the right of forming conspiracies by arrogating to herself the right of detaining her in captivity, and whom her minister, Walsingham, had lured into the perfidious snare of a plot which was betrayed beforehand, incapable of success, and able only to lead her to destruction.

CHAPTER XI.

FROM THE FRUSTRATION OF BABINGTON'S CONSPIRACY TO THE DEATH OF MARY STUART.

Deliberations of the English Privy Council—Appointment of a High Court of Justice—Transference of Mary Stuart to Fotheringay Castle—Mary refuses to appear before the Court—She at last resolves to defend herself—Her accusation and defence—Her discussion with Burghley—Her condemnation—Elizabeth hesitates to execute the sentence—Intervention of the Kings of France and Scotland to save Mary's life—Elizabeth signs her death-warrant—Paulet refuses to put Mary Stuart to death clandestinely—Mary's execution.

The trial of Mary Stuart was long canvassed before it was decided on. The idea of putting the unfortunate Queen to death had repeatedly suggested itself; and the English Government conceived that at length a mode had been devised for getting rid of her and of the dangers to which it had for nineteen years been exposed by keeping her a prisoner. The fate of Mary Stuart was first discussed between Elizabeth and Burghley,[1] and then submitted to the deliberations of the Privy Council. Some of the councillors were of opinion that it would answer the purpose to render her completely powerless by means of stricter captivity, while others, in the belief that they were protecting their Sovereign's life, and securing the triumph of Protestantism, argued for her death. Leicester is accused of having proposed the secret use of poison,[2] while Walsingham preferred a judicial sentence.

[1] Tytler, vol. viii., p. 347, on the authority of a letter of Burghley, in the State Paper Office. [2] Camden, vol. ii., p. 485.

This latter advice prevailed. Under what law, then, was Mary Stuart to be cited before a public tribunal? The statute of 25 Edward III., treating as guilty of high treason those who had conspired against the King, excited war within the kingdom, or held communication with his enemies, seemed applicable to her case. They preferred, however, resorting to the statute passed the year before [1] at the end of the famous Act of Association, by which power was given to prosecute capitally and to condemn to death any person who should lay claim to the Crown of England, or attempt to take it from the Queen Elizabeth, by means of a foreign invasion or a conspiracy against her person.[2]

In conformity with this statute Mary Stuart was indicted, on the 5th of October, 1586, before a High Court of Justice, composed of the most distinguished State officers and Peers of England, the principal Councillors of the Crown, and the most eminent judges and lawyers in the kingdom. This commission, over which Chancellor Bromley presided, consisted of forty-six members,[3] the greater part of whom proceeded to Fotheringay Castle, in Northamptonshire, where the final act of this long tragedy was to be performed. The royal prisoner was conducted thither on the 6th of October by Sir Amias Paulet, her keeper, Sir Walter Mildmay, a Privy Councillor, and Barker, a notary.[4] She there received a letter from Elizabeth, reproaching her with having been concerned in the conspiracy lately formed against her State and her person, and enjoining her to answer the charges which would be preferred against her before the judges invested with the powers of those laws under whose protection she had lived, and to whose rules it was her duty to submit.

Having, in the presence of Paulet and Mildmay, perused this letter, which was couched in severe and imperious terms, Mary restrained the feelings which agitated her. She told them with bitter irony that her sister was misinformed, so far as she was concerned, and she reminded them of the multiplicity of her own grievances, and the contempt with which her offers had been treated. Feeling hurt at the tone of command adopted towards her by the Queen of England, who seemed to expect her to answer to her judges as if she had been one of her own subjects, she exclaimed, while the blush of indignation suffused her brow, 'What! Does your mistress not know that I am a Queen

[1] The twenty-seventh year of the reign of Elizabeth.
[2] Howell, vol. i., pp. 1163–1166.   [3] Ibid., vol. i., pp. 1166–1168.
[4] Tytler, vol. viii., p. 348.
[5] MS., State Paper Office, 5th October, 1586. Tytler, vol. viii., pp. 348, 349

born? Does she think that I will degrade my rank, my condition, the race from which I spring, the son who is to succeed me, the foreign Kings and Princes whose rights would be injured in my person, by obeying such a letter as that?—Never! Humbled as I may seem, my heart is too great to submit to any humiliation!'[1]

She added, further, that she was deprived of her papers, destitute of advisers, and surrounded by enemies; that she was ignorant of the laws and the statutes of the kingdom, where she must look in vain for Peers competent to try her; and finally declared that she was innocent. 'I have neither,' she said, 'directed nor encouraged any attempt against your mistress. I am certain that nothing of the kind can be proved against me, although I frankly confess that, when my sister had rejected all my offers, I committed myself and my cause to the care of foreign Princes.'[2]

Mary's refusal to recognize the jurisdiction to which she was required to submit, was not only in conformity with her exalted rank but it was necessary for her personal security. Had she held out in this refusal to the last, it would have been difficult to condemn her without being heard, and it would have been impossible to lead her to the scaffold in virtue of a sentence pronounced by the incompetent subjects of another Queen. She seems to have been at once aware of this, and would only receive the Chief Commissioners in her own chamber. She had several interviews with the Lord Chancellor and the Lord Treasurer, both of whom she embarrassed by the cleverness of her answers and the energy of her recriminations.

On being made acquainted with her haughty replies, and her obstinate refusal to submit, Elizabeth directed the Commissioners to proceed with the investigation, but to delay the judgment until they should have returned and presented her with a full report.[3] She endeavoured at the same time, with great artifice, to shake Mary's determination, by tempting her with a ray of hope in the event of her showing greater deference for her wishes. 'You have tried in various ways,' she says, 'to take my life, and to ruin my kingdom by bloodshed. I have never acted so harshly towards you, but, on the contrary, have preserved you as if you were my second self. Your treasonable acts will be proved and made manifest. For this reason, our pleasure is that

---

[1] Howell's State Trials, vol. i., p. 1169. MS., State Paper Office, 12th October, 1586. The Scottish Queen's first answer. Tytler, vol. viii., p. 350. [2] Ibid.
[3] The English Queen to Lord Burghley, 12th October, British Museum, Caligula, Chap. IX., fol. 332. MS., State Paper Office.

you reply to the nobles and peers of my kingdom, as you would do if I myself were present. I require and command you to do this. I have been informed of your arrogance: act with candour, and you shall be treated with greater favour.'[1]

These last words, which could not but wound the feelings of Mary, succeeded in shaking her resolution. She was also worked upon by the insinuations of the Vice-Chamberlain Hatton. This favourite of Elizabeth, and presumed confidant of her intentions, conjured her to reply, lest her silence should be held as a confession of guilt, and judgment be proceeded with in her absence. 'You are accused,' said he, 'but not condemned.[2] You are, it is true, a Queen, but the royal dignity does not exempt its possessor from replying to the imputation of a crime, such as neither the civil nor the canon law, nor the law of nations, nor the law of nature, could save from prosecution. If you are innocent, the Queen's Commissioners, who are just and prudent men, will rejoice with all their hearts at your making your innocence apparent. The Queen herself will be no less pleased, I assure you. When I left her, she declared to me that nothing ever gave her greater pain than to see you accused of such a crime. Dispense, then, with that vain privilege of royal dignity, which cannot now avail you; appear in Court, maintain your innocence, do not lay yourself open to suspicion by avoiding the trial, and do not risk sullying your reputation with an everlasting stain.' Burghley added, that they would proceed against her next day, even in her absence.[3] After a night passed in all the torture of uncertainty, Mary consented to appear before her judges.

On the morning of the 14th of October, followed by a detachment of halberdiers, and supported by her maître d'hotel, Sir Andrew Melville, and her physician, Bourgoin, for she walked with great difficulty, she descended into the great hall of Fotheringay,[4] where the Commissioners were seated in the form of a court of justice. At one end of the hall, under a dais surmounted by the arms of England alone, stood, in an elevated position, an arm-chair, reserved for the absent Queen Elizabeth, and which remained unoccupied. On each side of the dais were ranged, in the order of their respective dignities, the different Commissioners: on the right, the Lord Chancellor Bromley, the Lord High Treasurer Burghley, the Earls of Oxford, Kent, Derby, Worcester, Rutland, Cumberland, Warwick, Pembroke, Lincoln,

[1] Life of Thomas Egerton, vol. i., p. 86.
[2] Howell's State Trials, vol. i., pp. 1171, 1172.   [3] Ibid., p. 1172.
[4] British Museum, Caligula, Chap. IX., fol. 333. Tytler, vol. viii., p. 354.

and Viscount Montagu; on the left, Lords Abergavenny, Zouch, Morley, Stafford, Grey, Lumley, and other peers, next to whom were the Lords of the Privy Council, Crofts, Hatton, Walsingham, Sadler, Mildmay, and Paulet. More in the front were placed, on the right, the Chief Justices of England and Chief Baron of the Exchequer, and on the left, the other judges and barons, along with two Doctors of Civil Law. In the centre were seated, around a table, the Queen's Attorney-General, Popham; her Solicitor, Egerton; her Law Serjeant, Gawdy; and Thomas Powell, Clerk of the Crown; together with two Clerks of the Court to write out the proceedings.[1] A few gentlemen of the neighbourhood, who were allowed to be present, stood at the bar.[2]

On appearing before this imposing assembly, Mary Stuart saluted the Lords with great dignity.[3] On being conducted to the velvet chair which had been prepared for her, and perceiving that it had not been placed under the dais, but lower down,[4] she seemed to feel the humiliation, and said proudly, 'I am a Queen, I was married to a King of France, and my place should be there.'[5] She then looked mournfully round on the grave assembly of lords, statesmen, and lawyers, adding, before she took her seat: 'Alas! there are a great number of councillors here, and yet not one of them is for me!'[6]

Chancellor Bromley then rose and stated the reasons which had determined the Queen of England to bring Mary of Scotland to trial, declaring that, had she neglected so to do, she would have deserved to be accused of slighting the cause of God and of bearing the sword of justice in vain.[7] The Clerk of the Crown then read out the Commission constituting the Court.[8] When he had concluded, Mary addressed the assembly, reminding them of the base and indignant treatment she had experienced in England, whither she had come as a friend and a suppliant, and where she had been kept a prisoner. She told the members of the High Court that she did not recognize the Commission by virtue of which they pretended to try her; that, as a free Princess and an anointed Queen, she was answerable to nobody but to God. She added that she would only reply to them under reserve of

---

[1] Howell, vol. i., pp. 1172, 1173.   [2] Tytler, vol. viii., p. 353.
[3] Ibid., vol. viii., p. 354.   [4] Howell, vol. i., p. 1172.
[5] L'Aubespine de Chateauneuf to Henry III., 30th October, 1856. MS. Biblioth. Nat., No. 9513. De Mesmes, *Collect. de lettres originales d'Etat*, vol. iii., p. 381, and Life of Egerton, vol. i., p. 86.   [6] Ibid.
[7] Howell, vol. i., p. 1173. Tytler, vol. viii., p. 355.   [8] Ibid.

this protest.¹ To this Lord Treasurer Burghley replied, that all persons within the realms were subject to the laws, which must not be maligned, and by which they were now about to try her.²

The Crown Serjeant, Gawdy, then entered into an account of the late conspiracy, maintaining that Mary Stuart had not only participated in the plan for invading the kingdom, but likewise in that for the assassination of Elizabeth, which she had known, approved, and encouraged.³ Morgan's letters, those of Paget, of Mendoza, of the Archbishop of Glasgow, of Englefield, of Dr. Lewis, of Dr. Allen, her own and the confessions of Babington and the other conspirators, certified copies of which were lying on the table, along with the written confessions of Nau and of Curle, were presented as evidences of her double complicity. Mary Stuart at once denied having had any communication with Babington. She declared that she had never seen him, that he had never written to her, and that she had never answered any letters of his. She asked how they could prove that she had received Babington's letters, supposing them to be genuine, and called upon them, if they maintained that she had replied to him, to produce her own letters.⁴

They then read out, from a copy merely, the long letter of the 6th of July, in which Babington had communicated to her the object of the conspiracy, and the means of carrying it into execution, together with the letter of the 25th of July, which, according to the accusation, she had addressed to Babington to encourage him in his design.⁵ After reading, in like manner, the written confessions of Babington, Tichbourne, Ballard, and Donne,⁶ the Attorney-General and the Lord Treasurer expressed their conviction that nothing could be more clear or more indisputable, than the Queen of Scotland's adhesion to the conspiracy.⁷ Without the slightest hesitation, and with the greatest promptitude, Mary Stuart replied, that this pretended evidence rested only on copies of documents, the originals of which were not produced, and on the verbal testimony of persons whom she had

---

¹ Camden, vol. ii., pp. 495, 496.
² Howell, vol. i., p. 1173. ³ Ibid., pp. 1173, 1174.
⁴ Ibid., vol. i., p. 1174. Hardwicke, vol. i., p. 233. *Advis de ce qui a esté en faict en Angleterre par M. de Bellièvre sur les affaires de la royne d'Escoce*, &c. MS. de la Bibl. Nat. Coll., Béthune, No. 8955; Coll. Colbert, No. 18, Mélanges; and Life of Thomas Egerton, vol. i., pp. 102, 103. Camden, pp. 496, 497.
⁵ Ibid., vol. i. p. 1174–1181. Hardwicke, vol. i., p. 233.
⁶ Ibid., vol. i., pp. 1176, 1177. ⁷ Tytler, vol. viii., p. 356.

never seen. Let the originals, she urged, be produced, and then she would examine and discuss them. Until this was done, she declared, that she solemnly protested against the imputations with which she was charged. 'I do not,' she added, with a sigh, 'I do not deny having wished for liberty, and having earnestly tried to regain it. Nature urged me to this; but I take God to witness, that I never conspired against the life of the Queen of England, and that I never approved of such a conspiracy. I confess that I wrote to my friends, soliciting their aid in delivering me from the wretched prisons where I have been held captive for nineteen years. I confess, too, that I have often written in favour of the persecuted Catholics, and that if I could have delivered them from oppression by the shedding of my own blood, I would have done it. But the letters produced against me were not written by me, and I cannot be answerable for the dangerous designs of desperate persons, who are unknown to me.'[1]

The skill with which Mary Stuart defended herself, by thus attacking the weak side of the proofs brought against her, determined the Lord Treasurer to reply. He went over the history of the conspiracy, dwelling on those letters which were least capable of dispute; he showed how, according to the declarations of Nau and Curle, Mary Stuart had carried on her secret correspondence, and in what manner she replied to Babington, maintaining the genuineness of the letter which Nau and Curle confessed to have sent, which Babington allowed he had received, which was known to Tichbourne, Ballard, and Donne, and which was written in the cypher found among her papers, and in Babington's room. He insisted that Mary's criminality was proved by the contents of this very letter, which was in entire conformity with Babington's confession, and the testimonies of Nau and Curle, showing not only her knowledge of the conspiracy but her approval of it.[2] The close argument of the Lord Treasurer failed to embarrass the courageous spirit of the Queen of Scotland.

Babington's declaration, she replied, was of little importance to her. She knew him not; nor could she tell whether what was presented as his confession was really his writing or not. Why had he not been confronted with her before being put to death? That would have been the way to discover the truth.

[1] *Advis de M. de Bellièvre*, in Egerton, p. 103. Camden, p. 497, 498. Tytler, vol. viii., pp. 357, 358.
[2] Hardwicke, vol. i., pp. 233-237. Tytler, vol. viii., pp. 358, 358. Howell vol. i., pp. 1183, 1184.

Did they wish to prevent her from clearing herself? The same might be said of her two secretaries, Nau and Curle. Doubtless, they were still living; why, then, were they not there, that it might be seen whether they would dare to assert in her presence what they had advanced behind her back? Curle was a simple, but, she doubted not, an honest man. Nau was a man of greater cleverness, and gifted with considerable talent; but, although he had been Secretary to the Cardinal of Lorraine, and recommended to her by the King of France, she was by no means certain that the fear of danger and the hope of reward might not have induced him to make a false deposition against her, to which he might have obtained the concurrence of Curle, who was entirely under his control.[1] Her secretaries no, doubt, wrote her letters, and put them in cyphers; but she was by no means certain that they had not inserted things which had not been dictated by her. Was it not possible that they might have received letters for her without delivering them, and that they might have sent away others in her name and with her cyphers without showing them to her? 'And am I,' she continued, with equal energy and dignity, 'am I, a Queen, to be judged guilty on such proofs as these? Is it not manifest that there must be an end to the majesty and security of Princes, if they are made to depend on the writings and the testimony of their secretaries? I claim the privilege of being judged from my own words and my own writings, and I am certain that none will be found against me.'[2]

In the course of this discussion Mary complained repeatedly and earnestly that she could not refer to papers which had been taken from her. She even seemed to insinuate that Walsingham had altered her cyphers, with which serious accusation the defenders of this unfortunate Queen, after the lapse of three hundred years, still load the memory of Elizabeth's unscrupulous secretary.[3] 'What security have I,' said she, turning towards

[1] Camden, vol. ii., p. 500.
[2] MS., Brit. Mus., Caligula, IX. fol. 383. Howell, vol. i., p. 1182, 1183. Hardwicke, vol. i., p. 233. Camden, vol. ii., p. 500. Tytler, vol. viii., p. 360, 361.
[3] Prince Labanoff formally accuses him, and Tytler also believes it. Not only Walsingham's unscrupulousness, and the perfidious means employed by him to ruin Mary, as already shown, but a discovery recently made by Mr. Tytler and Sir C Lemon in the State Paper Office, seem to confirm this accusation. It had been said by Camden (vol. ii., p. 479), that a postscript had been fraudulently added to Mary's letter to Babington of the 17th July, asking him for the names of the six gentlemen who had engaged to assassinate Elizabeth. This postscript was found by the gentlemen above-named in the State Paper Office, written in cypher by Philips, and scored out, showing that it was not sent. (Tytler, vol. viii., p. 326, 327.)

him, 'that these are my cyphers?' Then, addressing him with vehemence, she continued : ' Do you think, Mr. Secretary, that I was ignorant of the stratagems you so cunningly employed against me? Your spies surrounded me on all sides, but you are not perhaps aware that some of them made false depositions, and then informed me of it. And if *they* have thus acted,' she added, addressing herself to the whole assembly, ' how can I be certain that *he* has not forged my cyphers to procure my condemnation? Has he not already formed deep schemes against my life and that of my son?' [1]

This direct and terrible attack agitated Walsingham, who instantly rose and exclaimed with the greatest energy, "I call God to witness that I have done nothing, as an individual, not befitting an honest man, nor anything, as the servant of my Royal Mistress, unworthy of my office. I have declared my conviction of criminality, because the safety of the Queen and the kingdom concern me in an extraordinary manner. I have traced with the greatest care all the plans directed against the Queen and against the kingdom, and even if that traitor Ballard had offered me his

---

In fact, it does not appear in the certified copy of the letter of the 17th July, produced on the trial of Mary Stuart, nor in any of the copies which have been preserved. To account for the postscript not having been employed by Phillips and Walsingham, in whose hands the original cypher of Mary's letter remained more than a week before it was transmitted to Babington, Mr. Tytler and Prince Labanoff suppose that they had recourse to other means. They conjecture that in Mary's own letter there had been no reference to anything but the two plans of invasion and flight, and that Walsingham and Phillips, having abandoned the idea of mentioning the six gentlemen in the postscript, interpolated in the body of the letter the three passages which there appear relative to these persons, the last being of considerable length. (See Tytler, vol. viii., pp. 439–451. ' Historical remarks on the Queen of Scots supposed accession to Babington's conspiracy,' and Labanoff, vol. vi., p. 396–398.) In order to give credit to this supposition, it must be taken for granted that the whole letter was re-written by Phillips, who could not have found room enough in the original for the insertion of the three passages fraudulently introduced between the real ones relating to the invasion, the taking possession of England, and the deliverance of Mary; and further, it must be supposed that Babington did not perceive the alteration. It is also necessary to believe that Nau and Curle, in order to serve themselves, must have acknowledged as their own those pages which were inserted by Phillips,—must have given themselves credit for the work of the forger, which they acknowledged, the one to have written, and the other to have put in cypher,—must have attributed to themselves a share in the conspiracy against the life of Elizabeth, though all the while they were ignorant of it; and, finally, that they must have implicated their unfortunate mistress in it, while they knew her to be innocent.

[1] Tytler, vol. viii., p. 361, 362. Camden, vol. ii., p. 498. Howell, vol. i., p. 1182. *Advis de M. de Bellièvre*, in Egerton, p. 103.

aid to discover them, I would not have repulsed him.'[1] After some other discussions, the sitting of the High Court was adjourned till the following day.

At the second meeting Mary Stuart did not defend herself, as she had done the day before, by denying everything. She once more disclaimed the jurisdiction of the Court,[2] and then persisted in maintaining her innocence. 'I have been anxious,' said she, 'that the safety of the Catholics should be provided for, but I never wished that it should be obtained by means of bloodshed and murder. I have preferred the part of Esther to that of Judith, seeking rather to intercede with God for the people, than to deprive even the meanest of them of life.'[3] She however admitted her original letters to Morgan, Paget, and Mendoza, which could not indeed be disavowed, and even acknowledged that her secretaries, acting under her orders, had transmitted certain notes to Babington.[4] She endeavoured to show that these letters and notes referred exclusively to her deliverance and flight, which she would have favoured even by the invasion of England. But, said Elizabeth's lawyers, you could not have recourse to such means of obtaining your liberty without contravening the laws of the kingdom, and without endangering the Queen's life. The invasion of the kingdom and the death of the Queen are inseparably connected, and the one cannot occur without the other. By the mere success of the invasion the Queen would lose her kingdom and her life.[5] Though Mary Stuart acknowledged having entered into this plan of attack against England, urged by the dire necessities to which she was reduced, and even confessed to having meditated transferring the succession to the King of Spain,[6] she yet continued earnestly to disclaim the conspiracy against Elizabeth's life,[7] and persisted in rejecting the testimony of Babington, Nau, and Curle.

In this new discussion, in which her chief adversary was still the bitter Burghley,[8] she was noble and touching. The defence of her dignity inspired her with the most eloquent expressions, and the thoughts of her sad position repeatedly brought tears to

[1] Howell, vol. i., p. 1182. Camden, vol. ii., p. 499. *Advis de M. de Bellièvre*, in Egerton, p. 103.   [2] Howell, vol. i., p. 1184. Camden, vol. ii. p. 502.
[3] Ibid., p. 1185. Camden, vol. ii., p. 502.
[4] *Advis de M. de Bellièvre*, in Egerton, vol. i., p. 103.
[5] Hardwicke, vol. i. p. 245.
[6] Camden, vol. ii., p. 505. Howell, vol. i., pp. 1187, 1188.
[7] Ibid., vol. ii., pp. 504, 505. Howell, vol. i., p. 186.
[8] Howell, vol. i., p. 1185. Tytler, vol. viii. p. 365.

her eyes. 'With what injustice,' she exclaimed, 'am I treated! my letters have been picked out and perverted from their original meaning, and the originals have been taken from me. No consideration is shown for the religion which I profess, and the sacred character I bear as Queen. If my sentiments, my Lords, are personally indifferent to you, you might at least consider the Majesty of Royalty, which is injured in my person, and think of the example you are setting.'[1] She then appealed to God and the foreign princes against the injustice shown towards her,[2] and thus continued, 'I entered this country confiding in the friendship and the promises of the Queen of England,' and then, taking a ring from her finger, and holding it up to her judges, 'Here, my Lords,' said she, 'here is the pledge of love and protection which I received from your Royal Mistress. Look well at it. It was in reliance upon this that I came among you. Nobody knows better than yourselves how this pledge has been respected?'[3] She then demanded to be heard before Parliament, or to have an interview with Elizabeth,[4] and added, 'As one who is accused of crimes, I claim the privilege of an advocate to plead my cause; or else, as a Queen, I call upon you to believe the word of a Queen.'[5]

She never appeared again, however, before the Commissioners, nor was she admitted before Parliament, or before the Queen. The Commissioners would have pronounced judgment immediately, but for the secret orders of Elizabeth. In conformity with the instructions of that Princess,[6] whose indecision and delay provoked the impatience of Walsingham,[7] they adjourned on the 25th of October to Westminster. The *Queen of the Castle*, as Burghley ironically called the unfortunate prisoner,[8] was left at Fotheringay, with her intractable keeper. On the 25th of October, the Commissioners assembled in the Star Chamber at Westminster. Here they renewed the inquiry, and subjected Nau and Curle to a fresh examination in their presence. Thus, at Fotheringay they examined the accused without the witnesses, and at Westminster the witnesses without the accused.

[1] Tytler, vol. viii., pp. 363, 364. Howell, vol. i., p. 1185.
[2] Howell, vol. i., p. 1185. *Advis de M. de Bellièvre*, in Egerton, vol. i., p. 103.
[3] Courcelles, *Negotiations*, p. 18. Bannatyne, *Club Edition*. Tytler, vol. viii., p. 364. [4] Howell, vol. i., p. 1188. [5] Tytler, vol. viii., pp. 364, 365.
[6] MS. letter, British Museum, Caligula, C. IX., fol. 332. Camden, vol. ii., p. 506.
[7] Walsingham to Leicester, 15th October, 1586. British Museum, Caligula C. IX., fol. 415.
[8] Burghley to Davison, 15th October, 1586. Ellis, vol. i., p. 18.

In these proceedings, carried on in contempt of the usual forms, as they had been commenced in contempt of law, there was no confronting of witnesses. Mary Stuart's secretaries gave a *vivâ voce* confirmation to their former depositions, and the very same day the Commissioners unanimously pronounced sentence of condemnation against the unhappy Queen.[1] This sentence, signed by all the Commissioners, bore that, since the 1st of June of the 27th year of Elizabeth's reign, various plots had been framed by Anthony Babington and others, with the knowledge of the Queen of Scotland, who, making pretensions to the English crown, had taken part in these conspiracies, the object of which was the subversion and death of the Queen, their Sovereign.[2] Adroit as politicians, while they were merciless as judges, the Commissioners, at the instigation of Burghley, willing to spare the son while they sacrificed the mother, declared that their sentence was not to prejudice in any respect the honour or the rights of the King of Scotland,[3] for whom they preserved the prospect of the throne in the hope that his interests would blind him to his duties.

A few days later, the Parliament assembled at Westminster. It sanctioned the condemnation of the Queen of Scotland,[4] whom the vindictive but prudent Elizabeth desired not to put to death but under the sanction of an act, combining a judicial character with an expression of the national will. The Lords and the members of the Commons, with mingled feelings of thankfulness and fanaticism, of devotion and cruelty, expressed their gratitude to God's providence and the Queen's wisdom for having foiled the conspiracy which, as they said, threatened the life of their excellent and gracious Sovereign, in whose safety consisted all their happiness, which would have ruined the happy condition of so noble a kingdom, and subjected the true servants of the Almighty and the independence of the Crown to the tyranny of Rome,[5] and they demanded that the Scottish Queen should at length be brought to punishment for this detestable conspiracy, as well as for all those which she had previously contrived. 'By neglecting to do this,' said they to Elizabeth, 'you would incur the displeasure of Heaven, and expose yourself to the chastise-

---

[1] Howell, vol. i., p. 1188, 1189. Hardwicke, vol. i., p. 249, 250. Letter of Chateauneuf to Henry III., 5th November, 1586. MS. Bibl. Nat., No. 9513; Coll. of Mesmes, vol. iii., fol. 389, and in Egerton, vol. i., p. 88.
[2] Howell, vol. i., p. 1189. Camden, vol. ii., p. 506.
[3] Ibid.; Camden, vol. ii., p. 507.
[4] Ibid., vol. i., p. 1190. Camden, vol. ii., p. 508.
[5] Ibid., vol. i., p. 1190.

ments of God's justice, who has left us several severe examples of it in the Holy Scriptures.'¹

Elizabeth, in her reply, expressed her deep gratitude to the Divine goodness for having miraculously preserved her from so many dangers. She showed herself touched by the cordial devotion of her subjects, who, after twenty-eight years of her reign, exhibited more good-will towards her than the day she ascended the throne.² She spoke of the unfortunate lady, whose death they asked for at her hands, more in sorrow than in hatred, and concluded her speech by saying: 'Do not hurry my decision. It is an affair of great importance, and I am accustomed to deliberate longer on less weighty matters before making up my mind. I shall pray Almighty God to enlighten my understanding, and to show me what will be best for the interests of His Church, the prosperity of my people, and your own security.'³

Two days after, with a mind agitated by uncertainty, and with a seeming repugnance to adopt so terrible a resolution, she sent the Lord Chancellor to the upper Chamber, and the Speaker, Puckering, to the lower House, to entreat both of them to consider whether they could not devise some milder mode of providing for her safety, in sparing the life of the Scottish Queen.⁴ The two Houses deliberated again on the subject, and returned a unanimous answer, on the 18th November, to the effect that the Queen of England would be in danger so long as the Scottish Queen lived, because repentance on her part could neither be looked for, nor could it be sincere,—because a more strict confinement, with written promises and hostages delivered, would be vain as soon as the Queen of England should be killed,—and because her removal from the kingdom would immediately bring about an armed invasion of England. 'Therefore,' said they in their address to Elizabeth, 'unless the just sentence pronounced against her be executed, your Majesty's person will remain in great danger, religion cannot be long preserved among us, and the flourishing condition of these realms is threatened with early and disastrous ruin. In sparing her, your Majesty not only encourages the audacity of the enemies of God, of your own authority, and of your kingdom, but dispirits and discourages the hearts of your affectionate people, and provokes the hand as well as the wrath of God.'⁵ After citing the most cruel examples

¹ Howell, p. 1192.
² Ibid., pp. 1192, 1193. Camden, vol. ii., pp. 508, 509.
³ Ibid., p. 1194. Camden, vol. ii., pp. 509–511.
⁴ Ibid., pp. 1194, 1195.
⁵ Ibid., p. 1195. Camden, vol. ii., pp. 511, 512.

from ancient history, the Bible, and the middle ages, the Lord Chancellor and the Speaker, in presenting to their Queen, at Richmond Castle, this sanguinary supplication of the two Chambers, ended by calling upon Heaven to incline her heart to their just desires!¹

There is no doubt that this was exactly what Elizabeth wanted. It was her wish to be pressed, and to have the appearance of being forced, because it gave her the support of her subjects, who thus became her ardent accomplices, and enabled her to throw upon them the burden of this useful act of cruelty. She did not yield, however, even yet, and replied to them with embarrassing ambiguity. She told them that she felt more perplexed than she had ever done in her life before,—that she did not know whether she ought to speak or keep silence,—that she would have wished to have preserved her own life without sacrificing that of another, and that it seemed cruel to strike so great a Princess, and to dip the hands of the executioner in the blood of so near a relative.² Then, expatiating on the dangers of her position, the hatred of her enemies, the hesitations of her mind, and the troubles of her heart, she dismissed them with these words:—'If I accede to your request, I should say, perhaps, more than I think; and, if I reject it, I precipitate myself into the very danger from which you would save me. Accept, I pray you, my thanks and my perplexities, and take in good part an answer which is no answer.'³

In spite of the hesitation which she really felt, though she exaggerated it, and which belonged as much to her policy as to her character, Elizabeth despatched Lord Bathurst and Robert Beale, clerk of the Council, to Fotheringay, to communicate to the royal prisoner the sentence of death.⁴ Accompanied by Amias Paulet and Drue Drury,⁵ who had also been attached to Mary's guard, the bearers of the message announced, on the 10th November, to that Princess, whose tranquil courage equalled her extreme misfortune, that the judges had pronounced her sentence, that the Houses of Parliament had ratified it, and had moreover required its immediate execution, and that she must prepare to die, her life being incompatible with that of their sovereign and

---

¹ Howell, p. 1198.
² Ibid., pp. 1198, 1199. Camden, vol. ii., pp. 512, 513.
³ Ibid., pp. 1200, 1202. Camden, vol. ii., p. 513, and Parliamentary History, vol. iv., p. 298. ⁴ Howell, vol. i., p. 1202.
⁵ Mary Stuart's Letter to the Archbishop of Glasgow, of the 24th November, 1586, in Labanoff, vol. vi., pp. 466, 467.

with the maintenance of their religion. She listened to them without any signs of emotion, and thanked God for being regarded as a fit instrument to re-establish the Catholic religion, and for being called on to shed her blood in its cause.[1] Elizabeth's envoys having replied that it was impossible she could even pass for a saint or a martyr,[2] dying, as she was about to do, for having compassed the murder and deposition of Elizabeth, she continued with eagerness to repel that accusation. She also rejected, mildly but firmly, the offer made to her of the services of an English bishop or dean, and requested that she might be allowed the spiritual aid of her chaplain, of whom she had been for some time deprived.

From that day forward Paulet, regardless of her unparalleled misfortunes, conducted himself towards her with insolent harshness. He entered her chamber without ceremony, and told her that she should no longer be treated like a queen, but like any ordinary woman whose life was legally forfeited,[3] and ordered the dais surmounted by her arms to be pulled down. Mary showed him, instead of her arms, the cross of Jesus Christ,[4] and nobly told him that she held from God the dignity of Queen, and that she would deliver it up, along with her soul, to God alone.[5] Believing the hour of her death to be near at hand, and being still deprived of her chaplain, she wrote to the Pope asking his absolution, blessing, and prayers. Along with the salvation of her own soul, she commended to Sixtus V. the spiritual interests of her son; she remitted to the Roman Pontiff her own authority over him, beseeching him to act the part of a father to him, and to bring him back to the faith of his ancestors; she expressed a desire that her son, under the guidance of the Pope, the Duke of Guise, and Philip II., should render himself worthy to enter the family of the Catholic King by marrying his daughter. 'Thus,' she continued, 'I have laid before you the grief of my worldly desires .... Je les présente aux piedz de votre Saintete que très-humblement je bayse.'[6]

The secret messenger who was to bear this letter, after her death, to Sixtus V., ' was also charged with letters for Mendoza,

---

[1] Labanoff, vol. vi., p. 467.   [2] Ibid, p. 468.   [3] Ibid., p. 469.
[4] " Je leur ai monstré au lieu de mes armes audit days, la croix de mon Sauveur." Mary Stuart's letter to the Duc de Guise, November 24th, 1586, in Labanoff, vol. vi., p. 464.
[5] Mary Stuart's Letter to the Archbishop of Glasgow, ibid., p. 469.
[6] This letter from Mary to Sixtus V., extracted from the Archives of the Vatican, is dated 23rd November. Labanoff, vol. vi., pp. 447–456.

for the Duke of Guise and the Archbishop of Glasgow,[1] which could not be delivered till about a year afterwards.[2] In all of them the faithful and courageous Mary shows herself mindful of the interests of the Catholic cause, and solicitous about the fate of her desponding servants, while she views her approaching end with a resignation at once Christian and heroic, and takes leave of her friends with affecting tenderness. She had acquired an unwonted degree of mildness and serenity. Her eloquence, though great as ever, was divested of its spleen and its impetuosity. Her heart had rejected all the acerbities of life, and her thoughts had become imbued with the most religious elevation. She rejoiced to die for the Catholic faith. 'I am happy,' said she, 'to shed my blood at the instance of the enemies of the Church.'[3] She informed Mendoza that she retained the same sentiments towards the King his master, to whom she transmitted her rights, in the event of her son not returning to the true faith. In bidding him farewell, she thanked him for the zealous affection he had always had for her. 'You will receive,' she says, 'as a keepsake (*un tocquen*) from me, a diamond which I hold dear, as that with which the late Duke of Norfolk pledged his faith to me, and which I have always worn; keep it for love of me.'[4]

She also sent a ring set with a ruby[5] to the Duke of Guise, and in the letter which she wrote him, mingled effusions of affection with transports of religious faith. 'My good cousin,' she writes, 'more dear to me than any other in the world, I bid you adieu, being about to be put to death through an unjust sentence. . . . Though no executioner ever before imbrued his hands with our blood, do not feel ashamed of it, dear friend; for the sentence of heretics and enemies to the Church, who have no jurisdiction over an independent Queen like me, is profitable in the sight of God to the children of his Church; if I had adhered to them I should not have met with this blow. All those of our house have been pursued by this sect; as witness your father, along with whom I hope to be received into the mercy of the just Judge. And God be praised for all, and give you grace to persevere in the service of his Church as long as you live; and never may this honour depart from our race, that, men as well as women, we may always be ready to shed our blood to uphold the

---

[1] Labanoff, vol. vi., pp. 456, 461, 465.
[2] On the margin of Mendoza's are the following words, 'Reciviô-se en Paris á 15 Octobre, 1587." Labanoff, vol. vi., p. 461.   [3] Ibid., p. 458.
[4] Ibid., p. 460.   [5] Ibid., p. 463.

battle of the faith, setting aside all other worldly considerations; and as for me, I esteem myself born, both on my father's and my mother's side, to offer up my blood in that good fight, and I have no intention of degenerating."[1]

At the same time, she addressed her last wishes to Elizabeth in these pathetic terms:[2] 'Madam, I return thanks to God with all my heart, that it pleases Him to put an end, through your decree, to the weary pilgrimage of my life. I do not ask that it may be prolonged, having had but too long experience of its bitterness. I only beseech your Majesty that, as I cannot look for any kindness from certain zealous ministers who hold the highest rank in the government of England, I may receive from you alone, and not from others, the following favours:—

'In the first place, I ask, that—as it is not allowable for me to expect a burial in England, according to the Catholic solemnities practised by the ancient kings, your ancestors and mine, and as in Scotland dishonour and violence has been done to the ashes of my progenitors—as soon as my enemies shall be satiated with my innocent blood, my body may be carried by my servants into some godly land, especially France, where the bones of the Queen my honoured mother repose, in order that this poor body, which has never known repose since it has been united to my soul, may at length find peace when separated from it.

'Secondly, I pray your Majesty, from the apprehension I feel for the tyranny of those to whose power you have abandoned me, that I may not be executed in any secret place, but in the sight of my domestics and other persons who may be able to bear witness to my faith and obedience to the true Church, and to defend the remainder of my life and my last breath from the false reports which my enemies may spread.

'Thirdly, I request that my domestics, who have served me through so many troubles, and with so much fidelity, may be allowed to retire freely wherever they may wish to go, and to enjoy the small presents which my poverty has bequeathed them in my will.

'I conjure you, madam, by the blood of Jesus Christ, by our relationship, by the memory of Henry VII. our common parent, and by the title of Queen, which I still bear till death, not to

[1] Labanoff, vol. vi., pp. 462, 463, 464.
[2] This letter, printed in Jebb, vol. ii., pp. 91, 92, and in Labanoff, vol. vi., p. 444–446, is taken from the Vraye Histoire de Marie Stuart, by N. Caussin, published at Paris, in 1624. The phraseology, as there given, has been somewhat altered from Mary Stuart's, being that of the commencement of the 17th century.

refuse these my reasonable requests, and to give me assurance of that by a line under your hand; and thereupon I will die, as I have lived, your affectionate sister and prisoner.'

This admirable letter, to which no answer was returned, probably never reached Elizabeth,[1] who continued more than ever a prey to indecision. She wished to take her life, yet dared not. The whole world had been astonished and moved by the trial and condemnation of a queen. From France and from Scotland, where Mary had reigned, where her brother-in-law and son were still seated on the throne, where were her nearest relations and dearest friends, solemn embassies had been despatched to Elizabeth, conjuring her to spare her life, and threatening her, if she proceeded to extremities.

Chateauneuf, the ambassador of Henry III., immediately interposed in her favour, but in vain. Elizabeth had send Wotton[2] to France with certified copies of all the documents, which, as showing the reality and extent of the conspiracy, and the good understanding between Mary Stuart, the King of Spain, and the Leaguers of France, were best suited to convince Henry III., and to cool his ardour in her cause. Although not disinclined to admit the culpability of his sister-in-law,[3] Henry charged Chateauneuf to express all the interest which he felt in her. He considered her prolonged imprisonment an excuse for her conspiring, and recognized in no one the right of judging and punishing her.[4] He, therefore, charged Chateauneuf to beseech Elizabeth, in his name, as being her most perfect friend, and as having likewise his own reputation concerned, to manifest her kindness and clemency towards a near relation.[5]

On learning the sentence pronounced on Mary Stuart, he sent Pomponne de Bellièvre to England to try to save her life. Bellièvre arrived in London on the 1st of December. The audience, which he requested for the following day, was not granted till the 7th.[6] In the course of his long speech,[7] in which he accumulated every historical example and every political maxim in order

[1] Jebb, p. 92.
[2] Pacquet of Mr. Wotton's Despatches into France, 1586, October 4th. State Paper Office.
[3] 'Qu' encores que ma dite belle-sœur eut en quelque sorte participé à la conjuration . . . laquelle je suis pour ma part fort ayse et loue Dieu infiniment n' avoir point été executée.' Despatch of Henry III. to Chateaneuf of the 1st November, 1586. State Paper Office. [4] Ibid. [5] Ibid.
[6] Bibl. Nat. MS. 9513. Coll. de Mesmes, Lettres Originales d Etat, vol. iii., fol. 391. Life of Egerton, pp. 91, 99.
[7] Harangue de Sieur de Bellièvre. Bibl. Nat. MS. Dupuy, v. 844, fol. 450, et seq., in Egerton, vol. i., pp. 103–108.

to induce Elizabeth to show mercy, Bellièvre stated one reason, to which she ought to have been more sensible than to any other. Alluding to the ambitious designs and secret devices of Philip II., he said: 'If it is pretended that your Catholic subjects are less obedient to you on account of the support they find in the Queen of Scots, your good sense will enable you to see that there is no great reason to fear such a feeble support; and on this point, I will tell you, madam, what I have been assured is true by an honourable personage—that a certain minister of a Prince, whom you have reason to suspect, openly declares that it would be a good thing for his Master's greatness that the Queen of Scotland were already dead, for he is very certain that the English Catholic party would range themselves entirely on his Master's side.'[1]

Elizabeth did not appear moved, either by the merciful considerations, or the advice touching her own interest, which had been urged by Bellièvre. She broke out in invectives against Mary, and told Bellièvre and Chateauneuf, 'that she had been forced to the decision which had been taken, because it was impossible for her to preserve her own life and save that of the Queen of Scots also, and that, if they knew any mode of ensuring her safety, and at the same time sparing Mary, she would be greatly obliged to them.'[2] This same answer was made to Bellièvre a few days after by the Grand Treasurer Burghley, the Vice-Chamberlain Hatton, and Secretary Walsingham. They told him that the safety of the one was the death of the other.[3]

Elizabeth was equally inflexible at the second audience granted to Bellièvre and Chateauneuf, on the 15th of December, when they renewed their solicitations in favour of Mary Stuart. She complained, in a loud voice and energetic language, that Henry III. had failed in the treaty he had made with her, by refusing to deliver up Morgan and Paget, whose persons she had demanded.[4] She concluded by telling them, 'that though she had given them several days to think about it, they had not yet found out the means of preserving the Queen of Scots' life without risking her own; that she did not wish to be cruel towards herself, and that the King, their master, could not think it right that she, who was innocent, should die, and that the Queen of Scots, who was guilty, should be saved.'[5]

In order to obtain the enthusiastic support of her people

[1] Harangue de Sieur de Bellièvre. Bibl. Nat. MS. Dupuy, v. 834, fol. 450, *et seq.*, in Egerton, p. 106.
[2] Bib. Nat. MS., 9513; Coll. de Mesmes, vol. iii., fol. 399. Life of Egerton, p. 91. [3] Ibid. [4] Ibid. [5] Ibid.

against the solicitations from abroad, Elizabeth caused Mary's sentence of condemnation to be proclaimed in the streets of London. The Earl of Pembroke, the Lord Mayor, and the aldermen were present at this proclamation, which was accompanied by the ringing of bells and the most ardent demonstrations of joy.

For the space of twenty-four hours the bells were rung in London, and throughout all parts of the kingdom; and bonfires were kindled in token of approval and rejoicing.[1] The two ambassadors of Henry III., seeing this violent manifestation of popular feeling against poor Mary, feared that she would be put to death without further delay; and in the name of their master they immediately implored Elizabeth to postpone the execution of the sentence. Elizabeth granted them a delay of twelve days,[2] and they sent the Vicomte Genlis (son of the Secretary of State, Brulart,) to Henry III., to inform him how matters were proceeding, and to assure him that nothing short of his favour and his authority could now save the Queen of Scotland.

Henry III. wrote to his ambassadors, directing them to employ every means of persuasion to soften the severity of Elizabeth, and to intimate to her that if she should execute a sentence so rigorous and so extraordinary, it would be particularly felt by them, besides the insult which would thereby be offered to all the other princes and potentates of Christendom; and finally, to assure Elizabeth that he would, by all means in his power, prevent her being exposed to similar attempts for the future, and that the relations of his sister-in-law would pledge themselves in her name, and would promise on their faith and honour that neither she, nor any one for her, should make any attempt injurious to the Queen of England.[3]

On the 6th of January Bellièvre repaired to the Palace at Greenwich, where the Queen had spent the Christmas holidays. He conjured her to yield to the representations of Henry III., and to accept his offers, alleging that her safety would be much better secured by the life of Mary than by her death. 'The grand rule,' said he, ' for governing well and happily, is to avoid the shedding of blood; one execution leads to another, and these events usually have their train of evil consequences.'[4] In

[1] Bibl. Nat. MS. 9513; Coll. de Mesmes, vol. iii., fol. 399. Life of Egerton, p. 92. [2] Ibid., pp. 92, 93. [3] Life of Egerton, p. 95.
[4] Bibl. Nat. Béthune MS., No. 8955; Registers of Villeroy and Colbert MS., No. 18; Miscellanies; *Advis de ce qui a esté faict en Angleterre par M. de Bellièvre sur les Affaires de la royne d' Escosse en mois de Nov. et Dec.*, 1585, et Janvier, 1587. Life of Egerton, p. 109.

order to mingle threats with arguments, and to fortify sympathy
by fear, he added : 'If it be your Majesty's good pleasure to set
at naught such high considerations, and to disregard the prayers
of the King my master, he has charged me to tell you, madam,
that he shall resent this proceeding as a thing adverse to the
common interests of kings, and most especially offensive to him."¹
These last words roused Elizabeth's displeasure, and she angrily
exclaimed: 'Monsieur de Bellièvre, are you charged by the
King, my brother, to hold this language to me?' 'Yes, madam,
I have been expressly commanded so to do by his Majesty.'
'Have you,' rejoined the Queen, 'this power, signed by his
hand?' 'Yes, madam, the King, my master, your good brother,
has expressly enjoined and charged me, in letters, signed by his
own hand, to address these remonstrances to your Majesty.'
'Then I desire,' added Elizabeth, 'that you declare the same,
signed by your hand!'² Bellièvre then presented to her a copy
of the orders he had received, and he took leave without bringing
with him one glimmering of hope. Elizabeth merely said that
she would send to Paris an ambassador who would arrive there as
soon as he could, and who would make the King acquainted with
her resolution respecting the affairs of the Queen of Scotland.³

Bellièvre departed from London on the 13th of January; on
the 16th he embarked at Dover, and almost immediately Elizabeth addressed to Henry III. (whom she found to be at once too
weak to be a safe ally or to become a dangerous enemy) a letter
full of artful complaints and haughty reproaches. She asked
him whether he thought he was behaving honourably and acting
a friendly part in thus seeking to make an innocent person the
victim of a murderess. She told him that instead of thanking
her for having sought to defend him against the designs of those
who would end by ruining him, he was so blind as to yield himself to their counsel, and to address to her, through the mouth of
M. de Bellièvre, language the meaning of which she could not
well understand. 'To speak of resentment,' added she, 'because
I do not save her life, is the threat of an enemy, which, I promise
you, will never make me fear;—on the contrary, it is the surest
way to despatch the cause of so many misfortunes.' She requested Henry would explain to his ambassador how she was to
understand his words. 'For,' added she, 'I will never live to
see the hour when any prince whatsoever may boast of having

¹ Life of Egerton, p. 109.   ² Ibid., p. 101.
³ Ibid. Bèthune MS., No. 8955, and Colbert, No. 18, Miscellanies. Life of
Egerton, p. 101.

humbled me so that I should drink such a draught of my own dishonour.'¹

The efforts of the King of Scotland, in behalf of his mother, were not very strenuous. When Courcelles, the French envoy, went to Falkland Castle, to urge the unfeeling James VI. to intercede with Elizabeth, he found him engaged in hunting, and very little disposed to aid his mother.² James, whose affairs were conducted by Lord Hamilton, whose mind was directed by the perverse Master of Gray, and who had for his ambassador in London, the traitor Archibald Douglas, was aiming only to secure to himself the English succession, and to maintain friendly relations with Elizabeth. He had congratulated her on the discovery of the new conspiracy,³ and on being informed of his mother's sad position, he coolly observed that she had broken her promises to the Queen of England, and that she must drink the draught she had brewed for herself.⁴ Courcelles, Lord Hamilton, and George Douglas (the latter had remained faithfully attached to Mary Stuart, ever since he had delivered her from the Castle of Lochleven)—all represented to James, but at first ineffectually, the injury he would inflict on himself if he suffered his mother to be tried and condemned.

James VI., whom Elizabeth had informed by her envoy, Robert Beale,⁵ of the plot hatched against her by Mary Stuart, in conjunction with Claude Hamilton and the King of Spain, replied, 'that his mother was not better disposed towards him than she was to the Queen of England;—that she had been desirous of reducing him to the earldom of Darnley, of establishing a regency in Scotland, and depriving him of the sovereignty;—that he was assured the Queen of England would not have failed to apprize him if her life were at stake; and that his mother ought thenceforth to withdraw from all worldly affairs, and devote herself wholly to God.'⁶ He refused to send any one to London, or even to write thither to intercede in his mother's behalf. It is

---

¹ Bibl. Nat. MS., No. 9513. Coll. de Mesmes, vol. iii., fol. 421. Life of Egerton, p. 98.
² Letters from Courcelles to Henry III., dated Edinburgh, Oct. 4, 1586. MS. in the Bibl. Nat., No. 9513; Coll. de Mesmes, vol. iii., fol. 363; and Life of Egerton, p. 81.
³ MS. State Paper Office, Master of Gray to Burghley, Sept. 10th, 1586.
⁴ Courcelles to Henry III., Oct. 4th, MS. Bibl. Nat., No. 9513, and Egerton, p. 81.
⁵ Letter from Chateauneuf to Henry III., dated Sept. 11th, 1586; MS. in the Bibl. Nat., No. 9513; and Egerton, p. 76.
⁶ The same despatch of Courcelles to Henry III., dated Oct. 4th; MS. in the

true that he did not believe her to be in danger.¹ The Scottish nobles were indignant; and rather than submit to the treatment with which Elizabeth menaced their ancient kingdom, whilst affecting an insolent superiority over their country, Angus, Claude Hamilton, Huntly, Bothwell, Herries, and the principal barons, declared that they preferred to take up arms, and to risk the chances of war.

When Mary Stuart was brought to trial, and it was apprehended that her condemnation would ensue, a feeling of dismay pervaded nearly the whole of Scotland, and James VI. determined on sending William Keith to London, and addressing a firm letter to Elizabeth and a menacing note to Walsingham.² Keith was ordered to unite with the French ambassadors to save the mother of his King. He fulfilled his mission with fidelity, but without success. On acquainting James VI. that he had but little hope, he received from that prince a letter, teeming at once with the sentiments of a son and the menaces of a King.³ Keith immediately carried this letter to Elizabeth, who, on reading it, gave way to one of her most violent fits of rage, and declared she would banish Keith from her presence. On the following day she wrote in a tone of haughty displeasure to the young prince, who, subdued by her sternness, sent her, by the Master of Gray and Robert Melvil, some mean explanations.

In the new instructions which James transmitted to his ambassadors he confined himself to the request that his mother, by rigorous confinement and strict supervision, should be deprived of all power to injure Elizabeth.⁴ Though his assembled Parliament urged him to declare that he would attack England, should there be any design of sacrificing the life of the captive Queen, yet he refused to do so. He even did not scruple to avow to Earl Bothwell and to Lord Seton that, in the event of his mother being put to death, he would not break with Queen Elizabeth, unless she attempted to set aside his right to the English succession.⁵ That young royal sophist, alike devoid of dignity and feeling, presumed to maintain, before his assembled guests at

---

Bibl. Nat., No. 9513; and in Egerton, p. 82; and the despatch of Courcelles to Henry III., Oct. 31st, 1586, ibid.; and Egerton, p. 87. ¹ Ibid.
² Tytler, vol. viii., p. 379. ³ Ibid., p. 381.
⁴ Letter from Courcelles to Henry III., dated Dec. 31, 1586; MS. in the Bibl. Nat., No. 9513; Coll. de Mesmes, vol. iii., p. 407; and in Egerton, pp. 96–98.
⁵ Ibid., p. 97, together with the extract from the letter of the Sieur de Courcelles to the Sieur d'Esneval, Dec. 31st, 1586; MS. in the Bibl. Nat., No. 9513; Coll. de Mesmes, vol. iii., fol. 387; and Egerton, vol. i., p. 95.

table, that the ties of blood were less binding between relations than the ties of friendship between allies,[1] thus preparing himself, by cynical reasoning, to sacrifice the feelings of a son to what he alleged to be the duties of a King. This cold-heartedness began to be observed by the people, who, by murmurs, expressed their dissatisfaction whenever he quitted his palace.[2]

James VI. sacrificed his mother by entrusting her defence to the Master of Gray, who felt that his only safety was in the death of the Queen whom he had betrayed. He had already written to Walsingham, that it would be better to take her life by poison, than to have her publicly executed.[3] He arrived in London just at the time when Bellièvre was about to depart from thence; and he pretended, in public, to interest himself in favour of Mary, whilst in his heart he abandoned her. He frequently said to Elizabeth, '*The dead do not bite*,'[4] and he was wholly intent on securing the English succession to his young master. In concert with Robert Melvil, whose efforts in behalf of Mary were sincere, though unavailing, he demanded that the right of succession should be acknowledged in favour of the son, by the resignation of the mother. 'But how is that possible?' inquired Elizabeth; 'she has been declared incompetent, and therefore she cannot transmit anything.' 'If she has no rights,' returned the Master of Gray, 'your Majesty has nothing to fear; and if she has any, and your Majesty will permit her to transmit them to her son, he will then possess the full title of succession to your Highness.' No proposal could be more calculated to excite the jealous distrust, and to provoke the rage of Elizabeth, who exclaimed angrily: 'What! to be delivered of one, and find her place filled by a worse? Yes, indeed! I should put myself into a more miserable position that way than I was before. By God's passion! I might as well cut my own throat at once; and, for the sake of a dukedom or an earldom, you, or those like you, would not scruple to employ some of your desperate ruffians to kill me. No; by God! your master shall never be in this place!'[5] She then left them hastily, without granting the smallest delay in the execution of the Queen of Scots.[6]

[1] Letter from the Sieur de Courcelles to the Sieur d'Esneval. Ibid., and Egerton, p. 96.   [2] Ibid.
[3] Letters from Courcelles to Henry III., dated Dec. 31st, and Egerton, p. 97
[4] *Mortua non mordet.* Camden, vol. ii., p. 529.
[5] Robertson, Justificatory Documents, No. L. Memorial of the Master of Gray, January 12th, 1586-7.   [6] Ibid., and Tytler, vol. viii., pp. 383, 384.

More irritated than intimidated by the representations of the two Kings, Elizabeth, nevertheless, paused for a moment before them. She soon saw, however, that she had nothing to fear from two feeble Princes, whose people were divided, who would take care not to compromise, the one his inheritance, and the other his safety, and who would tolerate, after it was accomplished, the execution which they now sought to prevent. The better to attain her ends, she had, with artificial credulity and affected terror, laid hold of a story of a new conspiracy against her life, with which the French ambassador's name was mixed up, and denounced to her by the very persons who had had the signal audacity to propose it to him.

Shortly after the departure of Bellièvre, Stafford, brother to the English ambassador at Paris, whose mother had been for three and twenty years lady of honour to Elizabeth, and whose sisters resided next her person, presented himself before Chateauneuf. He was a young man of rather bad reputation, living in disorder and want. He stated that a prisoner for debt, named Moody, had to communicate to the ambassador of France something of interest touching the life of the Queen of Scots, and he offered to take the secretary, Cordaillot, to see the man in Newgate. Chateauneuf, who was at the time employing Cordaillot to write his despatches, was imprudent enough to send D'Estrappes, likewise attached to the embassy, to Moody, who, in the presence of Stafford, made to him the most criminal and most compromising proposal. If the French ambassador would pay the sum of one hundred and twenty crowns, for which he was imprisoned, Moody, on regaining his liberty, offered to assassinate Elizabeth.[1]

This overture was rejected by D'Estrappes, who instantly quitted Newgate, and also by Chateauneuf, who forbade Stafford to appear again at the embassy. Stafford, not succeeding in obtaining from him a hundred crowns, which he asked for to pay his debts and run off to the Continent, then accused him of having attempted to form a conspiracy against Elizabeth's life in order to save the Queen of Scots. The English Government[2] felt, or feigned to feel, the liveliest indignation. D'Estrappes was thrown into prison, Chateauneuf's despatches were intercepted, he himself was summoned to the presence of Leicester, Burghley, Hatton, and Davison, who accused him of being at least privy to a plot against the life of their sovereign without

---

[1] Chateauneuf to Henry III., Jan. 23rd, 1587 ; MS. of the Bibl. Nat., No. 9513; Coll. de Mesmes, v. iii., p. 427, and Memoir annexed to his Despatch, ibid. ; also in Egerton, pp. 112–114.   [2] Ibid.

revealing it,[1] and Elizabeth sent Wade into France to denounce him to Henry III., as guilty of criminal machinations towards her.[2] She, at the same time, ordered the English ports to be closed, and the country remained for several weeks without any communication with the Continent. In the midst of the emotion occasioned by the discovery of this chimerical plot, and whilst the most alarming reports were being spread, now of a descent of the Spaniards, now of the presence of the Duke of Guise in Sussex at the head of an army, now of an attempt on Fotheringay, and now of an insurrection of the northern counties,[3] the Privy Council held repeated meetings to urge the Queen to cause sentence of death to be carried into execution against her prisoner.

Elizabeth did not yield to the solicitations of Burghley, Leicester, and Walsingham, but she became thoughtful and gloomy. She neglected her usual amusements, indulged in solitude, and frequently muttered terrible words. She was heard to pronounce a Latin sentence, which served to indicate her anxiety; 'Aut fer aut feri ; ne feriare, feri.'—'Strike, or be struck ; if you would not be struck, strike.'[4] She would have been glad if any one would have relieved her, by a secret assassination, of the responsibility of a legal execution. She hinted to her ministers that they should put Mary to death, and spare her the cruel task of giving the order; and she reproached them with having promised largely when they took the famous oath of the *Association*, and yet doing nothing for her defence. But the responsibility which she hesitated to take upon herself, her ministers refused to incur. They knew her too well not to feel assured that she would disown them the very day after they had ministered to her passion; and that she would even punish them, so as to throw upon them all the odium of an execution, of which she desired the advantage without the blame. They turned, therefore, a deaf ear to her hints,[5] and the Queen was compelled to act directly herself.

On the 1st of February, Secretary Davison, for whom she had sent by Lord Admiral Howard, presented himself before her at ten o'clock in the morning, with the warrant for Mary's exe-

---

[1] Chateauneuf to Henry III. Jan. 23rd, 1587; MS. of the Bibl. Nat. No. 9513; Coll. de Mesmes, vol. iii., p. 427, and Memoir annexed to his Despatch, ibid.; also in Egerton, pp. 112–114.
[2] Letter from Elizabeth to her ambassador in France. State Paper Office.
[3] Tytler, vol. viii., p. 385. Camden, vol. ii., p. 529. Ellis's Letters, second series; vol. iii., p. 106–109.
[4] Camden, vol. ii., p. 532.   [5] Tytler, vol. viii , p. 386.

cution, which had been previously drawn up by the High Treasurer, Burghley. She took it into her hands, read it, asked for a pen, and signed it firmly, desiring Davison to cause the Lord Chancellor to affix to it the Seal of State. She recommended it to be kept as much as possible secret, and added, with an air of pleasantry, ' Show it, nevertheless, to Walsingham ; I fear the blow will kill him on the spot.'[1] She forbade a public execution, directing that it should take place in the great hall of Fotheringay, and not in the court of the castle, and she dismissed Davison with an injunction that she was not to be again addressed on the subject, having done all that the law and reason could require of her.[2]

Just as he was on the point of withdrawing, Elizabeth detained him, and complained of Amias Paulet and those who might have relieved her of this burden. She added, that she might still be freed of it, if he and Walsingham would write to Sir Amias, to sound him on the subject.[3] Whether from want of conscientiousness, or from excess of obedience, Davison did not reject this frightful proposal, but communicated it immediately to Walsingham, while he exhibited the Act signed by the Queen. That very day they wrote to Fotheringay, and in that age, when assassination was not disavowed by any sect, and was repugnant to no political party, two ministers of a powerful sovereign dared, in her name, to instigate the keepers of a prisoner to put her to death clandestinely. Here is the insidious and abominable letter which they jointly addressed to Paulet and Drury:—

' After our cordial greetings, we perceive, from some words lately spoken by her Majesty, that she remarks in you a want of diligence and of zeal in not having discovered of yourselves (without other instigation) some mode of putting that Queen to death, considering the great danger to which her Majesty is exposed, so long as the said Queen is in life. Not to speak of the want of affection towards her, her Majesty remarks further, that you do not consider your own safety, or rather the preservation of religion, of the public weal, and of the prosperity of your country, as reason and policy require you to do. Your conscience would be peaceful before God, and your reputation clear before the world, since you have taken the solemn oath of the *Association*, and since, moreover, the facts charged against that Queen have been clearly proved. Her Majesty, therefore, feels great displeasure at men who profess attachment to her, as

---

[1] Davison's defence, drawn up by himself. In Caligula, chap. ix., fol. 470; Tytler, vol. viii., p. 387.   [2] Ibid.   [3] Ibid.

you do, thus failing in their duty, and seeking to throw on her the weight of this affair, well knowing, as you do, her repugnance to the shedding of blood, particularly that of a person of her sex and of her rank, and so near a relative.

'We perceive that these considerations trouble her Majesty greatly, who, we can assure you, has repeatedly declared that if she did not feel a greater concern for the dangers which her faithful subjects and her good servants run, than for those which threaten herself, she would never consent that this Queen's blood should be shed. We think it very necessary to inform you of these sentiments expressed not long since by her Majesty, and to submit them to your good judgment, and so we recommend you to the Almighty's protection.'[1]

This letter, which Davison begged Paulet to burn after having read it, arrived at Fotheringay on the 2nd of February, towards evening. One hour afterwards, Paulet, who was a sombre fanatic, and a brutal gaoler, but not a dastardly murderer, replied to Walsingham in terms of deep concern and repressed indignation: 'Having received your letter of yesterday at five o'clock in the afternoon of this day, I could not fail to send you an answer with all possible despatch, as you direct. I send it you in all the bitterness which my heart feels at being so unfortunate as to see the day when, by the injunctions of my most gracious Sovereign, I am required to commit an act which God and the laws forbid. My property, my place, and my life are at her Majesty's disposal, and I am ready to surrender them tomorrow, if such is her good pleasure, acknowledging that I hold them from her sole and gracious favour; I do not desire to enjoy them but with the good will of her Highness. But God preserve me from making such a pitiable shipwreck of my conscience, or leaving so foul a stain on my posterity, as to shed blood without the authority of the law, and without a public Act. I hope her Majesty, with her accustomed clemency, will take my loyal answer in good part.'[2]

When Davison communicated this noble letter to Queen Elizabeth, she perused it with signs of strong dissatisfaction, and exclaimed with a passionate tone of voice: 'I detest those fine speakers, those stiff and punctilious persons, who promise everything, do nothing, and throw all the burden on my shoulders.'[3]

[1] This letter, extracted from Paulet's papers, has been printed in Nicholas's Life of Davison, p. 85, and in Robert of Gloucester's Chronicle, by Hearne, vol. ii., p. 674.
[2] Hearne's Robert of Gloucester, vol. ii., p. 675, and Tytler, vol. viii., p. 390.
[3] Ibid., pp. 391, 392.

Nothing now remained but to let the public execution take effect. The Act containing the order for it, which the Queen had signed with her own hand, after being invested by the Chancellor with the seal of State, had been returned to the Privy Council, the members of which, without again consulting Elizabeth, took upon themselves its execution. They addressed it, along with a letter signed by Burghley, Leicester, Hunsdon, Knollys, Walsingham, Derby, Howard, Cobham, Hatton, and Davison, to the Earls of Shrewsbury, and Kent, who were appointed to be present at the execution.[1] Armed with these two documents, Beale set off on his tragic mission to Fotheringay.

Mary had remained in a state of anxious suspense during the two months and a half which had elapsed between the announcement of her sentence and the order for her execution. Her almoner, Préau, had indeed been restored to her for a brief space, and the money, which had been seized along with her papers at Chartley, had been returned to her; but this favour, accompanied as it was by an ominous silence, led her to fear a sudden and secret death, similar to that of the Earl of Northumberland, which had occurred not long since in the Tower of London. Above all, she dreaded a death, under whose veil of obscurity the true dispositions of her soul would be left in uncertainty. Feeling a presentiment of the horrible project which threatened her, yet without suspecting its real author, she had invoked the aid of Elizabeth, who conceived it, against Paulet, who rejected it. On the 19th of December, 1586, she had addressed a final letter to the Queen of England in which she begged her not to allow her to be put to death without an order from herself, to permit her servants to be present at her execution, that they might bear witness to her faith, and her obedience to the Catholic Church, and to allow them to carry away her body secretly.[2] She concluded her letter by almost citing Elizabeth before her God: 'Do not accuse me,' she said, 'of presumption, if, in quitting this world and preparing for a better, I remind you that one day you will have to answer to your charge, as well as those who have been sent before you.'[3]

Such were the fears of Mary Stuart when Robert Beale arrived at Fotheringay on the 5th of February.[4] He had taken

---

[1] Ellis's Letters, second series, vol. iii., pp. 111, 112.
[2] Labanoff, vol. vi., pp 477, 478.   [3] Ibid., p. 479.
[4] Robert Beale left London on Saturday evening, Feb. 4th, according to the old calendar which was still in use in England, but the 14th according to the reformed calendar of Gregory XIII., which was adopted by the Catholic states of the Con-

along with him the London executioner, and after making known to Paulet and Drury the Queen's order and the wishes of the Council, he hastened to the Earls of Kent and Shrewsbury, to present the royal commission, which they were charged to see executed on the morning of the 8th. The two Earls, the Secretary of the Privy Council, and the Sheriff of Northamptonshire, proceeded to Fotheringay, where they were all assembled before mid-day on the 7th.[1] At sight of this unusual concourse, the poor servants of the Queen of Scots, suspecting the misfortune which awaited them,[2] were seized with inexpressible alarm. As for Mary, she was at the time confined to bed by her customary ailments.

About two o'clock, the two Earls desired to speak to her; she sent them word that she was indisposed, but that she would rise if the business they had to communicate was pressing.[3] Learning from them in reply that the business would not admit of delay, she dressed herself, and seating herself before a small work-table which stood at the foot of her bed,[4] she awaited their approach

---

tinent. 'He went to the Castle of Fotheringay, where the Queen was prisoner, on Sunday the 5th of the said month (15th according to the new style.') *La Mort de la royne d'Escosse, douairière de France*, où est contenu le vray discours de la procedure des Anglois à l'exécution d'icelle, la constante et royalle resolution de sa Majesté defuncte, ses vertueux déportements et derniers propos, ses funérailles et enterrement, &c. See Jebb, *De Vita et Rebus gestis serenissimæ Principis Mariæ Scotorum Reginæ*, &c., vol. ii., p. 612. I shall often have occasion to quote this writing, which was published at Paris in the beginning of 1589, from the recent recollections and circumstantial accounts of Mary Stuart's servants, on their arrival in France, particularly of Bourgoin, her physician, who never quitted her, and who is frequently introduced. The author, redressing the *Catholic reader*, thus refers to the pains he has taken to trace this *Histoire funèbre de la royne d'Escosse*:—'For to succeed in presenting to you the pure and sincere truth, without any varnishing or transports of private feeling, I have not left out anything that could be discovered, as well in Scotland and England as in France, even by the aid of those who could give true testimony from being present at all the acts, both during the life and at the death and funeral of her Majesty, of whom (having entertained them in familiar and ordinary conversation) I inquired minutely, along with the notes of reports verbally made by the servants of her defunct Majesty, to the King of France and great nobles of that kingdom.' Ibid., pp. 609, 610.

[1] 'The said Sieur Bele took with him the executioner of this city, who was dressed all in black velvet, as I am told, and they departed on Saturday night somewhat secretly.' M. de Chateauneuf to the King, Feb. 27th, 1587. Bibl. Nat. fonds de Bethune. No. 8880, fol. 7 and 'Advis sur l'Execution de la royne d'Escosse, by M. de la Chastre. Ibid., *Collection des* 500 de Colbert, vol. xxxv., pièce 45.

[2] *La mort de la royne d'Escosse*, &c., in Jebb., vol. ii., p. 612.

[3] 'All the servants were suddenly terrified, and fell into an extreme fear of what was to happen.' Ibid.   [4] Jebb, vol. ii., p. 612.

with the greatest calmness. Her women and the greater part of her servants were around her.[1] The Grand Marshal of England, accompanied by the Earl of Kent, and followed by Beale, Paulet, and Drury, advanced uncovered, and, bowing respectfully to her, informed her that the sentence which had been signified to her by Lord Buckhurst two months and a half before, must now be put into execution, the Queen their mistress being compelled thereto by the solicitations of her subjects.[2] Mary listened to him without exhibiting any emotion, and she afterwards heard the warrant read by Beale, containing the order for her death.[3]

When he had finished reading, she made the sign of the cross.[4] 'God be praised,' said she, 'for the news you bring me. I could receive none better, for it announces to me the conclusion of my miseries, and the grace which God has granted me to die for the honour of his name and of his Church, Catholic, Apostolic, and Roman. I did not expect such a happy end, after the treatment I have suffered and the dangers to which I have been exposed for nineteen years in this country.—I, born a Queen, the daughter of a king, the grand-daughter of Henry VII., the near relation of the Queen of England, Queen Dowager of France, and who, though a free princess, have been kept in prison without legitimate cause, though I am subject to nobody, and recognize no superior in this world, excepting God.'[5] Viewing herself as a victim to her religious faith, she experienced the pure joy of the martyr, partook of its sweet serenity, and maintained to the last its tranquil courage. She again disavowed the project of assassinating Elizabeth, and, placing her hand on the New Testament which lay on the small table before her, she solemnly declared: 'I never either conceived or sought after the death of the Queen of England, and I never consented to it.'[6]

On hearing these words, the Earl of Kent told her, with fanatic rudeness, that the book on which she had sworn was the book of the Papists, and that her oath was worth no more than her book.[7] 'It is the book in which I believe,' replied Mary; 'do you suppose my oath would be more sincere if I took it on yours, in

---

[1] 'To wit, all her damsels, Renée de Reallay, Gilles Maubray, Jeanne Keinedey, lamoiselle, and Elspeth Courle, Marie Pagets, and Susane Korcady; of men there were Dominique Bourgoing, her physician: Pierre Gonjon, apothecary; Jacques Gervait, surgeon; Annibal Stouart, *valet de chambre;* Didier Sifflard, butler; Jean Lander, baker; and Martin Heut, groom of the kitchen.' *La Mort de la royne d'Escosse,* in Jebb., vol. ii., p. 612.
[2] La Mort de la royne d'Ecosse, pp. 612, 613.
[3] Ibid., p. 613. [4] Ibid., p. 614. [5] Ibid., pp. 614, 615.
[6] Ibid., Jebb, vol. ii., p. 616. [7] Ibid.

which I do not believe?"¹ The Earl of Kent then advised her to renounce what he called her superstitions, and offered her the aid of the Protestant Dean of Peterborough, who would teach her the true faith, and prepare her for death.² Mary energetically rejected this offer, as being repugnant to her religious belief,³ and she requested that they would restore her almoner, who had again been removed from her for several days past.⁴ The two Earls had the cruelty and the infamy to refuse this religious consolation to a Queen on the eve of her death.⁵ Neither would they grant her the short delay she asked in order to write out her will carefully, and to make her final arrangements.⁶ Then, in answer to her inquiry as to the hour when she was to die, 'To-morrow, madam,' said the Earl of Shrewsbury, 'about eight o'clock in the morning.'⁷

When the two Earls had quitted her presence, Mary set about consoling her servants, who were bathed in tears.⁸ She ordered her supper earlier, so as to have the whole night for writing and praying. She ate but little, according to her custom.⁹ Bourgoin, her physician, waited on her at table; her *maître d'hôtel*, Andrew Melvil, having been removed from her at the same time with her almoner.¹⁰ She spoke of the Earl of Kent's attempt to convert her, and said, with a smile, that it would require a different sort of doctor to persuade her.¹¹ After supper, she summoned all her servants, and, pouring out some wine into a goblet, she drank to them, and, in an affectionate manner, called upon them to pledge her in return. They all fell on their knees, and, with tears in their eyes, replied to her toast with sorrowful effusion, asking pardon of her for any offences they might have committed against her.¹² She told them she forgave them with

---

¹ La Mort de la royne d'Escosse. Tytler, vol. viii., p. 395.
² Jebb, vol. ii., p. 617.
³ She said, 'that, rather than fail in it, she would lose ten thousand lives, if she had them.' Ibid., p. 617.
⁴ 'That they would send her her priest, whom they kept shut up in the house, to console her and prepare her better for death, for she neither desired nor asked for anything more in this world.' Ibid., p. 618.
⁵ 'She was answered that that could not be done; it was against their religion and their conscience.' Ibid., p. 618. ⁶ Jebb, vol. ii., pp. 622, 623.
⁷ Ibid., p. 621. ⁸ Ibid., p. 625. ⁹ Ibid. ¹⁰ Ibid. ¹¹ Ibid.
¹² 'At the end of supper she commanded all her servants to be called, and caused a cup of wine to be given her, and drank to them all together, asking them if they would not pledge her; caused wine to be given to them, and they each threw themselves on their knees, mingling their tears with the wine, drank to her Majesty, asking her pardon for wherein they might have offended her in time past.' Jebb, vol. ii., p. 626. Camden, vol. ii., p. 534.

good-will, and begged them also to pardon her for any uneasiness she might have caused them.¹ She exhorted them to continue firm to the Catholic religion, and to live in peace and friendship with each other.² Nau was the only one of whom she spoke with bitterness, accusing him of having often sown dissension among them, and of being the cause of her death.³ She then withdrew, and was occupied for several hours in writing, with her own hand, some letters, and her Will,⁴ of which she appointed the Duke of Guise the chief executor.⁵ As the greater part of the legacies she bequeathed could not be paid, except out of her dowry, which would revert to the King of France at her death, she earnestly commended to Henry III. her memory and her last settlements. 'You have always protested that you loved me,' she said; 'show it now by helping me, for charity's sake, in what I cannot do without you, which is to recompense my afflicted servants, by leaving them their wages, and in causing prayers to be made to God for a Queen who has been styled Most Christian, and who dies a Catholic deprived of all her means.'⁶

It was near two o'clock in the morning when she had finished writing. She then placed her will and her letters open in a box, saying that she would no longer occupy herself with the affairs of this world, and that she must think only of appearing before God.⁷ She had addressed a letter to her almoner, who was in the Castle, begging him to pass the night with her in prayer, and to send her his absolution, since she had not been permitted to confess to him, and to receive the last sacrament from his hands.⁸ She caused her feet to be washed,⁹ and searched, in the Lives of the Saints, which her damsels were accustomed to read to her every evening, for an account of a great sinner, whom God had pardoned. She paused at the affecting story of the good thief, which seemed to her the most encouraging example of

---

¹ Jebb, vol. ii., p. 626.   ² Ibid.
³ Ibid., p. 626. She had already, in her interview with the two Earls, made inquiries about Nau and Curle; and, learning that they were still alive, she said, 'What! I am to die, and Nau is not to die! I protest that Nau is the cause of my death.' Ibid., p. 621.
⁴ Ibid., p. 628, 630.
⁵ See her Will, dated 7th Feb., at night. Labanoff, vol. vi., p. 485 to 491.
⁶ Ibid., p. 493.
⁷ La Mort de la royne d'Escosse, in Jebb, vol. ii., p. 632.
⁸ This letter is in Jebb, vol. ii., p. 627, 628, in La Mort de la royne d'Escosse, and also in Labanoff, vol. vi., p. 483, 484.
⁹ La Mort de la royne d'Escosse, in Jebb, vol. ii., p. 632.

human confidence and divine mercy, and which Jean Kennedy read out to her. 'He was,' she remarked, 'a great sinner; but not so great as I am. I beseech our Lord, in memory of His passion, to have remembrance and mercy of me, as He had of him, in the hour of death.'[1]

Feeling somewhat fatigued, and, wishing to preserve or restore her strength for the final moment, she went to bed. Her women continued praying; and, during this last repose of her body, though her eyes were closed, it was evident, from the slight motion of her lips,[2] and a sort of rapture spread over her countenance, that she was addressing herself to Him on whom alone her hopes now rested. At daybreak she arose, saying that she had only two hours to live.[3] She picked out one of her handkerchiefs, with a fringe of gold,[4] as a bandage for her eyes on the scaffold, and dressed herself with a stern magnificence. Having assembled her servants, she made Bourgoin read over to them her will, which she then signed; and afterwards gave them the letters, papers, and presents, of which they were to be the bearers to the princes of her family, and her friends on the Continent.[5] She had already distributed to them, on the previous evening, her rings, jewels, furniture, and dresses;[6] and she now gave them the purses which she had prepared for them, and in which she had enclosed, in small sums, the five thousand crowns which remained over to her.[7] With finished grace, and with affecting kindness, she mingled her consolations with her gifts, and strengthened them for the affliction into which her death would soon throw them. 'You could not see,' says an eye-witness, 'any change, neither in her face, nor in her speech, nor in her general appearance; she seemed to be giving orders about her affairs just as if she were merely going to change her residence from one house to another.'[8]

These last attentions to terrestrial cares having been concluded, she repaired to her oratory, where there was an altar, on which her almoner, before he was separated from her, used to say mass to her in secret. She knelt before this altar, and read, with great fervour, the prayers for the dying.[9] Before she had concluded, there was a knocking at the door; she made them understand that she would soon be ready, and continued her prayers.[10] Shortly afterwards, eight o'clock having struck, there was a

---

[1] *La Mort de la royne d'Escosse*, in Jebb, vol. ii., p. 632.
[2] Ibid. [3] Ibid. [4] Ibid., p. 631. [5] Ibid., p. 631, 632.
[6] Ibid., p. 627. [7] Ibid., p. 631, 632. [8] Ibid., p. 632.
[9] Ibid. [10] Ibid.

fresh knocking at the door, which this time was opened. The Sheriff entered, with a white wand in his hand, advanced close to Mary, who had not yet moved her head, and pronounced these few words: 'Madam, the Lords await you, and have sent me to you.' 'Yes,' replied Mary, rising from her knees, 'let us go.'[1]

Just as she was moving away, Bourgoin handed to her the ivory crucifix which stood on the altar; she kissed it, and ordered it to be carried before her.[2] Not being able to support herself alone, on account of the weakness of her limbs, she walked, leaning on two of her own servants, to the extremity of her apartments. Having arrived at that point, they with peculiar delicacy, which she felt and approved, desired not to lead her themselves to execution, but entrusted her to the support of two of Paulet's servants, and followed her in tears.[3] On reaching the staircase, where the Earls of Shrewsbury and Kent awaited Mary Stuart, and by which she had to descend into the lower hall, at the end of which the scaffold had been raised, they were refused the consolation of accompanying her further. In spite of their supplications and lamentations, they were separated from her; not without difficulty, for they threw themselves at her feet, kissed her hands, clung to her dress, and would not quit her.[4]

When they had succeeded in removing them, she resumed her course with a mild and noble air, the crucifix in one hand and a prayer-book in the other,[5] dressed in the widow's garb, which she used to wear on days of great solemnity,[6] consisting of a gown of dark crimson velvet with black satin corsage, from which chaplets and scapularies were suspended, and which was surmounted by a cloak of figured satin of the same colour, with a long train lined with sable, a standing-up collar, and hanging sleeves. A white veil was thrown over her, reaching from her head to her feet.[7] She evinced the dignity of a Queen, along with the calm composure of a Christian.

At the foot of the staircase[8] she met her *maître d'hôtel*, Andrew

---

[1] *La Mort de la royne d'Escosse*, in Jebb, vol. ii., p. 633.   [2] Ibid.
[3] Ibid., p. 633, 634.   [4] Ibid., pp. 634, 635.   [5] Ibid., p. 634.
[6] 'Her clothes were of the handsomest she had, but yet modest, and becoming a widowed Queen.' Ibid. p. 639.
[7] See the description in Jebb, p. 639, 640 :—'She wore, besides a skirt of taffety, drawers of white fustian, stockings of blue silk, garters of silk, and morocco pumps.' Ibid., p. 640.
[8] 'The two Earls led her to the foot of the stairs, where they had caused to be brought the said *Sieur* Andre Melvil, a Scotchman, her *Maistre-d'hostel*, who had not spoken to her for about three weeks, having been separated from her, along with her Almoner.' Ibid., p. 635.

Melvil, who had been permitted to take leave of her, and who, seeing her thus walking to her execution, fell on his knees, and with his countenance bathed in tears, expressed his bitter affliction. Mary embraced him, thanked him for his constant fidelity, and enjoined him to report exactly to her son all that he knew, and all that he was about to witness. 'It will be,' said Melvil, 'the most sorrowful message I ever carried, to announce that the Queen, my sovereign and dear mistress, is dead.'[1] 'Thou shouldst rather rejoice, good Melvil,' she replied, employing for the first time this familiar mode of address,[2] 'that Mary Stuart has arrived at the close of her misfortunes. Thou knowest that this world is only vanity, and full of troubles and misery. Bear these tidings, that I die firm in my religion, a true Catholic, a true Scotch-woman, a true French-woman. May God forgive those who have sought my death! The Judge of the secret thoughts and actions of men knows that I have always desired the union of Scotland and England. Commend me to my son, and tell him that I have never done anything that could prejudice the welfare of the kingdom, or his quality as king, nor derogated in any respect from our sovereign prerogative.'[3]

She then expressed a hope to the Earls of Shrewsbury and Kent that her secretary, Curle, might be pardoned, and that her servants and women might be admitted to see her die. The Earl of Kent objected, that it was not usual to admit the presence of women on such occasions, and feared that they might give trouble by their lamentations, and perhaps cause scandal in their attempts to dip their handkerchiefs in her blood.[4] 'My Lord,' said Mary, 'I pledge my word that they will do nothing of the kind. Alas! poor souls, they will be gratified at taking leave of me; and I am sure your mistress, being a virgin Queen, would not refuse to allow another Queen to have her women about her at the moment of her death. She cannot have given you such rigorous orders. You would grant me more than that, even if I were a person of lower rank; and yet, my Lords, you

---

[1] *La Mort de la royne d'Escosse*, in Jebb, vol. ii., p. 635.

[2] 'It is to be remarked that the Queen was never used to employ this term "*tu*" to any person she spoke to.' Ibid., p. 635.

[3] See this speech in *A Reporte of the Manner of the Execution of the Scots Queene*, &c., taken from the MS. of the Cotton Libr., Calig. IX., fol. 465, with a dedication to Lord Burghley, by Mr. H. Ellis, published in vol. iii. of the 2nd series of *Original Letters illustrative of English History*, pp. 113-118. With the exception of a few words, it is the same as that in Jebb, p. 635.

[4] *A Reporte of the Manner of the Execution*, &c., in Ellis, vol. iii., 2nd Series, and *La Mort de la royne d'Escosse*, in Jebb, vol. ii., p. 635.

know that I am your Queen's cousin. You certainly will not refuse me this last request. My poor girls desire no more than to see me die.[1] The two Earls then, after consulting together for a moment, granted her wish, and Mary was allowed to call about her four of her male attendants and two of her women. She selected Bourgoin, her physician; Gorion, her apothecary; Gervais, her surgeon; Didier, her butler; Jean Kennedy, and Elizabeth Curle; the two last being those of her waiting-women to whom she was most attached.[2] As soon as they had come down stairs, the Queen, followed by Andrew Melvil, who bore the train of her gown, ascended the scaffold with the same ease and the same dignity as if she were ascending a throne.

The scaffold was erected in the lower hall of Fotheringay. It was two feet and a half high and twelve feet square in extent. It was covered with black English frieze, as were also the chair on which she was to sit, the cushion on which she was to kneel, and the block on which she was to receive the fatal stroke.[3] She seated herself on that dismal chair without changing colour, and without losing any of her accustomed grace and majesty. On her right hand were seated the Earls of Shrewsbury and Kent; on her left stood the sheriff; in front were the two executioners, dressed in black velvet; at a little distance, ranged along the wall, stood her servants; and in the remainder of the hall, behind a barrier which Paulet guarded with his soldiers, were about two hundred gentlemen and inhabitants of the neighbourhood, who had been admitted into the castle, the gates of which were closed.[4] Robert Beale then read the sentence, to which Mary listened in silence, and with such complete abstraction, that she appeared not to be cognisant of what was passing.[5] When Beale had finished reading, she made the sign of the cross, and said with a firm voice:[6]—

[1] *A Reporte of the Manner of the Execution*, &c., in Ellis, vol. iii., 2nd Series, and *La mort de la royne d'Escosse*, in Jebb, vol. ii., pp. 635, 636. Camden, vol. ii., p. 535. [2] Ibid., Ellis. p. 114, and Jebb, p. 635.
[3] Ibid., pp. 114, 115, and Jebb, p. 636. [4] Jebb, p. 636, and Ellis, p. 115.
[5] 'During the reading of which commission, the Queene of Scots was silent; listening unto it with as small regard as if it had not concerned her at all; and with as cheerful a countenance as if it had been a pardon from her Majestie for her life.' *A Reporte of the Manner*, &c., in Ellis, vol. iii., p. 115.
[6] 'The reading of the sentence or commission being ended, Her Majesty made the sign of the cross, as she had done the day before, and with a joyous air, and countenance of a fresh and lively colour, and a firm appearance and look, without any change, her beauty more striking than ever, with marvellous constancy, and her accustomed majesty, with a firm voice and sweet gravity, she began to say. . *La mort de la royne d'Escosse*, in Jebb, p. 636.

'My Lords, I am a Queen born, a sovereign Princess, not subject to the laws, a near relation of the Queen of England, and her lawful heiress. After having been long and unjustly detained prisoner in this country, where I have endured much pain and evil, though nobody had any right over me, being now, through the strength and under the power of men, ready to forfeit my life, I thank God for permitting me to die for my religion, and in presence of a company who will bear witness that, just before my death, I protested, as I have always done, both in private and in public, that I never contrived any means of putting the Queen to death, nor consented to anything against her person.'[1] She then proceeded to deny that she had ever borne towards her any feelings of hatred, and called to mind that she had offered, as the price of her liberty, such conditions as were best calculated to give confidence and to prevent disorders in England.[2]

After pronouncing these words in self-justification, she commenced praying. Upon this, Dr. Fletcher, the Protestant Dean of Peterborough, whom the two Earls had brought with them, approached her, wishing to exhort her to prepare herself for death. 'Madam,' said he, 'the Queen, my excellent Sovereign, has sent me to you . . . .' Mary, interrupting him, replied, ' Mr. Dean, I am firm to the ancient Roman Catholic religion, and I intend to shed my blood for it.'[3] As the Dean insisted, with indiscreet fanaticism, urging her to renounce her faith, to repent, to place her confidence in Jesus Christ alone, for he alone was able to save her, she repelled him with a resolute tone of voice, declared that she would not hear him, and ordered him to be silent.[4] The Earls of Shrewsbury and Kent then said, ' We desire to pray for your Grace, that God may enlighten your heart at your last hour, and that thus you may die in the true knowledge of God.' ' My Lords,' returned Mary, ' if you wish to pray for me, I thank you for it, but I cannot join in your prayers, because we are not of tne same religion.'[5] The struggle between the two faiths, which had continued throughout her life, was prolonged even to the scaffold.

Dr. Fletcher then commenced reading the prayers suited to the occasion, according to the Anglican ritual,[6] while Mary recited in Latin the psalms of penitence and mercy, and fervently kissed

---

[1] *La mort de la royne d Escosse,* in Jebb, p. 636, 637.   [2] Ibid., p. 637.
[3] *A Reporte of the Manner,* &c., Ellis, p. 115.
[4] Ibid., and Jebb, p. 637.   [5] Ellis, p. 115.   Camden, vol. ii., p. 533.
[6] Ellis, pp. 115, 116, and Jebb, pp. 637, 638.

ner crucifix. 'Madam,' rudely said the Earl of Kent to her, 'it is of little use for you to have that image of Christ in your hand, if you have not got him engraved in your heart."¹—'It is difficult,' she answered, 'to hold it in the hand without the heart being touched by it, and nothing suits the dying Christian better than the image of his Saviour."²

When she had finished, on her knees, the three psalms, *Miserere mei, Deus*, &c., *In te, Domine, speravi*, &c., *Qui habitat in adjutorio*,³ she addressed herself to God in English, beseeching him to grant peace to the world, the true religion to England, constancy to all suffering persecution, and to impart to herself the help of His grace, and the enlightenment of the Holy Spirit at this her last hour. She prayed for the Pope, for the Church, the Catholic Kings and Princes, for the King her son, for the Queen of England, and for her enemies; and, recommending herself to the Saviour of the world,⁴ she concluded with these words; 'Like as thy arms, Lord Jesus Christ, were stretched out upon the cross, even so receive me within the stretched-out arms of thy mercy!'⁵ So fervid was her piety, so touching her effusion of feeling, so admirable her courage, that she drew tears from almost all who were present.⁶

Her prayer ended, she arose. The terrible moment had arrived, and the executioner approached to assist her in removing a portion of her dress; but she motioned him away, saying, with a smile, that she had never had such *valets de chambre*.⁷ She then called Jean Kennedy and Elizabeth Curle, who had remained all the time on their knees⁸ at the foot of the scaffold, and she began to undress herself with their assistance, remarking, that she was not accustomed to do so before so many people.⁹ The afflicted girls performed this last sad office in tears. To prevent the utterance of their grief, she placed her finger on their lips, and reminded them that she had promised in their name that they would show more firmness.¹⁰ 'Instead of weeping, rejoice,' she said; 'I am very happy to leave this world, and in so good a cause.'¹¹ She then laid down her cloak, and took off her veil, retaining only a petticoat of red taffety, flowered with velvet. Then, seating herself on the chair, she gave her blessing to her weeping servants.¹²

---

¹ *La mort de la royne, d'Escosse*, &c., Jebb, p. 637.
² *Martyre de Marie Stuart*, &c., Jebb, vol. ii., p. 307, and also *Vita Mariæ Stuartæ, Scotiæ reginæ*, &c., scriptore Georgio Conæo, Scoto. Jebb, vol. ii., p. 47
³ *La mort de la royne*, &c., Jebb, p. 638.   ⁴ Ibid.
⁵ Ibid., p. 638 and p. 100.   Camden, vol. ii., p. 536.   ⁶ Jebb, p. 638.
⁷ Ibid., vol. ii., p. 639.   ⁸ Ibid., p. 636.   ⁹ Ibid., p. 639.
¹⁰ Ibid., and Ellis, vol. iii., pp. 116, 117.   ¹¹ Ibid., p. 639.   ¹² Ibid., p. 640.

The executioner having asked her pardon on his knees, she told him that she pardoned everybody.¹ She embraced Elizabeth Curle and Jean Kennedy, and gave them her blessing, making the sign of the cross over them, and after Jean Kennedy had bandaged her eyes, she desired them to withdraw, which they did weeping.²

At the same time she knelt down with great courage, and still holding the crucifix in her hands, stretched out her neck to the executioner. She then said aloud, and with the most ardent feeling of confidence: 'My God, I have hoped in you; I commit myself to your hands.'³ She imagined that she would have been struck in the mode usual in France, in an upright posture, and with the sword.⁴ The two masters of the works, perceiving her mistake, informed her of it, and assisted her to lay her head on the block, which she did without ceasing to pray. There was a universal feeling of compassion at the sight of this lamentable misfortune, this heroic courage, and this admirable sweetness. The executioner himself was moved, and aimed with an unsteady hand. The axe, instead of falling on the neck, struck the back of the head, and wounded her; yet she made no movement, nor uttered a complaint.⁵ It was only on repeating the blow, that the executioner struck off her head, which he held up, saying, 'God save Queen Elizabeth.'⁶ 'Thus,' added Dr. Fletcher,⁷ 'may all her enemies perish.' A solitary voice was heard after his, saying, 'Amen.' It was that of the gloomy Earl of Kent.⁸

A black cloth was thrown over her remains.⁹ The two Earls did not leave to the executioner, according to custom, the golden

¹ Jebb, p. 100, *La vie de l'incomparable Marie Stuart*, &c.
² Ibid., p. 308, *Le martyre de la royne d'Escosse*, and *La Vie de l'incomparable*, &c., p. 100.   ³ Camden, vol. ii., p. 537.   ⁴ Jebb, p. 640, and p. 308.
⁵ 'And on this the executioner struck with his axe, but failing to hit the joint, he gave her a great blow on the nape of her neck, but that which was worthy of her unparalleled constancy was, that one did not see any part of her body move, nor even did a sigh escape. The next blow was exactly on the first, by which the head was cut off from the body.' *Le vrai rapport sur l'exécution*, &c., MS. de la Bibl. Nat., fonds de Harlay St. Germain, No. 222, vol. ii., fol. 30, *et seq.*, and in Teulet, *Pièces et documents*, vol. ii., p. 880, 881. Ellis, p. 117.
⁶ Jebb, p. 641. Ellis, p. 117. 'He lift up her head to the view of all the assembly, and bad *God save the Queen*.'
⁷ 'Then Mr. Dean said with a lowde voice, So perish all the Queene's enemyes!' Ellis, p. 117. Jebb, p. 101. Camden, vol. ii., p. 537.
⁸ 'Yes, said the Earl of Kent, with a loud voice, *Amen, Amen*; would to God that all the enemies of the Queen were in that state.' *Le vray rapport*, &c. Bibl. Nat., Harlay Saint Germain, No. 222, vol. ii., fol. 30, *et seq.*, and in Teulet, vol. ii., p. 881. Jebb, p. 101. Ellis, p. 117.
⁹ *Advis sur l'éxécution*, &c., by M. de la Chastre, MS. Bibl. Nat. Coll. des 500 de Colbert, vol. xxxv., pièce 45.

cross around her neck, the chaplets suspended to her girdle, nor the clothes she wore at her death, lest these dear and venerated spoils should be redeemed by her servants, and transformed into relics. They therefore burned them.[1] They also took great pains to prevent anything being kept that had been stained with blood, all traces of which they caused to be removed.[2] Just as they were lifting the body to remove it into the state-room of the Castle, in order to embalm it, they perceived Mary's little favourite dog, which had slipped in beneath her cloak, between the head and the neck of his dead mistress. He would not quit the bloody spot, and they were forced to remove him.[3] The body of the Queen of Scots, after removing the entrails, which were secretly buried, was embalmed with but little respect, wrapped up in wax-cloth, enclosed in a leaden coffin,[4] and left aside until Elizabeth should fix the place where it was to be laid.[5]

The gates of the Castle remained closed for several hours, and nobody was allowed to go out until after the departure of Henry Talbot,[6] son of Shrewsbury, who bore to Elizabeth the report drawn up by Beale,[7] and signed by the two Earls as the chief witnesses.[8] He left on the 8th, and arrived on the following day at Greenwich, where the Queen then was. On the afternoon of the same day, the news was current in London, the inhabitants of which received the accounts of the Queen's death with the same transports of fanaticism which they had exhibited some months before on her condemnation. All the bells of the city were set a-ringing, and bonfires were lighted in every street.[9]

What was the effect produced by this tragical and audacious execution on the kings of Europe, and what were its consequences to Elizabeth?

---

[1] *Le vray rapport*, &c., Bibl. Nat., Harlay Saint Germain, No. 222, vol. ii., fol. 30., and in Teulet, vol. ii., pp. 882, 883.

[2] Ibid., and Jebb, p. 641. Ellis, pp. 117, 118.

[3] Jebb, p. 641. Ellis, p. 117.

[4] *Le vray rapport*, &c. MS. de la Bibl. Nat.; and Teulet, vol. ii., p. 883. Jebb, p. 645, 646.

[5] 'Her Majesty's body was embalmed carelessly, and put with the head into a lead coffin, and that into another of wood, and they left it in the said great chamber until the first day of the month of August, without anybody being allowed to approach it at all that time; the English perceiving that some of her people went to see it through the key-hole and pray to God, caused it to be stopped up.' *La mort de la royne*, &c., Jebb, vol. ii., p. 646. [6] Ibid., p. 641.

[7] *Le vray rapport*, &c. Bibl. Nat., and Teulet, vol. ii., p. 881. Ellis, vol. iii., p. 112. [8] Ibid.

[9] Chateauneuf to the King, Despatch of the 27th Fevr., Bibl. Nat., fonds de Béthune, No. 8880, and Teulet, vol. ii., p. 893

CHAPTER XII.

CONCLUSION.

Effect produced by Mary Stuart's execution—Elizabeth's pretended indignation—Anger of the Kings of France and Scotland—Elizabeth pacifies them—Philip II. resolves to avenge Mary's death—His preparations to invade England—The Invincible Armada—Its defeat—Triumph of Protestantism in Great Britain—Summary of Mary Stuart's life and character.

THE death of Mary Stuart delivered Elizabeth from a rival; but exposed her to violent hatred and to dangerous reprisals. Thus being rid of one cause of fear, she yielded to the influence of another; she blamed the execution she had permitted, seemed to regret the death of the Queen she had hated, and even punished the agents whom she had made subservient to her designs. By an audacious disavowal and by hypocritical grief, she sought to elude the vengeance of the sovereigns whose petitions she had rejected, whose feelings she had wounded, and whose dignity she had insulted.

During four days, she affected to be ignorant of the death of the Queen of Scotland, whilst the event was known throughout Protestant England,[1] where it was a subject of public exultation. Probably she was still undecided as to the line of conduct she should adopt, and the language it would be advisable for her to hold. On Monday, the 13th of February (23rd, new style), she pretended to have learned, with extreme surprise,[2] the execution of Mary Stuart, and with well-dissembled indignation, she gave vent to one of her most violent fits of anger. She pretended that the Queen of Scotland had been put to death without her orders and against her will; that her secretary Davison ought not to have carried into effect the warrant she had signed, before she had an opportunity of again speaking to him; that he had been guilty of precipitancy in transmitting the warrant to the Lord Chancellor for the purpose of having the great seal affixed to it; and that he had exceeded his orders in carrying it to the Privy Council, so that it might be executed without her knowledge; that the members of the Privy Council having presumed to send the warrant clandestinely to Fotheringay, had wounded her heart and trespassed on her authority. She angrily reproached them

[1] Chateauneuf to the King; Despatch dated the 27th of February. Bibl. Nat., fonds de Béthune, No. 8880; and Teulet, vol. ii., pp. 893, 894.
[2] Ibid., pp. 896, 897.

for a usurpation of the sovereign power, which must be regarded as an attempt to reduce her to tutelage.[1] She gave orders for the arrest of Davison, who was imprisoned in the Tower and brought to trial. She banished from her presence her old servant Burghley, who had given the warrant to Robert Beale, in the name of the Council, and he was so overwhelmed by her displeasure that he tremblingly tendered the resignation of all his appointments. Her two favourites, Leicester and Hatton, for having participated in the deliberation of the Privy Council, were, for a time, disgraced and banished from Court; finally, Beale, who had conveyed the warrant to Fotheringay was, a short time afterwards, removed from his post of Secretary of State, and installed in a subaltern office at York.[2] Walsingham alone was exempt from this violent and hypocritical disfavour, because a fit of illness, real or pretended, had prevented him from taking any part in an act, which Elizabeth at once took advantage of and repudiated. The Queen of England even carried her dissimulation so far as to wear mourning for her victim, and to order pompous funeral obsequies for the Queen of Scotland. Mary's remains were deposited in the Church of Peterborough, beside those of Catharine of Arragon, the first wife of Henry VIII.; where they remained until they were removed to Westminster Abbey by her son, on his accession to the throne of Great Britain.

By adding injustice to cruelty; by being false after having been relentless, Elizabeth hoped to mislead the judgment of the world, and, above all, to avert from herself the resentment of Henry III. and of James VI. In relation to them she felt uneasy; and not without reason. Henry III., in spite of his insensibility and weakness, had taken in very ill part the imprisonment of D'Estrappes, the examination to which Chateauneuf had been subjected, the arrest of his couriers and the opening of his despatches. He was offended at the charge of conspiracy brought against the people of his embassy, and he did not disguise from Wade (whom Elizabeth had sent to him on an extraordinary mission), how entirely he disbelieved the charge, whilst at the same time he manifested his dissatisfaction at the conduct of the Queen. Henry had sent to London one of his *valets de chambre* with orders to demand the release of D'Estrappes, that he might himself bring him to trial, and if he proved guilty, punish him. Taking re-

---

[1] Chateauneuf to the King; Despatch of the 13th March. Bibl. Nat., French Supplement, No. 3093/18, p. 71; and Teulet, vol. ii., pp. 902, 903.
[2] Robert Beale to Lord Burghley, April 24, 1595, in Ellis, third series, vol. IV., pp. 112-120.

prisals, he refused to grant an audience to the Ambassador Stafford; he arrested the couriers and despatches of Elizabeth at Dieppe, and put an embargo on all English vessels in the ports of France.[1]

The death of Mary Stuart increased Henry's irritation, by adding to his embarrassment. At the first moment, two of his ministers, the cold Bellièvre and the circumspect Brulart, were disposed to urge revenge. The former observed that it was imperatively necessary to show Elizabeth that the heads of sovereigns were to be held sacred; and the latter declared his determination never again to enter the council of Henry III., if that Prince did not demand satisfaction for the death of Mary.[2] The people of Paris manifested the deepest sorrow on being made acquainted with the tragical fate of the Queen whom they had known in her youthful days, when she was seated on the throne of France, and whom they regarded as a martyr to the Catholic faith. In the churches the preachers of the League fulminated their anathemas against the English Jezabel (as they called Elizabeth), and invoked upon her the vengeance of God and of Kings. Stafford and Wade dared not venture out of their houses in Paris.[3] Stafford, though his mother held a post in the English Court, was alarmed at the danger to which Elizabeth had exposed herself, and began to take precautions in anticipation of his own downfall. Through the medium of Mendoza, he made overtures to the King of Spain, to whom he offered his services. He assured Mendoza that he was wholly devoted to his Catholic Majesty, believing *that his mistress would not live but for a short time after having permitted the execution of the Queen of Scotland.*[4] Finally, Henry III. caused to be celebrated at Notre Dame, and in his own presence, a solemn service to the memory of his unfortunate relative.[5] He even showed himself disposed, in concert with the King of Spain,[6] to attack the Queen of England, who had transmitted to the Bank of Pallavicino at Frankfort, the sum of two hundred and fifty thousand livres, for the purpose of levying an army of German ritters to march to the aid of the King of Navarre.[7]

[1] Despatch of the 13th of March, 1587; Bibl. Nat., Suppl. Fran., No. $3\frac{993}{10}$, p. 71, and following; and in Teulet, vol. ii., pp. 903, 904.
[2] Mendoza to his Catholic Majesty, dated March 6th, 1587. Simancas Papers, Series B, packet 59, No. 35.   [3] Ibid.
[4] Ibid., Feb. 28, 1587. Simancas Papers, Series B., packet 59, No. 58.
[5] Ibid., March 26, 1587. Simancas Papers, Series B., packet 59, No. 14.
[6] Ibid. Simancas Papers, Series B, packet 59, No. 240.
[7] Chateauneuf to Henry III., dated London, March, 1587; MS. Bibl. Nat., Suppl. Fran., No. $3\frac{993}{10}$, fol. 7.; and in Teulet, vol. ii., p. 907.

Elizabeth now felt more than ever the necessity of conciliating Henry; and at length she received Roger, his Envoy Extraordinary, who had been a fortnight in London without having been able to obtain an audience of the Queen.[1] With a great show of grief, and almost with tears in her eyes, she spoke to him of the death of the Queen of Scotland; charging him to assure the King his master that the event had taken place contrary to her intention, and through the fault of Davison, who should answer for it.[2] Davison was, in consequence, condemned by the Star Chamber, on the 28th of March, to pay a fine of 10,000*l*., and to be imprisoned during the Queen's pleasure,[3] for having neglected her Majesty's commands and overstepped his own authority. Shortly afterwards Elizabeth had a conversation with Chateauneuf, and she also sent Walsingham to him[4] with the view of restoring a good understanding between England and France.

In her conversation with the ambassador of Henry III., Elizabeth displayed all her talent. She drew Chateauneuf aside, and taking him by the arm, said to him playfully, 'So this is the man who sought my life!'[5] She then admitted, that the plot in which he had been implicated, had been concocted by two villains, whose object had been to extort money from him.[6] Acknowledging the innocence of D'Estrappes, she added, that he was thenceforth free and might return to France. 'I am informed,' pursued she, good-humouredly, ' that he is a man of law, and that he intends to practise at the bar in Paris. I shall have my share of annoyance for what he has suffered, for he will owe me a grudge as long as he lives. You may tell him that I hope I shall never have to plead a cause in Paris, where he may have an opportunity of taking revenge for the wrong I have done him.'[7]

Coming to the subject which was uppermost in her thoughts, she spoke to Chateauneuf, with even more grief than she had evinced to Roger, of the death of the Queen of Scotland. That event, she alleged, was the greatest misfortune that had ever befallen her.[8] She maintained that she had signed the warrant

---

[1] Chateauneuf to Henry III., dated London, Feb. 27, 1587; MS. Bibl. Nat., fonds de Béthune, No. 8880, fol. 7; and in Teulet, vol. ii., p. 895.

[2] Ibid., and in Teulet, vol. ii., p. 897.

[3] Howell's State Trials, vol i., p. 1229-1250.

[4] Chateauneuf to Henry III., dated London, March, 1587. MS. Bibl. Nat., Suppl. Fran., No. $\frac{3993}{10}$, fol 71, and following; and Teulet, p. 902.

[5] Ibid., May 13th, 1587. MS. Bibl. Nat., fonds de Béthune, fol. 16; and in Teulet, p. 916. [6] Ibid., p. 92.

[7] Ibid., and Teulet, vol. ii., p. 917.

[8] Ibid., and Teulet, vol. ii., p. 918.

for the sake of satisfying her people; but that she had been firmly resolved not to take the life of the Queen of Scotland, unless a foreign force should have invaded England, or there should have been a considerable rising in the kingdom in favour of Mary. She added, that if the four members of her Council, *who had played her that trick* (which she alleged she could not have contravened), had not been so long in her service, and had not acted with a view to the interests of her person, and of her state, she would (she vowed to God) have had them beheaded.[1] She observed to Chateauneuf, that he ought not to believe her to be so weak and so wicked,[2] as to cast the blame on an insignificant secretary like Davison, if he were not guilty. In conversation with Chateauneuf, she observed, that it was the interest of the two crowns of France and England to unite for the purpose of eluding the designs of the Leaguers, and the ambition of Philip II., who menaced them both; she mentioned her intention of sending Drake to attack the coasts of Spain, and Leicester to support the Republic of the United Provinces. She proposed to Chateauneuf to secure for the King his master the support of four German Princes, who, on a single word from her, would fly to serve her with their troops, and she invited Henry to make himself instrumental in strengthening the bonds of friendship among them all. 'The times are such,' she observed, 'that both of us are more than ever in need of this friendship.'[3]

Without being deceived by the disavowals of Elizabeth,[4] but influenced by the same political reasons which guided her, Henry III. determined on not avenging the death of Mary Stuart. Interest triumphed over the ties of blood; and for fear of endangering his own crown, he abandoned the general cause of royalty.

He feared that if he helped the excited Catholics of the Continent in their designs on England, they might become triumphant in the Netherlands, and paramount in France; and that the downfall of Elizabeth would pave the way for the aggrandisement of Philip II., the elevation of the House of Guise, and his own ruin. After several months spent in dissatisfaction and

---

[1] Chateauneuf to Henry III., dated London, May 13, 1587; MS. Bibl. Nat., fonds de Béthune, fol. 16; and in Teulet, p. 916.
[2] Ibid.
[3] Ibid.
[4] Henry III. to Chateauneuf, May, 1587. Bibl. Nat., Registers of Secretary Pinart, French MS., No. 8808, fol. 28; and in Teulet, vol. ii., p. 913.

grief, he acted on the advice of the Queen his mother,[1] and he authorized Chateauneuf, in concurrence with Walsingham, to close the differences which had arisen between the two countries.[2] To break with Elizabeth would certainly have been to him a course no less difficult than dangerous. The necessity of repelling the invasion of the German ritters, who were penetrating into France in the summer of 1587, and of resisting the Leaguers, who were making themselves masters of Paris, by the barricades of 1588, withheld him from venturing to attack others, by obliging him to defend himself.

The King of Scotland seemed not so easy to be appeased. The death of his mother filled him with indignation, and he openly declared that the act should not pass unrevenged.[3] Elizabeth, fearing the resolution to which he might be urged by his own resentment, by the animosity of his subjects, and by the advice of the continental sovereigns, sent him a letter by Robert Carey, the son of her own cousin-german, Lord Hunsdon. Carey had already contrived to render himself agreeable to the King of Scotland. The letter of which he was the bearer, and which was written by Elizabeth's own hand, contained excuses and expressions of grief alike insincere. She spoke of the overwhelming sorrow she felt for the deplorable catastrophe which had taken place contrary to her intention,[4] and she called God to witness that she was entirely innocent of it. She begged James to believe that if she had commanded it, she would not scruple to avow it. She had not, she said, with dissembled pride, a soul so base that the fear of any prince, or of any living creature, should withhold her from doing what was just, or cause her to disavow it. The lineage whence she had sprung raised her above such vile thoughts. She added, that despite of any consequences that might result to herself, she would not cast the weight of her own acts on the shoulders of others.[5] She solemnly declared to James VI., that among kings no one was more attached to him than herself, and she expressed

---

[1] Despatch from Mendoza to Philip II., dated April 19th, 1587. Papers of Simancas, Series B., packet 59, No. 88, and MS. in Bibl. Nat. Original despatches of Chauvelin, vol. i., No. 95|3.

[2] Papers of Simancas. Series B., packet 59, No. 149.

[3] Lord Scrope to Walsingham, February 21st, 1587. Wright's Queen Elizabeth and her Times, vol. ii., p. 333, and Tytler, vol. xi., p. 4.

[4] This letter, which was written by Elizabeth on the 14th (24th) of February is extracted from Cotton MS., Cal. IX., fol. 161, by Mr. Henry Ellis; and is included in his 'Original Letters,' vol. iii., p. 22.

[5] Cotton MS., Cal. IX., fol. 161, included by Mr. Henry Ellis in his 'Original Letters,' vol. iii., p. 22.

the most affectionate interest for him and for the welfare of his kingdom.

In the first burst of his anger, James determined not to suffer Robert Carey to set foot in Scotland, where public feeling was violently hostile to Elizabeth. He obliged Carey to stop at Berwick, and thither Melvil and the Laird of Cowden-Knowes went to receive, on the part of James, the message with which Carey was charged. At the time when he offered this affront to the haughty Elizabeth, he was permitting the chiefs of the Scottish Border to ravage the English frontier, and suffering the inhabitants of the Isles subject to his dominion to succour the Irish rebels, who had risen under Tyrone.[1] He even appeared to be making approaches to the Catholics, by receiving the emissaries of the King of Spain, by lending ear to the Fathers of the Jesuits, by reinstating the Bishop of Ross in all his dignities, and by accrediting as his ambassador to Henry III., the faithful servant of Mary Stuart, the Archbishop of Glasgow,[2] who, in his name, solicited the aid of the French King, in avenging the death of his mother.[3]

Elizabeth was greatly alarmed at the state of things in Scotland. She, however, made no complaint of the devastations committed by Fernyhirst, Cessford, Bothwell, Angus, Johnston, and others, who, with the assent of the young King, were laying waste that part of the English territory situated in their neighbourhood. She feared lest these aggressions might be converted into a general war, all the nobility having taken up arms, and the men of the north, as well as the men of the south, were urgently insisting on carrying fire and sword to the gates of Newcastle.[4] Amidst this excitement of national exasperation, the odious Master of Gray was put on his trial for the crime of high treason, and he escaped only by perpetual banishment.[5] The partisans of Elizabeth were silent, and no one ventured to defend the alliance formerly concluded with her.

That Princess did not, however, despair of gaining over the ambitious James VI. She was the more interested in securing his friendship, inasmuch as she would have been placed in great peril, if, to the open enmity of Scotland, had been added the

[1] Tytler, vol. ix., p. 4-12.
[2] Ibid., vol. ix., pp. 4-12, and Papers of Simancas, Series B., packet 59, No. 111; and packet 58, No. 167.
[3] Papers of Simancas, Series B., packet 59, No. 77. Despatch from Mendoza to his Catholic Majesty, dated May 20th, 1587. [4] Tytler, vol. ix.. p. 7.
[5] Pitcairn's Criminal Trials, vol. i., part iii., p. 157; Tytler, vol. ix., p. 13.

rising of Ireland: such a state of things would have facilitated the invasion of England, for which preparations were being made on the coasts of Spain and Flanders. Elizabeth intimated to James that his succession to her crown would be secured if he remained at peace, but forfeited if he should go to war. By her command, Walsingham wrote to Maitland, Secretary of State to James VI., an adroit letter, in which he dwelt forcibly on the great inheritance that might await James.[1] In this letter Walsingham assured Maitland that a rupture with England would, on the part of the King, his master, be an act at once highly impolitic and dangerous; that it would revive the remembrance of old animosities between the two nations; that it would render James odious to the English people, in whose opinion he would irremediably compromise his rights; that he could not hope for the assistance of the King of France, who was but little disposed to support a near relation of the House of Guise, and who was naturally averse to the union of the two crowns of England and Scotland on one head; and finally, that he would be acting in the interests of the King of Spain, whom he ought to regard as a rival rather than an auxiliary.

These arguments caused James VI. to reflect, but did not bring him to a decision. Though he lent ear to the politic counsel of Elizabeth, he secretly maintained relations with Philip II., being alike reluctant to renounce the throne of England or to forego revenging his mother. He long held this equivocal position, and with well-dissembled duplicity he managed to keep on terms with the two great parties (who were ready to break into open hostility), but without declaring himself for the one or the other. He suffered the Jesuits free access to all parts of his kingdom, and allowed the Earls of Huntly, Morton, and Crawford (the leaders of the Scottish Catholics[2]) to concert with the Duke of Parma[3] for promoting the expedition which Philip II. was preparing.

The King of Spain was the only person who entertained serious thoughts of avenging the death of Mary Stuart. In this feeling he was stimulated at once by the necessity of extending the Catholic faith, and the desire of increasing his own denomination. He hoped thereby to restore the old religion in the Island, then the great focus of Protestantism, and the securest resting-point of the revolution raging in the rest of Europe; he flattered himself

[1] This letter is given by Spottiswood, pp. 359-362; Tytler, vol. ix., pp. 7, 8.
[2] Tytler, vol. ix., pp. 18-21.
[3] Papers of Simancas; Series B., packet 59, Nos. 94-161.

he might thus acquire a new throne, punish Elizabeth for the crime she had committed, call her to account for the aggressions she had so long sanctioned, and put down the rebellion in the United Provinces by the subjugation of England. Such were the great designs, for the accomplishment of which Philip II. employed all the power of his kingdom. When the interests of his ambition concurred with his feelings, he no longer wavered.

After the death of Mary Stuart, he did not conceal his claims to the double inheritance she had bequeathed to him. His ambassador, Mendoza, wrote to him as follows: 'God having been pleased to suffer this accursed nation to fall under his displeasure, not only in regard to spiritual affairs, by heresy, but also in what relates to worldly affairs; by this terrible event it is plain that the Almighty has wished to give your Majesty these two crowns as your own entire possession."[1] The Bishop of Ross wrote in French, in Latin, and in English, a declaration to prove that Philip II. was the lawful heir to the throne of England, the King of Scotland having rendered himself incompetent by his heresy.[2] The Spanish ambassador spoke to the Pope's nuncio of the rights of his master,[3] and even presumed to mention them to Catherine de Medici.[4] The Duke de Guise also admitted them. Writing to Mendoza, he says: 'Neither relationship, nor any other interest of mine, can with me outweigh the duty and the affection with which I devote myself to the humble service of the King of Spain. I regard his Catholic Majesty as the common father of all the Catholics of Christendom, and most especially of myself.[5] He consigned to the King of Spain the task of avenging Mary Stuart, and undertook to secure the triumph of Catholicism in France, whilst Philip II. re-established it in England.[6]

Having at his disposal ships and seamen, furnished by Italy, Portugal, and Spain, Philip, who had the best troops in Europe, and who was supplied with treasures from the New World, seemed to possess, more than any other sovereign, the means of succeeding in the enterprise he had resolved to undertake. He had conceived the scheme of invading England as early as 1570,

[1] Mendoza to Philip II; Despatch, dated 29th February, 1587. Papers of Simancas, Series B., packet 59, No. 58.
[2] Mendoza sent this document to Philip II., with the Despatch dated 9th of April, Ibid., Series B., packet 59, No. 73.   [3] Ibid., No. 38.
[4] Despatch of the 19th of April. Ibid., No. 91.
[5] Papers of Simancas, Series B., packet 59, No. 178. Note from the Duke of Guise under the name of Mario, addressed to Mendoza, and dated June 28, 1587.
[6] Ibid., No. 238. Despatch from Mendoza to his Catholic Majesty, dated March 28.

and had commenced his preparations in 1583.[1] These preparations gave occasion to the most vast maritime armament that had ever before been seen; and active exertions were made in all the ports of the Spanish monarchy. The Roads of Lisbon were to be the general mustering-place of the fleet. There the vessels furnished by Sicily, Naples, Catalonia, Andalusia, Castile, and Biscay, commanded by their most able captains, and manned by their most intrepid seamen, were to assemble in the spring of 1588. This fleet, which received the name of the *Invincible Armada*, consisted of thirty-five ships of various dimensions. Besides caravels, ourques, zabras, galleys (which were the general ships of the time), some with sails, some with oars, the Armada comprised a certain number of galleons, and four galeasses of enormous size. The galleons were round-built vessels, and the galeasses were vessels of larger size, having their forecastles fortified, besides carrying several tiers of guns. This fleet, which was manned by eight thousand seamen, carried twenty thousand troops, who were to land on the English coast. These troops were well supplied with arms and ammunition of every kind, and they had with them provisions for six months. They were also accompanied by a Vicar-General of the Holy Inquisition, and upwards of a hundred Jesuits and other monks, who were to work the conversion of the island.[2] The Armada was commanded by the Marquis de Santa Cruz, an experienced and successful admiral, who had twice, on the coasts of Terceira, defeated the Prior Antonio de Crato, who sought to render himself master of Portugal.

Whilst these vast preparations were going on in the Spanish Peninsula, the Duke of Parma was combining forces no less considerable on the coasts of Flanders. That able general was appointed military chief of the expedition. Besides the troops who were in his garrisons, or under his colours, five thousand men were sent to him from Northern and Central Italy, four thousand from the kingdom of Naples, six thousand from Castile, three thousand from Arragon, three thousand from Austria and Germany, together with four squadrons of ritters; besides which, he received forces from the Franche Comté and the Wallon country. By his command, the Forest of Waes was felled for the purpose

---

[1] Strada, who wrote a history *De Bello Belgico*, on the authority of good documents, especially the Papers of the Duke of Parma, concurs with what I have stated in this work (on the authority of the Archives of Simancas), respecting Philip's plan of invading England. Liber nonus, Antwerpi, 1648, vol. ii., pp. 630, 631.

[2] De Thou, book lxxxix.

[3] Herrera, vol. iii. pp. 87—93. Strada, vol. ix., pp. 633, 650-652.

of building flat-bottomed boats, which, floating down the rivers and canals to Nieuport and Dunkirk, were to carry an additional force of one hundred thousand men to the mouth of the Thames, under the escort of the Great Spanish Fleet. Gun carriages, fascines, machines used in sieges, together with every material requisite for building bridges, forming camps, and raising fortresses, were to be carried on board the flotillas of the Duke of Parma, who followed up the conquest of the Netherlands, whilst he was making preparations for the invasion of England.[1] Favoured by the dissensions which arose in 1586, between the insurgents of the United Provinces and Leicester, the Duke of Parma had recovered Deventer, as well as a fort before Zauphen, which the English commanders, Sir William Stanley, the friend of Babington, and Sir Roland York, had surrendered to him, when with their troops, they passed over to the service of Philip II., after the death of Mary Stuart, and he had also made himself master of the Sluys.[2] His intention was to leave to the Count de Mansfeldt sufficient forces to follow up an undertaking which had now become secondary, whilst he himself went at the head of fifty thousand men of the Armada and the flotilla to accomplish the principal enterprise.

That enterprise, which in the highest degree affected the interests of the pontifical authority, Philip II. had concerted with the Pope. Sixtus V. had promised to co-operate with his money; and he had pledged himself to advance a million of ducats the moment the expedition should reach the British shore:[3] meanwhile he had, at the request of Philip II., given the Cardinal's hat to Doctor Allen; the Doctor, who was director of the English Seminary at Reims, and a chief of the Catholic emigration, was chosen as legate from the Holy See to England. In a bull intended to be kept secret until the day of landing, Sixtus V., renewing the anathema fulminated against Elizabeth by Pius V. and by Gregory XIII., dispossessed her of the throne. The new legate, on his part, prepared a furious manifesto,[4] in which he reproached Elizabeth with the disgrace of her birth, the shamelessness of her heresy, the duplicity of her character, the dissoluteness of her manners, and the cruelty of her sentences. Copies of this manifesto were to be profusely circulated on the arrival

[1] Strada, vol. ii., book ix., pp. 640–644.
[2] Camden, p. 552. Lingard, vol. viii., chap. v.
[3] Sixtus V. to Philip II., August 7, 1587. Archives of Simancas, Neg. de Roma, leg. 950.
[4] Tempesti vita e geste di Sixto Quinto, vol. ii., p. 80.

of the Armada, in the hope that being shaken by the contempt and hatred of the English people, Elizabeth's government would speedily fall under the Spanish aggression.

Immense as was this armament, for the completion of which efforts were directed from all points, yet its magnitude and its destination remained alike unknown. The secret of the enterprise was known only to Philip II., Sixtus V., the Prince of Parma, Mendoza, and the Duke of Guise. It was carefully concealed from the Court of France, where it was not even known to the nuncio Morisini, who, being a Venetian by birth, was too much attached to the interests of Henry III., and too favourable to the policy of Catherine de Medici.[1] Thus it became a question in Paris as well as in London, whether the expedition was to subdue the Low-Countries, to invade England, or to proceed to the Indies. Mendoza artfully kept up this uncertainty, which was for a considerable time shared by Elizabeth herself.[2]

Notwithstanding her keen-sightedness, and the anxiety she could not help feeling, this Princess hoped that the storm which was gathering abroad would not fall upon her kingdom. As early as the spring of 1587, long before the Spanish fleet was ready to muster in the Tagus, she had sent Sir Francis Drake, with thirty-seven ships, to cruize off the coast of the Peninsula. This intrepid sailor, exceeding his instructions, had entered the Bay of Cadiz and the Lisbon Roads, where he had committed great ravages.[3] Moreover, during the summer of the same year, Leicester had returned to the Netherlands with five thousand men, in order to support the tottering republic of the United Provinces against the aggressions of the Spaniards.[4] These acts of offensive hostility, however, had not prevented Elizabeth from opening negotiations with Philip II., and even believing that she would be able to disarm his anger against her.

She had appointed, as her Commissioners, the Earl of Derby, Lord Cobham, Sir James Croft, and the two jurisconsults, Dale and Adams. These gentlemen had proceeded to Flanders in the beginning of 1588, and had had several conferences with the Count of Arenburg, Perrenot, Richardot, De Maes, and Greiner, the plenipotentiaries of Philip II. As great an adept in the arts of dissimulation as Elizabeth herself, and able to deceive with

---

[1] Under the title of 'Exhortation to the Nobility and People of England and Ireland,' Lingard has analysed it in the Note B B at the end of his second volume.
[2] Simancas Papers, Series 4, packet 56, Nos. $\frac{93}{550}$, $\frac{94}{551}$, $\frac{96}{552}$, $\frac{98}{555}$.
[3] Strype, vol. iii., part i., pp. 662, 663. Lingard, vol. viii., chap. v.
[4] Lingard, vol. viii., chap. v.

more calmness and as much ability, that Prince had accepted her overtures for peace, in order that he might lull her apprehensions, and thus take her at a disadvantage. The English Commissioners demanded that the ancient alliance between the House of Burgundy and England should be renewed; that the foreign troops should be withdrawn from the Netherlands; and that those provinces should be allowed liberty of conscience. The Spanish Commissioners accepted the first of the conditions, but rejected the other two, on the ground that they were at variance with the interests and the religion of the King their master, and were, moreover, in little conformity to the conduct of Queen Elizabeth, who claimed for the Protestants of the Netherlands a toleration which she did not grant to the Catholics of England. No better agreement was come to regarding the restitution of the towns pledged by the States to Elizabeth, and the repayment of the money advanced by Elizabeth to the States.[1]

This negotiation, which was carried on during the first six months of 1588, alarmed Henry III., who especially dreaded any accommodation between Spain and England, in consequence of which Philip II. would be enabled to subdue the United Provinces, and make himself master of France. In order, therefore, to divert Elizabeth from any arrangement, he offered to assist her, in case she was attacked by the Spaniards, with twice the number of troops which he was bound by the treaty of 1574 to send to her assistance. He had a long conference with her ambassador, Stafford, upon this subject, and told him that the Pope and the Catholic King had entered into a league against the Queen, his mistress, and had invited himself and the Venetians to join them, but that they had refused to do so. 'If the Queen of England,' he added, 'concludes a peace with the Catholic King, that peace will not last three months, because the Catholic King will aid the League with all his forces to overthrow me, and you may imagine what fate is reserved for your mistress after that.'[2] On the other hand, in order more effectually to frustrate this negotiation, he proposed to Philip II. to form a still closer union between the two crowns of France and Spain;[3] and at the same time he secretly despatched a confidential envoy to Constantinople, to warn the Sultan, that if he did not again declare war against the Catholic King, that monarch, who already pos-

[1] Camden, vol. ii., pp. 568-571. Strada, vol. ii., book x.
[2] Mendoza was made aware of all these propositions, and had informed the Catholic King of them. Archives of Simancas, B., 60, Nos. 117, 279.
[3] Ibid., B., 61, No. 62.

sessed the Netherlands, Portugal, Spain, the Indies, and nearly all Italy, would soon make himself master of England, and would then turn the forces of all Europe against the Turks.[1]

Philip II. was aware of all these intrigues, and proposed to frustrate them by the promptitude of his measures. He had carefully discussed the safest means of executing the enterprise which he had so laboriously projected, and which he was desirous no longer to defer. He had rejected, as productive of delay, very wise but very various counsels, which had been given him by men of great experience. In order to deliver so large a fleet as the Armada from the dangers of a stormy sea, Sir William Stanley proposed that a landing should be effected and a strong position secured in Ireland, from whence they would easily be able to invade England. Colonel Semple, a Scotchman, and Plato, an Italian engineer who had constructed a chart of the British coast, had pronounced in favour of a descent upon Scotland, where they would find the nobility ready to rise in arms, and the people desirous to avenge the death of Mary Stuart. Lastly, the Admiral Santa Cruz, and the Prince of Parma, had advised the King to make sure of some large harbour on the coast of Holland or Zealand, that the Armada, after having entered the Channel, might have a shelter in case of storm, from whence it could sail without difficulty for England. Philip II. adopted none of these prudent measures.[2] In the present instance, this cautious Prince, who frequently compromised his plans by temporisation, and annulled his preparations by uncertainty, exposed himself, by his precipitation, to failure in the greatest enterprise of his reign.

But, though he would not consent that the Prince of Parma should previously seize Flushing and the mouth of the Scheldt, he would not, on the other hand, allow the Armada to sail from Lisbon Roads until the Duke of Guise and the Leaguers had taken arms against Henry III.,[3] and thus prevented France from interfering in favour of Queen Elizabeth. With this object, the Commander, Juan Iniguez Moreo, was despatched by him, in the early part of April,[4] to the Duke of Guise at Soissons: and the Prince of Parma sent back to Scotland the Earl of Morton—who

[1] Letter from the Duke of Guise to the Duke of Parma, April, 1588; Archives of Simancas, B., 60, No. 12.
[2] Strada, vol. ii., book ix., pp. 634-637.
[3] This was the Prince of Parma's opinion. Strada, vol. ii., book ix., p. 634. March, 1588. See also the despatches of Mendoza to Philip II., 25th February, and 15th March, 1588; Archives of Simancas, B., 60, Nos. 254, 277.
[4] Despatch from Mendoza to the Catholic King, 5th April, 1588. Archives of Simancas B., 60, No. 35.

had come with Colonel Semple, to treat with him on behalf of the Scottish Catholics—to call upon James VI. to avenge the death of his mother, and the outrage done thereby to the whole Scottish nation.[1] The Commander Moreo met with complete success at Soissons. He offered the Duke of Guise, as soon as he took the field against Henry III., three hundred thousand crowns, six thousand infantry, and twelve hundred pikemen, on behalf of the King his master, who would, in addition, withdraw his ambassador from the Court of France, and accredit an envoy to the Catholic party.[2] A treaty was concluded on these conditions, and the Duke of Guise entered Paris, where he was expected by the Leaguers, and whence he expelled Henry III., on the 12th of May, by the insurrection of the barricades. A fortnight after this insurrection, which reduced Henry III. to impotence, and, to use the language of the Prince of Parma, did not even 'permit him to assist the Queen of England with his tears, as he needed them all to weep over his own misfortunes,'[3] the Spanish Fleet left the Tagus and sailed towards the British isles.

Elizabeth was utterly unprepared for this. Deceived by the negotiations which were still pending in the Netherlands, she had shared in the hopes of peace conceived by her Lord Treasurer, whose prudence and ability were for once at fault. Notwithstanding the advice of Walsingham and Leicester, who had represented to her that the invasion was imminent, she had sacrificed her safety to her avarice, and had made very imperfect preparations for defence. At the time when the Armada set sail, her fleets were still unformed, and not a single troop had been levied throughout England. Fortunately a tempest came to her aid. Before it was clear of the coast of Spain, the Armada was assailed, off Cape Finisterre, by its first storm, which dispersed it completely, and compelled it to take refuge, much shattered, in the ports of Biscay and Galicia. It was not, moreover, under the command of the Marquis of Santa Cruz. This experienced sailor, notwithstanding his diligence and success, had been unable to keep pace with the impatient ardour of his master. Philip II. had reproached him with his dilatoriness, and had said, with ungrateful harshness, 'You make an ill return for all my kindness'[4] towards

---

[1] Despatch of the Prince of Parma to Mendoza, 11th March, 1588. Archives of Simancas, B., 61, No. 105.
[2] Punctos de la Instruction, &c. Archives of Simancas, B., 61, No. 184.
[3] Archives of Simancas, B., 61, No. 62.
[4] 'Male tu quidem pro benevolentiâ in te meâ, mihi gratiam rependis.' Strada, vol. ii., book ix., p. 653.

you.' These words, from so absolute and reserved a monarch, had been fatal to Santa Cruz. Overwhelmed with fatigue and grief, he had died; and Philip II. had replaced him by Alonzo Perez de Gusman, Duke of Medina Sidonia, one of the most powerful of the Spanish grandees, but very ill adapted to command such an expedition. It is true that he had, as his lieutenants, two able seamen, Juan de Martinez Recalde of Biscay, and Miguel Ocquendo of Guipuzcoa.

While the Armada was refitting on the coast of Spain, Elizabeth had time to perceive the full extent of her danger, and to make preparations accordingly. Returning at once to her energy and foresight, she established a military council for the defence of her kingdom; directed that, in all the counties, every man capable of bearing arms, from eighteen to sixty years of age, should be enrolled;[1] ordered the formation of two armies, one of which, consisting of 31,932 infantry and 2400 cavalry, was to be placed under Leicester's command, to make head against the enemy; while the other, composed of 34,400 infantry, 1914 cavalry, and thirty-six pieces of artillery of different calibre, was to be led by Hunsdon, and employed in the defence of her royal person.[2] She thought of strengthening her position at Tilbury Fort, near the mouth of the Thames, where the Spaniards were to land; and she banished to the Isle of Ely and the midland counties, those English Catholics whom she most suspected, whilst she subjected the others to the strictest surveillance.[3] The two armies of Leicester and Hunsdon were summoned to meet, the first on the 28th of June, and the second on the 23rd of July. This would have been much too late to oppose the invasion, had it not been for the misfortune which occurred to the Armada; and, even under these favourable circumstances, they had not time enough to give their troops such a training as would qualify them to compete with the veteran Spanish bands. But the continued favours of fortune, and the intrepidity of the English navy, made up for Elizabeth's delay, and preserved her from the errors into which she had been plunged by her parsimony and credulity.

The number of vessels which she collected was very large. Assisted by the city of London, which alone placed thirty-eight ships at her disposal, and served with devotedness by all her subjects, who readily engaged in the defence of their country and their religion, she had soon a fleet of a hundred and ninety-one ships, most of them, it is true, of small dimensions, but carrying

---

[1] Lingard, vol. viii., chap. v. [2] Murdin, pp. 612-614.
[3] Camden, p. 566. Murdin, p. 605. Lingard, vol. viii., chap. 5.

in all, 15,272 men.[1] The largest vessels were commanded by Drake, Frobisher, Winter, Hawkins, and other bold captains who had distinguished themselves in distant seas, by their successful opposition to the power of Spain. This numerous and active fleet, to which volunteers belonging to the noblest families of England flocked in crowds, and which was officered by men of equal valour and experience, was placed under the command of Admiral Lord Howard of Effingham, with Sir Francis Drake for his lieutenant. Its rendezvous was Plymouth, where it awaited the approach of the Armada, at the mouth of the channel which separates the Island from the Continent; whilst a strong squadron, commanded by Winter and Lord Henry Seymour, joined the Dutch Admiral, Lonck, and the Zealand Admiral, Justin of Nassau,[2] on the other side of the Straits, and blockaded the coast of Flanders in concert with them, so as to prevent the Prince of Parma's flotilla from uniting itself with the Armada of the duke of Medina Sidonia.

On the 20th of July, the Armada set sail again; its navigation was at first prosperous, across a smooth sea and beneath a calm sky. This fleet, the largest the ocean had yet borne, advanced majestically forward, considered invincible because of the 7500 sailors by whom it was manned, the 19,000 soldiers who crowded its decks, and the numerous body of priests and monks whom it conveyed to the conquest and conversion of England. With its immense galeasses and formidable galleons, it seemed like a fortified town floating upon the water. After it had passed Cape Breton, exciting universal surprise and admiration, it hove in sight of the English vessels anchored before Plymouth. Being vastly superior in numbers, and impelled by a favourable wind from the south, it might easily have crushed Howard and Drake, and by a single blow, cleared the way into England. This the Spanish captains strongly urged their admiral to do; but the Duke of Medina Sidonia called them together, and showed them the King's order forbidding him to give battle until he had effected a junction with the Prince of Parma, and conveyed all the troops to the banks of the Thames. Don Juan de Recalde, nevertheless, maintained, that he ought to attack when he was sure to conquer, and that the King might be served by his obedience. But the timid Duke of Medina Sidonia, in scrupulous observance of the instructions he had received, sailed on to the coast of Flanders.[3] He obeyed too implicitly

[1] Murdin, p. 618.   [2] Thuanus, book xxxix, chap. ix.
[3] Strada, vol. ii., book ix., pp. 656-658.

an order which, given at a distance from the scene of action, and its occurrences, was in itself a fault, as it prohibited him from offering battle advantageously, without shielding him from being attacked at a disadvantage.

Howard and Drake, indeed, having escaped this danger, followed the Armada, which advanced slowly in the form of a crescent, and attacked its rear-guard with complete success. In this narrow channel, with the passages and quicksands of which they were well acquainted, their light vessels were always able to turn with the wind, and whilst avoiding a regular battle with the formidable fleet, which would have shivered them to pieces, they succeeded by their skirmishes, in capturing some important prizes. Thus, on the 4th of August, they engaged a squadron with triumphant success, before the Isle of Wight,[1] and continued to harass the Armada until it reached Calais, where it cast anchor on the 6th. It was now only a few leagues distant from Dunkirk and Nieuport, and seemed to have accomplished one of the objects of the enterpri .

At the approach of the Armada, the Prince of Parma broke off the conferences between the Spanish commissioners and the English envoys, and made preparations to join it. On the 7th and 8th of August, he had embarked 14,000 men on board the Nieuport flotilla,[2] and had hastened to embark the remainder of the army of invasion on board the flotilla at Dunkirk.[3] The Duke of Medina Sidonia intended to join him without delay, and to escort his flat-bottomed vessels to the mouth of the Thames. But Drake did not give him time to do this. With ardent and indefatigable perseverance, he had never ceased his pursuit of the Armada, and now lay at anchor at a short distance from her. The elements conspired to favour his attacks. During the night of the 8th of August, the sky assumed a lowering aspect, and gave notice of an approaching storm. Drake took eight of the least seaworthy and smallest ships of his fleet, filled them with saltpetre, bitumen and other combustibles, and had them towed, through the darkness, into the neighbourhood of the Spanish ships. At a certain distance, they were set alight, and the eight fire-ships, burning with lurid brightness, drifted on towards the Armada. The Spanish sailors were seized with terror. They feared their vessels would be all burned as another fleet had been, some years before, not far from Antwerp. Raising their anchors and cutting their cables, they precipitately

---

[1] Strada, vol. ii., book ix., pp. 659-661.   [2] Ibid., p. 665.   [3] Ibid.

left the coast and fled in confusion to the open sea. But they escaped conflagration only to be exposed to tempest.

A violent storm now burst forth, and the south-west wind began to blow furiously. Driven by the hurricane, the Spanish fleet, which was pursued and cannonaded on the next day by the English squadrons, was thrown on the shore, between Calais and the mouth of the Scheldt; it had great difficulty in getting clear of these quicksands, on which several galleons, and one of the four great galeasses, were stranded. The Armada had already lost fifteen vessels, which had 4791 men on board; and its only way to escape utter ruin was by leaving this dangerous channel. The expedition had failed; and the Duke of Medina Sidonia, driven from south to north by the tempest, which rendered it impossible to sail through the channel again, took a course scarcely less hazardous. He sailed completely round England, Scotland, and Ireland, and returned to Spain by way of the Northern Ocean.[1] During this stormy voyage, he scattered the wrecks of his fleet over the sea with which he was unacquainted, and left seventeen of his ships on the coast of Ireland alone.

Whilst the Armada met with this disastrous fate, and the Prince of Parma, considerably dejected by so great a defeat, was withdrawing his troops from his flotillas, the King of Scotland finally made choice between Phillip II. and Elizabeth. He had long wavered between the two. During the month of July he had given a favourable reception to Colonel Semple, who had been sent to him by the Prince of Parma; and he had written to the Prince in terms which might lead him to consider him one of his future auxiliaries.[2] But, when the Earl of Morton, in conformity with the agreement made in the Netherlands, gave the Scottish Catholics the signal of insurrection to support the Spanish expedition, James VI. perceived that he stood in as great danger as Elizabeth. In spite of the care which the agents of Spain had taken to be silent regarding the religious tendency of the enterprise, and to conceal Philip the Second's ambition beneath his desire to avenge Mary Stuart, the King of Scotland clearly perceived that it was intended to restore the ancient faith in England, and bring that country into subjection to the Catholic King. He displayed, therefore, no

---

[1] Strada, vol. ii., book ix., pp. 667-669.

[2] 'Et rex admisso perhonorifice Semplio, egit per litteras quarum autographum apud me est, gratias Parmensi duci, cujus humanitati adstrictum se in perpetuum profitebatur.'—Strada, vol. ii., book ix., p. 646.

further hesitation; but saying that the King of Spain bestowed on him the favour which Polyphemus granted Ulysses, that of being devoured the last,[1] he assembled an army, marched against Morton, captured his castle of Lochmaben, defeated him at Dumfries, and threw him into prison.[2] This vigorous act put a stop to the enterprises of the Scottish Catholics, and delivered Elizabeth from great anxiety regarding her northern frontier, which she had not placed in a state of defence. She immediately despatched William Ashby to the young monarch, whose creed and interest rendered him her ally, to congratulate him on his success, and to offer him an English dukedom, as a first step to the throne, with an annual pension of five thousand pounds, and the maintenance of a small body-guard of fifty Scottish gentlemen.[3] These promises, which the presence of danger induced her then to give, but which the return of security enabled her afterwards to break, completely gained over James VI. He renewed negotiations with Elizabeth, and as, in him, ambition was more powerful than consanguinity, the same reasons which had rendered him so accommodating with regard to his mother's captivity finally prevented him from avenging her death.

The Queen of England was now triumphant on every hand. Though she had not perceived her danger sufficiently soon, she had faced it with generous courage. She had inspired all England with her intrepidity and confidence; and had proposed to place herself at the head of her troops, whom she had visited in her camp at Tilbury, amidst enthusiastic acclamations. The English people, filled with gratitude and admiration, honoured her as their liberator, and believed that to her they owed the preservation of their independence, and the security of their religion.

As for Philip II., whose political prosperity had received a great check by this defeat, he learned the news of the destruction of the Armada with the tranquil pride of the most powerful monarch in Europe. His favourite minister, Don Christoval de Moura, undertook to communicate the sad intelligence to him. Don Christoval found him writing letters in his cabinet. Philip II. listened to him without change of countenance. 'I thank God,' he said, ' for having given me means to endure such a loss without embarrassment, and power to equip another fleet of equal magnitude. A stream can afford to waste some of its water so long as its source is not dried up.'[4] Then quietly taking up

---

[1] Camden, vol. ii., p. 583. Spottiswood, p. 369. Tytler, vol. vii., p. 340.
[2] Tytler, vol. vii., p. 341. Robertson, book vii. [3] Tytler, vol. vii., p. 341.
[4] Strada, vol. ii., book ix., p. 671. However, as we learn from a letter written

his pen, he went on writing his letters. The Armada, if we are to believe the statements of the ambassador Mendoza and the historian De Thou, had nevertheless cost him more than a hundred millions of ducats.[1] The remnant of this once mighty fleet arrived during the month of September, in the ports of Santander and Corogna, under the command of the Duke of Medina Sidonia, who received orders to retire at once to his estates without presenting himself at Court. His lieutenant Don Juan de Recalde, who returned with him, soon fell a victim to the fatigues which he had endured. Philip II. communicated this great reverse to his people in the lofty but submissive language of a Christian prince. He requested all archbishops and bishops throughout his dominions to offer up public prayers in their churches. 'The events of the sea,' he wrote, 'are variable, as every one knows, and as the Armada has just experienced.'[2] Attributing the misfortune which had occurred to stronger causes than could be met by human precautions, he requested them to invoke the assistance of God on his behalf. 'Recommend all my actions to our Lord,' he said in conclusion, 'that his Divine Majesty may turn them to the advantage of his service, to the exaltation of his Church, and to the welfare and preservation of Christendom. This is all that I desire.'[3]

Although his reply to Don Christoval de Moura seemed to announce the speedy equipment of a new fleet, and although Mendoza advised him to fit out another expedition,[4] Philip II. was unable to resume the plan, to which he had devoted five years of labour, and eighteen years of preparation, and which had failed in a few days. Circumstances did not permit him to do so. The Duke and Cardinal of Guise had met their death at Blois, towards the end of 1588, in the service of the same cause for which Mary Stuart had perished at Fotheringay: Henry III. had been assassinated by a monk at Saint Cloud, in the summer of 1589, and his death had for the first time separated Catholicism

---

by Don Juan de Idiaquez to the Prince of Parma, on the 31st of August, 1588, Philip II. felt more grief at this disaster than he cared to show. 'Su Magestad lo ha sentido que se puede creer; y si todavia no quedase alguna esperança en Dios de que podria haverse servido de responder por su causa, y que vuelta del Armada ha dado occasio à V. E. lo havià sabido tomar de suerte que no se escape de las manos, no se como se llevaria un sentimiento tan grande.' Gachard's Correspondance de Philippe II., vol. ii., p. lxxvii.

[1] Thuanus, lib. lxxxix., cap. 14.
[2] Herrera, vol. iii., p. 113.   [3] Ibid.
[4] Despatch from Mendoza to Philip II., 2nd November, 1588. Archives of Simancas, B., 60, Nos. 47, 48.

from the monarchy in France; and the Leaguers had for five years been engaged in an ardent and obstinate conflict against the Protestants and Royalists. These causes compelled Philip II. to transfer his attention from England to France. He employed his finances in supporting and his armies in defending the League; and whilst he was seeking to dispossess Henry IV., he was obliged to abandon his design of overthrowing Elizabeth. This Princess, after the death of Mary Stuart, and the dispersion of the Armada, had nothing to fear. No serious enterprise was attempted, or even contemplated, for depriving her of her throne, and overthrowing Protestanism in England. After having consolidated throughout her kingdom the revolution which her father, Henry VIII., had commenced, Elizabeth assisted Henry IV. to vanquish the League, and the Republic of the United Provinces to render itself independent of Spain. Wherever Philip II. attempted to restore the old creed, she felt it her duty to support the new faith: and this mission she accomplished with less power than her adversary, it is true, but with greater ability and success, for she secured the triumph of Protestanism in England, Scotland, and Holland, and prevented its suppression in France. Elizabeth's policy, like that of Philip II., was tarnished by deception and cruelty; but the decline of Spain dates from Philip II., while England's greatness began under Elizabeth.

Such was the issue of the protracted and unequal struggle of the two religions in Great Britain. Mary Stuart fell together with the ancient creed; Elizabeth became powerful with the new one. By maintaining a lost cause, Mary Stuart was neither happy during her life, nor avenged after her death. The position in which she found herself placed on her return from France to Scotland, and the creed which she aimed at restoring in her dominions, contributed to her misfortunes at least as much as her passions and her faults.

Scotland had in all times been difficult to defend and govern. Five kings of the house of Stuart had perished for having attempted to secure its independence of England, and to maintain the authority of the crown against the feudal nobility. The last who had sunk under the weight of this task was James V., the unfortunate father of the still more unfortunate Mary Stuart. By his death at thirty years of age, leaving as his successor a daughter only six days old, he predicted with melancholy foresight the fate of his country and his race. A conflict commenced around the very cradle of his infant heiress, as to whether she should enter the house of Valois or that of Tudor; whether she should marry the grandson of Francis I. or the son of Henry VIII.; whether Scotland should remain independent under the protectorate of France, or whether it should be incorporated with England by a union which had long been sought. The partisans of independence overcame the advocates of union, and Mary, still a child, was sent to France. In that country, her happiest and most delightful days were passed; but during this period, the tempest which was to destroy the peace of her future life continued to increase in Scotland. Governed first by the Duke of Chatelherault, a Regent devoted to the French party, and secondly, by Margaret of Lorraine, sister of the Guises, a Regent of French extraction, Scotland, at war with England and in alliance with France, plunged deeper and deeper into party divisions. To the old causes of quarrel, which still subsisted and were now revived, new ones were added; the reformation of religion occurred to strengthen the feudal independence of the nobles, and to mingle the ardour of a new belief with the energy of ancient interests. It allied the Presbyterian democracy to the territorial aristocracy. This great event took place during the absence of Mary Stuart, who, on returning to the throne of her ancestors, in the autumn of 1561, found herself exposed to dangers of a far more formidable character than those which her predecessors had been unable to resist.

In order to rule as a Queen over her powerful nobility, without provoking them to insurrection; to practise the Catholic form of worship, without exciting the aggressive distrust of the Protestants; and to preserve the plenitude of her sovereign authority in her relations with England, without exposing herself to the intrigues and attacks of the restless Elizabeth—in order to do these things, what qualifications did Mary Stuart bring with her into Scotland? She condemned the religion, and was unacquainted with the customs, of the country which she was called to rule. Leaving a brilliant and refined court, she returned, full of regret and disgust, to the wild mountains and uncultivated inhabitants of Scotland. More amicable than politic, very ardent and not at all circumspect, she returned thither with misplaced elegance, dangerous beauty, a quick but restless intellect, a generous but excitable temperament, a taste for the arts, a love for adventure, and all the passions of a woman combined with the extreme liberty of a widow. Although possessed of great courage, it only served to hasten her misfortunes; and she employed her mind in committing with better grace those faults to which she was urged by her position and character. She had the imprudence to present herself as the legitimate heir to the crown of England, and thus to become the rival of Elizabeth; she served as the support and hope of the vanquished Catholics in her kingdom, and thus incurred the implacable enmity of the Reformed party, who were determined to maintain at all risks the religious revolution which they had occasioned.

Nor was this all. The dangers to which she was exposed by the exercise of her authority, the pretensions of her birth, and the ambition of her creed, were aggravated by the errors of her private conduct. Her sudden liking for Darnley—the excessive familiarities which she allowed Riccio, and the confidence which she reposed in him—and the ungovernable passion which she felt for Bothwell—were all equally fatal to her. By raising to the rank of her husband and king a young gentleman devoid of all merit, except personal attractions—by the sudden aversion and disgust which she felt for him—by making a Catholic foreigner her secretary and favourite—and by consenting to become the wife of her husband's murderer—she gave the death-blow to her own authority. After having lost her crown, she inconsiderately exposed herself to the loss of her liberty. She sought an asylum in the dominions of her enemy, before she had been assured that one would be granted her; and after throwing herself upon the mercy of Elizabeth, she conspired against her with but little chance of success. From her captivity in the prison in which she had been iniquitously confined, she thought she would be able, in concert with the Catholic party, to provide means for her deliverance; but she only laboured for her own destruction. The Catholics were too feeble in the island, and too disunited on the Continent to revolt or interfere usefully on her behalf. The insurrections which she attempted in England, and the conspiracies which she framed until 1586, completed her ruin, by causing the death or exile of her most enterprising partisans. The maritime crusade discussed at Rome, Madrid, and Brussels, in 1570, and determined upon in 1586, for the purpose of deposing Elizabeth and restoring Mary Stuart, far from placing the Catholic Queen on the throne of Great Britain, only conducted her to the scaffold.

The scaffold! Such was then the end of a life, which, commencing in expatriation, was chequered by reverses, filled with errors, unfortunate almost throughout its course, and guilty at one period—but adorned by so many charms, rendered touching by so many sufferings, purified by so long an expiation, and terminated with so much dignity! Mary Stuart, a victim of the old feudalism and the new religious revolution of Scotland, carried with her to the grave the hopes of absolute power and of Catholicism. Her descendants, who succeeded to the throne of England sixteen years after her death, followed her in the dangerous course in which she had been preceded by so many of her ancestors. Her grandson, Charles I., was, like her, beheaded for attempting to establish absolute monarchy; and her great-grandson, James II., for endeavouring, like her, to restore Catholicism, lost his throne and was driven into exile. A foreign land witnessed the extinction of the royal line of Stuart—a family rendered one of the most tragic in the annals of history, by their inconsiderate spirit, their adventurous character, and the continued fatality of their career.

THE END.

www.ingramcontent.com/pod-product-compliance
Lightning Source LLC
Chambersburg PA
CBHW051850300426
44117CB00006B/342